*NOTES FOR PROFESSIONAL LIBRARIANS
AND LIBRARY USERS*

This is an original book title published by The Haworth Social Work Practice Press, an imprint of The Haworth Press, Inc. Unless otherwise noted in specific chapters with attribution, materials in this book have not been previously published elsewhere in any format or language.

CONSERVATION AND PRESERVATION NOTES

All books published by The Haworth Press, Inc. and its imprints are printed on certified pH neutral, acid free book grade paper. This paper meets the minimum requirements of American National Standard for Information Sciences-Permanence of Paper for Printed Material, ANSI Z39.48-1984.

Jessica K. Heriot
Eileen J. Polinger
Editors

The Use of Personal Narratives in the Helping Professions
A Teaching Casebook

"This book is a collection of short stories, personal essays, and poems covering a remarkable broad range of mental health issues. The book is organized into sections according to four stages of life, and further subdivided into sections addressing situations we encounter in practice. These range from the commonplace, such as women losing their sense of physical attractiveness as they age, to the unusual, such as people struggling with the urge to cut themselves. A variety of points of view are represented. The narrative style allows readers to gain first-person insight, as well as raw material requiring synthesis and analysis for clinical purposes. Questions are provided at the end of each selection to facilitate this processing. In addition, reading lists for more extensive learning accompany every major section. Editors Jessica Heriot and Eileen Polinger have assembled a unique and valuable resource that simulates practice experience and will help students hone their clinical skills."

Mary H. Semel, MSW
Co-Editor, *A Broken
Heart Still Beats:
After Your Child Dies*

"This is a moving set of first-person accounts of experience. The editors have assembled a broad range of short vignettes that capture some essentials of life experience. Each life story fragment is followed by discussion questions, making this volume a rich resource for courses in which students confront the issues of helping people adapt through the many challenges of life. It is a welcome and creative addition to the mental health literature."

Ruthellen Josselson, PhD
Author, *Revising Herself:
The Story of Women's Identity
from College to Mid-Life*

THSWPP

The Haworth Social Work Practice Press
An Imprint of The Haworth Press, Inc.
New York • London • Oxford

The Use of Personal Narratives in the Helping Professions
A Teaching Casebook

The Use
of Personal Narratives
in the Helping Professions
A Teaching Casebook

Jessica K. Heriot
Eileen J. Polinger
Editors

THSWPP

The Haworth Social Work Practice Press
An Imprint of The Haworth Press, Inc.
New York • London • Oxford

Published by

The Haworth Social Work Practice Press, an imprint of The Haworth Press, Inc., 10 Alice Street, Binghamton, NY 13904-1580.

"Lisa's Ritual" by Grace Caroline Bridges from *Resourceful Woman,* edited by Shawn Brennan and Julie Winklepleck, Visible Ink Press, 1994. Copyright © 1994. Reprinted by permission of The Gale Group.

Cover design by Marylouise E. Doyle.

Library of Congress Cataloging-in-Publication Data

The use of personal narratives in the helping professions : a teaching casebook / Jessica K. Heriot, Eileen J. Polinger.
    p. cm.
  Includes bibliographical references and index.
  ISBN 0-7890-0918-8 (alk. paper)—ISBN 0-7890-0919-6 (alk. paper)
  1. Social work education—Biographical methods. 2. Mental health education—Biographical methods. I. Heriot, Jessica K. II. Polinger, Eileen J.

HV11.2 .U73 2002
361.3'2—dc21

2001024340

CONTENTS

PART IV: OTHER ISSUES OF ADULTHOOD

PART V: PHYSICAL ILLNESS

Schizophrenia and Other Psychotic Disorders

Dissociative Disorders

Eating Disorders

Substance Abuse

PART X: OLD AGE

From the Perspective of the Elderly Person

From the Perspective of the Caretaker

ABOUT THE EDITORS

Jessica K. Heriot, PhD, has a bachelor's degree in English literature and a master's degree and PhD in social work. She has worked in the field for 35 years, with 24 years as a private practitioner with a specialty in women's psychology and therapy. She teaches in the clinical concentration at the University of Maryland School of Social Work as an adjunct professor. She enjoys writing.

Eileen J. Polinger, PhD, LCSW-C, has a bachelor's degree in English literature, and a master's degree and PhD in social work. Her early professional background was in writing. Upon completion of her MSW, she did agency-based social work for a number of years. Later, she went into private practice, specializing in adolescent and adult psychotherapy, which she engaged in during and following her doctoral studies. She presently divides her time between her private practice, her writing, music, and the study and teaching of Eastern philosophy.

CONTRIBUTORS

Barbara Adams is a professor of English at Pace University in New York City. She has published two books of poems and a book of literary criticism. Her poems, essays, and stories have been published in *The Nation, Free Association, Psychoanalytic Quarterly,* and other journals as well as several anthologies.

Lynore G. Banchoff is a writer, clinical social worker, and feminist in Providence, Rhode Island, where she provides training for the MS Society. As she moves into retirement, in an unretiring manner, she is exploring new avenues for activism and celebrating the gifts of grandmotherhood.

Kathleen Reiland Beck is an award-winning writer who has worked in the mental health field. She has a master's degree in creative writing from California State University at San Marcos and currently teaches at Cypress College in California.

Bridget Bufford is a writer living in Missouri. She is an affiliate workshop leader with Amherst Writers and Artists. Her short stories and poems have appeared in a number of journals and in an anthology titled *Pillow Talk II*.

Diane B. Byington has an MSW and a PhD in social work from Florida State University. During her twenty-five years in social work, she has been a therapist, educator, and researcher. Her hobby is writing. She lives in a small town outside Denver, Colorado, where she has a small psychotherapy practice.

Eleanor Capelle worked for over thirty years as a librarian. In May 1989, she received an MA in creative writing from San Francisco State University and has published in the anthology *Sexual Harassment: Women Speak Out.*

Edmund de Chasca lives in St. Louis, Missouri, where he is a senior editor of *Boulevard,* a literary magazine. He is a member of the National Alliance of the Mentally Ill.

Mary Clemens, CSW-R, is a social worker living in Albany, New York. She works with children in the Albany public schools. She writes fiction and nonfiction.

Elayne Clift is an award-winning writer, author, and journalist whose work has appeared in a variety of venues internationally. In addition to publishing several anthologies of essays and poetry, Ms. Clift has published widely on women and gender issues, international development, health, and the environment. She holds adjunct faculty positions at several New England colleges and universities and serves as a consultant to various international organizations.

Carol Cochran writes from the perspective of a parent of an adult son who has a serious and persistent mental illness. She holds an MSW and is active in the National Alliance of the Mentally Ill—Hennepin County, Minnesota. She is currently writing a memoir about mental illness.

Judith Beth Cohen is an associate professor at Lesley College in Cambridge, Massachusetts, where she teaches writing. She has published a novel, *Seasons,* and numerous short stories.

Mark Dalton is a licensed clinical social worker living in Chicago, who has worked in many settings, but "none inspired me more than working with the homeless mentally ill." The poems in this anthology are part of a larger work called the *Big Book of Delusions.*

Pamela Di Pesa, PhD, MSW, is a writer, clinical social worker, and teacher who lives in Baltimore, Maryland, with her husband and daughter. She is especially interested in the therapeutic uses of writing.

Rosemary DiStefano is the author of short fiction in the memoir genre. She lives in Baltimore, Maryland, working as a contract specialist for the University of Maryland during the day, and putting words on paper by night.

Ellen Fairey lives in Chicago, where she writes fiction, plays, and screenplays. She is a graduate of the Art Institute of Chicago. She currently works in advertising.

Robin Famighetti, a licensed independent clinical social worker, lives in Massachusetts and has been in the geriatrics field for twenty-five years.

Dennis Foley, a lifelong Chicagoan, a husband, and a father of three boys, has published fiction, memoirs, and poetry in a number of journals. He is a former prosecutor for the Cook County State Attorney's Office and currently works as an electrician for the city of Chicago.

Anderson J. Franklin, PhD, is a professor of clinical psychology at the City College of the University of New York and is in private practice.

Jamie Joy Gatto is a New Orleans writer whose short fiction, columns, and essays have appeared in numerous anthologies, periodicals, and online venues, including *Best Bisexual Erotica, Unlimited Desires, The Unmade Bed, Scarlet Letters,* and *Black Sheets.* She is editor-in-chief of the Webzine <www.MindCaviar.com> and is currently working on her first collection of short fiction: stories of sex, death, and loss.

Kathleen Gerard is a full-time author. Her work has appeared in literary journals such as *Lynx Eye, Christianity and the Arts, Mediphors,* and *Vermont Ink.*

Tami Gramont is a published writer living in Sedona, Arizona. Her writing includes short stories, fiction, nonfiction, and feature newspaper articles.

Anne Greene was born in Hollywood in 1939 and received her MA in English at Sonoma State University in 1972. She taught at Napa Valley College, and her poetry and short stories have been published in numerous magazines and anthologies. For the past fifteen years she has been teaching creative writing in the California Prison Arts Project.

Gary Guillot was brought up in a military family, spending most of his childhood and adolescence in Germany. Leaving home at the age of seventeen, he traveled as a musician for fifteen years before seeking a higher education. He is now living in Denver, Colorado, and attends Metropolitan State College.

Mary Hanson Carter is a pseudonym. Her real self lives in Washington State and has worked as an English instructor, a manager at Unisys in St. Paul, Minnesota, and a psychotherapist. A cancer survivor, she currently works as a freelance writer and has published poems and essays in several small journals and is working on a novel.

Janice J. Heiss is a writer, performer, and Web journalist who lives in San Francisco. Her writing has appeared in various publications, including *The Ecstatic Moment: The Best of Libido* (anthology); *Summer's Love, Winter's Discontent* (anthology); *Black Dirt; Frontiers: A Journal of Women's Studies; Women's Words; Proteus;* and the *Lullwater Review.*

Kathleen B. Henderson holds a PhD in literature and has taught at the college level for twelve years. She is an essayist and poet and was nominated for the Pushcart Prize in 1999. She is currently the director of the Academic Skills Center at Austin College in Texas.

Nancy Hewitt is a licensed independent clinical social worker who has a psychotherapy practice in Salem and Melrose, Massachusetts. She is enrolled in the Certificate Program in Creative Writing at the University of Massachusetts. Her poems have appeared in a number of literary journals.

Alan Howard, a graduate of the University of Michigan, is a retired English professor and newspaper columnist, a two-time Fulbright Scholar, the author of *Longing for Latitude* (winner of the 1999 MIPA Award for Poetry), and his writings have been published on three continents.

Elizabeth Howard is a teacher and writer with an MA in English from Vanderbilt University. Her family has struggled with a son's schizophrenia for twenty-five years.

George Jones is a retired businessman living in Leeds, Alabama. He was Chairman of the Leeds Welfare Cooperative and is active in the anti-death penalty movement. He authored a book, *Forest Home,* published by CeShore. He experienced a period of clinical depression and hospitalization, on which the story in this anthology is based.

Linda Kantner is a school social worker and writer living in St. Paul, Minnesota. Her stories have been published in several literary journals, and she received an honorable mention in the *Writer's Digest* fiction contest.

Linda A. Lavid has been a social worker for twenty-five years. She now works in the Buffalo Public Schools with children who have been suspended for violence. She has been writing for ten years and has published several stories in various literary journals. She is currently completing a novel.

David Levine is a medical editor for Pfizer Inc. and a contributing editor for *Physician's Weekly.* His articles have appeared in *American Health, Good Housekeeping,* and *Woman's Day.*

Debbi Lieberson is a writer living in Cambridge, Massachusetts. Her piece, "The Price of Admission," is an excerpt from a soon-to-be completed memoir. Ms. Lieberson's writing has also appeared in the *Boston Globe Magazine.*

Jeanne Loo was born in New York and lives in Carlsbad, California. She is a former concert pianist and dancer who also enjoys music and writing. Currently, she is involved in a residential treatment center for eating disorders.

Jim Lucas is retired from a career in public relations, publicity, and marketing. He is currently a print collagist, a serious amateur photographer, and a writer of poetry and short stories about affairs of the heart.

Bobbi Lurie worked as an occupational therapist for eight years but has always been a painter and writer and has always felt a need to question life through the process of art. Her essays, poetry, and short stories have been published in numerous journals and anthologies in England and the United States.

Michael E. Miller is a trial attorney representing the city of Washington, DC. He and his wife of thirty-nine years, Dawne, have three children, two grandchildren, and two dogs. His short stories have been published in *Wordrights!* and *The Arkansas Review.*

Libbi Miriam writes intensely about her primary family and now her secondary family, including stories about her adult children. She is the author of *Learning to Sit in the Silence: A Journal of Caretaking* and co-editor of a new international collection, *Here I Am: Contemporary Jewish Writing from Around the World.*

Diana K. Munson is a clinical social worker in private practice in Washington, DC. She is also an art therapist and an author of numerous articles, stories, and poems published in various journals and magazines over the years.

Frances Murphy works as a psychiatric clinical nurse specialist. She lives in Weymouth, Massachusetts. Her writing has appeared in *Reed Magazine, Lynx Eye,* and *Washington Square.*

Susan Olding lives in Kingston, Ontario, Canada, where she teaches at the Queen's University Writing Centre while writing fiction, nonfiction, and poetry. "Soldier Boy" is excerpted from a longer piece, "Wall of Glass," which received Honorable Mention in the *Prairie Fire* creative nonfiction contest and appeared in the magazine in 1998.

Vicki Pieser has published essays and memoir pieces in regional parenting magazines, *The Minneapolis Tribune, Minnesota Women's Press,* and *The American Jewish World.*

Maureen Porter graduated from the University of Rhode Island in 1990 at the age of sixty-four and has been a writer ever since. She is a grandmother and a great-grandmother living in Rhode Island.

Catherine Quigg is a freelance writer on environmental and health issues. She was a trustee of the Elgin Mental Health Center and is currently a member of the National Alliance for the Mentally Ill. She lives with her husband in Barrington, Illinois.

Rebecca Rees received a master's degree in creative writing from San Francisco State University. Her stories have been published in several literary journals. She is currently working on a book about a community activist and teacher. She worked for ten years in community mental health.

Sara Rife is a social worker, aspiring writer, and dedicated gardener living in Boston. She has worked in human services since 1973. She and her partner have lived together since 1991.

Elisavietta Ritchie is a widely published author both in the United States and abroad. She often works with adults and as a poet in the schools. Her home base is by the Patuxent River and in Washington, DC.

A. Rooney teaches writing at the University of Colorado and Metro State and writes fiction. He has an MFA from Naropa and has been a professional writer and consultant for over twenty years. He has been published in *The New York Times, Jumbo Shrimp, Alma,* and others. He also has an MSW and in another life was a therapist.

Juliana Rose has written fiction and essays that have appeared in such journals as the *Partisan Review,* the *Voice Literary Supplement, Tikkun,* and numerous anthologies. The author of many books on writing, Rose teaches writing and literature in New York City. Juliana Rose is a pseudonym that the writer uses for pieces of a personal nature.

Helen Ruggieri teaches writing at the University of Pittsburgh, Bradford, Pennsylvania. She has an MFA in writing from Penn State. "Daddy's Girls" is a chapter from a full-length memoir in progress.

Jean Sellmeyer Smith lives in the Cajun country of southern Louisiana. She is a grandmother of nine who fought and won lifelong battles with mental illness and alcoholism. At the age of sixty-six, she graduated from the University of Iowa's creative writing program.

Sybil Smith lives in Vermont and works as a nurse. Her work has appeared in many magazines, including *Yankee* and *The Sun Magazine.* As well as writing creative nonfiction, she writes poetry and screenplays.

Mary Sojourner, columnist, National Public Radio commentator, and author of the novel *Sisters of the Dream,* many short stories, and essays, lives in Flagstaff, Arizona, by choice and true luck.

Kimberly Sotiro currently works at the Danbury Superior Court as a monitor for the state of Connecticut. She has also been doing extensive work with a homeopathic doctor to try to pinpoint the causes and effects of her condition, and to find some solutions.

Stephen Stathis published a collection of short fiction, *Demons and Dreams,* in 1998. He teaches at Northeastern University in Boston and the Massachusetts College of Pharmacy in Boston. He is a licensed marriage and family therapist.

Sarah Sutro is a Boston-area poet and artist currently living in Bangladesh. She has taught at Emerson College, Lesley College, Museum School Boston, Ithaca College, and Cornell University. In 2000 she was awarded a Pollock/Krasner award in painting. Her work is included in several collections, including Harvard University Art Museums, Boston Public Library, and the Johnson Museum at Cornell.

Anita D. Taylor is an HIV/AIDS health care professional living in Washington, DC. She was diagnosed with manic-depressive illness at age thirty-eight. She is currently writing a book about her experience, *Mad Colored Woman: A Memoir of Manic Depression.*

Alison Townsend is an assistant professor of English, creative writing, and women's studies at the University of Wisconsin at Whitewater. Her poetry, essays, and reviews have appeared in a number of literary journals and anthologies. "At the Bottom of the Ocean" comes from *The Mental Illness Narratives,* a book in progress.

A Traveler, the author's pseudonym, is a teacher, editor, and writer.

Ellen Turner grew up in California and graduated from Stanford with a BA in English. She did graduate work at Yale and St. Mary's College, and has an MA in education. She is the mother of two grown sons. Her professional life has focused for over twenty-five years on work with teenage mothers and their families.

Bonny Vaught has written an industrial history, two books on religious education, and essays and fiction which have appeared in various literary journals. She lives and works in Hadley, Massachusetts.

Karen de Balbian Verster has published a novel, *The Way to Heaven,* and other writing. She has been awarded fellowships and holds an MFA in creative writing from City College of New York.

Louise Webster is a poet and writer. She lives in New York with her two children and husband.

Bill Weiner is a New Jersey-based writer and social worker.

Franz Weinschenk was born in Mainz, Germany. Except for a stint in the U.S. Army during the Korean War, he has been associated with Fresno City College in Fresno, California, as an instructor and dean for most of his professional life. Besides being published fourteen times, he is the creator of an award-winning radio series on National Public Radio called *Valley Writers Read,* which is currently in its eighth season.

Erin White is a twenty-five-year-old student from New York. She hopes the publication of her poem in this book will help to enlighten people about the emotions and thought processes involved in self-mutilation.

M. Elizabeth Wilson is the executive director of The Main Place, a consumer-run recovery center, near Columbus, Ohio. She is currently enrolled in a master's degree program in human services administration. She became a mental health advocate after being diagnosed with bipolar disorder.

Cherise Wyneken is a freelance writer with publications in various journals and periodicals, including anthologies such as *Filtered Images: Women Remembering Their Grandmothers; 2000: Here's to Humanity; Lessons in Love: Gifts from Our Grandmothers; Polyphony;* a collection by Florida poets, *Skinner House Books;* and Pig Iron's upcoming collection, *Religion in Modernity.*

Foreword

Each of us can recall events in our lives that brought us new insight or took us to crossroads where our lives changed forever. Eventually, these events become the stories that we tell to others and re-tell to ourselves. We become awakened to experiences and situations that might previously have been foreign to us. As we get to know the stories of other people, we are challenged to consider other perspectives, viewpoints, and ideas. We find our interest and passion aroused, and often we are even inspired to become socially or politically active.

Stories can be powerful because they speak directly to each of us, especially when the writer is asked to reveal something about her or his personal experience. Of the writer it requires significant reflection, often a hearty dose of courage, time, and a skilled pen. It is a true act of sharing.

The Use of Personal Narratives in the Helping Professions: A Teaching Casebook is filled with original, never-before published, first-person accounts. These narratives are presented chronologically, from the earliest stages of life through adulthood. In them we see key principles of biology, psychology, sociology, and social work. We see real people wrestling with the central issues of life.

The stories in this book portray vividly what is taught in the classroom. They give value and meaning to theory and research that is presented in textbooks and by professors during lectures. They are an excellent vehicle for teaching concepts in human behavior, psychopathology, and clinical practice.

The Use of Personal Narratives in the Helping Professions: A Teaching Casebook follows in the fine tradition of story telling. It is a wonderful collection of honest, personal accounts that readers will find delightful, challenging, and provocative.

David N. Sattler, PhD

Preface

Storytelling has its origins in humankind's earliest days, when we passed on life's information and mysteries to one another orally before we began to write things down. Based on the almost universal love of storytelling, it seems a logical step to make use of well-written stories in the teaching process. Traditionally, practice skills for the helping professions have been taught by the use of case vignettes, role-play, process recordings, or occasionally excerpts from established literature. These have tended, more often than not, to be dry and, by virtue of being in the third person, somewhat removed from and depersonalized for the student. In an effort to bridge this gap and make the learning of clinical practice more engaging, interesting, and immediate, the authors solicited personal narratives from writers who wished to share stories close to their hearts. Contributors wrote their own stories or stories about others. Some pieces come from therapists telling of their personal experiences. Pertinent literature was also reviewed and a few selections were made from there as well. Criteria for selection were that the editors found the material to be relevant for students in the mental health professions, well written, and applicable to the chosen format of the book. The book consists of a compilation of these pieces. Though it was our intent for the book to be wholly composed of original unpublished personal narratives, we were somewhat constrained by the responses we received to our inquiries. The content of the book reflects this.

The format of the book is based on the four stages of life: childhood, adolescence, adulthood, and old age. Each life stage is further divided into subsections, placing narratives with similar themes together. Issues of particular relevance to each of these four stages as they impact the people living through them and those surrounding these individuals are also addressed. The table of contents contains a brief synopsis of each selection for easy reference. Every piece is followed with study questions directed at stimulating discussion. Allowing for the uniqueness of each selection, questions address the issues presented in the narrative, assessment of the person and problem, treatment, skills, and knowledge. Suggested readings for further study and additional resources are provided following each section.

It is our belief that the personal narrative adds an important dimension to comprehending what people face as they deal with life's issues. These situations are often filled with richness, nuance, and complexity. It is our hope that this collection of narratives will help students achieve a broader appreciation for, and a more complete understanding of, their clients' experiences and, thereby, be better equipped to serve them.

Acknowledgments

In 1995, a small notice appeared in the newsletter of the National Association of Social Workers calling for personal stories about mental illness. In response, I sent Robin Famighetti a personal narrative about my mother's death from my child's-eye view. She liked it and kept me posted about the progress of the book, which she envisioned as a teaching casebook for students in social work. Life circumstances caused Robin to bow out, at which point I went on with the project and asked Eileen Polinger to be a co-editor.

A number of pieces in the book were collected by Robin when she was soliciting manuscripts. She started this wonderful project, and we thank her. A modified version of her fine play *Cerebral Dust,* about a woman struggling with Alzheimer's, appears in Part X of this book.

I also want to thank Nancy Aiken, John Biggs, and Hope Prosky for their expertise in suggesting questions and readings. Thanks to BeBe Bass for leading me through the thorns and underbrush of computer territory, to Dick for being the sounding board for my complaints and frustrations, and to Eileen, my co-editor, whose promptness, efficiency, thoroughness, and flexibility made our collaboration smooth and easy.

Jessica Heriot

I would like to lovingly thank my family and friends for putting up with me while I labored my way through this project. Their kindness, patience, willingness to listen, and helpful suggestions are valued beyond measure. I would also like to offer special thanks to those who have been my life teachers—who taught me how to be—so that I might be able to tackle something like this with enough internal resources to manage it.

Thanks also to Dave Porrazzo for his invaluable computer assistance and patience, to the staff at The Haworth Press for their unfailing cooperation, and to my co-editor Jessica Heriot for always doing her part.

Eileen Polinger

Finally, we both wish to thank all the writers whose fine work peoples these pages and brings to life our very human problems.

PART I:
CHILDHOOD

The Killing Jar

Jim Lucas

It is higher than he can reach: his father's glass case of butterflies. Sam pulls up a desk chair, stands on the seat, gazes into the compartments one at a time, and traces the impaled specimens. His damp fingers streak over the gallery of colorful wings. "Fly," he says. Sam is three. Beyond the case and through the summer screen, he sees Paul, his older brother, and a friend run through the coming twilight catching fireflies. Sam slides to the floor, goes downstairs to the kitchen cabinet where empty containers are kept. His dimpled hand hardly reaches around the jar. He grasps a lid in the other hand, runs outside, and collides with Paul.

"Look, would you just look, Sam? Four fireflies! One's in the grass on the bottom. The other three are . . . there . . . did you see it? Did you see it? Did you see his bottom light up? That one right under the lid," he says.

Sam stands on tiptoe, and the two boys huddle around Paul as he holds the glowing trap. All four fireflies light up in unison, and a bright shimmer washes over the boys' faces with their full, almost-ripe cheeks and eyes still large enough to accommodate wonder.

Sam is in awe. This seems like some kind of secret ceremony. His jaw drops, and drool forms on his lower lip as he gives the shining insects his full attention. Well, almost his full attention. Over his brother's shoulder, Sam sees a butterfly glide down in the last warm rays of sun on this mid-July evening, and land on the bottom porch step.

He breaks away from the other two boys and heads toward his quarry. It's a stare-down between Sam and the butterfly. Finally, Sam lunges with the jar in his right hand above his head. The butterfly tries for open air but sails into the jar, stunning itself as it hits the bottom of the jar. With his left hand, Sam claps the lid on unevenly, catching a wing tip under the edge. Pinned down, his captive flutters against the inside of the jar semaphoring for help.

Sam kneels on the ground holding his prize. By the time Paul and his friend join Sam, the flutter has slowed and the creature is barely alive. Sam sits on the grass with his nose pressed against the jar, watching. A transparent wall separates him from the fight for life going on inside. He begins to cry.

"What are you trying to do Sam, kill it?" Paul asks. "You don't have an air hole punched in the lid . . . don't you know about that? He's suffocating!"

Paul grabs the jar, removes the lid, and the limp butterfly slides down into Sam's hand. The air revives the butterfly, but not much. The wing that was caught in the lid seems to drop as the insect tries to take off. Sam cups his hands around the butterfly and carries it over to a low tree branch. It hesitates for a moment on an oak leaf.

"Go! Go! Go!" Sam calls out, and suddenly, the butterfly is gone.

The next afternoon, Sam returns to his father's specimen case and struggles to pull it off the shelf. The case is large, and his outstretched arms barely make the span of the box, but he slowly slides it down along the shelved books until it sits safely on the thick, hand-tied rug below. Silver latches at each end of the lid give way easily, and Sam lifts back the hinged glass cover, resting it against a row of books.

From the case, Sam carefully takes the butterflies outside one by one and places them at random on the boxwood hedges framing the front walk. He places a Compton Tortoiseshell low near the sidewalk, a Satyr Anglewing in among some leaves. A Resale Skipper, Falcate Orange-tip, Red-bordered Metalmark, and a Gulf Fritillary find resting places all up and down the hedges. Standing on his coaster wagon, Sam arrays a nearly perfect Kawasaki's Beauty, a Mountain Emperor, a West Indian Buckeye, and a Sonorant Blue along the top of each boxwood hedge.

When he has finished, Sam, hands on hips, regards his project from the front door. Then, while there is still plenty of warm sun for flying, he steps to each winged beauty and blows his trusting breath under their bodies. "Go! Go—ohhh!" he whispers over and over.

Questions for Discussion

1. At what age do children understand the concept of death?
2. Young children are magical thinkers. Their capacity for cause-and-effect reasoning has not yet developed. How would you explain to Sam why the butterflies in the case do not fly?

My Tenth Year

Jessica K. Heriot

Polio is everywhere. Polio is the reason I am still at summer camp, or so I'm told. The camp season is extended for two more weeks so children don't have to be in the city where it is easier to get polio. I only have to stay for one of the two weeks and am very relieved about this.

Camp feels empty, the row of green and white cabins silent and deserted, and those of us left behind cannot fill the space. We are marooned in a ghost town. The remaining girls are all bunked in the senior lodge, which is kind of fun. But I am thrown in with a bunch of girls I don't know, and they are not my age. I have just turned ten.

The days pass slowly. I am very anxious to go home. I have a feeling that something bad is happening at home and I desperately want to find out what it is. Finally, my week of captivity ends. I feel like a bird freed from a cage.

I am home at last. The problem is, Mommy is still sick. Her bedroom door is always closed, and she is in bed all the time. Dad tells me Mom is still sick and as soon as she feels a little better I can see her. I worry, but I am glad I am home, near her.

Mommy has been sick for a long time. She couldn't visit on parents' day in July. Dad came up alone and told me that Mommy was sick. She was still sick in August, and my aunt and uncle came up instead. We had fun. My uncle took lots of pictures, but I wondered why Mommy was still sick.

Daddy says I can see Mommy today. I am so happy. I open the door to her bedroom. She is lying in bed propped up on several pillows. She is a ghost person, a shadow of herself, gaunt, gray, and thin. Who is this person? Where is my mommy, strong and sturdy, the mommy with the big bosom and the long brown hair? Where did she go?

I want to scream out, "Mommy, what's happened to you? What's wrong with you?"

But I don't. Instead I start crying and run to her bed, "Mommy, Mommy."

She talks to me, asks me about camp. Her eyes are the same, but her voice is weak. She says she loves me and that I should go out and play now. She doesn't want me to stay. I know now that she is very sick.

I ask my father, "What's wrong with Mommy?"

I don't really know what he says, but I feel reassured and go to Gail's house to play.

The end of the summer drags on, hot and boring. I can't do anything because of polio. I can't go to the movies or swimming, or even visit friends. The only place I can go is Gail's house, next door. And then I can only stay for lunch.

Today, Gail's mother tells me that my father called to say that I can stay for a while after lunch. This is good because we are playing a game, and it is a treat to stay at Gail's house after lunch. By midafternoon my father has not called. I start to feel uneasy. Something may be wrong. I tell Gail's mother that I have to go home. She says that it is OK, I can stay. I tell her I want to go home, but she tries to get me to stay. Now I know for sure something is wrong. I run from Gail's bedroom, down the stairs, out the back door, across the side yard, through the big bushes onto our gravel driveway, up the steps past the lilac bushes, which my mother loves, arrive at our back door in a panic, and swing open the screen door.

My father is standing there. He looks defeated. I am crying hard. My father says, "She knows. How does she know?"

He is right, I know. But I say, "I want to see Mommy."

"Mommy is dead," my dad says. "Mommy is dead."

There is a party at our house. People are milling around our backyard on a cool sunny day. They are laughing, talking, and eating. Even my aunt Dora, whom I never see and whom my mother does not like, is there smiling and having fun. I think something is wrong. Why is a party going on? People should be sad; my mommy just died. After a while, my father comes over to me and says that all the people are going to the funeral, and I should go to Gail's house to play. I tell him that I want to go. He says I can't. I ask why, but his answer does not satisfy me. I feel angry. It is my mother who died, so I want to go to her funeral and I don't want all these people having a good time at my house.

No one talks about Mommy anymore. I want to talk about her, but none of the adults around me want to do this.

School starts. I am in the fifth grade. I do not say that my mother is dead, and no one mentions it.

A big fat woman named Sue watches me. When I come home from school, she is sitting in the living room listening to the races. The autumn sun streams through the front window illuminating a Milky Way of dust. The house is dirty.

My father does not come home after work like he used to. I wait up for him. The clock says 3 a.m. when I hear the front door open. This happens a lot. I beg him not to come home so late.

Daddy never talks about Mommy. I think he is glad she died because he didn't want to be married to her anymore. Mommy was trouble. She screamed and cried and was unhappy. I don't want to say this to him, because he will be mad at me and maybe he will leave me too. I feel scared a lot now, worried about what will happen now that Mommy is dead.

One day, I meet a nice lady named Hannah. She has pretty yellow hair and dresses in soft wool clothes. She is very attentive to me and smiles a lot. I like her.

Sitting on the landing, my feet on the top step of the stairs leading to the kitchen, I hear my father talking on the telephone in the dining room. He does not know I am there.

He says. "I don't care what she thinks; I deserve a little happiness in my life."

I know that "she" means me and that he is talking about Hannah. He doesn't care how I feel. I know now that I am right. He is glad Mommy is dead. He wants to forget her. I know I cannot talk about Mommy again and I should forget her too. I feel cut loose, a little speck, floating in space.

One winter weekend, shortly after Christmas, I visit my friend Valerie on Long Island. Her parents are friends of my father's. Valerie and I have fun and get to stay up late because her parents go to a party and leave us alone. The next morning, Valerie's father calls us into their bedroom. They are still in bed. Her father tells me that, like me, his mother died when he was a little boy. His dad remarried, and he really came to love his stepmother. "Stepmother." I hate that word. I know that he is telling me that it may not be so bad if my father married Hannah, and I guess that may be right, but I am a little puzzled. Why he is telling me this now? Then he tells me that my father and Hannah were married over the weekend and went to Bear Mountain for a honeymoon. When I get home, I will have a new mother. I am numb. I have no reaction or response. My mother has been dead for five months.

I hate this woman. She is taking my mother's place, sleeps with my father in my mother's bedroom, in my mother's bed. He sees her naked. I don't want them to close their bedroom door at night. She is getting rid of the furniture and rearranging the living room. They ask for my opinion. I tell them I hate it. I am mad all the time. Hannah tries to be nice to me, but I don't want her. She wants me to do things around the house. I tell her that she can't make me do anything. She is not my mother.

I am wild and unruly, sullen and nasty, indifferent and cold. One late June day, Hannah decides she has had enough. She tells my father that she can't take it anymore. She is in the bedroom packing her bags and is going to walk to the train station. I am listening from the top of the steps, overcome with terror. I have made her leave. My father will hate me. He will leave again and maybe not come home at all. It will be my own fault that I am all alone with no one to take care of me. I rush down the stairs into the bedroom. Hannah is in the bathroom combing her hair. I walk to the bathroom door and in a small voice beg her not to leave. No answer. I plead and ask her if she loves me. She looks satisfied. She stays.

Questions for Discussion

1. Speculate about how the secrecy (her mother's terminal illness, her father's marriage) and the prohibition against mourning may impact the narrator as an adult.
2. How does one talk with a child about terminal illness and death? When do you think the child in this story should have been told about her mother's illness and the possibility of her death?
3. If this child was referred to you for counseling for acting-out behavior following her father's remarriage, how would you help the family deal with the situation?

Land Where Our Fathers Died . . .

Maureen Porter

Another morning to live through. He gripped the pencil, holding it tightly between his fingers, trying to keep it steady enough to make a neat "Z." Once again the pencil wandered all around the targeted space. For the umpteenth time he wondered why the principal played that same song every single morning. What had he ever done to be picked on like this?

Mrs. Jackman was standing beside his desk and sighed as she saw his work. What was wrong with this little kid? In the afternoon he perked up and did quite well, but mornings were a disaster. She didn't criticize him. It was too soon into his career to destroy any self-confidence he had.

Zach noticed her out of the corner of his eye and shifted nervously in his seat. He knew she would never understand. Even his mother didn't know about his problem. He didn't know how to tell anybody. Why the school had singled him out from all the other children was a mystery to him, but they had.

Mrs. Jackman loved her job and the first-graders she encountered each year. There was usually at least one problem child in every class. Zach was not exactly a problem, but she noticed that he kept to himself during recess and lunch looking slightly forlorn. A first-grader who was so serious and introverted sent up worry flags in her mind. Perhaps she would give his mother a call. If he had a problem, maybe they could fix it while he was still young.

Mrs. Linstrom made arrangements to leave her office early and headed for Zach's school. What now? Mrs. Jackman had asked her to stop by to talk about Zach, her beautiful little boy. What was wrong with his little world now? Lord knows, he had enough to deal with already.

"Mrs. Linstrom? Hi. I'm Mrs. Jackman."

"Hello. What's wrong? Is Zach being a problem? I know he's an odd little guy, but he tries to be good."

"No. No. He's very good. I just wondered if we could figure out why he has such a problem concentrating and learning in the mornings. After lunch he seems to perk up and do better."

"I don't know. He's a very quiet kid who will not tell me or anyone else close to him what is bothering him. It's like he has a window that he will not open. He hides behind it. But before we go any further, you should be aware that last year when he was five, his father killed himself. A suicide."

"Oh my, how awful for you. And Zach. That helps to explain a lot, but his mornings are still a problem. Do you think you could talk to him and find out what the problem is? I want to help him now before his school behavior becomes a habit."

"I'll try, but he is a stubborn child when it comes to talking about his father and what happened last year. He has periods of raging anger every once in a while, but so far, he has done no harm. Other times he's so docile it troubles me." Mrs. Linstrom tried to hold back the sob, which bubbled up as she spoke.

"Oh, it's so hard. I have to work full-time and I know he needs me at home after school. I'm trying to hold it all together for him, but, oh God, it is just so hard."

"I understand. Of course your life is difficult. But let's try and help your little boy. As he grows older it won't be any easier to help him articulate his feelings. But now is the time to work on it. I'm glad you told me about his father. It will help me to understand him. So see if you can talk to him over the weekend. And I'll see what I can do on this end. It was nice meeting you, and I'm so pleased we spoke."

Zach was gobbling macaroni and cheese, his favorite meal, when his mother mentioned meeting his teacher that day.

"Did you like her? I like her. She's really nice," he said, talking with a full mouth.

"Oh, I thought she was very nice. She likes you too. She was wondering why you have trouble in the mornings but not in the afternoons. Is that true? Do you hate mornings or something?" She was trying to be nonchalant.

Zach's body stiffened and she thought, Oh no, now he'll never talk about it.

Maybe his guard was down because he had macaroni and cheese, because suddenly he gulped and sighed. "Well, I can't figure out why they play that stupid song every day."

"What song, love?"

"You know. That song that goes 'My Country 'Tis of Thee.' "

She ran the words through her head quickly, wondering what he meant. Then it hit her. The second verse began with the words "Land of the Pilgrim's pride, land where our fathers died." Oh Lord, here it was December and her small son had been living with this since September. "Oh, Zach." She wrapped him in her arms and just held him while his misery penetrated her world.

"Honey, why didn't you tell me before? They don't mean your father when they sing that song. It's a song about all the people who have died before us."

She wondered what the next obstacle would be and realized that life was not going to get any easier. But they would deal with it together.

On Monday morning she and Zach went to school together about an hour late. As arranged, Mrs. Jackman met them in the principal's office. Zach's mother cleared her throat and began to tell Mrs. Jackman and Mr. Romano, the principal, about Zach. As she spoke, both the teacher's and the principal's eyes were shiny with unshed tears.

Mrs. Jackman knelt before Zach and took his hands. "Zach, we won't play that song anymore. We had no idea how it was affecting you."

Mr. Romano put his arm around Zach and said, "Listen, pal, you and I need to have a little talk. We'll let these two go back to work while we chat."

Mrs. Linstrom murmured her thanks, gave Mrs. Jackman a hug, waved at Zach, and left.

Questions for Discussion

1. What symptoms was Zach showing in school and at home to indicate that he might be experiencing anxiety and grief? What other symptoms might a grieving child exhibit?
2. A perceptive teacher recognized that Zach was having a problem and called his mother. What do you think might have happened to Zach if this teacher had not been so observant?

The Orange Coat

Mary Clemens

The orange coat hung in the hall closet by the front door. It was cut full, with sleeves shaped like a cornucopia. My mother, whose coat it was, would say, "Now, Ruth, go play outside. It's too nice a day to stay in." And I would have to walk past the hall closet and the orange coat. As long as the closet door was closed, I was safe. But sometimes it was open.

My mother watched me carefully. "Now, Ruth. What are you doing? There's nothing in that closet but coats. You're much too big a girl to be afraid of a little, bitty closet. Just go on past it." And when I hung back, she'd raise her voice, "Go on past it, scaredy-cat. I said NOW!"

I did what she said but I kept my eyes on the floor. And yet I see it now in my mind's eye: yards of plushy, orange wool swaying to and fro on my mother's solid frame, the wide sleeves, the hem undulating around and around. There, against the deep blue sky of autumn, the coat stands out in my memory, like a pirate swaggering aboard his ship on the sea.

On those occasions when the door was open, I scuttled past the closet like a lower form of life, tripping and falling down the evolutionary ladder with each step. And with those words, I recognize how ashamed I was. It was as if the coat said, "Look at you. I am nothing. I am inanimate. But you are less than nothing because you are afraid of me." There were times when I could not go back to sleep, dreaming that the coat rose up and loosed its cornucopian sleeves over me, scooping my small self up and swallowing me in a smothering wave of thick, horrific wool.

"There's something wrong with Ruth," my mother said to my father one night as I played with my toys in the next room.

There was a long pause. My father rarely spoke.

"What's wrong with her?" He shifted and sighed on the sofa.

"She hates to go past that closet," my mother said. "I've told her a thousand times to just walk past it, but she won't."

"Why not?"

"She's afraid."

"Well, she's got nothing to be afraid of." The newspaper rustled.

"I know," my mother said. "That's what I keep telling her."

During the weeks that followed, I dragged like chains the knowledge that something was wrong with me because I was afraid. My mother saw that I was biting my nails. "Stop it," she would say whenever she saw my hand at my mouth. "Go outside and play." And so I would, gradually learning to hide my fear and, when I started school, at times, to forget it.

Shortly after I turned nine, I met a girl who became my first real friend. Her name was Penny and she had smooth blonde hair and narrow, straight blonde brows. I met her at the movies in Oakwood, which was the town next to ours and the only place within several miles that had a movie theater. Her mother knew my mother and the two of them chatted after the matinee. Penny eyed me solemnly, and when our mothers finished their good-byes, she smiled at me and said, "Come over."

I was lucky that Penny's house was on my side of East Oakwood Avenue, a busy road that my mother forbade me to cross without her. One day I walked just beyond my neighborhood and found Penny and her dad cleaning out their garage. Discards clogged their driveway: an old candlestick, a broken beach chair, stacks of paperback books with lurid covers, unusable tires, a baby stroller, a complete set of plastic dinnerware, and, at the bottom of a box which seemed to be filled with rags, stacks and stacks of empty bottles, holding the rags up like stilts.

Penny was standing next to a laundry basket filled with old toys. We didn't say much as she showed me what was there.

"He's from when I was a baby," Penny told me, picking up a discarded jack-in-the-box. "I used to play with him all the time."

Penny's dad disappeared inside the house. The street was deserted. Penny held the jack-in-the-box at arm's length, and then tossed it. It hit the driveway hard.

"My mom says I have to throw him away," Penny said. "I don't care."

She scooped up the jack-in-the-box and threw it on top of a box of color forms, which burst open like a broken kaleidoscope, showering shards of color on the driveway. I knelt to pick them up but Penny ran, yelling over her shoulder, "Come on. I don't have to work anymore. Once he starts drinking he doesn't stop."

She led me to a deep basin of bare earth surrounded by flimsy saplings at the very edge of her backyard.

"This is my hiding place," Penny said, looking at me over her shoulder. "Come on in."

"What do you hide from?" I asked her, eyeing the wide spaces between the young trees.

She looked at me. Her faced stayed as smooth as a stone.

My mother would have said that it was too cold to sit in the hideout, but we curled up in our jackets as if they were nests and talked about school and books and what we loved and hated, but not about what Penny hid from and not about the orange coat.

"I know," I said as dusk was falling, "let's make a club. It'll be you and me and we'll call it 'The Girls' Club' and we won't let anybody else in." I could barely see Penny's face in the dark. I knew only that she looked toward her house.

Suddenly, lights erupted from window after window as if they were on a dynamite fuse. The back door opened. I heard voices exploding—Penny's father and her mother, who said, "—the last straw! You said you weren't going to do this again!" In the same, harsh note came a call, "Penny! Penny! Time to come in."

"I got to go," said Penny, still looking away. But the door closed and she threw me the ball. We started playing catch and no one called again for Penny until my mother telephoned to tell me to come home.

Within weeks, the Girls' Club was a thriving institution. Penny's hiding place, now our clubhouse, required a certain vigor and staunchness of purpose in the membership as the cold now reached beneath our clothing. But these qualities were as good a requirement for membership as any; better than most, in fact, since Penny and I had them in abundance.

My mother never asked what I did at Penny's. She spent all her time "managing" the household. Had she known that most of my play hours during that Jersey autumn were spent on the cold ground she might have cared, if only for the impression her carelessness left on the neighbors. I never told her.

Penny's parents seemed oblivious to us. Mrs. McCracken stared out the window while she did the dishes. She seemed to be looking directly at us, but she never smiled at us or said anything to us, anything at all. Every evening my mother dutifully telephoned and then Mrs. McCracken would open the porch door and call us. She closed the door as soon as she finished calling. She never even looked to see if I was there.

One afternoon, when I arrived, Penny's house seemed deserted. All the blinds were closed tight and the newspaper still sat on the front porch. I remember that day as if I had lived it underwater. I felt suddenly out of my element. I walked up the driveway gazing apprehensively at the silent house, but Penny was my friend, the other member of the Girls' Club, and I could not turn back.

My legs moved slowly up the walk to the front door almost as if I were treading water. I looked down and saw my feet moving, half expecting the neglected yard to sway gently and wrap grass around my helpless ankles—like an undertow—something unseen waiting to pull me down. I rang the doorbell holding my breath.

As I waited, the corner of the curtain that covered the picture window lifted and a single, solemn eye stared at me. I shivered. Nothing could keep me in these terrible waters. Here were monsters, rocketing upward through silent slime, and I wasn't ready to have them on my hook.

I heard the door open behind me but I didn't stop until I was in the street. Then I looked back. Penny stood behind the storm door. Her smooth face was crumpled and spotted with tears like paper left out in the rain. She didn't move. Neither did I.

"I'll tell my mother," I yelled before I ran home. Penny's sodden face didn't change, but she raised her hands and pressed them against the glass.

My mother would, of course, manage things. She liked to tell people what to do and Penny was too helpless to object. In only hours, she had Penny installed in our house.

My mother told my father what had happened when he came home from work. He held a newspaper in front of him but his eyes looked inward. My mother's voice verged on tremolo, like a triumphant trumpet.

"I told him that we would take her. You should have seen her. When I got there she was still standing just where Ruth said she was. Well the mother had gone, of course. Just huffed out of there with breakfast half-cooked and the daughter not even dressed. She was still in just a slip, and it was cold behind that door. I told her father we'd keep her until he gets things straightened out."

My father still didn't look at her. He looked away. I thought it strange. He seemed to look right through the dining room wall. I think now, perhaps, he looked into another life, a life where my mother—and I—did not exist.

"I don't think you should have taken her away from her father," my father said.

"Why not? He wasn't fit to take care of her. He was drunk. Drunk!"

But my father had left the room.

Now, waking up at night, I would sense Penny in the bed next to mine. If I rolled over I could see her, curled beneath the fuzzy blanket, her mouth sagging open as if muscular control had abandoned her just as her mother had. I was not especially glad to have her there, not right there in the next bed, because she took up a lot of room that I felt was mine. But I was somehow heartened by her presence. It was clear. The worst had happened. And it had happened to someone else. I shook with relief almost as much as I once shook with fear.

I still could not ignore the orange coat, but I stopped dreaming about it. I knew whenever I passed the hall closet that the coat waited inside. But it no longer waited for me, no longer waited for the right moment to weave its woolly horrors. Sometimes I forgot it was there until I had passed the closet door. Then I would turn back briefly. It still deserved notice.

"Ruth, why don't you and Penny bake some cookies?" my mother would say. Or, "Go on down to Johnny's Market with Penny and buy some good hard rolls." Or, "If you two want to play on the playground after school it's okay, but be home by five." Suddenly, my mother was filled with enthusiasm for projects, things that Penny and I could do together, things that would be fun! She wanted us mixing and stirring, walking and talking, playing and singing all the livelong day. Someone could have written folk songs about us, we were so bewilderingly busy and lively and wholesome. But the Girls' Club was a thing of the past. Its mild rebelliousness could not survive the onslaught of my mother's management.

"You know, Penny shouldn't spend too much time thinking," my mother told me.

"Why not?" I asked.

"Because she'll miss her mother if she thinks about her."

My mother thought she was smart, but I knew that Penny could do nothing but miss her mother. All the activity in the world could not distract her. It was like expecting a surgery patient to substitute a floor show for anesthesia.

One night my father came to drive Penny and me home from a Scout meeting. We climbed the front steps slowly, Penny lagging behind. Before my father even opened the door he told us, "When you go in, go right upstairs, girls." Once in the house, voices drifted out to us from the kitchen: one was my mother's staccato, one was a man's, slurred.

The man's voice rose, hurried, liquid: a stream flooding its banks. Behind me, Penny stiffened. My father said quickly, "Go on, now." And we went. But Penny's face, at the top of the stairs, was tense.

"That's my father," she said, turning back. "I've got to go." The clatter of her descending feet rang upon the treads like an urgent code. But Mr. McCracken never got the message, for my mother appeared at the bottom of the staircase.

"Stay upstairs, girls," she chirped brightly. "Mr. McCracken and I are having such a good talk. Now, you don't want to interrupt us, do you, Penny dear?"

"Is he going to take me?" Penny asked.

"Of course he will," my mother cooed. "Just not today."

Penny sat down on the step.

"Now, you don't want to leave us so soon, do you, dear? We just love having you here. So good for Ruth. Why, she was scared silly of that hall closet until you came." My mother beamed equitably at each of us. I sat down then, too.

"Girls, you just have a nice time upstairs. Get ready for bed. I'm sure your dad will come up to kiss you good night, Penny. He surely will."

Penny got up heavily. She moved upward but her eyes looked down.

My mother became more efficient. "Now, you too, Ruth. You know I can't play favorites with you girls. Get a move on. I've got things to do." And she went back to the kitchen.

I stayed where I was. I was not intentionally disobedient. I wanted the emptiness I felt. After a while I began vaguely to remember that my mother had said something dreadful about me in front of Penny. Yes, about the closet. Penny had never known that I was afraid. Now she would know that something was wrong with me, too. Just like my mother and father did.

Of course, Penny had heard nothing once my mother said that Mr. McCracken wasn't taking Penny with him. Above me the bed creaked. I knew Penny was lying there hoping that her father would come upstairs. I imagined that we shared an aching bellyful of doubt. I sat on the stairs. Gradually, the grown-up voices penetrated.

Mr. McCracken slurred his words as if he were gumming them with honey. "She'll never come back. Never, never."

"Now, you don't know that, Mr. McCracken," my mother interjected briskly.

"Never, never, never," he moaned quietly.

"She just might. Especially if you pull yourself together. You have to show her that you can manage without her. That'll snap her head around."

"Never, never," he continued, as if my mother had said nothing.

"Look at me!" My mother's words cracked like a gunshot. There was a moment's silence. "Look at me," she demanded. "You sit there and complain and complain. You don't do anything."

Mr. McCracken was roused. "It's easy for you to talk," he said. "You have a husband, a daughter." His voice wavered. "While I—"

"You think I have it easy?" she shrilled. "You think I have it easy? Be a man. Listen to what I tell you. I know how to deal with trouble. You think it hasn't come to me? Oh, yes, it has, sir. Oh, yes, it has."

Mr. McCracken floundered. "Everyone has trouble."

"I had trouble, sir," she snapped at him. "Listen to me. I *had* trouble. I don't have it anymore."

Mr. McCracken sounded befuddled. "What are you talking about? What do you—"

"I beat it," my mother said triumphantly. "I would not let it get me." Her voice was fierce.

"I didn't have it easy," she continued. "Ruth was small and Ed worked in that box factory. Then he took the night school courses. We had nothing and he was never around. And Ruth was trouble. Oh, all the time. She cried and cried. I'd be sitting in the living room with her and she'd be crying about something and the landlady would come upstairs to tell me that my little girl was crying so loud her guests could hear it. Couldn't I make her be quiet?"

My mother paused and I heard the sound of breathing. It could have been her or Mr. McCracken. It wasn't me.

"You can't imagine what it was like. I'd come from farm country to marry Ed. Left a drunk of a father and a no-account mother and I thought things were going to be better. Here I was stuck in an apartment in the city. It was a long winter and it was cold. And then this landlady"—she sniffed disdainfully—"telling me I couldn't even manage my own daughter. And all that time the kid was driving me crazy, stuck with her inside those ugly four walls."

My mother paused. I could not hear any breathing now. I sat apart from them, chilled and stiff. They were as blind to me as if I were on a cold, dark planet, entirely out of their orbit.

"The next day Ruth started to cry over nothing, over nothing again. It was some small thing she wanted and couldn't have. I just decided that I wouldn't take this anymore. So I picked her up and sat her down right outside the closet door. And then I opened the door slowly, humming, enjoying myself. Ruth looked at me. 'Mommy's going out,' I told her. 'Mommy's had enough of your crying.' Well, she wouldn't stop. She tried to get to me but I sat her back down again every time, every time. I made her watch me. I took out my coat and slid my arms into it. That coat had nice, full sleeves. I took my time putting it on and all the while I hummed and sang. 'I'm going to the movies,' I sang. 'I'm going to have myself a good time.' And then I let her get up and come over to me but she was still crying. She grabbed at my wrist but she couldn't get a hold on me; the fabric was too thick. I just ducked away and kept on singing and humming and twirling my coat out like I was dancing. 'Mommy can have a better time without you,' I told her."

"What happened?" Mr. McCracken asked. His words sounded stuck, like he didn't want to know but had to ask.

"Well, I never had trouble with Ruth's crying again," my mother said. "She got all her crying out that day, I can tell you that."

There was a silence. Then the sound of chairs moving.

I stood up stiffly, like a piece of cardboard unfolding. I hurried up the stairs and got silently into bed. I could hear Penny breathing.

"Is he gone?" she asked me.

"I don't know," I said.

Penny's father didn't come up the stairs to kiss her that night. But he came back the next week. He'd hired a neighbor lady to watch Penny while he worked. "It'll be better for her to be in her own house," he said. "Missing her mother is enough. She doesn't need to miss her own house, too." He thanked my mother many times for all her help. But he didn't linger. And when she suggested that Penny could come to us after school sometimes, he smiled and nodded but ushered Penny quickly out the door.

My mother thinks it was her example that helped Mr. McCracken to "get himself together." Maybe she is right. But I never saw my friend outside of school again, and in a year, Mr. McCracken remarried and took his new wife and Penny to live in Pennsylvania.

It was many years before I could remember what my mother said while I was sitting on the steps listening to her and Mr. McCracken. I had learned never to remember as I had learned never to cry.

Sometimes, though, I dream about Penny. She is swimming toward me through a beautiful green sea where neither of us has any trouble breathing. But, when we reach land, the dunes rise up fantastically and smother me while she looks sadly on. As I fall backward, out of the corner of my eye I see the orange coat. It rises and wraps itself around me. It holds me firmly as the dune envelops me. In my dream, I can do nothing. But I do not cry.

Questions for Discussion

1. How are Penny and Ruth abandoned? What are the differences? What is similar?
2. The orange coat symbolizes abandonment to Ruth. Why do you think Ruth projected her fear of being left onto the coat rather than her mother? How do you think she felt when she found out the truth?
3. If you were to see Ruth and her mother in counseling because of a generalized fearfulness that Ruth has developed, how would you approach the issue? What questions would you ask?

Wanderer

Pamela Di Pesa

My father was restless. Itchy feet, wanderlust, spring fever—he suffered from them all. Strangely, he built houses for a while, as if he could settle himself by putting up structures of wood or brick, as if the rootedness of houses would somehow seep into him. His houses didn't do well—the people who bought them were displeased, and he was always running out to fix a leaking roof or flooded basement. It was the subcontractors' fault, he always said. He paid people for quality work, but they took shortcuts, using cheaper materials than he'd specified, charging him for longer hours than they worked. When one of the houses he'd built didn't sell, we'd move into it.

We moved six times before I was twelve. According to Mom, we always moved in a hurry, spurred by one financial crisis or another. And each time, Mom sold or gave away something she would later wish for—an old chest of drawers, an armchair, a rug that didn't fit the dimensions of the new house. Years later, she would lament these losses. "Why didn't I keep that rug?" she'd ask. "We could have used it now. But I was frantic with moving, with packing and unpacking every couple of years." She kept a box labeled "Necessities," where she'd pack the coffee pot and cups, cereal bowls, juice glasses, a few plates, and some flatware. On the morning of the move, she'd place a carton of eggs, a loaf of bread, some toilet paper, and our toothbrushes on top. That evening, we'd eat scrambled eggs and toast for supper, sitting at the kitchen table with boxes piled all around us. Mom would fall into an exhausted silence, Diane and I would chew glumly, and Dad would try to cheer us all up. "Girls, did you notice that brook across the street?" Or, "The family next door has two kids, and they've got a swing set. I'll take you over to meet them in the morning."

Eventually, Dad's construction business came to an end when a big developer swept through Massachusetts, putting up hundreds of identical tract houses. "People don't want quality," Dad would moan. "They're paying good money for a cardboard box with no basement." Every time we passed a road sign for a Harold Kenner development, Diane and I booed. Dad would turn to us in the backseat and ask, "What are those houses?" And Diane and I would always answer, "J-U-N-K, JUNK, JUNK, JUNK!" Dad would nod approvingly and predict that the next hurricane (we were getting one or two every fall, back then) would reduce the Kenner tracts to a pile of sticks.

But Kenner prospered and Dad had to turn to Sears for employment. After a few months of selling washers and dryers, he was unhappy. Not because he didn't like sales—Dad loved to sell people things. But after a while, he'd proved he could sell appliances to up-and-coming couples (probably the kinds of people who were moving into the Kenner developments), and he needed a new challenge. Jobs didn't excite Dad's imagination; schemes did. Investing in racetracks, becoming partners with someone who'd invented a new kind of can opener, buying filled-in swampland in Florida—these things swept him up. He made phone calls, paid visits, wrote out projections and plans, all in hopes of discovering something that would catapult him out of everyday life and into a world of wealth and prestige. When his schemes didn't work, he became depressed and drank.

I wondered where Dad did his drinking. Mom said he went to "flophouses." I hated that word: it made me think of a fish flopping about on the deck of a boat, blood oozing from the point where the hook had gone in.

Once I asked Mom why Dad drank so much. "God only knows," she said. "All I know is, he got started early." She told me how Dad, at the age of nine, had started working at night clearing tables in his uncle's restaurant. I imagined him moving down the aisles, stacking dishes on a large tray, and carrying the heavy tray back to the kitchen. Back and forth, back and forth, with little thanks from his uncle for what he was doing. After a while, he became curious about the wine pooled in the bottom of the glasses. He tried a little. At first it stung his throat, but then a warmth radiated through his neck and chest. The more he drank, the better he felt. Swallowing the wine for him must have been like licking an ice cream cone for me: it brought pleasure, comfort, even bliss, for a moment. I made a cone last as long as I could—half an hour was my record—because when it was gone, the world returned to its usual state. I could imagine how Dad must have felt when the glow of the wine faded, and all around him were empty seats and dirty dishes.

At some point whiskey replaced wine as Dad's drink. Wine seemed gentle and romantic: once I'd seen a picture in *National Geographic* of a couple eating lunch on a sunlit terrace overlooking the Mediterranean, raising their glasses of wine to each other. But when Mom said "whiskey," it sounded like the cold North, like a chilly wind blowing across gray rocks. Wine was to be savored and drunk with someone else, but whiskey was drunk quickly and alone.

Drink made Dad disappear. He disappeared for days, weeks, even months at a time. Often he chose the spring, when both Diane and I were born, for his major excursions. Mom, hoping to comfort us, would say, "Your father loves you. He just can't handle responsibility." Back then, I envisioned responsibility as a large metal box with razor-sharp edges—something Dad tried to hold on to but couldn't because the metal cut his hands.

When I was about to turn eight, Dad was still around. He assured me he would be at my birthday party. I was excited thinking about the role he would play: putting the blindfold on us and spinning us around when we played Pin the Tail on the Donkey, taking pictures of all the presents I would get, smiling proudly at me when I blew out all the candles on the cake.

The day got off to a bad start when I woke up to the sound of rain. Diane was already downstairs watching the Saturday morning cartoons. I pulled the sheet over my head, hoping the rain would stop if I waited long enough. Eventually Dad came upstairs to wake me. "It's raining, it's pouring," he sang, drumming his fingers on my back.

"Stop it," I said.

Dad picked up my doll, Rudy, and made him dance on my bottom. "Hey, Amy," Rudy jabbered, "did you know rain is good luck?"

I crawled out from under the sheet. "Is it really?"

Rudy's head bobbed emphatically. "Would I lie to you?"

I sat up and smiled. Rudy had been my favorite doll ever since Dad had bought him for me at the circus. He was dressed in a baggy orange and blue clown suit with a stiff ruffle at his neck. The real Rudy had made me laugh when he zoomed around on the sawdust in a miniature yellow car, honking his red nose. He was famous, Dad said, because he had recently defected from Czechoslovakia. "What's defected?" I'd asked.

"Oh," he'd replied absently, "it's when somebody leaves their country to be free."

Dad sat with me, smoking a cigarette, while I ate my bowl of cornflakes. Mom was busy making my birthday cake, three layers with chocolate frosting, as I'd requested. When I finished, Dad told me to go upstairs and get dressed. He had to go downtown to check on a business deal, he said. "Don't forget the party," I reminded him. "It starts at twelve o'clock."

"Don't worry," Dad reassured me. "I'll be back way before that."

One-thirty came and he hadn't returned. We'd played all the games and I'd opened all my presents. Mom wanted to bring out the cake. "Not yet," I said. "I want Dad to see me blow out the candles."

She looked at her watch. "It's now or never. The party's going to be over soon."

She brought out the cake with its eight yellow candles sputtering on top. Everyone sang. Diane's voice, high and slightly off-key, scraped the air.

"Now make a wish and blow out the candles," Mom said.

I took a huge breath; I had to blow out all eight or my wish wouldn't come true. I wish Dad would come back, I said to myself as I snuffed out the flames.

He returned at 9 p.m., when Diane was asleep and I was in the bath. "Thank God," Mom said, running downstairs.

I got out of the tub and listened at the door, shivering.

"Not fair . . . "

"Told you, I couldn't . . . "

"Drinking, I can smell it . . . "

I climbed back into the bath just before Dad appeared in the door. He was holding a pair of roller skates with a red ribbon around them. I'd been eyeing them for a couple of weeks at Randall's.

Mom pressed in beside him. "Wait until morning," she said.

His hand shaking, Dad held out the skates.

Mom pulled him back. "Dad's not feeling well, Amy." She steered him down the hall and into the bedroom.

I slid down into the tub and let the water cover my face, just for a minute, to see what it felt like to be totally submerged.

* * *

A few nights later, their loud voices woke me up. I could tell they were arguing about Florida. Dad had met someone who wanted him to invest in a housing development in an up-and-coming area outside Miami. He'd shown me the drawings of long, flat houses with flowering bushes flanking their front doors. "Why don't they have any roofs?" I'd asked.

"That's the way they build them down there," he'd said dreamily, as if the lack of a roof somehow made a house fanciful and carefree. Mom, however, had looked at the brochure and pronounced the houses to be cheap boxes. "And in a few years, they'll sink into the swamp you want to build them on." Dad had added another spoonful of sugar to his coffee and stirred it silently.

Now they were shouting at each other in the next room. Mom told Dad this was just another cockeyed scheme, and she didn't want to have anything to do with it. Dad said she lacked imagination, and if she'd just loosen up, she'd see what a great opportunity it was. "We could all be rich in a couple of years," he said.

"You're deluding yourself," she said. "But I'm not going to let you do a con job on me. Not anymore."

That phrase, "con job," made me wince. Mom had used it once before, when I'd asked her how she and Dad had decided to get married. "He did a con job on me," Mom had said. "He turned on the charm. What did I know? I was an innocent young girl. Or maybe stupid would be a better word." She'd gone on to explain that only after they were married did she find out that Dad didn't have a steady job, that he was eight years older than he had said, and that he had four children from an earlier marriage. "Four children?" I'd gasped. "Where are they?"

"Oh, they're all grown up now," Mom had said. "They live somewhere around here. Except for his oldest son, Mark—I think he lives in Florida."

I'd been so distressed by that news that I'd told Diane about it. "How could Dad have children who are grown-ups?" she'd asked. "It doesn't make any sense."

"Never mind," I'd said. The knowledge of Dad's previous family gave me a strange self-conscious feeling, and I had a harder time taking a deep breath from then on, as if those four oversized children were stuck in my chest.

Now, listening to him try to persuade Mom to move to Florida, I had a chilling thought: Was Dad's son in Miami? Was he part of the reason Dad wanted so badly to be there?

Suddenly I heard a loud thump from their room, followed by silence. Had one of them hit the other? Was someone hurt? I thought of getting out of bed to look. Diane was still sleeping, but her forehead was wrinkled, as if she somehow knew what was going on. She always slept through their arguments. It was unfair, I thought, that I had to be awake and listening to all this. I decided to stay where I was and pulled the blanket over my head. Later—I don't know how much later because I'd fallen asleep—I heard the scrape of the garage door going up, and the angry cough of Dad's car starting. This isn't really happening, I told myself. In the morning I'll find out it was just a bad dream.

But in the morning an after-the-bomb silence announced he was gone. When I went down to the kitchen, Mom slammed a cereal bowl and a box of Frosted Flakes in front of me. A note in Dad's handwriting was sitting on the table. I picked it up gingerly and read it while Mom was at the sink, noisily washing pots. "Am heading for Florida," it said. "Will contact you when I get settled." I pushed the note away. "Contact" was a strange word for Dad to have used: it sounded as if we were his business acquaintances instead of his family. Suddenly, I had a terrible headache, and the sight of the cereal made me nauseous. Just then, Diane came in and looked around the kitchen. "Where's Dad?" she asked.

Mom turned around at the sink. "He's gone to Florida."

"Florida!" said Diane. "What did he do that for?"

"Another one of his get-rich-quick schemes," Mom snapped.

"When's he coming back?" asked Diane.

"Eat some cereal," Mom said. "You'll be late for school."

I shoved my bowl toward Diane, who listlessly poured a few flakes into it.

On the way to school, I let Diane get ahead of me. I stared at her blue pants and red jacket as if I'd never seen them before. Her arms stuck out from her sides in their stiff sleeves; a brown paper bag dangled aimlessly from one hand. When she got to the corner, she waited for me. Crossing the street silently, I wondered where Dad was at this point. How long did it take to get out of Massachusetts? The autumn air was sharp against my ears, and my head felt like a giant aching globe teetering on my brittle shoulders. I walked Diane to the first-grade classroom and went upstairs to my room.

That day we practiced capital letters. I took great care to make each one exactly like the one before, slanted at precisely the right angle, and rigidly contained within the blue lines. Miss Bates came around, inspected my page of imprisoned letters, and gave me an A.

At recess I stayed seated while the other children rushed to the door. Miss Bates came over to me and asked, "What's wrong?"

"My parents had a fight last night," I whispered. "My father's gone."

She put her arm around my shoulders. "These things happen. I'm sure it will be all right when you get home. I bet your father will be back." When I didn't answer, she said, "Go on out, now, dear." I got my coat from the hook and slowly opened the door onto the noisy swarm of the playground, where the boys carelessly chased the girls, and the girls ran, hoping to be caught.

When Diane and I got home that afternoon, Mom was dusting the living room. "Thought I'd straighten this place up," she said. As she wiped under lamps and ashtrays and polished the end tables, she seemed energetic, almost cheerful. I hung up my coat and asked Mom if I could help. "You can empty the ashtrays into this bag," she said.

Carefully, I emptied the cigarette butts from three ashtrays. The butts, crumpled in messy heaps, had a stale, sour smell, something like the smell of Dad's yellowed fingertips. Smoking was a filthy habit, Mom said. And yet, it was so much a part of Dad: tapping the pack of Lucky Strikes against his palm to loosen a cigarette, pulling out his monogrammed lighter, smiling and sitting back when he took the first puff, picking a stray piece of tobacco from his lips. He liked to blow long strings of perfectly formed smoke rings to amuse me. I would laugh and try to hook them with my finger as they slowly twisted and stretched themselves out of shape.

"Do you think Dad is coming back?" I asked Mom.

"I don't know," she said.

"I think he might come back soon. Miss Bates said so."

"What!" Mom dropped her dust rag and gaped at me. "You talked to her about this?"

"Well . . . a little."

"What did you tell her?" Mom was looming over me.

"I just said you two had a fight last night, that's all."

"That's all!" Mom shouted. "Are you crazy, telling a stranger about our problems?"

"She's my teacher, not a stranger," I said in a low voice.

"Don't you ever do that again!" Mom grabbed my arm and squeezed. "That's family business. You don't ever talk about that to outsiders. Do you understand?"

I nodded.

"Give me that," she said, grabbing the bag of ashes from my hand. "I don't need your help."

*   *   *

Three weeks after Christmas, a crate of oranges arrived. Sent to you from Sunny Florida, it said on the side. We pried it open in the kitchen. "Wow," I said, picking up an orange. "These are huge."

"Are those oranges?" Diane asked. "I thought they were grapefruits."

A week later, Mom got a letter from Dad with a check enclosed. "A hundred dollars," she said. "How long is that supposed to last?"

"Can I read the letter?" I asked. Mom handed it over and I read it aloud. "I've got some good deals going," Dad wrote. "And a nice apartment only four blocks from the beach. Tell the girls they can swim in the middle of winter! Please come down. I want us all to be together."

"Can we go?" I asked Mom. In school, I often stared at Florida on the map, a fat pink finger of land beckoning me southward. If I closed my eyes, I could see the palm trees lining the streets of Miami, the abundant groves of oranges and lemons, the gentle ocean. For the moment, I forgave Dad his comings and goings. The thought of his son, Mark, was a bothersome little blotch on my mental picture, but I pushed it from my mind. The main thing was that Dad was asking me, Diane, and Mom to join him.

"We can't go down there," Mom said. "Your father's all excited because he's made a little money. But the crash will come. And then what? At least here we have—"

"What?" I asked. "What do we have here?"

Mom sighed. "A house we're used to. A school close by for you and Diane."

"But I could go to a new school. It would be fun."

"No," said Mom. "We just can't go down there. You'll understand when you're older."

"No, I won't," I said. I went to my room and lay down on the bed. Staring at the ceiling, I resolved never to understand Mom, no matter how old I got.

*   *   *

We didn't hear from Dad again for a long time, except for a few checks he sent. Mom took a part-time job at Klein's Bakery downtown, and we had all the doughnuts and blueberry muffins we could eat. I liked the white boxes she brought them home in, tied up neatly with blue-and-white string.

I began to get used to the house with just the three of us in it; things were more predictable. But at night, I missed Dad. He had been the one to tell me and Diane bedtime stories—long, preposterous inventions about a family of monkeys who rode the buses in Boston, and mysterious goings-on at a country inn named the Pig and Whistle. Dad could sit for half an hour spinning his stories, amusing himself as much as he amused me and Diane. When he turned the lights out, I fell asleep smiling. Now, with him gone, I tossed in my bed, trying to get comfortable. "Stop making so much noise," Diane would say. "I can't sleep."

One evening in early summer, when I went into the kitchen to get some milk, I saw his grinning face in the window. I dropped the glass. I hadn't seen him in over a year and a half. All I could do was watch the milk spread out on the linoleum.

"Aren't you going to let me in?" he called.

I stepped around the broken glass and opened the door.

"You scared me," I said.

His face fell. "I thought you'd be glad to see me."

I wasn't sure how I felt. I just started wiping up the milk.

"Tell your mother I'm here," Dad said.

"What?" she said when I told her. "Are you serious?"

"Dad's here?" Diane took off for the kitchen.

When we went in, Diane was hugging Dad and he was messing up her hair.

"What are you doing here?" Mom said.

Dad took off his hat and shook his head. "Is this the kind of welcome I get from my own family? I came up to tell you how well I'm doing. Look at that car out there."

In front of the house was a huge white Cadillac convertible.

"Oh, sure," said Mom. "You want me to believe that's your car?"

Dad looked hurt. "I want to take you all for a ride. How about an ice cream sundae?"

Diane and I looked at Mom. "Can we?" I asked.

"You can go if you want," she said. "Not me."

"But Lydia, I really want you to come."

"No," she said. "I don't need any more sweet talking. Things have been nice and peaceful since you left."

"Come on," he said. "How often do you get to ride in a Caddie like this?"

"I can live without it," Mom replied.

"Then the girls and I will have fun," Dad said.

We all sat in the huge front seat, and as Dad maneuvered the car down the street, I could see heads turning.

"Do you like the car, Amy?" Dad asked.

I nodded and stretched out my arms to the wind. Dad was really back, and for a moment I didn't think about how long he'd been gone, or how long he'd be staying.

He took us to the Redwood, a dusty little restaurant that nevertheless made great sundaes. While we were waiting for our ice cream, Dad took out his cigarettes and lit up. I thought about how I'd missed the smell of his smoke, how it used to permeate every corner of the house, how I could smell it even on my blouses and sweaters.

"So," he said, smiling brightly at me and Diane, "How have you been?"

"Fine," we both answered.

"And your mother?"

"She's been fine, too," I said.

"Does she miss me?" Dad asked.

The waitress came with our orders. I lifted up my maraschino cherry and dropped it onto Diane's sundae; she was very fond of them, and I wasn't. Then I scooped up a spoonful of chocolate chip ice cream, making sure to catch up some hot fudge sauce and whipped cream. "Mmmm," I said.

"About your mother," Dad continued, "I really want you girls to talk to her. Tell her I want us all to be together in Florida. It's a good life down there. Amy, are you listening?"

"Do you really own that car?" I asked.

Dad sighed, exasperated. "I'm trying to get something across to you here. Tell your mother she'd like it in Florida. She won't listen to me, but maybe she'll listen to you."

I swirled the melting ice cream around in the sauce. "I tried talking to her before," I said. "A long time ago. It didn't work."

"What do you mean?" Dad asked.

"After you sent the oranges," I said. "I asked her if we could move to Florida. But she didn't want to go."

"Maybe she'll want to now," Diane said. "Are you making a lot of money, Dad?"

He patted her hand. "Oh, lots. I'm selling houses like hotcakes."

I looked at his face. His right eye was twitching, as if a tiny restless insect were trapped under the skin.

Dad saw me watching him. "Talk to your mother again, okay? I'm counting on you."

Suddenly I realized I'd had too much of the sundae. I pushed the dish away. Dad waited for me to answer him, and when I didn't, he called to the waitress for the check.

None of us talked on the way home. Mom had given me a key so I could let myself and Diane in when Dad dropped us off. We stood in the doorway and waved as he walked back to the car. He sat for a minute and lit up a cigarette. Then, waving to us once, drove away.

Questions for Discussion

1. What does Amy's father provide for her that is lost when he leaves for Florida?
2. What does Amy understand as a result of her father's visit home from Florida?
3. What spoken and/or unspoken rules operate in this family?

Learning

Nancy Hewitt

Mr. Boyer was right on time when he knocked on the trailer door. I knew he would be. I could always count on him to do what he said he would.

Mom stubbed out her cigarette and got up from her chair at the kitchen window, where she always sat when she was waiting for Dad. She was wearing the blue dress that she wore when we went to town, the one that she told me brought out the blue in her eyes. She smoothed down her dress and gave me a look. "He's here," she said. We didn't often have company, and she looked nervous as she opened the door.

"Hello there Mrs. Miller. I'm Phil Boyer, Jimmy's teacher. I believe we met last fall at the school. Thanks for allowing me to come over tonight."

Mom smiled her for-company smile. "Jimmy talks about you a lot—you must be his favorite teacher." She stepped back as Mr. Boyer came in with his briefcase. The smell of his aftershave followed him. It wasn't a spicy smell like Dad's, but silky instead. This was a Tuesday—Dad only wore aftershave on weekends, and then only when he went into town. Never around just Mom and me.

Mr. Boyer smiled his big smile. "Well, I really like teaching. Guess it just comes naturally to me." He swung his briefcase onto our kitchen table and held me by the shoulders, a greeting somewhere between a hug and a handshake. I was glad he knew I was too old for a hug, but I wished he'd known I was old enough for a handshake.

"How are you tonight, Jimmy?" He had the best-looking crewcut of anybody I knew. The overhead light made his hair a shiny blond, like he'd been outside in the sun for a long time, or like he came from California.

"Fine, Mr. Boyer." I thought I should be polite, since this visit was almost a social situation.

"What's the matter, kiddo? Cat got your tongue?" His grin got even wider. "You know, Mrs. Miller, I really enjoy having Jimmy in my class. He's a little high-spirited at times, as we've discussed, but everyone likes him, and he adds a lot of energy to the class. I think with a little more tutoring in science, he'll come through this year just fine. And the *World Book Encyclopedia,* of course, will help him now and for years to come. Not that I'm prejudiced, or anything." He laughed as he patted his briefcase, the same way I patted Joey's new puppy.

Mom looked even more nervous. "Wellll . . . yessss." She stretched out her words like that when she felt out of place, or when she was afraid she'd say the wrong thing. She sat down at the table first, then Mr. Boyer, then me. "I don't know much about it." She smiled at Mr. Boyer, catching his eyes with her own bluest blue eyes. He smiled back at her, a quieter smile than usual, and his eyes stayed hooked into hers.

Mom had smoothed things over again, made it so that Mr. Boyer didn't care that she didn't know about the *World Book*. Mom was good at smoothing things over. It happened a lot, especially with men who would talk to us on the bus or at the grocery store on Saturdays, when Mom made me go with her because Dad wouldn't. I'd never seen her do it with somebody I knew, though. Usually that smile made me feel that things were going to be OK. This time, I wasn't sure.

Something in Mr. Boyer's face was different. He cleared his throat, cupped his hand around his mouth. "Well, here, let me show you what I've brought. I don't want to take up too much of your time. Will your husband be joining us?" He glanced quickly around the trailer, taking in the kitchen and living room and nodding toward the hallway that led to the two bedrooms.

"He's working late tonight—he's in construction, and they have to make use of all the daylight they have. You know how it is." Mom spoke slowly and carefully, so she wouldn't make a mistake. "But he should be home any minute now." Her hands were gripped together in her lap, like she was praying, where I could see them but Mr. Boyer couldn't.

"Sure. Let's get started, and maybe he'll be here soon. Now, I'm sure you've heard about the *World Book*. It's the best encyclopedia around. I've sold it to a lot of parents of Jimmy's classmates, and they all rave about it. I wouldn't sell something I didn't believe in."

Mom tried to look interested. "Ummh." She stared at me, trying to pull me into their conversation. She counted on me at times like this, when she didn't know what she thought she should know.

Mr. Boyer opened his briefcase and took out a book. He tapped one finger on the shiny red cover, then held it up for us to see. "You'd have a whole set of these handsome books to display," he said, his eyes flicking around the trailer but not lighting on a likely display spot. We didn't have much extra space.

I reached for the book, which said, in navy blue lettering sunk into the cover, "A-B." Mom stood up to look over my shoulder as I flipped through the pages. Mr. Boyer asked me, "What do you think of it?"

I looked at all the printed words in front of me, wondering why I would ever need to know about Antarctica or the aurora borealis. But to my teacher I said, "Nice book."

"You're pretty quiet tonight, son," he said. "Guess you used up all your talking in school today, eh?" He laughed, then leaned toward me, his elbow swinging out toward mine, like we had some kind of secret. Before then, I'd seen that happen only between grown men.

Headlights flashed in, then out, of the kitchen window. Dad was home. I knew without looking at her that Mom's looks had changed. When Dad came home this late, she had a way of looking happy and upset at the same time.

The door swung open, and Dad came in, grinning from ear to ear. "Looks like we have comp'ny." The smell of beer started to fill the room. Dad swayed too close to Mr. Boyer, then laughed that laugh which I knew would turn nasty before too long.

"I guess you forgot that Jimmy's teacher was coming over tonight, Harry," Mom said. Each word had the same weight as the one before it.

"What're you all dressed up for?" he asked. He was starting to sound nasty already.

Mr. Boyer stood up and stretched out his arm for a handshake. "Hi there, Mr. Miller. Nice to meet you." He dropped his arm when he saw that Mom and Dad were staring at each other and didn't even see him. It was the kind of look that I knew meant trouble as soon as Mr. Boyer left.

I coughed. Mr. Boyer got the hint.

"Sir, I was hoping to interest you and your wife in a set of encyclopedias. The *World Book* has helped many of my students." His voice had a question in it.

"You think there's some hope for this kid of mine?" Dad said, each word running into the next.

The next sound I heard was Mr. Boyer coughing. I felt his eyes fixed on me, but I was concentrating too hard on my reading to look up. To myself I read, "The aurora borealis is a luminous phenomenon that consists of arches of light in the sky at night. . . ." I was getting an idea for my next science project. Mr. Boyer would like that.

Questions for Discussion

1. How does the father's alcoholism affect this family's functioning? Specifically address the following: the mother's role, the marital relationship, and Jimmy's role.
2. What is your impression of Jimmy, specifically, his coping mechanism(s) and his strengths?
3. What might your approach be if you were seeing Jimmy in counseling? If you were seeing the whole family, how would you approach the problem of the father's alcoholism?

Mother's Savage Wait

Nancy Hewitt

Was the headline I read
in the Arts section lying
open on the kitchen table?
On closer inspection
it read "Moliere's
Savage Wit" but then
I began to wonder
what *was* savage
about mother's wait.

Was it the way she hunched
by the window, pulling
long drags from cigarettes,
then releasing the smoke
reluctantly as though her life
depended on it?
Or was it the screams
she pierced him with when
he finally arrived?

Or maybe he, under
the silken slurred words,
was really the savage.
But in the end the savage
wait and the savage
and the one who waits
become the same

and the child who must also wait
in the fog of mother's smoke
is sucked up in the cyclone
of the wait and disappears
perfectly
from sight.

Somebody Else's Making

Nancy Hewitt

The neighbor would drive my mother to the bars
where my father might be.   I was too young
to leave at home alone.   She took me with her
huddled in the backseat of the neighbor's car
while they searched the parking lots
the dark   the neon signs   the deadly quiet.
When she left me to find him in the smoky bar,
it was always cold and no lights in the car.
The neighbor didn't talk to me.
My stomach churned,   the cold vinyl seat
against my legs   my pale face   the curls
of cigarette smoke from the neighbor
at the wheel   my hands hugging something
a teddy bear   the car seat   or my own body in the quiet.
I might as well have been on another planet
as to be in this still dark room
of somebody else's making.

Questions for Discussion

1. What is the child's experience in these two poems? What might she be feeling?
2. Speculate about how these experiences, repeated over time during her childhood, could impact her life as an adult, especially her relationships with others.

A Father's Love

Linda A. Lavid

My earliest memory was at the kitchen table, in the morning, while I made Rice Krispies. I had to stand on the chair to pour the milk, partly missing the bowl, and when I sat back down, puddles of milk and cereal dotted the table from the overflow. Between mouthfuls, I blew on the scattered rice that looked like tiny boats sailing away. With my finger, I connected the puddles, making rivers, and when the spilt milk was too thin to spread, I'd spoon some extra from my bowl.

Dad appeared at the back door. At first, I thought, he was going to holler, but he grinned, lifting me high off the chair. "How's my little queenie," he said. He carried me to the living room, sat me on his lap and kissed my forehead, scratching my cheek with his prickly chin. After awhile I wanted to get up. Daisy was crying in another room. He didn't seem to notice, and with his arms locked around me, he said, "Daddy's got to sleep."

There were many times he didn't come home at night and we were left alone. Every morning, before going downstairs, I'd peek in his room to see if there was a mountain in his bed. It wasn't a problem though, because I knew how to take care of Daisy.

Then one night I woke up to a loud noise. At first I thought it was thunder. I curled up along the wall on the far side of the bed with a blanket nearly covering my head and waited for a flash of lightning. Instead, another sound pounded the walls, shook the room. It came from under me somewhere. I jumped up and bolted to the window. That's when I saw the shadows of two men throwing themselves against the back door. I got scared like never before. I ran shrieking to Dad's room and threw myself into his half-opened bedroom door. I blinked once, twice, wishing away what I saw—the bed was flat.

The house shook again with a loud cracking noise. I rushed into Daisy's room, gathered her the best I could, and dashed up the attic stairs.

I stood on the top landing, stuck, afraid to move. Daisy whimpered. I covered her mouth with my hand. I couldn't hear any more thuds and for a second I thought everything was over. But heavy footsteps and gruff, low voices echoed up the stairwell. They were in the house.

"We're going to play hide-and-seek," I whispered to Daisy. She looked at me wide-eyed. My heart pounded, but I knew I was good at this game, in fact, the best—one time I hid in a wastepaper basket with sheets on top of me.

The attic was dark. Still, I could tell from the outlines of things that on the other side of some boxes, two mattresses leaned against the wall. It was a perfect spot. I slid sideways between the cartons and jammed my shoulder into the middle seam. It separated. I held Daisy tight while I tucked in backward, pushing as hard as I could with my feet until total blackness and padding wrapped around us. Once inside, we collapsed to the floor, crunched up. I put my finger to my mouth with a "Shhh."

They were on the second floor now. Something crashed. A few seconds later, footsteps, the loudest I had ever heard, trampled up the attic stairs. Suddenly it became very quiet. A flash of light sparked by the tiny opening we had just made.

"Junk," a man said.

"This whole place is junk. Let's get outta here," said another, and they charged back down. The attic door slammed.

The next thing I heard was Dad screaming my name. A triangle of sunlight filtered in between the mattresses. "Here we are!" I yelled. But my voice was swallowed up by the thick padded walls. I shoved Daisy in front of me, forcing her ahead. Dad called me again, but he was sounding farther away. Desperate he would leave, I pushed Daisy so hard she popped out, falling flat-faced onto the attic floor. I clawed over her and sped down the stairs.

When Dad saw me, he ran and scooped me up, lifting me as high as I had ever been. He spun me around so fast my legs flew behind me. I crisscrossed my arms around his neck and closed my eyes tight. "Where's Daisy?" he asked. But I wouldn't let go. He asked me again and we tore up to the attic.

The police came with sirens blaring. Dad said we were all asleep when it happened. He told me he had to say that so he wouldn't go to jail. Later, after they had gone, he said I was very brave, the best daughter he could have asked for, and promised he would never leave us alone again. He carried us around all day. It was better than being on any ride, especially when we went up and down the stairs.

When they came to fix the door, they put in a metal one with screws as long as my middle finger. Still, it didn't seem enough to stop someone from breaking in.

After that Daisy and I went to sleep in his room and he slept on the couch—just in case. This went on for a while until Daisy wet the bed. Eventually, we ended up in our own rooms and things got back to normal.

I helped around the house the best I could. Dad taught me how to scramble eggs, make toast. I learned to set the table and pour beer without spilling any. When he had his friends over to play cards, I'd make sure the bowls were filled with potato chips and I'd take away the empty bottles and get cold ones from the fridge. It was fun, especially when they'd wink at me and give me quarters.

Back then I never mouthed off because I knew it was hard for him raising two girls. I tried to get excited with him about sports, but I wasn't very good at it.

Once we went to a hockey game but Daisy threw up after she ate a hot dog. We even tried fishing down by the river, except Daisy would scream over the worms, get tangled up in the line. He didn't have the patience for our outings. Under his breath he'd swear. But they were just words and I got used to them.

I don't remember us doing too much together except being together. Kids would talk about trips they'd taken with their parents or going for rides in the country. We just stayed home. But that was fine for us. Soon, I forgot about the robbery and stopped worrying that it would happen again. In a way, I thought, the whole thing was a blessing.

Then one night for dinner Dad made us noodles with green specks in them. Daisy never liked different foods to touch, and she especially didn't like her food all mixed up.

At first, Daisy tried to scrape the flecks away with her fork but they wouldn't come off. Dad told her to cut it out but she didn't listen. Instead she started to pinch out the spots with her fingers. Her hands got all gummy and when she picked up her fork, it slipped to the floor. He yelled, "Eat it!" but she shook her head and said, "No." He reached over to her plate, grabbed it, and flung it against the wall. The dish shattered but the food stuck to the wall like a clump of dangling white worms and I laughed. Snatching my plate away, he said, "So you think this is funny!" and he hurled it toward the sink. It cracked the kitchen window. He then stood up, lifting the corners of the kitchen table. Glasses tipped and tumbled, milk spilled, silverware crashed to the floor. "Get out of here!" he roared.

We ran into the living room, and that's when we heard it—"I'm leaving you kids," he said. "Tonight!"

Daisy started to cry and asked if he was going away again. I told her no, that he was just talking. But I said that to make her feel better.

Suddenly he kicked open the kitchen door and ripped toward us, red-faced. "Didn't I tell you to get out!" Daisy gasped for air and I froze, not sure what to do, where to go. He lunged at us and, twisting both our arms, threw us toward the stairs. "Go to your rooms!"

I helped Daisy with her pajamas and told her everything would be all right in the morning. Then I went to my room and sat on the bed listening for sounds from downstairs. I couldn't hear anything so I crept into the hall. I still couldn't hear anything. Slowly, I inched down the steps until the rush of running water became clear. I crouched down on a stair near the wall where he wouldn't be able to see, and listened to the clatter of dishes. After a while he came into the living room and turned on the TV. I slipped back to my room, and before going to bed, I opened my window so I could hear if the car was being taken out of the garage. Then I got into bed and fell asleep.

In the middle of the night I woke up. Dad was in my bed with his arm around me. Stroking my hair, he told me that he was sorry for what happened earlier and that he loved me. I told him I loved him too. He stayed there for a long time, rubbing my leg and being close to me. I smelled beer on his breath and, soon, I fell back asleep. In the morning, he was gone.

The next day when I went downstairs, he and Daisy were talking and laughing. He kidded me about being a sleepyhead. I sat down and had some toast. It was a spring morning. We finished breakfast, grabbed our lunches, and headed out the door. He kissed Daisy and she skipped out in front of me. He then told me he acted silly the night before. I said it was okay.

As I left the kitchen, he slid his hand from my waist to my backside and gave me a pat. I turned around and looked at him—he had never done that before. He smiled. I waved good-bye.

After that things changed between us. He would come to my room every so often and lie down beside me. It was usually after I was already asleep. When I was too young to realize, he made funny noises and would rock in the bed. It didn't bother me all that much, I suppose. Besides, anything was better than to have him leave us.

Now when I think back to when it started, it was more like a dream than anything else.

Questions for Discussion

1. What factors put this father at risk for child sexual abuse?
2. What is the narrator's role in this family?
3. If, for some reason, this family was referred for counseling, do you think the sexual abuse would come out? On the basis of what you know from this story, what would cause you to entertain this as a possibility? Without knowing about the abuse, what family problems would you want to treat?

Lisa's Ritual, Age Ten

Grace Caroline Bridges

Afterwards when he has finished
lots of mouthwash helps
to get rid of her father's cigarette taste.
She runs a hot bath
    to soak away the pain
        Like red dye leaking from her
           School dress in the washtub

She doesn't cry
When the bathwater cools, she adds more hot.
She brushes her teeth for a long time.

Then she finds the corner of her room.
curls against it. There the wall is
hard and smooth
as a teacher's new chalk, white
as a clean bedsheet. Smells
fresh. Isn't sweaty, hairy, doesn't stick
to the skin. Doesn't hurt much
when she presses her small backbone
into it. The wall is steady
while she falls   away:

    first the hands   lost
arms dissolving   feet gone
    the legs   dis- jointed
      body cracking down
        the center like a fault
       she falls inside
          slides down like dust
          like kitchen dirt
            slips off the dustpan into
            noplace

    a place where

nothing happens
nothing ever happened.

When she feels the cool
Wall against her cheek
she doesn't want to
think about it.
The wall is quiet, waiting.
It is tall like a promise
only better.

Questions for Discussion

1. What happens to Lisa when she curls up in a "corner of her room"?
2. Name some of the problems you think Lisa will face as an adult as a result of the incest?

Willie and Winston

Dennis Foley

The mousetrap screamed. I looked across the kitchen table at my friend, Willie. His eyes were spread wide, starin' at me. His brother, Winston, grabbed my arm.

"You hear dat?" Winston said.

My mother stood just a few feet from us, cooking our lunch at the stove, a frilly, blue apron that matched the color of the kitchen walls bow-tied 'round her waist. Grilled cheese sandwiches hissed in the butter.

I said nothin'. We all knew the sound. Willie and Winston lived just down the street with their mom and gramma and they sure as heck had mice, just as we had mice. I jumped from my chair and ran to the fridge, my glass of pop in hand. On the floor, in the one-foot space between the fridge and the big window that looked out over the back porch and yard, I found the mousetrap.

I bent over to take a look and Winston bumped into me. A single ice cube spilled out of my glass and landed directly on the mouse's head. It did no further damage. The mouse was already dead. I pushed the cube away and took a closer look.

"Lemme see, lemme see," Winston said. This mouse would never sing or dance or play catch again. The bar came right down across his neck. I'd seen other mice in traps before, squirming and squeaking. Not this one. His neck was crushed, forcing his mouth to open wide. He displayed the tiniest of teeth.

Willie and Winston were breathing hard over my shoulder. I grabbed the mouse and trap and stood up, making certain I didn't touch his furry black body. I pulled him to me and held him up like a show-and-tell piece. Willie and Winston both moved in for a closer look. Winston shot his right hand at the mouse and touched his fur with his brown finger.

"Ick," Willie said.

"Get rid of that thing and wipe your filthy mitts," Mom said. "The sandwiches are almost ready."

"But don't ya wanna see 'im, Ma?"

"Does a bear poop in a toilet?" That was Mom for ya. She liked to answer a question with another question that provided the obvious answer. Willie set both of his hands on the back screen door and pushed it open. His arms and hands were darker than his brother's. They were the color of the mouse. Winston grabbed a pack of matches from the window sill as he walked out the door onto the back porch.

"Lemme see, lemme see," Winston said again. I liked being in control. Again I held the mouse at waist level. Willie and Winston moved closer. Winston dropped to his knees to get a better look. His light gray shorts seemed to melt into the battleship-gray porch floor. His eyes were at the same level as the dead mouse.

"See the blood?" Winston said, pointing at my mouse. I missed that. I raised the mouse to my own eye level. Then I saw it. Winston was right. One lonely speck of blood rested on the corner of the trap. It was the size of half a teardrop.

"C'mon," I said, "let's bury it." Willie and I moved toward the stairs.

"No," Winston shouted.

I turned back. Willie's eyes were fixed on his younger brother.

"Let's burn it."

"What?" Willie and I both said.

"Burn him," Winston said, his face filled with teeth. "I done it befo' to an old squirrel I found squished in the alley." Winston stopped for a second to stick his finger in his ear. He twisted it back and forth and then pulled it out. "At first, he started to burn real slow. Den, his bushy tail got to goin' fast and he was a complete scorcher in no time flat."

"You crazy," Willie said.

I shook my head and aimed a mean stare at Winston. "We ain't gonna burn him."

"He's my mouse so we'll—"

"Why's he yo' mouse?" Winston said.

"Cuz he was in my house."

Winston stapled his hands to his hips. "Well, he coulda been in my house befo' and then followed me here to visit. So, he might just as much be my mouse as he is yo' mouse."

"No he ain't," I said through tight lips. I pushed my face right up to Winston's and hawked my eyes. Only a few inches separated us. "He died in my house so he's my mouse." I shoved Winston back. "We'll dig a little hole and bury him."

"Time to eat boys," Mom yelled through the kitchen window.

I set the mouse on the porch bannister. "Let's leave him here for now." His furry, black body looked cozy atop the gray-everywhere bannister. I kept my eyes on Winston. I knew he wanted that mouse bad. I made him go through the back door before me. "We'll get him later," I said. Winston didn't look too happy.

We plopped ourselves in the kitchen chairs and feasted on my mom's food. Grilled cheese, pickles, and applesauce. Me and my friends were all smilin' again. I liked it better this way. But still, who ever heard of burnin' a mouse, or any dead animal. That's sick. We passed around the glass of Pepsi, all of our lips not mindin' that the others' lips touched the glass.

The back door flew open. My father stood there, the dead mouse layin' in the palm of his hand—looking very small and lost. Dad was back from the sanatorium but he was trying to catch up on the time he lost at Papp's Tavern by goin' even more now.

"Who the hell left this on the porch?" The smell of Mr. Papp's place climbed offa his lips. He raised the mouse and trap in the air like the guys do at weddings, when they're makin' a toast.

"Mind your words, Jack," Mom said. My father glared at my mother. My mother glared right back.

"Who?" Dad said.

"I-I-I did, Dad." I had to squeeze each word out. Willie and Winston stared at my father, their eyes wide and unblinking. My father stared back.

"Whatcha lookin' at?" my father said, pointing his bony, right index finger at Willie. Willie's eyes fell to his plate. Winston's eyes did the same. My dad looked at my mother. "I told you before about these two," he barked. Again he pointed. This time his index finger wavered like a sword back and forth from Willie to Winston. "I don't want these goddamn nig—"

"Jack!" my mother screamed. My father stopped talking.

"What," he snarled.

"I'll give you 'What'." She knotted her hands across her chest. Her face was pinched. "Go to bed and sleep it off." Lines raced across my mother's face and her teeth were showing, like a growling dog. "We don't need to hear this crap."

Willie and Winston kept on starin' holes into their plates. My father kicked open the back screen door and, before the door had a chance to close, tossed my mouse out onto the porch. I watched him somersault and turn and twist in the air before he finally clanked off the porch floor. My father then backed away, circling his way through the kitchen like a boxer in the ring. I watched him until he finally made it to his room, where he slammed the door shut.

I looked at Willie and Winston. Their eyes hadn't moved yet. I wanted to say something to make everyone feel better. My mom did, instead.

"Eat up and share your pop, boys." She took off her apron, balled it up, and tossed it atop the fridge. "And be glad that you're drinking pop, too, instead of whiskey like Mr. Foley." Willie and Winston lifted their eyes from their plates. My mother was smiling. I smiled too. "That's right, boys. And when you get to be an old geezer like my husband, don't go 'round drinking whiskey all the time." My mother laughed. "Mr. Foley's a fine example of how whiskey melts the brain." We all laughed. My mother took a seat at the table and watched us eat. I was glad she was on our side. We ate our food and drank the pop, and all of us were glad that it was pop we were drinkin' and not whiskey. We all knew my mother was full of wisdom. When we finished, we stuck our plates in the sink.

"See ya, Ma," I said. "We'll be in the alley."

"Thanks, Mrs. Foley," Willie said.

"Me too, Mrs. Foley," hollered Winston. My mother patted both of my friends on their fuzzy heads.

"You're both very welcome."

We buried the mouse and Winston didn't seem to mind much. Only thing was, I couldn't stop thinkin' that Winston was gonna dig the mouse up later and burn him. With the mouse planted, we played with Winston's Super Ball in the alley. You had to be a good shot to play with a Super Ball in the alley. There wasn't much room. Not only did you hafta smack the ball off the cement and make it sail high into the sky, but you hadta make sure it landed on the cement again, avoiding the garages and garbage cans that lined both sides of the alley.

"My turn," Willie said.

"No it ain't. It's mine," Winston said.

"It's Willie's turn," I said. I liked being the judge.

Willie tossed a good toss. The striped ball bounced off the concrete, sailed about forty feet into the sky, and landed about twenty feet from us. We chased it down.

"Dat ain't nuthin'," Winston bragged. He showed us his teeth and twisted the ball around with his fingers. "Watch dis." Winston lifted his left foot high into the sky, like Giants pitcher Juan Marichal, brang that foot down, and whipped the ball into the cement. The ball exploded into the sky. I lost it in the sun. Then I saw it again—rising, rising, rising, and then falling, falling, falling. "Here it come," Winston yelled. As the ball neared the ground, Winston shot his right hand out and snatched the ball like it was the easiest thing in the world to do. Only I knew it wasn't.

"Dang," I said. Winston was the best. And Willie and I knew it.

"Fergie Jenkins, man," Winston said. "Fergie Jenkins. That's who I'm gonna pitch like when I'm growed up. I'm pitchin fo' the Cubs too." We all loved Fergie. He was the best pitcher on the Cubs. We shoulda been White Sox fans since we lived on the south side, but all three of us were Cubs fans. Mostly cuz of Fergie and cuz of Ernie Banks, the Cubs home run king.

Willie and Winston's gramma came down the alley. She didn't get too close but I still knew it was her. She had that same ol' spotted-red bandanna tied over her hair like Aunt Jemima on the pancake box, and she had a tiny piece of a cigarette glowin' between her lips. She probably just found that cigarette butt on the ground. I never saw that lady with a full cig. She had a way of findin' the little half-smoked ones on the ground and savin 'em like pennies for when she needed 'em.

"C'mon home boys," she hollered.

When Willie and Winston left, I went back to my apartment. Dad's door was still closed but Mom was gone. I figured she went to the store. Sharon and Donna were in the front room watchin' somethin' on the TV. But I wasn't in the mood for TV. I grabbed a 100-piece puzzle and started snappin' it together on the kitchen table. I was kinda thirsty, too. But there wasn't any more pop in the fridge so I grabbed a glass of water. I don't know how long I was workin' on the puzzle but it musta been a while. It was more than half done. Most of Soldier Field—where the Bears play—was laid out flat on the kitchen table, starin' me square in the face. My dad was awake now, only I didn't know it.

As I pieced in part of a fluffy white cloud floating above Soldier Field, I felt a tremendous tear at my hair. My head was being yanked backward. I almost fell outta my chair. Instead, the chair teetered on its hind legs like a dog beggin' for a treat. My father leaned over me. He was standing directly behind me, peering down. His face was red, his forehead crinkled. His lips were twisted open and I could see his snarling teeth pressed tightly together.

"Don't ever bring those little niggers 'round here again. Ever." He shook my head back and forth and then stopped. "You gottit?"

I said nothin'. I could really smell the whiskey on him. The stink was wrapped around each one of his growling teeth. I just looked at him, wondering what to do or say. He pushed his face even closer and yanked my head again. "You gottit?" he screamed, louder than before.

"Yeah, Dad," I whispered. "I got it." He let go of my hair and my chair came back to the ground. As he walked from the kitchen, I started to cry and wished my mom was home. Dad stopped moving and turned toward me.

"Quit with the tears," he said. His face was no longer so twisted, so ugly. He almost released a smile. Instead, he just turned and walked back to his room. He closed the door, but there was no slam this time.

The word "nigger" was almost never said in our apartment, least not when Mom was around. I could count the times of its usage on two hands. When one of my older brothers used the word, Mom always treated the situation the same. She'd grab 'em round their collars and threaten, "You say that word one more time, just one more time, and you'll be eatin' a bar of soap for dinner." She'd then shake 'em like they were boneless dolls. I never said the word. Never. Truth be told, back then, at that age, I didn't really know what the word meant. I know that might sound stupid, but it's the truth. Heck, I was only seven years old at the time. There were a lot of things I didn't know. I knew it was a bad word, though. As bad as motherfucker, even. I said that word once, when I was little. I didn't know what that word meant either but I knew it was bad. I heard Johnny call one of his friends a motherfucker when he was mad. So when I got mad at Tim, I called him a motherfucker. My mom was in the same room. She scrubbed my tongue with Dial soap till it was good and clean. Then I was sent to my room. Motherfucker was a bad word. I knew it. Nigger was just as bad. But like motherfucker, I didn't know what the word meant.

My dad said the word sometimes. Whenever we moved the two blocks from one apartment to the next, Dad said it was because "there's too many niggers on this block." I knew there was something or someone that was a nigger and it was a bad word, bad enough to get soaped for saying it and bad enough to make us move. After my father nearly ripped my hair from my head, I knew for the first time what the word actually meant. And I wondered why my dad didn't like my friends. Just cuz of their color? Heck, my father loved Fergie Jenkins and he was black, too.

Questions for Discussion

1. What point does this story make about race and bigotry?
2. What do you think about the mother in this family?
3. What part does social class play in this story?

Two Mean Boys

Linda Kantner

Ma was hungover when she woke up, and as soon as she saw me, she started yelling, "Eddie, turn off that goddamn TV. Can't you see I'm trying to sleep? Hey, I'm talking to you. Are you deaf or stupid?" She went on like that but she wasn't really mad. Her head hurt like a nail'd been jammed between her eyes. She hates me to see her this way.

I grab up the rest of the pizza from last night and a bottle of beer from the case next to the couch. I snare her pack of smokes just before she hits me. A fingernail slices the top of my ear like a needle sliding across a record. "Didn't hurt, didn't hurt," I yell as I run out the door.

"Don't come back, you little shit."

About half the time she wakes up this way, mad and needing to hit somebody. The other half of the time it's worse. She wakes up crying. She'll say she's no damn good and she wishes she were dead. She says, "I got nothing to live for." I hate it when she does that. She pulls me into her bed, smelling all boozy and smoky and funky. She'll hold me too close, rub my hair, and run one of her fingers up and down my arm until I'm covered with little bumps. She'll say I am the only thing that counts in her life. The only one who has ever loved her. She'll whisper into my ear, "You're my man, aren't ya, honey?"

It makes me feel good for about a minute, but I know better. I have heard her tell lots of guys they're the best and she'll love 'em forever, but they never say it back. She makes me. "Do you love your mamma? Tell Mamma how much you love her."

If I don't do it just right or if I start to squirm she'll cry even harder and talk about jumping off the Washington Avenue Bridge near our house.

I walk over to that bridge sometimes. It crosses both the Mississippi River and the highway. I look over the edge and wonder which part she plans to hit. Real late, one night around Halloween, I stole this big pumpkin and carried it to the bridge. It was dark except for a far-off streetlight. I balanced the pumpkin on the railing of the bridge, wondering but not really thinking. And then I pushed it. The pumpkin took forever to fall and yet it was over in a second. The top came off and a candle fell out and I imagined this was just how it would be with Mom. Her glasses would fall off and the cigarette would slip out of her hand and she wouldn't make a sound.

Just before the pumpkin hit I shut my eyes, and when I opened them, there wasn't a piece left. A car must have hit the damn thing and sent it flying. I kicked that bridge till my foot ripped through my sneaker and slammed the steel. Next time my eyes would be wide open.

There is a strip of swampy woods behind our apartment. People throw their old couches and garbage and car tires there. It's not like the junk is hidden; they might as well drop it in the street. My friend Jimmy and I have a place there. It isn't a fort or a camp—that's kids stuff. It's just a hole someone dug and left. We pulled branches and a tarp over the top and covered it with leaves. We call it The Place.

This morning Jimmy got here first. He looks like he's spent the night but I don't ask him. His mom, Gloria, must be with some guy, one who doesn't like kids. Once a dude gave Jimmy five bucks to go play video games and disappear for awhile. Another time a man with a snake tattooed on his neck gave Jimmy two joints and let him sleep in his car while he was with Jimmy's mom. Jimmy thought the guy was pretty cool until the next morning. His mom had a black eye and a fat bloody lip.

She stopped going out for a few days and Jimmy stayed home with her. He didn't even have to go to school. She wrote a note saying that he was needed for a family emergency. When her face got better she started up again, but she didn't look as good. That cut on her lip stayed purple and puffy. The men she brought home were meaner and crazier and almost never gave Jimmy presents. My mom said that Gloria looks like the kind of woman a man could hit and nobody would care.

Jimmy doesn't have it all bad. He can take anything from Tom Thumb and not get caught. One time he walked out with a whole bag of Doritos and a six-pack of Mountain Dew. He just told the cashier he was carrying them out for his mom. We watched through the window as some lady with about six kids tried to explain that Jimmy wasn't one of hers. Also he skips school all of the time and Gloria doesn't even care. She says school is "up to him."

The extremely cool thing about Jimmy is that he's got a real live monkey. His name is Skeeter because he's always scratching like he has mosquito bites. I don't know where Jimmy got Skeeter. He won't say. Jimmy likes having secrets and being mysterious. Mom says there's no mystery about where Skeeter came from. She said, "Gloria picked him up at the bar and didn't realize her mistake until the next morning. You know, she'll go home with anything." Ma and me laughed about that.

Skeeter lives in the attic of Jimmy's apartment. The attic is bad but it's safer than the apartment. His mom said he could have Skeeter as long as she never sees him and he doesn't cost her a cent.

In the winter, the attic walls and windows are covered with ice. I'm surprised that Skeeter doesn't freeze. I asked Jimmy if I could take Skeeter home with me when it's really cold, but he said no. He said he couldn't take

Skeeter out too much or mean kids would try and mess with him. This is pretty funny because everyone thinks me and Jimmy are the mean kids.

When it's too cold, Jimmy skips school and sits in the attic with Skeeter. They make a nest out of old coats and blankets. Jimmy brushes Skeeter's thick sticky hair. He reads to him with a little flashlight and tells him private stuff. Stuff he won't tell any human, not even me. He's crazy about that monkey.

I don't know anyone else who has a monkey, but I know a lot of kids would like one. As a matter of fact, one day last year Jimmy brought Skeeter to school. Everyone in the whole class, no, I could say the whole fifth grade, wanted to touch that monkey. That day everyone was really nice to Jimmy even though usually they won't get near him. They say he stinks. Some kids say his mom is a whore and a boozer. I know they say the same things about my mom, but not so I can hear it. One kid talked about my mom, one time, and I broke his arm. Jimmy should do the same thing but he won't. He doesn't get mad, not like I do.

For that day Jimmy was the coolest kid in school, and because I am his best, actually his only, friend, some of the kids were even nice to me. They wanted to hold Skeeter and feed him little bits of banana and sunflower seeds and make him dance. It got crazy. Skeeter was on a little red leash and about thirty kids were standing around him in a circle holding out bits of food. Someone reached out and grabbed his tail and Skeeter turned around to bite 'em. At the same time someone else snatched the red baseball hat off his head.

Finally Skeeter jumped right into a window, trying to escape. It was funny to watch, but it looked like Jimmy was going to cry. His face turned red and he smashed his knuckles into his head. The teacher made Skeeter stay in a closet the rest of the day for being a disruption. I said, "Hey, no fair. It was the stupid class's fault," but the teacher just ignored me. Jimmy laid his head on his desk with his arms covering his face, not saying a word for the rest of the day.

When I try to talk to Jimmy about how great that day was and how he should bring Skeeter back again, he never gets excited. He just says, "Yeah, right." Like I'm stupid or something. Sometimes I don't think a kid like Jimmy deserves a monkey. If Skeeter were mine that would have been the best day of my life.

The top of Jimmy's greasy black head is sticking out of the sleeping bag. I kick the bag to wake him up. When he sees the pizza, he grabs for it. "Don't cha got no manners?" I say, holding the pizza away until he's out of the bag. I settle into the warm space he's left. When you put the bag over your head it smells like piss and beer, cigarette smoke, and other things that could make you gag. But only for a minute, then it just feels cozy.

I watch while Jimmy eats. He's a jumpy kid, ragged as a winter squirrel. He gulps the pizza, jerking every few seconds like he's dodging bullets. When he's done, he catches me staring. "What, fucker?" he says.

"Good morning," I say, giving him a big smile. Jimmy rolls his eyes like I'm some hopeless case.

The sun is pushing through the heavy leaves, warming up splotches of ground. I crawl out of The Place wearing the sleeping bag over my shoulders like a king's cape, royalty in a Mud Puppies T-shirt. Jimmy joins me and we light up Mom's Winstons. He chews his thumbs as he smokes and picks his nose and looks at what he finds. He's a pretty gross kid.

I work at prying off the beer bottle cap with a rock. It's not easy. Ma should get twist-offs like most people but she don't trust 'em. The metal gouges my hands bloody before the top finally flies off. Skunky foam gushes from the bottle and I gag a few swallows down before choking it through my nose.

"You drink like a lady, Eddie. I could finish this bottle and another one without stopping for air."

Course I say, "No way, you woman." And Jimmy guzzles the rest of the beer. He doesn't smirk or nothing, just tosses the bottle at a rock, where it explodes.

Jimmy goes back to digging in his nose. I toss a couple of matches by his head and he doesn't even move. He's crouched down like a kid ready for leapfrog. It takes about an hour for him to raise his head and look at me. He don't have to do nothing but look and I feel like dog shit.

"I need something to burn," I say, holding the match under my thumb.

Jimmy goes over to The Place and gets our magazine stash. Mostly crumpled *Hustler*s and *Playboy*s and one called *Warm Furrys* where a guy pretends to have sex with rabbits. At least I think he is pretending. Together we rip out the pages with no pictures and crunch them into balls. I light a book of matches and drop it on top. At first the fire just smokes, we take turns blowing on it and looking at the pictures of tits.

"Which is your favorite month?" I ask, and Jimmy thinks it over for a long time, like it's going to matter.

"Miss July, I guess."

"What would you do to her?"

"Nothing. Well, maybe I could bring her here."

"To The Place? Miss July?"

"I like her mountain bike, but I'd get baskets for it so that Skeeter could ride too."

"You really are a pitiful puke, Jimmy."

First, I hear their voices. "We'll get the eggs for Mom . . . " "And baking powder." And then I see them, a fat girl from school and her little brother walking on the path. They're talking about the Tom Thumb store. "And then we get a treat, each of us get our own, Mom said." The fat girl says, "We could get Sweetarts or Snickers or Baby Ruth . . . "

"We could get Fritos or Red Hots or orange pop or bubble gum, candy cigarettes, or how about real cigarettes." The little boy giggles.

"Oooooo . . . I'm telling mom," says the girl, and they both laugh.

I hate them. I grab Jimmy's arm, "Come on. It's a girl." Jimmy follows me, running close behind. I start screaming, these weird horror movie sounds. I grab the front of the fat girl's shirt and jerk it once, but nothing happens. I jerk it a second time and two buttons pop. I ram my hand into her shirt and squeeze her. With my other hand I grab at the zipper of her pants. I'm not sure what I'm doing, but my hands go wild, ripping at her clothes, digging into her skin, jamming into the tight band of her underpants.

"Jimmy, help me get her."

But Jimmy's no help at all. He just stands next to me screaming and waving his arms like he's seeing a ghost.

"Help me, fucker!" I shout at him. "You're going to miss it."

Right then the fat girl goes wild. Her mouth stretches into a scream but nothing comes out. She reaches past me and jams her fingers into Jimmy's eyes. He never even touched her. She scratches long red welts down his skinny white face. He stumbles away like a drunk, puts his hands over his eyes, and starts to cry.

In the sudden quiet I see the little brother standing back against a tree. He's wearing a Barnery windbreaker, a cowboy hat, and a little gun holster with a pistol. He's crying and rocking from foot to foot. "Don't hurt my sister, please don't hurt my sister."

What a fuckin' baby. I hate him more than the girl, at least she fights. I move to slap him and the fat girl bites me, really hard on the soft inside part of my arm. She doesn't let go; it's like she doesn't even care that I'm bleeding into her mouth. Then she kicks me right square in the balls. All I can do is bend over and try not to throw up. The fat girl holds her pants together with one hand and shakes her little brother with the other. "Run, Nicky, run!" she screams, dragging him after her.

I could puke. Nobody has ever kicked me like that, not even a boy. I can already see seven red teeth marks where her braces caught my arm and ripped it open. My heart is ready to crash out of my chest.

Jimmy is standing in a single spot of bright sunlight. His face looks bad. Just like when Ma gets after me with a coat hanger. He's still crying, sucking air like he has the hiccups. He's got snot smeared all over his face and it's shiny in the sun.

"Wasn't that great. Can you believe that? I grabbed that girl's tit. I ripped open her pants and got her pussy. Boy, you know what I would like to do to her." Jimmy doesn't say anything. So I say, "Did you see how she squirmed around and went crazy. It was kind of like the day you brought Skeeter to school and everyone was poking at him. Remember how he just went nuts. Shit, that was funny."

"Shut up, you fucker. Would you just shut up about the monkey and the girl and everything. What's wrong with you?" And then he crumples to the ground like a stamped-on beer can.

A shiny blue button from the fat girl's shirt is lying in the leaves. I pick it up and rub it between my thumb and finger. It's cool and smooth in my hand like a medal. I put it into my pocket to look at later. "I got a piece of that girl. You saw it. I got me a piece and you didn't."

I slam my tennis shoe into Jimmy's ribs but he doesn't even look up. He pulls himself into a tight ball and keeps crying. I think about the night I took the pumpkin; I remember the thrill of stealing it and running to the bridge, the weight, heavy in my arms. Then balancing it carefully on the railing and waiting until just the right moment. I remember the cool madness when I pushed it with the tip of my finger and how the pumpkin looked as it fell.

This time the fat girl's button is in my pocket and my eyes are wide open.

Questions for Discussion

1. Describe the differences between Eddie and Jimmy?
2. If Eddie and Jimmy were referred for counseling, consider the following:

   - What issues/problems would you want to address with each?
   - How would you engage Eddie? Jimmy?
   - Whom else would you want to talk with?
   - What resources could be mobilized to help each of these boys?

3. Without intervention, what future do you envision for Eddie? For Jimmy?

SELECTED READINGS AND ADDITIONAL RESOURCES

Death and Loss

For Children

Brown, Margaret Wise (1995). *The Dead Bird.* New York: Harper Trophy (children ages four to eight).

Viorst, Judith (1976). *The Tenth Good Thing About Barney.* Alladin Paperbacks (children ages four to eight).

For Professionals and Caretakers

Altschul, Sol (Ed.) (1988). *Childhood Bereavement and Its Aftermath.* Madison, CT: International Universities Press.
Edelman, Hope (1994). *Motherless Daughters.* New York: Bantam Doubleday.
Kennedy, Alexandra (1993). *Losing a Parent.* New York: Harper Collins.
Kroen, William C. and Espeland, P. (Eds.) (1996). *Helping Children Cope with the Loss of a Loved One: A Guide for Grownups.* Minneapolis, MN: Free Spirit Publications.

Alcoholism in the Family

Black, Claudia (1991). *It Will Never Happen to Me.* New York: Ballentine Books.
Black, Claudia, et al. (1996). *Children of Alcoholics: Selected Readings.* Rockville, MD: National Association for Children of Alcoholics.
Hastings, Jill, M. and Typpo, Marion, H. (1994). *Elephant in the Living Room: A Leader's Guide for Helping Children of Alcoholics.* Minneapolis, MN: Comp-Care Publications.

Sexual Abuse

Pryor, Douglas, W. (1996). *Unspeakable Acts: Why Men Sexually Abuse Children.* New York: New York University Press.
Silbury, Joyanna, L. (1996). *The Dissociative Child: Diagnosis, Treatment, and Management.* Baltimore, MD: Sidron Press.

Child Neglect

Garbarino, James (1999). *Raising Children in a Socially Toxic Environment.* New York: Jossey-Bass.
Karr-Morse, Robin, Wiley, Meredith, and Brazelton, T. Berry (1999). *Ghosts in the Nursery: Tracing the Roots of Violence.* New York: Atlantic Monthly Press.

PART II:
ADOLESCENCE

Bonfires

Diane B. Byington

Eva arrived at her best friend Sarah's house an hour before the boys were expected so she could help with the party preparations. Eva and five other girls had been invited to a sleepover for Sarah's sixteenth birthday, and each of them had been allowed to invite a boy to join them until midnight.

"You did ask John, didn't you?" Sarah asked Eva as they carried the card table outside.

"Of course I asked John. What kind of dorky question is that?" Eva sounded irritable, even to herself. This wasn't how she wanted to start the evening of her best friend's birthday. She lowered her voice so none of the other girls would hear. "Sorry. It's just that Betty is coming with Greg."

"But you dumped Greg for John. What's the problem?"

"Oh, I know that, but it gets me mad that Betty jumped on Greg so fast. She's just out to get him because he used to be mine. She'd better leave John alone."

"Well, if I'd known you had such a problem with Betty, I wouldn't have invited her," Sarah said doubtfully.

"No, it's OK. We'll just sort of ignore each other. It'll be a great party, don't worry. Besides, you won't notice anything else after Jerry gets here." They giggled in excitement because Jerry was one of the most popular boys at their school, and it had amazed them both that he had accepted Sarah's invitation to the party. Giving each other a satisfied hug, they joined the other girls in hanging Japanese lanterns.

After setting everything up, the girls paused to admire their handiwork. The party was to be held in Sarah's backyard, which bordered on some woods. Card tables were stacked with sandwiches and soft drinks, the stereo was set to blare rock music through the neighborhood, and lanterns were ready to be lit. Most exciting, though, was the large brush pile Sarah's dad had built toward the back of the yard that would be turned into a giant bonfire as soon as the boys arrived. The party would be held by firelight, which turned even ordinary people into romantic figures.

"Why did you make the bonfire so far back in the yard?" Eva asked. "It seems a little close to the woods."

"Isn't it obvious? My parents are going to be watching us out the kitchen window all night long, so we can't make out in the yard without them seeing. I figured if the fire was close to the woods, the couples could just slip away for a while without my parents noticing. At least that's what I'm hoping to do with Jerry. You can do what you want."

Eva eyed the woods speculatively and wondered if she and John would be able to sneak away together for a few minutes. She certainly hoped so. She had known John for three whole weeks and hadn't yet been alone with him. Because he was three years older and in college, her parents had insisted that they double-date. They had barely even kissed up to now.

Eva had daydreamed a lot about what it would be like to be alone with John. She was still a virgin and hadn't even done any heavy petting. The guys she had gone out with before John had been as timid as mice. Her images of lovemaking came from romance novels, which she devoured whenever she wasn't in school. The heroines and heroes in her novels usually stopped just short of "doing it" until they were married, but they were always in a state of high excitement over each other. That was the way she felt about John. The two of them seemed to have stepped out of the pages of one of her novels. They had fallen in love at first sight when they met at the mall, and everything had been perfect ever since. John was very sophisticated and gentlemanly. He opened car doors for her and took her to fancy restaurants. This was a new world for her and she was thrilled, even though a little uncomfortable. When she wasn't sure how to act, she fell back on her novels and did what she thought her heroine would do. Everything had worked out reasonably well so far.

Would she let John touch her breasts tonight? She thought her heroine would probably let him get that far, but no further, and it seemed like a good plan to her. She wondered what other girls did with their boyfriends, but they never really talked in specifics. Everyone thought they knew who was a virgin and who wasn't, but she wondered if that were really true. Betty and some of the other girls had reputations as sluts because they slept with their boyfriends, and she was mildly sorry that she was seen as a Goody Two-shoes. "Oh, well," she thought as the boys began to arrive, "I'll just have to see how it goes."

John was the last to arrive, and he made quite an entrance as he wheeled his new sports car into the driveway. "He sure is *fine*," Sarah whispered to Eva as the other kids gathered admiringly around his car.

"I know," Eva answered, with a certain smugness. He was by far the best-looking guy at the party, even better than Greg, who was ignoring her and making a fuss over Betty. John was tall and blond, and he really did resemble a romance novel hero. "I should remember to tell him that tonight; he'll think that's funny," she thought as she hurried to his side.

The bonfire lit with a whoosh! and Sarah's backyard was transformed into a magical place. Couples danced around the fire and made crazy shadows out into the yard. Eva was having a wonderful time—she felt beautiful and dramatic and very much like a romance heroine. She danced seductively close to John.

After a few minutes, John quietly led Eva back into the woods, away from the others. He pulled her to him for a passionate kiss. "You've been driving me crazy all night," he whispered huskily. "That T-shirt is so tight that your headlights show through, and I've been dying to kiss them all night."

Eva was thrilled by his pleasure in her but she was slightly disconcerted. None of the other boys she had been with had talked like that. She wasn't sure how she was supposed to respond. Was there something her heroine would say? She giggled nervously. He kissed her again, and she felt even more excited and disturbed.

John took Eva's hand and pressed it into his crotch, which was hard and lumpy. Eva had never felt a guy's crotch before, but she knew that the hardness was because of her. John moaned when she touched him and she jerked her hand away. Meanwhile, Eva could feel his tongue in her mouth, searching. For what, she wondered? It felt like it would go all the way inside her.

As they became more involved, Eva felt her resolve to control the situation wavering. Vaguely she thought that she would stop it in a little while, but she was enjoying herself too much right now.

His hand moved down her shirt and up again inside it, and the feeling of flesh on flesh made her giddy. Although she hadn't realized it at the time, his other hand had reached inside and unhooked her bra. He seemed so expert at it. She wondered if this were due to experience or age. Suddenly her bra was loose and his hand moved to her bare breast. She had never experienced such excitement at the forbidden pleasure. Her knees were so weak that when he moved to pull her to the ground, she gratefully gave way.

Time passed in a blur. John's hands continued to explore. When he lowered the zipper on her jeans, she inhaled sharply and thought, "That is going too fast. I can't handle this." But she only held her breath and stiffened, without being able to think of words that would make him stop without pissing him off.

Suddenly John sat up and away from her. He pulled down her shirt and looked at her solemnly. She could barely see his eyes in the moonlight; they looked a little wild, she thought. In a low voice he said, "I can't do this to you. You're still a virgin. I can't take the responsibility."

Everything was moving so quickly! Eva frantically wondered what she was supposed to say. She was so confused; this was beyond anything in her past experience. Finally she managed to say, "Oh," and wondered how she could sound so dumb. She was usually able to handle situations; why had her brain failed her now?

The moment lengthened as they stared at each other. Finally John said, "Listen, you'd better get up and walk away right now. Because I'm afraid if we stay here I won't be able to stop myself."

Here it was, her big moment. Her world really did seem to pause for an instant, as the novels described. But what was she supposed to say now? Her lines weren't clear. She knew he was just being considerate, that he didn't really want her to leave. But what did she want? She wasn't sure. She felt as though she were floating above herself, watching and wondering what would happen. So she sat, still and silent, as the moment lengthened.

Finally John smiled. "All right," he said. "I'll be gentle. And I love you."

In a trance she let him lay her down and remove her jeans. He did some things but she hardly noticed. When he entered her it felt like a knife piercing, and she bit her lip to keep from crying out. "What is he doing?" she thought wildly. "Does he know what he's doing? Oh, God, this hurts. What is happening to me?"

After a short time he stopped moving and lay beside her on the ground. "How was it?" he asked anxiously. "Are you OK?"

Her thoughts were wild and confused; she was upset and angry. Without saying anything, she groped frantically for her clothes. John said softly, "It'll be better next time. I'm sorry if I hurt you." He hugged her and helped to straighten her hair and clothes. As they walked back toward the bonfire she thought, "It wasn't at all what I thought it would be. Why does everybody make such a big deal about it?" She shuddered in disillusionment.

They rejoined the others and tried to act as if nothing had happened. Sarah hurried over and hissed, "John's going to have to leave. My parents caught on to what was happening and they're making the guys leave early." She noticed Eva's dazed look and asked, "What have you been doing for so long? I was getting worried."

Eva smiled vaguely and said, "Not much. I'm OK. Don't worry." She didn't know whether she could trust Sarah with this experience, even if they were best friends. What if she thought Eva was stupid?

Eva walked John to his car. He was concerned that she was all right. "I'll call you tomorrow, OK?" She just nodded, kissed him briefly, and turned away. She felt numb, and the last person she wanted to talk to was John. Maybe she could deal with him tomorrow. She wanted to be alone to think about this thing that had happened to her, but she had to get through the rest of the sleepover first.

After the boys left, the girls settled down in Sarah's living room to analyze the evening. They giggled just loudly enough to hopefully keep from waking Sarah's parents.

"John sure is nice," Betty said to Eva. "How did you two get along? You must have had fun out in the woods—you were gone long enough."

Eva realized that Betty was trying to trap her into revealing something that could be turned against her. "Oh, it was fun, but no big deal. I'm surprised you even noticed. I saw you making out with Greg all night."

Betty began to chatter about how great Greg was and how lucky she was to have ended up with him. Eva didn't care a whit what Betty had to say. All that foolishness was far behind her now. She kept wondering if something was wrong with her that she hadn't heard bells and whistles during her first time making love. "Making love" didn't seem to be the right phrase to describe their hasty sex act. She wondered if she had just had a bad experience or if the romance novels were lying. But why would they lie about such an important thing? She heard Betty whisper to Sarah, "Boy, Eva must really be in love. I've never seen her so out of it."

She wasn't sure if there was something she should do after this experience. Take a bath? She certainly felt dirty and grimy. She knew she couldn't tell the other girls, because it would be all over the school by morning. Suddenly her goody-two-shoes reputation didn't look so bad. She wondered if she could trust John to keep their secret. The thought that her reputation was in the hands of a guy she barely knew troubled her.

Slowly another thought surfaced, and she was aghast. Oh no, could she get pregnant from that tonight? She thought she had seen him fumble with something in the dark, but she wasn't sure. She had been too embarrassed to look closely. And what about AIDS? Oh, my God, could I have gotten it from him?

Eva didn't sleep at all that night. Something had gone terribly wrong with her romantic scenario. She thought she understood why the characters in romance novels usually stopped at the crucial moment. The fantasy might be better than the reality of sex. Or maybe, she thought, she just needed to try again. The two ideas battled in her mind—should she go back to her old life and wait a while longer for any more sex, or should she dive into the experience to see if it got better? She knew that something in her had changed forever, that she wasn't the same innocent girl she had been yesterday. But she didn't know whether she liked being this new person. Can people tell by looking at me that I'm . . . *experienced,* she wondered? Would John be willing just to kiss me without having sex? What would he do if I got pregnant? What would her parents say? How would her friends react? The whole thing just seemed too overwhelming to be possible.

Before she went home the next morning she made a deal with God. "God, if you just give me my period next month, I swear I won't do it again until I'm out of high school. And if I change my mind, I'll try to figure out a way to get on the pill beforehand, or at least I'll make him use a condom." Her period was due in a week, and she knew it was going to be a long seven days.

As she walked out to her parents' car in the morning, Eva's attention was drawn to the area in the yard where the bonfire had been. It was just a big patch of blackened earth now, with no grass. So much had happened since yesterday.

Questions for Discussion

1. Eva got her messages about sexuality from romance novels. Today where do most teens get their messages about sex? What are these messages? How are they different from the ones Eva got?
2. John gives Eva an either-or choice: go "all the way" or stop making out. Do you think this was manipulation on John's part? Give your reasons.
3. Did Eva really make a choice to have intercourse? If not, what kept her from choosing? What do you think Eva really wanted?
4. What type of sex education program is needed for teenage girls? What topics would you include?

Double Fuselage Model

Barbara Adams

I was ten years old, a tomboy, and quite content with my own company when Suzie sat on the wings of my P-40 fighter plane. The wings crunched under her butt like a baby bird's. Suzie had invited herself because her mother and my mother were always making us play together. The P-40 was my first attempt at building a model plane. I planned to make a P-38 next, with its sleek double fuselage; it was the fastest fighter plane from World War II. I didn't know it then, but it was also the last one of its type—the jet engine came along and made the P-38- and P-40-type planes with conventional piston engines obsolete. After Suzie dive-bombed my P-40 wings that day, I slugged her, and gave up building airplane models.

Suzie and I lived at opposite ends of a dirt road outside of Huguenot. We were supposed to have a lot in common because our parents had known each other in Manhattan, where we used to live and where I'd been born. Everyone in Huguenot, except Suzie's family and mine, was descended from French and Dutch Huguenots who had arrived in 1697.

Suzie wore frilly dresses, usually pink, and whined just like her mother to get what she wanted. Her father, Sol, gave up his job in Manhattan and got rich in Huguenot real estate. The only one I liked in her family was her grandmother, Mrs. Schwartz. She made apple fritters for Suzie and me and spoke a language I learned was Yiddish, with words so chewy I could almost taste them.

My silent mother and garrulous father, though attractive and youthful, had even less in common than Suzie and I. On most weekends, my father brought his city friends to our house in Huguenot to provide him with company, an audience, and drinking buddies.

Our mothers finally gave up forcing us on each other. Autumn turned to winter and the dirt road became a bowling alley of hard-packed snow and ice where cars skidded like ninepins. I read my books and comic books, contented to be by myself. Daddy and his buddies provided me with all the company I needed. On Sundays, when everyone slept late, I got up and tiptoed downstairs to listen to forbidden church music on the radio. I had discovered Bach.

By the end of our second year in Huguenot, Daddy stopped coming home from Manhattan every weekend. He had to stay in town to finish a job, he said. I heard Mommy say on the phone that he must have a new model. I thought she meant an airplane, maybe a B-52. Then I saw Daddy's model in a picture that was in the pocket of a suit Mommy was getting ready to send to the cleaners. The model was all white skin and long black hair.

Just before my eleventh birthday, Daddy sold the house. My mother, baby sister, and I moved into a rented house in the village of Huguenot. I still went to the same school, walking three blocks instead of taking an hour bus ride. The best part was that I didn't have to play with Suzie anymore. I made new townie friends and they came to play in my house and we listened to Frank Sinatra and Perry Como records.

One day, I came home from school and found Mom asleep in her darkened bedroom, snoring and blowing out smelly fumes. I changed Deirdre's clothes and fed her cookies and milk. Mom was sent to a hospital in Manhattan. It seemed more peaceful when Mom was away. Daddy sent a check for my allowance and groceries; Deirdre stayed with him and his new model. When Mom finally came home, she was all right for awhile. Then the afternoon naps started again, and she had to go back to the hospital, a cycle that repeated. By the time I started high school, I saw so little of my parents I began to think they were figures in a dream. Each new day I woke alone. But I loved school and knew what I wanted—to write and teach. My absent father had left me one important legacy: "Girls can do anything boys can do," he told me, over and over. I believed him. I would never be like other girls, especially Suzie.

I had not counted on seeing Suzie again. She was a year ahead of me in high school, and in the "career" track where they put the "dumb" kids. I was the class "brain," in the "college" track. Never the twain should meet, at least in classes. Suddenly, though, we were forced into each other's company again, by having undergone puberty, I suppose. Suzie's steady boyfriend, Dutch, was the crewcut star of the basketball team. Peter, my new steady, was the son of a Greek diner owner—and the only other non-Huguenot in school besides Suzie and me. Peter had asked me to the junior prom but he didn't have a car. Dutch had a Chevy, blue and white with lots of chrome. So the guys arranged a double date. As a junior, I felt very mature to be going out with three seniors.

My mother, who happened to be sober and between hospital visits at this time, proudly took me to buy my first prom dress. Mom had never been to a prom, having dropped out of school at sixteen to marry Daddy. In a shop filled with fluffy dresses that looked like paper cupcake holders, she picked out a moss green taffeta with a fitted bodice and full skirt—and strapless. I had no idea how it would stay up on my flat chest. I hated the color too, but I was too embarrassed to mention my lack of breasts to the blue-haired saleslady. I slunk into the dressing room and took off my padded bra, then dropped the yards of rustling taffeta over my head. I emerged holding up the bosom, so-called, to let my mother zip up the back. The zipper pulled the bodice tight—and flat. The dress suited my tiny waist and wire held up the bodice, but the cups where my breasts should have been punched inward like deflated balloons. My mother sighed, "You're so skinny!" But she bought the dress, disregarding my glowering silence. At home, she made me try it on again. Squinting over my flat chest, she stuffed two pairs of white socks into the bra cups. "There! No one would guess they weren't yours!"

On the night of the prom, Mom restuffed the bodice with the socks, then spread a thick layer of pancake makeup over my face and back to hide my acne. It dulled the brightest pimples, but the color made me look sunburned. At a distance, I could pass for a fairly pretty girl, with Peter's gardenia corsage around my wrist and a Bobbi home perm that gave a lift to my stringy brown hair. My mother's eyes glistened happily as I left, my arm hooked properly through Peter's, my feet wobbling in new three-inch heels.

Dutch sat drumming the steering wheel of his shiny new Chevy. He had picked up Peter first, then me, since we all lived in town. Dutch smelled of Brylcreem and looked like Mickey Mantle, only meaner. Suzie still lived outside of town in the beautiful stone house overlooking their lake. As we drove to her house, I remembered her grandmother Schwartz and her apple fritters, and that she still had a father who lived at home. I felt a pang of something like homesickness and envied Suzie, who was so lucky.

In the backseat, Peter stole a quick look at my strapless top, eyeing the peculiar lumps where my breasts should have been. I pulled a yellow chiffon shawl around my pimply back. Dutch grunted hello without turning his stiff neck.

It took twenty minutes to get to Suzie's. Frank Sinatra wailed from the car radio, "The girl that I marry will have to be / As soft and as pink as a nursery . . ." A pimple on my bare back rubbed against the harsh cloth, feeling like a wasp sting. Peter's aftershave clashed with the spicy scent of my gardenia, making my delicate stomach queasy. We sat with twelve inches of blue upholstery between us. I stole a look at Peter in profile. Black straight hair dangled over his narrow forehead to the bridge of his enormous Roman nose. But from this angle, I couldn't see the space between his front teeth. Suddenly, he turned his black eyes on me—his best feature besides his straight-A average. "Are you warm enough?" he asked, putting his arm around my back. It was a lovely May evening, seventy degrees. "You have goose bumps on your arms," he noted.

Dutch pulled up the long gravel driveway in front of Suzie's house and honked repeatedly. The back of his short neck bulged over the tight collar of his white shirt. Frank Sinatra's perfect girl was gone, and now the Andrews Sisters were "drinkin' rum and co-CA co-LA."

Dutch hit the horn again. "Women," he growled. The side door opened finally and Suzie stepped out, dazzling in a skin-tight short white dress. Her white high heels clicked firmly on the stones as she sashayed toward us. Peter leaped out to open the passenger door for her. The whiteness of her dress was blinding, set off by her tanned skin. Peter leaned over her chest as she bent forward to get in the front seat, her bosom straining for release from the halter top. Dutch grabbed her with his right arm resting on the back of the seat and pulled her close for a loud, wet kiss. When they broke for air, his face was smeared with blood-red lipstick. Suzie wiped her mouth indifferently before applying a thick new layer of lipstick. Dutch wiped his face with his handkerchief, grinning proudly.

I knew envy of another female for the first, if not the last, time in my life. Suzie had never made it on the honor roll. *I* was used to being the object of envy, the one always with top honors, always the teacher's pet. Obviously, this did not matter to Dutch and Peter, who viewed Suzie's overstuffed body with hormonal admiration. Suzie half-smiled a hello. "Um-um," I murmured. We drove in silence to Huguenot High. The gym was decorated with pink and white apple blossoms which I had helped make by the hundreds out of crepe paper. Pink punch—lemonade mixed with Kool-Aid—was sickeningly sweet. Mrs. Sullivan, my favorite English teacher, stood with her husband, the math teacher, beside the punch bowl to guard it. Dutch had already talked of spiking the punch as we got out the car, flaunting a pint of Teachers scotch hidden under the front seat. "Having a good time, dear?" asked Mrs. Sullivan.

I nodded, hoping she approved of my date. Peter was one of the smartest seniors in Huguenot and was trying for scholarships at several good colleges, but his father wanted Peter to take over the diner. Peter, like me, was an outsider: he was not Dutch Reformed. Mrs. Sullivan, though Irish like my mother, was otherwise nothing like her and filled a huge hole in my heart at that time.

The band played soft, slow music and Peter and I danced a foxtrot. I could lindy, but he couldn't, so we sat those out—much to my frustration. After the first three numbers, the socks had slipped down and now bulged like wandering tumors over my ribs. I pulled the yellow shawl over my front and we went to get some punch. Mr. Sullivan turned to Peter, "Made up your mind about college yet, young man?" he asked.

"I've joined the Marines. As soon as I graduate, I leave for Camp Lejeune. When I've served my hitch, I'll be a lieutenant and can go to college for free."

"Oh, Peter!" said Mrs. Sullivan, putting her hand on his arm, but he pulled away.

I was unable to hide my dismay. The only reason I dated Peter was because of his brains. The Marines! My father, a die-hard socialist, taught me to hate the military, especially the elite class of officers. My father would have turned over in his grave—had he been dead. In fact, he was still alive, still in Manhattan, proven by the allowance checks he sent every month.

We danced and drank insipid punch until midnight when the King and Queen were crowned. Voted most popular by the class, Ian Lefevre was headed for Yale, and Betsey Deyo, looking like Shirley Temple, was going to Wells College. The King and Queen of Huguenot High led the promenade around the gym. Dutch came up to Peter and whispered loudly, "Let's get out of here and have some *real* fun." We left childhood behind and went out to Dutch's car.

Perry Como moaned of unrequited loved from the car radio. Peter put his arm stiffly around my sweaty shoulders as we sat like two mannequins posing for a teenage love scene. The drive took an hour, up the state highway toward Kingston, then veering off onto a winding road that snaked through pitch-black pines. An occasional dot of weak light blinked through the dense needle forest, marking some sort of human presence. Dutch kept swigging from the pint of Teachers, driving with one hand. He handed the bottle over the front seat to Peter without looking. Peter took a small sip. Suzie gazed out her window into the dark blank night, refusing a swig. I had not drunk alcohol since I was six, when a playmate's mother from Hungary gave me a glass of homemade wine. It made me dizzy and then I threw up. My mother's drinking made me hate alcohol with a passion. I mused about Suzie's boyfriend, pure Huguenot, and already a partner in his family's plumbing business. After they married, Suzie would no longer be thought of as a New York Jew. She could join the exclusive Garden Club. Ugh! What a bore! I was still a tomboy—I'd never fit in. Suzie fit in. Lucky Suzie.

Finally, Dutch pulled up in front of a long, low building covered in dark shingles. Pine Brook Inn said a dimly lit sign. My feet hurt in the high heels as I stepped onto the gravel and tripped on the hem of my skirt. Dutch got out and slammed his door, ignoring Suzie, who helped herself out of the car in her spotless white dress. Her high heels seemed part of her natural foot anatomy as she glided over the gravel. Peter held my arm as I wobbled toward the door, to keep me from falling on my face.

A whining cowboy droned from the jukebox at one end of an empty dance floor. The only decorations on the knotty pine walls were neon signs that buzzed Pabst in blue, Miller High Life in yellow, and Budweiser in red. A row of dirty, dangerous men sat at the bar. "Well, looky at that!" said a fat one as Suzie swung her ample hips. They glanced at me and turned away.

We picked a table in back of the empty dining room. "What'll you have?" asked Dutch when we settled around the red-checkered tablecloth with cardboard beer coasters. "The usual, honey," whined Suzie. "A beer," said Peter. "A Coke with lemon, please," I said.

Dutch drew back, his mouth agape mockingly. "Coke?! They don't proof you here. That's why I picked this joint—so we can have a good time."

"But I really want a Coke," I said, feeling like the wandering Jew. Peter's face had turned red. "OK," I relented, to spare his embarrassment. "I'll have a glass of white wine."

Dutch walked up to the bar, shaking his crewcut head, whispering to Peter with sympathy. The guys came back carrying glasses. Dutch set down the Seagram's and 7UP for himself and Suzie. Peter put down a beer for himself and a Coke with ice for me. "They don't have wine here—just beer and whiskey." Gratitude made me feel warmly toward Peter for the first time since hearing he'd joined the Marines.

"This is more like it," croaked Dutch.

"Good stuff," said Peter, sipping his glass of beer.

Dutch scraped his chair back and walked toward the jukebox, pumped in a quarter, and punched six selections. Swaggering back like John Wayne, he was the image of macho. Perry Como came on first. "I know what women like," Dutch said, pulling Suzie out of her chair and clutching her tightly.

"Lucky stiff," one of the barflies chuckled.

"*Stiff* is right," another one guffawed.

Peter asked me to dance without enthusiasm. We had already discovered at the prom that his huge feet moved in a tight square, and that my tiny feet in unaccustomed heels could serve as lethal weapons. I wanted to lindy, but "steadies" were supposed to slow dance, tight as two pieces of chewed bubblegum.

Peter, imitating Dutch, pulled me close. I stiffened and jabbed a heel in his instep. He yelped. Suzie and Dutch rocked back and forth, feet barely moving, their lips locked in an unending kiss. Dutch's hands slid over Suzie's backside. "Tonight we love," sang Perry, to the tune of Tchaikovsky's First Piano Concerto. I was the only one in that room who knew Tchaikovsky deserved credit for the music.

The song ended, the record swung back into the stack, and we sat down. "Powerful thirsty, ain't you, gonzo?" Dutch asked Peter. "My turn," said Peter, handing him a five. Dutch walked up to the bar and ordered another round. The barfly closest to him slapped him on the back and nodded, laughing raucously. Dutch preened, basking in his fellows' approval. He returned with a tray of drinks and set them down, one at a time. My fresh drink was not a Coke.

"It won't bite," Dutch said.

I let it go. Maybe I *was* being too prudish. Everyone in high school drank. I lifted the Seagram's and 7UP, took a tiny sip, and gagged. I tried another and managed to choke it down. A ribbon of fire scalded my throat and landed in my stomach like hot lava. "That-a-girl! See, it don't hurt," said Dutch triumphantly. "Hey, Pete, let's put some more music on that there jukebox. We need to warm up these ladies."

They bent their heads together making selections, their faces lit up with the orange glow like devils in hell. Dutch whispered something to Peter, who blushed. "Make an easy lay," I thought I heard, but my head was buzzing from the whiskey. He could have said, "Make a lazy play" or "Make a lady lay." The jukebox thumped like a drum signaling a sacrifice. A silver foil packet passed from Dutch's hand to Peter's. "Time to go, girls," he said. "Don't want to get you too tired—yet."

I dozed on Peter's shoulder. Crunching gravel woke me. We weren't home, but on the overlook near the Mohonk Golf Course. Dew had settled, silvering the grass in the moonlight. Dutch left the engine running, the radio turned low, and the heater humming against the cool night air. I was exhausted and wanted to go home and to bed. The announcer said, "Two o'clock, fellow night owls." Dutch pulled Suzie close and kissed her. Peter pulled me close and kissed me, sticking his tongue between my teeth. I yo-yoed between a thrill of pleasure and a feeling of disgust—not unlike my reaction to the whiskey.

"Here's old blue eyes again, folks out there in radioland," crooned the announcer. Dutch switched off the engine before Frank Sinatra could sing a note. He got out of the car, opened the trunk, and took out a blanket. Opening the door for Suzie for the first time that night, he pulled her out of the car. They disappeared into the heart of darkness near the ninth tee.

"It's three o'clock in the morning, / We've danced the whole night through," sang Rudy Vallée, a crooner from my mother's generation. Dutch and Suzie reappeared out of the moonlit darkness and got in the car, Dutch slamming his door and Suzie climbing into the passenger side by herself. He revved up the engine, backed up with a squeal, spewing gravel as he sped down the mountain road. I had pulled down my dress, feeling filthy as Peter zipped up his fly and wiped his hands on his handkerchief. When we got to Suzie's house, she jumped out, and I saw her in the floodlights—her hair in wild disarray and her white dress spotted with dirt, ripped down the front, letting her breasts hang out, sagging like an old woman's. Without speaking, she raced toward the house, limping on a snapped heel, jerkily, like a broken toy. At the door, she turned, and the cruel light of Dutch's headlights pinpointed dark bruises on her cheek and dried blood on her lips. A handprint circled the soft white flesh of her arm like a brand. Dutch honked twice, then did a squealing U-turn out of the driveway.

Later that summer, Suzie and Dutch got married in the Dutch Reformed Church. Peter was in Marine boot camp, not allowed leave, saving me from a copycat fate. I skipped the reception and packed to move into my father's summer camp in the Catskills, sleeping on a straw mattress on the porch like Cinderella. I found my old P-38 model kit and decided to try to put it together. It was boring, so I gave it up and read my father's books—James Joyce, Tolstoy, and Fitzgerald.

Peter gave me an engagement ring on his first leave. He wanted me to skip college and marry him that fall. The day before Labor Day, I packed up my belongings and left for college. I wore Peter's ring to keep from being labeled a grind, but I knew I'd never marry him. I was still my father's daughter—I could do anything a boy could do. I was going to be a writer and professor of English and marry a man who liked literate tomboys.

Questions for Discussion

1. What do you think prevented the narrator from taking the road that Suzie took?
2. Though the narrator's father encouraged his daughter to achieve, he chose women for their youth and beauty. How do you think this mixed message could cause conflict for the narrator as an adult woman?
3. What happened to Suzie on prom night?
4. Why do you think Suzie married Dutch after what happened on prom night?

Liberty Seventeen

Ellen Fairey

On my seventeenth birthday Mark gives me a miniature metal Statue of Liberty. It fits in the palm of my hand and sinks to the bottom of my waitress apron when I drop it in the pocket.

"It was either that or the Eiffel Tower," he says, stirring his drink with a straw.

I smile, flattered that he would associate me with international landmarks.

"Here's your oysters," Christine, the bartender, says. She slides him the icy plate and raises her eyebrows. Mark is the brother of the owner of Hazy Janes, where I've been working since dropping out of high school last fall. He's forty, divorced, and in between jobs. He sits at the bar in his brown leather jacket and drinks Bloody Marys, beer, or, if he's with a girl, martinis with olives.

Hazy Janes used to be a vegetarian restaurant, but they were going out of business, so last year they changed: they built a bar, added a stereo system, allowed smoking, and put New York Strip on the menu. Now it's busy. They still have plants hanging all over the place and stained-glass light fixtures with fairies on them; it's just now you can wash down your tofu cutlets and mixed steamed vegetables with a gin and tonic and a Marlboro.

I ask Mark how he knew it was my birthday.

"I know these things," he says, looking at me in a way no guy in high school ever could, like he knows what's going on, with me, with him, with the world. He's always at Hazy Janes, at the bar or hanging around the employee area. He stands in the kitchen and smokes and watches us work. He probably saw my name written on the calendar in the back: Molly's B-day—gifts accepted.

Mark doesn't have the attitude that some people do when they find out I dropped out of school. "Don't sweat it," he said when I first told him. "Some of the world's smartest people dropped out. Shit! Einstein for instance!" He comes by in the evenings, after record shopping, and shows me what he bought, mostly imported stuff from Europe; his favorite is Miles Davis, the King of Cool.

Sometimes he comes in with girls who look like they're from some place where everyone is beautiful and interesting and the last thing on their minds is high school or college. They wear things like ponchos and high boots outside their pants, clothes I know for a fact they did not get in this preppie college town. They all have high cheekbones and exotic names; I remember hearing him call one Alexa and how she smoked cigarettes from England and clicked her fingernails on her champagne glass in time with the music.

"You want to try?" Mark asks, holding up a tiny fork with an oyster dripping from it.

"No thanks, I'm working."

"You sure? It is your birthday after all." I shake my head no and start spearing olives.

"Thanks for my present," I say, wondering if the Statue of Liberty is a wonder of the world. "I love it." He slips the oyster in his mouth and grins.

"Do you know you're beautiful when you're embarrassed?" he asks.

He thinks I'm beautiful and international.

"Hey, you know what?" he says to me. "My kid is out of the house tonight, and I was thinking of having a little get-together." His kid is John and he was in my class in high school. Mark doesn't know that.

"That sounds cool," I say, trying to be easy, kicked back like him.

"Maybe someone who's working on her birthday could use some special treatment later, a nice glass of wine, maybe a little jazz. If she doesn't have plans."

"Who knows, maybe she could." I don't have plans because my friends from high school aren't my friends anymore; the only people I spend time with are here at work. I press too hard with an olive spear, stick my index finger and swallow a yelp of pain, smiling at him.

I go to the bathroom to check how I look. Lately, I don't know why, I sometimes have to look in a mirror to make sure I'm still there. I put some Rum Raisin lipstick on and take my hair out of the mini ponytail it's been in. I try to remember Mark's son from high school. All I can picture is tall and plain and quiet, no face, and a deep voice. I remember he was in my art class and he made a giant papier-mâché spaceship and painted the entire thing black. He left it on a table in the back of the art room all semester, abandoned and covered in dust.

Dropping out was no big production. It was simple and quick. I called up the school, told them I wouldn't be coming back, and dropped off my books a few days later. That was it. My counselor, Mr. Jackson, called me at home wanting to know what happened. Nothing, I told him, I'm bored. He had a big afro and a pot belly. In his office was a poster of a fist painted red, white, and blue—*Right On,* it said. I felt bad that he felt bad. My parents had a talk with me in the living room; they didn't know what to say. Me dropping out seemed more of an inconvenience to them than anything else. They sat and looked at me and said they wished I wouldn't do this. My mother sighed and said she was a failure. I explained to them that they had been letting me do what I wanted for so long already, what made this any different? They looked relieved when the talk was over; those kinds of things made them uncomfortable. If you're not going to be in school, they said, then you need to get a job, you need survival skills. Now I pay them one hundred dollars a month for rent and call home if I'm going to be out after two. What I wanted to know was, if my mother was a failure, then what did that make me?

After my shift, Christine sets a piece of carrot cake on the bar with a candle in it and everyone sings "Happy Birthday." Mark sits with a cigarette dangling out of his smile, clapping along, holding up his drink in a cheers at the end. I look at his face to see if I can see signs of John, something that would make me remember him, but nothing comes up. We all do shots of tequila and lean against the bar, laughing with limes pressed against our lips. Mark holds the back of my neck for support as he drinks another one, his fingers gripping my shoulder as he shoots it down his throat. This is a great birthday, I think; this is me.

"So, you ever been to New York?" Mark asks me. We're walking to his car parked up the street. It's Thursday night at Doogin's, the frat-boy bar across the street. People are always vomiting or peeing or fighting outside of it. I'm glad I'm over here with Mark, walking next to him, us having a conversation about New York.

"Yeah, but I never went to the Statue of Liberty," I tell him. Up by his car, a big black Oldsmobile, he opens the giant passenger door for me, swishing back his arm saying, "Madame." I get in and notice the way I look against the velvety interior, pale. It smells like smoke and some kind of cologne, maybe from the bottle of Aramis that's laying in the backseat next to a pair of socks.

"What's so funny?" Mark asks. His car is like a huge ship; it has to be ten years old.

"Oh, nothing," I say. "I'm just thinking about stuff." I'm thinking how bizarre it is that here I am with one of my classmates' fathers and what Mark, me, and John might look like flying around in that black papier-mâché spaceship.

"Just stuff huh? Cool." He pulls a small folded paper rectangle out of the inside pocket of his jacket. "Hey, speaking of stuff, you into this stuff?" he bounces the packet in his palm.

"Sure," I say. I take the Statute of Liberty out of my jeans and start to balance her on the dashboard. Mark coughs. Directly in the center, taped on the pebbly vinyl surface, is a small red square of velcro. The velcro's mate, zillions of tiny plastic loops, are on the base of my statue, the same exact size as the square on the dashboard. I'm embarrassed that I thought he got her for me but don't want him to know that I noticed so I put her back in my pocket and fiddle with the radio. I wonder how long she has been riding around with him. A Talking Heads song comes on that sounds like it was recorded underwater, "Same as it ever was, / Same as it ever was."

We drive past the street that my parents and I live on and I don't look down it. Dad would be doing the crossword right now, in the kitchen, with his glasses at the edge of his nose, and Mom would be reading in the corner of the living room, both with their own little lights on above their heads, the rest of the house dark.

We pull into an old apartment complex located on the edge of the city, where it goes from pretty college town to gray industrial town. It always seems like it's fall over here, craggy old trees hunching over, leaves on the ground, no matter what time of year. The apartments are set up as a kind of mock village—one-story brick cottages with white window panes and fake black shutters. The shutters are cut at an angle and pasted to the brick to give the effect that they are flung open, letting all the sunshine in. The freshly paved parking area makes the car feel like it's floating.

"You'll have to pardon the mess," Mark says as he opens the door to his place. But other than some mail lying around and a plate with a piece of toast on it, it doesn't seem messy. What surprises me is how ordinary it is; I had expected his apartment to be different, cooler or something. There's a stereo, TV, and a futon in the living room, a tiny kitchen, and a bedroom with a glass-topped table in it. The only thing on the walls are some fairy paintings I recognize from Hazy Janes before the update.

Mark directs me toward the round table in the bedroom and says he'll be right back. My feet are aching from work so I toss my shoes off, figuring I might as well get comfortable, no big deal. I take Liberty out of my jeans and set her in the middle of the table and wonder who the woman is they modeled her after; she stands there, with her arm up, looking patient or bored. Mark puts on a Miles Davis record and brings in two glasses of Mumms champagne. With a single-edged razor he scoots the cocaine out of its packet and onto the top of the table and begins chopping and drawing lines.

"To you," he says, sniffing up half the pile with a rolled-up ten, "and I would never be so rude as to ask a woman her age." This last bit is directed to my statue, which is staring at him from the center of the table. He cracks up, pinching his nose between his fingers, cleaning it. The dim overhead light makes his face look gray.

"To me," I say, sniffing up the other half of the pile. I'm surprised by my reflection in the mirror; I look like one of Mark's wavy-haired poncho girls. Mark closes his eyes and leans back in his chair, getting into Miles Davis. I try to do the same, but each time I close my eyes all I can see is my mother and father in their dark house, not saying a word. The music sounds foggy and slow and doesn't match my mood. I hate being so still. I look around the room and sip my champagne. Mark gets up and takes off his jacket. He does a couple side bends with his eyes closed and makes a little whew sound as he walks over to the bed.

"Happy birthday, Ms. Molly," he says, patting a space on the bed next to him.

I go and sit next to him and touch his arm. Mr. Jackson, my high school counselor, always called students by their last names, Ms. This or Mr. That. "Ms. Walker," he'd said to me, "You don't want to end up working at Joe's Diner do you? I have higher hopes for you."

"Happy birthday," I say too loud, trying to change the mood. It feels sludgy in here, like my parents' house.

Saying what I do next is out of my control is not completely true, but I don't know how else to really describe it. It's like when I have to look in the mirror to make sure I'm still there. I mean, of course I know I'm here, but there's part of me that's somewhere else, maybe at home with my parents or back in school being bored out of my mind, or maybe traveling to the top of the Eiffel tower. When I'm missing like that, something else makes my decisions for me, and a lot of times they surprise me.

Mark is looking at me like I'm the most beautiful thing; his hair is messy; he is slouching. In a way, he looks almost frightened. I push the hair off his face and lift my Hazy Janes T-shirt over my head, tossing it to one of the chairs at the table. I want him to stop looking frightened. I climb onto his lap, put my arms around him, and kiss his neck. My heart is beating fast. I feel light and invisible as he put his arms around me, lifts me up and around so that we're lying next to each other on the gold and green plaid comforter. He is so quiet as he touches me. The music sounds like it is going in circles. I want to brush my teeth.

A door opens and someone sets down some keys. Mark grunts and gets up off the bed, dragging the comforter to the floor with his weight.

"Dad?" a voice says.

"Shit. Hold on hon, sorry," Mark combs his fingers through his hair and kisses my cheek. "Just a sec, bud!" he yells to John.

I bounce off the bed and go and stand in the triangle of space behind the open bedroom door, against the wall. I can hear John and his father discussing something about the time, and a pizza in the freezer. They're talking and laughing about something, calling each other dude. Through the crack, where the door hinges, I can see my shoes lying on the hallway floor; they're boat shoes, the kind all the popular kids in school wear that cost seventy-five dollars. I have never been on a boat. I look around the corner of the door at the statue on the table; she is surrounded by the champagne glasses, a little pile of cocaine, and an ashtray full of butts. A wad of cellophane from the Miles Davis album Mark opened envelops her like a huge crinkly robe. She looks tiny.

"Ms. Liberty," I whisper toward her, "I had higher hopes for you, you know."

I wait to try and hear what Mark or John will do next. The Miles Davis record has ended; the needle is going back and forth near the center making a scraping sound. No, I do not want to end up at Joe's Diner, I think, and I am pretty sure I don't want to end up in this apartment either. I walk quickly and quietly to the table, jam my T-shirt on over my head, pick Liberty up out of the mess, and shove her into my jeans' pocket. I reach into the hallway with my stockinged foot and scoot my shoes toward me with my toe, thinking if I can just stay inside the parameters of the bedroom I will remain invisible.

I am sitting on the floor tying the thin leather laces when John walks by to change the record, or turn it off. He stops, looks at me, then the rest of the room in a kind of survey. For a minute, I swear I can smell high school on him: the mopped hallways and metal lockers, the cafeteria and gym and sleep-inducing auditorium that's painted mauve. I remember him all at once, right in front of me: his clean, round face and sandy brown hair that falls into his eyes. I remember him always tilting his head up to see from under those bangs, like he's doing right now. And his eyes: dark, gray-blue just like mine, the kind you can't tell what they're thinking, I remember those now too. And all I can think of is how young he looks, like a kid, and how someone should worry about him and watch out for him, and that he still needs to be taken care of. Then, he doesn't say a word; he just walks into the living room and turns the record over, making me wonder if he remembers me from high school or if I am just a girl on the floor in his father's bedroom.

Questions for Discussion

1. What impact did Molly's encounter with Mark have on her?
2. If Molly decided to seek counseling shortly after her experience with Mark, what would you want to know about her life and circumstances? What questions would you want ask?
3. What are Molly's strengths?

Drive

Michael E. Miller

My mother has been in a state insane asylum, a booby hatch, for over two years, and they want me to go see her.

"Patrick, you're the man in your house now, and someone has to go see your mother. She's better and it's time for you to see her. You and Uncle Alex can go to Mandeville Saturday. He says you can drive there," Nannie Deese says.

She's Mama's sister. She taught me to drive and let me use her car to get my driver's license when I turned sixteen in January. She took me out in the park, on the fairway of the old golf course, and I started driving. I almost didn't need to be taught. I don't remember any struggle. I drove in my mind for years before I actually did it.

I love being behind the wheel. I love the feeling of a car, of the engine, the resistance to turning, learning the limits, controlling the thing. I love it. Nannie let's me use her car sometimes to go off by myself. I can pick up the guys, and I do the driving. I don't really know why I love driving so much, but I do. And I'm good at it.

We never had a car at home. Everyone else did, but we didn't, until one day my father parked an old prewar town car, which he had bought, beside the house. The car was long and black, with outboard fenders, plush upholstery, and curtains. It was very exciting for me to be able to climb in and tell the other kids, "This is our car." That car never ran and one day, like my father, it just disappeared.

Mama didn't exactly disappear two years ago. She just started acting strange, and seeing things no one else saw, and being scared, and crying a lot. Then Nannie and Uncle Alex came. Nannie told Mama she had to go away to a hospital.

"What about my children," she cried.

"They'll be OK," Nannie said. "I'll see about them. You've got to go."

"NO, NO, NO, I can't. This is a plot. You've been planning this to take away my children. You're trying to get rid of me. Help me. Help me. Somebody help me!" Mama screamed.

Nannie stepped to the bedroom door, looked into the next room at me, and said, "Patrick, leave now. You shouldn't be here for this."

I left. I left my mother, who was terrified and begging for help. I turned my back on her and walked out the door. I just kept walking down the street until I couldn't hear her anymore, then I walked farther. When I came home she was gone. I got her room, her bed. I got to do what I wanted. No one, at least no one in this town, could tell me what to do. And I haven't seen Mama since.

* * *

On this Saturday morning Uncle Alex and I leave Opelousas, with me driving as promised, going east on highway 190. I drive over the Bayou Courtableau Bridge, the first high bridge I ever drive over. Twenty miles farther I manage the higher Atchafalaya River Bridge at Krotz Springs, driving next to the right edge, with the meanest river in the world boiling past below. I drive past the young sugarcane in the fields west of Baton Rouge, and over the really big bridge across the Mississippi. I keep watching the road, feeling the excitement of driving over a road somewhere for the first time, but then I think of where I'm going. Mandeville. My mother in the nuthouse.

A black liquid fear oozes up from my gut, like dirty oil with colors streaking through it, rising like it'll get to my lungs, stop my breathing. This road doesn't have a curve on it, and at times I'm so stiff, that if it did, I'd run straight off. I answer my uncle's questions as I drive, without even hearing what I say.

I just drive, like I've got to, to the end of the road. To a gatehouse where we've got to be approved for me to see my mother. To a low white building where my uncle leaves me in the car to go get Mom.

She comes out, dressed like she's going to church. She's always been skinny, but now she's even thinner. Her eyes are deeper and darker than ever, and she approaches me as though she's afraid of me. I get out and stand in front of her. I don't want her to touch me. I don't know what to say. I don't know what to feel. I just know I've got to do this. She's staring in my eyes, and I look away.

"I missed you every day," she says.

"Yes, ma'am."

"Did you get my letters?"

"Sometimes."

"I wrote you every day I could. I really did think of you and Beth every day. It's all that got me through. How is Beth? I wish I could see her."

"Elaine, we better go to lunch. We don't have that much time," Uncle Alex says.

I drive to the restaurant. It's just a restaurant.

"When are you coming home?" I ask.

"I don't know for sure. It's not up to me, but my doctor says I'm doing so well on this new drug I may be able to try it in a couple of months," she says.

I don't even know the name of this doctor, who decides if my mother can come home.

We drive back to the hospital. She gets out and I stay in the driver's seat. She looks at me.

"You seem to be mad at me. Why are you mad at me?" she asks.

"I'm not mad. We just need to go."

"I'm trying as hard as I can to come home. I hope you want me to come home."

She turns, with her head down, and walks straight through the side door of the building with Uncle Alex.

He walks back to the car and says, "You want to drive back too?"

"I don't care," I say.

Questions for Discussion

1. Patrick's aunt and uncle tell him to leave the house while they make his mother go to the mental hospital. What do you think Patrick was feeling after he left the house?
2. How do these emotions affect his interactions with his mother at the mental hospital?
3. How do you think his mother's hospitalization could have been handled by the adults?

Soldier Boy

Susan Olding

My office walls are made of glass. Gregory Fell is a tall boy, whose Crayola-orange hair seems to vibrate under the fluorescent lights, so that long before he taps on the door, I can see him awkwardly approaching. He hunches, shoulders almost level with his ears, and frowns, averting his face from everyone else's.

"Hello," he says, bowing and dipping like some strange old-fashioned toy, one of those stiff-necked plastic birds that bobs perpetually for colored water.

"I know you're busy, but . . ." His lip twitches.

"Come in. Sit down." I brush away crumbs and swallow the last of my milk.

He shrugs, buckling the stripes on his pullover. Then, closing the door behind him, he peers furtively under the desk and into the farthest corner of the tiny, triangular room. Finally he sits on the edge of the molded plastic chair, releasing his iron-fisted grip on the dark green gym bag he always carries with him. It falls to the floor with a thud. Gregory is not good at sports, so whatever this bag's intended use, it has never, in fact, held athletic equipment. Instead, it contains books—every text for each course he is taking— and also all his binders. Unlike his classmates, Gregory will not leave these in his locker and pick them up during breaks between periods or at lunchtime. Lately, he will not go to his locker at all.

"Counselors are always busy," he observes. "People coming by. People needing help. Yes, I understand." His voice trails off.

Then he clears his throat. "You know, I was wondering. I need to make a few phone calls. Just a few calls." A sly gleam ignites his eyes. "I have an interview, you know, for a job. A government job. I have to call them immediately."

I have been warned to refuse this request. In the past few months, Gregory has been "doing the rounds" of the counselors, taking over our offices for hours at a time. (*Just one more. Just one more!* he will insist, if interrupted, shielding the phone with his elbows.) He has made at least a hundred calls, racked up a huge long distance bill on the school's account. The secretaries in our main office are tired of fielding angry and confused complaints from the various officers in obscure federal and provincial subdepartments who, so far, have been the main casualties of his delusions.

"Gregory, I'm sorry, but no. I can't allow you to tie up that line."

It's true. Any minute now, someone else may call—a desperate teacher, a despairing parent, a counselor from another school, a probation officer. At the same time, as Gregory knows, and I know, my excuse is also a lie. I *could* let him use the phone, if I wanted to.

Abruptly, he starts to cry. I stand to close the blinds—a recent, much needed addition to the room supplied by a sympathetic principal—but no sooner have I done so then he stops.

"It's okay," he says. "I understand. Of course, of course, you're busy." His skin has flushed a blotchy pink. He stands as if to leave, but then does not.

"I think my parents are trying to hurt me," he blurts. "I think they're after me. I found a trail of papers on our lawn. And then . . . and then . . . "

"Yes?"

"They don't want me to pass my courses. There is too much noise there. You know what I mean? Too noisy."

"Do you have younger brothers and sisters? Is that it?"

"No. It's them. Just them. They're always *talking*. They wouldn't talk like that if they wanted me to do well. They wouldn't. It isn't right. It isn't *fair*. I have a lot of courses—they know that—a *lot* of difficult courses this term. So it's pretty obvious, isn't it. They want me to fail." He smirks.

"It sounds as if you're feeling anxious, Gregory. As if you are under a lot of stress."

"Stress, that's it. I'm stressed. I need to find somewhere else to work, somewhere quiet. Do you know some place I could go? Could I stay at the school overnight? In Mr. Ross's room? Or maybe here, instead." He looks around again, as if considering the best spot on the floor for a sleeping bag. "In here would be fine. Would the janitors kick me out?"

"Gregory, have you tried talking with your parents?"

"No. *No!* I can't talk with them."

"You know you can't stay here at night." I hope my voice is gentle.

"Do you remember what we talked about last week? Have you thought some more about going to see your doctor?"

He is eighteen. Even if they wanted to—and I am not sure they do—his parents could not force him to go. I cannot force him. He has to decide this for himself.

But he grabs his bag and lunges toward the door.

"You *could* let me use the phone, you know. You *could* let me use it. It wouldn't really be so hard for you at all. *You* could use somebody else's office. You *could*." By this time, he is shouting, and if the blinds were still open, I know I'd see the curious faces of his peers, smudge-nosed against the pane.

He slams the door behind him. I long to lay my head on the plastic walnut finish of the desk and cry.

Three years ago, when I was still a classroom teacher, I worked with Gregory as his tutor. Even then he was rigid and vigilant and stiff; our students called him "Soldier Boy." He prided himself on his reliability. As obsequious as Uriah Heep, as punctual as the Inspector of Schools, I can still see him racing against the bell, his green gym bag held out stiffly in front of him, and an odd, self-satisfied smile on his pale face.

Later, we had a falling out. On Fridays, I had been giving him lifts into town, driving out of my way to take him to McDonald's, where he worked. We had agreed that he should ask me for these rides in advance, and at first he was religious with his requests. Then, he started forgetting. He would show up at my door at three o'clock and stare pointedly at his watch, while distractedly, clumsily, I gathered up my things. *Hurry, hurry,* he would say. *I don't want to be late!* Or he would neglect to ask me at all and simply wait by my car in the dusty lot. Meanwhile, I'd have promised rides to four or five other students or teachers, and there wouldn't be any room. Sometimes I had weekend plans that would prevent me from going into town at all. One day I had to rush to make a dental appointment. "I can only take you to the traffic lights at Princess," I warned him. "I can't take you all the way this time."

Gregory at first agreed, but as we drove, he began to argue about it. His voice took on a hostile tone I'd never heard in him before; he was rude and obstinate and demanding. In retrospect, I see this as a warning sign, a symptom of his breakdown, but at the time, I was preoccupied with my own worries and indignant at his ungratefulness. I asked him to put himself in my shoes: Would he want to do favors for people who complained and took him for granted?

He was not open to reason. He clenched his jaw and started shouting at me. His pale hands trembled. I pulled over to the curb then and asked him to get out. Thereafter, he avoided me in the halls, looked down when he caught my eye, consumed his library lunches in a carrel hidden from my office. So when he suddenly appeared at my door again and asked to make his phone calls, I knew he must be desperate. Who could deny humiliation like that, except in direst need?

*   *   *

Summer, and I am walking across the campus of the university. First, the new library, with its wide stone plaza, wooden benches, and its freshly planted trees; next, "Fort Jock," the big athletic center, surrounded by beds of vivid flowers. Students spill out of doorways, glide by on bicycles, shout to one another from across the street. I am enjoying this walk—the sense of freedom any holiday brings, the feeling of sun on my skin, the beauty of the young, fresh faces all around me.

Suddenly I hear a familiar, yet unplaceable voice. Someone is calling. Someone is calling *me.*

Missus. Missus!

I am not a "Mrs." Nobody calls me that. It must be a former student, one of those sweet, old-fashioned, well-meaning ones who can never get *Ms.* out of their mouths. I stop and spin around, my sandals scraping the pavement.

Gregory?

I recognize the red hair, which seems to shiver in the sunlight. Otherwise, he is greatly changed. His illness has swollen him. Or perhaps this new puffiness is a side effect of medication.

Has he started taking medication?

In less than a month, he has gained at least twenty pounds, and his striped pullover, too heavy for today's heat, strains at all its seams. His skin gleams with an unhealthy sweat. His suffering is so palpable, and so incongruous here in the warm sun, among these glowing young bodies and faces, amid the brilliant flowers, that I want to look away. I *do* look away and then force myself to turn back. His own eyes dart and flicker. He drops the green gym bag on the ground.

"Have you been working out?" I ask, astonished.

"I have, I have," he stammers. "I graduated, you know. Even passed chemistry. I'm taking a couple of courses. Part-time. My marks aren't good enough for full-time. But they let me use the facilities."

"Congratulations, Gregory. You had a rough term. I'm really glad you made it."

Maybe he will be all right.

"Yes." He sighs, scuffing his shoe against the sidewalk, a smile dawning at the corners of his pale and blistered lips.

Maybe he'll be fine after all.

Then he chuckles. "Well, you know, got to get in shape. Got to get myself in shape, to take that government job."

Questions for Discussion

1. What behaviors might alert a school counselor or social worker to the possibility that Gregory may have a severe mental illness?
2. What diagnosis, based on the information in this story, would you assign to Gregory?

3. If you were a school counselor or social worker, how would you intervene to try to get help for him? What steps would you take? How
would you approach the family?

SELECTED READINGS AND ADDITIONAL RESOURCES

Brown, Eva, M. (1989). *My Parent's Keeper: Adult Children of the Emotionally
Disturbed*. Oakland, CA: New Harbinger Publications.

Byers, Sandra and O'Sullivan, Lucia (Eds.) (1996). *Sexual Coercion in Dating Relationships*. Binghamton, NY: The Haworth Press.

Dunn, Bonnie (1993). Growing up with a Psychotic Mother: A Retrospective Study
American Journal of Orthopsychiatry 63(2), 177-189.

Easson, William (1996). *The Management of the Severely Disturbed Adolescent*.
Madison, CT: International Universities Press.

Gutkin, Lee (1995). *Stuck in Time: The Tragedy of Childhood Mental Illness*. New
York: Henry Holt Publishers.

Leeming, Frank, O'Dwyer, William, and Oliver, Diana (Eds.) (1996). *Issues in Adolescent Sexuality: Readings from the Washington Post*. Needham, MA: Allyn
& Bacon.

Lieberman, Susan (1999). *Venus in Blue Jeans: Why Mothers and Daughters Need
to Talk about Sex*. New York: Dell Books.

Pipher, Mary (1995). *Reviving Ophelia: Saving the Selves of Adolescent Girls*. New
York: Ballentine Press.

PART III:
FAMILY RELATIONSHIPS IN ADULTHOOD

On Not Being Seen

Bobbi Lurie

The desire to be seen is what falling in love has always meant to me. As a child I bought into the fairy tales which crescendoed toward a glorious climax: the meeting of some handsome prince, that one special person in the world who would see me as special. But I could not hold on to this fantasy. I knew, through my mother's unhappy marriage and from the sense of hopeless passivity which surrounded her, that my chances of reaching any type of "happily ever after" were slim at best. It was obvious that a long-term relationship with that magical, faceless prince could only spell disaster.

In those early days of my childhood, it was enough for me to long to be seen by my mother, to have her love, and for her to recognize me. But this was also an impossibility. My mother was turned in on her own unhappiness. She often told me she wished she never had children. So I entered my own private dreamworld and invented my own imaginary mother who would find me some day and reward me for my diligence. Since I could not identify with the plight of the princess and I could not find a way to have my mother see me or respond to me, I made a gallant effort to be my mother's prince. I believed, and still believe, I was the one person in this world who saw my mother's unseen beauty, who looked at her in a way my father and brothers never did or could. This was my specialness, to see my mother's specialness. I felt my role as a woman was to see deeper than the men did. In this way I found a way not to be faceless. I was determined to stay by my mother, imbibing her sadness, her untold story. I was determined to feed her story back to her in the shape of recognition. I only wanted to be seen in return. But to this day, I do not know if my mother ever saw me.

This is my story: seeing, not being seen. It is the story of the writer trying forever to communicate with an unknowable lover. And it is the story of anyone who loves someone with Alzheimer's disease. Those with Alzheimer's disease are clearly alive, walking on the earth, appearing as people. As diminished as they are, they remain alive to us. It is we who have died. We have died to them. They do not connect with us or see us. And when I see my mother now, seemingly more happy than she ever was during her life before senility, I realize that Alzheimer's disease is *my* disease.

Alzheimer's disease is the end of reciprocation. There is no continuity, no shared history. We are not seen, and ultimately we see that we also cannot see. We cannot see or know those with Alzheimer's disease. Their bodies are familiar to us but we are unable to connect with them. Alzheimer's disease is the disease of the human being who longs for connection and recognition.

All the parts of myself which were given to me by my mother, all the parts I gave to my mother are as if vanished through our mutual disappearance from each other. I know I will never be seen by her and that, although she lives, I can never again be a part of her mysterious world.

My mother seems at peace. It is I who live in sadness. It is I who mourns my mother's life. Yet, I cannot help but learn from my mother's newly found innocence. For the first time in her life, I see that she is open to whatever life might bring. I take her to eat ice cream with my six-year-old son. She tries to sip the strawberry ice cream out of the top of the plastic spoon. She laughs when I show her how to hold the spoon and eat from it. I wait for her comprehension. Usually it does not come. What I mostly wait for is my mother's connection to this world finally to be severed and end.

Being with my mother exhausts me. Still, I see her. Seeing her is still my task. I suspect it will always be my task to see her or at least try to see her. What I think now is that we all live in symbols and that once the brain can no longer make or digest these symbols, there is only emptiness, a vast unknowing.

Someday I, too, may fall into a state of unknowing. I believe that, like the smooth morning lake undisturbed by waves of habit and description, my mother might be living in a realm of newness and surprise I am too closed to see.

I watch her eat her strawberry ice cream. She smiles and repeats over and over, "This is good. This is good."

Questions for Discussion

1. In what ways would treatment with this woman be similar to grief-after-death counseling?
2. In what ways, other than the way this daughter coped, can feeling unrecognized by a parent impact personality development?

Mother Stew

Lynore G. Banchoff

You tell me
how to make stew
although I am forty-two.

You yell:
put the carrots in whole
    as I am chopping,
throw in entire potatoes,
    while I am quartering,
toss in whole onions,
    as I am slicing.

No matter how
I chop, quarter, and slice my life,
you tell me how to make stew
although I am forty-two.

Question for Discussion

1. What components of this relationship would you address in treatment? After you have listed the obvious ones, list another one.
2. How can you help an adult child deal with a controlling parent?

Elaine

Michael E. Miller

"Pat, your mother died tonight," Tim says, after picking me up at New Orleans International Airport.

I don't answer. I sit for a long while, until we find our way to I-10 and head west to go home. I think, "My mother died. This should feel terrible, but I feel nothing. No, that's not quite right. I feel blank. How the hell am I supposed to be feeling? What am I supposed to do?" Tim drives on in silence, over the dark land. Over the flat dead landscape. No color. Black and lighter black, that's all.

As we near the town of Eunice the edges of the headlight beams start to soften, and we emerge from the dark into light gray. I see Eunice approaching in monochrome over the old rice fields. The square, spare, wooden houses on the edge of town. The water tank still standing guard above the buildings. The silent corrugated tin rice dryers, doing their continuous work, night and day, summer and winter. We pass the low sprawl of Wilson Memorial Hospital where Mom just died.

Dead. She's dead. Is her body still there as we go by the hospital? Or is it at Ardoin's Funeral Home, lying on one of those damn tables, being drained, and injected, and preserved, and decorated. And where do I go now, to her house where she lived with her mother, Sweet Mama, or to Ardoin's?

The sun is up. The town is still dull. How come I didn't notice how ugly this town is when I was a kid? When I prayed, I would thank God for letting me be born here. I thought everyone else was disadvantaged. I might have been born in Massachusetts, or Russia, or some place like that, but I was lucky.

At age five I would sit like a puppy at Mom's feet, under the floor lamp, while she read. More than anything, I wanted to be able to sit and read with her. I knew then that she loved me completely. I never, ever doubted that she loved me, no matter what I did.

Tim turns the corner and pulls to a stop in front of the house. I still feel nothing, but I know a great, yawning emptiness is just out of sight. I'm beginning to feel it the way I can feel the thirty-five thousand feet below an airborne jet if I pay attention, but I'm not going to pay attention.

My sister, Beth, sees us and comes through the screen door to the front porch, where we meet.

"Where is she?" I ask without greeting.

"She's at the funeral home. We're going there now. Want to come?"

"No, not yet. I'd like to come later."

"Here's the keys to her old car. Just come when you want to," Beth says.

I thank Tim and watch Beth and Sweet Mama drive off.

I walk into the empty house directly to her bedroom. The room is furnished with a 1950s modern blond suite, the finish now darkened and cracking. The double bed, which we shared when I was a child, is covered by a chenille bedspread, one which has been washed until the knobs are worn and the once pink color is almost gone. Above the chest of drawers is a crucifix, and on the chest, images of the Blessed Virgin and the Sacred Heart of Jesus. On her dresser, on doilies, are her bottles of cold cream and cologne, and brushes, and mirrors, and a framed picture of me. Of me with the sweet, round, freckled face of an eight-year-old. This is all waiting for her. She left for the hospital feeling a little bad, expecting to be home by now. In a month she is to be visiting with me in Maryland. She has her ticket. She'll love my new home. A California contemporary on a lot with big trees. She'll love it. Oh shit! She'll never see my house.

I take out my camera and start shooting the stark, colorless bedroom. The gauzy curtains are yellowed with age. The rug is beige. The black and white shots will be flat and grainy because I am shooting them that way, and I will blow them up and print them that way.

Why did she have such a shitty life? Why? What did she do to anyone? She just loved me more than anyone else. I'll never be loved like that again. Where do I replace that? What fills the hole? Who do I call? Who, no matter what I do, will be there when I call? I've got to get out of here.

I take the car and drive around town, by my old school, by my childhood friends' houses, and finally to the house we lived in through the biggest part of my growing up. I park in front and stare at the oak that Mom and I planted twenty-seven years ago. It is a beautiful oak, tall and straight and full.

Why was her life so pitiful, so painful? Why did she marry a raging alcoholic, whom she loved until the day she died? She left him. Took the kids and left him when I was six and moved in with her crazy, mean mother, with whom she fought the rest of her life. In her twenties she had early, experimental periodontal surgery and a total hysterectomy. I remember her lying in bed, in the afternoon, moaning in agony from the gum surgery. It was futile, and she lost all her teeth anyway. In her thirties she became psychotic, spent two years on a ward in a state mental hospital, and came home a guinea pig for Thorazine, which she took until yesterday. It probably killed her. What the hell kind of life is that?

Someone should have taken care of her, loved her. For all she gave me, I never learned to show love and affection for her after she left for the state mental hospital. I hated her for leaving me. I hated her for making me ashamed of her. I hated her for having to see her that way. I love her.

What to do now? I'll go to the funeral home. All my life there have been funerals at Ardoin's. They were Sweet Mama's greatest social event. They were exotic. They were for others. Now Mom is there, in that damned room, in that damned casket, with all of those damned sweet-smelling flowers, and all of those damned hypocrites who are just glad it's not them.

I go in. I don't go look at her. Just sit down in a chair next to Beth. Mr. Matt Fruge comes up. I stand and shake his outstretched hand.

"She was a wonderful woman. We'll all miss her. She never said anything bad about anyone," he says, as he leans forward solicitously.

"Thank you," I say.

What I want to say, what I terribly want to say, is, "She complained about what an awful boss you were all the time, you pious, hypocritical, sanctimonious old son-of-a-bitch. You overworked and underpaid her all those years, and going to mass every goddamned morning didn't do you, or anybody else, a goddamned bit of good."

Fuck him. I'll go to the back room.

I sit here for a long time by myself. Somehow I can sit and not feel, but if I move, if I do anything, I might break. I just sit in this suspended animation. This is all right.

Then the door opens quietly, and Dad's brothers, Uncle Billy and Uncle Whitney gently walk in.

"Hi, Pat. How ya doin'?" asks Uncle Whitney softly.

I stand and face them but hold my ground. "I'm fine," I say.

"Pat, we're real sorry, son. You know we always loved Elaine. She was a fine woman," says Uncle Whitney.

I nod.

Then Billy says, "Pat, we brought your Daddy from Baton Rouge. He wants to pay his respects, but only if it's all right with you."

"Tell him to go fuck himself," I say.

Billy stands and looks at me as Uncle Whitney lowers his head and turns to leave the room. Billy takes one step toward me and, in the softest voice I have ever heard him use, he says, "Son, you've got to give this up. It's not good for you."

I stare him down until he also turns and leaves, closing the door behind him. I sit alone again.

Questions for Discussion

1. What emotions is the narrator experiencing?
2. What unresolved issues does the narrator have in relation to his mother and his estranged father?

Daddy's Girls

Helen Ruggieri

The humidity is so heavy I can barely stand upright. My head aches and there's a circle drawing tighter and tighter around my right eye. I wash my hair and sit directly in the path of the fan, and when my hair dries, I wet a washcloth and sit with that on top of my head. Heat helps, but it is too hot for heat. I don't want to think about it because it hurts.

I deserve to suffer. Suffering makes me feel better. Since my mother died I haven't had time to suffer properly. I haven't grieved enough or I've grieved too much, but not as one should, not formally. When Daddy died, I couldn't write, not for a year or even more. Every morning I would sit to write and start to cry. I knew it was too much. "Unseemly," my mother would say. "Don't carry on so!" He was ninety-six. But I couldn't help it. Nobody ever loved me like he did.

My mother didn't really care. I was just someone who provided transportation because she was too cheap to call a taxi. I could have been anyone. Half the time she called me by my sister's name. She disapproved of me since the day I was born. Nothing I did pleased her. She was "fair affronted" by me and never failed to tell me or to indicate that disapproval.

If I think of my father I can cry, but I know it's unseemly, irrational even, to grieve like this. He died in July. It will be two years soon. See, I'm crying already, but that's all right. I can cry and type at the same time and it may help my headache.

He called up one night from Arizona, where they spent the winter, and said he loved me and hung up. I didn't know what to think, but I started crying. He could always make me cry with his maudlin expressions. I thought maybe he'd been drinking; he talked funny, slurring his words.

Then my mother called to say he was in a nursing home dying. I charged the plane tickets. I was angry because she hadn't told me sooner. I couldn't afford the ticket at the monthly rate, and now I would be paying it off until Christmas.

The day I got to Phoenix was the fifth day in a row the temperature had been over 115. My throat was dry way down between my breasts. I couldn't breathe right from the plane and then the wind began to blow, making grit and dirt into miniature tornadoes. Dust devils and sheets of newspaper hovered in the air like giant birds of prey. The transition from my cool mountain town to this kiln, this maelstrom of sand and sun, was too much. My sinus apparatus began to pull tight around my forehead, my eyes. No mercy.

When we got to the nursing home, Daddy was tied in a wheelchair. Without his glasses and his teeth, I couldn't be sure. "This isn't Daddy," I said. The aide left the room. Daddy's eyes didn't focus. "He's been like that for two months," my mother said. "Let's get something to eat." I had such a headache from the sand, the storm that seemed to be coming, and the wind, I thought something to drink would settle my stomach, all wretched with airplanes and sinus and Daddy sitting there like a sleeping stranger.

When we got back to the trailer, there was a phone call from the nursing home. They said Daddy had taken a turn for the worse and we'd better come back. We sat in the room and listened to him breathing. It sounded loud in the silence, each ragged breath, frailer and frailer. Outside the window a giant mesa sat like a purple bruise on the horizon. The clouds got darker and darker until the mesa disappeared, but there was no rain, only wind and grit thickening the air. The windows didn't open, and the breaths went on, and Daddy didn't know me, and my mother kept asking for a doctor though there was nothing any doctor could do. "Aren't you going to do something?" she demanded of the nurse.

The nurse and I made eye contact as if we understood, which I did and didn't. I knew he was dying and I had been crying all afternoon and my nose hurt and my sinuses ached and Daddy struggled. Then he raised his hand as if he were hitchhiking and I took it, and he closed it around mine like a baby does, and then he stopped breathing.

The professionals came and did what they do. I kept on crying for three days, stopping occasionally to sleep and eat, but every time I'd think of his hand, feel that cool hard flesh of his palm next to mine, I'd start to cry again. I'm even crying now, though I know it's silly, indulgent, probably psychologically unhealthy, morbid, ridiculous. An old lady myself crying for my daddy. Daddy's little girl, daddyless. Death enters my life. The only person who ever loved me enough, for no reason other than that I was me, is dead and I'm alone.

Mother died in January and I cried, but not like this, not still, not now. I'm crying for Daddy again, for me. The grief of orphans is for themselves. Selfish brats.

The roots of this extreme grief are so tangled, so knitted up with my childhood, my genes, my psyche, there's no way to untangle it. The subjectivity of it, the fearing to tread on angel ground, all my weaknesses, nightmares, hates, fears, guilts, bad seeds, wants are coated with this emotional haze and Daddy is there at the center of it, not a giant spider, but one of those cysts that send out tentacles spinning themselves around the ligaments and veins, trying to be a part of you so badly, there's almost no way to uproot them. One tiny cell left, and they begin to grow again.

That's how it is for all us daddy's girls. We didn't want to be like our mothers, God forbid we should wear aprons and schlepp around the house all day doing boring things—dusting, watching soap operas, playing bridge. We wanted to go out like Daddy did, drive away and come back with stories, paper umbrellas, chopsticks, glass cocktail stirrers with the names of famous clubs, fascinating artifacts of the life out there where exciting things were done while we waited at home.

Our lives were structured like that—waiting for Daddy. Everything was geared to his leaving and his return. Meals, holidays, vacations. If your daddy was unreliable like my daddy, stopping off for a few, forgetting it was Christmas Eve or Friday night, forgetting presents or that we were going out for a fish fry, forgetting us completely, you began to rebel. As I became a teenager I could see clearly that my mother's inability to drive kept her a prisoner. Worse than Rapunzel, she waited in front of the TV set all dressed up and no way to go.

I refused to wait. Nobody would leave me waiting like that. I would go out and work. I would be independent, drive, have my own car, my own job.

It's complex. It was wanting to be like him, and not wanting to be like him. I wanted to be independent and I wasn't. I wanted to be dependent and I couldn't be because I saw what came of it—eternal waiting. Leave me waiting on a street corner, you're lucky if you have fifteen minutes. I would be so overwrought by then, I would explode into tears and not speak to you for a week. "They also serve who only stand and wait." Not in my book, although I have mellowed some. It took me years to make the connection between those interminable Friday nights waiting for dinner, those holiday eves, bags packed or presents wrapped, sitting around, waiting to begin being happy, and my irrational behavior when someone kept me waiting.

That's why I get so wacky. Daddy's little girl is being betrayed again. Waiting means you don't love me enough to come home. Silly, but one small ganglion unraveled.

Some of us make the unraveling a lifetime's work. We pay listeners to help us thread our way through the connections of our lives and find meaning in the events of our childhood. But I've heard that the cure rate is better for self-exploration—51 percent to 49 percent for paid listeners. I worked on myself. When I did something irrational, I tried to find the pattern. Once I found the pattern, I'd work back into the past or ask my dreams to give me a solution. I'd read Jung, buy junk dream interpretation books, approach strange psychologists at parties (mostly ignorant behaviorists) looking for opinions, comments.

I got out into the world, the independent sort of person I am, because I couldn't stand waiting around. I learned that I couldn't rely on anyone, not even if they loved me. Daddy was responsible. He gave me the role model and he gave me the reason—to be independent emotionally and to work.

I probably write poetry because I can't express my emotions or even understand them easily. I have to think about them, analyze them, look for causes, offer myself probable solutions. I write poems because I can put into images how I feel and then I can better see what's happening. Emotions suffuse me, like a mist, wrap themselves around me, obscure everything. They're the invisible winds that circulate weather over us. All I can do is respond in some physical way—scream, cry. All the subtlety is gone. And that subtlety is what I'm looking for.

Daddy's girls are love-hate dichotomies. We love Daddy and we hate him. We forgive him and we wait for him to die and we dissolve ourselves. We don't get over it. He wouldn't like it if we were crybabies. The hell with him. Oh, my God! I don't know who or what I'm mourning for. I'm that damn bird, that stupid dove who mourns for everybody.

His old friends at the funeral said he knew I was there, said he waited for me. That's what I wanted to believe, so I did. I took pine cones from the tree over his grave. I know he's down there in that beige suit wearing that grim smile the undertaker gave him, making a fossil in that desert memorial park burned beige by the sun, studded with explosions of plastic flowers, the only kind allowed.

One of his card-playing buddies said to me, "You look just like your daddy." I see him in the mirror sometimes, just catch a glimpse of him as I turn away, like a ghost, a view of him, one gene at a time.

I'm always on time, frightfully punctual, and I always have to have the car, and I watch my drinking, and I usually have a job or I'm looking for one. I'm learning to forgive what I am and why I am. The crying doesn't make any difference. I think right through it. I ignore the weather, my own pain, anything else that gets in the way. That's how Daddy's girls are. We're tough, determined, or so we like to think. We don't cry easily, but when we do, we can't stop.

Questions for Discussion

1. What are the relationship dynamics between the narrator and her father? The narrator and her mother?
2. What part do gender role prescriptions play in the narrator's ambivalent relationship with her father?
3. How do you think her relationship with her father may impact her adult relationships with men?
4. If this woman were to go into counseling to deal with her protracted grief, how might you help the narrator deal with and understand what this loss means to her?

Coffee, 7 a.m.

Diana K. Munson

"Would you like some coffee?"

"No. Thank you."

"I'm having some. Sure?"

"I wouldn't want to bother you . . . "

"No bother. I'm having some. It's instant."

"No. That's all right."

"Are you sure? Easy as boiling water."

"I don't want to put you out!"

"It's just as much trouble to boil water for two as it is for one. Quick, tell me. I have to go to work."

"Oh, that's all right. You go ahead. You have your life and I . . . "

"This has nothing to do with my *life*. You are my mother. I am your daughter. You are visiting me. Granted, you didn't tell me you were coming, but you *are* here. I trust you slept well? It's morning. We both have coffee by habit in the morning to wake up. I have to boil the water anyway. I *know* how to boil water. I do it every morning. So what is the problem? *Have some coffee,* for God's sake."

"Well, if you insist, maybe a cup . . . but you *are* shouting."

"I am not shouting. Why every otherwise normal, simple thing becomes so complicated when we get together, I'll never know. Let's start over again: *please,* have some coffee with me. I INSIST."

"Huh, sure, thanks . . . if it's not too much trouble."

"I give up. I give UP! I give up. All right, don't have any. See if I care!"

"But I said I'd have some . . . "

Questions for Discussion

1. Describe the mother's behavior in this interaction. What is the daughter's reaction?
2. What components of this relationship need to be addressed in treatment?

Cigarettes

Diana K. Munson

SHE: I had cancer . . .

HE: Oh, yeah. . . . What kind?

SHE: Lung cancer.

HE: Come on! Why wasn't I told?

SHE: I didn't want to bother you.

HE: Hell, I'm your husband. You had cancer. Come on. Why, you smoke a pack and a half a day!

SHE: I had lung cancer. Why don't you believe me?

HE: Well, for starters, you waited ten months to tell me.

SHE: I didn't want to upset you . . . or the child.

HE: Well, why are you telling me now? To make me feel good?

SHE: To see if you care. I sometimes think you don't care about me.

HE: Hell. Sure, I care; you're my wife. But I don't believe you. I think you're playing games. I think you're . . . hallucinating. I think you're schiz or something, just like your mother.

SHE: You think I'm crazy! You don't believe me! [Weeps]

HE: It's hard. Prove it. Show me a bill, a lab report, anything. A doctor's bill. No one waits ten months to tell folks, "Oh, by the way, I had cancer last year."

SHE: I could, but I won't. You don't believe me.

HE: Prove it.

SHE: Forget it.

HE: What do you mean forget it? You brought it up.

Questions for Discussion

1. The wife here repeats the behavior of her mother in the piece called "Coffee, 7 a.m." How can you explain the repetition of the mother's behavior on the part of the daughter?
2. What defense mechanism is the daughter using with her husband in this interchange?

Paper Plates

Libbi Miriam

On Tuesday I flew in from California and headed right for the hospital. Sheila was already in a thin gown barely covering her huge body, her eyes wild with fright. She grimaced and repeated the same questions she must have asked her doctor a hundred times: *What treatment will I follow? Will it hurt? Will I lose my hair? Will I die?*

For forty minutes we sat in the admitting room waiting for Dr. Aherns; the second Sheila dragged herself to the bathroom, he stormed in.

"Well, where is she?" His gray eyes were cold, and his handsome tight face, tense. Instantly, I became protective toward my big sister.

"I hope you'll be patient with my sister.... She has ... uh ... some sort of ... uh ... personality disorder." I spoke calmly to show him *I* was different. I've been trying to prove it all my life. "I've spoken to my therapist about it and that's what she says," I added quietly. I didn't know what else to say. Her personality problem was deeper than the runaway cancer cells.

"Look, I'm here to do surgery, Ms. Harris, not to get involved with your family's personal problems."

I was furious. How could he separate the two? At the same time, I wished my sister's growth might be slightly serious, not anything that would kill her, just something to make him more understanding.

"She's in the bathroom. She was anxious about missing you and wants to ask if—"

"I've already spent a full hour answering her questions—several times. She repeats herself, you know. "

Yes, I know. I felt my shoulders hunching up with tension, and old habit. "That's not the point."

Finally she walked out of the bathroom, ignored my presence, and grabbed his hand. "Oh, Dr. Aherns, do you think I'll make it?"

"You'll do fine, Sheila. I told you, you're having a lumpectomy, not a mastectomy," he mumbled. "It's not a radical procedure. Hundreds of women go through this. Are you ready now? I'll get you through it." His voice softened a bit. "You'll be dancing out of here in no time."

That night I slept alone in her place uptown, remembering our childhood. I turned down the thermostat; I was no longer used to East Coast overheated apartments in winter. All night I tossed, the heat and smells of Sheila's quilt reminding me of the awful "games" we played as kids. Once, she locked me in the closet. When I howled my head off, she apologized and kissed me all over, but I was still angry for a long time. In adolescence I kept my distance from her. I went away to school at seventeen. Mom, always after me to phone her from college, begged me to call Sheila on her birthday every year. Reluctantly, I did.

She claims she always "adored" me while I remained aloof. Now we're thrown back together again.

Aherns discharged her only two days after surgery. I couldn't believe it, *two days,* but that's hospital policy, and Aherns agreed. On the morning of her discharge she drove the aides crazy. She wanted more heat, less heat, water, diet Coke, Diet Pepsi, extra gauze, her bed straightened, a bigger wheelchair, a special lunch, a permit for me to park in front of the hospital, which I ended up paying for.

When I left to pick her up, I'd forgotten to turn up the heat. After we arrived home, she took off her coat, stomped over to the thermostat, and started raving.

"You broke the goddamn heater; you broke it. Look, it says forty-five. I never heard of such a thing! I'm sick with breast cancer, I come home from the hospital, and there's not a drop of heat. This is New York, not California. It's Thanksgiving, and you turn off the heat."

"It's three weeks *until* Thanksgiving, and it says sixty-five, not forty-five. I was going to start it as soon we came in. I can't breathe with all that heat."

"You're sick!"

That did it.

"I'm getting out of here," I said, gnashing my teeth. I hated those words and her accusations. I grabbed my purse while she stood there blubbering, "I have nobody. Norman's with that bitch he married, and I can't even get our kid on the phone. Brad doesn't care if I live or die. Mom and Dad would never abandon me."

"I'm not Mom or Dad. Get that into your head. They've been gone over three years."

My eyes stung as I jogged up to my old college buddy Trudy's place. Outside, in the air, strength seeped into my body; I wasn't scared of the neighborhood; I wasn't scared of anything. I could have strangled two muggers at a time.

I reached Trudy's; we hugged and got blurry-eyed. I've always loved my women friends the way I wished I could love my sister. I hung out with Trudy for hours, grateful she didn't ask too many questions. At midnight I took a cab and crept into Sheila's apartment feeling rotten. How could I leave her alone her first night home from the hospital? Why did I have compassion for everyone but her? She was dozing but heard me. "Nina?" I didn't answer. She called out insistently again, this time by my childhood name. "Nini, is that you?"

"Go to sleep. I'll see you in the morning." No reply, only a faint moan. Thank God there was no time for her to grill me with her usual questions— Did I still love Arthur? Were my kids respectful? Was I "happy"?— or to sentimentalize how all of us, even failing old Grandma Essie, piled into the Ford and drove to the Catskills years ago. And no time to rehash the details of our parents' deaths or which one of us loved them more. Yes, I, the younger one, had become more responsible toward her since we'd lost Mom to breast cancer right after we lost Dad. She couldn't overcome their loss.

On Friday a woman from Ahern's office called. Someone from the American Cancer Society would take Sheila to the outpatient clinic for her breast check. She wanted me to go along, but I said one person was enough. She said that was lousy of me, making her go with a stranger, but I stayed and made up for it by cooking a great dinner: wild rice, broiled chicken, and eggplant that I'd bought. Then I grabbed her shopping list of things she wanted and ran out before she came home. On my walk, I read her long, embellished writing on a crumpled note:

> *Nina, get this food—don't tell me it's bad for me.*
> *Lox and bagels, hot dogs, Swiss Miss, coffee, and sweet rolls.*
> *Also pick up some hair color, L'Oréal, Royal Black, Number 13.*

Cringing, I bought everything, except the hair color, and stashed it away. More than the breast surgery nagged at me. What it was, I didn't know, but I felt in an odd way that I myself was at risk.

When she returned, Sheila recited every detail of her day, how nice the oncologist had been, how he didn't put her down like Aherns, how he held her hand and answered all of her questions, how he understood women and the effect of mutilating their breasts. I listened with relief. Was she sensible because of a stranger's kindness? Her terror was understandable. We went into the kitchen to eat.

"Why did you make this?" she hurled at me with disgust.

"I thought you'd like it."

"You knew goddamn well I wouldn't like it. *You* like this kind of food, not me. You made it to please yourself. You left the kitchen a mess, too."

I controlled myself. She just had breast surgery; besides, there was some truth in what she said. I *was* a bad cook.

"Why didn't you bring the hair color I asked for?"

"Because it's not good for you, especially now."

"Don't start that California crap. Can't you bring what I ask for? You didn't bring the L'Oréal, and now there's nothing to eat. I'm having hot dogs."

"What! You're eating hot dogs? At least wait until you recover."

"Don't lecture me. I'm the one with cancer, not you. All you ever do is lecture."

She opened the cupboard and dragged out the paper plates I hated.

And our first week together was over.

On Tuesday, our second week together began. I rented a video about George Sand and Chopin to keep her mind off herself. She hated it.

"Why is she always dressed in men's clothes like that? Maybe she's a lesbian," she kept repeating irritably.

"She's in love with Chopin. How can she be a lesbian? And so what if she is?" I was even more irritable.

Disgruntled, she'd finished watching and was getting ready for bed when she made an odd request.

"Let me see your breasts."

Defiantly, I pulled up my sweater and T-shirt and showed her my 34A bra.

"Let me see them without your bra."

I pulled up the bra.

"Your breasts, they're so tiny. You're lucky," she sobbed, trying to embrace me.

I pulled away. "Listen, breast size has nothing to do with cancer. It's more related to lifestyle."

She looked at me tearfully. "Remember who taught you to drive, your big sister. Remember who taught you about sex? You always were luckier than me. You're still young. Color your hair strawberry. You'll look better. Pretty soon you'll look old and gray like me."

"Your neighbor thought I was older than you," I said. She acted as if she hadn't heard and went right on her track.

"I'll tell you right now, I'm not going to lose my hair. I can't handle that. I won't take chemo, no matter what."

"Aherns told you it would be okay. It wasn't invasive. Don't you believe him? Just the radiation and tamoxifen. Your chances are good. The growth was small."

"Yeah, but three lymph nodes were involved."

The next morning we got up early to go to the doctor's. We dressed in front of her mirror lined with old photos of Mom and Dad that I'd never seen. I wanted copies, then thought it better not to mention them and open up old wounds. My eyes went to her obsolete wedding portrait of Norman and her, snaps of Brad as a baby, and, in a corner, old black-and-whites of the two of us as kids. Despite our different coloring and size, the snaps showed we definitely looked like sisters.

As she struggled into a gold-beaded blouse, I glanced at the long complicated drain pinned to a bandage wrapped under her breast.

She began to cry. "I can't take it. I'm all swollen. How am I going to stand this? How will I get dressed? I don't want anyone to see me. I'll never make it for the radiation. I won't be able to handle it."

"Look, you're not going to a party. You don't have to put on a bra and makeup. Just get ready. I'll help you."

She started to paint her face.

"C'mon, let's go."

"Let me put on my face. I need it. After you leave, I'll never make it."

"Lots of women make it. You'll make it."

Impatiently, I waited in the living room, my eyes taking in the pink floral design of the couch and wondering if I'd be sitting *shiva* here in two years, listening to people praise her. Trudy would remember when Sheila taught us the two-step on the old living room carpet. Our one living aunt would cry about how she sent her flowery birthday cards. Would Brad come, or would he continue to search for his birth mother?

She finally finished her face. "How will I get to the hospital after you leave?"

"The American Cancer Society has trained volunteers who drive."

"I don't want to go with strangers."

"Come on, we're late. You know how Aherns is."

"I'm the one who might die, not him."

"Sheila, you've got to stop this. Calm down. You'll join a support group, take one day at a time, be grateful for every moment you have—"

"Bullshit. Look at you. You can't do it. You're running off to Trudy's all the time to get advice from her."

I forced an attempt at cheerfulness. "Dinnertime, come on; we'll have this stir-fry I picked up. It's pretty good. Vegetarian. I'll set the table. Put on some music. Let's eat on real dishes tonight." We'd been eating on those hideous paper plates ever since I'd arrived.

"Get the paper."

"It's just as easy to wash two dishes."

"I'm not washing dishes."

"I'll do them."

"Can't you do what I ask just once?"

"It's not ecological."

"Did you hear me? Don't give me that California crap."

I exploded. "I won't eat here again if we eat on paper plates."

"I always knew you were sick. Go ahead and leave again. Leave me without a soul."

Sick. That did it. That word always did it.

For the first time in my life, I tried to smack her, but even after her surgery, with drains hanging from her breast, she was stronger than me. She blocked me with her hand, and I fell against the kitchen wall.

"I'd rather die than ask you to help me ever again," she cried hysterically.

I was screaming by now. "I left my family and my job and flew across the country. I thought I could help you change, but it's impossible, even when your life's at stake."

She sat down at the table, her head in her arms, and wept. "You always destroy my last bit of confidence. You know how alone I am with Mom and Dad gone. Brad hasn't come once since he found out. You're the only one I have."

I heard myself screaming like a maniac. I couldn't stop. "We're all going to die some day." I slammed the door and started running toward the bus that would take me the three miles up to Trudy's. I ran with the power of an Amazon.

"You feed into her; pretend she's not your sister. Set boundaries, tell her what you'll do and what you won't. Sometimes when I run into her, she's actually pleasant."

"I can't seem to manage that."

"Why not? You know, she still has her old sense of humor. I saw her a few months ago. She sounded so proud of you."

Sense of humor? Proud? Pleasant? Friends? My God, why couldn't I see that side of her? Had she become more bitter since our parents' deaths? Was Trudy right, had she just become a social worker after all these years? I didn't respond.

"You should have come for just one week, not three," she said.

Silence. Finally I answered, "I'll stay until the end of the month. Then I leave. Talk to me like a friend, like you used to before you got your degree."

"I am. I'm telling you exactly how I feel. Why take it like that? Why punish yourself?"

"I think we better not discuss Sheila right now."

"Okay, but remember, you're the one who keeps bringing her up."

We went out for dinner and over pasta, Trudy and I talked about everything—except Sheila— for two straight hours. My heart felt full and warm, the way it never does when I'm with my sister. It reminded me of what I still liked about New York. But I didn't want to go back to Sheila's apartment— ever.

"I found a woman to help you after I leave."

"Who is she? Where'd you drum this one up?"

Instantly she caught my hesitation.

"I asked you where you found her."

"Talking to an old neighbor of yours."

"Are you crazy? You don't know a thing about this person and you ask her to help me? Do you think I'm going to take a strange woman into my house because some neighbor I don't know uses her? The woman could be a drug addict."

"For God's sake, why would the old lady hire a drug addict? Trudy said she'd drop by after I leave to check things out. Maybe she'll come up with some ideas. I've consumed myself with this for three weeks. I've a life to get back to."

"Maybe *I* won't have any life to get back to. Trudy's your friend, not mine."

Momentary silence. We glared at each other. Then she tried to touch me again—"Do you care? Say you care."

"I care, okay?"

"Say you love me."

"Goddamn it. Enough."

"Did you ever say it to Mom or Dad?"

"What are you, a child?"

Silence.

Quietly she said, "You're really cruel."

I breathed deeply and didn't reply. I pretended to busy myself with laundry.

In desperation, she paused, and then said, "Why don't you leave me tonight?"

I got up, unsure of what move to make. And then she floored me with that off-the-wall way she connects things.

"Hey, how come you never thanked me for the birthday card I sent you?"

I put on my coat.

"Go ahead, just go ahead. You're sick anyway."

And I left.

The last three nights I calmed down. I figured I could take it now that I was leaving. In the mornings I'd talk to the visiting nurse, who insisted everything was "just fine," then I clung to my routine: hit the avenue; stop at the ma-and-pa grocery for bagels and nonfat milk; walk around the block for forty minutes with heavy shopping bags, pretending they are weights. I would stay out in the cold, biting air as long as I could, a relief from the stale apartment.

The morning before I left, the wind picked up and began to blow hard in my ears. I entered the old neighborhood library where a handful of unemployed Russians found refuge reading the foreign newspapers. I picked up a book on surviving breast cancer. Shakily, I dropped into a chair next to a snoring man, a magazine covering his head. The rhythmic sound of his snoring, the close heat, and the smells of the room made me claustrophobic. I couldn't wait until I returned home to go for my foggy morning jogs. I wanted to know how my kids were. I needed Arthur now. My nose was running. I reached into my pocket and took out a crumpled note I hadn't seen before:

Dear Nini,

I'm sorry I caused you aggravation. I know you were trying to help me. Mom and Dad would be upset if they saw us now. Let's try not to fight.

Love Always, Sheila

Questions for Discussion

1. How would you describe the relationship dynamic between these two sisters? What part does each sister play in this dynamic?
2. If these sisters wanted to get help to improve their relationship, how would you begin? What would you want to know? What approach would you take to help each of them be more respectful to the other?

The Answer Is: Grocery Bags

Rosemary DiStefano

We are having a quiet lunch together. Jon and I sit on the side of the hill by the old station building. We don't touch. We don't say anything about the way things stand between us. But this time spent together in silence convinces me to feel an unspoken connection, and to expect a deeper union. I'm not conscious that this is a pattern. We discuss who will pick up the kids, and who will buy the groceries. Jon and I appear as a modern, liberated couple—two people committed to sharing the duties of child care and breadwinning. The simple word *share* stands alone. The defining word *equally* gets left out. The parent who picks up the kids gets the car, and the one who picks up the groceries gets the bus. Jon gets the car and the kids. I get the bus and the groceries. I'm sure a good reason exists for this assignment of duties and assets, but I don't remember.

Waiting in line at the Super Saver, I scan the tabloids. I read the headline "AIDS Cramps Vampires' Lifestyle" and convulse with laughter. I guess life's rough for everyone. The story registers as another sign convincing me not to feel badly about my situation. Punchy and tired, I have a hard time snapping back. So what if I had to stand up all the way on my bus ride home! My fellow shoppers don't appreciate my outburst, and I make the tactful decision not to share the reason.

The day turns colder and becomes night as I walk home from the bus stop. I reach the top of my block and dread making the trip from the main street down the deserted sidewalk to my house. The paper bag I carry feels light, but the distance, cold, and my apprehension are heavy. The mass I try to support weighs down on me. The edge of the package digs into my arms, which ache with a numbing pain that I talk myself into enduring. How did the human spirit rally to survive the frigid march to the death camps? People on the verge of physical and mental breakdown—living in the moment—carrying their weight and the near-death weight of loved ones.

I put the bag down when I get to the front door. Our porch light hisses, pops, and then goes out. In the dark I start to dig through my purse for keys. I can't find them, so I sit down on the steps and wait for Jon and the boys. Again I start to feel hope. I have set down my load. I wait in the quiet evening watching for my family. I'm okay, even happy, waiting.

Jon pulls up with Gabe, Paul, and a bag of groceries. The kids spill out of the old VW like clowns out of a circus car. Coats, blankets, stuffed animals, painting projects, and laughter follow the boys. I look past them at the bag of groceries Jon carries. We somehow got our wires crossed. He starts to yell at me before he hits the steps.

"What the hell are you doing sitting in the freezing dark?" he asks.

I tell him I can't find my keys.

"Why isn't there any light out here? I guess you forgot to turn it on before you left this morning. Tell me you missed the bus, too, and were late again for work," Jon finishes. His eyes drop down to my bag of groceries. The kids hit the steps and run to give me monkey-neck hugs and fish-lip kisses.

"I can't believe you. You are so stupid sometimes. How could you forget your keys?" he asks.

He's quiet.

I know more is coming.

"And what the hell is this?" He kicks my bag.

"Did you buy groceries too?" Jon yells.

I block this out and focus only on my two sweet boys. The verbal assaults continue, and I can't respond. Each one of them drives me farther and farther out of my physical place. I concentrate on busying myself. I get Gabe and Paul settled. Each boy sits in a high chair. As Jon's rage grows, our bags of groceries wait on the kitchen table. I start to unpack them and see that we have bought exactly the same things: bread, milk, eggs, cheese, fruit, and a green vegetable. I somehow think this is a sweet and romantic moment.

Jon goes berserk—ranting and raving about how we don't have any money, and what a foolish girl I am.

His screams fall on the boys. They don't understand, but the scene repeats itself as one that has become too familiar.

I don't know when, but I move out of the kitchen onto the steps in the living room. My eyes close. The looks on the kids' faces live in my mind. Jon's irrational behavior over something as insignificant as our buying the same groceries explodes behind my eyes. I can no longer ignore that this marriage operates against a backdrop of verbal and mental abuse. Jon has too much anger, and an irrepressible need to be in control. What I have not been able to change for myself becomes easy when it protects the boys. This angry man cannot sabotage the loving and nurturing parenting of our sons.

I sit on the steps. I want to rock here, numb to the pain for a long time. I wish someone would come to take me to a safe place. I know that other people get to go there because they act crazy, but once there they become calm and seem safe. I wish I could just give in to the yearnings inside of me and let myself go crazy. Crazy people are spoken to with kindness and patience. I want to let go—to go crazy—to go to this place. I choose this. I think this is the only way that I will be treated better. But I have my sons, and I could never leave them.

Questions for Discussion

1. How would you help this woman to find options, other than going crazy, to help herself?
2. Discuss the impact, both short and long range, on children who hear verbal abuse in their home.

Downstairs Apartment

Nancy Hewitt

His shouts erupt
In a mushroom cloud of sound,
and the dull thud that follows
could be a fist hitting a wall.
He slams out of the front door
and the aftermath is quiet,
like the surrender of sound
before the fallout.

I hear her steps, tentative at first,
as if they belonged to someone
newly blind. Then the whir
of her washer, the whish
and shush of wet soapy clothes
as the machine twists them clean.
The whine of her vacuum
persistent as a dentist's drill.

Her steps become brisk and steady
as she completes her tasks.
I imagine her bending,
kneeling, stretching,
maybe humming as she cleans.
She dusts and polishes so well
that when he returns, her mind,
too, will be immaculate.

Questions for Discussion

1. What function does housekeeping serve for the woman in the "downstairs apartment"?
2. What, if anything, should the upstairs neighbor do?

The Gravity Machine

Barbara Adams

The personality of an individual is hard to explain in terms of genetic inheritance, especially when there is a hint of mental illness. And if you are deeply involved with that person in a long marriage, it becomes even more difficult to interpret events and behaviors in terms of what seems "normal" and what slides over the line into "abnormal."

Working backward into the years of his unromantic, Frostian New England childhood, I wanted to find out what made my husband El so odd: the origin of his black rages, angry silences, and jealous accusations. I wanted to know why he could turn from being the gentlest, kindest, and most loving of men into one who hated everyone, especially me, but most of all himself.

His unpredictable shifts of mood tormented me and our four children. He would leave the house for work in a sweet, cheerful mood, kissing me good-bye passionately. But by the time I got back from work, he would be sitting at the kitchen table glowering in a rage that was palpable in the air around him. He would not speak to me or explain why he was angry. He would not tell me if he was angry at me or someone else. Or if something had happened at work. In this mood, he would sit up till dawn, smoking and drinking cup after cup of coffee—not reading, not writing. Just staring into space and glowering.

In forty years of marriage, I often asked myself if these black moods were indeed my fault, as El claimed. When they first became apparent, we read books of psychology together, trying to determine what was wrong. El would read one, say, "That's it," and start analyzing himself. "Thank you for helping me understand," he'd say to me, but within fifteen minutes, he would twist and turn his thoughts until he was again blaming me. "You made me do it," he'd mutter darkly. "It's all your fault."

I desperately wanted to know why El could love me one minute and hate me the next. I wanted to know why he could give up drinking so easily when a psychiatrist told him he was an alcoholic but could not stop smoking even after surgery for an aortic aneurysm, even after being diagnosed with lung cancer. I wanted to know why a man who was a born storyteller could not finish writing his stories. I wanted to know if his behavior was caused by mental illness and, if so, its name. I had to resurrect his family ghosts to find some answers.

I met El in college, where his car, "Sweet William," a 1930s Chevy coupé, was our "home" together until we married. Neither of us cared about going to our parents' homes. I was an unwanted guest in my father's small Manhattan apartment, where he lived with my stepmother and baby half-sister. El's family lived in a mill town in New Hampshire. Six of his seven siblings were still in school (El was the oldest, his mother's favorite). Going home meant another mouth to feed. El cheered his mother up by fixing things—he was the only repairman she could afford. His alcoholic father just laughed at every broken thing, knowing he couldn't afford a new one. El was also his mother's protector, defending her against his father's drunken brawls.

In high school, El had been placed in the mechanic arts program because his father was a bricklayer, the family poverty-stricken. El told the guidance counselor that he'd rather take the college preparation program. The counselor smiled patronizingly and said it wasn't appropriate and would be too difficult for him.

El hated the shop courses, making useless picture frames. He did make a bookcase for his precious copy of *Shakespeare's Complete Works,* several *Reader's Digest* books his mother had bought for a dollar, and a few classic paperbacks.

After graduating from high school—the first in the family for as far back as anyone could remember—El joined the Army just as World War II ended, to get the G.I. Bill. He finished his hitch and, based on his very high score on the entrance exam, was accepted at the University of New Hampshire. He packed his old car, Sweet William, with his precious books and few clothes, leaving poverty behind forever, he hoped.

Unable to plunge into an intellectual environment so different from anything he had ever known, El flunked most of his classes at UNH, except one in creative writing with Dr. Scudder. El had begun writing stories about his family which Dr. Scudder read to the class saying, "Now that's *real* writing." El was terrified of the praise and cut the final exam, but Dr. Scudder gave him a C instead of an F or the A he had earned to that point. El spent most nights drinking in local bars.

After a terrible summer at home, El was rescued by Dick, a neighbor of his grandfather, who had earned a PhD in biology. Dick had been offered a job at a state college in New York, and he invited El to come along. El leaped at the chance and was admitted to the college, thanks to Dick, in the fall of 1950.

When we met at this college, I was immediately taken by the stories El had written about his New England relatives. They were colorful, eccentric, and exotic people to a girl from the big city. Outwardly, El and I were opposites; inwardly, we were much alike—the ugly ducklings in our inhospitable families. We were drawn to each other and never looked back—or so I thought.

By far the most fascinating of El's family was his grandfather "Sammit," the legendary fierce patriarch. He'd died the year El and I met, and though I never saw Sammit, it was clear that he had ruled the family like a biblical patriarch, riding herd on his four middle-aged sons whom he called "the boys" until he died. He'd bullied his overworked farm wife, May, who had been a schoolteacher before they married. He also claimed suzerainty over his first grandchild, El, in his high chair, pinching the baby's cheeks hard to correct playing with his food, so hard El never forgot. Nor could anyone protect him from Sammit, especially his powerless, poor mother and father. I imagine that Mary suffered for her beloved first son. I also imagine that Reat, El's father and the second eldest of Sammit's "boys," would have grinned slyly, happy that Sammit was tormenting someone besides himself.

El's stories of Sammit outweighed all the others, and despite Sammit's fiery temper that could lash out when least expected, El preferred staying with his grandparents most summers when he grew old enough to help on the farm. El loved nature and working outdoors, and as long as he didn't do anything to cross his grandfather, he was treated kindly. His grandmother, May, cooked chicken pies and homemade rolls and doted on him. Compared with home and siblings who arrived year after year, Sammit's farm was peaceful. Except for Sammit's outbursts. "May, you know I can't drink from a cracked cup," he would say sweetly, then smash it to bits on the plank floor. May's hands shook as she ran to get a clean, uncracked cup and a dustpan to sweep up the shards. El trembled, watching, over his dinner plate. "Eat up, boy," said Sammit, frightening El to a loss of hunger. "Sit up, boy," Sammit would say, slapping El on the back to make sure he would follow instructions.

When El's one-room country school teacher Mrs. Tuxbury sent a note home that said, "Elwood cannot see the words on the blackboard. He needs glasses," the roar of protest from Sammit could be heard all the way to Hanover. Dr. Dunbar, the optometrist, said, "Flat as a pancake, those retinas. This boy is nearly blind. He'll have to wear glasses for the rest of his life." No one wanted to break the news to Sammit. "No!" he roared, when told by a brave Mary, "No Adams boy is gonna be a sissy and wear glasses!" and smashed the table with his fist. El got glasses from the Lions Club and Mrs. Tuxbury was happy. No one else was.

But the worst crime Sammit committed against El happened when he was a teenager. Always a loner, El had for company a slingshot he'd made for hunting rabbits and, as a birthday present from his favorite uncle, Allen, a twelve-gauge shotgun. He hunted for food for his mother to cook and became an expert shot. One day, a stray dog followed El home from the woods. Any dog not a hunting dog was a "cur," in the Adams parlance. El fed it, and his mother smiled. When Reat stumbled home that evening, he laughed at the shivering beast. "You call that a dog?" But he let El keep him. El had a friend at last, a pet he named Scout—one he could trust as no human being.

Several months later, El came home from school and called for Scout, who didn't come immediately, as usual. He looked everywhere. "Ask your father," was all his mother would say, not looking at him. Reat finally came home, drunk, and El ran out to the car. "Where's Scout?" Reat said matter-of-factly, "Sammit shot him. He's dead."

El reeled and ran away crying. Had he been bigger, he might have beaten his father and grandfather. Had he been crazy, he might have shot them. But he was a child, weak and lonely. He cried. His father looked away in disgust at this sissy son. El hid in the woods for days.

I was dumbfounded when El told me this story. "Why?" I asked "Why did your grandfather shoot that innocent animal?" El had tears in his eyes as he explained, "They said he'd killed some chickens. A lie. Mostly, my grandfather hated nonworking dogs, and he'd just been appointed dog catcher in Etna. Scout was a chance to exercise his new authority—the 'execution' of a stray."

Every time El told me this story, as he did often, he was just as full of sorrow as if it had happened yesterday. I wondered if Reat and Sammit wanted to teach this "sissy" boy a lesson, make him take it like a "man." Or puff up their own flimsy manliness by hurting the boy.

The only thing that counted with Reat, Sammit, and Ben (the oldest of Sammit's boys), besides brute manhood, was money. When El went off to college, they regarded it as more "sissy" behavior. But if he'd come back rich, all would have been forgiven. He would be like the rich Boston doctor that Ben and Allen took hunting every fall. But El had given up hunting as soon as he moved to New York. He'd never liked it, but he had to go along to win praise from the Adams men. El eventually published one story, a satire that slyly described his family and the pretentious Dartmouth crowd they'd held in contempt. Titled "Life Among the Hogslop Barbarians," it was published in *The Saturday Review* in 1972.

In college, El read his stories to me and our friends. We admired his talent and laughed at his wit. I thought he'd be a great writer one day. He was majoring in biology, however, thanks to his friend Dick, the biology professor. El did well in lab work, got all A's in his major, and cut classes in everything else. So he nearly flunked out again, cutting classes he didn't like. He sat up all night drinking beer and writing stories that he'd read to me the next day. "Wonderful!" I'd say. "But how does it end?" "It needs a little polishing," he'd say, blushing, and a little angry. El rarely finished a story.

In the second year of college, when we were unofficially engaged, a strange obsession took hold of El. I did not understand it, but I felt uncomfortable whenever he brought it up. He hated a physics professor who had made fun of him in class one day for reading the barometer "incorrectly" too low. "That's impossible," the professor had smirked. But it turned out that the low barometric reading had been correct, a fluke of weather. El wanted revenge, to prove he was smarter than this professor. Of course, a gravity machine was impossible, though many, many scientists had tried to invent one. El set out to prove *he* could invent a gravity machine. El's manhood was at stake; he had to prove he wasn't the sissy and idiot his father, grandfather, and uncle Ben made him out to be.

For several months, El filled notebooks with odd diagrams. He'd draw them at night, in classes, and show them to me with excitement. They looked something like waterwheels, or swastikas with legs chasing each other inside a circle. Portions were blackened to indicate they were filled with water. The water was supposed to slosh out from one part to another somehow, as the device spun on an axis—the movement of the water in the legs causing perpetual motion of the wheel. "But how would it start?" I asked, unable to comprehend. I knew nothing of physics and thought that El knew a lot about it. I sensed that his device wouldn't work, but I couldn't explain why. El was defensive, poor at the actual math, and said, "I'll have to build a working model." That would take years, I thought, a lot of money, and special equipment. He had no backing from the physics department. At the same time, El neglected his successes in biology, certain he had discovered the secret of the universe. He would become famous overnight! He had found a means of supplying unlimited clean energy! Mankind would bless him! He'd go down in history! This he'd say to me as if from a great distance.

The gravity machine notebooks piled up and the semester ended. We were getting married the day after my last final exam, leaving college after two years and moving to New Hampshire. I was depressed and exhausted and wanted to get away from my alcoholic mother, who had come back from Florida to see me. I wanted to forget my father's rejection of me. I wanted to go where no one knew me, to start life anew and have children. I thought El would be a great writer and maybe a great scientist. My own career plans meant nothing to me anymore.

Living in New Hampshire taught me otherwise. I saw firsthand the stories of El's family. He hadn't exaggerated. After four years of misery, we moved back to New York to finish college, with three children, and one on the way. I was depressed but determined to get my teaching license for the sake of independence. It took all my strength to take care of the children, take classes, and, most of all, keep El from sliding off the rails every day. His masonry work got us through college. But he came home drunk and angry, every night, so that I was almost grateful when he was drunk enough to pass out. We finally finished our bachelor's degrees and got teaching jobs. Our marriage was strained to the breaking point, however, and I wanted to get a

PhD to teach college and write. I urged El to get a master's degree. He started three different MAs, and, despite getting all A's, dropped every one. He became brilliantly successful teaching children with learning and emotional disabilities and could easily have obtained an advanced degree in psychology. But the principal caught him smoking several times in the hall and campaigned to fire him. El instead got an extended sick leave, spending three weeks in a psychiatric ward before signing himself out.

Out of desperation, I had begun psychotherapy, and El soon followed me out of jealousy. The psychiatrist told him he was an alcoholic, and he stopped drinking. But we grew further and further apart, as I stopped putting up with El's tantrums. One day, in a very stressful family therapy session, I spoke of what I liked about El, how we met in college, mentioning El's gravity machine idea in passing. The doctor looked up, immediately. "Gravity machine? That's a sure symptom of schizophrenia." I was shocked. El seemed not to notice the implication of the doctor's observation. I'd known for years that *something* was wrong with El, but couldn't name it. *Schizophrenia* seemed unreal, too drastic a diagnosis. Yet, over the years of therapy, the doctor persisted in this diagnosis. I was never quite convinced. The field of therapy was changing rapidly, the Prozac generation of drugs just around the corner, and Freudian theories weakening their grip. Genetic research was advancing rapidly, finding "markers" for various emotional and physical problems, from cancer to schizophrenia.

What was wrong with El? I still couldn't figure out if his unpredictable mood shifts and behavior were some form of brain damage (he'd been thrown from his grandfather's horse when he was twelve and was in a coma for a week from a badly fractured skull); some inherited Adams mental quirk, like Sammit's vicious temper; or caused by the cruel assault on his manhood by his father, grandfather, and Uncle Ben. I hadn't decided which of these elements was to blame when El was diagnosed with terminal lung cancer at the age of sixty-six. The question of his mental condition seemed moot, but I couldn't let it go, even after he died. I needed to know, for my children's sake as well as mine. El had often said to me, "You're the only one who can figure me out."

Five years after his death, I remembered a book I'd first heard about in high school. I found a library copy, then bought one from an out-of-print Internet company. *A Mind That Found Itself* was first published in 1908, written by Clifford Beers, a young man who suffered from severe mental illness and decided to describe it and his less-than-ideal treatment in various mental hospitals. Beers had jumped out of a third-floor window in New Haven and was put in an asylum, where he lapsed into depression and delusions. After two and a half years of confinement, he apparently made a complete recovery. Upon his release, Beers made reform of the treatment of the mentally ill his life's work.

As I read this gracious, self-effacing book for the first time, I soon began to notice eerie similarities to El's behavior. Beers had been diagnosed manic-depressive, though I believe diagnosis was then—and still is—a very inexact science. In the depressed phase, Beers became mute and unresponsive, hating himself to the point of suicide. In the manic phase, Beers became ebullient, certain he was a genius—the greatest the world had ever seen. In the midst of the manic phase, he was confined to a cold, padded cell, for his own protection. He was also stripped of clothes, except for underwear, and had no furniture—nothing but a "drugget," a mat made of felt to sleep on atop an iron bed. Though he was freezing and half-starved, Beers felt full of energy and craved to expend it. Having nothing else, the felt mat became his material: he tore it into strips and wove it into a crude suit. That was taken away, and a new drugget given to him. Every day, he tore the mat and made a new suit—twenty all told, which his family had to pay for. Finally, one day, he tore the mat into strips again, but this time he tied the ends to the bed and secured the other ends to the transom and window bars. Then he pulled the bed up to the ceiling. He climbed in, feeling like the king of the world. Beers said he was certain that he had succeeded in overcoming gravity! He told the doctors and attendants that his "gravity machine" would make him famous:

> My sensations at this momentous instant must have been much like those which thrilled Newton when he solved one of the riddles of the universe. Indeed, they must have been more intense, for Newton, knowing, had doubts; I, not knowing, had no doubts at all. . . . For weeks I believed I had uncovered a mechanical principal which would enable man to defy gravity. . . . Gravity was harnessed—that was all. (Chapter XIX, pp. 127-128)

Today, we know much more about mental illness than when Beers wrote his terrifying memoir. New drugs and more humanistic therapies have transformed the treatment of people suffering from painful mental distress of all kinds. Beers luckily got well, given the limitations and cruelties of the time, perhaps because he had a loving and supportive family, and plenty of money for the best treatment available.

El and I had no one but each other. My family had failed me completely and his was downright destructive. The psychoanalyst who treated us in family therapy for nearly nineteen years eventually prescribed Trilafon for El, a psychotropic drug to allay the symptoms of schizophrenia. It dulled El's mood, certainly, and abetted—if not caused—impotence. I wonder, sometimes, had El lived ten years more, if a new antidepressant and better therapy would have been able to cure him, or at least, to relieve him of the worst of his rages and black moods. But he died, without any clear diagnosis of what ailed his mind. I am still not sure what caused his destructive behavior; I don't know if it has a name in the DSM-IV vocabulary.

Questions for Discussion

1. In a situation such as the one described in this story, how would you help the surviving spouse achieve viable closure?
2. Given that diagnosis is an inexact science, what would yours be in El's case?
3. What kinds of treatment would have been helpful in this case—both for El and for his family?
4. Connect the events of El's history to his adult behavior.

SELECTED READINGS AND ADDITIONAL RESOURCES

Mothers and Daughters

Cohen, Edward M., Cohen, Susan Simon, and Cohen, Ed (Eds.) (1997). *Mothers Who Drive Their Daughters Crazy: Ten Types of 'Impossible' Moms and How to Deal with Them*. Rocklin, CA: Prima Publications.

Koppelman, Susan (Ed.) (1985). *Between Mothers and Daughters: Stories Across a Generation*. Stony Brook, NY: The Feminist Press.

McGregor, Denise (1999). *Mama Drama: Making Peace with the One Woman Who Can Push Your Buttons, Make You Cry, and Drive You Crazy*. New York: St. Martin's Press.

O'Reilly, Andrea and Abbey, Sharon (2000). *Mothers and Daughters: Connection, Empowerment and Transformation*. New York: Roman and Littlefield.

Rubin, Lillian B. (2000). *Tangled Lives: Daughters, Mothers, and the Crucible of Aging*. Boston, MA: Beacon Press.

Sons and Mothers

Gurion, Michael (1994). *Mothers, Sons, and Lovers: How a Man's Relationship with His Mother Affects the Rest of His Life*. Berkeley, CA: Shambhala Publications.

Fathers and Daughters

Wright, H. Norman (1989). *Always Daddy's Girl*. Ventura, CA: Regal Books.

Sisters

Ariel, Margaret Lannamann (1998). *Sisters: The Unbreakable Bond.* Kansas City, MO: Andrews & McMeel Publishing.

Spouses/Domestic Abuse

Gottman, John and Jacobson, Neil (1998). *When Men Batter Women.* New York: Simon and Shuster.

Koppleman, Susan (Ed.) (1996). *Women in the Trees: U.S. Women's Short Stories About Battering and Resistance, 1839-1994.* Stony Brook, NY: The Feminist Press.

PART IV:
OTHER ISSUES OF ADULTHOOD

The Invisibility Syndrome

Anderson J. Franklin

At forty-seven, Bill was part of the first wave of black men who broke down race and class barriers and made it into the middle class. He graduated from Yale in the late 1960s, served as an Army officer in Vietnam, and is now a highly paid manager in a major American corporation. He and his family came to see me because their son was having trouble in school, but it quickly became obvious that the family was having trouble with Bill. He frequently came home from work withdrawn and impatient. When he talked to his wife about his difficulties on the job, he felt misunderstood and unsupported. He ranted and raged at his son and daughter when they fought, minimized their conflicts, and told them to solve their problems on their own. He and his wife had grown increasingly distant, and the atmosphere at home was charged with tension and stress.

One day, about five weeks after family therapy began, Bill revealed a disturbing incident. The night before, he had taken a white business client to an expensive restaurant in midtown Manhattan. When Bill told the maître d' they were there for dinner, the man had looked right past him and asked his white guest whether they had reservations. When the meal was over, the waiter placed Bill's American Express Gold Card and the charge slip in front of Bill's client. Bill imagined how his father, a tough, city bus driver who never let such racial slights go by, would have exploded at the waiter. But Bill, fearful of creating an embarrassing scene, simply reached over and signed the slip while continuing to chat amiably with his client.

The two men walked out into the night and shook hands, reaffirming their agreement on a major contract. It should have been a sweet moment: the agreement put Bill in line for a major promotion. The white client stepped to the curb and effortlessly hailed a cab. Fifteen minutes later, Bill was still at the curbside with his hand up, while white men and women flowed around him to hail cabs of their own. Finally, after yet another cab passed him up in favor of a white couple, Bill flung himself across the hood, swearing and flailing his attache case against the driver's window. All evening, he had struggled with a sixth sense that he was not being seen for himself, but as a

---

This article first appeared in the *Family Therapy Networker,* July/August 1993, and is copied here with permission.

stereotype—first, as too insignificant to host a client at an expensive restaurant, and, then, as too dangerous to be let into a cab. And in the end, he told us, he felt his explosion of rage had just reinforced those very stereotypes of invisibility and menace.

This was hardly the first time that an African-American* man in therapy has told me of such indignities. All black men, if you ask them, can describe the small social slights that accumulate to create what I call *invisibility,* after Ralph Ellison's powerful description of this experience in his 1949 novel *Invisible Man.* We are not literally invisible—that might sometimes be preferable. But on the streets, in stores, on elevators, and in restaurants, we are seen as potential criminals or as servants, not as ourselves.

Within a single hour we may be viewed as a potential rapist—hugely frightening—and as a doorman—absolutely insignificant. I am an African-American man in my fifties with a PhD, a father, a husband, and a tenured full professor. But, I, too, experience humiliating "levelers," reminders of the old-folk phrase "You can't get too big." I, too, have stood on street corners fruitlessly trying to hail cabs. Security guards have followed me around department stores. Sometimes, white women clutch their pocketbooks and flinch when I enter an elevator where they stand alone. Sometimes, I hear car locks click as I stand at an intersection, waiting for the light to change. I didn't need to be convinced of what Bill was talking about. The mirror the world holds up to me often does not reflect my human face.

These daily experiences are often as much a part of our lives as the air we breathe, and they shape the dynamics that occur within black families. Black men in America have always suffered such indignities, and worse, but the struggle today is particularly poignant for middle-class black men who have successfully jumped through the academic and corporate hoops that society promised would guarantee respect. They may go for days before a random encounter reminds them once again of their "place." They wonder how much to rely on their families' traditional ways of coping with racial slights and how much to believe that times have changed.

They often don't speak of these things with their wives and children, caught up in an obligation to present themselves as strong and successful men, capable of protecting and caring for their families. As a result, black men often have nowhere to go to tell their stories. Their indignation can move along a destructive pathway, the initial anger becoming internalized, smoldering rage. They feel disconnected from their families, and the anger eats away at them inside. In adolescents and some adult men, this manifests itself in what police and teachers call a "bad attitude," and what black psychologist Richard Majors calls the "cool pose"—the aloof, distant, tough, impenetrable veneer that often passes for black masculinity and is used to buffer pain and channel overpowering indignation and rage.

---

*The terms African American and black are used interchangeably.

Black men need something better. They come into therapy needing someone to hear their stories and recognize their pain. All too often, however, when they talk about the accumulation of indignities in their lives, white therapists minimize them or explain them away. When black men feel as invisible in therapy as they do in daily life, they don't want to bother.

One white therapist suggested to a black man I know that he should be more understanding of the fearful looks he gets on elevators, given what people read and what they see on television. Another client, a refrigeration technician, told his white therapist he had been given all of the company's most difficult business clients. In the patient's mind, it was a win-win situation for his white supervisor: If he failed to satisfy the clients, the problem could be blamed on his incompetence, in part alluding to his being black. If he succeeded, the supervisor looked good and the white technicians were grateful for not having to handle the problem jobs. The white therapist naively tried to reframe this positively, as a sign that the supervisor saw the black technician as more competent. He quit therapy with her and looked for a black therapist.

Another black man I know, an investment banker, complained that he had been steered away from corporate business and into state and municipal government accounts because so many government officials are black. Perhaps, his therapist suggested, his boss was acknowledging his area of expertise. "No," the banker said, with a smile, "It's not only me; all of us [African Americans] are working in the public sector. And that's not where the money is." He got his point across, but he was tired of spending his sessions educating his therapist.

Faced with responses like these, it's not surprising that black men hesitate to describe to white therapists our "sixth sense," the sensitive antennae we deploy to detect racism when we face rudeness or injustice. Nor is it surprising that black men—even more than most men—are skeptical of therapy. They are willing to come to therapy to help their children or their families, but they don't have much faith in the process. Therapy isn't a traditional source of help for black men or women; we are much more likely to turn to relatives, friends, doctors, ministers, and fellow churchgoers when our kids are in trouble or times are rough.

While out on the street, black men are perceived as invisible or dangerous; inside the therapy office, many black men feel ignored by therapists who find their anger or assertiveness frightening. Jim, a stock clerk and concerned inner-city father with a booming baritone voice, dominated the first ten minutes of his family's first session. He was furious with the way his son's teachers and the school psychologist were dealing with his son's problems. Whenever his son got in trouble, the school called his wife at work and never called him—assuming, he thought, that he was just another absentee black father. When he and his wife went to a meeting at the school, he said, the school psychologist, a white woman, had repeatedly solicited his wife's advice and hadn't even asked his opinion, even though he was sitting right next to her. When he got frustrated and said what *he* thought, the psychologist sat up straight, crossed her arms, and pulled away in her seat, seemingly annoyed and a little frightened by the interruption from "this tall, big, black man." As he related this to me, Jim became more heated. He waved his arms, raised his voice, and stood up out of his seat. Therapy, he made it clear to me, was a family decision. He expected to have his views respected as much as his wife's. He didn't want what happened with the school psychologist to happen again in my office.

Jim's experience with the school psychologist is not unusual. For years, white therapists I have supervised have come to me with some embarrassment and admitted being uneasy and fearful of black clients during sessions. They often don't know what to do with their feelings and are afraid of being perceived as "racist" if they express how unsettled they feel.

I usually advise them to work on their feelings in their own therapy. I also suggest they discuss them with me, enroll in a course in cultural sensitivity training, or read Nancy Boyd-Franklin's *Black Families in Therapy,* William Grier and Price Cobb's *Black Rage,* or sociologist Andrew Billingsley's *Black Families in White America.* I often ask them what past incidents are triggering their feelings: Have they had personal experience with black-on-white crime? Did they grow up in a family where racist attitudes were encouraged? When their discomfort is mostly the result of unfamiliarity, I suggest they admit their ignorance to their clients and ask the clients to help educate them about African-American life. As long as you're genuine, there's no harm in admitting your ignorance. It is far worse to pretend the discomfort isn't there than to simply lay it on the table and deal with it openly and honestly.

Some therapists routinely ask families right at the start of therapy how they feel about seeing a therapist who is of another race. When I am working with white clients, I don't. I want to see how things go, and I raise the question if or when I think things are stuck. I suggest that white therapists who are working with black families try something similar when they reach an impasse, perhaps saying something like, "I feel we're not really moving and I wonder if you have some concerns about seeing a white therapist."

Once the pervasive impact of racism is acknowledged as a force in a black family's experience, the family can move on to confront other issues. But if the impact of racism is ignored, it's unlikely that therapy will go anywhere. Jim, for example, was full of rage when he thought of how discouraging teachers had been about his own dreams of being an entrepreneur. When his son had problems in school, he was enraged that the school did not have the interests of young black men at heart. Sometimes he was right and his son was being treated unfairly, but sometimes his son exploited his father's rage to avoid responsibility for his schoolwork and to drive a wedge between his parents and the school. Therapy provided an opportunity to explore the crossroads where family dynamics and racism met. It was crucial that Jim make the distinction between the realities of racism and his son's adolescent flair for manipulating a situation to his advantage.

In the hands of an unknowing and racially insensitive therapist, these fine distinctions can be blurred. In Jim's case, for instance, I began by listening to him vent his anger about his son's situation and his own treatment by the school psychologist. I let him know I understood the social landscape he and his son moved in. If I had quickly leapt to the interpretation that his son was engaged in a kind of adolescent "get something over on your parents" manipulation, Jim would have perceived me as "blaming the victim" and as discounting his realistic observation about institutionalized racism within the schools.

So we started with what was on Jim's mind. After a couple of sessions, when he seemed to have fully expressed his original sense of the situation, I began normalizing the way teenagers tend to justify themselves and hide things from their parents. I talked in a general way about how "kids in school tend to be always offering explanations for their behavior and their disagreements with the teacher's interpretations." I talked about my own children, and my own school days, and asked Jim what he'd done in school. He readily acknowledged the ways that he had tried to get out of trouble when he was a teenager. "But you still have to watch out for the way schools treat black kids," he said.

As the atmosphere relaxed, I thought about the teacher's complaints about Jim's son—that he clowned around, talked in class, and sometimes hit other kids. "Could it possibly be that your son actually did these things?" I wondered aloud.

"Well, yeah, that's possible . . . "

"Have you ever asked him whether that was the case?"

Jim turned to his son and said, "You didn't do any of those things, did you?"

The son, not surprisingly, said, "No," in a tone of injured innocence.

I chuckled. "Come on," I said to Jim. "When you were his age, would you admit to your father that you had messed up? In front of your mother, too? And if you did, what would have happened?" We all laughed, and the son was off the hot seat, but without having succeeded in playing either his parents or me for a sucker.

Black men need to learn how not to wallow in self-pity, or to be so buried in anger and frustration that they self-destruct. Therapists who hope to serve black men must learn how to draw on their main sources of strength—extended families, family rituals, and community folk wisdom—to help their clients fight the alienation that public invisibility produces. It is not enough simply to listen to and acknowledge the frustrations of black men and their families. It is important to empower them, to help them clarify their goals and clear away the obstacles to achieving them. When my clients are stuck in the quicksand of hopelessness, looking around and pointing at all the indignities and injustices they see, I have to counter that despair and tap into their inner strength, wherever it may live. Often, the source of inspiration comes from strong religious and spiritual beliefs, or from the African-American tradition of survival.

We African Americans have a history of drawing upon inner and extended-family resources to survive from one generation to the next, no matter what the obstacles and indignities. When I ask people what they remember of the survivors in their families, they may recall elderly members of their Baptist congregations when they were growing up. I ask them to notice how the same survival strengths are present in them and help them to draw on and amplify them. When people reconnect with this history, it gives them heart, and a sense of self that is empowering.

I may help people reconnect with their history by quoting Langston Hughes's poem, "Mother to Son," which contains the phrase "Life for me ain't been no crystal stair." The message behind the poem is this: Nothing is guaranteed and it's not going to be easy, but others have done it before you. I also talk about great African-American leaders—from Frederick Douglass to Malcolm X to Martin Luther King Jr.—they are powerful examples of black men who converted their frustration and anger into an indomitable will to succeed in their vision or life mission. Sometimes I quote from King's "I Have a Dream" speech or from the autobiography of Malcolm X. These writings evoke the vision of a better world with self-respect. The way I see it, it's not enough to make the precarious climb into the American middle class or to be accepted on white terms—I want my clients to connect to a deeper sense of self. Stories from the lives of great African-American leaders act as teaching tales, and they help my clients answer the questions I often pose: "What is your vision of yourself? What is your vision of your life? You have got to have a dream."

When Bill told his family about the incident in the restaurant, he massaged a clenched fist, stabbed his finger in the air, and made riveting eye contact with me. I met his gaze. Behind his look was a message: Can you stand my fury? This is the assertiveness white men and women fear and misinterpret as aggression. Many white women cringe at it, and many white men either become combative or defensive or seek to suppress it. In the wider world, attuned as it is to expect some degree of submissiveness from all people except successful white men, Bill's kind of assertiveness always runs the risk of being taken as threatening. And there was another, rarely discussed factor at play in the room: riveting eye contact between black men is a test of manliness known as the "stare down." I suspect that Bill was also testing to see if I still had any "street smarts" or whether my training had purged me of them.

Besides being angry, Bill also was hurt, although he did not want to appear vulnerable in the eyes of his children, especially his son. He wanted to show his son that he could handle situations of subtle and blatant discrimination, but there was an air of defeat in the room. "When does this shit ever end?" he asked softly. There was silence in the room, as his children and wife absorbed the full impact of his anger and bewilderment.

After a moment, I felt that it was crucial to challenge the atmosphere of hopelessness, so I asked Bill whether he wanted to share any lessons from his experiences with his children. The incident became transformed into a parental lesson for the children, uniting Bill and his wife in a shared concern. Softly, Bill told his son, much as his father might have told him, "You need to watch your back." Bill drew parallels between his experience and the past experiences of his father. He began to recall family and African-American history to teach his children about race relations. He talked about the types of treatment they might encounter in different situations. He coached them on how not to become discouraged, how to carry themselves with dignity. Through teaching, he not only restored his self-respect but found comfort in assuming the family mantle of protector. This was an Afrocentric translation of Bowen's family system theory, passing the family legacy about race relations along to the next generation. Over the next several weeks, Bill brought the message home to his children over and over: No matter what circumstances you get yourself into, don't allow your personal sense of self, your self-respect, to be compromised.

In later sessions, he talked about hearing his own father describe his racial confrontations as a way of teaching his children to "watch their backs." Bill's uncle had lost his job when he stood up for himself, and Bill had been taught that dignity and integrity were worth a high price. His response to the humiliation in the restaurant was linked to old family lessons he had absorbed about the importance of vigilance. By not confronting the maître d' in the restaurant, Bill felt he had betrayed his ancestors as well as himself and other black men. And yet he was unsure how the old family lessons applied to the new social contexts he found himself in. What would be the cost if he became confrontational in front of a corporate client?

Over many weeks of individual, couples, and family counseling, Bill teased out the answers to these questions. Sensitive to slights, he spent a lot of energy figuring out whether disrespectful behaviors by his co-workers were naive or intentional. Now that he was in touch with his feelings about perceived slights, I did not want him to ignore those reactions, but to develop a wide range of responses that both maintained his sense of dignity and allowed him flexibility. We discussed which battles Bill wanted to fight, and I coached him on some alternatives to the style of direct confrontation that had once served his family well in different circumstances. His wife, Gloria, and the children also offered suggestions. One of the strategies Bill developed was to speak directly to co-workers and educate them about behaviors that he found disrespectful.

Earlier in his life, Bill would have shared such troubling incidents with his brothers and sisters and his best friend. They would have helped him blow off steam and offered a reality check about his reaction. But Bill had abandoned that source of support when he became a corporate success. Although he still perceived his daily surroundings as hostile and unsupportive, he no longer felt free to talk to his extended family about this. He was the first member of his family to go to college and enter the corporate business world, and he had become the family's great success story. To confess that he was still troubled by racial indignities felt too much like an admission of failure. He was afraid to discourage his relatives with less education: If he could not succeed, with all of his education and opportunities, what could they expect out of life? But most of all, he was ashamed to reveal that he was no longer as outspoken and confrontational as his family traditions had taught him to be. He had become overly cautious about how he appeared to others. The pressure to succeed had transformed him into a conformist in spite of a strong family legacy emphasizing self-respect and honor above all. In the face of this conflict, he had found no role models or mentors he could turn to in the business world.

Cut off from other support, Bill had only his wife, Gloria, to turn to. But Gloria had been raised in a Southern family that had traditionally dealt with racial slights in a more relaxed and accommodating way. Trying to contain Bill's anger, she often minimized the incidents he described, and she frequently complained that Bill and his whole family were too preoccupied with race.

On the day that Bill first talked about the incident in the restaurant, I asked Gloria to repeat what she had heard from Bill. This time, she did not minimize what had happened. She had heard his complaints before, she said, but now she heard his despair. Throughout the process, Gloria was attentive. She was supportive of Bill and saw his storytelling as an important experience for him.

Clearly, part of Bill's anger was a feeling that Gloria did not understand and ultimately care about what he was going through. I told Gloria that in order for them to resolve the family problems, it was extremely important for each of them to understand what the other was saying. She agreed with this. I then began a process of having her repeat her understanding of Bill's thoughts and feelings, using him as a resource for clarifications. When there was confusion or misunderstanding, I would act as translator or as a buffer for loaded emotions.

In the following weeks, I encouraged Bill to reconnect with his brothers and sisters, and he found that his fears of being judged by them for not being confrontational enough were just fears. The strength of black families has traditionally been the extended kinship network, including fictive kin and church family. Bill is a familiar case as an African American, consumed by pressures of a new status, losing sight of how family can still be a vital support. At first, Bill could not see that he did not have to create an infallible image for the family. In fact, they proved to be eager to advise him as a way of participating in his success.

Some therapists might find this case overly focused on Bill and Bill's problems. The reality in this family was that Bill's suffering was causing everyone else to suffer. Bill's sensitivity threatened not only the emotional stability of the family but its economic survival as well. If he messed up on the job and was fired, the family would lose its major source of income. And black, middle-class families like Bill's face far more precarious prospects than white families at the same income level. There are no major assets or inheritances to fall back on, and no extended network of family and friends to help out with money or job offers when a job is lost.

At home, Bill and Gloria became closer, and the children, too, made more of an effort to understand their father. No longer did he come home ranting and raging and feeling dismissed by his wife. The atmosphere at home relaxed and, for the first time, Bill and Gloria began to talk openly with their children about their experiences with racism. For Gloria, the open discussion of the problems of racism helped anchor the family. For Bill, these discussions reframed the demeaning experiences of invisibility into visibility with dignity and self-respect.

Bill realized that by keeping his daily struggles to himself, he had deprived his children of the lessons others had painfully taught him about managing racial slights. When his son told him that he wasn't being called on in class, Bill encouraged him to go to the teacher after class and discuss his feelings. And he let his children know that he would come down to the school and support them if they were unable to resolve things on their own.

None of this, of course, changes the invisibility that black men suffer on the streets, or the invisibility I may suffer after I end a session and walk out the door. But it gives me great satisfaction to reconnect a man like Bill with the traditional sources of support that have always sustained the black community, and to stop the world's racism from tearing another family apart. Family therapists—black and white—have much to offer African-American men and their families. But only if most white therapists abandon their almost willful naivete. And only if the invisibility that black men suffer ends when they open the door and step into the therapy room.

Questions for Discussion

1. What stopped Bill from sharing with his family the humiliations he experienced in the world?
2. According to the author, what are the ways a white therapist can thwart therapy or even cause African-American men to terminate therapy?
3. What suggestions does the writer make about how therapists can not only empathize with their black male clients, but empower them?
4. If you are seeing a client of a different race, would you bring up this difference right away or wait until something came up to address it? Give your reasons.

Against the Odds

Sara Rife

At the age of thirty-four I finally accepted the fact that I am a lesbian. Coming out was a long journey of twists and turns in strikingly different worlds. The journey began in my early adolescence and led me into adulthood. Along the road there was exposure to many forms of sexuality and a process of coming to terms with myself. The process involved accepting my sexuality, wrestling with demons of homophobia, taking a real stand for myself in my family, and embracing the question "Why be normal?"

It's hard to know when the process began. Memory tells me that it was sometime in junior high school when I longed for a depth of contact with one of my girlfriends that was not reciprocated. I quickly began to contort my feelings into acceptable forms of outward behavior, with inward desires taking shape in dreams. My best friend in school was Annie, a girl who loved Bob Dylan. Every day after school we would go to her house and listen to Dylan while eating popcorn and slices of American cheese and drinking Coca-Cola. I loved Annie. She had a great imagination and made up a fantasy lover. She told stories about her lover. In an attempt to stay connected, I copied her and created a fantasy about love, but it had no passion. She was interested in sex and older guys. She would talk about getting a reputation for letting guys go to third base. I was fascinated, grossed out, and jealous. I didn't know exactly what I wanted, but I wanted to be with her, to press up against her, maybe even kiss her. I found sneaky ways to make little bits of physical contact but was careful to keep up a front of interest in boys. We stayed friends for a few years but drifted apart as she became a high school jock and I became a budding hippie.

Somewhere in those same years, and maybe a little before, a member of my family used me for sexual exploration. This secretive activity happened over a period of time that is a haze to me now. It added confusion to my already confused brain. I was fighting off intercourse while feeling my body aroused by the pressure of him huffing and puffing against me. This secret occurred in my family where there was really no sexuality except male sexuality. The unstated rule was that girls/women were to be interested in sex mainly to please men. *Playboy* magazine was a gift in my teenage brother's Christmas stocking, and this was thought to be a liberal gesture by my parents. Meanwhile my sister, the oldest of the three of us, was always in trouble for staying out late with boys. As the youngest, I had a vague sense of sex being good for the males while shaming for the females. I didn't tell anyone about the sexual things being done to me. I was too afraid of getting into trouble. Instead, I held it against myself and learned to associate arousal with fear and shame.

In high school, I became friends with Julie, a girl whose single mom was an alcoholic. Her mom was involved in amateur theater. She took us to plays and bars and let us drink and smoke. Sometimes her mother would pick up men in bars and bring them home for sex. Many nights there would be screaming conclusions to these escapades, with drunken men tumbling down the carpeted steps. Nobody paid much attention to us. We stayed out all night on weekends in their Pontiac convertible sipping rum and Coke and flirting with each other and with guys. I was fascinated with Julie's large breasts. I really wanted to cuddle up with her. Sometimes she would let me get close while we listened to Carole King's *Tapestry* album. When Julie figured out that I wanted more than friendship, she made it clear that she liked me as a friend but wanted a boyfriend. We hung out a lot with her older sister, Vicki, and her fiancé. I began to fall in love with Vicki. She was beautiful, thin, and tall with one blue and one green eye. Her fiancé was Jewish, and together they introduced me to a new world of good food and radical politics. At their wedding he wore a Nehru jacket, she a miniskirt, and Jefferson Airplane played in the background. They were exotic to me, as a WASP girl coming of age in the late sixties. Julie and I drifted apart as she moved on to college and I stayed in high school. Vicki and her husband began to be my friends. I stayed overnight at their apartment and they introduced me to pot, ideas about encounter groups, and Woodstock. I was excited, stimulated, confused, and drifting far from my conventional family. I began to live two lives. The emerging, typical high school student and the "hip" girl hanging out with older people who were immersed in the evolving culture of the sixties. Vicki and I grew tighter, and one night she took me into the woods. In what was an evening of magic, she put my hands on her breasts and kissed me. I was thrilled beyond belief. We continued to have periodic touch sessions for the next several years. These sessions expanded to include her husband. I was never interested in her husband, but I played along for the moments when I could touch her.

After high school I moved in with them because my parents would not send me away to college. I quoted Kahlil Gibran to my mother—"Your children are not your children . . . "—and later went off to live in a country farmhouse with a group of counterculture characters. The image of my mother sitting sadly on our living room sofa as I moved out at seventeen haunts me still. I began to attend college and to support myself. Money was a struggle so Vicki led me to work in a bar. It was a sleazy joint with women dancing on a stage for money and men drooling over them. It was a world of prostitutes, heroin addicts, underground crime, and exploitation. But it was also a hotbed of lesbians. Over the next two years, I worked three nights a week dancing and avoiding sexual encounters with men while going to college and studying philosophy. I spent nights in the bar talking to all kinds of men. Vietnam vets, traveling businessmen, men of all ethnic backgrounds, sleazy men, kind men, addicted men, kinky men. I saw strip shows and watched prostitutes work their johns. This was a world of sex for sale. Most of the younger women, like me, had histories of sexual abuse and were lost souls on a confused path. The older ones were tough gals who scared me. Some of the younger ones were gutsy and fun and outrageous. I slept with a few young women and learned about lesbian sex. My experience in the bar ended with a dispute with the owners over racist treatment of a co-worker. My sense of justice saved me from a world where I was always in danger.

Vicki and her husband and I drifted apart after I began to feel judged by them for my lesbian behavior. I left the farmhouse, quit college, and moved to a city apartment with an old friend. I decided I wanted to be heterosexual, to go straight and get back with my family. I clung to some of my hippie identity but I wanted to settle into the mainstream. I started to work in a flower shop. I dated a few guys and attempted to have sex. But sex always got stuck for me in a place that was mixed up between anxiety about arousal and fear of being queer. Still I wanted to please my parents, who knew nothing about my shadow life of the bar and sex with women. This phase lasted a short time, until I was introduced to the Women's Movement.

The Women's Movement came to me through a feminist neighbor called Ruth. She was a woman I quickly admired. Ruth led me to a consciousness raising group. I was twenty at the time, the youngest member of the group. We met each week, talked, laughed, and supported one another. This was my first experience with a group of women, some of whom proudly identified as lesbian. The group opened doors to new friends and lovers. This was a time of relief and joy. I came to the group after having returned part-time to college. I was taking a psychology course, and the textbook told me that homosexuality was deviant and that if a person had not resolved such longings by the late teens, there was something pathological going on. The CR group was the antidote to my fear that the textbook was right. It was a temporary reprieve from the wellspring of shame that had started with incest, grown bigger in the aftermath of the bar, and fed by the textbook. While enjoying the company of feminist women, I began to work in the field of human services, the start of my career path. The CR group adventures and related pals led me to my first serious lesbian relationship.

My first committed lesbian love affair moved me from Maryland to Massachusetts. After being introduced by mutual friends, our romance began passionately. Sex was great, mutually intense, steamy, and loudly orgasmic. It was my first real taste of physical intimacy. I was twenty-one and at last sure I was a lesbian. I moved to Boston in 1975 to be with my lover, a medical student. We set up house in an apartment and the relationship was quickly tested. She was gone most of the time and I was lonely in a new city. She was somewhat closeted among her school peers and I was naively thinking everyone would delight in our passion. I came out to my older sister and she was horrified. She begged me not to tell our parents because "it would kill them." Out of the haze of my sexual bliss I was shocked by this response and further isolated from my family. My loneliness in a new city coupled with longing for my family led me to develop a deep crush on a work buddy, Becky, who was straight. Becky came from the type of WASP family my parents really approved of, old New Englanders with quiet, understated, extremely polite affluence. At the same time, I entered therapy with a therapist who was convinced I was straight. Things began to fall apart in my love nest. Sex became conflictual, incest ghosts began to haunt me, and the homophobia of those around me smothered my lesbian pride. I left my girlfriend in a painful and abrupt manner. I vowed to be straight.

The decision to be straight came out of a desire to fit into my family and into my new friend's WASP world. I loved and admired Becky. She introduced me to the pleasures of sailing, knitting, and using hand tools. She was my boss and my pal. We hung out, traveled together, and avoided talking intimately. I wanted to be like her. She had a close, supportive family, had attended good schools, and was always in control. For the next twelve years, I lost myself in hard work and repressed feelings. Becky was supportive of my professional development. While working hard, I dated some men and kept them frustrated. They were mostly kind, smart guys with whom I would have sporadic, controlled sexual contact. I dreamed of having sex with Becky. My heart was broken when she had boyfriends; I became angry and jealous. I smoked a lot of pot, hazing my discomfort, and at times thought of ending it all. I channeled my passion into my work in human services. Work was my substitute for intimacy. During this time, incest and shameful memories began to haunt me. I had not told Becky a lot of things about my past, including the real reason I had moved to Boston. She had made it clear that she was homophobic. The truth would have ended the friendship. I was alone with haunting memories, and my misery was beginning to wake me up at night.

For my thirtieth birthday Becky gave me a party. There were three men at the party who were courting me. I appreciated their attention but I was locked in my own closet. I was thirty and alone, frozen in my fear of being lesbian. That year I developed another friendship with a straight artist named Liz. The process began again. I had a crush on her that tormented me. Liz was available for emotional discussion and cozy physical contact. She was married and in charge of the distance-closeness factor in our relationship. I was a longing soul trying to pass as straight. People around me were confused about why I was not in a relationship. I made up stories about why and believed them myself. Finally my sleepless nights and a friend's suggestion led me back to therapy.

My second experience in therapy was far different than the first. My therapist was warm, available, and open to my confusing process. I eventually told my incest secret and the story about working in a bar. She supported me, encouraged me, and let me take my time telling my story. But this therapist was straight and I wanted to please her. I wanted to be a good heterosexual client, someone she would respect and want as a member of her family. I don't know how I would have come back to my sexuality had it not been for the good fortune of working on my incest experience. I heard about a book called *The Courage to Heal* and told my therapist. Although she may have been straight, she was extremely open to anything that would help me get out of my loneliness. She encouraged me to follow my curiosity about the book and its authors. One night I went to a book promotion and heard Ellen Bass and Laura Davis talk about their work. They opened a door that had long been closed. They were both lesbians, and they were out and proud. My heart opened and my next crush was on Ellen Bass, an accomplished, radical lesbian. I attended several workshops for sexual abuse survivors led by her. These workshops were a mix of lesbian, bisexual, and straight women. While on the surface I worked on past shame, underneath my sexuality reawakened. If someone as attractive and bright as Ellen Bass could be a lesbian, then why couldn't I? Without even knowing it, she was opening a door of liberation for me. I was, after many years of lonely drought, preparing to leave the desert and enter the forest.

It took me a few years after meeting Ellen Bass to fully come out. My therapist was curious and helpful and encouraged me to be myself. I slowly started to tell my straight friends about bits of my past and I began quietly to date women. At thirty-six, I met my partner, Linda. I fell head over heels in love immediately. A gorgeous, feminist carpenter and proud lesbian, she let me into her heart and we began our journey together. Sex, sexuality, and intimacy returned to my life in new and deepening ways. I was so thrilled I came out everywhere, including telling my parents. They were very unhappy. My mother said she thought I had been dating a black man and that was why I had never gotten married. My sister thought I should never have told them. My family did not want us to come to holiday celebrations. When my brother married for the second time, I was invited alone.

My parents refused to meet my partner for four years. This time I did not cave in to their rejection of me. My partner, the depth of our relationship, and the support of old and new friends kept me going. I was not going to be pushed back into the closet.

My mother died when I was forty. She met my partner only once, three months before her death. I was alone with my mother when she died, touching her, seeing myself in her body, mourning the loss of all we could have shared. Had she been willing to know Linda, I am sure she would have liked her. After my mother's death, my family finally began trying to accept us as a couple. A gap remains in worldviews and social experience. I am a lesbian social worker in a family of Republicans.

Being lesbian is a central part of who I am. It has always been a defining factor, but one I denied out of fear and shame. I regret those closet-bound years. The good that came of them was my professional development, working in human services, finishing undergraduate and graduate school. In many ways the rewards have been worth the struggles, but life is short, and on a melancholy day, I wonder what else I might have done if I had accepted my sexuality earlier. Still, given the variables of my life, things have turned out well. Homophobia is a force in the world, but it no longer rules my life. I am through with the shame and have moved on to the pleasure.

Questions for Discussion

1. What does this narrative say about the process of "coming out"?
2. What role did each of this woman's therapists play in her development?
3. In what ways can family members support or hinder gay or lesbian loved ones?
4. What do you think the current status of homophobia is in today's society, and what are some of its effects on those who face it?

Hag

Mary Sojourner

Mariette tells me we still have beautiful legs, both of us, even if our faces have gone to seed. She is fifty-three and doesn't come from this country. I am fifty, and the day we have this conversation, which is about discovering that our faces and bodies, in men's eyes, no longer exist, I am heading into town to dye Easter eggs with my best friend, Deena, and her wild boys. I see a woman walking along the road. She is dressed in brown tights, a cherry-pink top, and a turquoise headband. There is sunlight all around her, clear mountain light, and she looks wonderful. I am jealous.

I pass her and realize it is Mariette, walking the five miles into town to do her shopping. She has made herself up beautifully, in that subtle way European women seem to know. I beep. She ignores me. I go back to get her.

"It's you," she says. "You didn't have to turn around for me."

"True," I say.

"I'm glad you did," she says. "There are lots of assholes driving this road."

"You look wonderful," I say. "I am so jealous of your legs."

"Thanks," she says, "about my beautiful legs. Let me tell you a story."

She cracks open the window, lights a cigarette, and aims the smoke delicately out into the slipstream. Not for one second, while she talks, does she turn to look at me.

"I had just turned fifty," she says quietly, "in Atlanta. My daughter had given birth to her third daughter and I was helping out. I walked to the big mall to buy some Pampers. A truck came up behind me in the parking lot. The driver going slow, staying behind me. He was saying things that were dirty and they were also said so gently that they were turning me on. I was wearing tights and one of those big shirts that hides everything but your legs. I kept walking. He finally drove up past me. He was young and cute. Like a carpenter maybe, one of those guys. When he saw my face, he made this ugly, ugly look and he flipped me, you know, that middle finger."

I bow my head.

"I wanted to disappear," Mariette says.

"I know," I say.

"Right then," she says, "I was gone. As a woman. Gone till the day I die."

Up until now, though we live in a half-acre collection of cabins, trailers, and sheds a few miles south of a small Arizona mountain town, we have not talked that much. We are two of three women in the place. The third is Darlene Jackson. She's half Northern Paiute, half Chicana. Darlene works at Mille's Café and she has some interesting views on men and sex. If she's going to fuck him, he's got to have a car and a job, and if he doesn't make her come the first time, she doesn't answer the phone for a few days. The guy always disappears.

"I can tell right away," Darlene says. "If they don't have willpower in the sack, they haven't got it anywhere else."

Darlene does manicures on the side, somewhat unlicensed. She has little business cards printed up that say *Darlene Jackson . . . when it's touch that counts . . . 637-9910.* She weighs two hundred pounds—"two hundred beautiful pounds," she says. "We Jacksons are big scrumptious women," she says. She wears Levi's cutoffs, fuschia tank tops, silver cowgirl boots, and when you see her heading out in early twilight for a date, you know she's right. All that mocha skin catches the last sweet rose of sunset. She wears eye shadow the same blurred lilac as the mountains. She pauses to wave before she climbs into her truck, and you can see how some horny guy would be grateful for all of her, for a woman big and scrumptious, bright and shadowed as the moon.

All our other neighbors are guys, three of them steady tenants, the other four a floating crapshoot. What we do, Mariette and Darlene and me, in the rare instances when we meet by the community shower house, is compare notes on the lovelies the fellows bring in. We were going to organize a pool on average age difference between guy and girlfriend, but Darlene said Mariette and I tended toward bitterness and it wouldn't help to see the truth in round figures.

For instance, Amy's twenty-three and Rick's forty; the redhead's thirty to Dale's fifty, and, cruelest cut of all, Tina Rae's twenty-seven to the sober doper's fifty-seven. Thirty fucking years. Damn near Grandpa and Grandpet.

"Round figures?" Mariette said mildly. "Yes. *Round* figures."

"You bet," Darlene said. "Life on life's terms." She goes to self-esteem meetings where she hears stuff like that. She likes it. It's a small price to pay for no longer waking up next to strangers, looking down at her round dark arms, and counting the bruises that blossomed there.

"You would not believe the way my romance hangovers were," she told Mariette and me, "just like sitting on your paralyzed butt, looking down a tunnel, and the light at the end of the tunnel is the Midnight Express . . . aiming for you."

"I believe you," Mariette once said. "It sounds a lot like getting fifty to me."

"Don't talk about that!" Darlene says, whenever *that* topic comes up. "I'm twenty-eight and I'm not going to think about being fifty till I get there."

"You turn around, darling," Mariette will say in her throaty Latvian or Belgian or who-knows-what accent, "and you are there."

Mariette leans back and rests her feet on the dashboard. I open my window. Spring is cooking the pine oil out of the trees. We both take deep breaths.

"So foolish, so sentimental," she says. "When I smell those trees I could be twelve again. We would go to the mountains, to a tiny lake. The summer evenings were so long. We would sit by the lake, my father pretending to fish, my mother doing nothing, just sitting, watching him. Those were the only times I saw her still, even when she was an old woman. Always something in her hands, always something to keep her occupied. But not there at the lake."

"Do you think she worried about losing her sexiness?" I ask.

Mariette laughs. Cold. An ancient sound.

"The war came," she says. "And then, being refugees. And then . . ."

I signal, pull into the shopping center, and park. I don't know what to say.

"You going to Fairway?" are the words I find.

"I'll get back OK," she says.

"I didn't ask if you'd get back OK," I say. "I asked you if you're going to Fairway."

"I am. I don't need much. Potatoes, some milk. I can carry everything."

I stop, pull in next to a brand-new cherry-red Bronco. Blonde mom swings out of the driver's seat. She's wearing Day-Glo aerobics gear, her hair pulled back under a visor that reads *Lake Powell*. Two cute kids scramble out of the back and they all bounce into the store.

I don't move.

"No," I say. "I'll take you back. I want to talk more."

"You have something to do," she says. "Yes?"

"I'll call Deena," I say. "I hate Easter anyhow."

"Yes," Mariette says vaguely. "Easter is for witches, and it got all turned around." She lights another cigarette. "Spring. Fertility. Making love in the fields . . . that is Easter. That bunny is not about cute. It is about fucking."

I laugh. I watch normal life go on outside the truck. I like that I am in this movie where a gorgeous, silver-haired witch is telling about holy sex.

"Did you see that mother?" Mariette says. I turn. She is a smiling 1920s German film sorceress. Her green iceberg eyes look straight into mine.

I nod.

"I used to look just like her." Mariette sticks out her chest. "Except my breasts were more beautiful."

Even without a bra, even with what nursing four kids, and with what irresistible gravity has done, she is impressive.

"They still are," I laugh.

She doesn't alter her gaze. She pulls up her shirt. It's eleven in the morning in the middle of the busiest shopping center in West Flagstaff on Wednesday, the day the bonus coupons are in effect. I look at her breasts. Ivory bells. Burgundy nipples. Stretch marks silvery against her pale skin. I think of the moon, half full, how its surface is scarred and perfect.

"Mariette," I say, "they're beautiful. You should see me."

"Go ahead," she says, "show me." Her voice is harsh. She looks down at herself. "No one will bother to notice two old hags." She looks flat into my eyes.

I remember driving the lake road back from my ex-lover's when he was my lover. A young eagle dropped out of the sky and raced alongside my truck, pure light between me and the dawn-dark trees. Somehow, I kept the truck on the road and studied the bird's cold bright eye for what felt like hours.

Mariette's eyes are the same. I look past her. I don't know what I expect to see. People are schloomphing along, cars and trucks pulling in and out of parking spaces, the bag boy gathering in a dozen carts. A raven perches on a lightpole and screams.

"No," I say, "I can't do that."

She nods. Smiles. "Gone," she says, "both of us. Every woman our age. Disappeared till the day we die."

"Mariette," I say, "go buy your groceries. I'll wait for you."

"Sure," Mariette says. "Thank you."

She pulls down her shirt and climbs out. I bend to put a tape in the deck. When I straighten, I see that Mariette is waiting. She taps on my window. I open it.

"Hag," she says, "was once a holy woman."

The tape starts. Annie Lennox. Mariette smiles.

I watch her walk away, her legs perfect as a dancer's, her back straight, her pewter curls escaping from the knot into which she's gathered them. If I were a man, I would fall down at her feet.

The raven flops down, scavenges what's left of a bag of Chee-tos. I close my eyes. Mariette's scent lingers. Belgian. Expensive. What's left of the last gift her last lover gave her. Once a day, just before sleep, she puts one drop at the pulse in her throat.

"It is for me," she says. "Otherwise I will forget."

Questions for Discussion

1. What does this story say about our culture's view of older women?
2. Did the women in this story buy into this view?
3. What concrete changes could be made to alter our cultural views of youth, beauty, and the value of women?

Telling Mr. M.

Elisavietta Ritchie

"You and Dad are di-a-me-tri-cal-ly opposed."

Tim drops his hockey stick on my bedroom rug.

Like it or not, *my* bedroom now.

Tim's six-syllable word, picked up wherever, is startling. This year, his twelfth, he's become as monosyllabic as his father. After a childhood loquacious and gregarious, nowadays he won't invite friends. Embarrassment over my recent single-mother status? Or his desire to emulate John? John prides himself on few, but good, friends, whom he sees every six months, for bridge.

"Not *opposed,* Tim. Or exactly *opposite.*"

"Yes, you are."

I've bent over backward not to mention differences, to keep everything *so* civilized, make sure Tim understands: both parents, even apart, form a united front regarding his welfare and conduct . . .

I'm in my closet wondering why Persephone chose last Christmas's saved wrappings to birth three kittens in this morning. May she keep quiet now!

"Make me a two-column list, Tim. Diagrams. Parabolas."

They're learning to chart parabolas. Among the few aspects of math concrete enough to make sense: *What goes up, comes down, though it may have a high flying interlude en route.*

I spin down my own mental chart: John is compulsively tidy, while I like others to be orderly but can't attain neatness myself. John keeps excellent accounts; I balance neither checkbook nor budget. John likes bridge; I'd rather talk or read. Or am I scared of competition? Hostility, from others, even from myself? Skip on to listening habits: I tune in to news and classical music on the radio, tune out—turn off—commercials; John keeps the TV on, indiscriminately. John is brilliant, ambitious, thrifty, sensible, organized, etc.

In bed, all dichotomies dissolved . . .

One does not spend one's life in bed.

"For heaven's sake, Tim . . ."

But I mustn't imitate John now and complain of tracked-in snow, untied shoelaces, dirty face, tardiness . . .

"I was watching the movers unload a houseful down the street," he volunteers.

Because I want this litter of Persephone's (the first John hasn't been around to drown immediately) to surprise Tim on Christmas morning, even if he'll be hurrying over to John's, I close the closet door.

Because Tim remains standing here, apparently awaiting further discussion, I say, "You've heard the cliché *opposites attract*."

Addition to *my* two-column list: I hate clichés; John argues clichés are a normal part of speech, essential—how could knowledge be handed down without clichés? Increasingly our last year together, he brought home New Age psychobabble like "warts and all," "bottom line," "self-actualization," "interfacing." Apparently not just with computers. Once "Have a nice day" slipped out.

Though nowadays I only shop at thrifts and no-frills outlets, the postman brought our old department store bills addressed "Mr. and Mrs." for ladies' intimate apparel I'd neither charged nor received. This suggested John was acquiring his new speech patterns, and new habits of generosity, with another lady, one who presumably watched television frequently and needed a change of underwear. Enough additional clues in other domains, that when he announced her existence, I wasn't surprised.

Traumatized, probably. Isn't that the purpose? So one will be too passive—numb—to indulge in a royal row?

Yet—the thought whacks me now like a stepped-on hoe—I felt strangely relieved. Nothing like Another Woman to serve as—*catalyst* isn't the right word: a catalyst causes other elements to change without itself changing. The lady in question must find her life at least slightly transformed through wrecking one marriage and gleaning the leftovers for another.

If not *catalyst,* how about *crowbar? grenade? dynamite?* The match to ignite existing gunpowder, blast apart—what maybe needed sundering? I was too dumb—I'd like to say *loyal, devoted*—to notice.

But when a child is involved, parents should stay together. Should*, should.* Too late for shoulds. But I've always said, about other people's breakups, "One should *not* deprive a child of paternal presences." So I dutifully urge Tim to spend more time with his father and the new wife, whom Tim is expected to like and, sooner or later, to love.

Although John doesn't care about holidays, and she isn't accustomed to kids, it's logical they'll make a big thing of their first Christmas together, with big presents for Tim. Don't we all try to overcompensate, for our guilts, those of others. . . . My presents for Tim this year will not, alas, be big or exciting: a few clothes he needs anyway; a basic tool kit which is at least symbolic of his entry into the adult world; some books and games, picked up at a going-out-of-business sale last summer. At least he will have the surprise of the kittens.

"Yes, Tim, possibly we *are* different—though Dad and I enjoyed a happy decade. . . . I'm curious what differences you notice."

"Oh, I dunno . . . "

Resuming his sullen expression, abandoning boots midhall, he disappears into the bathroom. The shower runs. He reappears into the kitchen wrapped in my towel and spilling armloads of his dirty clothes.

John would be bellowing, "Pick up after yourself, young man!"

In surprise, I watch Tim fill the washer, retrieve dropped socks and shirts, stuff everything into the rising tide. Have John and . . . my replacement . . . enforced some sense of responsibility?

"The new kids down the street," Tim shrugs, "wash their own laundry, and they're younger."

I almost say, "Whoa! Less detergent!" But why spoil it, and anyway, this helpful phase won't last. Normal—deliberate?—preteen carelessness will return once Santa's done his thing.

* * *

The whole interval before Christmas, Tim washes his laundry, stuffs it in the dryer, even takes it out and carries it back to his room. That, of course, remains cluttered.

Another new development this week: his classmates, the boys anyway, troop in. Afternoons a teepee-like structure of junior-sized hockey sticks rises outside our door, a giant game of jackstraws bent at the tips. Wet boots freeze outside or steam inside. Mugs sloshed with cocoa sometimes reach the dishwasher, though as I enter the kitchen Tim is explaining to his guests that with only two of us now, we wash by hand to save electricity.

"More companionable to do dishes together," I interject, not wanting to show how miserly I have, of necessity, become.

"I'll wash them all later," Tim shrugs.

The boys nod, rinse their cups in the sink. Around grown-ups, they've entered the Age of Taciturnity. En masse the noise level spirals.

Later Tim says in passing, "I knew you're the only mom who'd let everyone come over at once."

I manage half days off this week and, to create some ideal image of A Competent Mother, bake sixteen panfuls of Christmas cookies to decorate the tree. This year I've bought the tree I always wanted: a live, if miniature, blue spruce to plant afterward in our slip of a garden.

Most cookies disappear before reaching a twig. Tim blames Persephone. "That cat'll eat anything, no wonder she got so fat." He hasn't commented that she's long and lean again. But baggy. Too busy with his new social life to notice. As a former stray accustomed to hiding in odd places, Persephone normally keeps a low profile anyway.

What to do with all those kittens? John was correct about overpopulation. But I love cats. So does Tim, unless he's outgrown pets the way he lost interest in his cactus collection. Neglect becomes cacti, but . . . I won't mind looking after his kittens. But *three?* Soon enough, *four* grown cats. John will be horrified when Tim tells him. Maybe I should have done . . . the necessary . . . and had her spayed.

Obviously Tim will go to John's for Christmas; they're phoning back and forth. Tim, rightly, refuses to be a messenger between John and me, and I must heed the admonitions of our elderly neighbor Henrietta Costwich: "Stay out of it, dear. Let them settle their own plans."

Still, I dread another holiday alone. Thanksgiving, I stayed home feeling sorry for myself, then found an unopened gallon of white paint in the cellar, sent it rolling around the floor until I guessed it must be agitated enough, and repainted the living room.

As Tim unpacks today's groceries, preparing to challenge my choices of cereals and vegetables, I remark, "I'll be roasting a turkey anyway. Christmas is for gathering, so I'm inviting several others without families."

"Like who?"

"Mrs. Costwich, who isn't perhaps that interesting to you, but you hit it off with her Dutch student boarder Jan. My old English teacher Mr. Boatwright because he always joined my parents' parties, a widower now. My secretary Suzanne whose fiancé is overseas—she's lively enough—and maybe some others from work, though I think everyone else has a family or is already invited somewhere."

"What about those new people down the street?" Tim asks.

"I don't know them."

"I do. The kids go to their mom's Christmas Eve, but Christmas Day they'll be back with Mr. M., their dad. Niko is only eleven but plays hockey okay. Angela's eight and a crybaby, but Mr. M. says she'll outgrow it when their lives settle in more. They'll start at my school in January. They haven't had time to buy a tree and their mom got to keep the old ornaments anyway. So can I invite them for Christmas dinner?"

Normally I greet new neighbors with cookies and lemonade or sandwiches on moving day, even a supper invitation. But a divorced father? In my situation, it would be forward to play welcome wagon. As I've told several colleagues who want to date me, "Thanks very much, but I fear it is too soon for my son to deal with . . . extra men."

Rather, is it too soon for *me* to cope . . . even, or especially, with single male neighbors.

I don't expect them to come but, rescuing a piece of last-year's Santa paper spared by Persephone, wrap a new Monopoly set in case. Tim can always take it over the next day.

Tim just opened his Christmas stocking, has eaten all the camper's snacks I meant him to save for summer, skimmed all the little books on frogs, snakes, jokes, and space aliens I could stuff in, and is deep in the anthology of sports stories I gave him. Anything to turn him on to reading. Apparently he is in no hurry to leave for John's. They must be holding their celebration there tonight.

As soon as I baste the turkey, it will be a good moment to unveil the kittens. I can imagine John's reaction when Tim tells him.

Someone knocks. An hour early! Like the witch in *Hansel and Gretel,* I'm half in the oven, hands heavy with turkey in a hot roasting pan. No space to put it down, no time to put on lipstick, no time to change from jeans into the red dress I've ritually worn every Christmas since John gave it to me a decade ago.

Tim runs to let in—the M.'s. He's warned me he never caught the name and it's too late to ask. "Too long anyway, but everyone calls him Mr. M."

Mr. M. is slightly bent, as if ashamed of his height—six-four? Skinny. A hurt look in his eyes, black. Two black-eyed children follow in silence. All three wear green sweaters, sleeves shrunk, must have been knitted several Christmases ago by a grandmother or aunt. Or mother?

I foresee a dreadfully heavy afternoon, and no piano for carols.

The man clutches several bottles.

"Not very fancy champagne, I'm afraid." His hands are too full to brush back an unkempt lock of brown hair. Grey at the temples. "I thought that since—your Tim has explained this is your first Christmas alone—and sparkling grape juice for the children."

He stands on the kitchen threshold as if unsure what to do with the bottles. I stand equally encumbered, mulling over the word "alone." Perhaps even married, I was . . .

"Thank you," I stammer. "There might be room in the fridge if I move the salads."

"Let me." He opens the refrigerator door but drops the bottles. The champagne rolls across the linoleum like an oversized rolling pin. Only the sparkling grape juice smashes, fortunately the clear kind that won't stain the floor more irreparably than it is.

So Mr. M. starts our acquaintance by mopping the mottled linoleum. Finally I settle him in the living room with a bowl of celery and apple slices intended to keep everyone alive until dinner. The children are already on the floor bending over Monopoly. Tim occasionally murmurs "Park Place," "Marvin Gardens," or "Wanna buy a railroad cheap?" The M. kids are silent.

Mr. M. runs his fingers over my books. He strokes Lawrence Durrell's *The Alexandria Quartet,* then leafs through a large Gauguin collection. "We have similar tastes."

Trying to figure his accent—something European—I hurry to change. Persephone meows as I reach into my closet for the red dress. Damn, the skirt still bears last Christmas's stains. Christmas was the day John chose to announce, "This, son, will be our last family Christmas because your mother and I . . . " And I dropped that turkey, which, being slightly over-cooked but still nice and moist, fell apart when it skidded under the kitchen table. Things moved rapidly thereafter.

The green silk dress, a hand-me-down from Henrietta Costwich because she bought it on sale and it didn't fit, is too springlike but more becoming. And new. And she will be pleased.

Approaching the living room I overhear Tim telling the M. children, "My mother will get the shock of the year when I bring out my surprise. Shhhh—kittens. Three. I know where Persephone hid them. We can't keep them all, so, in a few weeks, would you like one? Or two?"

Squeals from Angela and Niko, they are actually talking, begging to see the kittens, but Tim continues his monologue. Astonished to hear him hold-ing forth at length on any subject, except perhaps hockey, I can't help eaves-dropping.

"Now, Angela, don't you spoil the surprise. Keep quiet when she comes in the room. Kittens—that's one of the differences between my parents I ex-plained to your father last week. My father likes dogs; Mom likes cats. She doesn't dislike dogs, but Dad hates cats. He likes steaks; she likes vegeta-bles. Turkey today because it's Christmas. And when I tell Dad stuff like, oh, 'I made something in shop,' or 'I got an A yesterday,' he says,'Good,' then goes right back into his newspaper. Or his honeymoon bridge game with Doreen—that's his new wife. But my mom—at six a.m. today she went out in the snow in her bathrobe and boots to nail up the birdfeeder I made her. She frames my A papers. But . . . " his voice trails off, "no A's lately."

"Me neither," mutters Niko, and they go back to Monopoly.

Mr. M. stands as I pass the door. He seems to be looking me over. Without thinking I straighten up. Ingrained instincts.

"Need help?"

"Oh, no thanks. I mean, yes thanks, the turkey's heavy. The other guests are due soon. Mr. Boatwright's a feisty old bird, the Dutch student seems lost but writes one sonnet daily to improve his English—they'll get along. Henrietta, Suzanne—"

"Yes, Tim recited your list."

"Oh . . . I wasn't sure Tim would even be here, or—but we'll all squeeze around. . . . Sorry about his springing the kittens on you; he should have checked with you first."

"Already cleared," Mr. M. says. "Tim discussed it privately with me last week. He mentioned his father wanted him to fly to Florida and Tim was torn but decided to stay to distribute the kittens."

I feel a flash of . . . something like jealousy? Once again I've been left out. No one mentioned Florida.

As if sensing my disconcertment, Mr. M. adds, "Sometimes it's easier to talk with someone else's parents than one's own."

I guess I should be glad Tim is still here. Yes, of course. Nonetheless . . .

A knock. Henrietta and Jan, chocolate Yule log and gouda, Suzanne and fruitcake, Mr. Boatwright with guitar for carols. A snowy frenzy of boots, poinsettias, cookies spilling sprinkles.

Mr. M. introduces himself: "Constantine." Perhaps in time he will reveal more. For now, he carries in the turkey and automatically begins to carve. I arrange cranberry sauce, string beans, sweet potatoes, salads. Colorful, at least.

Mr. M. pours grape juice and champagne. His children are delighted with the bubbles on their tongues.

"Wait!" Tim clinks a spoon against a glass. "I will make a toast."

What follows is more speech than toast. He didn't learn either from John.

"My mother has another present. From Persephone. Called that because she purrs. Actually, three presents for three people. Mom chooses first, then Angela and Niko. Please keep silent."

I hope Persephone hasn't chosen to move her nursery.

Trailed by a perturbed cat, her belly drooping almost to the rug, Tim returns cradling *four* tiny kittens: black, white, tabby—plus one spotted as a Dalmatian.

"Merry Christmas! Qua-dru-ple surprise!"

Tim hands me the tabby. The white goes in Angela's lap, the black to Niko. They're chattering like chipmunks. Tim holds the spotted kitten. Beside the turkey, Mr. M. is beaming. Only Persephone looks perplexed.

I can't help laughing. First time in months? Maybe in time laughter replaces bitterness. Bitchiness.

Mr. M.—Constantine—catches my eye, raises his glass. "To a happier New Year?"

Statement? Question? Even a veiled invitation to celebrate together? Whichever. Christmas, at least, is turning out something close to happy.

Questions for Discussion

1. What sorts of issues arise for separated spouses at holiday times?
2. How do you prepare the children of separated parents for such situations?

Dance Away

Stephen Stathis

Rada was her name. She was twenty-two and worked as a waitress at an all-night truck stop. She had long thin black hair and a dark complexion and a nervous energy that ran through her slender body. During her travels, she brought along her pot and drinking binges and self-recriminations. She greeted strangers with the glazed stare of an owl and a reddened face—not because of the drinking, but because of the heat that whorled up inside of her body. She punished herself for feeling unloved; she punished herself for being unable to love. She was hesitant around men; most of them were concerned only with her body shape; some of them looked like the family friend that had raped her years earlier; a few were unable to deal with her vulnerabilities, her need to squash anyone who got too close. She came to store away feelings, building a fort around herself as she was cast adrift into the future.

Her twisted past has followed her during the years she worked as a nanny and the months she greeted people as a hostess to the time she came to a small town in the center of Maine where the winter months strained and strove toward springtime. She spent nights grabbing food lined up under heat lamps and rattling off blackboard desserts. She became fond of an older waitress with reddish hair and nervy musings.

"I like tall guys," said Sherry, clearing the counter of the dirtied plates left behind by a series of customers. "My last boyfriend was barely my height. He was thin, too. That bugged me."

"My last boyfriend wasn't rich," shot back Rada. "He wasn't a dream man either. He was a regular guy, nothing special."

"You seeing anyone now?"

"I met this truck driver. I suggested we start dating, then he got defensive; sometimes I say it like a joke; sometimes I'm serious. He likes the bar scene."

"What about that guy you were taken with at the counter a few weeks back?" asked Sherry.

"His girlfriend moved to Philadelphia. He said that he was leaving the area in March and wanted to see the world. 'I don't want to string you along' were his final words. There was no real intimacy. He still cares for his ex. He was the only guy I remotely felt for." Rada skimmed the edge of the coffee cup. She glanced down at her ruby red nail polish on each finger. "Even his voice made me feel good."

"What color was his hair?"

"Sandy brown."

"Was this guy taller than me?"

"Tall and slender with a long nose. A really nice guy. Nice. It could be something about me. I was really nervous, each time. He was a good person. He even called me back to say he had a nice time as soon as he got home. He stood between me and the traffic when we walked to the movie."

"Rada, you can't go on about this guy if he's leaving. Let's get together after work. We got customers waiting."

The stream of customers, frenetic and unbroken, disturbed her: she became testy with people who bored her, nasty with the ones who flirted, frustrated with old men who told her how important it was to serve the public. One, a stocky college professor, asked why she left high school. "I only liked my geology class. I didn't have any interest in my other classes." She set down a plate with slices of pot roast and mashed potatoes. "It must be nice to teach at a college," she continued, "and have a real career." The gray-haired professor reached for the pepper and said, "I call it surviving. Not a career. I work at a glorified high school."

Another one, a man wearing a collarless shirt and faded jeans, came in with a group of friends. She waited near their table, overhearing a comment about babies and marriage and how men needed to avoid both. She glared at them and muttered, "I could tell you're afraid of women. There's a big sign over your head."

She worked solemn and hard-hearted. She hurled invectives from her threatening voice time and time again. The indifference and callousness estranged her from people. She came to cast a jaundiced eye toward Sherry during a late-night conversation.

"It's not my bitchiness this time, Sherry. People set me off. They try to use me," she snarled and jabbed her index finger into the air.

"You do it to yourself, too. You would be this way no matter what. Someday this act of yours will really wear thin on others."

On the days that brought out ice fishermen and cicadas hibernated under the frost line, she took refuge in sleep; it was here that memories came together, memories that zigzagged across her mind as family and friends and strangers melded into one another. She recalled childhood walks with her father and brother to the store for penny candy; the Halloween nights when the family dressed up as witches and pirates and ghosts; the holidays when she decorated the family dog's tail with tinsel. She pictured her untouched bedroom in her parent's home, the room probably still considered hers even though she had not slept there for more than six years; the closets still stuffed with left-behind clothing and trophies; the dresser topped with a glow-in-the-dark Madonna and a plaster Cat Woman and Lamb Chop next to Ehaw.

She was the youngest child: an older brother by five years had left for college when she entered high school. He would be labeled the success in the family while she was left behind to mediate the tensions between the parents. She bore the scars of the sacrificial acts of her family. She was the "problem" child, the "bad" one, the "failure" around which the others danced. Her teenage years turned nightmarish. She stopped seeing herself as voluptuous. She no longer waited for her Prince Charming to appear. On her final day at home she screamed at her parents, "I'm not some hootchie. I'm the daughter you two sowed." She flew into a rage. She told them how insecure they made her feel, how they would not know how to miss her when she left home. It was on that day her voice flattened out like a crumpet; her false bravado and illusions collapsed on all sides of her.

She had strayed far looking for a place of solitude away from the rancor and divisions left behind. She hated her need for other people's approval. On her thirtieth birthday she would come to see that approval by those left behind was not needed to create another kind of life for herself. Today her lack of composure distanced her, kept her from having a wider view of where she might fit in. She recalled Sherry's words from one of their meetings. "It's all one life, Rada. You can't cut off where you came from. But you can be different from those you started out with."

Rada lived in a time when the young were free to indulge themselves: they exercised daily at the gym; they drank barley juice in the morning; they moved to a major city and planned successful parties and attended cocktail socials; they built careers and vacationed in exotic places. She wondered how others were able to take apart big dreams and break them down into doable parts, how one connected gossamer passions with an actual life. It was this that frustrated her: this disconnectedness between her dreams and reality.

For weeks she remained indoors. She grew impatient with her days. Her shift at the diner became insufferable. She spent these days listening to country-and-western music; she caked her face with layers of makeup and admired the lizard tattooed on her forearm; she vacuumed paint chips dropping from peeling ceilings; she flounced around on the frayed green carpet in her sweat pants, blue flannel shirt, and an old sweater. Her slovenly dress covered the excess weight that started to appear around her hips. She created diversions that encouraged being a loner. Being alone eased her insecurities. She had hoped for a smoother, more forward flow of time in this place. Time only ran slow during this period. More time only created more disorder. She felt stuck in reverse, standing guard over her secrets, preserving them as if they might shatter and leave her totally desolate.

She would live with these hurts and disappointments through a series of other jobs; jobs she would quit, followed by periods when she obsessed about a lack of money and then scrambled about to find new work. An outsider looking over this time in her life might wonder how she survived the pain. Rada was coming to see that life's painful moments never killed you: life went forward with the pain in tow.

Springtime came like the sweet sap that slowly awakened to the cold nights. Rada brought herself out of a long silence one Saturday afternoon and walked out of her apartment. She headed for a church not far from the diner. She slowed her pace as a wedding party appeared in the distance. She watched lynx-eyed as the bride and groom came into view. By the time she arrived in front of the church, the couple had entered through the front door along with guests. She waited outside until a greeting line formed. She headed over to the couple once the stream of well-wishers thinned out. She embraced Sherry and pulled away. "I'll only get married when I'm old. Really old. No teeth. Guy's too old to hurt me." Her eyes softened as she took Sherry's hand. "Good-bye."

Rada strolled past the guests milling on the sidewalk. She pined to become part of that dance where people joined hands and moved in a line to the same tempo and in the same direction even as others cut into the dance. She walked away from the fieldstoned church and shifted onto the cobblestoned street. She headed down to the pier. She continued on until a long, pink, cloudless sunset appeared like the ones seen after a volcanic eruption. The northern pintails, silhouetted against the sunset, and a calm wind that fell across her face made this moment seem like a blink of an eye compared to the long winter that was over. She sensed the past and present colliding in new ways. The shrouded slumbers were being altered somehow by a far-off future that would become part of her past, too. Seagulls flew above her with their silent and graceful movements. They beckoned her to follow as she walked along the shore. They were like escorts to her as she searched for her voice and path in this place. She was being led to places unknown and powerful.

Questions for Discussion

1. What might bring Rada into treatment?
2. What areas would you stress in working with her?
3. Is this typical postrape behavior? Discuss the ways rape impacts a person's capacity for relationships.

The Self Family

Tami Gramont

I grew up in a household that was chock full of dream thieves, inspiration eaters, and self-esteem suckers. And I'm not even talking about the parents!

When I first learned how to write a sentence, I was so delighted that I proudly announced I would write a book. I was only about five or six, but that was what I wanted to do. I could draw the pictures and with the new knowledge of how to write a sentence, I could write a book. Well, the one who called herself "Mom" said, "You're too little. You can't write a book."

I tried anyway. When I got stuck, I asked her for help. She said she didn't know the first thing about writing a book. "You'll have to do it on your own," said the mom. I gave up not long after that, as I didn't know how to make it like a "real" book. I did have some of the text and some pictures in a notebook, but no real direction.

I remember a few years after that being asked what I wanted to be when I grew up. I said, "A horse trainer, as I'm going to be too tall to be a jockey." I loved horses! I thought I would be praised for my sound-mindedness and for my logic. The mom laughed in a condescending way. The dad said, "You have to have a lot of money to train horses. Where are you going to get that kind of money? It takes money to make money, you know."

After much consideration, I felt it would be just too difficult to battle the "parents" on that issue and would choose something easier. So, soon after that, I chose "artist." I would use my painting and drawing abilities as a job.

"An artist?! You'll never make any money as an artist. Haven't you heard of a starving artist?" one of them shouted. Jeez!

So, I went back to the drawing board. I don't know exactly what happened after that, but I do remember thinking that I'll decide later. Maybe they can pick out what I should do, since they don't like what I choose.

Now, that wasn't the really bad part; it was just some of the picture. See, the whole time all of this was going on, the one who called herself Mom would tell me I was stupid or that something was wrong with me because I forgot everything. Now, I'm sure other mothers do the same thing, but day after day and year after year, it soaks in eventually. Being ignored didn't help much either.

I began seeing imaginary friends. My friends were what many people consider monsters. I never outgrew my monster friends. They are still with me. Well, some of them anyway.

They hang around and won't get out of the way. I have to yell at them to shut up and go away. Many days they just sit in the corner eating junk food, telling me I'm stupid and I won't amount to anything. One in particular, Pro Crastination, tells me, "I told you! You can't do anything! Don't even start; you won't finish it anyway." He talks a lot but doesn't do too much else but watch TV and eat.

I know these monsters well. As a matter of fact, they're like family. They have helped me grow up and taught me how to survive. One was Miss Pression. I can call her Dee; she taught me how not to cry. She said if I just stand still and don't cry, the one who is called Mom will stop hitting me. She told me that was the mom's goal—to make me cry. She said, "Just watch, when you don't cry, she will stop hitting you. It's what she wants. So don't give it to her and she will stop hitting you altogether."

So, the very next time the mom slapped me in the face, I just stood stock still. I felt my eyes sting like pepper, but I made the feeling dissolve before the tears came out. I emptied my mind and pretended I was nothing. Empty. Numb. Nothing. It wasn't too hard because, deep down, I knew I was nothing. Before the second blow came I was numb. I didn't feel any of the slaps. It was much easier then I thought it would be. Then the mom said, "Oh, so it doesn't hurt, huh? Well, this will." She went into the kitchen, came back, grabbed my arm, and . . . WHACK! It had a nice warm burn, after the initial sting subsided. Cripes! Dee was right! She never used the bread board before. How many more times is she going to—Whew! Thank goodness it broke, cuz it was starting to make it through. It might have made me cry. Dee told me if I cried it was all over. The mom stopped that time. But she never did stop hitting me altogether. I just stopped crying. Not crying made me feel safer . . . not so weak.

Dee stayed with me for a long time. She introduced me to other friends. I have said good-bye to many of them. They moved. I chose not to. I have never been out of the country and was a little afraid to go with them.

They aren't as bad as I have made them out to be, though. There is one main monster; his name is Ad Iction. I have met many of his cohorts, like Al, the one who was drunk all the time and made promises he couldn't keep. He was a lot of fun in the beginning. We would stay out all night and have some pretty fun times. By the end of our relationship he was kicking me in the stomach. When he got so destructive that I had to eat a whole roll of antacids before we met, I knew it was time to go our separate ways.

There was the controlling thin child who was afraid of everything. Her name is Anna Rexia. She didn't want to grow up. Anna was afraid of re-sponsibility and of not having a say-so in any part of her life. And boy did she have weird eating habits!

Oh, can't forget the sad fat girl who read all the time and has a constant headache. Some call her Bulla. She has a disorder. All those Emias think they're fat. I knew for a fact that Bulla would look in the mirror and see herself as fat. She had this odd thing about not having any food inside her . . . ever! Oh she'd eat, but she just wouldn't keep it down. I have been her friend the longest. The Emias are hard to spot; most are average weight, but you wouldn't know by how much food they eat and the baggy clothes they wear.

Of course, the sneaky paranoid one who will do anything to maintain her cool image is called Addy, the sister of Ad. Her friends call her "Druggie" or sometimes "Freak." All of these monsters are now living somewhere in the Fiji Islands. I haven't had any contact with them for about eleven years. It is said that if you recite these certain twelve spells and add willingness, powerlessness, and sincerity, they will all go on vacation. I still say those spells and they haven't moved back. Yet.

They do send postcards to say they are alive and well, having a great time and wish I was there. They even try to talk me into going out there. I can go if I want. I just don't want to . . . today. I keep telling them "maybe," just not today. They are great like that though; they don't ever forget me. And I never forget them either.

Then their crazy old aunt moved in next door. Her name is Lowe Esteem. She had an illegitimate child called Self Loathing. Self's father was from the Loathing family. Now I have occasional visits from Lowe Esteem and Self Loathing. I have asked them repeatedly to find another place to live. They keep coming over to borrow things. Once it was a shovel and they still have not returned it. I see them in their yard, using it, but I don't have the guts to ask for it back.

Oh, I almost forgot Lowe Esteem's cousin. She is from the Doubt family. Auntie Self Doubt is a nagging old broad. She wears gray and it looks like her whole body droops. Her gray hair is always falling out of her bun and she has usually forgotten to button at least one button on the front of her dress. She won't come right out and say what she thinks, but she just sort of whines. If I don't listen to her, she will nag me a little every day until I finally give in and spend the day with her. That isn't enough. I have learned that if I spend one day with her, she will want to stay a week, and then I won't get anything accomplished.

I don't hate the neighbors. I just want them gone. I have tried to scare them out, yell at them, and even bake cookies for them. Well, they love cookies! They will eat the cookies, borrow another garden tool, and be quiet for weeks, sometimes months and then—Bam!! In the middle of the night they will bang on my door, demanding I get up and entertain them. On occasion they will show up right before a job interview and want to go along. They always want to ride along to parties, and once in the middle of . . . well . . . in the middle of sex they marched into the house and right into our bedroom. Can you believe?! They walked right in on us and we had to stop. I felt terrible. They stayed for weeks that time.

Then there are those new exorcism books. You know the ones, in the self-help section. They don't work either.

All of this is not as terrible as when they come over for coffee in the morning and won't leave. If they know I'm going to write, they will purposely cause an argument and won't leave. For some reason they hate it when I write. Maybe because they know how important writing is to me. I don't know for sure.

I'm safe today; they went Christmas shopping. You know them, Self Loathing purposely gives gifts that shows she doesn't care. She will do whatever she can to get someone else to acknowledge what a rotten person she is, where Self Doubt takes all day to choose one present. She also has to have constant reassurance that she is purchasing the very best gift she can give. So I imagine they will be gone most of the day.

I have made a new friend. She used to work on a newspaper I freelanced for awhile ago. I really like her and enjoy her company. She is thinking of moving here but now lives out of state. I have invited her for a long-term visit. I sneaked a phone call! Oh, her name is Acceptance de la Self. I think she is from aristocracy, but she won't say. You can just tell by the way she carries herself. I don't think my current neighbors will enjoy this houseguest. Especially if she brings her husband, Luv.

So, now you know of my recent discovery. I met Acceptance and Luv de la Self and now I don't want to let them go. I can't smother them; they have clear and definite boundaries. I respect them for that. I have met others like them before but they fooled me. Usually they talked the talk but didn't walk the walk. Soon after I met them I discovered they were fair-weather friends.

But not Acceptance and Luv! I'm so excited! It's so much fun having new friends! I know they will stay; they are calm and humble, and somehow subtly wise. They sip not slurp, they use the salad fork but don't care what fork I use, and they listen when I speak without interrupting.

I didn't realize how my childhood monsters kept these types of friends away. Keeping my old friends, like my neighbors, I missed out on so much fun and so many opportunities. Well, that's really disappointing. Now, I want to make up for lost time. If they become permanent houseguests, I think it will work out fine. I'll do whatever it takes to make them happy and comfortable.

Questions for Discussion

1. What does Tami Gramont's story say about our internalized negative self-beliefs?

2. How do you think Miss Pression may have affected the writer's life as an adult?
3. Self Loathing buys gifts so she can get others "to acknowledge what a rotten person she is." What are some other ways self-loathing can manifest itself?

SELECTED READINGS AND ADDITIONAL RESOURCES

Divorce

Stewart, Abigail, Copeland, Anne, Chester, Nia Lane, Malley, Janet, and Barenbaum, Nicole (1997). *Separating Together: How Divorce Transforms Families.* New York: Guilford Publications.

Wallerstein, Judy and Kelly, Joan Berlin (1980). *Surviving the Breakup.* New York: Basic Books.

Homosexuality

Falco, Kristine L. (1991). *Psychotherapy with Lesbian Clients.* New York: Brunner/Mazel.

Greene, Beverly (1994). Lesbian Women of Color: Triple Jeopardy. In *Women of Color,* Comas-Diaz, L. and Greene, B. (Eds.) (pp. 389-427). New York: Guilford Press.

Gray, Mary, L. (1999). *In Your Face.* Binghamton, NY: The Haworth Press.

Johnson, Bret K. (1997). *Coming Out Every Day: A Gay, Bisexual, or Questioning Man's Guide.* Oakland, CA: New Harbinger Publications.

Penelope, Julia and Wolfe, Susan J. (Eds.) (1989). *The Original Coming Out Stories.* Freedom, CA: The Crossing Press.

Vargo, Marc. E. (1999). *Acts of Disclosure.* Binghamton, NY: The Haworth Press.

Aging and Attractiveness

Greer, Germain (1992). *The Change.* New York: Knopf Publishers.

Racism

Bell-Scott, Patricia (1994). *Life Notes: Personal Writings by Contemporary Black Women.* New York and London: W.W. Norton and Company.

Davis, Larry, E. (1999). *Working with African American Males: A Guide to Practice.* Walnut Creek, CA: AltaMira Press.

hooks, bell (1993). *Sisters of the Yam: Black Women and Self Recovery.* Boston, MA: South End Press.

Jacobs, Bruce (1999). *Race Manners: Navigating the Minefield Between Black and White Americans.* New York: Arcade Publishing.

Pinderhughes, Elaine (1989). *Understanding Race, Ethnicity and Power: The Key to Efficacy in Clinical Practice.* New York: The Free Press.

West, Cornel (1994). *Race Matters.* New York: Vintage Books.

PART V:
PHYSICAL ILLNESS

When I Was Old

Bonny Vaught

For twenty years I was old.

Old age crashed into me at forty-four. It held me fast until I could partially reverse the process two decades later. At both ends of those decades— and indeed, in all the years between—I was amazed by the relationship between old age and disability. Today I am not "young," nor was I "old" at forty-four. I was, in fact, disabled. However, as changes abruptly struck me, people rushed to pin me down with stereotypes of old age.

After much agonizing, I pinned a label on myself: disabled. I am disabled, I would say. Often I qualified it, saying *partially* disabled. But no matter how I tried to define myself, people saw disability—and thought *old age*.

I moved gingerly through examination after examination, while doctors looked me over and registered *old age*. Ruptured cervical disks were hard to diagnose before CAT scans and MRIs, but at least one neurologist or orthopedist should have realized I was hobbled by pain, not age.

When I was old, I was stunned by an onslaught of peculiar neurological symptoms. Common sense told me not to aggravate the pain, but doctors dismissed common sense. If they could not have a docile patient—a heavily medicated little old lady—they would find yet another reason to encase me in yet another neck brace. They immobilized me.

Several specialists thought the cause of pain was emotional, but a psychiatrist was certain it was not. "They just haven't found the real cause," he said. His support proved invaluable.

I had expected aging to be a series of gradual changes. I'd expect to have a little stiffness here, a little soreness there. I thought I'd work till seventy and still play Bach every day when I was eighty-three. What was the "old age" I suddenly encountered?

It was a shutting down. A terrible cutting off.

Whether I called it disability, or others thought I'd careened into old age, it meant no more full-time work, no more steady employment. I was not hireable. There would be no more long, productive days of research and writing. No more late nights preparing to teach. It meant no more driving. No more walking in the city, playing the organ, directing a choir. I couldn't even curl up in a chair to read. Now I required a straight, hard, wooden chair placed just so in front of a reading stand. Now I fumbled with clips and backing sheets to anchor printed material. For the first time in my life, I gauged the size of a book to see if it was too heavy to handle.

When I was old, I could not be spontaneous. I had such limited strength—limited endurance before the pain spiked again—I had to anticipate every action. Time shrank. I parceled out my strength. I tried to gauge my stamina. I'd seen elderly men and women look fearful at the end of an outing, and now I knew why: they had miscalculated. They'd just realized the price they were about to pay. When I was old, I joined them in distress.

At first I was surprised to see women in their seventies and eighties calmly welcome me as their own. Then I saw that they, too, had lives closing in. They, too, coped with limits on all sides.

When I lost my driver's license, I lost my freedom. The end of driving made old age official. Jolting, vibrating buses made pain skyrocket, and cabs were rarely available where we lived; I couldn't walk, couldn't fly in a plane, couldn't do all the taken-for-granted things that had shaped my life. My independence disappeared.

I was stunned by the saccharine tone people adopted. Did they really see me as a not-too-bright, uninvolved, out-of-touch individual? Since when? They seemed to think I'd changed drastically. I didn't realize their approach to me was society's approach to old age. In their eyes, I had joined the ranks of "nice old ladies," and they treated me accordingly.

"Niceness" posed a problem. Apparently, old age is sanitized so much that we—they—are all supposed to be lovable. Evidently we—they—are all to be tolerated. Indulged. Smiled at, smiled about. I could grapple with physical pain, but sweetness and light baffled me.

When I was old, people saw my husband come through the door carrying a ladderback chair, and they fluttered. Was I warm enough? Did I need better lighting? (Better *lighting?*) They rushed to find soft cushions—the last thing I needed. What were they thinking? Why so nervous?

Sometimes I winced, remembering how I'd show concern for friends who were twenty or thirty years ahead of me. But personality doesn't change with disability, nor does it change with old age. I wanted to be treated as always.

When I was forty-four, my father was eighty, suffering from Paget's disease. Dad was angrily aware of his crumbling vertebrae. He tried hard to draw himself straight, pulling against his shoulders as they curled forward. When I was old we had spinal problems in mirror image. I was straight and stiff, Dad was bent and stiff. We were equally frustrated.

I know a pastor who saw a woman every week for more than twenty years, through her seventies and eighties, into her nineties. One day when he called on her in a nursing home (she was by then a widow), Clara eyed him from her rocking chair and said, "You don't know me at all." He was startled. "You think I'm ninety-three," she said. "You don't know that inside I'm a girl of seventeen."

The pastor often tells that story. He keeps her chair in his office—a reminder of a woman who insisted she be clearly seen.

"You don't know me at all." I muttered that to myself time after time, when I was old.

For years I'd teased my husband about his way with elderly people. Now I knew why they liked John so much. He assumed they were alert and engaged. He joked with them, saw them as real people. He also took them seriously. He was solicitous if they needed a steady arm or special care, but that sprang from courtesy.

What I learned in those years of limitation and pain—what I see now, finding myself with somewhat better mobility—is a great mix. I struggled with anger and frustration, but I gained perseverance. Bewilderment led to insight.

In other words, a great deal happened when I was old. My life didn't stop. I didn't ossify. Both disability and old age bring challenges that seem endless, but there's an occasional triumph as well.

Values do change with age. I watch the struggle of an eighty-three-year-old friend in a nursing home. In her room she has nothing personal but her clothes. Her descent into illness was so rapid, friends had to dispose of her apartment and furniture, and they made a clean sweep. She's left with no comfortable chair, no tapes or CDs to enjoy. She lacks even her address book. Slowly, painfully, she has come to terms with her new life. She says quietly, "You know, as you get older, you don't want so many things. You don't need them." I listen to her steady voice and do not hear sadness. I do not hear her grieving for possessions. I wonder if I will be like her in twenty years.

Right now, suspended between my forties and my eighties (I am hopeful; I come from sturdy stock), I feel younger than I have in years. Natural progression has been upended again. An effective treatment has sent me lurching back toward the land of the living.

And yet . . . and yet . . .

"Doing my normal act" is what I call my life today. I am not willing to disclose the pain. I don't want people to see how bad things are.

I wonder if this is part of aging—part of old age—for everyone. At sixty-seven, should I admit I'm in pain? Should I confront an impossible task and say, "I can't do that." Why is it hard for me to be open about my limits?

I wonder if it would be different if I'd not had two decades when I was perceived as old. Might I have aged gradually, gracefully? I'll never be sure.

Today, what seems arbitrary to an onlooker may be crucial to me. I can ride back and forth in an unfamiliar car, sit through a meeting, look all right at the end of an evening. Then the pain wakes me at 3:00 in the morning, again at 4:00 and 5:00. I groan, knowing how the next day will go, and maybe two or three after that. Raised in the Midwest, I know how to put the best construction on whatever bears down. But am I overdoing it? Why? Maybe I'm simply resisting. I don't want to be put in a category. Or maybe it's hard to acknowledge actual old age.

In Chang-Rae Lee's novel *A Gesture Life* (1999), a seventy-year-old man says, "This is the first instance I've had of feeling my age, which does not seem so beleaguering a notion but rather a strangely comforting one, as if a voice inside me is trying to proclaim, *I accept. I accept.* It's the way one relents when walking the last half-mile of a hike in light rain, to taste the sweet of the water on your face, and not just feel its chill" (p. 129).

I warm to those words. I want to acknowledge their wisdom.

I see old age filled with contradictions. My husband looks down the road twenty years or more and thinks old age won't come until he needs constant care. I think old age comes every day, every time I must admit my body can't do what was routine, years ago.

Surely old age means something different for women than for men. In a society that prizes physical appearance—youthfulness is all!—women too often accept a youthful standard. We try to measure up. I hope today's young women benefit from mothers' and grandmothers' efforts to change the world. I hope they feel free to say, "No, that's not me. Don't expect *me* to meet *your* expectations." When Gloria Steinem says, "This is what sixty looks like," I cheer. Hours later I catch myself wishing I didn't look so old. It's hard to apply her words to my face in the mirror.

My father was flinty and feisty in his mid-eighties. He still played with numbers in his head. He added and subtracted so quickly I marveled at his agility. His body failed, his world shrank to a nursing home room, but Dad kept his mind agile.

When I was old, I committed to a year of rigorous treatment, and I was determined that at the end I'd be the same as the day I started. *I will not change,* I told myself over and over. I can think of no other time, no other reason, that would make me take such a foolish stand. Looking back, I'm proudest of the changes I *did* make. It takes courage to change. The adage rings true: Old age really isn't for sissies.

Far more important than the physical aspects of old age are the mental and emotional changes. Slowing bodies (yes, it does happen) afford time to think. To reflect. To ponder. And always, to question. The task of old age, psychologists tell us, is to synthesize our lifetime experience. We need, as never before, to make sense of our existence.

Spiritual growth comes more readily, I think, in old age, than during any other time in life. Looking toward the end of our days plays a part in reassessment. We hold fast to friends in a new way, enjoying them, knowing—really knowing—they will not always be here, nor will we. We reevaluate traditions that have been meaningful. Which ones should we continue, which set aside?

When I was old, and now that I truly am older, the way I spend time takes on added meaning. Just as older people often speak more freely, I choose more freely. I'm not going to waste time on what, to me, is a meaningless pro forma event. I've become adept at refusing invitations. This is my way of gaining time to do what I value; others may need to socialize more. But old age is a time to sharpen preferences. Figure out what's essential. Strip away the rest.

Pay attention to the soul.

I fear being dependent, but I dread becoming narrow or rigid. These days, I'm pleased to discern much more gray in issues. Tolerance—understanding—is to be cherished in old age. In a youth-oriented culture, wisdom can still accompany age.

It's easier, when we are old, to take the long view. Crises impact differently. We've seen it before, we've been there and handled that. Or we know that this, too, will soon end.

On the other hand, old age brings the freedom to be passionate. Sexual passion may be governed by physical strength. Nothing stops emotional passion. I care deeply about racial issues. I long to see racism dismantled. I cannot teach or travel, but I can stand at my computer and handle the complexities of finance for a national antiracism organization. It's not what I'd prefer to do, but it's what I can do.

Doing what I can: the major task of old age.

Jesus' disciples wanted to get rid of the woman who gifted him with extravagantly expensive oil, but Jesus stopped them. "She did what she could," He said.

While minds are clear and bodies still function, old age offers time. We do what we can. When disability pushed me into old age, I did what I still could do. With actual old age comes the chance to do what we've always wanted to do. One former president jumped out of a plane; another works on trouble spots around the world.

For me, disability and old age tumbled together, inextricably entwined. I cannot unbraid the strands of my own existence. But I do know that freedom comes when we accept the reality of our situation, however tough it may be. Only then do we gain freedom.

I don't wish I could be young again. I simply want to savor each day and year that is to come. This awareness—this sweet savoring—is the gift I will cherish all the way through old age.

It is, in the end, the very best thing to come out of those twenty years.

Twenty years, when I was old.

Questions for Discussion

1. Describe the ways the narrator's disability impacted on her life.
2. What does this essay say about how people with disabilities and old people want and need to be treated?
3. If this woman had been your client, what sort of support services, emotional and concrete, would you have offered her?

Beauty Shop

A. Rooney

Aleen Water never wanted to own the HairHaven. All she ever wanted was to do hair and then go home. At the shop, she and Deeda Pangburne did hair for older women, as well as for girls who needed big hair for proms and weddings. Rudy and Desmond did all the special cuts and "style" hair for the younger women. Rudy owned the beauty shop and among the four of them, they did a lot of the hair in town. It was an arrangement Aleen and Deeda liked.

One weekend Rudy went away with Desmond and didn't come back. When Aleen came in Monday morning, Rudy had left them a note:

> *Girls—Desi and I have gone off to Denver. This town is just a little too . . . The shop is yours. The equipment, the supplies, everything. And the rent's been paid. Take care of all the ladies and babies. Luv, Rudy.*

Ladies and babies were what Rudy called the older and younger women. Aleen picked up the phone and called Deeda. Deeda came right down and sat in one of the upholstered chairs to study the message. After she said "hmm" twice, she walked to the liquor store and bought a pint of schnapps. Aleen drank a little in her coffee and watched Deeda consume the rest between appointments.

When they closed that evening, Deeda kicked off her shoes and said, "Aleen, I believe Sister Rudy done left us a nest egg." And it was true, he had. That night Deeda talked Aleen into going country dancing with her and they stayed out late and ate breakfast together. For the first time in a long time, the HairHaven didn't open until after noon.

During the first eight or nine years after Rudy left, the HairHaven continued to be as busy as it ever was. Aleen and Deeda added two young women to do the style hair and they continued to handle their old customers. Eventually the two young women left and started their own shop and Aleen and Deeda hired a succession of stylists after them.

The day Deeda turned sixty-seven, she announced she wasn't going to work as hard anymore and began coming in half days three days a week. It was just as well, Aleen thought, because there wasn't that much big hair business anyway. When the last style girl quit, Aleen didn't bother to hire another one and business dropped off even further.

One day after closing up, Boyd, a trucker Deeda had been seeing a lot of stopped by to pick her up. Deeda announced she and Boyd had decided to move to Palm Springs to retire and live in senior housing. It was quite a surprise to Aleen but the two women hugged and kissed and called each other sweetie. Then Deeda was gone.

Aleen stood in the dark looking out through the neon HairHaven sign wondering what she was going to do. She had done hair since she was eighteen, and at sixty-eight, she didn't know any other way to make a living. Her husband was dead and she didn't have any children, and now her best friend was moving to Palm Springs.

During breakfast at the Solar Inn, Marvelle, the owner, told her to close up the shop and put it in her house, "Cut back on all that overhead."

Aleen thought about it and the next morning began moving the things she needed, one at a time, to her enclosed porch. During the weekend she had a garage sale and sold off pieces she didn't need. At the shop she taped a large sign in the window that said the HairHaven was closed and for appointments they could call her at home.

Within a few weeks, many of her regular clients had called and made appointments. Most days she saw two or three customers and that was plenty. She knew some of them made appointments just to have somewhere to go and someone to talk with. Aleen wasn't ready to sit on the sofa and do nothing, so she didn't mind fixing their hair.

Before Mr. Water had passed he enclosed the front porch so that it was a comfortable place in summer and winter. Aleen kept the equipment there because she didn't especially want people inside her house, touching things, prying into her life. In a window on the porch above the mailbox, Aleen put a simple black and white sign that said "Beauty Shop."

Everyone who came to the house wanted to know how Deeda was doing, and she told them, "Fine. Deeda's just fine." She and Deeda talked about once a week on the phone and sometimes she got postcards from Palm Springs and southern California. Sometimes she showed them the postcards.

One day when she was doing a permanent, a customer noticed how scabby and discolored her hands were and suggested she have them looked at. "Overgrown liver spots," Aleen said, "nothing to worry about."

While the woman sat with her hair pinned, she went on to tell Aleen how her niece had to have some kind of cancer taken off her neck and one of her lymph nodes removed. Aleen wasn't really interested in the story but the woman chatted on anyway about the niece's skin graft from her buttocks and how the first graft didn't take very well and they had to do it again and now she can never wear a bikini and she had such a cute shape.

But the spots on Aleen's hands got bigger and turned dark and irregular and then she finally made an appointment to see the doctor. The doctor himself was dark, Dr. Gupta. In the exam room he rubbed the back of Aleen's hands with his thumbs and asked his assistant to prepare a biopsy slide. With a small surgical knife, Dr. Gupta removed a piece of skin from one of the spots and placed it on the glass slide. He told his assistant to make another appointment for Aleen in three days. Aleen's bones had been aching for weeks, but she didn't share that with Dr. Gupta.

That night when Aleen called Deeda, Boyd answered the phone. He told her Deeda was out at bingo and he would tell her to call when she came in.

"Anything wrong?" Boyd asked. "No, no," Aleen said, "just wanted to catch up."

Three days later, after he had taken X rays, Dr. Gupta sat with Aleen in a small conference room, not the exam room. He had literature in front of him that explained the different types of skin cancer.

"Normally when we do the biopsy," Dr. Gupta said, "it takes a week. When I saw your hands, I had the lab rush the biopsy because I was very concerned. There are three types of skin cancer, Mrs. Water: basal, squamous, and melanotic. Mrs. Water, you have the most serious form of skin cancer. You have advanced melanotic cancer."

Liver spots, Aleen said to herself, they're liver spots. I'll rub them with cream every night and they'll be gone in a week. A real doctor would recognize that. She never should have come to this clinic, with foreign doctors. Skin cancer. She would go home and take a hot bath, and rub her hands.

When Dr. Gupta had finished talking with Aleen, he asked her if she had friends or family around. She said no and he gave her the number of the hospice and suggested she call them.

"I am very sorry to tell you this, Mrs. Water," Dr. Gupta said patting Aleen's hands, "but after looking at your X rays I must tell you; you are dying and I'm afraid we cannot help you." Before she left, the doctor wrote out a three-month prescription for pain medication and told her she would need it over the coming days and weeks.

On the drive home, Aleen wept quietly. She had never been much for emotion, not even with Mr. Water when he was alive. She watched people coming and going on the streets and sidewalks and thought how most of her life she had taken care of others but never found time for herself. Aleen was familiar with loneliness, but now she was dying, and she heard the drone of her imminent death in her ears. She wished Deeda was there because Deeda always knew what to do and how to handle things. She wanted to call Deeda, but she didn't want to bother her or Boyd.

Aleen parked in front of the HairHaven and sat in the car. The store was empty and there was a "For Lease" sign hanging from the old neon. Maybe she should just go home and call the hospice, she thought, get it over with. Aleen drove the car down the block to the Solar and went in for coffee.

Marvelle came and sat with Aleen and asked if she was feeling all right. "Hon," Marvelle said, "you don't look so good. You want some soup or something?" Aleen struggled to tell Marvelle what was wrong but could not. She put her hands flat on the table, around her coffee.

"Girl," Marvelle said, shaking her head, "you better get you some cream for them hands."

Aleen smiled and asked Marvelle if she had a gun.

"Sweetheart," Marvelle said, "what's an old gal like you gonna do with a gun?"

Aleen explained that there was a coyote in the neighborhood that had been eating some of the cats, and the other night he almost got hers. She wanted to wait up a few nights to see if she could take care of the problem.

"Aleen, you ever use a gun?" Marvelle asked.

Aleen lied and said Mr. Water had showed her all about guns.

"Well," Marvelle said, "I got a little popgun .22 I'll let you have. But you got to promise me you're not gonna go right over to the First National and use it to make a withdrawal."

Marvelle wrapped the gun in a white pastry bag and brought it out to Aleen when she'd finished her coffee. Aleen set the bag next to her on the seat in the car and tried not to look at it. She examined her hands on the steering wheel as she drove and wondered how it was that these damned dark spots could cause so much trouble. She wanted to be angry at something or someone but didn't know how.

That night Aleen brewed a pot of strong coffee, took some of the pain medication, and sat in her chair on the back porch with the gun. She'd never really seen a coyote around her house, but neighbors had told her they'd seen one.

With her cat, Stripes, in her lap, Aleen dozed and began to look at parts of her life on the yellowing pages of a photo album. Mr. Water in his army uniform, home from the Korean War. Mr. Water, with his big feet and ever-present grin, standing in front of their house in Walsenburg. Aleen's mother and two sisters at her wedding, standing arms folded, looking serious at the camera. Her brother Thomas, visiting them from the seminary in St. Louis, looking serious at the camera. Aleen standing in front of the beauty shop in Walsenburg, looking serious at the camera.

Aleen got up from the chair and went into the bathroom for more of the medication. Everything inside her rib cage hurt and her body ached. Aleen made another pot of coffee and wandered through the house, looking in each of the meticulous rooms. Shouldn't there be pictures and knick-knacks, she thought. Deeda had pictures and knick-knacks everywhere in her house. Where are my pictures and knick-knacks?

Aleen brought the pills out of the bathroom, took four more, and set them on the kitchen table. She held up her hands and spread her fingers and was surprised to see them glowing brightly. The dark cancerous spots now formed beautiful circles that were moving up her arms and over her body in waves. She went to the porch for the gun.

When Aleen returned, she took the remainder of the pills and lay down on the sofa in the living room. She thought about covering her glowing hands with rubber dishwashing gloves but didn't feel like getting up to get them.

Aleen held up her left hand, pointed the gun at it with her right, and tried to pull the trigger but could not. She found the safety and released it, then fired the gun at one of the circles. The bullet burned through the back of her hand and exited through her palm. The glowing stopped.

Aleen was pleased and folded her hands together across her stomach. When she closed her eyes she could see Mr. Water, grinning, in his uniform. She could hear the rise and fall of the blood in her veins and feel the warm wetness on her hands. In the morning she would call the hospice.

Questions for Discussion

1. What kinds of questions would you have asked her before letting her leave the clinic?
2. What other services or resources would you have suggested for Aleen following her diagnosis?
3. Explore the concept of intentional and inadvertent suicide.

The Price of Admission

Debbi Lieberson

In October 1991, at the age of forty-two, my husband, Rich, died of AIDS. In the last year of his life, he was admitted to the hospital six times, spending eighty-nine days as an inpatient. There were times, when Rich was feeling better and we had had too much to drink, that we could find humor in hospital insanity. As I look back and write about one of our experiences, I find it hard to remember what it was that we were able to laugh about.

For several days, Rich's fever persisted. Despite Tylenol every four hours, it never dropped much below 101 degrees. Sometimes it rose to as high as 104 degrees. After forty-eight hours of oral antibiotics, his cough wasn't worse, but it wasn't any better. It became increasingly obvious that Rich had not simply caught a cold from our 2½-year-old son, Ben. For the third time in three days, Rich went to see Dr. Epstein and Vicki Nolan, his nurse practitioner. For reasons I cannot recall, I was not working and was with him for his appointment. Ben was in day care. Dr. Epstein, Vicki, and Rich agreed that it made sense for him to go into the hospital where he could be given intravenous antibiotics and have diagnostic tests done more quickly.

They discussed the options. Rich could be admitted to the hospital "directly to the floor" or "through the emergency room." Each route involved different logistics, people, and paperwork. They decided that in this situation, on this given day, an emergency room admission would be more efficient.

Rich and I left Harvard Community Health midmorning and drove to Brigham and Women's Hospital. I pulled up to the door of the emergency room, stopped, and looked at Rich. He looked pale. His skin was translucent.

"Let me run in and grab someone to give you a hand," I suggested.

Rich wearily shook his head.

"Then at least let me get a wheelchair to bring you in."

"Deb, let me walk in myself. I'll be OK."

I had learned long ago that no amount of arguing ever changed Rich's mind once it was made up. I watched as he slowly got out of the car. I waited until the automatic sliding door closed behind him before pulling away.

There was a line of four or five cars in front of the entrance to the hospital's multitiered parking garage. One car would pull out of the garage and then the next car in line would pull in. I knew better than to try to find a parking space on the street. Several times in the past, I had abandoned the line assuming there had to be a metered space somewhere within a mile of the hospital. I was always wrong and would return to a line that was longer than the one I had left. After about ten minutes, I pulled onto the roof deck of the garage.

I walked quickly through the mazelike corridors of the hospital. I passed through the main lobby and then followed the blue lines on the wall that pointed the way to the emergency room. I had walked this same labyrinth many times before but still needed to focus on the lines or I would get lost. I saw the words, like blurry road signs along the highway, on the doors I passed—Vascular Surgery, Infectious Disease, Neurology, Pediatric Oncology. I tried, unsuccessfully, not to look into each waiting room. Each time I did, a face would capture my attention. I could not stop myself from imagining that person's horrors.

I looked at my watch. I had dropped Rich off nearly a half hour earlier. I wondered if I would arrive in the ER only to find that he had already been transported up to the floor. I shouldn't have worried. When I got there, Rich was still standing with an intake clerk who was collating and stapling some of his paperwork. It didn't seem to matter that he had filled out the same papers less than six weeks earlier, at the time of his previous admission. With the exception of the date and the "Reason for Today's Visit," nothing had changed. His address, phone numbers, employer, health insurance, next of kin, doctor, medications, and the answers to fifty or sixty other questions were exactly the same.

I sat down next to Rich. I knew by looking at him that his temperature had gone up. His skin looked pasty, his eyes glazed. He looked much older than forty-one.

"I'll take you back in just a minute, Mr. Cahalane."

"Isn't there any way they can just Xerox the information from a previous admission and just change anything that's different?" I naively asked.

Rich rolled his eyes and shook his head. The clerk shrugged.

"Makes sense to me," she said. "It would make my job a whole lot easier. But nobody asks me."

She paused and looked at Rich.

"I'm sorry this is taking so long."

A few minutes later, she returned with an orderly who was pushing a wheelchair. I gathered up Rich's things and stuffed what I could into his canvas shoulder bag. The orderly was a very tall, wide-shouldered black man who towered over us. His hospital scrubs were too short and I could see that he was wearing white socks.

"Would you like some help getting into the wheelchair, Mr. Cahalane?"

Rich smiled weakly and thanked him. Unlike many of the doctors and nurses who told patients what to do and what they needed, this man had asked. And then waited for a response. I knew that Rich, as I, had noticed.

I walked behind Rich and the orderly and could hear bits and pieces of their conversation. By the time he wheeled Rich into exam room eleven, Rich knew the man was from Haiti, had two children, a boy and a girl, had worked as an orderly for over a year, and had come to the United States three years earlier. He handed Rich two johnnies. Rich extended his hand.

"Good luck, man," the orderly said as the door closed behind him.

This man had no name for us to know. The clinical staff all wore clearly visible name tags on their uniforms and lab coats. Their tags were identical: one-by-three inch rectangles with the hospital logo in the upper lefthand corner; first name, last name, title, printed in red capital letters. The clerical staff wore smaller tags. Theirs were printed in black and had their first name, last initial, and department. The transport orderly's identification consisted of a large piece of laminated plastic that was clipped to the waistband of his scrubs. From several feet away, when the light was not reflecting off of it, I could see a one-inch-square DMV type photo. His name probably was somewhere on the tag, but short of putting my face six inches from his crotch, there was no way I or anyone else could read it. Obviously, no one seemed to think that the name of the minimum wage orderly mattered to patients or staff. But it mattered to Rich, who later commented that he felt badly that he hadn't asked the man his name.

It took a long time for Rich to undress. I resisted the temptation to ask if he wanted my help. I folded his clothes and placed them in a white plastic drawstring bag that was on the gurney. He had learned from past experience that anything left behind in an emergency room was unlikely to be recovered. Rich's large, heavy hiking boots did not fit into the bag. He wore those same boots every day of the year, regardless of the weather. They were the only style big and sturdy enough to accommodate the bulky orthotic device that he wore in his left boot to compensate for the difference in the length of his legs.

Rich put the first johnny on with the opening in the back and then put the second over the first, with the opening in front, tying it like a bathrobe. Veteran patients knew that this was the only way to avoid inadvertently exposing themselves while walking around. I thought that the orderly knew this and had intentionally given Rich two.

Rich climbed onto the exam table. After a few minutes of sitting with his legs dancing over the edge, his back unsupported, he asked me to raise the head of the table. After I did, he stretched out and closed his eyes. I realized then that I had not brought anything with me to do or to read. I closed my eyes.

About fifteen minutes passed before a medical assistant came in. She mumbled something unintelligible. The only word I recognized was "vitals." The woman was massively overweight. She moved slowly and looked down a lot. When she walked, her feet never lost contact with the floor. She looked suicidally depressed. Getting the normal adult-sized blood pressure cuff to stay on Rich's emaciated arm was a problem. Twice it slid down to below his elbow. He grimaced but said nothing when she quickly pumped the cuff pressure up to over 200 before slowly releasing it. Her digital thermometer beeped and blinked at 103.4 degrees. She wrote down her numbers and left without saying a word.

"Deb, can you get three Tylenol out of my bag?"

I glanced at the clock on the wall but made no comment. Rich had taken three Tylenol less than three hours before. I found a paper cup on the counter and Rich swallowed all of the tablets at once with one gulp of water. Again, he lay back on the exam table and closed his eyes. I stared at the ceiling and then at the floor. I looked around desperately, hoping that someone had left behind a magazine or newspaper. But the room had obviously been cleaned prior to our arrival.

The room was about nine by eleven feet and totally devoid of color. The institutional off-white walls were adorned with medical equipment. There were no photographs, paintings, or educational brochures. The floor was dark gray, speckled with flecks of black and a lighter gray. Nearly every item in the room was black, white, gray, or made of stainless steel. The small, bright, plastic yellow cap on some bottle of chemical solution on the counter looked garish and out of place.

There was a knock at the door, but before either of us could answer, a nurse came in. She held Rich's chart, which was nearly three inches thick. It contained information from his previous admissions. She moved quickly, crisply. She was either extremely efficient or cold. Or both. I couldn't yet tell.

"I'm Carol. . . . I spoke with Dr. Epstein earlier. She wants you admitted to Infectious Disease. Probably Five West. Have you been there before?"

She seemed to be asking the questions to Rich's chart. She turned the pages as she spoke, never once looking up at Rich. She didn't seem to notice or care if he answered her questions.

"Yes, he has," I thought to myself. "Twice before. Nice of you to ask."

"There probably won't be a bed available for another few hours so we'll keep you here. When did you last take any Tylenol?"

"About fifteen minutes ago," Rich answered.

She shook her head but made no comment. No one in the hospital had given him any so she knew that he had taken his own. Clearly, she was not pleased.

"How long have you had the fever?" She jotted down Rich's answer. "The cough?" She wrote some more. "A fourth-year medical student will be in shortly to get your history and do your preadmission workup."

She knew, Rich knew, and I knew that an experienced resident could do this piece of the process in less than fifteen minutes. A medical student could take an hour or more.

"Is there any way we could have the resident do his admission?" I asked plaintively. "Rich has a temp of over 103 degrees and he feels really lousy."

"I know what his fever is," she snapped impatiently. "Look, this is an emergency room. No one here feels great. As I'm sure you know, this is a teaching hospital. Medical students are part of the territory."

Rich dozed and I stared mindlessly at the ceiling. I looked at the clock again. One-thirty. No wonder I'm so hungry. I quietly opened the door and looked both ways, hoping to spot a vending machine in the hall. There was none. The cafeteria was in the next building and I didn't want to leave Rich, even if there was nothing for me to do. Even with a fever of 103 degrees and barely able to lift his head off the pillow, Rich, I knew, was a better advocate for himself than I. He had been maneuvering his way through medical mazes since childhood.

I heard Rich's chart being slid out of the box on the outside of the door. Someone turned page after page for about ten minutes. Then there was a knock.

"Come on in," I said. The sound of my voice woke Rich.

"Hi. I'm Brian. . . . I'm a fourth-year Harvard med student." Brian looked at Rich. "I need to ask you some questions."

Brian looked very young and very earnest. Rich suggested he pull up a chair.

"Thanks, Mr. Cahalane," he began.

"Call me Rich."

"OK. I'd like to start with your past medical history. I see from your chart you're a hemophiliac and have AIDS."

Rich nodded.

"So, how old were you when you were diagnosed with hemophilia?"

Oh God, I thought. If he starts there we'll finish next March. I'll have died of starvation. They'll have found a cure for AIDS by then.

"I was diagnosed at eighteen months."

"Do you have any other medical problems?"

"You mean besides hemophilia, multiple orthopedic problems from the hemophilia, AIDS, and all the problems as a result of having AIDS?"

Brian looked embarrassed.

"I guess that was a stupid question. Your medical history is just so long and complicated I don't know where to start. Sorry."

"It's OK."

There was an awkward silence. Brian flipped through Rich's chart as if he were looking for something in particular. He closed the volume and stared at the blank sheet of paper clipped to the front. It was then that he noticed the card with Rich's vital signs.

"Did you know your temperature is over 103 degrees?"

Rich nodded.

"You must feel awful."

"I do."

Brian looked down at his sheet of paper again.

"Maybe I should start with your past hospitalizations. Can you begin with the most recent? Or maybe it would be better if I got down your medication list first."

If Brian had been one of the many arrogant, rude medical students he had had to deal with over the years, Rich would have been uncooperative and uncommunicative. But Brian's uncertainty, honesty, and humility made Rich want to help him. Rich knew what would happen if Brian returned to the "attending" physician with a disjointed, incomplete medical history. Both of us had seen and heard doctors criticize and humiliate students, often in front of their patients.

"Let me see if I can give you a hand," Rich said.

Within five minutes, he provided Brian with a concise, streamlined, yet appropriately detailed "past medical history" and "history of present illness." An experienced physician could not have done a better job. Brian scribbled frantically trying to keep up with Rich. When he finished writing he took a deep breath and smiled.

"How'd you know how to do that so well? Do you work in health care or something?" he asked.

"Lots of practice I guess."

Brian's smile disappeared. "I guess you've been through this a lot. I really am sorry."

Brian seemed suddenly to realize that Rich was something more than an impossibly complicated patient. For the first time, I think it occurred to him that Rich was a man not much older than himself who was dying. He extended his hand and thanked Rich again.

"I'll try to write this up as fast as I can so they can get you up to the floor."

A few minutes after he left, Rich fell asleep. About ten minutes after that I heard his chart being slid into the plastic rack on the outside of the door. Brian had finished. Another twenty minutes passed. Afraid that we had been forgotten, I opened the door a few inches so that my chair and Rich's feet, which overhung the edge of the exam table, would be visible to anyone who walked by.

I slipped the chart out of the door rack, curious to see how well Brian had done with his write-up. I was also so bored by this time that I would have happily read the phone book if that had been the only printed material nearby. I had already counted how many holes there were in a half dozen of the acoustic ceiling tiles and calculated the average.

I read Brian's notes. Then, I read about Rich's previous hospitalization. I read consultants' reports, nurses' notes, and discharge summaries. I was so thoroughly engrossed that I was unaware of nurse Ratchet's presence until I heard her voice.

"What do you think you're doing?" she screamed as she grabbed the chart out of my hands. Rich woke up with a start.

"I was just reading—"

She didn't let me finish my sentence.

"How dare you? Medical records are confidential. I don't know who you think you are, but in case you didn't know, it's against the law to—"

This time I interrupted her.

"I'm sure Rich doesn't mind if—"

"I don't care if he minds or not. This is a medical record and you have no right to touch it, read it, or be anywhere near it."

It had taken Rich a few seconds to awaken completely and move beyond his initial disorientation.

"It's fine with me if she wants to read my chart," he said softly. His fevered lips were cracked and dry. He looked really sick.

The nurse glared angrily at him.

"It's not your decision."

Rich sat up stiffly. His body posture was as close to confrontational as he could manage, and I'm sure it took tremendous effort on his part. He raised his voice only slightly and spoke slowly and deliberately, as if speaking to a child.

"Look. A patient has a legal right to have his medical records made available to anyone he wants. And I'm giving consent for her to see mine in their entirety."

"If you want her to have a copy of your chart, you can go over to medical records and sign a release form."

She stormed out of the room still clutching the chart. She slammed the door loudly behind her.

"Asshole," Rich and I both said simultaneously. We started to laugh. But within seconds, my laughter turned to tears. I was sobbing and I didn't know why. For a long time, tears continued to stream down my face. Without saying a word, Rich took my hand. A short time later a resident whom Rich had met before came into the room.

"I hear you two really pissed off the nurse," he said with a big grin. "Don't worry. She's an asshole. Anyway, let's get you upstairs. The folks on Five West are anxiously awaiting your arrival."

Questions for Discussion

1. Discuss the issues of administrative red tape and inappropriate staff behavior and how you would advise patients in handling them.
2. If you were a social worker or patient advocate in a hospital and a patient expressed his or her anger to you about the rudeness of staff, the endless waiting, and the bureaucratic procedure, how would you respond?
3. The two lowest people on the hospital totem pole showed the most respect for Rich. Was that a coincidence, or do you think there are reasons for that?

Stroke

Bobbi Lurie

The bed is wet again. She has to take off his diaper, move him off the bed, bathe him, change his pajamas, change the sheets. "Damn it," she mutters. She feels tears pour into her eyes. She hasn't a moment to herself. The only way to endure it is to stop thinking, to take each obligation moment by moment, step by step.

She looks down at him. There are tears in his eyes. Somehow he knows how hard this is for her. There seems to be an apology lurking there. "OK, darling," she says. "It's OK. It's OK." The sun's harshness sneaks in through the slats of the shuttered windows. These striking beams of light mock her indoor existence. The smell of stale urine is easier to endure on a rainy day.

Outside their door people are walking along the beach, lying in the sun. She can hear the hazy sounds of portable radios coming from below their apartment window. She can picture the children on their roller skates, the lovers holding hands. She walks over to the shutters and closes them more tightly, annoyed by the remaining lines of light reflected on the bedroom wall.

She leans down and lifts his head off the pillow. It's a dead weight, a repository of thoughts which can never be retrieved. His eyes look up blankly at her; his mouth is drooping to one side; spittle runs down his chin. This once domineering man whose handsome charm seduced her into marriage has found a way to torment her into her old age.

It had taken her years to find the inner strength to assert her rights against his powerful rage and control, and now that she had finally made him understand, now that he had softened into the sweet understanding man she knew during their courtship, fate had struck its blow. Like a mockery of her constant wish for a more passive, tender man, he was now paralyzed and helpless, mild-mannered and totally dependent. Her back aches as she manages to get him into a seated position on the bed. She moves his hips forward, straightens out his legs, places his good arm against the bed to keep him from falling. His head droops forward.

Questions for Discussion

1. If this woman were to seek counseling, what would be the focus of your talks?
2. What services could you secure to lighten her load?

Dear Doctor

Cherise Wyneken

Dear Doctor,

It was good to see you today and hear you say I've got at least 50,000 miles left on me. But when you reached to shake my hand—somehow I knew just what that meant. He's retiring.

How can you do this to me—after all we've been through together? You're still a young man. You've got so much to give yet. What are your fifty years compared to my ninety-three?

Forgive an old woman's presumption in offering her opinion. It's just my way of saying how much you mean to me—how much I appreciate the kindness and care you've given me and my late husband, Joe.

Oh, I know that's a sore subject with you. You always blamed yourself for insisting it was better to let the sleeping cancer lie dormant than to roil it up by trying to cut it away. But you did what you thought best. What more can anyone do? Who can know which way was right? We never blamed you for it. My husband thought the world of you.

And all that business with your wife—in the news and all. It must have been terribly disturbing to you. Yet you kept right on seeing to your patients' needs. That's the kind of thing people notice—not how many degrees are plastered on your wall—or if your belt matches your shoes. Like that time I had my appendix out and my granddaughter brought me a bouquet of sweet peas. I can still see you bending over them and sniffing their sweet scent. It's things like that that make a person real. And when you're sick in bed you want someone real taking care of you. Not some robot in a white coat.

And that time after Joe had his radiation. The treatments did reduce the tumor in his esophagus, but in the meantime he'd not been eating much and was sinking fast.

Then his friend from the pool hall came to see him and said, "Hey, Joe. How'd you like a nice cold beer?"

"Sounds good to me," Joe said.

"Give it to him," you said. "Anything to get him eating again."

I know alcohol is against your religion and all, so I'm doubly grateful for that extra year you gave me with Joe. I figure it was the beer that gave him back his appetite.

When I came to see you about a year after Joe died, I could hardly believe it when you asked me if I was still sleeping on the sofa—like I told you I was doing when he was first gone. How did you remember such a thing?

And after all that, when I started losing my sight, how you sympathized and helped me find my way around. I can still hear you tell your nurse—the one I liked so much—"Help her. See to it she finds her friend in the waiting room."

Oh, Doctor. I can't tell you how much that meant to me. You seemed to understand how frightened I could feel, not seeing where I was. It's an awful thing—going blind in one's old age. It happened too late for me to catch on to reading Braille. I kept thinking I would die soon and it wouldn't matter. Yet here I am with your predicated 50,000 miles left. Except for these arthritic knees, I'm in the best of health. But what's going to happen now when I get that bronchial cough next winter? Will the new doctor know what to give me?

And that brings up another subject. You gave me a list of doctors' names to choose from but said you couldn't tell me which one you would recommend. So I chose the one on top—a woman. (I figure that's why you put her there.) I never had a woman doctor, though I might have liked one early on, when I was birthing my children. What I'm trying to say is, Will she understand an old lady's problems? She never lived through them like you have with me.

And I think how much I always wished you'd be there to hold my hand when it's time for me to go. Then I tell myself, "Hey, old lady. Isn't it wonderful that young women are able to become doctors now?"

Then in the darkness of my blindness, I see light. I think, Isn't it just like you to give me such a gift—a purpose in my old age—to help a young woman understand old age and help us all to grow? Thank you, Doctor, for everything.

Your patient and your friend,
Lydia

Questions for Discussion

1. What elements of her personality enabled this woman to cope so positively with her serious losses?
2. What does this physician offer the narrator that is so often lost in this era of managed care?
3. What support services would be appropriate and available for this woman?

What If?

Cherise Wyneken

"I'm sorry to hear about your mastectomy," I said to my mother's German friend.

"Ach, ja. And at mine age!"

In her eighties at the time, I had to agree—not an appealing resolution at the coda of one's life. Now—seventy myself—I wonder, "What if it happens to me?" A question at the tip of every woman's mind.

I've been told I have beautiful breasts. (Aren't they *all?*) They weren't always so. As a young woman they were scrawny buds. Age has blossomed them. A bonus I never expected from the passing years. How *would* I react to losing one or both? And how would my husband react? Now, as I wait for the doctor's report of a biopsy taken from my right breast, my first thought is to run out and buy a roll of film. Have my husband take some pictures for his future fantasy and recall.

But he seems more concerned about keeping me than my breast and I end up consoling him. "Don't worry. It's probably benign."

Benign? What if it isn't? Is he right in worrying? Is it a fast-growing kind—too far gone already? Should I write my farewell letter to my kids? Then reason returns. Even if it *is* malignant that doesn't necessarily mean radical mastectomy. But—What if?"

We women often say, "Love *me*—not my body." Yet we do drastic things to keep our bodies beautiful—starve, binge, purge, risk losing our hair by dousing it with dyes and chemicals; clip, oil, shave; expose ourselves to cancer-yielding gamma rays; spend more precious time making up our faces than clowns at a circus. And the older we get—the more time it takes.

Edging closer to the end, one begins to realize that physical change and deterioration are inevitable. Being able to see, hear, walk, and laugh become major events. In my seventy years I've had several major surgeries: appendectomy, leg veins stripped, hysterectomy, gall bladder removal. I recall saying to my doctor, "There's nothing left you dare take out." "Not so," he replied. "You've got two kidneys and two lungs. One of each could be removed." He didn't mention breasts. As I wait to hear from the pathologist, my philosophical reasoning departs—leaving me devastated at the thought of it actually happening to me. How or would I cope?

I am brought short by the news from an acquaintance—much younger than I am, wife, mother of two young children. At her regular checkup, without time for a reflective "What if?" she was slapped into the hospital for a radical double mastectomy. How and will *she* cope?

And then she shows me. Actually writing a lovely note in the middle of her problems, thanking me for my concern and prayers. By being open about her condition. Keeping her sense of humor. By her determination to look the best she can—choosing reconstruction with C cup dimensions this time around. Anticipating short hair—a thing her husband had always vetoed. Trusting God to help her cope as always with the problems life offers.

It might not be as simple as her seven-year-old implies: "It's okay, Mom. We don't need those things anymore, anyway. We're big kids now." Not simple, but she's managing. Managing because she's moved beyond her own loss to "What would happen to my husband and children if I lose my life?" What if?

As I discovered long ago, breasts are a bonus in life, not life itself. Anaïs Nin put it this way, "I postpone death by living, by suffering, by error, by risking, by giving, by losing."

Questions for Discussion

1. How does this essay show the importance of input from others? Discuss this in relation to its positive and its negative possibilities.
2. What coping strategies could be used to help both the patient and her family during their wait?

When Your Surgeon Is the Muse

Sarah Sutro

When Your Surgeon is the Muse
for the time being.
when the scalpel
is the pen,
poised,
to cut off the
breast.

when the one who saves
your life
is the one
who cuts into it.

when you wait—
in a darkened room
in a large brick building
with many other people
—for the news

when the one who brings bad news
is
the one you most want to hear from
the poetry gets sharp as steel.

Questions for Discussion

1. How would you go about making a list of available supports for cancer
   patients in your area?
2. How would you familiarize yourself with both the medical treatments
   and counseling options for breast cancer patients?

SELECTED READINGS AND ADDITIONAL RESOURCES

Chronic Illness/Disability

Frank, Arthur W. (1995). *The Wounded Storyteller: Body, Illness, and Ethics*. Chicago: University of Chicago Press.

Jacobs, Pamela (1997). *500 Tips for Coping with Chronic Illness*. San Francisco, CA: Robert D. Reed Publishers.

Kotarba, Joseph A. (1983). *Chronic Pain: Its Social Dimensions*. Thousand Oaks, CA: Sage Publications.

Matthews, Gwyneth Ferguson (1983). *Voices from the Shadows: Women with Disabilities Speak Out*. Toronto: Women's Educational Press.

Register, Cheri (1987). *Living with Chronic Illness: Days of Patience and Passion*. New York: The Free Press.

Zola, Irving Kenneth (1982). *Missing Pieces: A Chronicle of Living with a Disability*. Philadelphia, PA: Temple University Press.

HIV/AIDS

Aronstein, D. and Thompson, B. (1999). *HIV and Social Work*. Binghamton, NY: The Haworth Press.

Gabriel, Martha A. (1996). *AIDS Trauma and Support Group Therapy: Mutual Aid, Empowerment, Connection*. New York: Free Press.

Shilts, Randy (2000). *And the Band Played On*. New York: St. Martin's Press.

Stroke

Burton, Carol and Donnan, Geoffrey A. (1992). *After a Stroke: A Support Book for Patients, Caregivers, Families and Friends (The Family Health Series)*. Berkeley, CA: North Atlantic Books.

Caplan, Louis R. (1994). *American Heart Association: Family Guide to Stroke Treatment, Recovery, and Prevention*. New York: Random House.

Breast Cancer

American Cancer Society (ACS) National Headquarters. Access information on: Patient services, types of treatment, cancer survivor's network, education, local resources. 1599 Clifton Road NE, Atlanta, GA 30329.

Haber, Sandra and Acuff, Catherine (1995). *Breast Cancer: A Psychological Treatment Manual*. New York: Springer Publishing Co.

Kahana, Deborah Hobler (1995). *No Less a Woman: Femininity, Sexuality and Breast Cancer*. Alameda, CA: Hunter House.

PART VI:
SURVIVING AND HEALING
CHILDHOOD TRAUMA

The Ring of Truth

Jean Sellmeyer Smith

Too soon, I'm an old woman and I'm tired. Bone tired. In a Dallas park, I slump onto the bench under the Chinese elm, and there I sit, listening to distant thunder and staring at the dingy-watered duck pond. A nearby swing set squeaks. From the merry-go-round, children's squeals swirl through the air. I was never carefree like those kids. Even as a child, some nagging fear, some miserable feeling of inadequacy crept over the happy times.

Absentmindedly, I turn the class ring on my finger. I gaze skyward and search for answers in the thunderclouds. With each turn of the ring, an odd assortment of memories comes staggering back. It's strange. How could I have spent a lifetime in denial? I wrinkle my brow and squeeze my eyes shut. And how many years had my ring been missing? I shake my head. Dear God! Forty-five, at least.

Today, although my daughter Kathy told me where and when she'd found the ring, I still can't recall the exact circumstances of its disappearance. I know only that one morning when I was a freshman at the University of Oklahoma, I woke and the ring was gone from my finger—not dropped, not mislaid, not hidden. Gone. The loss of my class of 1950 ring has always been a mystery, a major concern.

"Yaaahooo!" Now I hear the high, bubbly giggles of the little girl on the swing set. I watch her ponytail flying out behind as the young father pushes his daughter higher and higher. How I'd loved my own daddy! I adored the daredevil barnstormer whose small airplane had dodged thunderheads and looped and spiraled through the sky—and whose stunt pilot's license was signed by Orville Wright himself. Later, when Daddy settled down a bit, he was equally as charming and dashing in his Braniff Airways uniform. His cool blue eyes reflected the cloth's color. His light brown hair glistened around the cap that perched on his head at a cocky angle. My father carried himself proud and tall in the tradition of his German heritage. But his mouth wore a superior, arrogant smirk.

"Jeanie, I'm home!" Smiling, Daddy strode through the door. With a dull thud, he dropped his suitcase and flight bag to the floor and held his arms wide as I leapt into them.

"What'll it be, girl?" he said. "How 'bout we go dove hunting in the woods across the road? Just the two of us. And if your mom fixes fried chicken this evening, I'll arm wrestle you for the pulley bone. Later, we'll snuggle up on the backyard cot and gaze at the stars. Okay?"

"Okay!"

"I'll teach you the constellations. One by one. You've got a lot to learn, girl."

"And will you tell me one of your Pinocchio stories?" Laughing, I held my hand in front of my nose as far as my short arm would reach. "I want to see your nose grow long."

At dinner he and I pretended to fight over the pulley bone, then gobbled our food. After dessert, we raced for the sofa. As Mother clanked around in the kitchen washing dishes, I giggled while Daddy tickled my tummy and . . . and what? I go blank. I sigh.

Sighing, Mother looked up at Braniff's big DC-6 and hugged me before I boarded it for Chicago. Tears beaded in the corners of her eyes.

"Bea!" Daddy said. "Don't worry. Jean's in good hands. Rita Romero is a topnotch stewardess. She'll keep an eye on your little girl during the flight—and in the morning, too. Rita's going along with us to the planetarium. With Jean starting school in the fall, this'll be a great educational trip for her."

From the small square window, I waved to Mother as Daddy taxied the plane down the runway. Once we were airborne, Rita served the drinks and food, her shapely legs in silk hose swishing up and down the aisle as she walked. Her dark hair flowed evenly around her cap. She had a big tropical smile—and that night, Daddy had a big slash of orange lipstick on his collar when he got back to the hotel room. Having long finished the bag of cherries and stack of comic books he left for me, I'd grown terrified as the night wore on. But Daddy said big girls don't cry. So I didn't. Eventually, I heard his key turn in the lock. I pretended to be asleep.

He leaned over the bed and tried to kiss me good-night but lost his balance and tumbled down beside me. His breath was hot. The smell was strong and strange—like a combination of cigar and that golden drink from the small, flat bottle hidden in his flight bag. He stroked my hair and said I'd come to understand many things someday. And he would teach me. He kissed me on the mouth and . . . and that was all I remember.

That was all. No more memories of my father until high school. At fifteen, Mother got me my first pair of high heels. Ballet lessons had taught me balance and grace, and I walked easily in the new black suede sandals. Daddy smiled and looked me over from head to toe as if I were a young racehorse he wanted to purchase. What's he doing *that* for? I felt strangely ill at ease. And at the dinner table, I pretended not to notice when Daddy slipped off his shoe and rubbed his foot over mine.

"Hey, Bea. I see you bought Jeanie a pair of heels," he said. "They're beautiful!" Both confused and proud, I mumbled a word of thanks.

Again, I look down at the ring on my finger and remember when Dad stepped on my girlfriend's fingers. A group of us were lolling about on the living room carpet, looking at the Highland Park High School yearbook when Daddy appeared in his uniform. As he walked through the group to get to the door and on to the airport, he stepped on the hand of the prettiest girl, Judy Kelley. I knew it was crazy, but for a second, I thought the accident was intentional. Judy yelled and pulled quickly away. Daddy apologized profusely, bowed, and kissed her hand as though he were some knight in shining armor. Comically, Judy pretended to swoon. I was puzzled. I'd never before realized that he was attractive in a sexual way, much *less* to my friends. To me, Daddy was Daddy—nothing more. Still, alone with him, I always felt weird. *Oh, how silly,* I told myself. *How stupid!*

And how stupid of me to be wondering why Daddy's copilot stared at me in my new red sweater. And what did Daddy mean? "That one's *mine,* Virgil." How *silly!* My father said it in a proud way, of course. Nothing more.

Nothing could be more fun than our trip to South America, where Braniff had just opened a new route. Me (at sixteen) and Mother and Daddy. They'd let me try all the wonderful, exotic alcoholic drinks of the many Latin countries. I might not go there ever again, Daddy said. Besides, I was growing up fast, and it was high time he taught me how to drink. Bourbon with water, he said, was best—adding Coke or 7UP was concocting a sissy's drink. Daddy didn't like sissy drinks or sissy women.

The first night in Lima, Peru, we dined at our elegant hotel with my parent's airline buddies from the States. One man, a nice person, had been my ballroom dancing teacher back home. It was great fun to be whirled around the floor, dancing rumbas and sambas and tangos. But when a second man (who'd tried to feel my leg under the table) asked me to dance, I refused. Mother's face reddened. She said flatly that I was rude to refuse Daddy's friend, Braniff's senior pilot. "He's had a bit too much liquor—that's all," she whispered. "He's a fine man." She glared at me. "A *fine* man."

In the wee hours, we went up to our rooms. I fell into bed and it started spinning. I knew enough high school Spanish to understand Daddy when he'd ordered rum punches—"doble." But had the double shots been for *me,* as well as Mother and him? *Oh,* I thought, *here I go again with my stupid, suspicious, overactive imagination. My own father would never try to get me drunk. How silly!*

I heard the door to my parent's adjoining room open and perhaps footsteps and . . . I passed out.

At dawn Mother woke me to prepare for the flight across the Andes to Rio de Janeiro, but before I could even say, "Mother, I'm sick," it was as though I'd been kicked in the stomach. Vomit flew from my mouth across the bed and hit the wall. For the rest of the two-week trip, I continually fell into a dead sleep with my head in Mother's lap. In my few waking hours, I stared blankly and didn't speak.

Upon returning to the States, Mother took me from doctor to doctor. Finally, a woman in a dirty little office misdiagnosed an underactive thyroid and prescribed pills. Gradually, I emerged from the stupor and seemed normal, though by now I'd become a real misfit at Highland Park High, and when alone with Daddy, I was intensely uncomfortable. *How odd.* I berated myself even more. *How strange, how dumb, how totally paranoid I've become!*

My first menstrual period had been a month before the trip, and when I had no second period for several months, Mother whisked me off to the regular family doctor. She stood at the end of his examining table, frowning, watching Dr. Munford stick his hand and his instruments inside me. Embarrassed? I felt like dying. Later I realized that Mother, ever suspicious of everyone but Daddy, probably thought I was pregnant. In college, when I really did first have sexual intercourse, I didn't bleed at all. Since I wasn't particularly athletic, it's unlikely that sports participation had somehow broken the hymen. Still, it never crossed my mind that I wasn't a virgin.

At twenty-six, after marrying and having four children, suddenly I became comatose and was carted off to the mental hospital, where I had a single shocking dream: Daddy was in my bed, trying to seduce me. I was attracted but resisted. In answer to my timid question about whether the *unspeakable* had happened—and incest *was* unspeakable in 1960—the psychiatrist said, "No, of course not. All young girls are attracted to their fathers. Don't be silly." His incorrect Freudian attitude, which I accepted as the total truth, put my recovery on hold for two decades. While in the hospital, I also began having recurring nightmares. I was strapped in the tail section of an airplane as it crashed and burned.

The dreams kept on and the truth lay dormant until I was in my late forties. At that time, my friend Beverly and I decided to visit my parents. On a hot summer day, we drove from my home in south Louisiana to Scurry, Texas. By the time I turned the car onto the long gravel lane leading to my parents' ranch house, Bev and I were hot and dry and thirsty for a tall, cold beer.

After greeting us and lugging our suitcases upstairs, my father mixed highballs. We four sat at the kitchen table and talked and drank for hours.

Even Mother, who seldom had more than a couple of cocktails, imbibed heavily that night. No one mentioned dinner or even snacks. We all drank.

The room started swimming. I left the table, stumbled upstairs, flung my clothes over a chair, and the minute I hit the mattress, I was out. Sometime later, I sensed a presence. I opened my eyes. I felt the hot breeze blowing in through the balcony door. Earlier, it had been closed. My father was kneeling by the bed, staring at me. The light from his eyes glowed red. They didn't seem red or look red; they actually *were* red. Not bloodshot, but the strangest color I'd ever seen. I know it sounds dramatic, but his irises and pupils both emitted an odd reddish glow—almost like devil's eyes.

Even at *that,* my automatic response was to kiss him—just with my lips closed like any small child would kiss a father. He started to kiss my breast. I remember seeing the back of his balding head bending over me, and I remember saying, "No, don't." And . . . I blacked out.

I woke in the middle of the night and was lying on my stomach. I tried to push up. Without warning, a forceful stream of vomit spewed out—exactly like it had that early morning so long ago in Lima, Peru.

The next morning, only the slightest trace of the night before was in my memory, along with the conviction that I'd had another horrific nightmare. I may never have known the truth, except the next day riding in his truck, my father made a fatal mistake.

He took my hand and smiled. "Well," he said, "what do you think about an old man and his daughter?'

Oh God! I edged closer to the door. *It's true!* "As far as I'm concerned," I said, jerking my hand away. "Nothing happened."

"Okay!" His eyes glinted with anger. "Have it your way. But we made tracks on the sheets. You better wash them."

"I already did—in the middle of the night," I said. "I had to. I threw up on them."

"Good!" he said. "And remember, if you tell anyone about this, they'll never believe you. After all, you've been in the loony bin—more than once."

For a long while, I thought it was my fault. Had I been seductive? Dressed too sexily, perhaps? Then I thought the incident could be buried, forgotten. *Real* lunacy! Although I'd been in mental wards three times (complete with shock treatments) I checked myself into a fourth mental hospital to try to retrieve memories. In my confused and vulnerable state, I chose unwisely. The national, well-advertised facility preyed on the weak and offered minimal help with sexual trauma.

I joined a recovery group. SIA (Survivors of Incest Anonymous), summoned my courage, and wrote my parents letters of confrontation. Their answer: silence.

I didn't communicate with them for five years, during which time my sweet Kathy learned through therapy and hypnosis that my father had raped her, too. The bastard!

Then, my mother had an operation (for a growth on her uterus, probably malignant), and I reinstated the relationship. When I thought she would die, my emotions ran strong. I found that I still loved her, and, truthfully, as an only child, I also felt deserving of an inheritance. God knows, I'd earned it. I wanted it for my nine grandchildren who had good brains, few funds, and a longing for a college education.

Mother's growth was benign; our reconciliation was malignant. It lasted only two and a half years. After the first blush of reunification, the relationship grew ever more intolerable. Her criticism and domination still ran strong. Also, I became disgusted at having to pretend to like my father in order to be near her. Bit by bit, she chipped away at my hard-won sanity. When finally she first mentioned the past, I made a permanent break. I had to. Her words, "I forgive you for seducing your father," were more than I could bear. Her detailed lies concocted to blame me and protect him were so ludicrous even a child wouldn't have believed them.

There are still many missing parts to my life story puzzle. Today, one more piece fell in place. Before I came to the park, Kathy surprised me with the missing class ring. Thirty years ago, she said, she'd found it in my father's bureau drawer, and without realizing its significance, she'd stolen it. Kathy remembered that she had taken the ring when she was fourteen, shortly after my father had asked her to ride in his truck with him to the far back pasture of his ranch—where he raped her.

Now, rising from the bench under the Chinese elm, I'm again aware of the happy shouts of nearby kids—and I feel cheated, betrayed, robbed of a childhood. A life! And I'm angry. Furious!

On wobbly bird legs, I totter forward. For a moment, I imagine the duck pond to be the vast Pacific where all truths ebb and flow, where all wrongs are righted, all filth washed clean. To wet my finger, I lick it, and over my swollen knuckle, I twist off the ring. With all the strength I can muster, I hurl the damned thing into the pitifully insignificant pond and watch while murky water rings ripple out from where the ring strikes the surface and sinks, appropriately, into the muck and mire.

At age sixty-three, *true* recovery begins. *Finally!*

Questions for Discussion

1. It is not uncommon for adults who were sexually abused as children (particularly if the abuse occurred when the child was young) to forget the details of the abuse. In Jean's case, what could account for her "forgetting"?

2. Jean eventually got verification of the abuse from the perpetrator himself. Even if this had not taken place, what data in the narrative would cause a clinician to suspect that sexual abuse had occurred?
3. What are some of the long-term effects of intrafamilial childhood sexual abuse?
4. How would you diagnose the perpetrator?
5. The Freudian idea that little girls have sexual fantasies about their fathers kept women from disclosing sexual abuse and clinicians from believing in and treating it. What changes occurred that brought this problem to public recognition and finally gave victims such as Jean a shot at treatment?

Letter to Margaret

Jean Sellmeyer Smith

Dear Margaret,

I write to you, my dearest daughter-in-law, who has survived the horror of incest, for we have a special bond. As you embark on your road to recovery, I share some thoughts.

Ages ago when I started my journey, I expected too much too soon. The way is long and winding with countless roadblocks. Trust yourself. Listen to your counselors, but be guided by your own stars. Trust the readings of your own inner compass.

Like you, dear Margaret, my main roadblock came from the least expected source—Mother. For so long, my recovery was sabotaged with her negative words that encouraged constant dependence. I fell into eternal self-doubt, refusing to believe anything except the "fact" that I was worthless and Mother was wise, beautiful, and unreachable.

Finally, I broke off relations with both my mother and my father, the abuser. Severing ties with Dad was unexpectedly easy. With Mother, unexpectedly difficult. I wanted to hang on, to wrench some drop of understanding from her, to make her into someone she wasn't and never would be.

In my first meeting at SIA (Survivors of Incest Anonymous), one young woman was crying desperately. Theresa, eight years into recovery, was one of the group's senior members. She had just returned from a family reunion that she attended at her brother's invitation. Theresa had gone expecting a reconciliation with her mother and when she found that, after all those years, her mother still refused to believe her, she was devastated. Listening to Theresa's painful outpouring, I vowed never to allow my lack of realism to resurface.

After five years without parental contact, my youngest daughter, Libby, called me with the news that Mother was being admitted to Baylor Hospital in Dallas. A growth on her uterus. Likely malignant. Instantly, I knew I'd been fooling myself. My love for her existed as strongly as ever—right alongside the hate. I sent flowers. I sent a special book. I went to see her.

But . . . I also remembered Theresa.

Her growth was benign. We picked up where we left off—no mention of my abuse, no mention of my letter of confrontation, and no mention of my five-year absence. It was an odd relationship, on her terms, as always. Our relationship ended when I found that she was *not* in complete denial, as I'd thought. Instead, she was dead set on protecting my abuser at all costs. Perhaps that's the only way she can survive. Even today, a small part of me longs for a mother who could have nurtured me instead of sacrificed me for her own emotional and financial needs. I know she won't change. Finally, I'm finding more comfort in accepting reality than in wishful thinking. Strangely, with the last shred of unrealistic hope fallen away, I'm truly at peace.

Margaret, all incest survivors with nonsupportive mothers say the same thing: the betrayal by a mother is worse than the deed itself. Accept that fact.

I wish you well on your road to recovery. As you stumble, walk, jog, stumble again and fall, and pull yourself up to go again, I hope that Theresa's story and mine will help surmount one of the biggest road-blocks—hanging on to Mother. I pray for a true and lasting healing from your grief and anger.

Love,
Jean

Questions for Discussion

1. In her letter, Jean says that the "betrayal by a mother is worse than the deed itself." Why do you think this is the case?
2. What are some possible reasons a mother may deny, fail to believe, and side with the perpetrator in cases of intrafamilial child sexual abuse?

Hurt

Louise Webster

Even in my earliest memories, it has been with me. I remember standing in my bedroom. I remember the exact way the sunlight looked coming through the window, and I remember a terrible urgent feeling that crept up my spine, making me feel like I would burst out of my very skin. Then I remember looking down at the back of my hand, now imprinted with marks of baby teeth. The indentations were deep and purple and did not bleed or hurt. I watched them until they disappeared, and then my memory stops.

As I grew older I began scratching at my arms when the feeling came on. Now I was better at identifying it as self-loathing, but it also felt primitive and raw. I did not feel embarrassed about the scratching unless someone saw the marks when a sleeve might pull up. But then I would also feel annoyed and violated should they ask, "What happened?"

It seemed to go away for a while after I married a very kind man at the age of nineteen. I was finishing school, married, and happy. After we had our first child my symptoms returned, only stronger. I now took to cutting myself with scissors, razors, and sharp metal. I still tried to keep it secret but now experienced profound guilt about my actions. I was supposed to be a normal mother with a wonderful baby boy and my actions were bizarre. Still I couldn't stop.

I began to see an excellent psychiatrist due to obsessive-compulsive disorder and tremendous anxiety. He was very helpful, but I did not mention the cutting. One session he noticed cuts on my wrist. I was immediately hospitalized, which came as a shock. This psychiatrist believed the cutting was either an attention-grabbing device or a suicide attempt. It was neither. I used cutting as a way to manage stress that seemed overwhelming. With two small children at home and the legacy of an abusive childhood etched in my psyche, I had not developed healthy coping skills.

Eventually I made contact with a doctor who understood why I cut. I believe the reasons for cutting are as unique and diverse as the cutters themselves. There is no one simple answer or treatment plan. Luckily my doctor addressed the cause of my cutting—unrelenting anxiety—and not the cutting itself. He encouraged me to talk about the feelings without acting on them. He prescribed antianxiety medication which helped me deal with the intrusive negative thoughts and channel the overflow of energy in a more positive direction. I now use writing and painting as a release.

I am still in therapy and still have moments when the urge to hurt myself is quite strong. My new doctor is more understanding than I imagined possible, and I hope I am finally able to cut no more.

Questions for Discussion

1. The author began hurting herself as a small child and says that it was "the legacy of an abusive childhood." Why do you think this coping mechanism develops in the context of an abusive environment?
2. What may account for the reoccurrence of the author's self-hurting after the birth of her first child?

A Sharp Feel

Erin White

No more razors
Haven't I said this before?
Nothing is worth the blood
No one commands a scar
I have control

Hello?
Am I experiencing déjà vu
Or something
Because I know I've said
This all before

No more "good pain"
Hiding bandages under long shirts
Trying not to flinch when someone
Pats my arm and I just want to roar
"Hey, asshole, watch it!
I'm still healing . . ."
Won't say a word
Can't say a word
This shouldn't be happening . . .
But it is

Didn't I throw out the blade last time,
Swearing the cold metal would never
Drag across my skin again?
Did I swear?
Well, swears to myself
Don't count

I feel the urge
I know my choices
All choked up with my
Silent promises of "next time"

What about this time?
Forget last month
Smoothing over old scars
Tell me about now
How I have control
How I can pick up the phone

Well, fuck that!
I won't talk
I can't talk
I'm too busy crawling backward
I know my choices . . .
But I feel the urge

This shouldn't be happening
But it is

I've said it all before

Questions for Discussion

1. What is the key feature of cutting behavior described in this poem?
2. What would a clinician want to know about the author's cutting behavior to develop a treatment approach?

Sacrifice

Bridget Bufford

I cut myself because I wanted to feel. I cut myself because I needed to be punished. I cut myself so I could be in control. I cut because the urge grew upon me like a shadow that approaches and encroaches, turns everything black until it is easier to split skin and let the blood flow than to fight it any longer. I cut because it worked; once blood spilled, I became relaxed, relieved, and present.

In September 1995 I went to therapy. I had seen counselors and psychologists and social workers and psychotherapists before, seventeen separate attempts. Working with Dr. Karen Johnson was different.

Prior experiences had left me skeptical, without much respect for therapists, but I liked Karen from our first session. That day, she told me she typically gives homework assignments to provide continuity between sessions. Instead of an assignment, she pointed out that I was already doing the things she considers important: exercising, writing, exploring other venues of creativity, attending a support group, working on a moral and spiritual inventory.

I had just spent the previous weeks being reviled and rejected by those I cared about, as a result of my own choices and actions; I came to Karen none too confident in my ability to make good decisions. Karen recognized how hard I was working, and then I could see it, too. I left her office with a glimmer of hope.

Karen encouraged me to continue to write, meditate, exercise, pray; frequently she offered both personal experience and printed guidance. Her candor impressed me. The risk she took—telling me some of her spiritual beliefs, the initial skepticism, the practical results of the practices—made it easier to share my own experiences. With Karen, therapy became a mutual process.

I hadn't cut since I had begun seeing her; I wanted to stop. After the release, the shame and guilt remained, and the lies. When the urge to cut struck, I called Karen or my close friend, Janet. I talked to someone till the tension dissipated and I found an alternative method of expressing my frustration or my rage.

Still, I carried a pain like a vestigial organ, a rudimentary adaptation to a relationship I needed to abandon. Pam and I had been good friends for years.

We shared a passion for books, music, and movies. She encouraged me to start writing and edited some of my early pieces. The mutual support deteriorated with Pam's escalating addiction to drugs and alcohol. Instead of invitations to go out for coffee, I was getting late-night calls to pick her up from jail. She wouldn't allow me in her house because of the abusive man she kept. I saw Pam only during her periodic psychiatric admissions, and the strongest connection we had was my pain. I wanted it gone.

I had tried before to step back; I got frantic phone calls at home, at work, even at a coffeehouse I frequented. Pam wasn't ready to let go. I missed the friend I once had but was miserable in her presence.

I resolved to sever ties. In many cultures, rituals of mutilation and scarification are bound to healing. I needed a ritual of my own. It seemed right, but radical. I decided to seek some other perspectives.

I went to Janet's house on a Tuesday night. We met in the sparsely furnished basement, where I explained my resolve to cut ties with Pam, to ritualize the letting go by severing my flesh as I would sever the connection. The scar would remind me not to choose that path again.

I said that in the past, compulsion drove me. Tormented by the urge until I could no longer resist, cutting released the scream inside that drove me to it. "I don't feel that way at all, now. I have time. I can plan it and then wait until it's right."

"Tell me how that ties in with your resolve," Janet said. "This is the first thing you've said in eons that I really don't understand."

I told her a visible scar would symbolize my resolve, like a tattoo, or like the antithesis of a wedding ring. I chose my ring finger for the mark.

Janet nodded, mulling it over. I told her that the taboo against ritual cutting, as opposed to self-mutilation, is largely cultural.

"I don't know that much about other cultures, but it's probably true," she said. "When do you see Karen?"

"Tomorrow afternoon."

Janet hoped I would wait a day and get Karen's perspective. She said, "I do understand it, though. You've always worked in a different realm. I would never do it myself, and I couldn't support any kind of frequent use of such a tool, but in this one situation I really don't have a problem with it."

Janet's support reassured me, but I marveled at it. How did I convince a friend to sanction self-mutilation? Do I live that far from the norm?

Late Wednesday afternoon I saw Karen. I described my desire, then told her that I hadn't anticipated Janet's acceptance.

"Did you want her to try to stop you?" Karen asked.

"No." I hesitated. "I guess I expected some debate, I didn't want her to think this ritual was just a bid for attention, and she didn't, but she said she doesn't have a problem with it."

Karen frowned, started to speak, then hesitated.

"I can't say without reservation that I consider it a good idea," I said. "I would never suggest it to anyone else, and I would probably lie about it."

"There must be some shame with it, if you feel like you have to lie about it," she said.

"Shame doesn't seem like a part of it," I said. "Cutting's a difficult thing to explain. It's very private."

She asked if the act would represent a continuation of an old, dysfunctional pattern.

"No; it's the tool I used with that pattern, but the desire is different. This is not compulsion. I want to use a ritual of cutting my hand to symbolize cutting ties."

Karen is generally forthcoming with her ideas. Now she was holding back, measuring her words carefully. I missed our usual free-flowing dialogue. Was she appalled by this inspiration?

Karen did say she wasn't comfortable with a ritual that involved hurting myself. "Why add pain to pain?"

"It won't hurt any worse than it already does." I paused. "It would feel better to control the pain." I'd always been so worked up from fighting the urge that by the time I actually cut it never hurt. I would watch the skin part and the pale edge of the wound redden and spill blood, but I didn't feel anything. I had reservations about my ability to control the damage, though, because cutting requires a degree of agitation. Stitches wouldn't bother me, but I hoped to avoid surgery.

"If you injure yourself seriously, it would defeat your purpose of trying to control the pain," Karen said.

I designed the ritual to objectify the wound as much as to control the pain. I told her I wanted the scar—an immediate, accessible reminder.

Karen urged me to find alternatives for externalizing my resolve. She suggested getting a piece of wood and carving it, applying the cutting to something else.

Wood could be lost. Besides, I was unlikely to carve without cutting myself. "If I do this, I want it to be volitional."

Karen also suggested that I find or make a really beautiful piece of jewelry, telling myself, "I choose beauty over this pain."

I just looked at her, and thought, *You really don't get it.* She was struggling to help me find an alternative. Why? Did she know how serious I was? Did she know how much damage I was capable of doing? I clenched my right hand; I'd had a tendon repair ten years earlier.

Karen leaned forward. She looked concerned and worn out. I could continue to reject her suggestions, or I could drop it. "I'll pray about it," I said.

"Good," she said. "I think that's a really good idea."

At that time, I came in only twice a month, but we agreed to meet the following week. As I stood to leave, Karen said, "I can't support your method, but I respect the integrity of your ideas."

She knew my history of cutting, since our first session. Other therapists had made it a focus of treatment with behavioral contracts, action plans. One intake ended when I told the therapist I cut myself; he said he could not work with me. Karen said she's not so bothered by cutting, that she doesn't try to take that away from people. She recognizes cutting as a tool for expressing emotions, and she believes in developing a greater repertoire of skills and choices for dealing with feelings.

Now she did seem bothered. Because it involved hurting myself? Was it her training?

At home that night, I prayed for guidance, then meditated. It heightened my certainty that this sacrifice would be beneficial.

Pam called Thursday from a medical detox ward, desperate to see me. I got to the hospital and she said, "Who asked you here?"

Her face was swollen and flushed from vomiting. Despite heavy sedation, she shook so much she couldn't lie down. She'd try to curl up, draw her knees to her chest, but the violence of the tremors threatened to fling her from the bed. "So nice that you could come for this," she said.

Her pain was palpable, weighty; it immobilized me. "Hi, Pam," was all I could manage.

"Go ahead, say your piece," she said. "Get it out. No holds barred." She wanted me to yell at her, call her a lowlife. I shook my head.

Unable to goad me into a fight, Pam began screaming abuse at her nurse. The noise drew a doctor; Pam got another shot.

I went home and called Karen. She seemed angry, though not at me. More than ever, I longed to sever ties. "You think the cutting is a bad idea, don't you?" I asked.

"Yes, Bridget, I really do. I have a problem with you hurting yourself. I respect the integrity of your ideas, but I'm torn. You've had enough pain in your life," she said.

"You looked kind of appalled when I talked about it Wednesday."

"I'm bothered by the idea of you hurting yourself, but I'm not appalled by you or your thoughts," she said. "This is my reaction, based on my feelings. I wouldn't expect you to make decisions based on that. If you choose to cut yourself, I would not be appalled."

I wondered if she wanted to protect me from Pam or from myself. Usually I hate that; I don't trust it. With Karen, it's so rare I don't need to struggle against it. I'm grateful for her vulnerability, for the humanity I see in the woman. So many therapists hide their reactions behind a veneer of professionalism. Karen doesn't use a role to shield herself from involvement.

"I appreciate that you're telling me how you feel about it," I said.

"I will be honest with you."

Talking about the ritual was a relief to me, but it disturbed Karen. In session, she had looked drained, on the verge of frustration. I regretted her distress on my behalf; it didn't seem right to apologize, though. I said, "On Wednesday it looked like you'd had a hard day."

She had been struggling with some issues of her own, she said, and she was trying to take good care of herself. "You're perceptive, though. You may notice some fluctuations, some changes of mood."

She suggested I get a leather cord, tie widely-spaced knots in it to represent the entanglements I wish to avoid, and wear it as a bracelet. I did that. A friend saw the bracelet and asked about it; two days later, a knotted cord of purple embroidery thread circled her wrist.

Saturday I purchased some butterfly bandages. I planned to cut on Sunday morning, when I had the house to myself.

Saturday night I contrived some explanation for the impending wound, then began sharpening the knife. Honing a blade to a razor edge has been my accustomed preparation for mutilation. The blade scraped the whetstone, over and over, a hypnotic sound. The lock-back Buck knife had a satisfying heft. I watched the edge grow bright, trued the angle of steel to stone. Passing the blade across the stone aroused the familiar urge, the unbearable tension that demands immediate release. I had my story straight; I had the bandages; the knife was sharp.

It's not supposed to go this way. Sweat pricked my scalp and my armpits. I might do considerable harm. I called Janet.

"You need to calm down. There's no urgency," she said.

True; I needed to be calm and certain before I acted. Taking a wild slash at myself in the midst of emotional turmoil was an old behavior and likely to bring back old feelings. If I found it necessary and helpful to cut ties in this symbolic way, I needed to treat myself with respect, and I needed to treat the act with respect.

Janet thought I should call Karen. I promised to consider it and thanked her for her help.

I grappled with the idea of calling Karen. I didn't want to bother her, didn't want to ask for help, didn't want to admit that I was in over my head. Beyond that, though, loomed the image of Pam in the hospital—the scene she made, the nurse and doctor in disorder around her self-created crisis. I've done that; I don't ever want to do it again.

I prayed, then put on some loud rock music and washed my few dishes from dinner. Guidance, for me, can be quite mundane. I bellowed along with the music, turned my intensity toward cleaning the kitchen, then ran a bath. Bathing has been a frequent alternative to cutting; once I'm soaking in hot water, I get too relaxed to hurt myself.

Sunday I got up early to a gray, cold morning, and journaled for a long time. I wrote:

> *I want it to be an affirmative use of an old tool. Cutting myself used to be punishing. I want to know, in my mind, in my emotions, in my body, that I will not choose to continue perpetuating the lies and false hopes around this relationship. There is a depth of intimacy that I am not willing to give.*

I structured my morning with an attitude of reverence, building toward the ceremony. I prayed, then listened to music as I cleaned my study. I selected elements of ritual that seemed appropriate and reinforcing, then covered the table with an old towel. I readied the bandage, briefly sharpened the knife.

Once the altar was laid, I focused on emotional and physical preparation. I put on a tape of drum music, danced till my body was loose, my mind empty. Then I did a sitting meditation for about twenty minutes, going into a deeper trance. Afterward, I stretched until I was relaxed.

I sat cross-legged before the table, took up the knife in my left hand, made a fist with my right. I tucked my thumb against my ring finger, pushed it higher than the others. I said a quick prayer, closed my eyes, and cut. It stung, an itchy sensation as blood spilled. I kept my focus, didn't let the blood run down my wrist. I approximated the edges of the wound and closed it with two butterflies. I had a half-inch-long gash through the skin and fascia.

I stood up, laughing, with tears running down my face. Cutting always brings profound relief. This time, instead of a numb calm tainted by incipient shame, I felt euphoric, victorious.

When the wound no longer seeped, I took off the butterflies so that a more prominent scar would form. I didn't care whether anyone else could see the mark, but I wanted to be able to find it. I looked once more at what I had written.

> *I won't do this again. I don't think I'll ever want to or need to. I want to remember forever the decision I make today. It's a hard choice, but it's mine.*

The following Thursday, Karen started the session in a buoyant, irreverent mood. She grew still, intent as I read the passage about preparing to cut myself. She said, "You handled that well."

I described my distress Saturday night and told Karen that I had been reluctant to call because I knew my intent bothered her. "I know it's not my responsibility to take care of your feelings," I said.

"That's right."

I said I'd thought also of Pam, her chaotic scene in the hospital. I'm capable of that, but I don't want to draw people into my turmoil.

She nodded. We moved on, talked about the sorrow of losing a friend.

The cut left a small scar that has faded to white. I don't need to look at it much anymore. Karen and I have not discussed it further.

My desire to cut myself disturbed Karen, but her strong belief in personal autonomy created a conflict. Her unease tempted me to jerk her around, scare her a little. It would not have worked; she's got the skills to stay out of that trap, or to extricate herself quickly.

More important, *I did not do it.* Karen told me how she felt, but she treated me with respect. She believed that I would act with integrity. Her honesty overcame the lure of manipulation. I knew she cared about me, regardless of my decision, and that knowledge took away my urge to create a power struggle. I realize now that our interaction marked me more deeply than my ritual.

Questions for Discussion

1. From the writer's point of view, what was the positive aspect of her choice to ritually cut herself? Do you think she achieved her goal?
2. What about Dr. Johnson's approach helped the writer stop cutting?
3. Though Dr. Johnson did not approve of the author's choice to ritually cut herself, she came down on the side of client self-determination. Do you agree?

SELECTED READINGS AND ADDITIONAL RESOURCES

Sexual Abuse

Courtois, Christine (1998). *Recollections of Sexual Abuse: Treatment Principles and Guidelines.* New York: W. W. Norton.

Edwards, Tess and Derouard, Mary (1999). *Hope in Healing: A Guide for Survivors of Sexual Abuse Written by Survivors.* Niagara Falls, NY: Source RE Source.

Herman, Judith (1992). *Trauma and Recovery.* New York: Basic Books.

Hooper, Carol-Ann (1992). *Mothers Surviving Child Sexual Abuse.* New York: Routledge.

Johnson, Janis, T. (1992). *Mothers of Incest Survivors.* Bloomington, IN: Indiana University.

Self-Hurting

Alderman, Tracy (1997). *The Scarred Soul: Understanding and Ending Self-Inflicted Violence.* Oakland, CA: New Harbinger Publications.

The International Society for the Study of Dissociation (ISSD). Guidelines for treatment, education, books, conference information. <www.issd.org>.

Many Voices: Words of Hope for People Recovering from Trauma and Dissociation. (Newsletter) Cincinnati, OH: Many Voices.

Miller, Dusty (1994). *Women Who Hurt Themselves: A Book of Hope and Understanding*. New York: Basic Books.

Putnam, Frank, W. (1989). *Diagnosis and Treatment of Multiple Personality Disorder*. New York: The Guilford Press.

Ross, Colin (1996). *Dissociative Identity Disorder: Diagnosis, Clinical Features, and Treatment of MPD*. New York: John Wiley and Sons.

West, Cameron (1999). *First Person Plural: Life As a Multiple*. New York: Hyperion.

PART VII:
MENTAL DISORDERS

ANXIETY DISORDERS

The Color of Disorder

Jamie Joy Gatto

Angie sprawled on the sofa and stared at the fuzz balls tumbling across the old oiled-wood floor. It gleamed in such a way that her mother would have proudly said you could eat off of it, but the cat had begun to scratch and preen, causing a tiny whirlwind of white billowing fluff to litter it. A knot began to rise in her belly; she felt as if she were choking on cat hair.

Angie had spent the entire afternoon after classes moving every piece of furniture in the apartment to catch the dust, skim the baseboards, vacuum every rug, every inch of the now lemon-scented apartment. Her apartment was always clean during exams—too clean.

She felt the pressure rise again in her stomach, and her heart began to beat loudly in her ears.

I'll just rest for a few minutes more, then I'll start writing again," she said. "That work wore me out."

Mark laughed softly. He had heard this routine every day for the last week. "What do you think, Ange? You think old Professor Collins will give you an A in mopping technique? You should bring him over instead of handing in your thesis."

She pouted and noticed a line of red thread caught on his navy sweater near his collar. Her temples throbbed.

"When's it due, hon?" he smiled, hoping to cushion his last remarks.

"Don't ask." She folded her arms and leaned back, head falling over the arm of the tightly covered white wool sofa. It felt hard and scratchy, causing her neck to ache in sync with her head. As she looked backward in the awkward and painful position, she noticed dust she had missed under the glass side table.

"Well . . . " She sat up. "I guess I'd better start on the bathroom. The sink is really gross. Have you been using something blue in the bathroom?"

"Blue?" Mark thought about it. "Yeah, that new whitening toothpaste you just bought me."

"Well, it's gunked up all over the sink. I'd better buy some new toothpaste."

"Ange, if you don't start researching . . ."

She cut him off. "Mark, for the last time—don't bug me! You know I can't concentrate if the house is dirty. How can I think if the sink is blue and the cat keeps shedding?"

Mark wanted to reason with her. He wanted to take her and wrap her in a great big sanitized hug. He wished he could take her hair out of that tight ponytail and let it lose, shake it out. Do whatever it takes to make her wrinkle up her nose and give him her crooked smile. Take her to bed and keep her up past midnight, make her scream out loud. But, what could he say about a toxic blue sink? About monster cat fur? He turned on the TV instead.

"Tomorrow, when you go to the grocery, would you pick up some of those scented garbage bags? I want pink ones, okay? To match the bathroom. And get some white toothpaste."

He flipped from channel to channel: Infomercials on dehydrators, "How to Lose Weight in Thirty Days or Less! Guaranteed!," a black-and-white classic barely watchable on the public station.

"Write it down, okay? You'll forget."

He flipped and flipped: *Dracula, 1,000 Flushes, Elvis in Las Vegas.* "Uh huh," he answered.

She put on her yellow Playtex Living Gloves and scoured the blue from the sink with a pale green powder. She lifted the lid to the toilet. The throbbing began again.

Questions for Discussion

1. Most compulsions have a significant function. What does compulsive cleaning symbolize?
2. This woman uses cleaning as an avoidance mechanism. How would you approach this in treatment?

Step on a Crack, Break Your Mother's Back

Janice J. Heiss

Mother will pull through, Mother will make it, he recites to himself like a nursery rhyme on his commute home along the Dan Ryan Expressway. He rolls the words around in his mouth like a baby lozenge. It doesn't help. As the kaleidoscopic shapes of a migraine coat his vision, he feels smaller and somewhat nauseous. Squeezing the steering wheel helps ground him. Somehow, he makes it home. As he pulls into the driveway, he notices, with some surprise, that his large three-bedroom Colonial suburban home is where he left it that morning. His wife appears in the den window in front of the TV, exactly where he would expect her to be at this time of day.

How can Mother be dying? She can't! He loves her with the tender vehemence a toddler has toward a favorite teddy. He finds himself in his bedroom. Looking around. Taking a deep breath. *Ah!* The familiar mix of household cleaning solutions permeates his lungs. It collects him like a magnet gathering iron filings. Everything looks the same, is in order. Clean, neat. *No, of course, Mother . . .*

His visit that afternoon was not reassuring. She had been so listless. He had tried to bolster her with his resolve. "I asked the nurse if they could move you. It's taking a while because I'm so picky about rooms. Room 707 or room number 522 looks possible, Mother." She groaned. "No, you'll like it. They have much better views—much better than a parking lot." *Much better room numbers. Get her out of Room 323. Bad number—three. Unstable triangles. Terrible number, three. So much suffering in the world caused by threes!*

"Would you mind picking up some Ngaio Marsh books for me at your library, sweetie pie?" And then she had dozed off. When he rose to leave, kissing her good-bye, he snatched the newspaper beside her. "Three Die in Car Crash" had been staring at him since he had arrived. He folded the paper in half, covering the dreaded D word, and put it in the wastebasket. *She won't miss it. Death will miss—damn!* He said it. He bit his tongue five times to get rid of the D word. He placed a breath mint on his tongue, but then spit it out since breath and death rhymed. He'd brush his teeth as soon as he got home.

First, he brushes his teeth. Then he puts his wallet in the top drawer of his secretary. Next, he washes his hands. Then he removes the black-onyx-and-diamond ring that his mother gave him when he was sixteen. He rubs it tenderly, holding it to his chest. He sighs so slightly that the ticking of his wristwatch obliterates the sound. Then he kisses the ring. Just as he had kissed her good-bye several hours ago as she lay like cardboard in the hospital bed. Little rapid-fire pecks five times in a row, his lucky number. The perfect number. *Two always being good—meaning love and marriage—plus two and add one for good luck.* He hesitates putting the ring down. He kisses it five more times, five times each. Five times five—doubling of good luck. *Good. Good. This should do it. This should pull her through.*

"In my will—"

But he cut her off immediately. "Mother," he whined, "come on, it's premature to be discussing your will—"

Ignoring him, she continued, "You'll see that I'm leaving my entire miniature set to you and Eleanor. You do realize that it is one of the best collections outside the Art Institute's Thorn Collection. Remember when I'd take you there when you were a little boy. We were two peas in a pod. . . . I'm sure that Audrey and Hilary will not be happy, but you and Eleanor appreciate fine things.

When he was a little boy growing up in her house, he spent countless hours staring into her collections. Tiny, rich-colored, orange and royal blue glass teacups, no bigger than a fingernail, sat on dainty, Lilliputian saucers. Rooms and rooms of exquisite oriental rugs, rich brocade drapes, Queen Anne and French Empire chairs, and meticulously reproduced Georgian and Hepplewhite period furniture adorned her sanctuary. No one could disturb her world inside her flute glass English mahogany breakfront. So refined, so flawless—like her. He fantasized becoming small enough to climb into the breakfront to live surrounded by these divine objects, in this pure space. He didn't dare. He had to be careful around her fine, valuable Waterford and Limoges collection, the Baker mahogany and the Royal Doulton glass. No one but she was allowed to touch her expensive breakfront. Only she, with the softest chamois cloth, shined the wood every day. When she wasn't looking, he would take the fragrant cloth and touch it to his cheek. It was as soft as nothing.

Next, he removes his old, lucky U.S. Navy cufflinks that got him through the war. Absentmindedly, he starts to kiss them too, but stops, recognizing that this isn't part of his routine. *What was she doing talking about her will? My goodness!* Next, the Rolex watch. "Where did I put the cufflinks? Darn it. No, not that way. What am I doing?" he mumbles. As a dog marking its space before sitting, his carefully manicured fingers circle the leather top of his secretary for the proper landing. *Place the cufflinks strategically; they link everything; they are good; then everything will be all right,* he tells himself. *Put the cufflinks in the center of the secretary in a perfect row, little soldiers at attention, at a right angle to the watch that will stand watch over the soldiers with the ring intersecting the angle so that it rings true.* He shifts the objects on his secretary with the concentration of a chess Grandmaster. Queens, pawns, bishops, kings, and knights—all pieces must be placed just right for him to win. *Position them all a few more times* (his fingertips touch down lightly on each object) *forward and backward: watch, ring, and cufflinks; now backward and forward: cufflinks, ring, and watch. Ah, yes. But best to cross-examine them. Make sure. The ring. Touch the ring. The ring guard. Make sure. Yes. Make sure. Checkmate.* He stands for several minutes touching the pieces, almost petting them. Finally, he steps back to confirm all players are in position, his laser eyes scanning the secretary.

"Will you stop by the house to check on whether the girls are polishing the furniture? . . . " She kept fading away. "And, Samuel, make sure the Biedermeiers get polished; they're such lushes for furniture oil!"

"Of course, Mother," he assured her. *Now, I won't be able to play golf on Friday,* he thought, hating the thought simultaneously. *What kind of a son am I, anyways, thinking of golf?* He bit a hang nail until it bled.

Where's my wallet? Didn't I just put it—better check. Top drawer of my secretary. Count the money. Wash your hands. Oh, now wait. Did I?. . . Count it again. I'm tired; shut up. Do it. Count it again! This is the fifth or sixth time since lunch. No, count it backward too. Close out for the day. Put it away. Wash your hands. I'm not certain I counted right . . . and make sure the money's in order. Here's one fifty-dollar bill, then two twenties, two tens, and five ones. Remember to give Eleanor thirty, but, of course, don't break the fifty—your age, good luck. Check the bills. They should all face the same way. Go the extra mile. This is not a game, boy, this is your mother! *Do it right, and Mom will be all right. So right, be right, right is right and left is wrong. Wash your hands. Step on a crack, break your mother's back. Don't say that? What's wrong with you? It's not funny. Bite your tongue. Yes. Five times five. Close the drawer. No, open it. Just check the wallet one more time to make sure. Now close the drawer. You can do it! Now wash your hands.*

Things look good; everything is in order. He sighs, satisfied. His hands, big birds, glide over his construction. He then points them at the window where they fly on special wings above the traffic on the Edens Expressway to his mother's hospital room where they bless her.

"How're the kids?" she had asked on Wednesday. She was more alert, even a bit chipper.

"They're fine, Mother. They said to send their love," he fibbed. "I'll bring them this weekend." *What a mother! They don't make them like that any-*

more. So ill, but so selfless she asks about the kids. He loved her like an athlete who wins a race but keeps running around the track again and again not knowing when to stop.

Oh no! Did I forget to wash my hands when I left the hospital? If so, I've contaminated everything since leaving there—the steering wheel, the front door, my wife, and everything that I've touched since arriving home! Well, he sighs, *better retrace your tracks with alcohol wipes.* But then he remembers washing his hands. *Oh, yes, of course. . . . Thank goodness!*

You must bring the kids to the hospital soon, he orders himself. He cringes as he recalls taking the kids to the hospital when they were toddlers. *They were so difficult. They crawled all over the hospital floors and put their hands on everything.* No matter how many times he told them about germs, they just didn't seem to care. *They should care. They are part German. German-Jews. Germans are antigerms.*

I'd have to bring them on the weekend. No golf. He bites his tongue on the word golf, hard, so it hurts, so he winces. *I should be arrested for such a thought,* he thinks and looks sideways suspiciously.

Just remember to warn them about cancer. The word cancer is a no-no kids, he prepares to say out loud. *Cancer—out-of-control cells—impossible? Mother is in control of everything.*

"Mother, the room change should come soon. It will be a good thing. Oh, and all the gals from your canasta group want to come visit. Levora called."

"No, I don't want them to come . . . "

"But why, Mother? Levora's your favorite. It would cheer . . . "

"Yes, but that group can't come here. Christian Scientists can't go to hospitals, and I don't like the way Heddie dresses anyway."

"Oh, Mom, please. Maybe if Levora hadn't gotten you all involved in Christian Science, you would have gone to a doctor and been operated on sooner."

Affectionately ignoring him, in a way only a mother can ignore her child, she playfully tossed her arm over the side of the bed. She smiled her perfect heart-shaped valentine smile. He sat wondering at her rosy-marbled, cherubic skin. He took her hand. She was almost too fine, too pure to touch, like her treasured, Victorian grande-dame figurines inside their glass bell jars.

Christian Science, damn Christian Science almost killed her! What am I babbling about? He asks himself. *Concentrate on what you can see and understand!* He traverses the rest of the room with his laying on of hands. He touches the bedpost, the picture frame, the valet, and the dresser, lightly as a feather, as he had been doing for the past twenty-five years, as if to say, "Hello, I'm home," and to ask, "Are you OK? Do you need an adjustment?"

He is almost done. He flattens an aggravating crease in the bedspread. Everything is in order. He flushes from the familiar rush. *This is the next best thing to a hole-in-one. Of course, Mother will pull through. She can't possibly d—and leave all this . . .*

"Honey, dinner's ready," his wife calls from the foot of the stairs. Over an hour has passed since he arrived home.

His name is Samuel but only his mother calls him that. Everyone else calls him Sam. Because he loves his mother, he never tires of hearing others say, "Sam is his mother's son," words that go down like warm milk.

In the spring of 1972, when he was fifty and she was seventy-five, he went to Old Friend's Hospital on the north side of Chicago almost every day after work to visit her. He was a good son; he meant to be. She was dying and was ill a long time, into summer and the golfing season. During the season, Sam routinely played on the weekends and occasionally on weekdays after work. Sam loved the game of golf. Once, he made a hole-in-one on the fourth hole at their country club. For a man fixated on fabricating new symmetries between his thoughts and the world, a hole-in-one was an especially magical event. For a 1 3/4" diameter ball to travel over 175 yards and gracefully land inside a 4 1/8" cup in the ground was proof positive of truth, beauty, and order in the world. He lived for these perfect moments.

Sam is torn. How can he golf when his mother is in the hospital? His wife, Eleanor, lifts him out of this dilemma delicately, like a baby out of a high chair. Throughout the summer of 1972, every Thursday and Friday, they have the same after-dinner conversation.

"Go ahead," she advises, "Sam, go ahead and play a couple of holes. It will take your mind off it. What can you do? Come on. I'll play with you." She is decisive and confident. At the same time, she is patient with her husband. Sam makes good money, and she has grown accustomed to their country club lifestyle. Despite her periodic good-natured gibes, such as, "Sam is like a car someone else is driving," Eleanor believes her husband is a sweet, well-intentioned man.

Although deteriorating, Sam's mother hangs on into the fall of 1973, way past the doctor's predictions. Is it because of the Christian Scientist faith healer who has agreed to come to the hospital? (A nurse informs Sam of this.)

His mother's extended illness is hard on Sam. In order to get to Old Friend's hospital on the north side in time for visiting hours and then home to the southern suburbs at a reasonable hour, Sam has to leave work early. To avoid being seen in the elevator, he often uses the emergency exit and walks down thirty-five flights. Although a vice president, Sam constantly worries about losing his job. The worrying becomes part of the job. Over time, the worrying becomes job security.

"Are the girls attending to my antiques, especially my crystal?" she asked.

"Of course, Mother, and I've been checking on them," he replied. She was so certain about the way she wanted things, he knew she must be right. Every day, they grew more and more alike.

"Now, you shouldn't have come with the weather report the way it is, dear. Look out there—there's a terrible storm brewing."

After squeezing his mother's hand, Sam slumped into a corner chair. The hospital white emitted a blinding glare. He breathed in deeply to regain his equilibrium. The commanding smell of alcohol whipped around his face like a cat's tail. It pulled him back to the antiseptic potpourri of his childhood, of Spic and Span, Old English Lemon Oil, Murphy's Oil Soap, Wright's Silver Cream, Goddard's Copper Polish, and Windex. He remembered the whoosh of the woody, distilled air locked inside his mother's huge breakfront, how it dazzled him—the vapor from pampered possessions, the soothing scent of the inert.

"Samuel, come on, put on your coat, honey, it's time to go. It's starting to rain, just like I said," she faintly scolded him, stirring him from his daydream.

The rain turned to sleet on his way home on that bottomless, gray September day. The golf season will end early this year, he lamented.

"How was work?" his wasting mother asked weakly as he entered room 522 the following Monday. On her death bed, as when giving birth to him and almost dying, she offered whatever was left of her to see him through. "Fine, Mother," he lied. So distracted was he by her failing health that when she offered her hand, he stared at it as though it were a foreign object. It took all her strength to reach out to him, and she grazed his left hand before he knew what was happening.

"No don't!" he cried, surprising them both. "I'll be right back. My hands are dirty—I went to a scrap yard today," he lied and dashed to the men's room down the hall. When he returned cleansed, she had drifted off. He sat in a chair squarely facing the side of her bed. He looked reverent, like someone in an art gallery gazing at a Rembrandt.

Oh, if she only knew, if Mother only knew how work was! She wouldn't last a day there!

That day at work, Henry Sapir had made one of his inevitable visits. "Sam, what in the hell did you put in that financial report you armed Larry-Baby with? We've been trying to sell to Listner Iron and Metal for God knows how long! Congratulations!"

The decimation began immediately. *Oh my God, why does he have to lean on the leather divan?* Henry's malignant hand grabbed the shoulder of the couch. *First hit!* said Sam silently. Lysol or alcohol will ruin leather. Sam mentally marked the desecrated spots. *I should ask him to sit down. What financial officer do you know who doesn't ask THE BOSS to sit down?* He charged himself.

"We've tried to get in there for years, and we couldn't sell them an ounce of anything! Larry-Baby got a really good order—2,000 tons of number two bundles and 5,000 tons of number one busheling." Sam offered Henry a seat to minimize the damage, but Henry was in a roaming mood. He picked up a one-pound scrap-iron memento shaped like a crushed automobile and tossed it back and forth in his piggy hands.

Oh Lord, Sam said under his breath: *The Lord is my shepherd; I shall not. . .* Henry picked up Sam's lucky gold pen. *He maketh me to lie down in green pastures . . .* Sam's puppet mouth opened but no sound came out. Henry ignored this and picked up the picture of Sam's mother that Sam had just brought to the office that day. *Yea, tho I walk through the valley of the shadow of . . .*

"Sam, this is a really nice picture of your mother." Not waiting for a response, Henry said, "I want you to take over the . . . "

He leadeth me beside the still waters. He—You bastard, put her down, put her down! You are killing her, you son of a . . .

"Sam, Sam did you hear that? Are you OK? I just offered you the Ridge Farm account."

"Oh, sorry, Henry, I was lost in thoughts of . . . " Henry drummed his stubby, bitten-down fingernails ("booger" fingers, Sam dubbed them) on Sam's leather desktop. *He restoreth my soul . . .*

"For Christ's sa—!" Sam cried, surprising himself, when he saw that Henry was about to touch the Seth Thomas clock that his mother had given him.

"I beg your pardon?"

"Oh, excuse me," said Sam, jumping up, "I get so mad at myself for not taking better care of this clock—there's a smudge here," and he peered at the clock while delicately shooing Henry away. "Sorry, what did you say?"

"I asked you to put me on your calendar for lunch," Henry responded, a bit nonplussed. "This order calls for a little celebration. Choose when and where . . . " Henry held out his hand. Sam had to offer his hand. Like some trapped animals who tear themselves loose by self-amputating a snared limb, Sam imagined abandoning his infected hand, which no longer felt a part of him. Sam stood with a smile on his face while Henry's clasp made a deep impression on Sam's palm and unleashed a recurring scene in Sam's mind. Sam saw Henry reading *The Wall Street Journal* in his plush office behind his stately desk in his limousine-black, executive-size leather chair encircled by seven sizable but subordinate black leather chairs. Occasionally, when a corner of the *Journal* hung down, Henry Sapir's fingers, now linked to Sam's, were exposed in all their splendor—vigorously, vaingloriously, and enthusiastically picking his nose and then flicking it! "Thank you, thank you very much," Sam said as they shook hands. Henry remained clasped, lingering.

Will fear no evil . . . Henry finally let go and exited. Sam felt a gumminess on the inside of his fingers. *I will dwell in the house of the Lord for ever, I will dwell in the house of the Lord for ever . . . Repeating it again and again calmed him.*

Sam, though shell-shocked, went into emergency mode. With brisk decorum, he strode to the executive washroom, gingerly holding his hand out from his side as if it were a pooper-scooper.

He marched back to his office to assess the casualties. His photographic memory had registered all of Henry's contact points. They appeared like glow worms. He promptly proceeded to his reserves—several cans of Lysol, alcohol, and paper towels hidden under his desk and at other strategic points.

Upon opening his eyes, a dangling hand sprung into Sam's view. At first, Sam recoiled in his chair, but, realizing that the hand belonged to his mother, Sam leaned down and kissed it. *Gosh, I'm tired. Huh! If she only knew how work was.* "Mother, I'm going now," he gurgled, knowing that she was fast asleep.

Sam's mother, Sheila Weissman, died October 15, 1973, after a protracted fight with colon cancer. Dr. Edwin called Sam at the office. At least he wasn't on the golf course. "She's dead, she's dead," Sam announced almost accusatorily to Henry Sapir, who happened to be on hand. Why couldn't the son-of-a-bitch bastard keep his dirty little hands off her clock? Henry, in condolence, put his arm around Sam's shoulder. Sam hit bottom.

After his mother dies, Sam doesn't play golf for two calendar weeks. It is very late in the season anyway. Then, when the weather allows, he plays incognito at an out-of-the-way, little-known city course, finishing the year there. Eleanor continually reassures him that it is appropriate. After all, it is only half playing, not playing at their country club, Alyssum Fields.

As he approaches the eighteenth hole in late October during the last game of the season, Sam studies the cultivated fairway, its gleam of cut-glass kelly green. It soothes Sam to think about how his mother would appreciate it, nature at her finest. As he retrieves the ball from the cup, Sam cannot tell whether it is sweat or tears that anoint his silky cheeks.

Questions for Discussion

1. In what ways does this man's compulsion both aid and complicate his handling of the loss of his mother?
2. What are the current treatments for obsessive-compulsive disorder?
3. What would you do with or for the family of an obsessive- compulsive?

Prone to Panic

David Levine

If I had to choose the defining moment of my life, it would be a Sunday morning in May 1972, when I woke up afraid that I was dying. I was nineteen, and my life has not been the same since.

I was a junior at Johns Hopkins, spending the year at University College, which is one of the colleges that comprise the University of London. I had just returned from traveling through France, Italy, and Switzerland over spring break and was about to begin my final trimester of classes. I was looking forward to going to Greece for the summer. I never made it there.

I woke up that Sunday morning and felt an impending sense of doom. The feeling was very powerful, yet I was in no pain and was not disoriented. At first I thought I was dreaming, but the feeling that I was going to die did not go away. It became stronger and stronger. I stayed in bed, afraid to move, and called out to my French roommate, François, for help. His first reaction was that I was joking. When he saw I was not—he told me my face was ashen and that I was shaking—he said, "You must have had a nightmare. Come get out of bed, wash your face, and eat something." I followed his directions because I was unable to make any decisions for myself. We went for a long walk, and, gradually, I calmed down. I don't remember anything else about that day, except waiting for it to end. I hoped that a night of sleep would help me and I would wake up feeling normal again. But just like in the movie *Groundhog Day,* the next day was the same day. I woke up with that same sense of impending doom. I should add that I was not on any drugs, legal or illegal, nor suffering from any illness.

François had to teach on Monday. I had classes to attend. I was afraid to leave the apartment, but more afraid to be alone. So I went to school that morning, where I ran into a friend and told her how I was feeling. She looked at me with great concern and took me to the infirmary. The doctor examined me and, except for my racing heart rate, found nothing wrong.

I told her, "I'm scared I'm going to die," but she assured me that these feelings would go away soon. I went to see her a few days later because I felt no better, and she referred me to the school's psychiatrist. He said I was anxious and prescribed Valium to ease my nerves. He advised returning home to the United States as soon as school was over, ascribing my anxiety to being homesick.

François decided I needed to get out of the city. Driving was good therapy. When I felt anxious, I felt paralyzed. So as long as there was movement, I knew I was alive. But, the beauty of the English countryside was not a lasting tonic. I was always relieved to get back to the city, back home to familiar sights and sounds. This proved to be a pattern of behavior I would repeat for many years. Somehow I always felt safer being in my own house, whether it was my apartment in London, my parents' home in Long Island, or my apartment in Baltimore.

When I finally returned home to New York in June, my parents did not know what to do. They were puzzled by my feelings, disturbed by my attacks. Unable to believe that my problem was a mental illness, they sent me to their internist. I hated him. Without taking even a second to talk with me about my feelings, he nonchalantly informed me that sudden changes in behavior were often due to a brain tumor. Hardly a very comforting thought. He referred me to a neurologist, who found nothing wrong, and an endocrinologist, who gave me a glucose tolerance test. Hypoglycemia (low blood sugar) was a popular diagnosis in the 1970s, thought to be a cause of anxiety, but I didn't have it. My medical file was getting thicker and thicker, but doctors could find nothing wrong. Finally, by midsummer, my internist said I should see a psychiatrist—a big source of embarrassment for my parents. They warned me against telling my friends, my aunts and uncles—even my own sister.

According to the psychiatrist, taking Valium was a mistake. "By now you know the attacks, as bad as they are, do not kill you, even though you believe they will," he told me. "The more attacks you have, and the more you see that they won't kill you, the faster they will go away." He was dead wrong. In fact, life got worse without Valium. I had attacks daily, up to five in one day, and even less confidence than before. I would later learn that anxiety attacks are a throwback to our ancestors' "fight or flight" response. But an anxiety attack turns that power inward. Because I was not burning up the energy by running or fighting, it's no wonder that every attack left me exhausted to the core.

By some cruel twist, the attacks often came during those rare moments when I felt relaxed—when I was daydreaming, for instance, or taking a walk. The worst attacks struck at the end of dreamless naps. I woke up completely drenched, disoriented, my heart pounding. During an attack, which would last for minutes, sometimes an hour, I felt detached from myself, as if it were happening to someone else, not me. Objects looked strange, even unreal. I felt no sense of the past or future. I was totally in the moment, except instead of feeling one with the universe, I felt terribly alone and afraid.

Because the attacks were so devastating, I began to live in fear of losing control, of having the next attack. This is not unusual, it turns out. Many people become so paralyzed by this fear that they never leave the house, a condition known as agoraphobia. I have a friend whose mother has not left her home in twenty years.

Since I was living day to day that long, nightmarish summer, I didn't prepare wisely for my senior year at Hopkins. It wasn't until late August that I started to make housing arrangements. I belatedly called my two apartment mates from sophomore year, Jack Thayer and David Stevenson, but, not surprisingly, they had already made their own plans. I ended up rooming with two fellow juniors who needed a third person to split the rent.

It became obvious very quickly that the situation wasn't going to work out. Both of my roommates were frightened and puzzled by my behavior. I tended to stay in the apartment most of the time, giving them little time to themselves. I asked for their help when I had attacks. At first they were sympathetic, but after a while they got tired of it. Finally, after one particularly bad attack, they told me they could not cope with it anymore; I would have to move out at the end of the semester. I did not know what to do. I wanted to call my old friends and beg them to take me in, but I was afraid to let them know or see the new me. I felt disappointed, angry, abandoned.

I missed Jack and David—among the best friends I ever had and probably ever will have. We met as freshmen, when we were all living in Baker dormitory. Jack came from a prep school in Rhode Island, but his parents had scrimped to get him in school. David grew up in Lancaster, Pennsylvania. He liked to get into long conversations, usually trying to dominate the floor with his point of view. If I was a little to the left of David, Jack was more conservative, making for a nice balance. We got together each night and took turns getting Cokes and french fries from the snack bar to accompany our discussions on the meaning of life, the Vietnam War, and women.

Our close friendship continued into our sophomore year, when we shared an apartment on St. Paul Street. The tradition of taking turns continued each night at dinner, as one of us would cook a meal, the other had to clean up, and the third got the day off. Dinner was always at 6 p.m. sharp—the time for *Star Trek* reruns. The three of us bonded completely and lastingly, probably because we were going through so many major life events together— deciding on majors, or falling in love for the first time.

Jack felt abandoned when David and I decided to go abroad for our junior year. Even worse, his girlfriend dumped him that fall. He wrote me a letter describing his loneliness, telling how he stared down the quad, wondering where his best friends were when he needed them most.

Once I became ill, I understood how he felt. But I held back from telling Jack and David about my illness. Each had found their niche that senior year. They never called me, never invited me over. When we bumped into each other on campus, we talked for just a few minutes. Many years later, Jack told me he could see something was wrong, but since I never said anything, he didn't say anything either.

As angry as I was about being abandoned, a large part of the blame was mine. I was distant, simply too embarrassed to talk to them about the anxiety that gripped me—an embarrassment no doubt instilled in me by my parents. Many times I picked up the phone to call my old friends, but I hung up. Since the best experts in the world were baffled by my illness, what was I going to say? It took me twenty-five years to tell Jack my story. I never got a chance to tell David, and never will. He unexpectedly passed away this spring from a heart ailment. He was only forty-seven years old.

At Hopkins, my case was baffling to the staff of the "White House," the aptly named building that housed the social workers, psychologists, and psychiatrists who dealt with students who had mental and emotional problems. I became well-known there. It was frustrating for everyone because I did not respond to psychotherapy or to any of the drugs that were given to me. I was referred to a private psychiatrist, who saw me twice a week. A traditional psychotherapist, she tried to root out the underlying problems. But, despite long conversations in front of her fireplace, the attacks continued.

My life at Hopkins was reduced to seeing doctors and going to classes. I never stopped going to my classes, which, looking back, took a lot of courage. In fact, I threw myself into my work, and my grade point average was higher that year than any other. I enjoyed the subject matter but couldn't wait until each class was over so that I could go back to my apartment (where I was now living alone) and hide. Although I feared being alone, I feared having an attack in front of others more.

My tiny black-and-white TV set served as my entertainment and social life, as well as my connection to the world. My favorite night was Thursday, when I watched *Kung Fu, The Streets of San Francisco,* and *The Waltons.* (Yes, I hate to admit it, but I liked the series a lot. There was a family and the people were not alone.)

Though I had studied literature during my year in England, I was determined to try something new when I returned. So I signed up for a course in playwriting—Problem Drama. For my first assignment, I wrote a comedy about a man bringing his boss home for dinner. To my amazement, when the class read the play out loud, people laughed, including me. The play was one of five chosen to be presented before a combined student and alumni audience. Elliott Coleman, the founder of The Writing Seminars was in the audience, and he invited me to apply to their graduate program, a great honor.

Writing became a salvation. After all, writers are supposed to write alone. None of the students in my playwriting classes were people I knew from before, so they had no preconceived notions about me, nothing to measure me against. I was the mysterious loner, the writer who never went out for drinks after class or stayed for a cast party. I remember one woman who found this intriguing at first, but she later divulged that, although others in the class admired my dedication to writing, they considered me aloof. I don't remember what I said in response, but I knew I was not aloof. I was afraid. If you can imagine holding your breath for as long as you can, and then being asked to hold it in longer, that's how I felt. I held my anxiety in as long as I could. When class was over, I had to get away and breathe.

By the late 1970s, researchers had seen enough cases like mine to realize that they were dealing with an illness that did not fit the pattern of traditional anxiety. People had attacks "out of the blue," unrelated to stresses in their lives, to the effects of a drug, or to another medical condition. And the attacks could not be treated through traditional medicines for anxiety or talking therapy. They called this new illness panic disorder. However, neither I nor my psychiatrist knew about this. The results of the studies took years to be published.

After finishing up my master's at Hopkins I went back home to Long Island to live with my parents. I stumbled into a career in public relations, working for the county's department of drug and alcohol addiction. Many of the people I worked with were ex-addicts, ex-alcoholics. I felt right at home, another impaired person.

Then in 1977, five years after my first attack, a strange thing happened. The severity of my attacks dramatically declined. I was able to go into New York City, to begin dating again, to start enjoying life a little more. I rediscovered a sense of play. When your every thought is of dying, you lose your sense of humor and enjoyment over little things—the pleasures of having an ice cream cone, enjoying a sunny day, or reading a book.

This is not to say, however, that I was completely back to being my old self—the David Levine of my teenage years who loved tennis, rock music, politics, and travel. The David Levine who had no trouble making friends or attracting girlfriends. Though my severe attacks disappeared, I continued to have minor attacks after napping. I became very vigilant, ever waiting for the first signs of anxiety that would signal the return of my illness.

In December 1981, I went on a job interview in Brooklyn. I was standing on an open-air subway platform when the heavens opened up, soaking me to the core. I jumped on the first train that came along and got off at a central station. There was hardly anyone around, but I managed to find a woman who could give me directions back to the city. Her name was Janet. Four months later, in April, we got engaged.

In June, my illness returned with a vengeance. My attacks continued and got worse. Over the years, I had learned to hide the effects of my attacks quite well, so for a long time Janet did not know how bad they were. By coincidence, Janet's brother was a psychiatrist studying panic disorder, and he was looking at the effects of beta-blockers (which actors often use to temper performance anxiety) on panic attacks. I spoke to him about what was happening to me. He was the first medical specialist to give a name to my illness and he showed me a book listing all its symptoms—the very same symptoms I'd been experiencing all these years: fear of dying, shortness of breath, dizziness, etc. Best yet, he told me there were ways to treat panic disorder. He referred me to a colleague, who confirmed the diagnosis and began treating me.

I still see the same psychiatrist today. In doing my research for this story, I asked him if getting engaged had triggered the return of my attacks back in 1982. His answer: No. He pointed out that during those years my attacks disappeared, my parents divorced, and I changed jobs, apartments, and girlfriends. The basic answer is that the attacks would have come back anyway.

Having an undiagnosed illness is very frustrating. I have worked at a cancer organization and have interviewed many cancer patients for stories. I was very surprised to learn that they felt better once they had a diagnosis, even if it was cancer. The uncertainty is more frightening to them than being told they were going to die.

I felt a similar sense of relief when my future brother-in-law diagnosed me. But I was also very angry. All those tests, doctors, drug treatments, and therapy I had endured over the years had been a waste of time. The drugs given to me did not work because they were the wrong drugs. Today, doctors know that panic disorder is most effectively treated with antidepressants, such as Tofranil and Prozac. Although antidepressants like Prozac and Zoloft are relatively new, tricylic antidepressants, such as Tofranil, and MAO inhibitors, such as Nardil, were used in treating depression as far back as 1972.

There is no question that my illness has affected my marriage. Panic attacks are not cured by medicine or therapy, only controlled. Drugs have side effects; the worst for me is insomnia, and I often wind up using my weekends to catch up on sleep. The drug I take, Nardil, has significant food restrictions; for example, I cannot eat cheese or have red wine or chocolate. If I unknowingly eat a food that has been marinated, smoked, or dried, I run the risk of sending my blood pressure to dangerously high levels. Over the years I've tried going off my medication and experimenting with other drugs, but no other drug has worked for me.

I worry, too, about my children, Rachel, who is fourteen, and Ben, who is eleven. When I see them get worried about something or seem a little down, I worry that I have passed on genes that will cause them trouble in the future.

Janet and I went for counseling to deal with many of the issues surrounding my illness, and I have made progress in some areas. I've started flying again, for instance—an activity I had given up for life, or so I thought, after my return flight from London in 1972. I now fly all over the United States and the world, alone, with the whole family, and on separate trips with my children.

My hope is that by writing with candor about my own experience, I can help dispel some of the stigma that continues to cling stubbornly to mental illness. To those who have suffered, or are suffering, mental illness, please realize that you are not alone.

One of my friends at Hopkins, who called me when David became ill, confided in me about the struggles he has had with mental illness as an adult. He said I must have had tremendous courage and strength to deal with it at such a young age. In fact, many mental illnesses strike young people when they are college age. Most cases of panic disorder begin in young adulthood, as do depression, obsessive-compulsive disorder, schizophrenia, and manic depression. To develop mental illness in college—without the social support of family and friends—is very difficult.

My generation was brought up to think that we can solve all our problems (and the world's) without help. But that is not reality. You cannot wish a panic attack away, and you cannot order a depressed person to cheer up. I know, I've been there. But, I feel that I am a lucky man because I survived, and I'm still here. There are many who are not.

Postscript

Although I've traveled to France several times over the past few years, I never returned to London until this past June. Finally, the time felt right to return alone and face my personal demons. If there was a key to the puzzle of my illness, I thought, it might lie in London.

I spent several hours strolling around the grounds of University College, and many memories did come rushing back. But they were good ones. I was happy to see my old school. I was happy to be back in London. Being there did not summon up the terrible memories I had feared.

The key to the puzzle was not in London. In fact, there is no key to the puzzle. The current thinking is that I was genetically programmed to have panic disorder on that May morning in 1972. A morning I just happened to be waking up in London.

Questions for Discussion

1. Describe the ways the narrator's panic attacks affected his life and functioning.
2. How would you advise the spouse of a person suffering from panic attacks?
3. Would you advise a person with panic attacks to tell his or her employer? What would you advise him or her to say and when?
4. What are the current treatments for panic disorder?

Going to Pieces

Kathleen Gerard

In the dream, there's always a test.
Fill in the blanks:

> 1. People are lonely because they build walls instead of _____.
> 2. London _____ is falling down, falling down.
> 3. *The* _____ *on the River Kwai* is only a movie.
> 4. To burn one's _____ (behind one).
> 5. _____ is merely a card game.
> Extra Credit Question—Finish the phrase:
>> Love many, trust few, learn to paddle your own _____.

I rack my brain: Nothing. Vacant. Void.
Blank lines: Tedious. Flat.
Empty spaces.
Simple questions. One-word answers.
Answers that evade.
And yet, it's all within me. Within my grasp. In the forefront of my mind. On the tip of my tongue. But from thought to action is a leap—a chasm I can't seem to cross.

George Washington, Tappan Zee. Goethals. Brooklyn. Verrazano-Narrows. Bayonne. Cross Bay Veterans Memorial. Queensboro. Willis Avenue. Alexander Hamilton. Macombs Dam. Henry Hudson. Bronx-Whitestone. Throgs Neck. Triborough. Pulaski. Kosciuszko. Manhattan. Marine Parkway. Williamsburg. Outerbridge Crossing.

Sweaty palms. Sweaty armpits. Sweaty brow. Dizziness. Vertigo. A sinking feeling. Nausea. Vomiting. Loss of bladder control. Palpitations. Perspiration. Tachycardia. Arrhythmia. Hyperventilation. Diarrhea attack. Panic attack. Heart attack. Death.

These are only some of the reasons why I've been going three times a week to see Dr. Mendham for the past year. He's a phobia specialist. He scares me.

There's no plausible explanation for what I feel about bridges—or Dr. Mendham, for that matter. In my sixty-two years, I have never really had a traumatic experience on a bridge. I have never had an accident, fallen, tripped, or been stranded on, or rescued from, a bridge. Occasionally, I have had suicidal thoughts—but always involving unsensational things like pills, sharp objects, and bristling rope. I have wanted to throw Dr. Mendham off a bridge several times over the course of the past year. But the worst that ever happened to me was getting stuck in a traffic jam—for seven hours—on the Tappan Zee Bridge a year and a half ago. A barge smashed into the massive steel. Poor barge, poor me. The saddest part of the whole ordeal was not that I missed an important meeting with a tax client, blew a big money-making account, was yelled at by my boss, or that I was ultimately forced into an early retirement. No. The most notable thing to come out of that experience was that I learned that there are no bathrooms on bridges. I was forced to urinate into a plastic bag in the backseat of my car.

"So, where do you think my fear of bridges comes from, and why is it getting worse?" I asked Dr. Mendham at our first session over a year ago.

He answered, "Maury. Where does cancer come from and why does it get worse?"

$$* \quad * \quad *$$

My wife, Gloria, calls in to me as I'm toweling off in the bathroom on Monday morning. She says, "Honey. Don't forget—Stephie's place is opening this Saturday night . . ."

I swallow hard.

". . . The poor thing," Gloria goes on to say. "I think she's getting herself all keyed up."

"Well, it's a big commitment," I tell her, "but if anyone is going to be a success, it's our little girl."

"Can you believe that she's finally going to be a restauranteur?" she says, shaking her head, reminiscing. "There she was, the kid who used to burn things on the stove and set off the smoke alarms in home ec, and now she's at the helm of her very own kitchen? Talk about coming a long way—"

"—Well, I sure hope she took out a good fire insurance policy," I say to Gloria.

She chuckles. "I guess all that money we invested in her education is finally paying off."

"Yes. Yes. Yes, indeed," I say, as I sprinkle on some powder.

"So, what time do you think we'll need to get on the road Saturday night, Maury?"

"Where are we going again?" I ask.

"Maury!" My wife gasps. Her eyes are wide on me. "You're so wrapped up in yourself lately!" Then, she looks at me sideways. She studies me in a doubtful, worried way. She knows that I really haven't a clue. "We're going to Stephie's restaurant opening in Tarrytown Saturday night. I just told you. Remember?"

Then, it hits me. My skin burns, hot and flushed. I can't speak. Tarrytown. We'll have to cross the Tappan Zee Bridge to get there. And the Tappan Zee is a long bridge, a narrow expanse—one that sweeps and curves and hovers close to the Hudson River for almost three miles. Breathe, breathe, breathe. I tell myself. Then, I do the math. It's only Monday. You've got six whole days, 144 hours, 8,640 minutes and counting . . . I begin to hyperventilate. Relax . . . Breathe . . . But it may take as long as five minutes to get across that bridge . . .

"I know you don't like to talk about it, and I don't want to pry, but how are your sessions coming with Dr. Mendham?" Gloria asks.

"Oh. Okay, I guess. We're still in the early stages."

"The early stages? You've been with that shrink for over a year, Maury—"

"—I know. But these things take time," I tell her.

"Well, perhaps this trip up to Stephie's will be a good gauge to see how you're progressing . . . " She treads lightly, cautiously, as if on eggshells.

"W-well," I stutter. "I still would like it if you'd drive."

"Of course. Of course, I'll drive honey," my wife says. I look at her loving smile. She slips her hands around my spare tire and presses her warm, soft lips against my bare chest. She kisses me. I am unable to lift my arms to hug her back. They feel tired, burdened, heavy with fear. My heart is beating so hard, I wonder if it will leap out of my chest—maybe it will hit Gloria in the head, knock her out, give her a minor concussion, or at least a killer headache. Then maybe we won't have to go anywhere Saturday night.

* * *

Dr. Mendham tries to calm me when I lose my cool with him at my last session of the week on Friday. "Trying to unravel the human psyche is a process, Maury. And phobias are irrational, excessive, and persistent—"

"—And so am I, Doc. So what does that mean?"

"Maury," Dr. Mendham says. His tone grows quieter while mine grows more intense. "Are you practicing the biofeedback techniques and your breathing exercises?"

"Yes. Yes. But once I'm on that bridge Saturday night, forget it. I'm not gonna be able to find the center of calm. I might even forget how to breathe . . . "

I look across the desk at Dr. Mendham. For a moment, I swear I see a twinkle in his eye and the corners of his mouth curling upward. He has an amused look on his face—dollar signs glowing in his eyeglasses. I hate that I'm paying him $150.00 an hour to be amused by me.

"And what about the rubber band therapy?" Dr. Mendham asks. "Are you putting them on your wrists and snapping them when you feel the phobic fears rise up inside you?"

"Those rubber bands almost cut off my circulation last time," I tell him. I undo the cuff of my starched white shirt and show him the scars—long, deep slashes and gashes on my wrists. "I was so focused on plucking and twanging them, I drew blood."

"Next time," Dr. Mendham says, "try putting them over the cuff of your shirt. Not against the bare skin, Maury."

I inhale deeply.

"So, how about we take this step by step and look at this calmly," Dr. Mendham says. "Fact one—Gloria is going to drive Saturday night. Correct?"

I exhale. "Of course. She always drives when we go over a bridge."

"Good," Dr. Mendham says, as steady and even keeled as a flat line. "And this time everything will be fine, Maury. Because you will tell yourself it will be fine. Right?"

I nod as my answer.

"Now, let's practice visualizing you going over that bridge and feeling calm . . . ," Dr. Mendham says, bringing his voice down nearly to an inaudible whisper. "Let's take the three steps: You'll concentrate. You'll breathe deeply. And you'll focus on a positive image . . . "

I look at Dr. Mendham. I do the drill.

". . . You see, Maury—you'll cross that bridge when you come to it."

"Great," I yell, as I sit bolt upright in my chair. "I'm paying you the big money so you can spit out clichés?"

Dr. Mendham peels off his eyeglasses. He says, "Maury, you know that we've discussed that anger is a barrier to healing—"

"Oh, cut the crap. You'd be angry, too, if a phobia was overtaking your life, your job, and your relationships," I bark at him, rising to my feet. "I wanna know the bottom line, Doc. What you are gonna do to help me gain control so I can get on with my life?"

"What do you think I should do to help you?"

"Goddamnit!" I say, flailing my arms with fierce determination as I point to the wall of diplomas, commendations, and awards hanging behind his desk. "You're a trained professional. Why can't you offer me a solution to this problem?"

"Living is the only creative solution I can offer," Dr. Mendham says, as he whips out his prescription pad and lifts the cap from his fountain pen. "I don't like to resort to medication, but I'm writing you a prescription for a tranquilizer—Xanax. Take two before you leave Saturday night . . . "

Dr. Mendham reaches across his desk and hands me the slip of paper.

* * *

I am on the elevator headed for the lobby when I realize that I have left my raincoat on the couch in Dr. Mendham's office. I hit the button for his floor and up, up, and away I go again.

As I step back inside his office, I see a half-empty glass of water and a large, open bottle of Xanax on Dr. Mendham's desk. Then I hear the sound of whistling. It is coming from Dr. Mendham's bathroom. It's echoing out to me. After a few bars, I recognize the song. Simon and Garfunkel. I sing the words in my head. "When you're weary / feeling small / when tears are in your eyes / I'll dry them all. . . . Like a bridge over troubled waters."

If I were a contestant on the game show *Name That Tune,* I would win the big money, I think to myself, as I reach for my raincoat. But instead, I'm paying the big money. I'm paying Dr. Mendham the big money—and he's humming tunes about my phobia? I wring my raincoat between my hands like a sponge, one I'd like to rip into pieces. It's big money I don't have because I'm living on a fixed income because I'm retired. And I didn't even want to retire. They forced me out . . .

On my way home, I stop at the drugstore. I think I will need that prescription for Xanax before tomorrow night.

* * *

In the dream, I am sitting next to Dr. Mendham. It is dark. It is night. We are sipping cocktails at a table in the middle of the south side of the Tappan Zee Bridge. He is popping a few Xanax, eating them like candy. The traffic is zooming by us. I feel no fear.

Dr. Mendham hands me that test—that same test again—and a pencil.

This time, I answer questions one through five easily. But I keep drawing a blank on that last one.

Love many, trust few, learn to paddle your own _____ .

And then Dr. Mendham says, "I'm sorry, Maury. Time's up."

I am flustered. Out of breath. My palms are moist. Perspiration beads up on my brow. I'm a perfectionist. An overachiever. I will cry if all the blanks on that test paper are not filled in. I won't be able to drive home. I won't sleep for a week. I will pace the kitchen at dawn and eat a pint of rum raisin ice cream straight out of the carton for breakfast. I will tuck the evidence into my briefcase before my wife even wakes up. Like a criminal, I will look over my shoulder as I dispose of the flattened cardboard ice cream container in the trash in the men's room of my office . . . But then I remember. I don't even go to the office anymore. I'm retired. And I didn't even want to retire. They forced me out . . .

It is then that my thoughts are suddenly distracted. I look up from the test paper and stare out at the water. I see it. I see it clearly. I see a canoe on the water. I see a man in a sports jacket with a wrapped package on his lap. He is paddling that canoe across the Hudson River, over to the New York-Westchester side.

Ah-ha! Canoe. Canoe is the extra credit answer.

Dr. Mendham reaches for my test, but I yank it from his grasp. I quickly press the pencil down on the paper to scribble the answer, but I push too hard. The lead snaps.

Dr. Mendham stares at me blankly.

"How does this make you feel, Maury?" he asks, peeling off his eyeglasses and looking at me sideways. (I hate it when he does that.)

"Frustrated," I say. "But I think all I need is another pencil with a point, so I can finish this test and get on with my life . . ."

Dr. Mendham looks at me amused. "Why does there have to be a point, Maury?"

* * *

It is Saturday. I am dressed and ready to leave. I am holding a wrapped package in my hands. It is a gift I intend to give to my daughter to celebrate the opening of her restaurant. Her restaurant up in Tarrytown. The one on the other side of that creature—the Tappan Zee Bridge.

"I'm sorry, Gloria. I wanna go, but I can't go. I'm just not capable," I tell her.

"Did you take the Xanax?"

"Yes, I took *three*. But I don't feel any different."

"Well, give it time to kick in and don't anticipate, Maury. By the time we hit the bridge, it may start working."

"No," I shout, my hands balling into fists, my pulse frenetic, unsteady. "We're not going. I can't go." I am pacing the floor of the foyer—back and forth and forth and back—as if trapped in a small, locked cage.

Gloria stands at the front door with her coat on. "I can't live like this, Maury. Tonight is the most important night of our daughter's life. She's worked years for this. We need to be there for her—"

"—I'm doing the best I can," I shout. "Why can't anyone understand that?"

"Your world is shrinking, Maury. It keeps getting smaller and smaller. Tonight is Stephie's big night. And I'm going—with or without you—"

"—I just told you, Gloria. I just can't go."

"You *can't* or you *won't*?"

"Why are you badgering me?"

"Why can't you move beyond this, Maury? Do you want to spend another year nurturing your neurosis?"

"What I'm doing," I tell her, through clenched teeth, "is trying to overcome my fears."

"No, Maury. You've made your phobia your passion, your life's work. Don't you see? It's consuming you—"

"—Gloria, how can you be so insensitive? How can you speak to me this way?"

"Because, maybe this is the way you need to be spoken to," she says, as she buttons her coat and heads out the front door.

I feel helpless like a frustrated child who can't get his way. "But we're a team," I remind her as she gets into the car.

"No, Maury. You're a team of one." I watch as Gloria's eyes moisten. She slips the key in the ignition and starts the car. "Don't you see, Maury? You've become an island . . . "

I am still holding the wrapped package, a gift I long to give to my daughter. "Can't you at least give this to Stephie?" I say, thrusting the package through the window toward Gloria. But she begins to back the car out of the driveway.

"If you want her to have it, then you'll have to give it to her yourself," she says, as she throws the car in drive and imposes a distance between us.

My mouth falls open. I can only stand idly by, watching the rear, red taillights of the car. Thick, red bars. Minus signs. Bright red slits. Blank lines. I stand there alone, watching them fade, growing smaller and smaller, more narrow and dim. Distant. They are dwindling from my sight—moving away from me—until they disappear.

*   *   *

Thirty minutes and three more Xanax later, I feel my sweaty hands gripping the steering wheel. My arms outstretched. White knuckles. My deodorant's working. I am searching for my center of calm. I am breathing—Lamaze breathing. I have six rubber bands around each cuff of my sports jacket. I am plucking away. Twanging my heart out. I am focused on hurting myself. Pretty soon, I am popping another Xanax. Five minutes later, another . . .

I see the sign: Last Exit Before the Tappan Zee Bridge.

I do not take it. Yet, the closer I get, the more the feelings begin to rise up inside me.

Sweaty palms. Sweaty armpits. Sweaty brow. Dizziness. Vertigo. A sinking feeling. Nausea. Vomiting. Loss of bladder control. Palpitations. Perspiration. Tachycardia. Arrhythmia. Hyperventilation. Diarrhea attack. Panic attack. Heart attack. Death.

But now, I am on the bridge. I can hear the car tires drumming over the expansion joints. *Thump! . . . Thump! . . . Thump!* I am on the inside track. I am hugging the divider. I am not crashing. I am doing it. I am on my way. I am cruising along. I can see the water. I am under all those steel girders. I am halfway there. I can see the green lights flashing. Signals. Toll booths at the other end of the expanse. I have almost made it. *Put that in your pipe and smoke it, Mendham.* I'm doing it. *Wheeee!* Look at me.

I breathe in.

I reach in my pocket, pull out a couple dollar bills. I am back on concrete land.

I exhale.

And just as I go to slow down at the toll booth approach, it happens. I misjudge the distance. The space between us. I rear-end the car in front of me.

I slam my foot on the brake. Too late. I stop the car. I try to get out, but it's an effort to hoist myself up. Once I'm on my feet, I feel woozy and dizzy, dopey and drugged. Yet, happy—for a change. Without a care in the world.

"What the hell's the matter with you?" an older woman says, as she inspects the damage to the bumper of her car.

I don't know if it's my elation from crossing the bridge or the overdosage of Xanax, but I don't see a thing.

"My husband's gonna kill me when he sees this," she says, pointing to what looks like a line as thin as a spider's web. "This is a brand-new car, you know." I look at her squarely. I see dollar signs in her eyes.

"I understand," I tell her. I feel distant and separate, apart from life. I open my wallet and pull out seven twenty-dollar bills and a ten. "Here's $150.00. It's all I've got," I tell her. "Take it and let's call it even. I'm supposed to be someplace."

I don't have to force her.

On her way back to her car, she turns to me. I can see in her face, she appears amused. She holds up her own arm, points to her wrist and asks, "What's the deal with all those rubber bands, anyway?"

I glance down at the cuff of my sports jacket. "Oh, these?" I call out to her, raising my arm and taking a few stray plucks and twangs. "They're holding me together."

She shrugs her shoulders and shakes her head. I can see she is laughing.

And as I get back in my car, I, too, begin to laugh. I pay the toll. I can't stop laughing. I'm on Route 9. I am hysterical laughing.

I don't stop laughing until I get to Stephie's restaurant in Tarrytown.

As I walk in and see my daughter in her apron, I hand her my wrapped present. A gag gift. A smoke alarm. She is amused. She takes one look at it and then at me. She smiles. And as she puts her arms around me and hugs me tight, I can't remember the last time that I held her, my little girl. I never want to let go. And later, as I lift my glass of champagne, to toast to her accomplishment and wish her success, I can tell she is as proud of me as I am of her.

And then, I look to my wife, Gloria. Her eyes are beaming. Her face is glowing, radiant, vibrant, and alive. She is so surprised and pleased to see me. And as we gaze at our daughter and then at each other, my empty heart fills with relief and love and life again. It wells up until it's overflowing. And I know that she loves me—that my Gloria still loves me—even more now that I have come this far, traveled all this distance, and bridged the gap between us.

And then, one hour, two glasses of champagne, and a total of eight Xanax later, I finally collapse—right onto the bathroom floor of my daughter's new restaurant.

* * *

And in the dream, I am standing in the middle of the Tappan Zee Bridge at dawn. Suspended. Confident. Quiet. Calm.

Dr. Mendham meets me halfway.

Fearless. Unafraid. I rip that test paper into pieces, and I throw them up into the brightening sky like a spray of confetti.

I look Dr. Mendham in the eye. And as I hand him his pink slip, he peels off his eyeglasses and glances at me sideways. "How does that make you feel, Maury?" he asks.

And, this time, I wear the amused look on my face as I tell him, "Sometimes you have to stop searching for answers."

Questions for Discussion

1. What treatments, other than the ones mentioned, are used for phobia sufferers?
2. Discuss the importance of incentives in overcoming phobia and the reasons why incentives sometimes do and sometimes don't work in cases such as this.

Through the Woods, Darkly

Mary Hanson Carter

It's hot. Hot and humid, completely still. Mosquitoes whining unbearably, infiltrating the netting along with the predawn dark. I wake up, notice for the tenth time that I'm wallowing in a puddle of my own sweat, try to go back to sleep.

"They're coming in."

"Who?"

"The patrol. They made contact. They're coming back in."

"Are they all right?"

"Yeah, they're OK."

"You are, too. The war is over."

"Oh, OK."

We hadn't done much camping together yet. While every spare minute of my life between 1969 and 1984 had been spent in the woods, he hadn't done so much as go for a walk in the park since deer season of 1969, the year he got out of the Marine Corps.

Fifteen years. Before that, as a kid, he'd run wild in the fields and wooded ravines near his home in Wisconsin. He's shown me those places—the culvert where he slipped off the edge running for cover in a game of hide-and-seek and knocked himself out; the highway embankment where they'd ambush unsuspecting motorists with rocks and gravel, then melt into the underbrush; the site of the now-demolished one-room schoolhouse where he began kindergarten. But after 'Nam, deer hunting with his uncle, walking the yellow woods of northern Wisconsin with a thirty-ought-six, looking for a sign—some recreational killer sends a stray round cracking past his head, and in one fluid movement, a beautiful testament to his training, he lets off the safety, slams the bolt home, and returns fire. Back in North America, he unloads, walks out to his car, puts the rifle in the trunk. There will be no more hunting today, nor any day, nor walks down roads in yellow woods. One year, 1967, has made all the difference.

When we first started going to the woods together, he'd hold my binoculars and look out over the landscape, telling me how the next ridge would look lit up by napalm, how the F-4s would look roaring down the valley like huge birds shooting fire from their bellies. Why is he trashing my landscape? I'd wonder. After a while—a long while—I realized binoculars mean one thing to a birdwatcher, another to a forward observer. It's another language—the meaning of mosquitoes, binoculars, getting lost.

A week of fishing from a canoe taught me something more about that vocabulary. First of all, we had to "get there" ASAP. When I pointed out, in midportage, that we were already "there," the veins bulged in his forehead as he grabbed the fishing tackle from my hands and raced ahead. "Stuck for a week in the middle of nowhere with this asshole," I thought, fighting tears.

Looking for the next portage was a nightmare. The shoreline was tricky, with strange perspectives, the map hard to translate. I'd have been happy to stop early and go on the next day, but something about not knowing where he was—somewhere on Lake Insula wasn't a sufficient account of our position—drove him to a rage. It was years before we figured out why getting a bit lost in the woods, or even in the middle of Kansas, was a minor inconvenience to me, a looming catastrophe to him.

How do you learn from your mistakes when mistakes are fatal? When is a walk in the woods not a walk in the woods? The Vietnam campus is a school of hard knocks, a claustrophobic green classroom where to err is to die, or worse, to err is to live forever with the memory of your mistake. After ten months in-country, after a monthlong siege, after an ambush by overwhelming numbers of North Vietnamese Army regulars, he gets a week's R&R. Ah, the choices, the ignorant choices that make us who we are: he was scheduled to go to Bangkok, alone, but at the last minute his girl-wife and the baby son he'd never seen arranged to meet him in Hawaii instead.

He's walking in the woods, in the dark before dawn, counting off the paces to the spot where he's to call in a preset fire mission, when his mind takes him back to Hawaii, to soft nights in a soft bed with the wife of his bosom, thoughts of that had kept him sane through the mosquito-bitten nights on listening post and the rat-ridden nights in a muddy hole at Con Thien. He's there with her, with the baby, thinking of the future and of how the hell to stay alive long enough to see them again, when he realizes he's lost count of his steps, has been walking—for how long?—without knowing where he is. Heart beating now with fear and self-reproof, he stops in the dark to get his bearings. By the time he's reoriented, the lieutenant—the only one he's ever had who gave a shit about his guys—decides the fire mission must have been called off and starts repositioning his people for the ambush. By the time he realizes his error, the North Vietnamese, their numbers and organization unscathed by the delayed mortar attack, catch them in the open and the lieutenant dies. He replays that morning countless times, lying awake in hot nights, cold nights, in beds of various descriptions, lying next to four different wives of his bosom, wondering, trying to make it turn out another way, trying to learn from this mistake, lost in a wood of error and remorse. It's always darkest before it gets darker.

* * *

It is 1991, and I sit in the Marine Corps Archives at the Washington Navy Yard, reading the command chronology, looking for anything that would suggest the fury of a ground attack, the terror of being surrounded and cut off, but there is nothing especially evocative about the account I've just read. What the hell is it like to wake up and realize the "little guys" aren't Out There anymore—they're *In Here,* inside the perimeter, in some places they're in guys' foxholes, fighting hand to hand? I find a summary, written in the tranquillity of hindsight:

> During period 9-21 May the units at CON THIEN . . . began receiving artillery fire daily from the north and northeast direction. . . . Resupply by helicopters . . . artillery and mortar fire so heavy the re-supply had to be effected by aerial delivery. Engineer work on the clearing around CON THIEN was slowed considerably due to harassing enemy artillery and mortar fire. The frequency of artillery fire increased almost daily through 17 May.

A fuzzy black-and-white photograph comes to mind, one of his last from Con Thien before his film ran out. A plane flying low, tail to the camera, specks hanging from parachutes falling out of its belly. It was history being made: the first aerial resupply of marines of the Vietnam war.

What does it mean to be resupplied by airdrop?

It means the engineers can't keep the road open because they keep getting killed, so trucks can't get in. It means the rockets are flying so thick in the landing zones that choppers can't land. It means you can't medevac the wounded, so the dead pile up, bloat, and stink in the morning heat: 105 degrees by noon, then a few hours of downpour. If it gets much worse, your unit will run out of supplies. Replacements won't make it in. It'll be a war of attrition, as they used to say, delicately, in the Pentagon, and you'll do the attritting.

The language of helicopters is the indelicate language of fear. You use them for air assaults, watching the tracers as they shoot up at you, trying to take you out; you watch the door gunner do his mad dance to the tat-tat-tat of the machine gun as he clears the landing zone. You use them to evacuate the wounded, to carry away piles of dead guys like some huge motorized vulture. Even when a chopper means you're going home, your fear isn't over, you're afraid of dying just as you lift off because the landing zone is hot, no one but the dead and wounded have left in days, and when they finally start taking live guys, the panicked marines make a mad dash for the bird, leave you feeling ashamed to be a marine even if you weren't one of the panicky ones. It's small consolation that other guys have been on choppers so swamped by terrified South Vietnamese troops that the crew chief had to shoot them to lighten the load. Choppers are the way in and the way out, the way up and the way down, lunatic darning needles stitching the frayed interface between life and death. You may love them or hate them, but you always fear them.

DATE 13 MAY 1967

TO: NINTH MARINES

CONFIDENTIAL

ANTI-AIR: 121655H – RE-SUPPLY HELICOPTER HIT IN AIR BY SUSPECTED LARGE CALIBER WEAPON. HELICOPTER CRASHED IN VILLAGE AT YD16694. 2 FR WIA. ¼ CP (FWD) PERSONNEL SEARCHED WRECKAGE APPROX 130940H AND FOUND 2 BODIES.

He and his buddy Willie help unload that chopper, rockets exploding all around. As the bird lifts off, they run for cover in a nearby amtrack. Guys are inside, yelling for them to hurry. The chopper gains altitude, swings up and to his right, then flies ahead of him and behind the amtrack. Then a rocket explodes right below it and the bird, a C-34, turns end over end, gushing fire. The pilot and the gunner are surely dead. As he dives into the amtrack he can see the chopper come full circle, go down in a final burst of flame as the ramp closes behind him. Then, just seconds later, comes a pounding on the ramp— "Let me in! Let me in!" It's the crew chief, thrown free but horribly burned by the explosion. The whole left side of his face is raw meat. Somehow they get a battle dressing on him. They never know if he lives or dies.

* * *

I wonder, sometimes, what it must be like to get shot at. When a car engine backfired and he jumped, or when a helicopter flew over the house and his pupils flared wide with the 1,000-yard stare of a man seeing a ghost, I'd ask myself, what's it like to have rounds from an AK-47 cracking around you?

A sniper ambushes them as they climb a ridge through some trees. The best cover he can find is in the open, next to his radio operator. The AK-47 is on full auto, and the sniper squeezing the trigger sends a spray of bullets in his direction—they always shoot at the guy next to the radio operator. He can see the clouds of dirt kicked up by the impacting rounds, see the path they make straight for his legs as he lies on his back by the log. "This is gonna hurt a lot," he thinks dispassionately, watching slow-motion jets of dirt fly around and between his legs.

Nothing. The guy missed.

He watches as a machine gunner, trapped in the open field of fire twenty feet away, plays dead, his M-60 lying nearby. The lieutenant asks the man if he can get to it, and, knowing how desperately they need the firepower, the gunner starts creeping toward it, lays his hand on the weapon as the sniper draws a bead on him. The bullet goes in clean from the back of his head and comes out in a spray of blood and brains. The gunner, prostrate in the killing zone with the retrieved M-60 in hand, rears up once on all fours, then collapses, the nerves in the limbs firing automatically, without meaning, the brain gone.

Watching, feeling like an automaton himself, he thinks, "I need a cigarette," and sleepwalks from his scrape in the dirt to bum a smoke from somebody fifteen feet away. He doesn't notice the sniper's next bullet as it misses him. Someone is yelling "Get down!" as he leisurely returns to his view of the dead gunner.

"Didn't you hear him shooting at you?" somebody is saying.

"No. I just wanted a smoke."

The mind is its own place. One minute you're watching the front of a guy's head blow out, then—snap!—your whole being is focused on getting a cigarette. You can't do a thing about the final, out-of-reach, slow-motion paroxysms of a nameless machine gunner, but a cigarette—now *that's* manageable. At least you can touch it, feel its effects, make sure you're not dead. Or years later you can be standing by the sink, talking to your wife, when in the air over her right shoulder you see three new guys get vaporized under that exploding chopper. You mean you've never remembered those guys before? And how many times have you seen that bird blow up in the last thirty years? And you thought you remembered everything. Or you could be in the shower, talking to your wife while she brushes her teeth, and suddenly you see some beleaguered crew chief pick up a wounded guy with all the tenderness of a mother for her infant, you see the rockets' red glare, hear the rifle bursts and the bloop-bloop of the Doopers, while the water pours from the showerhead like a monsoon and washes away your tears.

My father used to say that we're the sum of our memories, a kind of mental calculus: I remember, therefore I am. But that which I would remember, I cannot, and that which I would not—that I remember. I try to imagine what it must be like to open a cupboard and have a pile of memories come cascading, like so many toppling cans of beans, into the middle of your life.

"What was I looking for?" he asks.

"You were looking for some milk."

"Oh. Well, I guess I'll try the refrigerator."

One of the ironies of post-traumatic stress disorder, or PTSD, is a blithering inability to remember things in the present—such as your intention to get milk out of the fridge—combined with an unrelenting recall of things from long ago: smells, sounds, sensations, sights, savors come back uninvited and bring with them a wake of grief and fear. But however many times the images come back (and they do, like the endless reruns of some low-budget TV station), you can never be sure you're remembering all of it, or even that what you do recall is what really happened. If you think of your own experience—a car accident, perhaps—you find that you remember what happened as you perceived it at the time. The driver or another passenger may recall the event very differently because that person's attention was focused on something else. As the saying goes, "A thousand soldiers, a thousand bridges."

He has a bridge, too, his moment of memory poised between two unknowns. The way he recalls it, the platoon was getting ready to cross a jungle river—the kind you see in the movies or in your nightmares—bamboo poles lashed together to form a log across an abyss. Crossing a river, like crossing a road, or any open area, is inherently hazardous: anyone caught out in the open is a target, so instead of bunching up into one big bull's-eye and dying all at once, the group spreads out and goes one at a time. On this crossing the lieutenant went first. When he reached the halfway point his radio operator started over, and when he got to the middle, it was the forward observer's turn. So he was the third, just short of halfway, when a sniper opened up on the lieutenant, alone on the other shore.

"Go back!" he yelled to the two on the bridge behind him.

The radio operator, already most of the way to the lieutenant's side, fell into the river. Caught in the middle, the third turned back, and the sniper, seeing a suitable target, directed his fire at the running figure on the bridge. He made it, AK-47 rounds passing so close to his head they didn't even whine, landing in plumes of dirt right in the spot he was headed for, place of safety, place of peril. This is the kind of thing you wonder about years later—how it could have been any other way, how maybe he'd be dead if he'd kept going, how maybe he should have kept going anyway. Maybe, maybe, maybe.

It was different the morning after the ground attack at Con Thien. He was assigned to a working party on a landing zone when a truckload of dead South Vietnamese soldiers rolled up and stopped. It was late morning, closing in on 100 degrees, and the corpses and assorted body parts, stacked like so much cordwood in the back of the truck, dripped blood from the tailgate. They'd already begun to bloat and stink in the heat. "No way," he said to himself and headed off in the opposite direction. So there he was, watching, as the last poncho-full of miscellaneous arms, feet, and whatever was carried up the ramp of the chinook, watching as the last marine walked down the ramp, a severed head rolling after him. With something like amusement, as if from a long way off, he saw the fellow pick it up by the hair, toss it overhand into the closing tailgate of the departing chopper. Hysterical, he thought, just like a goddamn football.

*   *   *

"Let's eat someplace new tonight."

He looks at me. "Like where?"

"The 'Nile Delta.' It's Ethiopian. They serve the food on big sheets of pancake and you use it to eat with."

So we went there that unseasonably cold November night and ordered whatever it was we ordered. It came, as promised, on a huge crepe that you tore off with your hands and used to scoop up meat and vegetables. During dinner I noticed his pupils were flashing all over the place.

He was nice about it, let me smack my lips and keep chowing down, but he stopped eating.

"Let's get out of here," he said finally.

Outside, I said, "What was the matter?"

"The bread—it felt like dead flesh that's been out in the rain a while."

"Oh Jesus."

*   *   *

"What are your hands doing?" asks the group leader.

He sits in the "focus" group, a small squad of vets at the VA hospital grappling with their memories.

"Holding the corners of a poncho."

"Where are you?"

"Inside a chinook."

"What's the next thing you see?"

"I'm outside. I see a head."

"What now?"

"I can't see anything after that. I just feel something slimy in my hand."

"Then what?"

"I think it's me, throwing the thing back up the ramp."

"How'd it get in your hand? Where are you when you pick it up?"

"Oh shit, we're walking down the ramp, all the stuff is loaded, and this head comes rolling after me."

As Macbeth said, there was a time when the dead stayed dead, but now they rise up and push us from our stools. That's what's so disconcerting about flashbacks—they have a way of barging in on your life, your plans, with a kind of visceral realism that overwhelms the cooler, more slowly unfolding story that you project from the past into the future, the one you call your life. These moments, dismembered, undigested, void of context as they are—with the immediacy of present experience, not the *re*-membered quality of things recollected in tranquillity—seem more real than "reality."

I think sometimes of Ingmar Bergman's movie *Hour of the Wolf,* a horror story about a writer whose nightmares become real, a wolf chasing and devouring him in the forest on the island where he and his wife are vacationing. In the course of the movie, the wife keeps watch with her husband through his nightmares—as I have—and is finally so consumed by his reality that she now waits on the island for the demons to devour her in turn. At the end, the camera dollies back to reveal her face as she finishes her tale to the police; her look is anguished, that of a person so caught up, so mastered by her empathic identification with her husband that she has no nightmares of her own—only his, and they will eat her up as well. I saw this movie thirty years ago, and it has always represented to me the peril that awaits people when they mingle their story with another's. I wondered, then, were I in that woman's position, could I shape the story toward a more positive end than she could? I guess I have my answer: we're divorced now. After thirteen years, I was getting secondary trauma.

For a narrator of fiction, the problem of suffering is chiefly a formal one, a question of genre. You find ways to acknowledge the tragic in the midst of comedy or to inject comedy in the midst of tragedy. But an essayist is not just a narrator. Far from it. I wanted a happy ending—I have a sort of psychotic optimism about the possibility of finessing a decent outcome from a lousy hand, or I wouldn't have become a therapist, wouldn't have married him. But life is the most unforgiving medium of all, and I'm just another mortal, struggling to make sense of contextless factoids that erupt out of the past, struggling to make them mean something, knowing, in the end, that you play the hand you're dealt, and wrestle with the meaning in the darkness before dawn.

Questions for Discussion

1. Using the DSM-IV, identify the symptoms of PTSD exhibited by the veteran in this essay. Are there sufficient symptoms to make this diagnosis?
2. What evidence is there in this essay that the narrator was, in fact, developing secondary traumatic stress? What would you need to ask her to confirm a diagnosis?
3. What treatment modalities are presently being used for PTSD?

MOOD DISORDERS

Karen

George Jones

Jenny was their only child. A little girl with an almost unworldly beauty. The photographer's art with light and shadow giving the blonde hair almost a halo effect. Karen showed the picture to every newcomer to the open adult unit. It was almost like part of their initiation to the unit. She showed it over and over to all of us, as we sat together in the bullpen. Everyday. She'd sit, legs tucked under her, chain-smoking one cigarette after another. Staring into nothing, into something behind and beyond us, into a limitless horror and shock. We'd heard the story so often. We were sorry for Karen. We really were. Every time. But to Karen it was happening right now. A videotape in her mind that just played on and on. Over and over. Could she make it? Maybe if she could, some of the rest of us could hope.

She arose early, a sun-drenched, flower-bright, Hawaii morning. The promise of another lush tropical day. Johnny, a straight-up, effective noncom at Hickham Field, was due to be off early. The three of them were planning a picnic together on the white sands of the beach. How soundly little Jenny was sleeping, Karen thought. A surge of love for their only child overwhelmed her. Brought tears to her eyes. She touched Jenny, tenderly. Jenny was so cold.

"Oh my God! Jenny! Johnny, Johnny, oh my God. Johnny come here! Jenny isn't breathing!"

Karen would shriek the very words she screamed to her husband that obscenely beautiful Hawaii morning.

"They could never even tell us why she died. There was nothing wrong with her. She was just dead and we never knew how." Karen would relive the terrible event with us. Eyes beseeching us to tell her how, why, this tragedy happened to them. Knuckles white as she ground her fingers together. We wondered how she kept from breaking them.

"It was just God's will," Miss Lorena would tell her. Miss Lorena carried her Bible with her everywhere. As we sat in the bullpen of the Open Adult Unit, Miss Lorena would read her Bible.

Occasionally we'd hear her mumble, "Oh, how true, how true." No one ever paid much attention to what Miss Lorena had to say. It was probably that way all her sixty-plus years.

"No," Karen would explode at her. "There's no reason. Just tell me how my baby died. There was nothing wrong with her. All the doctors said so."

The leg that had been hidden under her would now be touching the floor. Foot beating an involuntary staccato tattoo on the institution's tiled floor. Fists now tightly clenched. We'd always check when Karen got to that point to be sure the cigarette was safely in the ashtray. When she got that way she could burn the whole place down, and all of us in it.

"We never even went back to the house," Karen would relate. "They had us back home to Alabama in three days."

Maybe, we thought, the military bureaucracy wasn't as bad as we'd always heard. It was certainly nice of them to do that for Karen and Johnny. We all thought so, and that helped make it so.

When Karen wasn't there, we'd talk about how sad it was. But then we talked about everybody at one time or the other. It gave us something to do. The therapy sessions took only a few hours per day, and the rest of the time we just waited for another day to be over. Waited till the nurses brought us the assortment of pills so we'd be knocked out through another long night.

I knew they talked about me, too, when I wasn't there. There was a sudden silence when I came to the bullpen. The half-guilty expressions. One part of me wanted to know, but another part was terrified. We all had our secret places. It was private. No one else's concern.

Jenny would have grown up to be just as pretty as Karen, we'd tell each other—curly blonde hair, clear blue eyes, a pert little nose, and a generous mouth with ripe lips. Except she kept them in such a taut and grim line. Sucked in tight and drawn against her teeth. You couldn't see her even white teeth because she never smiled.

We all agreed about Karen—Miss Lorena, and Ken, Sulu, and all the rest of our locked-up community.

Maybe we talked more about Karen than most of the rest of us. She was so young, so attractive, and so troubled. For me, there was a special attraction. I'd lost—my business failed, and I fell deeper, deeper into a black hole of despair. She'd lost. Not the same. But then again, the same in some way. Maybe if she could pull out of it, just maybe I could.

The doctors said being a community, sharing pain, and coming to consensus agreement was some of the best therapy we could get. And who were we to disagree with the doctors? Besides, it didn't pay to disagree with the doctors, or let the demons in us show. It would delay the day we got out.

Karen's husband Johnny visited her every time he could get off from his military duties. He was very devoted that way. We all thought so. But Karen told us that she and Johnny were going to get a divorce. Since Jenny died, things just weren't working out. But when Johnny would come visit, Karen didn't act like a divorce was pending. She'd grab his arm with both hands. Squeezing, holding hard. Like it was all she had to hold on to. Maybe it was.

We could tell Johnny had things well under control. He was organized, professional military and good at it. Just as he was a good husband, he had been a good father. He adored Jenny and Karen, had loved Karen since they were high school freshmen. The shock of Jenny's sudden death had shaken Johnny badly. But he handled it. Got it under control. Lived through and with it, though the pain was still there and would be always.

Johnny was friendly and polite to all of us, but a bit uneasy and not quite sure how to handle us. He probably was concerned we might act in some abnormal way. He never said that. But we agreed he probably thought it. We'd laugh about it sometimes.

Johnny's puzzlement about Karen was transparent. He was a simple, direct man who handled things as they came. Why couldn't Karen handle it? Why couldn't he get Karen organized, straightened out before she ever got to the point of a mental institution?

He really did love her. We could all see that. Did he have a sense of guilt because he'd been unable to stop her swift descent into madness? That made sense, we sagely nodded to one another. And besides, he felt the same embarrassment all our families felt at having someone in the family locked up.

When Johnny would be ready to conclude his visit with Karen the tension would build. Karen wanted him to go, but wanted him to stay. Hurt and anger would be in her eyes and voice. Her answers would become monosyllablic. She was prepared to explode at any one of us.

"Do you suppose she's afraid she'll lose Johnny like she did the baby?" That was Ken talking. A really pleasant guy. One day he'd burned his home to the ground. He could no more explain the reason than any of us could understand.

"Maybe she's afraid he won't come back."

"Kind of a protective thing?" I hazarded.

"Yes," Ken agreed. "And she threatens divorce so she can't be hurt so bad again."

All of us in the bullpen nodded agreement. We were proud of ourselves for figuring it out. We were almost as good as the doctors. It showed we'd probably soon be getting out.

"Such a sweet girl," Noonie voiced to no one in particular. It sounded like she was going to cry. Everything she said sounded like she was going to cry.

A lot of times she did. Noonie was a fiftyish, plump, frazzled lady who lived with her domineering mother when she wasn't an inmate. She was a repeater. Had been here before and probably would be again. The same went for some of the rest of us.

After Johnny left, Karen would go to her room for a few minutes. Then she'd join us in the bullpen.

"It's just not going to work out. I'm going to divorce him," Karen would announce to us. Her tension, her barely contained explosiveness made us very uncomfortable. We had enough troubles of our own without this being dumped on us. A lot of times we wished Johnny wouldn't come. It made things harder on Karen and, we thought, on us.

Sometimes, if you behaved yourself, the doctors would give you a furlough. It would be for a few hours or a whole weekend. Kind of a trial run to see if we could handle the outside world. It was something we all desperately wanted, but we were desperately scared too. A furlough, maybe several of them, always preceded a discharge. So you could get out for good. When someone would be discharged it gave us hope. It could be us the next time or the time after. Sometime anyway. Even though we all agreed we were a lot more sane than some of those people on the outside, we were unsure how they'd react to us. Or us to them in the very different environment.

We knew Karen was going to get a furlough. She was terribly frightened. We were frightened for her, more than for most of the rest of us if we got a furlough. So much seemed to hang on Karen doing well on the furlough.

Johnny and Karen were a handsome couple that day as they left. He was tall, with open brown eyes. Ramrod stiff military bearing and a chest full of ribbons. Yet a tenderness and gentleness toward Karen showed another person beneath the organized military demeanor. Karen's eyes and manner showed the hurt and fright of a wounded little bird, but also a barely awakening pride in getting to go home, in her husband, and, we hoped, in herself too. She'd fixed herself up. How pretty she looked! Johnny's pride showed in little gestures. A smile, a touch on the arm. Karen smiled. We all saw her smile as they boarded the elevator going down and outside. It was the first time we'd seen her smile the whole time on the ward.

We told one another the whole weekend that we really wanted it to go well for Karen. We worried about her. That was good for us. We could feel for someone else's pain besides our own. Even Jeff, the great hulking teenager from the diagnostic unit, asked if we'd heard how Karen was doing. We were all frightened of Jeff. He was so big and rough looking. And the diagnostic unit people, well, you couldn't be sure of them. They really were locked in, and sometimes acted crazy. We didn't know he could feel concern for others.

The bullpen was situated where we could see everyone who came and went in the whole adult mental health facility. Our eyes would follow them from the time they exited the elevator. Occasionally it would be a visitor for one of us. That was always nice. We liked visitors. It showed someone cared. We even enjoyed it when someone else had a visitor. We'd talk about it. We were always looking for a topic of conversation to avoid those awful quiet times.

We were all in the bullpen Sunday afternoon. Karen was due back at 6:00 p.m. At 6:10 p.m., she and Johnny came before we could get really worried about her. Just looking at them we knew it had gone well. We actually grinned at one another. They had their arms about each other. Johnny was looking down at her with all the tenderness and love in the world. Karen was looking up at him. There was still hurt, confusion, and pain. But something new. Maybe Karen was close to ready to chance loving and being loved again. We really hoped so. All of us. Almost as much as we hoped for ourselves.

Karen didn't come back and join us that evening. The next day Karen was back with us in the bullpen.

"Oh my God, Johnny, Johnny, the baby—!" She was back into the story again. We looked at one another and shook our heads.

But we noticed, almost imperceptibly, the story wasn't quite as tense, not as violently explosive as it had been before. And she didn't tell us she was going to divorce Johnny a single time that day.

Questions for Discussion

1. Today, in the world of managed care, Karen would be hospitalized for only a few days, and only if she was a danger to herself or others. Do you think Karen's problem could be handled on an outpatient basis? What are the advantages of an extended hospital stay?
2. The death of a child is a devastating experience, and who can say what is a "normal" time limit for grieving. Besides medication and hospitalization, what other interventions might have been helpful in Karen's situation?

Dry Dock

Kathleen B. Henderson

I have already learned perhaps the most valuable bit of information I will glean from the experimental drug trial for treatment of depression in which I volunteered to participate. This most important information is simply that I have been, for quite some time, clinically depressed. Endogenous depression, the doctor called it, after having ruled out other causes, menopause, or diabetes as the root cause of a symptomatic depression. I am depressed, as the term is clinically defined.

This information leads to other revelations that, taken together, may help me begin to salvage the shipwreck of my life. I am, as the expression goes, cautiously optimistic. The optimism springs from the realization that a neurochemical imbalance causes the disorder, and the imbalance can be successfully altered with medication. The caution comes from the realization that the disorder can be controlled only through continuous use of the medication, like high blood pressure or diabetes. I am underwhelmed at the prospect of taking those little tablets indefinitely.

A more serious concern also makes me cautious, a concern that arises from the realization that external factors are not the cause of my depression. Like most everyone, I suppose, I believed that the mental state I have been in for so long was a result of a series of devastating personal losses and setbacks that I had undergone. I believed I was a failure, but I also believed that if I could rectify the circumstances of my life, both personal and professional, that I would be fine again. I had heard the bromide that I was responsible for my own happiness, and I had paid lip service to its veracity. Yet I believed my depression was precipitated by circumstances beyond my control.

I was wrong to think that, just as wrong as I would be if I thought that taking those green pills would magically fix everything that needs to be fixed in my life. I had the order of operations backward: I thought I had to first salvage the wreck before I could emerge from the depths; now I know that I must emerge from the depths before I can salvage the wreck. This is the second most important bit of knowledge I have already acquired, and the source of caution. I may be able to control the depression, but there is no assurance I can repair the damage done to my personal and professional lives. Yet there is some cause for hope: I made the effort to seek help. It was very difficult, and at several points I nearly blew it off, thinking it would lead to just another in a long line of failures. More to the point: at least if I get the depression under control I will be better able to reclaim the rest of my life, something I could not possibly have done in the state I was in.

I still have some reservations, some real fears of failure. I would like very much to believe that the need for medication is temporary. I would like to think of it as a life jacket to keep me afloat until I can raise the wreck and get it back under way under its own power. This may be wishful thinking. I may be stuck taking medication forever, a situation about which I have serious qualms. And it is harder by far to painstakingly restore a life to wholeness than it is to concede responsibility to events beyond my control and to surrender to the depths.

I was very close to doing that. In retrospect, I clearly see that it is the path my own mother took. In her sixties she was diagnosed with depression, but refused to be treated for it. To her and to many of her generation, mental illness of any kind was perceived as a shameful weakness. I remember her telling me about the diagnosis and her refusal to take the prescribed medication. She was angry and defiant; she insisted that she could "put a board up her back" and fight on. She could not, of course, but instead of taking the shame-laden antidepressants her physician prescribed, she became more and more dependent on what she considered an acceptable and preferable alternative, alcohol. In her view it was better to pour larger and larger quantities of cheap bourbon into a glass of ice and drink herself unconscious every night than admit to the reality of a mental illness that exerted ever tighter control over her as she got older.

I came very close to making the same decision at an earlier age. Honestly, I know I could find myself in the same condition without much difficulty. It would be easy. The irony is poignant: I had a difficult relationship with my mother while she was alive; the sadness I felt at her death was mixed with a sense of relief. We share the same demon; I understand this now in a way I could not when she was alive. Would she castigate me for confronting the same "weakness" and seeking medical help as she castigated me for just about everything I did? Or would she be able to acknowledge the damage, the corrosive effect her mental state had on the rest of her family? This is perhaps her legacy to me: I vowed that I would never make my own children feel as unwanted as I felt as her child, that I would not be the cause of the kind of pain I and my siblings suffered at her hand. I think that was the reason I finally sought help. As I said to the psychiatrist and supervisor of the study, "I want whatever is wrong with me to end with me. I do not want my problems to become their problems." For a long time I thought the way to ensure this was to extricate myself from their lives, either the easy way or the hard way. I have seen the deleterious effects of suicide and of slow death.

I am willing to try another way for their sakes. Rest in peace, Mother, the peace you could not find in this life.

Questions for Discussion

1. How does knowing that her depression is due to a chemical imbalance change the writer's perception of herself?
2. Though she says that her little green pills will not "magically fix everything," she feels that her life circumstances were not the main culprits in her depression. Do you agree? What part do life circumstances play in the life of someone with chronic depression?
3. Do you think that counseling has a place in helping people with chronic depression? How?

Mad Colored Woman:
A Memoir of Manic Depression

Anita D. Taylor

I'm in a wrestling match with fire. It dances around me, through me, in me, singeing, making me scream obscenities and weep pain. For years the fire has chased me into and out of college, to the doorsteps of doctors, into and out of apartments, to funerals, weddings, through England and Spain, the Netherlands and France, and even to the Cape of Good Hope, where I climbed a mountain, only to look out into despair. I jogged the streets of Bermuda, walked the hills of Barbados, slept on the shores of Mexico—all to escape the burn. I drank to quench it, cognac and champagne, Budweiser and Merlot; ate to sooth it, fried fish in Soweto and lima beans picked by my grandmother's hands—all in search of a resting place, a nestling place, a comfortable place to be numb.

There's no rhyme or reason to any of this, no episode that says, "This is the reason life is unbearable." Every day is like every other. Drive the fifty miles back and forth to Rockville, Maryland, close the office door, stare out the window overlooking a vacant field. Vacant, like how I feel. Go to work, come home, lock myself in a room, cry, eat copious amounts of food, nurse the cognac bottle, sleep nightmare-filled dreams, go to work, come home, start the routine again, lying in wait of the sudden explosion. No warning, no brush fire. The napalm is dropped. I'm a near-casualty looking for a way to die.

I call Aetna. There's a telephone number on the back of the insurance card for all subscribers in need of psychological help. Help from my insurance agency. I sit behind the closed door of my office staring into a Matthiesen lithograph of Charlie Parker, number nine of 500. Charlie Parker, jazz artist extraordinare, drug addict, manic-depressive, slow suicide victim. Slow suicide. That's my ride. I'm hitched to the back of the cart and it's dragging me along.

"Well, Ms. Taylor, we do have a database of pertinent information about possible therapists. You do understand that there is a $25 deductible for each of up to twenty visits annually." An invisible woman outlines my limitations before agreeing to help.

Twenty visits. That's probably about five months of therapy. Napalm-inflicted wounds healed after five months? Very unlikely.

"Would you like me to search the database for you, Ms. Taylor?"

What are my options? "Yes. Thank you." Impatiently I wait, listening to the clicking of the keyboard through the phone, strangely, as if it's a woodpecker at work on a lazy afternoon.

"Would you rather a social worker, psychologist, or psychiatrist?"

"A psychologist is fine. I don't want treatment centered on drug therapy. A PhD is fine." I don't tell her that I've already made indentations into the sofas of six shrinks. I've tried Jewish female, elderly black Baptist (too elderly, she died on me), middle-aged gay black male, black Muslim, and a couple of WASP males. Three of them prescribed antidepressant medications right off the bat, one suggested I let my hair grow (I punished her by withholding payment), one sent me to God and the gym, one said absolutely nothing, and one cocky soul actually gave a diagnosis of schizophrenia.

"Is there anything else that concerns you? Does gender or race matter?"

"Race matters. Black. Gender? Female. And generation. My own. Common ground in hope of basic understanding." I feel like I'm ordering a car—black as the night, Saab 900, please. Eight-cylinder engine, four-wheel drive, compact disc player, air-conditioning, electrically warmed seats, and convertible top a must. Big black power machine complete with escape hatch!

"My computer shows three therapists who fit this profile, but one seems to have much higher qualifications than the others. The computer also shows her success rate is high. Her name is Kim Singleton. She's located in the northeast quadrant on Tenth Street. Why don't you call her, have a preliminary meeting, see how she feels to you, and if it's not a match, call us back and we'll consider the other two."

"Does this preliminary meeting count as one of the twenty?"

"Yes, unfortunately it does."

It figures. In medicine, a second opinion is generally advised. In mental health a second opinion is punishable.

Singleton had converted a lovely townhouse into an office. The atmosphere is homey; exposed brick walls, two working fireplaces, hardwood floors, Caribbean and African-American folk art, plush leather furniture, and soft white carpeting upstairs where the sessions are held in a quiet room surrounded by books on depression, Christianity, affirmations, and Jungian philosophy. For close to a year I become Kim Singleton's patient, sneaking out of work an hour and a half early, pretending to get away unnoticed. Every Thursday afternoon at 5:00, I relax on her sofa, flip through her books, find something new in the beauty of the art around me, and talk or listen or cry or sit still.

Singleton says, "Anita, have you noticed that somewhere in the course of our last three sessions you've steered each conversation toward a discussion of your grandfather? Didn't your grandfather commit suicide?"

"Yes." I sit, rocking, squeezing a pillow, staring at the blank surface of the cocktail table. I think of my Grandpa Doc sitting in his favorite wooden side chair, a taste of alcohol in his mouth, the barrel of a shotgun against his chest, pulling the trigger. I can imagine the blood beating the bullet to splatter against the wall behind him. I see him fall forward, pain searing through his chest, struggling like a wounded animal toward the telephone to call— who? I imagine his dog scratching fiercely against the back door to reach his loyal companion, to save him from invisible demons. I see my grandmother hurrying from her mother's house, having heard the ringing shot, knowing what it is, who it is, knowing before she reaches him all that has happened.

The room is cool. The fireplace burns downstairs in the waiting room but the one up here has instead a little electric box that kicks dry heat through the chill.

"Are you having suicidal ideations?" She waits for me to answer, seated at about a forty-five-degree angle from me in a tiny little chair where only a woman of her petite frame could fit. Ankles crossed, hands stretched out to rest on the blank yellow legal pad that sits on her lap, one hand resting in the other, palms up. I think she must be secretly praying.

I can't look at her. "Am I going to kill myself? No. I have to wait until my parents are dead. One suicide in the family is enough. They won't survive mine. They're still struggling with Grandpa Doc's ten years after the fact." My mother wants to know if her jealous God has spared his soul from hellfire. My father buries himself further in drink.

"Are you struggling with his suicide? Do you have those questions? Are you angry with your grandfather ten years later?" Her body twists just a little. I can tell she's worried. I don't concern myself with searching for the words that will ease her worry.

"No. I was never angry with him. I always understood. I understand it completely. The unquenchable fire eventually consumes itself." I say this so matter-of-factly that I surprise myself. Singleton is quiet. Just for a moment everything in the room is right. The air is not chilled or warm or dry. The prodding has stopped. I've said it aloud for the first time in ten years.

I understand the all-consuming, unquenchable fire. It's that thing that makes you want to run through the streets in the middle of the night because you can't get enough air where you are, no matter *where* you are. It's the thing that creates that love-hate relationship with alcohol and sleeping pills and any over-the-counter antihistamine that warns of drowsiness. It's the thing that makes a car a lethal weapon, playing Russian roulette with the edge of the Chesapeake Bay Bridge. It makes your heart rush and your body shake and your eyes bloodshot red with pain. It breaks your skin out in hives and shuts your throat too tight for speech. Your hands shake and you lose your appetite or you eat until you can't eat anymore and then you purge and eat again. It hides in your office, forcing paranoia at every turn. It shatters your dreams, destroys your confidence, and gnaws at your friendships until they cease to exist. It turns your family into your enemy and yourself into your own prosecution. It eats you alive.

"Anita. I want to raise something with you. We've spent a lot of time together over the past several months. Generally at this point my patients are ready to move on. They've learned the skills they need. But with you it's not happening. I fear you may be having more trouble than either of us originally thought. How do you feel about being evaluated by another doctor, a psychiatrist? I know that your internist dispenses your medication but I've worked very closely with a psychiatrist, a woman, whose work I have great faith in. Now, before you say anything, I want you to think about this. I'm *very* concerned about you. I want us to continue to work together but I really think there's something going on that I'm not quite seeing. Another doctor's evaluation may help us."

"I'm fine with that," I lied. Was she upset that I couldn't be added to her list of successful patients in and out in twelve months? Gee, was her record in jeopardy? Bitch. Fuck her! Now I'm about to be passed on to incompetent number eight. Isn't there anyone who can tell me how to smother this shit? The fire is coming. I feel it welling up inside me, smell it's putrid odor, feel the tinge of the first sparks. Oh God, it's happening again. A private whisper betrays me. "I just want to die." I don't look at her. Too scared. I hadn't meant for that to slip.

"Anita, would you rather go to a hospital?"

Oh my God. She doused it. That quickly it's out. I can breathe. I can look away from this damned empty table. I can look at her face. I can say, "Yes. I want to be put away."

We sit silently for a moment. Tears form in my eyes. The stoicism that I tried so hard to grab has eluded me. "I want to go away. Someplace quiet. Someplace where the world won't bother me."

There is quiet. Singleton gets up from her chair, moves to her desk. She shuffles papers behind me. She does this, I think, more in an effort to give me a little space of my own than to look for anything in particular. I sit there grateful for this small gift. I shiver a little. I had a friend once who feared being put away. We discussed it periodically, how her depression might just boil over one day and she'd be sent away. I'd listen to her, but inside I always thought this would never happen to either of us. But here I am sitting in Dr. Singleton's office agreeing to go away, a mad woman after all.

"Dr. Singleton"—I never referred to her as doctor. Why now?—"I can't go to a DC public hospital. I can't be around a bunch of lost and turned-out street people."

"You don't have to, Anita. One of the best facilities on the East Coast is right in Baltimore. I'm just checking my records to make sure Aetna will cover your treatment." The shuffling continued. She's still behind me. I don't turn to look at her. There's something comforting about this. I'm alone but I'm not. There's space to breathe. I look down at my hands, pick at my fingers. I've never been one to bite my nails or rip them, but right now I find myself picking at skin on the sides of my thumbs, drawing blood.

"I need to go downstairs for a few minutes, Anita. Will you be okay up here by yourself? I just want to make some phone calls while you're still here."

I shake my head yes. Suddenly I'm numb, like a robot lost in space.

Three days later. Sunday. Tomorrow I leave for the hospital. I sit waiting for the bathwater to cool. Kathleen Battle is singing me lullabies. Candles burn. A yellow rose stolen from my neighbor's garden appears to open in the mist. I sip a glass of Australian merlot. The smell of the sea salts rising from the bathwater is soothing. I wait. It's 7:00 p.m. The day is gone, my last day. Fear rises. I should call someone. No. No one can rescue me. That's what Singleton said, but I should never have told Kevin that I needed some time alone, that he should go out. I'll sit here, soak. I'll write in my journal, acknowledge what's happening. Try to move on.

At 7:50 p.m., Hilda calls. I'm glad. She's always been supportive of me, particularly regarding depression. Over time, I'd learned to be careful in the telling. *"You need to go to church. That's your problem. You've turned your back on God."* Some would shake their heads in wonder. *"What have you got to be depressed about? You don't have chick nor child."* Or, *"Psychiatrists are for white folks. Black women don't get depressed. They're the strongest people on earth."* That one particularly enraged me. Mules of the world lack the capacity to collapse under pain. But Hilda knew differently—seventy years of keloids encasing her spirit. Hilda knew.

I tell Hilda about my session, that I've agreed to go to Sheppard Pratt. "Good, Anita." I hear the richness of her voice, imagine her soft brown eyes, know that I have her full attention and I trust her. "It sounds like you have a good therapist. She's heard all that you said and she's made a wise choice about the best place for you to do your work. I've visited Sheppard Pratt. It's a beautiful place, looks like an old Ivy League campus. Bring the novels you've wanted to read and some small familiar things to decorate your room, things that will help you feel safe." I think about this. Do black women ever feel safe?

It's 5:30 a.m. I've awakened three times from horrible dreams about people vanishing, favorite belongings stolen, lovers revealing courtship with others. Damn it, why can't this one last night in my own house, my own bed, be restful? I've done everything I can to anesthetize myself. Hot bath, glass of merlot, Xanax. Shit, just get up, Anita. Get up, take a shower. Pack.

I find Kevin's half-empty glass of cognac. Certainly this isn't healthy, waking before dawn with the warmth of cognac in my throat.

My brain says, "This is the point of no return, Anita. You go to this hospital you commit to live. You commit to health. You have a choice. You can stay here, not move, not pack. You can sit in a hot bath with a bottle of very good cognac and one by one, you can take every Xanax, Paxil, Serzone, Ludiomil, Ativan, Zoloft, and Prozac you've stashed for just this moment. By the time your bathwater turns to ice you will be in a sleep no one can wake you from. You can do that. It's your choice."

I sit here numb on the sofa, staring at nothing. Maybe I am dead already.

The front door opens. It's Kevin. Neither of us speaks. He takes off his coat and takes my hand. We walk upstairs to his room. He pulls back the spread, motions for me to get in. I crawl into my familiar space near the wall. He showers and soon climbs behind me. I cry a little. He holds me. Slowly I fall into sleep. I sleep soundly.

The phone rings. He answers, gets up, he's gone. I move into the space that was his. I smell his smell, warm and soapy. He comes back, sits on the edge of the bed. "Anita, this is Singleton." She tells me it's all right to be a little anxious and tries to reassure me. I will be safe. I don't say much, make inaudible sounds.

Today is Monday, October 16. I have made my choice.

What the hell do you pack when your journey is to the nuthouse? I take a month's supply of clothes, a dozen yellow legal pads, number 2 pencils, cigarettes. I don't know if I can have matches but stick them in the glove compartment with a stash of Xanax. Books, stamps, my grandparents' wedding photograph.

"Here's a list of everything, Kevin. I sent these people letters telling them what's happening. The attorney shouldn't need me for anything. I signed everything for the bankruptcy already. Here's a bunch of signed checks for my portion of the bills. I'll call you to let you know how I'm doing."

I can tell he's hit with panic, probably wondering if I'm going to flip out one more time before leaving the house, just to remind him of the hellhole I've made of this place. "Everything's going to be all right, Anita," he says. "You're not going away forever. You're not crazy." He's not looking at me. Instead he is pacing like he can't wait until I get out of here. He can't even bring himself to drive me to the damn hospital, can't hold my hands in the daylight hours the way he does at night.

I say, "I know. Just please put my bag in the car for me?" What I really know is just the opposite. I'm surrendering to madness. The facade is crumbling. Those screaming fits in the bathroom, driving through the city at 4:00 a.m. because I can't sleep and can't stand still, feeling trapped and itching like someone suffering from burns over 90 percent of her body. The jig is up. I'm being institutionalized.

DAY 1

The first sixteen hours are gone. It's nearly 4:00 a.m. and I'm exhausted from intake interviews, too exhausted to sleep. What do I do with myself except lie here and wait for first light? If I could concentrate I'd read but I can't so I won't. If I felt free I'd take a walk but I don't so I can't. I'm barricaded in this room with all my nameless demons. Why did I come here? Did I let Singleton talk me into this? Did I beg her? I don't remember. There's so much I don't remember. That day, that awful day when Kevin and I stood next to each other in the kitchen, not looking at each other, him recounting what happened the night before, how I screamed and cried in the bathroom so loud the neighbors could hear. How he didn't know whether to kick in the bathroom door or let me scream it out. How neither of us had a clue what "it" was. How he walked me to my room and put me to bed. How I rocked myself to sleep like a frightened kid. And then how he found the empty vial of Ativan, the vial that was full the day before. And he didn't know whether to let me sleep or wake me but I'd overdosed so he woke me and made me walk around for hours and hours and hours. And he bathed me and talked to me and forced me to drink water and coffee and juice. God. How can I not remember this? He told me every little detail and as he told me I stood there, not looking at him, and I cried. And he cried. We just stood there crying because we were both scared. He couldn't lie to himself anymore. I couldn't either. Overdosed on sleeping pills. Deliberately. Tried to kill myself. Again.

DAY 2

Dr. McIntyre shuffles papers behind his desk. Short, skinny, bespectacled and gray, he looks like a tired traveling salesman. I'm tired too, sitting and waiting for the same series of questions already asked and answered. But we only have twenty minutes together and he uses his time wisely.

His directness is refreshing. "Debilitating depressions, anxiety, rage, spending sprees, sleeplessness, racing thoughts, irritability, increased sexual activity, poor judgment. This list accurately describes your state of being?"

"Yes."

"How is your driving? Have you had any accidents?"

"I've hit a couple trees, a couple cars. Nothing major."

"Can you tell me how often your moods change?"

"I'm like a roller coaster. I don't know how often. The feelings of despair are long lasting. In a year's time, I've had feelings of intense pain at least half a dozen times. But then it changes and I'm ridden with anxiety that is weird, different from the depression. I have to move, drive, run. I feel like

I'm on fire. I can't sit long or read or watch television or sleep. The worst is that I can't read—anything. And I used to read everything. I just have to move. Sometimes I find myself on the beltway driving round and round the city at 3:00 in the morning, wondering why I'm there, crying hysterically but unable to get off."

"Ms. Taylor, I've read your file and I've talked with your therapist. I am certain that you are suffering from bipolar disorder, manic depression. I am prescribing lithium to be taken in conjunction with an antidepressant. Here is the prescription, which the staff at Weinberg House will have filled for you. But in the meantime, here are some pills to begin taking immediately."

Like the news of my grandfather's suicide, I am stoic. I am stiff, deliberate, and direct. My eyes are fixed on his, back straight, shoulders square. "No lithium, Doctor. Sorry. I can no longer depend on my mind. I will not give away my memory. And I am fat. I cannot handle any more weight gain. You're going to have to dig in your grab bag and find something else."

The chair creaks. Dr. McIntyre sits back, startled, like I've punched him square in the jaw. Silence for several awkward moments. My eyes do not move from his. I have not finished with my demands. *Don't check your brain at the door.* "I will also need access to the most recent DSM and the *Physician's Reference Guide.* Until I can do my own research, I will not take anything."

He seems to have recovered from my near boorish tone. "I'll arrange for you to get the necessary reading materials from Jeannie. And we can try Depakote rather than lithium. But you can't play with this, Ms. Taylor."

I stop him. "I'm not playing with anything. But I'm also not stupid. I'm not challenging you, I'm just telling you. Until I feel confident that you're making the best recommendations for my care, I cannot accept the diagnosis or the treatment. So the sooner I have the reading materials, the better." But the truth is I know and I'm putting up a stone front to keep from turning brittle. I know without reading one word of technical medical jargon that I am manic-depressive. And I'm petrified. I have a disease, a brain disease. It has a name. I am certifiably mentally ill.

Dr. McIntyre phones the nurse. I sit. Silent. Three remaining minutes on the clock but both of us have taken our last shot. Nothing more to say. So we wait. A timid knock, a relieved "Come in," and Jeannie stands, disheveled, books in hand.

"Here you are, Doctor," she says as she steps forward to unload this mass in his hands.

"No, not for me. For her." He waves his hand in my direction as if shooing away a pestilent fly.

"Oh." She looks from him to me and back and forth again. Then, finally, as if some voice has told her to compose herself, she sets the books on the edge of the desk and begins to explain their contents.

I put up my hand to stop her crash course. "That's not necessary. I'm familiar. I requested them."

Our session ends. McIntyre stands, having accomplished in twenty minutes what nearly a dozen other therapists couldn't do in months and years. I stand, heavier than I've ever felt, like my body has turned into boulders. I drag it down the long corridor and flee the hospital grounds. I flee to Hilda. Bayleaf Court is my refuge.

DAY 4

All day I recount Hilda's words. "Now that you have a diagnosis, treatment can begin in earnest."

Hilda talked with me for hours, both of us lying across her bed, books and pillows surrounding us. Safety. This is safety. This is where I must be to decipher these words that I wish were foreign. Bipolar. Manic depression.

"Dr. McIntyre has an excellent reputation. I know him. It wasn't a twenty-minute diagnosis. I'm sure he poured over your records and talked at length with your therapist before meeting with you. He recognized the spending sprees, sleeplessness, intense highs, suicidal lows, rage, and anxiety for what it is. You are one of thousands who live with a biochemical brain disorder that can be fixed. Do you hear the last part, Anita?"

"Hilda, I'm scared. I'm scared shitless. I was perfectly comfortable believing that I was just depressed. I was willing to experiment with psychotropics, go through therapy again, fall completely apart, and have someone put me back together again. But bipolar? Manic depression? The visuals are incredible here. Vincent Van Gogh slicing off his ear, Virginia Woolf kissing the floor of the sea, women dancing naked on the streets of Paris without ever knowing how they got there. This can't be me."

"That isn't you. Don't get dramatic. Yes, I understand that you're frightened. But you've read enough to know that no one need suffer the way that Van Gogh or Woolf did. It's not necessary. You can live a perfectly normal life with manic depression, a life free of all the pain you're currently feeling. Imagine your life without sleepless nights, without suicidal thoughts, without edginess or rage or paranoia. Imagine being able to sit down and read Toni Morrison again. When is the last time you've read a novel or written an essay? What's the last movie you saw? How many days of the week are you productive at work? How much alcohol do you consume? On the phone you said you had so many thoughts running rampant, you felt like you were constantly chasing your brain. Talk about frightening visuals. You don't have to live like this. Hear me, Anita. You don't have to live like this."

I can live a perfectly normal life. How many times over the course of this disaster will people tell me this? It's a platitude I will grow to hate as it becomes clearer and clearer that there is no such thing as normal, not after one has once lost her mind. I can never again trust it to be solidly with me. My brain is its own entity to beseech me whenever it chooses, whether or not I pickle it with anticonvulsants, antidepressants, and antipsychotics. I must find something sturdier than me to cling to. I choose Hilda's seventy years of wisdom.

Hilda rises from her place on the bed to stand next to me, rub the stubborn stiffness out of my shoulders. "I'm going to make you some hot tea and then I want you to rest. But you're not going to spend the night. You have to get in your truck and drive back to Sheppard Pratt. Your healing begins there."

I drink the tea in the dining room, staring at my reflection in the black grand piano, wishing I could hear music, but instead hearing Dr. McIntyre say "manic depression" over and over in my head. Slowly this brain disease with a name is claiming me, determined never to let go.

DAY 4

I was lightly reprimanded for leaving the grounds without permission, but I wasn't locked up so I took it in stride. I sat in Dr. McIntyre's office again, conceding defeat, having taken the first of a lifetime dosage of the anticonvulsant Depakote. McIntyre looked none too pleased when I told him I'd run to a friend for refuge from his monstrous diagnosis. That look of displeasure on his face is totally incongruous with his words. "Well, it seems you have a strong support system." Then quickly he moves on.

"Anita, I'm not sure there's sufficient reason for you to stay here. You've talked at length about your relationship with your therapist. It seems to be solid. You trust her. You're clearly very bright, capable of participating in decisions about your care. You're past the crisis that brought you here. There's no indication that you are suicidal. I feel comfortable releasing you if you feel you're ready. Technically you're an outpatient. Continued individual therapy, possibly combined with group, should work well as long as you stick to the medication regimen we've agreed upon here. How does that sound to you?"

Stunned. I was prepared to stay here for at least a month, prepared for an institution to take care or me, prepared to collapse, go crazy. But as it is, I'm being released, thrown out, three days short of a full week. "Can I think about this for a while—a few hours or perhaps a day?" He shakes his head yes, and I am relieved. The dismissal doesn't have to occur just yet.

Fear about returning home grips me. I'm incapable of taking care of life's little details. Bankruptcy, foreclosure, short-term disability from work, Kevin—all weigh far too much. A familiar, suffocating feeling makes my head feel dense as a brick, my chest hard, incapable of receiving air, or so it seems. My skin tells me that the air is cool. My eyes register a bright sky. A gust stronger than any southern October wind slaps my face. I turn my back to it and, in defiance, attempt to light a cigarette, but the fire disappears much as it has in me. The wind wins. Cold and breathless I make my way to Weinberg, where I climb the stairs to weep.

The drive home from Sheppard Pratt is as difficult as the drive there. I am not sure what I'll find when I get home. Diagnosed now with an illness, a disease, I tell myself that I should feel relief. At least the demon has a name. Now all I have to do is find the right arms to slay it. But quenching the dragon's fire is not an easy task. Instruments as common as garden hoses just won't do.

I return to Dr. Singleton with a commitment to be totally honest. If we are the team summoned to beat this thing then she needs to know everything.

I am blunt. I have not told her that Kevin is my first cousin, and we have been lovers. I tell her now.

"I can't believe you didn't tell me that. Now it's all beginning to make sense." I wait for her to say more. She looks incredulous, like a betrayed lover. "Anita, I have a problem. Obviously I have failed with you somehow. You don't trust me."

I'm trusting you now. Isn't this what therapy is all about? Slowly we build trust, slowly we share confidence, slowly we bare our soul? So it took me a year to come clean with the truth about Kevin. How much of your ego is in the way of my therapy?

"I think you should see someone else. I don't know a lot about manic depression. You need a specialist. I can give you the names of three psychiatrists. Each is good; I highly recommend them. Until you begin seeing one of them, I'll continue to work with you."

Wait a minute. You tell me you're angry that I don't trust you. You tell me you know nothing about manic depression and pass me off to a colleague. You tell me you'll work with me until. Goddamn it! There's nothing you can fucking do for me.

"No, that won't work. There's no need for us to continue to work together. I won't be coming back." I rise to leave. I'm not sure if she's surprised by my decision. Perhaps she's even a bit relieved. Weeks later I receive a form letter in the mail saying that she's released me. I also receive a letter from the insurance company handling my disability saying that upon conference with Dr. Singleton they have learned that I am now medically ready to return to work.

What kind of shit is this? Get out of a mental institution with specific instructions to continue treatment with a psychopharmacologist and therapist for bipolar illness with no doctor to provide medical care, and I'm ready to jump back into the workforce. Is the dragon dead?

I call Aetna. I need a psychopharmacologist and I need one fast. "None are registered in your area with Aetna; however, a psychiatrist can perform the same tasks. Would you like a list of doctors?"

"Yes. I have no specific concerns except that they be extremely competent. Give me a list of your top ten."

I call ten doctors and leave messages, requesting twenty-minute appointments to ascertain whether they are qualified to serve me. It is Dr. Ellen Kilmartin, certified psychiatrist and former heart surgeon, whom I choose. The message on her answering machine comforts me with its practicality. "If this is an emergency, please go immediately to the nearest emergency room. Otherwise, leave a detailed message and I will return your call as soon as possible."

It is 9:00 p.m. The ring of the phone disrupts my nervousness. It is Kilmartin. "Anita, I'm sorry to be calling so late but I just got in and received your message. You sounded frightened. I wanted to make sure you are okay. Would you like to talk for a few minutes?"

"I've just been released from Sheppard Pratt, diagnosed as manic-depressive, dumped by my therapist. I'm confused and scared."

Our sessions begin that same week. Finally, in a middle-aged, Irish, surgeon-turned-psychiatrist, I find my savior.

Questions for Discussion

1. What is Anita's reaction to learning her diagnosis? What feelings and thoughts does being diagnosed with manic-depressive illness evoke for her?

2. What part does being African American play in Anita's story?

3. What thoughts do you have about Dr. Singleton's reaction to Anita's revelation about Kevin? What do you think was the basis of Dr. Singleton's reaction? What might have been a different response?

Madwoman: A Mental Health Professional Living with Mental Illness

M. Elizabeth Wilson

To My Friends and Family:

Many of you know already that I was diagnosed with bipolar disorder (manic depression) two years ago, but only recently has the severity of the disorder made itself undeniably clear to me. This letter is my attempt to explain some things, apologize for others, and ensure that you do not dismiss me—or the disorder—without further thought. Like life, the reality of bipolar affective disorder and the lack of a clear distinction between my disorder and my personhood are infinitely more complex (and far more profound) than an adjective like "crazy."

A few weeks ago (just days after leaving my husband of eleven years and my two children), I systematically and intentionally overdosed on a medication I had just begun taking (Depakote) for my manias. The dosage (3,000 mg) was significantly high, but I decided not to succumb to the impulse to die, and I had someone call poison control. What resulted was easily the most horrific and humiliating experience of my life: At a local hospital, I was forced to drink twenty-four ounces of liquified charcoal and laxatives (and was given only a bedpan to deal with the purging of the medications and charcoal from my body), had blood drawn repeatedly, was given an IV of a thick, painful solution (saline), and was treated by the nurses as both an annoyance and a "crazy." My concerns were invalidated and I was condescended to by the staff, who all but forced me to admit myself to a psychiatric facility. On Saturday, I was put in the uncomfortable position of having my son visit me on his tenth birthday at that facility. You can imagine how terrible that was for everyone involved and how much of a loser I felt like for having to forego our plans for a birthday party at the park.

However, at the psychiatric facility, the care was given by learned professionals and was catered to my individual symptoms and needs, which ensured that I received a proper assessment and committed to a plan for my future mental health. The psychiatrist and counselors there were able to answer questions and point out things that I knew but refused to believe (like the fact that my impulsivity and heightened sexual needs were biological, not psychological) as well as things I'd never known (like the fact that I also met the criteria for a personality disorder from the incest and wife assault I had experienced). Understanding that leaving my current husband, a culmination of ten years of struggling with a severe psychiatric disorder, was a two-edged sword: I received great relief in knowing that many of my behaviors (which had caused me and many of you everything from irritation to enormous grief) were wholly biological, but I also had to accept that I'm not strong enough or smart enough to "beat" this disorder. As one patient said, "Nothing in my upbringing, character, or education prepared me for this!" Bipolar disorder is severe, it is chronic, and it is incurable. It is completely biological in nature and primarily psychological (mood, affective states) in expression (Goodwin and Jamison, 1990). I am now accepting that I will need to remain medicated for the rest of my life in order to control the disorder's expression. Being a counselor has not, and will not, protect me from the bipolar illness. I am committed to remaining medicated by traditional means while I explore other treatments (like nutrition). I have also begun a counseling program to deal with the stress the disorder has caused (dysfunctional coping patterns, denial, etc.) in my personal and financial life, and to assure that I am coping with this tremendous loss of control over my life (those of you who know me closely realize that the loss of control is the single hardest part for me).

I want to tell you what this disorder has been like for me over the last ten years (possibly my whole life), and I've done that by using quotes from other bipolar disorder patients and some medical information, primarily taken from the clinical text *Manic Depressive Illness* (Goodwin and Jamison, 1990). Bear in mind that, even though I was able to choose quotes that reflect my experience, all mental disorders are experienced somewhat differently by different persons, as our experiences shape our realities—even our delusional ones.

An abridged description of bipolar disorder is this: patients experience neurochemical changes that precipitate manias/hypomanias, which are marked by three stages of mental, emotional, and sensory heightening. Stage one represents clarity of thought, gleefulness, high productivity, and various sensual heightening. Stage two involves an increase in all the aforementioned and the presence of irritability, distractibility, and flights of thought. Stage three is the peak and—depending on the severity of the episode—can involve severe irritation of the senses, jumbled thoughts, outrageous behaviors (caused by impulse-control loss), and even delusions, paranoia, and hallucinations. These manias/hypomanias are often followed by depressions that are, clinically, the worst known to medicine. Between or after these episodes some patients may be completely normal for months or years before another episode hits (I'm a rapid cycler, which means I have two or more manias or depressions a year).

For me, the hypomanias and manias are the worst and best of life. They are where I experience creative rushes (at the beginning stages of them), where I feel powerful and resilient, and where I don't get afraid or feel aimless. One bipolar patient anonymously describes experiences similar to mine in Goodwin and Jamison (1990):

> I have felt more things, more deeply; had more experiences, more intensely; loved more, and been more loved; laughed more often, for having cried more often; appreciated the springs more, for all the winters; worn death "as close as dungarees," appreciated it—and life—more; seen the finest and most terrible in people, and finally learned the values of caring, loyalty, and seeing things through. I think I have seen the breadth and depth and width of my heart and mind, and seen how frail, and ultimately unknowable they are. . . . I have been aware of finding new corners of my mind and heart. Some of those corners were incredible and beautiful and took my breath away and made me feel as though I could die right then and the images would sustain me. . . and when I am my normal self—I cannot imagine becoming jaded to life, because I know of these limitless corners with their limitless views. (p. 22)

My manias resemble being high on pot or LSD in the way that my senses become heightened (Goodwin and Jamison, 1990, make the connection with LSD on p. 26). However, as the mania progresses, irritation becomes the norm. Another anonymous patient explains this phase eloquently:

> There is a particular kind of pain, elation, loneliness, and terror involved in this kind of madness. When you're high it's tremendous. . . but, somewhere this changes. The fast ideas are far too fast and there are far too many . . . you are irritable, angry, frightened, uncontrollable, and enmeshed totally in the blackest caves of the mind . . . there are only others' recollections of your behaviors . . . mania at least has some grace in partially obliterating memory. What then, after the medications, psychiatrist, despair, depression, and overdose? All those incredible feelings to sort through. . . . Who knows what? What did I do? And, most hauntingly, when will it happen again? . . . Credit cards revoked, bounced checks to cover, explanations due at work, apologies to make, intermittent memories of vague men [what did I do?], friendships gone drained, a ruined marriage. And always, when will it happen again? Which of my feelings are real? Which of the me is me? (Goodwin and Jamison, 1990, pp. 17-18)

This is a very accurate description of my manias. I become very agitated because of the overstimulation of my senses. My thoughts race uncontrollably and I experience frequent distractibility and flight of ideas. To simply hug or hold one of the kids is agonizing, and the thought of having them squirming on me or even being in the room (where, being kids, they move a lot) is like sandpaper being rubbed on the inside of my skin. This is the hardest part for me because I want to comfort and nurture my children, but to do so would mean a torturous—and very legitimate—physical irritation for me. I become highly impulsive and shoplift, drive recklessly, listen to music loudly, skip classes, etc. I also act on things that have been visualized during the earlier, sexual stages. Sexual promiscuity is a hallmark of both stage two and three for many patients. I have done and said a lot to justify the infidelities in my marriage, going as far as to completely deny things I firmly believed in and restructuring my entire theory bases to justify my impulses.

However, the manias do not change my emotions; they simply exaggerate and enhance them. This is important to point out because the nature of bipolar illness is physical—they are still my thoughts and emotions, but my words and feelings are just not tempered or rationalized because they are coming too fast to filter. What I say during those times is always based in fact or reasoned opinion at its inception, but it is overstated (and felt) to the extreme.

Another common part of my manias are delusions (the presence of delusions or hallucinations being the distinguishing criterion between bipolar I and—the less severe—bipolar II). The term delusion has very negative connotations, but in my case it usually means that I believe more strongly in my ability to read hidden messages in people's words and gestures. A generally perceptive person anyway, the omnipotence I feel during manias becomes all-inclusive and I second-guess everyone's motives and actions, often building elaborate ideas about what is being said or done behind my back (paranoia).

I'm very careful and have become skilled at not letting many people see the disordered me. The me who is irritated and mean, who says and does things that she regrets. I'm sorry for whatever of the latter has been forced upon you. If I had known what I do now, I would have been medicated and insisted on good care a decade ago. Some of you have been cut off from me because of the disorder, and some have had their entire lives shaken by it, and "I'm sorry" seems like the lamest possible thing I can say in the face of that, but I truly am sorry.

*   *   *

This letter—written after my release from the mental hospital—garnished little reaction from anyone. Many of my friends had already abandoned me after I committed myself to a psychiatric hospital, and many others changed the way they viewed me. This made me angry, and were it not for the three steps that my mental health team worked on with me, I would not have chosen life these past years. Those not-so-simple steps were (1) insisting on a good mental health team, (2) finding a good support system, and (3) being open to learning as much as possible about my disorder.

The need for a good mental health team (MHT) is listed first because it has been the most immediate, if not most important, predictor of my success. A minimal MHT would include a psychiatrist whom I see monthly and a counselor (either a psychologist or social worker) whom I can see as needed. A larger MHT would include the aforementioned, a good insurance agent who understands the ins and outs of mental health parity and community mental health clinics, and a social worker who serves as an advocate for my care and coordinates the team that works with me. No professional in this chain is more important than another, though each serves different needs. However, each individual has to know my case, know my disorder, and—most important—view herself or himself as an advisor (not an authority figure) in my mental health care. Even a great psychiatrist who meets these criteria rarely has time to discuss anything other than my medication. She or he cannot spare the time (as most psychiatrists—especially at community mental health centers—are scheduled in fifteen-minute blocks) to discuss personal topics like my mother's death or another trauma I may be experiencing, except in the context of how it has affected the efficiency of my medications. Similarly, my social worker cannot change my medicines, but she or he may be able to help me understand where added anxiety or depression is coming from and suggest behavior management techniques to combat the added symptoms (eliminating the need for higher doses or different medications). The main need I have when working with my MHT is to feel secure that each individual is willing to acknowledge my nuances (as they relate to that professional's role in the MHT) and recognize that every disorder manifests itself in subtly different ways from patient to patient. I have had doctors overmedicate me because they were unwilling to take my concerns about side effects seriously "because this is the normal dose for someone like" me. Refusing to accept that a book of dosages could accurately reflect everyone's medical needs, and unable to perform my job because of side effects, I went off my medication completely and became clinically depressed. Had the doctor validated my concerns and reduced the medicine (I am with a new doctor on a lower dosage and having no side effects), I would not have been subjected to an unnecessary ultimatum of oversedation verses noncompliance with the medication. I have also had counselors condescend to me when I have presented various concerns, a certain way to ensure that I close myself off emotionally to them (thus severing the relationship emotionally, if not literally).

Moreover, I currently see a physician who encourages my input and participation in the process of finding the right medications for me. Knowing that I research any changes I am considering, he weighs my opinions with me and the ultimate medications I take are mutually agreed upon. My counselor also supports me without creating a hierarchy between us. I feel comfortable demanding good care because I know that—if I demand it loudly enough—I will receive it. However, it should be the goal of anyone who works with the mentally ill to value their personhood and validate their opinions (and their family's opinions, secondarily), even if they are undereducated about their illness and too afraid to demand what they need.

A good support system springs either from existing support (e.g., family and friends) or through the referrals of members of a patient's MHT. Let there be no mistake, being mentally ill is still very stigmatized. I am dismissed, ignored, mocked, and openly made fun of because of my mental disorder. I also experience larger than normal mood swings, despite the medication, and can have "breakthrough" manias at any time. In addition to that, my son has attention deficit hyperactivity disorder. This volatile mix can wreak havoc on a family of four, especially on the two members who struggle to understand my son's and my disorders. Fortunately grassroots organizations and large advocacy networks like NAMI (National Alliance for the Mentally Ill) provide "living with mental illness" meetings for my son and I and family-centered groups for my daughter and husband. NAMI frequently hosts free workshops for families and friends of the mentally ill that explain a particular mental illness in-depth. The value of such groups cannot be overstated, and it behooves mental health professionals to know these organizations and to create liaisons with them so that they can confidently refer patients for additional support.

Learning about my disorder has been the single most liberating part of my illness. I have asked permission to do research papers on the disorder, spent summers reading clinical reference books, sorting through abstracts, and spending time listening to both professionals who treat mental illness and individuals who are living with mental illnesses to understand what may be happening inside my head when I cycle into a mania or depression. Because my disorder is being continually researched, there is always something to learn. Much of my interest in learning more stemmed from brochures lying around my physician's office. Instead of reading about how I needed to lose ten pounds or how to do my makeup perfectly, I read about Paxil, Zoloft, Zyprexa, bipolar affective disorder, schizophrenia, and other mental health topics in brochures displayed next to the *Glamour* magazines. Every patient won't want to read clinical research, but many can benefit from brochures, books written for (and by) patients, and Web sites that explore mental health issues (many of which include chat rooms for empowering patients through the exchange of ideas).

As I look back over the last few years, I find myself thankful for the wonderful mental health professionals I have met, and I also feel proud that I was able to insist on the proper care when I did not get it. However, as a mental health professional myself, I realize that many patients are not college educated, do not have good insurance that allows them to choose their providers, and lack the resources to get the care they need. This is why America faces a mental health epidemic, and why each mental health professional needs to advocate for clients' rights. In recent years, we, as mental health professionals, have become legally liable for ensuring the proper care of our patients, but with one out of every four or five bipolar patients successfully committing suicide, somehow our human liability still seems a much higher priority.

Questions for Discussion

1. One problem in treating people with bipolar disorder is noncompliance with medication. What are some of the possible reasons a person with this disorder would not want to take or might discontinue the use of medication for this illness?
2. What strategies could a helping professional employ to assist a client with medication compliance that do not involve threats, humiliation, or "pulling rank" (e.g., "I am the expert and I know best")?
3. What does the author consider to be the components of a comprehensive treatment plan for bipolar illness?

SCHIZOPHRENIA AND OTHER PSYCHOTIC DISORDERS

The Sleep of Reason

Alan Howard

When it came, and it was bound to return sooner or later, it struck suddenly, unexpectedly, mercilessly, and with great violence, just as it had so many times before. This time, though, the timing was all wrong.

Actually, the day was meant to be one of those minor milestones in a contented life. Craig Townsend awoke early so that he could drink several cups of his special Kenya AA coffee and smoke one of his high-quality cigars. Today, the last day of February, he would teach just one more class at Ultima Thule College, and then the institution would close for winter vacation. Following a weekend of homework he would say good-bye to his daughter, Amy, and the brutal Michigan winter and fly to Alabama for six days of relaxation on the Gulf of Mexico. That was the plan, and he was happy.

That is perhaps why the first hour of class went so well. Craig lectured on the background of Victorian English literature, and if his presentation was not inspiring, it was humorous, and the students took well to it.

During the break he mingled with his students in the hall, explaining several times that Amy would not accompany him on his trip because her high school was still in session. He tried to keep his mind on the task at hand, banishing thoughts of beaches and palm trees. After a few moments he eyed the hall clock and prepared to herd his charges back into class, but before he could, his worst nightmare was actualized. Out of the next classroom stepped Tricia Winchester, his research writing student, and she was dressed in pink. The experience of seeing her was horrible beyond imagination! She stepped to the drinking fountain, and Craig could see that she sported a pink top, pink pants, and pink shoes. Completely unprepared for this assault on his senses, he steadied himself against the wall and wrestled with an unnameable agony. He was already late for class, but he ran to his office and retrieved an Ativan, which he kept for an occasion such as this. His heart raced precipitously, and after he swallowed the pill, he felt the wall all the way back to the classroom.

"Class," he said, approaching the lectern as if he had not left it, "we were considering the impact of the utilitarians upon . . . upon . . ."

"Carlyle!" chirped one of the men in the back row.

"Carlyle, yes," Craig continued. The class was changed in a strange way, and an electric charge of malevolence crackled in the air. "Yes, as I was saying, Bentham and Mill created the philosophy of utilitarianism to correct the evils of society, but Carlyle . . ." In the third row Jessica Hanley scratched her eye, throwing Craig even more off balance. "Carlyle rejected the anti-spirituality of Bentham and . . . Bentham and . . ."

"Mill!" offered Sissy Smith.

Craig tried to control his thoughts, but he was completely devastated when Susie Snodgrass in the front row whispered to the girl in the next seat, "Hey, Di, slip me some Juicy Fruit, will ya?"

He knew then that he could not continue. "Class," he mumbled, "it has come to my . . . to my attention . . . that I don't feel so well, so I'm going to cancel—"

The class erupted with screams of joy before he could finish his sentence, and the students began to gather their books. Craig added his last thoughts. "Finish *Sartor Resartus* for the day after vacation . . ." but his words were lost. Most of the students had already left the room.

A moment later, feeling the first effect of the tranquilizer, he walked numbly to his office. Collecting his composition papers, he slipped out a side door without speaking to anyone and drove home the most inconspicuous way.

Driving cautiously down Thirtieth Street he felt the comfort of the drug and tried to concentrate, but his mind raced with a jumble of disconnected, unrequested thoughts.

Coming to the end of the street he turned on Third Avenue North and drove as slowly as he could past the ShopKo store. Just as he neared the parking lot, a rusty Oldsmobile pulled out in front of him and decelerated suddenly so that their bumpers almost touched. As Craig stepped on the brake pedal he caught sight of the car's license plate: 124DTY.

If he was horrified before, he experienced sheer panic at this moment. He pulled to the side of the road, stopped the engine, and clutched his chest in anticipation of a heart attack. He may have been confused, but it took less than a second to decipher the message that the Oldsmobile driver had sent him. One plus two plus four equals seven. Seven is the number of deadly sins. The Bible says that the wages of sin is death. Therefore, DTY means Death To You.

A half hour later Craig regained some composure and putted home. Amy was still in school, he knew, so now he would be able to collect his thoughts. He sat in his favorite easy chair, petting his beagle Gargantua, and lit a cigar. Then he began to weep. His dog, looking as quizzical as the RCA Victor dog hearing His Master's Voice, stretched to meet his face, whimpered sympathetically, and licked his eyes. Craig responded with a heartfelt hug, squeezing the one creature who was not intelligent enough to hate him.

After a few kisses and puffs of smoke, Craig sat back to review the evidence, which he categorized methodically:

1. Tricia Winchester wore pink today. She is writing a term paper on suicide. Therefore, the Conspiracy wants me to associate self-murder with the color pink, which I will see everywhere, of course, and that will drive me to destruction.
2. Jessica scratched her eye with her middle finger. That was obviously an obscene gesture aimed at me.
3. Susie called Diane Rutherford Di. She never does that. She always calls her Diane. Obviously she meant die.
4. The driver of the Oldsmobile expressed his wish for my death with his license plate. That proves that the Conspiracy has spread beyond Ultima Thule. Someone in the secretary of state's office in Lansing is cooperating.
5. Co-workers have been lending me books and articles about suicide and talking about skiing at Suicide Hill in Marquette.

Satisfied that he had marshaled enough proof of the Conspiracy, Craig reassured himself that he only needed to endure for three more days and then he could flee to a safer clime in Alabama. And yet, there remained a lingering thought that the Conspiracy might not be real after all. Since it was remotely possible that his suspicions were merely the product of an overactive imagination, he decided to phone his psychiatrist for a prescription for Loxitane, just on the off chance that he was experiencing a relapse of mental illness.

That afternoon, having obtained his medicine, Craig felt too agitated to correct papers, so he brooded in his study over the evidence of hatred. At 3:30 Amy came home, but he didn't greet her. Enshrouded in loneliness, he kept to himself all evening, took his Loxitane at 11:00, and retired to a night of fitful sleep.

Saturday morning Craig awoke from uneasy dreams and spent an hour in his chair, drinking ordinary coffee and smoking an ordinary cigar. When Shakespeare spoke of the thousand natural shocks that flesh is heir to, he anticipated Craig's miseries. At 11:50 the professor collected the mail from his postal box. Twelve envelopes were held together with a rubber band, and the top envelope displayed a bright red "D" sticker—D for Death.

That afternoon he decided that, come what may, his homework needed to be completed, so he sat down to correct a batch of composition papers. He glanced at the first paper, but he couldn't finish it. He didn't know what it was about, but it mentioned the word "hang" six times. The next paper, though, raised the art of subtlety to new levels. If one looked at the first letters of the sixteenth, seventeenth, eighteenth, and nineteenth lines, they spelled out D-E-A-D. At length Craig recognized the futility of his attempts and put the project off. The rest of the day he spoke to Amy and Gargantua a few times but otherwise hid in his study.

Sunday morning Amy visited a Lutheran church with a friend, and Craig went to the Methodist church alone, hoping the solace of religion would pacify his mind. This attempt, too, was futile. He felt the hatred of the other parishioners, a loathing that made it impossible for him to concentrate on the sermon. Over and over he mumbled, "Bless them that persecute me," as a mantra, but he didn't achieve the desired effect of reconciliation. Deeper and deeper into the innermost core of his mind he went. It was ironic, too. Years ago his wife had left him because he was uncommunicative and too much within himself, but Craig felt that her judgment of him was not valid. How can one communicate when his mind is a black hole that sucks in every detail like a gigantic Hoover and lets nothing out? How can one reach out to others when his mind is imploding? Or, perhaps better put, how can one share his thoughts when others are stealing them and replacing them with new, unwanted thoughts? In the end, the everlasting arms did not reach out to support him.

After lunch Craig made a serious attempt to read the *Detroit Free Press* in his easy chair. He could not comprehend it, so his thoughts were not interrupted when Amy walked in with her friend Tammy. "Look, Dad," she said. "I've brought you the videotape of *Amadeus*. I know how much you love Mozart."

He thanked her for her thoughtfulness and placed the tape in the VCR but was surprised to learn that the girls were not going to watch it with him. "Enjoy yourself, Dad," Amy remarked. "We're going skating." And then they left.

This could be just the right diversion, Craig thought, as he lit an expensive cigar and settled in to enjoy one of his favorite movies. This time, though, he saw it differently. First came a jumble of noise and then the driving strings of the Symphony no. 25 in G Minor, and a number of people ran through snow-covered streets, and then two peasants climbed some steps, and then, following an agonizing scream, Craig saw Mozart's rival, Salieri, lying in a pool of his own blood, the result of a self-inflicted wound. Craig arose, shut off the VCR, and sat back down in the deepest despair imaginable. His own daughter had joined the Conspiracy. The baby he had cradled in his arms now desired his death. Oh, how sharper than a serpent's tooth.

Hours later Amy returned to find her father depressed. Having learned the valorous part of discretion years ago, she kept silent, tiptoeing through the house to accomplish her activities. Later, Craig hugged her and informed her that he would not be taking his trip to Alabama after all. She accepted his pronouncement knowingly, and he retired to another restless night.

For the next week Craig remained in his study, coming out only for meals, while Amy looked after herself. The next Sunday night, feeling braver, he stepped out onto the front porch and watched the neighbors walking by. One woman wore a pink jacket, but Craig did not feel threatened. And then it hit him—he was being ignored, the most wonderful feeling a person could have. No one wished him ill. All was well again.

Then he looked across the street. The sun was going down, spreading fingers of orange and yellow across the western sky. Craig had survived once more. Once again the sun came up, the sun went down, and Craig was none the worse for any of his experiences. Like Tennyson in *In Memoriam A. H. H.,* Craig felt that he knew virtually nothing. Why these spells appeared, why they disappeared—he had no idea. Yet he could live with ignorance if only the world would let him live. No one hated him now; in fact, no one had hated him before. He would die, of course, but the hour of his death would be chosen by fate, not by an imagined conspiracy.

Craig returned to his kitchen and took a sip of coffee. It tasted rich. Life was good and would continue to be. He would silently apologize to all of those he had wronged with his suspicions and vow to live a good, decent, mentally sound life. He would join the human race once more. Yes, life was very, very good, and it would remain so, at least until the next time.

Questions for Discussion

1. What treatment would you like to see this patient receive in addition to the medications he was prescribed?
2. Using the DSM-IV, what diagnosis would you assign to the narrator?
3. What might have been going on in his daughter's mind and how might she have been counseled regarding her own and her father's well-being?

Searching the Headlights

Gary Guillot

This is how I remember it. There was a convenience store across the street from a high school, and at lunchtime the students would converge on the store, and as they left, they would throw their pennies on the parking lot. When they were gone, I would pick them up and take them to a small room I rented at a rooming house, just big enough for a bed, a nightstand, and a broken suitcase containing a powder blue tuxedo from another life. There were never enough pennies, so I made a shoplifter's coat out of an old army jacket and taught myself how to steal.

The hospital made me move close by so they could grab me if they wanted to. So they could snatch me off a flagpole or pull me from the jaws of death, as long as they felt in control. But all I did most of the time was lie in the dark and talk to the past.

At first I yearned for people. I ached to talk to someone, but I didn't think any of my old friends wanted to see me. I had grown ugly and forgetful, but I think they would have come to visit if they knew how bad it was for me. I may not have known them anyway . . .

At the end of the day I would lock myself safely in my room and go a little more insane. I really had no control over my emotions and all I did was rock back and forth on my bed.

One day a fat woman came to see me. I didn't know her, but she knew me. She took her clothes off. Then she took my clothes off. She laid ten dollars on the bed before she left. I looked at the money when she was gone and rubbed it in my fingers. I felt the sheets. She had been real.

One day I got lost while taking a walk and decided to take a nap on somebody's lawn. I was tired and I didn't know where I was. It made perfect sense to me.

I was glad to see the two policemen who grabbed me by the arms and pulled me to my feet. "Man, I am so happy to see you guys; you're heroes, you know." There was a couple standing half the yard away staring at me and I asked the policemen, "Who are they?"

"They're the owners of this property," said one of them.

"Peachy," I said and waved. "Once you guys saved me from a giant dog."

"What are you doing here?" asked one of the policemen.

"I was lost, but now I'm found. The boys in blue have come to take me home."

"The boys in blue are taking you to jail," said the other policeman.

"That's all right. I like cop cars. Cop cars are cool. I'm insane you know."

"No kidding," said one of them.

"And you're a pig," I burst out. "You're nothing but amoeba. You're slime. You're robots with guns. You're idiots. You're assholes! Did you hear that? You're nothing but worthless sons of bitches."

The next morning the judge let me go, considering the fact that it was my first offense and because I think he thought I was stupid. He told me to try sitting down when I got tired. He seemed to be a good man. I could tell he cared about me. He was a real swell guy.

It was snowing when I walked home, the heavy wet kind that children chase with their tongues. Someone had pasted a long ribbon of flypaper on the sidewalk. It was covered with little human being things and everybody walking on it made a sucking sound.

Not one person was looking at me though. At best, they seemed to be looking through me. This told me that I was invisible. There was only one thing I didn't like about being invisible, that was stray bullets. Can you imagine if I caught one, being invisible and all? A stream of crimson blood would pour out of thin air and form a puddle of black and red vital fluids on the sidewalk. The pedestrians would walk around it in case it was even worse than it appeared to be. They would walk around it as if it were a big steaming pile of dog shit, but it would be me.

I knew I was in trouble when I found an open bottle of beer sitting on my nightstand, still full, and a cigarette burned to ashes, lighted but unsmoked. To waste a beer is a grave and personal crime in that state of mind. To waste a cigarette is another crime.

One 4:00 a.m. I woke up wearing my powder blue tuxedo. It was saturated with blood. I closed my eyes and searched my mind for an explanation, but my mind was just an empty place. Then I began to hurt. Then I began to yell. I yelled until somebody found me.

When I awoke, standing above me was an extremely ugly woman, wearing a nurse's uniform and torturing me.

"That hurts, you know," I said.

"Oh, shut up. We'll never stop the bleeding if we don't get this gravel out of your face."

"There's gravel in my face?"

"Like you don't know."

"I don't know."

"Well, you've got gravel in your face. Lots of gravel."

"What's wrong with me?"

"Your arms are broken and you're in pain."

"Excuse me, but I have to ask. Are you the enemy?"

"I'm the head nurse."

"If that's so, what's the enemy like?"

"She's just like me."

"You can go now, Nurse," said the doctor as he entered the room.

"She's not very nice, is she?"

"She's a witch, but she has a contract."

"May I ask you a personal question, Doctor?"

"Certainly."

"Does it mean you're crazy if you go looking for God in the headlights of automobiles?"

Questions for Discussion

1. What diagnosis would you give this person?
2. What combination treatment would you recommend for him?
3. What community support services could he benefit from?

Dissociative Identity Disorder

Jessica K. Heriot

She cannot speak the words
to say what happened
Trapped in her throat,
She talks in nods and whispers

"When I turned to stone,
pieces of myself,
chunks of me,
flew into orbit
too far to touch

The child cries lost tears,
pleading for cocoa and poo bear.
her sobs, like the hum of traffic,
always present, barely noticed

The tough one rages and roars
prowling empty midnight streets
courting danger
when we are weak with fear

The watching one
who never sleeps
on duty by my bed
my soldier of the night

A twelve-year-old grabs the wheel
and drives to unknown places

Who are you?
I want to know, and don't."

She must reel them back
bring them home
till she is solid as the earth,
till ordinary day
turns to ordinary night,
and the earth circles the sun
in glorious monotony
till she is whole again.

Questions for Discussion

1. How many parts does the person describe in this poem? What is the function of each?
2. Why do you think the person is ambivalent about knowing who the twelve-year-old is?

A Narrative of Survival

A Traveler

I was conceived because of a lie. I was born of the union of greed and desperation. How could my name have been anything other than Shame? That one deadly word has haunted me all of my life—the feeling that I had no right to be here, that something was bad about me. My mother was a fading former beauty queen born into a patrician family that had lost its great fortune but not its pride. My father was a philanderer who married for money and then couldn't abide his wife's superiority. My mother met him on the rebound after the breakup of a ten-year relationship with an ambassador; she was desperate, getting older, feeling lonely, aware that all of her friends had long since married. The philanderer was estranged from his wife, awaiting a divorce, and claimed that he could not have children. He told his parents of the "rich" beauty queen he had met; they were prejudiced against her from the beginning—assuming her to be haughty from his description. My mother, who found my father's machismo too powerful to resist, became pregnant, and they married as soon as his divorce was final.

My mother's family despised my father from the start; they found him vulgar, boisterous, and a fake. It wasn't long before my mother began to agree with them. For his part, my father soon realized that his new partner had more style than money and that he had been forced to marry her because she was pregnant with me—thus he resented me from the beginning. He saw her and her family as effete, domineering, and haughty. These judgments dominated my childhood. Anytime I displeased my father, I was demeaned as being like my mother; when I displeased my mother, I was described as the spawn of the cad who was my father. I was, at age four, put out of the car by mother and her sister and left on the roadside for acting like my father. Eventually, they came back for me—but not before I had become desperate, frightened, and totally ashamed. My father threatened constantly to send me away to military school. He pointed out the orphanage in our town, saying if I did not do what he wanted, he would send me there. The threat of abandonment was always a part of my young life. Thus, the emotional abuse began. Had this been all I suffered, I should have been like millions of children of bad marriages—the unhappy offspring of disappointed people ill suited to each other. Unfortunately, the members of my family had their own pathology that ran much deeper.

My father was an angry man, repressed and frustrated, locked into a deal he had made that did not offer the benefits he expected. My mother was too proud ever to divorce him. The stage, of course, was set for violence. My father beat me unmercifully and on the slightest pretext. I cried the first time I saw the film *Mommie Dearest* when Joan Crawford dragged her daughter out of bed and beat her with the wire hanger because a dress was hung improperly. It was my childhood all over. Once my father yanked me from sleep and beat me viciously because I had drawn in a new magazine—all the while shouting obscenities at me. I have come to see that his capricious anger and attendant violence were always the result of his being furious with my mother and transferring the anger to me because he could not get away with hitting her. On the night of the magazine incident, my mother had gotten drunk at a party and treated him with disdain—something his overweening pride could not stand.

The older I became, the greater my father's violence. He would beat me and tell me that, if I cried, he would hit me harder. On one occasion, he had beaten me so severely that I was a quivering, red, shaken mess, barely able to walk or make sense. He forgot that we were expecting guests and when the doorbell rang, he panicked. He told me I must go and wash and come back downstairs and act as if nothing had happened. I begged to be allowed to stay in my room. He refused. He said that if I let the guests know anything was wrong, he would kill me when they left—I truly believed he would. That evening was pure hell. The people who came to visit never returned to our home.

By the time I was a teenager, I was in fear of my life. When my mother and I traded her car in on another one while my father was out of town, he fairly seethed with rage. When there was a small problem with the car we bought, he flew into a rage. My father screamed that I had no right to make deals with "his" vehicle and began to slap and throw me. He hit until I said that I wished I were dead. He then put a loaded pistol in my mouth and told me to pull the trigger. I broke down completely and he kicked me. I lay curled up and crying in a ball on the floor. And, where was my mother in all of this? Often she stood and watched, with terrible pain in her eyes, and let me take the blows that were meant for her. At other times she would send me away—to stay with friends or to stay with my aunt. She was my sometimes savior.

My father began an affair with his secretary when I was a preteen. My mother knew, her family knew, his family knew—none of them approved. The hotter this affair got, the more difficult my mother became to handle and the greater the rage she poured out on my father—she used her one powerful weapon: a very sharp tongue. She demeaned him over and over, reminding him how common she thought him. She usually did this when she was drinking; the alcohol changed her from a loving mother into a wicked, haughty, and vicious witch. His anger was unleashed through more and more violent attacks on me.

When my mother was diagnosed with terminal cancer, there was a lull in the rage. He was afraid she would leave him and he would not inherit what money there would be. Soon enough, however, she began to outlive the one year given her by the doctors, and he got frustrated and very violent. She quickly sickened and died. After she was gone, he was very kind to me—until I had signed all the papers necessary to see that I got nothing and he got everything. He married his mistress and soon left me to survive alone in the world at the tender age of seventeen.

I grew up. I put myself through college, earning a degree summa cum laude. I decided I was gay, moved to a large city, and came out. I worked in corporate and investment banking. I met a kind, gentle man and settled down with him to build a life together. We were both highly successful and quite affluent. I hoped to be free of the past, but who can ever be free of it? My dreams were haunted by hurt and pain. I had terrible memories of ghosts entering my room in the dark—not knowing what this meant, I accepted the notion of the supernatural as real. I had terrible bouts of depression and made a few unsuccessful suicide attempts when I was at my lowest. My lover always helped me through—he was the strength that helped me hang on, the one who believed in me and loved me no matter what.

Then, most unexpectedly, my lover died a horrible and premature death. I was completely shocked and vulnerable. He had provided a love and stability that had always been lacking in my life. With his death, I was more alone and lost than ever. I returned to the town where I was born—I think I was seeking answers from the past. There I met the person who has literally saved my life, my psychologist. Although I had been in therapy on and off for years, I never made much progress. As soon as things got too painful, I would run away.

My depressions were becoming more and more severe. I would also find myself in situations that were violent and destructive. I would find myself dressed in clothing that was not at all like me and in sexual situations that were terribly dangerous; I began to lose time. It was as though I wanted to be punished. I needed help and I knew it. I sought out and found my therapist. After a number of sessions, she wisely insisted that I begin to take antidepressants. I worked with a psychiatrist to find the right medicine, which for me turned out to be Remeron. Once the drug had begun to work in my system, I could handle the difficult times in therapy without going into the "hole" or running away from what was too painful to think about.

After doing a lot of work with the emotional and physical abuse I suffered as a child (more severe and more frequent than I have outlined in this brief narrative), I opened up about some of my odd memories. I spoke of the ghosts I remembered and of floating around my house. As we delved deeper into specific memories, the "ghosts" began to disappear and I saw what was behind them. The memories, even now, are almost too painful to describe. The earliest dissociated memory was of me lying in my baby bed at the age of three or four: a white light began to fill the room, I heard a bell toll, something large and white was coming toward me out of the white light, I floated up and away. After time passed, I heard the bell again and floated back into my bed—where I felt hurt, afraid, and lonely. As the real memory emerged, it was my father coming toward me, he was naked, he had a horrible and lustful drool, he forced his penis on me. At that time, I slept in my parents' bedroom and in the background I could see my mother asleep in the bed.

Once this first awful memory was revealed, a cascade of memories returned. I also began to realize that some of the "games" my father made me play were sick. He would make me play a game where I had to sit on the floor and stick my head up through his legs while facing him. The object was not to let him pinch his legs together and catch my head—of course, he always did and would rub my face against his penis.

Sometimes I had bad feelings about memories that were partial and seemingly innocent, such as the memory of my father driving me to school one morning when I was in second grade. I had on short pants and was cold because he had the window down. I remember feeling ashamed. Going back, I recalled why. At that time, my mother, who was a teacher, would leave home early in the morning. I would be fed and dressed and told to wake my father, who would take me to school on his way to the office. I was always afraid to wake him. On the morning of this memory, I woke him and he pulled me into bed with him. He slobbered all over me, forced me to perform fellatio, and rubbed his penis between my legs until he ejaculated. Then, disgusted with me, he pushed me out of bed and told me to get cleaned up.

All of the sexual encounters with my father were abusive. He would do horribly sadistic things, such as rubbing my face with the washcloth he had used for cleanup after defecating. He would lure me into sexual games and then express his disgust afterward by shaming and blaming me.

As an adult, I have come to realize that my father wanted to beat and rape my mother because of his resentment of her, yet he knew that he could not. So, he did these things to me. I became his shame. He always said I was not man enough, I was not good enough.

At the same time that I was suffering this abuse, I was also the pawn of a classic pedophile—my mother's sister. Although she was always the relative who did the most for me, even as an adult, I felt repugnance each time she touched me and felt guilty about this. The memories that emerged here were less violent but equally sick. My aunt was an alcoholic who would entice me to her house; sometimes I was sent to her to protect me from my father—how ironic. She would feed me all of the treats I was not allowed to have at home and then pull me into her bed and fondle me—forcing me to fondle her as well. Often, she would be so drunk she would throw up on me. In her sober state, she emotionally abused me—calling me lazy, weak, not man enough, just like my father. How odd that she and my father hated each other.

All of these memories (those hidden and those not) had a devastating effect on me. I became an adult who remembered none of the sexual abuse but acted based upon it and the other wickedness I had suffered. From the emotional abuse, I felt I had to be better at everything so as not to be abandoned or worthless. From the physical abuse, I developed an oversensitivity about justice and terrible rage. From the sexual abuse, I felt confused about sex, unsure how it went with love. It was in this last area that everything broke down. When my lover died, I felt ashamed to live on. I began to involve myself with sadistic men and to feel pleasure from being punished. This is when I entered therapy seriously: I knew I would get myself killed otherwise.

After two years of therapy, I had remembered most of the sexual abuse. Then, the most devastating memory came—that my mother, my only defender (however occasional) in that mad household, had begun a relationship with me as a teen. All of the shame returned. I felt that I had made the choice to become my mother's lover, that I was old enough to have known better. Suddenly, I knew why Oedipus gouged out his eyes. It has taken a great deal of emotional work to make peace with this memory. My therapist was gentle in helping me to see that where there is no choice, there can be no moral judgment, that I was living in a nightmare, a madhouse where the only person who tried at all to protect me gave me no choice but to become her lover. This was the most difficult betrayal. My mother, I think, did this out of her loneliness and out of a kind of love (albeit a sick one). She did not do this with the intent to hurt, as had my father. She did not do it from pathology, as had my aunt. Nonetheless, it was wrong of her, and I lost the only "hero" of my childhood.

Throughout my therapy, I had described my moods as "inner parts." I began to name them. I also began to recall memories that made no sense: flashes of myself in relationships with people I had no other memory of; too many memories for the same time period; not enough memories of a time period. We began to explore these memories, how I felt in recalling them, changes in the way I behaved. One day after we had been working for months to synthesize some of these extremes and deal with my inner conflicts, I said to my therapist, "My diagnosis isn't just severe depression." She said very gently, "No." I said, "It's dissociative identity disorder." Very quietly, she said, "Yes." She had let me come to this in my own time and in my own way. We talked about how, even before I named it, we had been working to explore this dissociation and to integrate parts. I said, "I had many, many parts—not just a few." She admitted, "Hundreds." We talked about the times I had been my alters and confirmed her witnessing them. It was only after I had healed enough, after a dominant and integrated personality had begun to emerge, that I could recognize what my life had been.

It was through this dominant personality emerging, more centered, more at peace, that I realized I am essentially heterosexual. I had felt very emasculated by the women who raised me and remembered my aunt's sexual abuse first (yet only in a vague way) while I was in college. Homosexuality was, therefore, a safe haven for me. However, with my lover's death, the abusive father within had emerged and made homosexuality unsafe, too. Only when I set sex aside altogether and began to work on my mental healing did an innate and gentle sexuality appear. It could have been homosexual or heterosexual—I make no judgment on that: either orientation can be healthy. In my case, it just happened to be heterosexual. Yet, I pay a great gratitude to the human ability to experience the continuum of sexual orientation since being gay probably saved my life for many years.

As we explored my "pockets" of memory, I realized that there were points (especially right after college and before I met my lover) when I was extremely dissociated—living several lives unknown to one another. One of those, which lasted briefly and then was buried until I began to integrate, was a very "together" man dating a lovely woman. My therapist has often spoken of how there was a will to live in me, a part that wanted to be all right—I think this was the one. He was often overwhelmed and submerged, but as I began to integrate, he became the core of that integration.

I have healed to a great extent. I have gone from being totally unaware of my alters to knowing them as "inner parts" to being aware of the alters and feeling the shifts to integrating these characters. It has been a long process and one that really never ends. I have been in weekly therapy for some years. I know that, in a severe crisis, I run the risk of shifting. But, I have learned to recognize what that shift feels like. I am still recovering memories. To integrate, I have had to learn to love or at least accept each alter. This has, at times, been horribly difficult. Some parts are very unlovable; nonetheless, to become whole, these alters must be accepted—otherwise, they remain separate parts with the power to take control. My psychologist has helped me to see this. I know that, to some extent, I shall always be in therapy.

I feel very fortunate to have found my therapist. She is an expert in working with abused children. She is able to let me make my discoveries in my own time, yet to encourage me gently. She knows when to urge me forward and when to let me rest with what I have learned, giving me time to process it. She has been able to help me see what is or was destructive without shaming me or allowing me to shame myself. Her approach to therapy is diverse. Although we primarily use a cognitive or talking therapy based upon my daily journal, she has had me work in clay, create sand trays, dialogue between inner parts, read (the stories of others, poetry, affirming works, and so on), and write letters (which I choose to send or not). She has encouraged me to work through relationships and helped me heal enough to end destructive ones.

Perfectionism and shame have been the two sides of the dangerous coin I have spun all my life. I am learning to be kinder to myself and, thus, to others. Expecting the impossible was the lesson I learned as a child—yet no one could be both what my mother wanted (the urbane, civilized, elegant, mannerly intellectual) and what my father wanted (the athletic, outgoing, tough guy). Failure meant shame. I have learned that shame is never good because it says, "I *am* bad." Guilt can be good; it is an appropriate reaction at times because it says, "I *did* something bad." With guilt comes the ability to make amends. With shame, the only amends would be death—hence my old suicide attempts. Shame is now a warning signal for me. When I feel it, I realize that it is only a feeling and begin to assess why it has occurred. Usually, I can work through the cause and let go of the shame. I no longer live by the motto "Win or die."

I was not brought up to trust. I was betrayed all my young life. Yet the only way I have made the great strides that I have in therapy has been through trusting—myself and my therapist. I feel so incredibly fortunate to have found a therapist of such high integrity, such gentle wisdom, and such keen insight. She has taught me how to trust wisely.

My journey of discovery and becoming and healing is far from over. But, I have reached a turning point, the vantage of which shows me hope, brings me peace and healing, and leads me to the future. I just now am able truly to believe I have a right to be here and that no one, including myself, has the right to shame me or hurt me. Even though my therapist tells me I have done all the work, I know that I could not have done it without her.

Questions for Discussion

1. Look up dissociative identity disorder in the DSM-IV. What symptoms does this person display that would substantiate this diagnosis?
2. The author describes hundreds of inner parts or alters, how do you think this can be?
3. Several important guidelines exist for working with people with DID: developing a trusting and collaborative relationship; being clear that sexual and physical abuse is wrong; and helping the patient to put together a coherent narrative of fragments of memory and to work toward integration of the patient's inner parts. Where in the narrative does the therapist do these things?

4. What are some countertransference issues that therapists may experience in working with someone with DID?
5. Considerable controversy surrounds recovered memories and whether people actually dissociate memories that are held by separate parts of the person. What do you think?

EATING DISORDERS

The Shape of Things

Jamie Joy Gatto

I used to tease him when I stroked his belly. I used to say that he must have come from a pod. At the smooth, oblique spot where his navel should have been, but wasn't, he had instead what looked like the part of a cantaloupe where it was once joined to the vine. No delicate blond fuzz would grow over the scar tissue left from a herniated umbilical cord at birth—the only thing soft in the middle of a marine-made washboard stomach.

When he reached for my center, to touch mine in reciprocation, I shuddered and folded myself up small. Laughing, he tried to tickle and taunt at what he called the perfect "in-ey." I just stiffened corpselike and climbed from the tangled mess of sheets.

If I was smaller, he would love me, really love me. But I am a blob.

On the first of our last dates, I positioned the car visor's mirror in such a way that I could view my middle as I drove to his house, messy fat melting like wax as I held in my belly.

Don't breathe. Maybe then, he'll never notice.

Smiling as he saw me, trying to hide the fact that he didn't notice the atrocity, he just couldn't keep salt off the wound. He touched me at my waist, slipping a finger into my belt loop, testing the density of my girth, kissing my cheek and laughing with sadistic pleasure at my weakness. He told me I looked beautiful. I called him a liar and left.

I went to the gallery opening without him. I ate one strawberry and three grapes. The box wine made me dizzy. A man with a silver tray offered me some Brie on a cracker. It wiggled like lard, reflecting in the shine of the metal tray. I held my breath and swallowed the bile that came up in my throat.

Another message on my answering machine with sweet lies. How could he be sorry when he knew he had found the ache and shoved it in my face? Size three may be a small number, but it's the shape of things that counts.

Questions for Discussion

1. What might eventually bring this woman into treatment?
2. How would you address the issue of distorted body image with a client who has an eating disorder?

Two Raisinets and a Corn Flake

Jeanne Loo

I was proud of one thing. I had control over my weight. I stepped on the metal scale in Sue Luke's nutrition office. Even though it was a scorching hot Tuesday in July 1989, I wore my heavy Nike aerobic sneakers, bulky black sweat pants, long woolen underwear, red cotton turtleneck, and gray J. Crew cable-knit wool sweater. I watched Sue move the big metal weight to 50 and the little metal weight up toward the right end of the bar. The small cold balance hovered at number 19. I squinted my eyes to get a closer look. Did it land just precisely on the number 19? Yes! I was down one more pound from last week's weight of 70.5. I knew Sue Luke would not be pleased. But I was secretly delighted—the last thing I wanted to do was gain weight. I cherished being as thin as a bird—it was like I had the world wrapped around my little finger with my life zipped up straight and safe. It didn't matter whether or not anyone said I was "too thin." With each pound lost, I gained tighter control over my weight; no doctor or nutritionist could free me from my obsession to be bone thin. At times, I found my quest somewhat disturbing, but I was so caught up in this caged world of mine that I didn't care what anyone did or said to take care of me.

Sue shook her head and said, "You weigh 69.5. This is terribly serious. You could die of heart failure. You must gain at least two pounds by next week or I will have to put you in the hospital for an eating disorder refeeding program."

I pretended to share her concern by nodding my head in agreement. Part of me knew she was right—that my life was in jeopardy. So I meekly asked, "OK, what shall I eat?" But deep inside, I was already thinking of how to lose more weight. It didn't matter to me if Sue thought that I could very possibly, very soon, die from malnutrition.

"Ideally, you should be eating about 4,000 calories a day consisting of protein, carbohydrates, and fat at every meal. In addition to your meals, I'd like you to eat three snacks: midmorning, midafternoon, and bedtime. A woman in your extreme underweight medical condition should also be drinking four cans of nutritional supplements a day, such as Ensure or Sustacal."

I pretended to appear motivated by smiling half-heartedly. "OK, I'll try. What's a snack? Do five plain M&Ms count as a snack? How about carrot sticks?"

"Of course not. By 'snack,' I do not mean candy or rabbit food like carrot and celery sticks. Veggies are mostly water, and candy is all sugar. I mean real snacks containing nutritious calories and nutrients: peanut butter and whole grain crackers, yogurt and cereal, or oatmeal cookies with a glass of whole milk."

I nodded, pretending to cooperate by agreeing. I really didn't see Sue's point at all. I didn't see anything wrong with snacking on low-calorie veggies or nonfat food. After all, these were the foods that people snacked on when they were trying to lose weight. "I see what you mean. Can I drink a can of Slim Fast as a snack? How about one of those low-fat SnackWell's cookies or Hershey's Sweet Escapes candy bars?" I thought to myself, "OK, if I absolutely have to eat, I'll get fat and blow up like a balloon . . . but if I eat commercial fat-free and traditional low-calorie diet food, I'll still feel like I'm dieting and maybe won't get fat."

Sue sighed in frustration. "Absolutely not! NO diet products allowed. I need to get you off of your dieting mentality. You need to be eating real food, not diet food."

I lied, "OK, I promise this week to make an effort. It's hard for me to eat though. I just don't get hungry anymore." The real truth, however, was that I was hungry all the time: morning, noon, and night. Within the hollow emptiness of my stomach, there crouched a hunger beast ready to jump out like a roaring tiger. If I tempted it with one cookie, the animal would gobble up all my efforts to suppress my appetite for food, and for anything else related to a healthy body, including love, human relationships, care, and nourishment. For twenty-five years, I had been compelled to eat less than 900 calories a day to remain skeleton thin.

I permitted myself to eat only two Raisinets and one corn flake for breakfast; four pieces of hard candy, fifty plain M&Ms, and one pack of sugar-free gum for lunch; and a bag of microwave 94 percent fat-free popcorn for dinner. I was also very good at distracting the hunger beast with hours of compulsive exercise, shopping, cleaning chores, and running errands throughout the day. I would put all my waking time, and mental and physical energy, into these elaborate starvation rituals. I simply could not wake the sleeping beast that dwelled in the cage made inside the bones of my skeleton.

I noticed that Sue was watching me for any changes in expression or enthusiasm. She handed me a stack of meal plan sheets, the American Dietetic Association's exchange lists for foods, and a food diary to record my feelings about eating during the day. I knew I didn't want to eat according to those guidelines. I was convinced that my own 900 calorie "diet" was the best game I ever played. I thought if Sue ever knew what I really ate, she'd put me in the hospital and force-feed me. I will establish a game plan: I will think of something to fill in all those blank boxes on those sheets before my next appointment. My next move is to go home and reach into my bookshelf, pull out one of my diet books, and copy the diet down in the empty boxes. I told myself I should have no difficulty with this scheme of making up seven sheets of "pretend" meals to be eaten for breakfast, lunch, and dinner, one for each day of the week. Yes, my goal would be to have these sheets to show Sue and tell her that I ate what was written down on the papers. If she accepted my maneuvers, I would win my game. I vowed to keep this secret lie to myself as my way of competing with Sue. And I was determined to win by losing more weight.

It was 3:30 p.m. It was so hot and sticky out—the temperature was in the nineties, and I was sweating profusely underneath my long underwear and gray wool sweater. My face was beet red from the tension I felt after Sue's appointment. In the taxi going home from her office, I felt terribly nauseous and dizzy from not eating anything all day except two Raisinets and one corn flake with coffee for breakfast, and four Life Savers, two pieces of chewing gum, one Hershey's Chocolate Kiss, and ten M&Ms for lunch. I knew I had to get home fast so I could drink some diet Coke before passing out. As much as I loved the high from self-starvation, at times I thought I was losing my mind. I forgot things easily and sometimes couldn't think straight. I remember trying to fill out a financial aid form for Katie and not being able to read the simple numbers or perform the basic calculations of adding up my taxes. I kept telling myself, "Something could be wrong with this game of mine . . . my brain doesn't seem to be functioning right. But I still have to win, so let me play just one more trick; let me see if I can deceive Sue into thinking that I really did try to put on some weight. Then I'll gain weight "for real" . . . umm . . . maybe sometime next year. But this week? No!" I closed my eyes and fantasized about the two bags of Chips Ahoy! cookies in my kitchen cabinet. I imagined myself standing over the kitchen counter rapidly stuffing the soft chewy rich morsels into my mouth until both bags were empty. But this was only a fantasy, as I would never allow myself to indulge in such binges. I possessed such an overwhelming fear of trying to eat even one cookie; I knew I could never be satisfied with just one or two. Instead, I would lose total control of the hunger monster inside myself. If I ate just one cookie, I knew that the monster would come out like a roaring beast, ready to kill all my efforts to lose more weight. By eating both bags of cookies, I would have lost my game and lost all control of my body.

The taxi continued on toward my home. I opened the window, desperately needing some fresh air, or I felt I would faint. I shut my eyes and recalled the first day I stopped eating. I would never forget that day twenty-five years earlier. I was eighteen years old. My Chinese friend, Cathy Chen, and I were trying on new designer coats. Cathy looked gorgeous and classy in the brown Bill Blass wool A-line garment. When I put on the same coat, the lines of the style didn't cover me as fashionably as they did Cathy. My dad was there and when he saw me, he commented, "Jeanne, you're getting a little fat, aren't you?" That did it. From that day on, I vowed to become as slim and attractive as all my Chinese friends. I constantly reminded myself to put my hand on my stomach to make sure it was flat, and to check that my two hip bones were jutting out to the side. I thought, "Cathy Chen has a flat stomach; well, my stomach is going to be flatter than hers." I was trying both to compete with Cathy and to get my dad's approval.

I began to eat less and less at meals. No desserts, ever. I would put my chopsticks down between bites to make my meal last longer and to prevent myself from eating too much too fast. The first week of this new ritual, I lost two pounds from my normal weight of 103 and felt the first thrill of victory over my body weight. I had a game of control over both my appetite and my weight. I figured, "The less I eat, the more weight I'll lose. It's that simple— less food in, more weight off." What a fantastic feat of starvation! All I had to do was just will my mind into denying my hunger. I managed to concentrate on intellectual things, like sitting at my wooden desk reading Dostoyevsky's *The Brothers Karamazov* until 3:00 in the morning. Somehow this type of mental concentration distracted me from the growl of my hunger pangs. Periodically, I would close my eyes and fantasize about all the food I could have been eating. But no. I would not allow myself a single bite.

My mother would make me hamburger for lunch and steak for dinner. Since I was all alone during my meals (my mother was running a Chinese restaurant during this period of my life), I would eat one corner of the juicy red meat and wrap the remainder in Reynolds Wrap. Then I would run down the wooden stairs to the basement, open the gray door of our garage, and dump the ball of tin foil into the garbage can in the driveway. In ten months, I must have thrown away over 250 hamburgers and 250 steaks. Not to mention the scoops of rice and English muffin halves that my mother had made to accompany my meals. Part of my game was to deceive my mother. I would lie to her, "Yes, Ma, the steak was so juicy, I ate the whole thing and sucked the meat on the T-bone too." The real truth was that I felt like a hungry dog that finds a bone in a garbage can after starving all day, only to throw it back into the garbage again. What I was really doing was throwing away my life and my desire simply to laugh and play like a normal human being.

I continued to eat like this for ten months. At times, I wanted to cry out loud, "I'M HUNGRY!" I would feel this awful knot of emptiness in my stomach, straight through to the small of my back—a deep, dull, hollow ache that sometimes bordered on actual physical pain. But, no, I would not let myself give in to this hunger monster. I felt it was more important that I continue to win the game with myself, to stay as thin as a bird. The more weight I lost, the greater my chances of winning. How long could I keep this up? The scale read 88 pounds, then 79 pounds, then 75 pounds.

When I got to 72 pounds, I caught bronchitis and was rushed to the hospital because the doctor feared I would lose my life. In the hospital, I learned some new strategies for my food game. For two torturous days, nurses poked needles into both my arms and took X ray after X ray. They tried feeding me foods from the high-calorie menu—buttered mashed potatoes, cinnamon Danish with icing—with no success. I managed to wrap all the food from my tray in napkins and throw it in the garbage can by my bed when I knew the doctors and nurses weren't looking. "I'm still winning," I thought. "They will think I've eaten everything on my tray . . . Little will they know that I dumped everything in the trash." I kept saying to myself, "I am OK. I've a strong will and mind, and I will triumph over all my body's natural instincts and desires." It became a game of deception and denial all at once that would waste my life away.

On the third day I weighed 69 pounds. The doctors and nurses came into my room, sat by my bed, and calmly stated, "Jeanne, we've discovered your problem. According to all your blood tests, X rays, and physical examinations, we have diagnosed you to have a disease called anorexia nervosa. It's an eating disorder that is very complicated to explain and involves your inability to eat and maintain a normal, healthy body weight." I was on the verge of tears. "But I am eating . . . ," I said. "No, you aren't. We searched your trash cans and found all your food wrapped up in paper napkins." I began to cry and felt totally ashamed of myself. I certainly was not happy that all my efforts to hide my food disposals had been made in vain. My tricks no longer worked. I felt humiliated at the thought that I had been discovered.

I was required by my doctors to see a nutritionist to help me regain weight to a medically safe number of 85 pounds. Since I wanted more than anything else to please my doctors, I actually began the refeeding process with a great deal of zeal and enthusiasm. In many ways, I welcomed the permission to eat again; yet at the same time, I was frightened of eating real food and putting on weight. What would become of my scheme of trying to be thin? What could I do in place of my reliable, bedtime ritual of eating only a bag of microwave popcorn after not eating a single meal all day? Would I no longer have the comfort and pleasure of counting exactly 240 pieces of Cheerios at the end of my evening as a "bedtime snack"? What about cutting up my bread into neat one-inch squares and placing one-inch square slices of nonfat cheese on top of the bread pieces? These rituals were reliable; the food was safe and harmless. I was torn between accepting the permission to eat versus the safety and security of being as thin as a skeleton. Being thin was a way for me to wrap up my life into a simple coat of nothingness, free of the feelings and desires that any normal human being would want. The coat's layers smothered me until I was an emotionless walking zombie, no longer human, foreign to the planet Earth. I believed I was superhuman and did not need food, water, or love to function. The dangers of starvation didn't phase me in the least. If deprived of nourishment and care, I would not be malnourished like a normal earthling would be. I was way beyond all that.

Twenty-five years later, I was still obsessed with my game to be as thin as a bird. Over the course of those twenty-five years, I lost six jobs because my malnutrition did not allow me to think straight. I made serious computer errors, which cost my employers a lot of money, and I felt like I never got along with any of my co-workers. I never socialized, laughed, went out to lunch, or attended parties. At times, I thought, "Maybe I'm missing out on something by not eating."

So I decided to try to keep my promise to Sue, the nutritionist, to gain one pound. When I arrived home, I walked straight to my bookshelf and took out the most recent issue of *Weight Watchers Magazine.* I opened it up to the Weekly Planner Menus for Seven Days and copied the foods for each meal, word by word, onto Sue's meal-planning sheets.

But then I changed my mind. I couldn't bear the thought of gaining weight. I was frightened to death of my body resembling the figure of a woman and had stopped getting my monthly periods. I was scared of forming intimate relationships. I didn't have a clue how I would cope with grocery shopping, cooking, and taking care of myself. I didn't know how I could possibly sit by myself without that secure feeling of having triumphed over my natural appetites. So I decided to put aside Sue's meal-planning sheets and to eat hardly enough to feed a scrawny chicken.

I knew why I wasn't eating as Sue had requested. I feared the hunger monster inside myself getting out of control and eating until it would burst like a balloon full of hot air. To play it safe, I tried to burn calories by exercising as much as my body could tolerate. Every morning at precisely 3:30 a.m., I woke to my alarm. I put on my dance leotard, splashed cold water on my face, and walked into my exercise room lined with dumbbells, a barbell, a Plyo Ball, a Pilates Performer, and a collection of over 200 exercise videos. At 3:45 a.m., I turned on my VCR and exercised to my heart's content until 6:15 a.m. I had to ensure that my body fat remained below 10 percent, so most days, I hoisted heavy dumbbell weights and did weight-training exercises in addition to my hours of dance aerobics. Even though 10 percent body fat was considered way too low for an adult woman, I was petrified of my body being at a normal 17 to 22 percent body fat. Being "normal" meant having monthly periods, PMS, sexual desires, and intimate friendships with men. I did not know but came to understand later that I could not cope with all of the conflicts and problems associated with relationships, nor could I allow myself to experience the joys and pleasures of being close to someone. So rather than open a can of ugly worms, I chose to shut my life out. Exercising by myself kept me lonely, but at least I was burning body fat.

At 7:00 a.m., after my tough exercise session, I wandered into my kitchen to eat "breakfast," a ritual that included black coffee, my typical two Raisinets, and one corn flake. First, I brewed the coffee, then I put the two Raisinets side by side on my plastic plate with the golden yellow corn flake placed right in between the two chocolate-coated raisins. I sipped my coffee and felt the hot liquid slide down my throat. I read the morning newspaper, finishing by 8:00 a.m., page by page, sip by sip, and chewed the crunchy corn flake and sweet chocolate Raisinets piece by piece between my teeth. This pattern was so reliable and familiar that I wondered if I'd ever be able to give it up. Or want to.

Lunch was equally unproblematic, only because I limited that to a pack of Life Savers, thirty Cheerios, two packs of gum, and seven pieces of hard candy. I didn't bother so much with the time frame. Less ritualized, lunch required less solitude and I had grown relatively comfortable letting my co-workers fancy me, quite simply, a candy freak. I loved sucking Hershey's TasteTations—their sweet sugared liquid melted in my mouth as I bit down on the round morsels. My colleagues would ask me to lunch, but I would tell them that I feasted on huge, starchy breakfasts and didn't eat much for lunch. Or I would say, "I have to finish this monthly asset report by 12:30 p.m. today, so I'm just going to eat at my desk." My co-workers had stopped questioning the contents of the little Ziploc plastic sandwich bag that I carried with me everywhere I went—and they eventually stopped inviting me to lunch.

When my work day ended, I walked home passing by Rebecca's Bakeries, Au Bon Pain, Finagle a Bagel, Burger King, DeLuca's Gourmet Groceries, and the food court in the Prudential mall. Depending on the time of day, the right combination of wind direction and open doors sent in my path alternate whiffs of honey-glazed doughnuts, french fries, teriyaki chicken wings, and homemade oatmeal bread. I wished so much to eat this simple food but would contract my stomach to deny my hunger. Instead, I thought that smelling their aromas would fulfill me the same way as eating them, except I wouldn't get fat by just sniffing homemade barbecue sauce and freshly baked corn bread. Some days—bad days—this was an experience I simply could not bear—so potent and real were the scents, and so painful was the sight of women shopping, of menu-planning women with their cake boxes, tins, and bags packed to the brim with cheeses, breads, and specialty jams. I envied them. I was jealous of the beautiful, attractive, healthy women dining so casually, sipping wine and eating shrimp cocktails with their boyfriends. I just couldn't stand the feelings inside my aching body—the overwhelming desire to eat and laugh like them—so I forced myself to go home on the subway, a considerably more boring route, faced with people rushing home from their jobs to their families. I would rather smell the foul odor of a train station than be tempted by the sights of people feeding themselves with Dunkin' Donuts and Papa Gino's pizzas.

But on good days, I marched up the same street feeling agile and lithe. I felt a certain secret satisfaction on my journey past food and beyond it. Walking up the street, my hands cupped in my coat pockets and resting against my hip bones, I would pause in front of Rebecca's Bakeries' display window and size up the day's array of chocolate mousse cake, pumpkin cheesecake, cheese tortellini salads drenched in creamy Italian dressing, and overstuffed smoked turkey club sandwiches. As I continued walking, I liked to peer at people eating with the fascination of a person eyeing a foreigner in a foreign country. Watching these people, and then pressing on, reinforced a combined sense of rigid detachment—this business of looking at food, noticing young men wine and dine young women, then feeling my hip bones and flat stomach, then moving away—I considered this feeling essential to my daily existence and sense of power and self-worth.

I knew these "normal, foreign" people ate meals in homes and restaurants and went grocery shopping every week. I never ate meals. When I went to the supermarket, I walked up and down the aisles with my empty blue basket, eyeing all the food and nutrition labels on the jars of peanut butter, boxes of cookies, and the cartons of ice cream in the freezer compartment. But I went through the cash register with just a six-pack of Diet Pepsi, 94 percent fat-free popcorn, and an occasional package of day-old bread or cheese sold at half price. I felt I did not deserve to feed or care for myself.

As I ended my walk at the door of my condominium, I madly tried to avoid my hunger signals screaming for food. I frantically paced from bathroom to bedroom to living room, looking for magazines and old mail to tidy up or throw away. I even sprayed Windex on my mirrors; cleaning chores kept me occupied and distracted from the roaring, hungry voice of the beast inside me. I'd count out thirty Cheerios while I got ready for my evening exercise session. Then I hurried myself into putting on my blue cotton dance leotard. I again walked into my workout room, pulled out another exercise video and exercised my body to exhaustion. I was compelled to burn more calories for another hour and a half before turning off my VCR and calling it a night, feeling totally worn out and depleted of energy.

At 8:30 p.m. every night, I put on my white nightgown, washed my face, and made my lovely pink bed ready for sleep. At 8:45 p.m., I put a bag of 94 percent fat-free popcorn in the microwave and restlessly tidied up my kitchen while listening to the monotonous "pop-pop-pop" of the popcorn. When the popping died down to more than two seconds between pops, I took the bag out of the microwave, emptied it into a big bowl, and began my favorite evening ritual. This was my most reliable time of day and most secure form of eating behavior. The solitude was safe and consistent; the popcorn ritual was perfect and precise. From my kitchen drawer, I pulled out a china plate. Then I went into my pink bedroom and propped myself up on my frilly lace pink pillow. I began by counting out twenty pieces of popcorn—first the smallest pieces, and then gradually picking up the larger kernels. I lined these yellow pieces up in a perfect six-inch diameter circle on the china plate. Then one by one, I picked up the popcorn pieces and put them in my mouth, nibbling slowly, feeling every salty yellow piece on the roof of my mouth and surface of my tongue before swallowing it. When the entire yellow circle on the plate had disappeared into my mouth, I marked a check in my journal notebook. Seeing the check marks made me feel even more in control of my ritual. Then I counted out the next twenty pieces, placed them in a circle, picked them up, put them in my mouth, and marked off another check. When I reached fifteen check marks, the bag would usually be empty.

This procedure, well rehearsed and perfectly timed, lasted ninety minutes. As usual, I was not concerned with what I had planned to read—most of the time my eyes were fixed on the yellow circle of popcorn, as I counted out each group of twenty in precisely the same manner. When it was over, I washed the china plate, put it back in my kitchen cabinet, and threw out the empty microwave bag. Then I put my bony hands on my stomach, slightly protruded, and got into bed. I lay flat thinking about the bag of popcorn I would eat tomorrow night, then rolled onto my side, legs tucked up in a fetal position against the cold pink sheets. Lying there, I hoped that sleep would come easily, or I would be up all night thinking about the chocolate tortes in Rebecca's Bakeries' window, or the coconut doughnuts displayed on the Dunkin' Donuts shelves across the street. And I hoped, anxiously, that tomorrow would be a good day too.

*   *   *

Friday came, and I was scheduled to see Sue Luke again the following Monday. Every day that week, I was supposed to have eaten three healthy meals at 700 calories each, three nutritious snacks worth 200 calories each, and four cans of Ensure worth a total of 1,200 more calories. If I ate according to these instructions, I was supposed to gain at least one to two pounds.

The last thing I wanted to do those past five days was gain weight, even though I had promised Sue I would try. Every day had been a good day because I had kept my calorie count under 600 calories a day.

On Monday, I left work at 11:30 a.m. and hailed a taxi to drop me off at Sue Luke's office. It was hazy, hot, and humid outside, and I felt sweaty and sticky underneath all my layers of wool clothing. I carried my black bag, which contained Sue's meal-planning sheets, and noted that it was actually quite heavy. I decided that I would eat a lunch consisting of a green garden salad made up of three cups of romaine lettuce, four cucumber slices, and three half-inch slices of tomato. No salad dressing. I also drank two twelve-ounce cans of diet Coke. Before going into Sue's office, I stumbled into the ladies room to tidy myself up. I stood in front of the mirror eyeing my pointed chin, sunken eyes, and dry, brittle hair. I clumsily applied light makeup blush to my pale, lifeless cheeks and pink lipstick to my cold blue lips.

I walked into Sue's office with a huge smile on my face. "Hi, Sue!"

"Hi, Jeanne. How are you?'

I muttered, "I'm fine. I did great this week. I planned out all my meals and wrote them down on these sheets you gave me." I had practiced this lie all week long and hoped to heaven that it sounded as if I were really telling the truth.

She started the session by asking how my eating patterns were that past week. I opened my bag and took out my sheets. "Well," I said, "I have all my menus written down here on the sheets you gave me. I had some trouble trying to eat it all, but I disciplined myself and forced myself to eat, knowing that my nutritional health would improve if I tried. I just 'willed' myself into doing it."

"That sounds good. Do you want to step on the scale now and see what you weigh?"

"Sure!" I was really anxious but wanted to get the whole ordeal over with. I stepped over to the scale and took a cautious step onto the small black platform. Sue moved the larger weight to 50. Then she started maneuvering the smaller weight up toward the number 20 and slightly past it.

"Let's see, you were 69.5 pounds last week. This week it looks like you've gained 2.5 pounds. Good for you!"

I was secretly pleased. I walked over to the chair. I noticed my hands were shaking a little but tried to hide my nervousness by sitting on them.

Sue asked, "Well, how do you feel about your weight gain?"

"I feel fat. And I feel like I'm eating too much. I hate eating sandwiches and cookies, cheese and meat. But I forced myself to eat according to these menus I wrote down. Plus, I don't want to go into an eating disorder hospital feeding program. So I decided to cooperate. I'm glad that all my efforts resulted in this 2.5-pound weight gain!"

"Well, keep up the good work. Do you think you could continue eating like this for another week to continue the weight gain?"

"I guess I could try." I wanted to bolt out of Sue's office in a flash and wished that she would just let me go home rather than sit and talk about menus.

I picked up my coat from the couch as Sue continued, "You look anxious. Are you OK?"

"Yeah, I'm OK. I just want to go home. I'm really tired."

"You keep up the good work with your eating, OK? You're doing great!"

Like lightening, I bolted out of Sue's office and ran to the nearest ladies room down the hall. I locked myself in a stall and quickly took off my sneakers with a huge sigh of relief. I was sweating. I saw that my feet were painfully red and burning from the small, square, half-pound weights I had hidden in both my sneakers. Then I rolled up my wool sweater sleeves and removed the other two half-pound weights I had attached to both of my triceps with packing tape. I cringed as I noticed the furry hair that had grown on my arms sticking to the tape. I had just one more to remove, and that was the one taped to my protruding stomach, which looked so fat. After taking that one off, I threw all five gray metal weights into my bag, put my sneakers back on, and sighed, "Ahhhhhhhhhh." I felt much lighter not carrying those extra gray weights on my body. Best of all I thought, "I tricked her!! She didn't have a clue that I had weights on."

I hailed another taxi and got in, grinning with a sigh of relief. "I'm still winning!" I told myself. I looked forward to another evening propped up on my bed with my bag of popcorn and china plate and hoped that next week, every day would be a good day.

Questions for Discussion

1. How are eating disorders similar to compulsions and addictions? How are they different?
2. Given that eating disorders are often resistant to treatment, to what factors would you attribute this difficulty?
3. What societal influences contribute to the development of eating disorders?

SUBSTANCE ABUSE

That Goddamned van Gogh

Sybil Smith

It started when I was born, but let's skip that part. My mother was distracted, depressed, disappointed, and abused. My father was a charming, eccentric, violent drunk. Fortunately, that elusive quality the psychologists called resilience was mine in spades. And so, by hook or by crook, I crawled my way up the ladder of what we call success and found myself, at forty-five, a little-known but kick-ass writer, the proud mother of a completely normal and beautiful child, a professor of nursing, a good neighbor, a homeowner, a searcher, a reader, and the proud partner of a loving man.

Meanwhile, the little girl inside me was kept quiescent through a series of substances, including Percocet, alcohol, Darvon, morphine, Demerol, Tylenol 3, pot, acid, and anything else I could get my hands on. Obviously, this was a problem. Being a responsible person I was seeing my umpteenth shrink and gradually admitted I was an alcoholic. I left the other stuff out.

I tried to quit drinking, but AA didn't take. The concept of God eluded me. I had no loving higher power introject, as it were. I gave it some thought and—Eureka! I realized the best higher power of all was Antabuse. This was concrete enough for me. Wake up, blunder downstairs full of good intentions, take the pills, and—Voila!—you couldn't drink. You couldn't drink even if you'd had a bad day. You couldn't drink even if lots of smart people drank, like Ernest Hemingway, like F. Scott Fitzgerald, like Raymond Carver, like Meriwether Lewis, like Ulysses Grant, like Winston Churchill. You couldn't drink no matter how many cool people were at this moment sipping margaritas. You couldn't drink because, if you did, you would sweat and puke and froth and convulse and any number of nasty things.

My dear shrink, whom I adore, told me to stay sober for three days before I took the first pill. Pah! Impossible! I managed twelve hours. I dry swallowed the pill in the pharmacy. Then all hell broke loose. The pill was fine, no side effects whatsoever. The problem was I went into withdrawal. I decided to do what I call my Florence Nightingale thing and went to bed. Florence Nightingale has the record I think; she stayed in bed for twenty years while writing twelve hours a day, and all this without computers, cell phones, and faxes. The problem was, I had no family money, and no faithful maid and general factotum to minister to me. I had no adoring public.

Of course, I had some tranquilizers stashed away for a rainy day, and I took them. Lots. This helped. I listened to Beethoven, Mozart, and Mahalia Jackson. Mahalia Jackson was not a good idea. In my befuddled brain I came up with the idea I was a sinner and needed to punish myself. I got out of bed and promptly shit myself, a side effect of alcohol withdrawal. I cleaned up scrupulously (as Florence would have, or as Florence's maid would have) and wobbled downstairs, noting to myself that I was suffering from ataxia. I got a knife and began to hack at my arm but the knife was dull. I got angry at my boyfriend for not sharpening the knives, because my father was always scrupulous about this household task. I called my psychiatrist. She didn't answer. I called my sponsor; she didn't answer. I got angry at them all and went out in the shed, where I found an X-Acto knife. I worked on my arm for quite some time, till it looked really lacerated and mutilated and all those other nice clinical words. This pleased me. Things were getting fuzzier by this time but it seemed that rubbing chicken shit in the wounds would help, by possibly producing an infection which would require round-the-clock care and perhaps amputation. I went out to the chicken yard and they were doing their scratching, flapping, happy thing. This cheered me up so much I almost stopped the whole borderline scenario. But then one pooped, and I scooped up the fresh waste and rubbed it on my arm. It stung like a bastard. By now I was really tired so I went to bed and listened to Beethoven's "Ode to Joy" and cried so much I almost shorted out my Walkman with tears. In the midst of this my shrink called. I told her all about my adventures and she decided I wasn't safe. My boyfriend came home and concurred. They plotted against me. The booby hatch was next.

Oh, canny me! I gave the phone to Peter to make his nefarious plans, and while he was distracted, I gathered up a blanket and leapt into the car. I roared away with him receding in the distance making O's with his mouth. I knew they'd call the police, so I took the back roads, hid the car, and found myself a safe place to curl up in the ferns. I stayed there for hours. Then I got thirsty. I had been crashing around in swamps for a while so I looked like a proper special forces operative. I did the low crawl home and checked out the scene. I peeked in the windows of my house and evidently I was not as stealthy as I perceived because my boyfriend Peter caught me. He told me I had to go to the ER to make sure I was okay, or get slammed in the booby hatch. Since I'm a psychiatric nurse (you laugh), I chose the ER. The doctor found out what I already knew, 20 mg of Klonopin had barely slowed me down. Aside from the ataxia I was fine. My blood pressure was bang up. My pulse was regular and strong.

The doctor was annoyed to have me in his emergency room because I was dressed in a ragged nightgown and my feet were dirty. He was rather cold, I thought, but then, people who misbehave in spectacular ways tend to be annoying.

I went home and slept. I woke up the next day.

My boyfriend is being cold.

My shrink will probably blow me off.

My family thinks I'm a crazy bitch.

My computer, on the other hand, is hot.

* * *

So this morning I'm walking around the house talking to myself. My boyfriend is ignoring me. My daughter is looking sad. I called my sister and she declined a civil conversation. So I'm walking around and I'm muttering stuff like, "That goddamned van Gogh. He was such a pain in the ass. Can you believe he cut his ear off? Just trying to get attention. Left blood all over the kitchen. Why didn't he think of anyone else. Jeez."

"What in the Sam Hill was wrong with Ulysses Grant. He got so drunk one night he started throwing crystal wine glasses and then threw up on the Persian carpet in the Oval Office. What a loser."

"Virginia Woolf was such a hysteric. She was so self-dramatizing. She always walked around with this martyred look on her face, scribbling in notebooks. And now she's gone and drowned herself. She probably thought it was symbolic, with all its Ophelia overtones. She never gave a thought to her poor family."

"And Beethoven. Don't get me started on him. What a narcissistic sadist. Everyone in town hated him, he was so mean. How he wrote the Ninth Symphony is beyond me."

"D. H. Lawrence? Everyone knows the scoop on him. Marrying that fat creep Frieda and having fistfights all over town. No dignity whatsoever."

"Edgar Allan Poe? An opium addict. Freud? A cokehead. Darwin? A depressive. Ethan Allen? A drunk."

"And that creep John F. Kennedy. He'd fuck anyone in a skirt. I don't know how he managed to get elected president. His father's money, no doubt. Sure he could turn a phrase now and then, but he broke a few commandments, let me tell you."

"Sylvia Plath? I wish she'd never started this confessional shit. Airing all this dirty laundry. Oh, isn't madness cute! All those poems, nothing but poor me, poor me. Then she sticks her head in an oven and leaves her two little children. Poems schmoems. I hope she rots in hell."

So far, no one seems amused.

Fuck 'em, I say. It was goddamn fun being crazy. I remember lying on my blanket in the ferns and the breeze blew across my face like a long kiss. God was my midwife. I remember gathering ferns to make a soft bed, and looking up at the swaying pines. Like an Indian. I bore the little girl onto the earth, and she never cried. She looked at me with her dark surprised eyes and let me go.

I'm in trouble now, I suppose. They're still plotting. Oh well, they won't catch me. I have my Antabuse. I have my words. I have my freedom, tenuous as it may seem. I am fierce now. I'm ready to live.

Questions for Discussion

1. The writer conceals the use of any substance other than alcohol from the therapist. Is this significant in her diagnosis and treatment? How? If you suspected other drug use would you confront it?
2. What part does the author's chaotic childhood play in her substance abuse? Do you think this would have to be addressed as part of her recovery?
3. What is the prognosis for this writer? Would you expect relapse? Would you treat her if she continued to use?

I Lost You to Liquor

Nancy Hewitt

So long ago you'd think I'd
Be used to not having you around.
Sometimes, in fact, I almost forget
you haven't died yet. But then
you lure me with a witty remark,
snag me with a shared joke
and I'm hooked again, speared
by the you that's like me,
so that for a little while
I'm authentic.

But then your beery words
begin to slur. You chuckle
in that way you have
and before I know it
I'm the cheap object
of your grin. Another
fraudulent transaction.
I think I find myself
only to find
I want to lose you again.

Questions for Discussion

1. What is the poet describing in this poem?
2. What does she mean when she says, "I almost forget you haven't died yet"?

Mother, We're Going for a Ride

Maureen Porter

The shiny black shopping bag with white lilies gracing its side banged against Diane's knee as she flew down the brick walk. The October gale whipped her long brown hair across her determined face.

Today was the day of her exorcism. All her ghosts would be put to rest. She carefully placed the bag on the passenger's seat, even pulled the seat belt around it. Satisfied, she ran around and wiggled into the driver's seat.

"Well, here we are, Mother. We're going for a ride, a long one, and you have no say in the matter." Diane smiled to herself. She was in charge and it felt good, even though she half expected her mother's voice to float eerily from the black bag.

Last week as she had watched the lonely, helpless, old woman gasp for breath in the nursing home, she had been overcome by a sense of detachment. Why hadn't she been able to feel sorrow while witnessing her own mother's travail through the throes of dying? The only emotion she had been able to summon was pity.

"Is there something wrong with me? Have other daughters ever felt like this?" These questions had raged through her mind as each heaving intake of air racked the old lady's frail body. Diane's misery increased with her realization that she couldn't feel sadness, just that damned pity.

When the phone had rung at four-thirty the next morning, she had muttered, "Thank you," as Larry said, "She gone?" After she had nodded, they had both turned over and gone back to sleep.

"Okay, Mother, we're off. Our first stop is Weymouth Street. Remember that? It was my first experience being a substitute mother. David was only three years old, too young to be without you, so I took your place.

Oh, yes, you may say that you were there all the time, but I'm talking about mind and heart, not just body. Today you cannot change the subject or walk out of the room. You're my captive audience and you are going to finally listen.

There it is. Remember those front steps? Do you know how many times we sat there, me and David, waiting for you to come home and wondering if you would?"

Diane pulled up in front of the old three-story tenement house with its yellow flaking paint, parked, and gazed at the first-floor windows, mentally traveling back in time. Once again she was ten and mostly in charge of her brother. Their father, injured in a fall at work, was confined to his bed in the back of the house.

"I know you had to go to work, Mother. You held it all together and that was a brave thing, but why did you have to get drunk all the time? Why couldn't you have come right home from that restaurant? Did you have to go with the other waitresses to the bar after work?

Do you know how hard it was to fetch for Daddy and keep track of David and feed everybody? I was only ten and while all my friends were out riding bikes and playing games, there I was, child homemaker.

Did you ever think about how scared I was when you were late? Did you think I never heard the fights when Daddy wanted to know where you had been? Did you know what insecurity I felt, never being sure David and I would have someone to take care of us?

Then that time you got yourself a boyfriend. I'll never forget those days, and I'll never forget his name . . . Roy. I hated Roy. I don't care how many times he took us to the beach or bought us ice cream. He was a creep and Daddy used to get so angry and upset when you said Roy was just a friend. Even David, in his childish ignorance, knew better.

The worst day, Mother dear, was after Daddy went back to work. It was cold and snowing. We came home from school and the door was locked. Nobody was home. To this day, I don't know what happened. We played outside and got all wet and cold, so we sat on those steps right there and shivered together.

Mrs. Farrell, next door, finally called us over and invited us to have supper with them. I remember their house. It was warm and steamy and we had creamed tuna on toast. They had seven children, so I guess that's why she served water to drink. It was cozy and peaceful in that house and we sat in the parlor until Mr. Farrell told us that there was a light on in our house. Looking back, I realize they must have been aware of our family problems and took pity on us.

Well, Mother, when we came into the kitchen we could hear you throwing up in the bathroom. You never even knew we were home and didn't care either. Daddy came home the next day. Where had he been? Nobody said. And life just went on as though nothing had happened. And those, dear Mother, are my memories of that house. Shall we continue our tour? Oh, I forgot. You have to continue because I'm driving."

Diane was unaware of the tears streaming over her cheeks as she drove away. The little boy in the window regarded her with fascination. He had never seen a grown-up lady talking to herself and crying before.

She rolled the window down. The fresh autumn air blew against her wet face, drying the tears. They were headed for Algonquit Beach in Esquetog. The stunning scenery failed to register as the car sped along Route 8.

"How many times we rode this route going home after a day at the beach. I don't think you ever knew how terrified we were. Daddy would be furious, you would be drunk, and we would be sunburned and cowering in the backseat waiting for some dire accident or explosion.

I very seldom come here now. It's still too painful. Remember the time we rented that cottage for two weeks one summer? It could have been such a wonderful vacation, but once Daddy left for work in the morning it was all downhill . . . every day.

We would start out for the beach around eleven, but on the way we had to pass Callahan's Bar. That was always your undoing, wasn't it? After three highballs, you would tell me to go on ahead with David and you would come over later. It's a wonder we didn't drown that summer. I guess the lifeguard watched us; he was always blowing his whistle and waving us in to shore.

What would you have done if we hadn't picked you up on the way home? Would you have gone off with one of the sleazy guys in the bar? And don't ever think that those stupid Sen-Sen tablets kept your breath from smelling of alcohol. Well, they did, of course, but the Sen-Sen odor was a dead give-away.

Look, there it is. The wild roses are still climbing all over the porch, and someone is living there. I always loved that little cottage, you know? It was for sale about five years ago and I looked at it and almost bought it. But as I walked through the small rooms I knew I could never be happy there. Too many awful memories that I thought were dead kept surfacing.

Can you see it, Mother? Can you see those too little kids cringing under the covers every night? You always thought you were having fun, a wonderful time. Well, that's what you thought, I guess. The reality evidently never reached you, but that's what this ride is all about. To let you know what our reality was."

Diane dawdled in front of the cozy cottage wishing she had gathered the courage to buy it, but no time today for unmet wishes. Time for driving past the bar on Main Road.

"Callahan's has been long gone Mother. It is now a clam cake and chowder diner, but I can still see you perched on that stool with your highball and cigarette, happy as a clam—no pun intended—and pretending to be the belle of the ball.

All those scruffy bedraggled men swarming around you like bees around a flower, laughing at everything you said and teasing you. I realized even then that it was easy to be popular when you are the only woman in a roomful of men, but why would any intelligent woman want that? Did you need something that Daddy didn't give you? Maybe it was the same thing that you didn't give us . . . a caring attitude, love, respect . . . what?

But there it is, Mother. Take a good long look and try to remember how we two kids looked sitting outside on the bar doorstep waiting for you to go to the beach."

Diane spun off from the gravel curbstone and sped away. She was feeling curiously drained. Maybe this was a bad idea. She changed her mind about making all the stops she had planned on for this painful journey. But there was one more she needed to face before she met David at the cemetery tomorrow morning.

She had never told him about that escapade. He didn't need to know. He had been hurt enough. Why add to his heartache. Her hands shook as she entered Westbury and turned onto the long boulevard where they had lived during their teenage years. The huge graceful trees still spanned the road and the homes remained stately and well kept. The whole appearance of the neighborhood screamed prim, proper, well-bred people.

"The house still looks nice, doesn't it, Mother? How proud we were when we were able to move into this neighborhood. It was like we had finally 'made it.' And I know how hard you and Daddy worked to buy that house. What a thrill it was to have our own bedrooms. If only we had found happiness or peace there, but as always, there was the drinking, arguing, and unfaithfulness.

He would leave. You would leave. You would both come back eventually and life would go on. One time, when I was visiting you at the nursing home, you accused me of being a 'cold fish' with no emotions. Years ago, I erected a wall between myself and a world that could bruise me. For a long time I lived behind that wall. It took Larry to heal me.

Yes, Larry. The one you didn't approve of because he was 'dull' and lacked that superficial glitter that you always fell for. But he is real and would die before he would ever cause me pain. Good old solid, steady, easy-going Larry."

Diane stared at the home of their dreams. A soft yellow paint covered the walls and white shutters decorated the windows. A wreath with corncobs and pampas grass hung on the black door. It had a contented look, with mail sticking out of the box and a child's tricycle waiting on the walk.

"When I think of that day, even now, I get so angry I could spit. Will you listen now, Mother? Well, you have to, don't you? How could you have taken a chance on being found like that by a little kid? I guess at that point you didn't care, but when I ran up the walk that morning and pushed open the door just before you could lock it, I didn't care what you felt. All I knew was that David was due home for lunch at noon and he would have discovered his mother dead.

When your friend Eleanor called me at work and warned me to get home right away, I grabbed a taxi and made the driver speed. At that stage of the game I didn't ask questions. I was always prepared for any outrageous emergency. You must have seen me and rushed to lock the door. Thank goodness you were already groggy and couldn't move fast. I remember the overpowering odor of gas. It filled the house. I ran around opening windows and doors, screaming at you about David, but you were almost out of it by then. Thank goodness you didn't light one of your cigarettes or we both would have been blown to smithereens.

I was so damned mad and frantic I made you go sit on the porch and called Daddy and told him to get his fanny home pronto. He must have heard the rage in my voice because he was there pretty fast. I told him to take care of his wife and to get your lives straightened out because I was through picking up the pieces. I remember how he looked at me. Puzzled. As if trying to figure out how I knew anything was wrong. You two deserved each other. Yes, you did, that's for sure.

It wasn't easy to meet David at school and surprise him with a special lunch at the little hot dog stand. He was thrilled. I wanted to wrap him in my arms and protect him. He was the nicest little kid, so good and smart. He never knew what happened because, as usual, life went on, and on, and on . . .

But you know what, Mother, somehow it's not important anymore. I'm sorry you had a rotten life. I'm sorry that your marriage was so chaotic. All of a sudden I feel free of some invisible burden of anger. I've spent my life being angry and I no longer intend to do that. I've said my piece and you had to listen and it's over. It's really over."

She glanced over at the bag, half expecting it to twirl around or something. "Okay, Mother, let's go home."

Trees in full autumn array swayed in the bright sunshine of October. Diane drove through the winding lanes of the cemetery while David looked for the small headstone marking their father's grave.

"You don't think we'll get caught, do you?" Diane worried.

"What else can we do?" answered David. "Do you have $3,000 to spare? I know I don't. Besides, she's the one who wasted her money. She's the one who cashed all her insurance policies and blew every cent. I don't feel the least bit guilty."

"Yes, I guess it has to be this way. If we act casual it should be fine. There, over on the left, that's it."

The two strolled over to the stone. David knelt and dug up a square of sod, then placed it to one side while he scooped out a hole. Diane stood in the praying position, head bent "in prayer" as he worked. Any one passing by would see two reverent figures paying their respects to a departed loved one.

"Okay." David whispered. "Hand me the ashes. I'm ready." He poured the ashes into the hole and replaced the square of grass carefully. There was no evidence to show what they had done. They stood for a minute in silence.

Diane shivered. "You know, I think we had better hightail it out of here before Daddy realizes she's here."

"I think you're right," said David, and the two walked arm in arm to the car.

Questions for Discussion

1. Why did Diane take her mother's ashes on a ride through places from her childhood? What did Diane want from her mother as an adult?
2. What role did Diane play in her alcoholic family?
3. What problems/issues could Diane's familial childhood role have created for her in adulthood?

DIAGNOSIS PROBLEMS

Look So Normal

Anonymous

People tell me I look so normal. That's good. I'm glad that my history doesn't show on my face. I don't want people to be able to guess the horrors I have experienced in the past. And I have worked hard to create a facade behind which to hide. It protects me from your judgment. But it also protects you from truths you may find offensive.

To all appearances I am a middle-aged, middle-class woman. I struggle with my weight but am not grossly obese. I am clean and well-groomed, but usually unconcerned with hands roughened by hard work. I am intelligent, though not highly educated—more than high school but less than a college degree. I used to believe that finishing that degree would make me feel OK about myself. Just like I used to believe that I would feel OK if I could just get thin enough and keep the weight off. Or if I had the right job or the right spouse or the right religion, all my anxiety would leave and I would be happy. The depressions would go away and never return. I would be content and cheerful and have lots of friends.

It has been difficult to give up my illusions. And it is difficult to face that this is probably as good as it gets. I can smile and nod and briefly make idle chatter. But I am uncomfortable in crowds and even small groups if I don't feel I belong. My anxiety is evident in the constant motoring of my restless feet and my shifting gaze. When things are bad, and they are more often than I care to admit, I avoid both large crowds and intimate gatherings.

I can hold a job . . . sometimes. And when I do, I am bright and competent and conscientious. But there was the time I stood in the corner, hiding behind a door, and sobbed in despair. And the time I curled in a ball beneath a conference room table, plotting my suicide and avoiding the walk down the hall, through the locked doors and into the psychiatric unit. And that time, many years ago, when I slapped a confused old man who then grabbed me and scratched my face. I've had a long list of jobs, and I left each one with well-justified reasons: I didn't like my manager, there was no room for advancement, their management style was too rigid, I had a better offer, etc. But with each job change I grew more desperate. My search for the satisfaction I thought just out of reach grew more frantic. My anxiety over my performance and my sense of inadequacy sent me job hopping again and again. Or I would go into the hospital or into treatment or on extended medical leave, and then be unable to face my co-workers again. The shame I carried grew more burdensome. My depression and anxieties became more difficult to hide.

Have you begun to understand? Are you watching me with alarm, waiting for sign of a fresh breakdown or a slip of propriety? How can I tell you what it is like? I try to enjoy any peaceful stretch while keeping a watchful eye for dangerous drops waiting just out of sight. The doctors toy with labels. Manic-depressive? No, not quite. Major depression with anxiety disorder and panic attacks? Perhaps. Ah! Borderline personality disorder! But how do you explain those long spells of functional normalcy? So the doctors and I play roulette with pills. They come in a vast array of shapes and colors. Green, white, pink, or purple; tablet or capsule; oval, square, round, rectangle— the variety is endless. The doctor pushes a white script across the desk. Try this one. Not sleeping? He doubles the dose. Still sobbing and screaming at my husband? He adds a new pill to the mix. I have a basket of failed drugs beneath my bathroom sink. I save them. It gives me a sense of security to know that they are there if the pain becomes too much to bear. Kind of a security blanket in reverse, you know?

I spent a few years in a sedated haze. Stumbling through the barest of obligations while longing for a return to my bed, I often slept fourteen to sixteen hours a day. I finally put my foot down and stopped the class of drugs that sapped my energy to that degree. I told my doctor, "I can't function. I can't think. I won't take those anymore!" Puzzled at my recalcitrant mood, the doctor adds "noncompliant" to my list of labels.

Just for now I've found a balance. I take the drugs that seem to help without crushing my spirit. I spend my hard-earned money in a therapist's chair. She's wonderful, but I long for her to say I don't need her anymore. I work part-time, guarding against too heavy a load. To overcommit puts me at risk for another crash-and-burn episode. I exercise in the gym and in the pool, forcing my chubby body to keep moving and avoid the inevitable weight gain that plagues my life. They tell me it helps my mood. Sometimes I believe them.

I'm torn between wanting you to understand who I am and my fear of your rejection. One sad truth of mental illness is its isolation. People rush to your side with chicken soup and words of comfort if you break a bone or suffer a heart attack. Offers to help pour in. They wish to cook you a meal, mow your lawn, or sit by your bedside in gracious oblivion. But who knows what to do for someone who confesses mental disease? When faced with that uncomfortable fact, people blush and stammer or stand in awkward silence. They don't know what to say. Even worse, some of them offer to pray for healing and suggest that some day you'll be able to throw those pills away! I've challenged that foolishness defiantly and asked if they would advise diabetics to discard their insulin. Their discomfort is understandable, but suggestions stemming from ignorance cause more damage than can be excused.

I keep most people at arm's length. I don't want to offend anyone. Or worse yet, in a moment of weakness, expose myself to yet another loss of dignity. It's a lonely life, but infinitely safer than the risk of rejection or abuse. My secrets remain secret to all but a few. And often, after revealing a piece of myself, I will have a panic attack in response to my bold disclosure.

I have come to a place of resignation. No longer believing that if I change my circumstances I will find happiness, I struggle to stand quiet and live each day as it comes. I fight my bitterness, trying to prevent disappointment from making me a sour old woman. I try to accept that I will never live up to my intellectual potential because emotional turmoil stands in my way. My tolerance for stress is limited, and I must save my emotional energy for the essential pieces of my life. Living with these restrictions is frustrating, and at times I am furious at God, and fate, and my crummy genetic mix, and my sheer bad luck for having this particular curse on my life.

Questions for Discussion

1. Would you consider treatment options other than individual therapy for this woman?
2. How would you conceptualize her feelings other than the obvious frustration at not having symptoms that fall within a clearly defined diagnosis?

In Search of a Diagnosis

Kimberly Sotiro

During my recent participation in a research study conducted by a well-known hospital in the state where I live, I made some discoveries about something I have been struggling with. The study is focused on people suffering from post-traumatic stress disorder (PTSD), which I was diagnosed with in 1990. It has included countless questionnaires, and other various physical studies. I am no medical doctor and am not claiming to possess expertise in psychology. What I have been experiencing in my life has been difficult to live with, especially because it has been quietly going on and is not recognized, possibly not even by others who may suffer from it. In presenting my discoveries, I am merely trying to shed some light on what I see as an undiscovered problem in our society. It may or may not help others, maybe only myself.

As I participated in the research study of PTSD, I encountered many occasions of awareness of the things that have gone seemingly unnoticed for most of my life, by myself and those around me. During one part of the study, I was asked to have an MRI done. I was asked numerous times if I have ever suffered from claustrophobia. My answer was repeatedly "no" because I never believed myself to be claustophobic. I went through the MRI without a problem. In fact, I felt the sensation of freedom more than anything else. I was without the burden of conversation, answering questions, or participation of any kind. I could just lie there and let it happen. The independence I had from not feeling pressured allowed me to come up with a new way to make chicken for dinner that evening, which my family responded to enthusiastically!

As I thought back on this, I realized that I am indeed claustrophobic, but not in the sense that the doctors were questioning. I am claustrophobic in an emotional sense. I will try to state examples to explain this theory the best that I can, as a layperson.

In the town where I grew up, I saw countless individuals and families fail at what they strived for. I always knew as I grew up that I would not let that happen to me. I sort of obsessed over that, and still do. I was born in 1972 and grew up in the prosperous, "greedy" (as it's often referred to) 1980s. I witnessed the rise of what is known as the "yuppie," though my family was never quite in that category of living comfortably. I suppose this is the

American dream: to at least achieve comfort in a monetary sense. I became trapped in the mind-set: at whatever cost, I will succeed. Yet I was never too ambitious. I slipped through high school seemingly unnoticed and have always resented my sense of obscurity. I never had the desire to go to college because my mind sort of froze when I was expected to complete certain assignments, and I could not imagine going to school for four more years, once again being trapped in the river of unending expectations. I accepted this as adolescent rebellion. But I am no longer an adolescent. I am twenty-six years old, a married mother with no career, a repertoire of only miscellaneous jobs, and I still feel complete opposition, almost disgust, at the thought of going to school again. My mind has finally put all this together to form an idea, possibly a discovery, that I am emotionally claustrophobic.

The American Heritage Dictionary of the English Language defines claustrophobia as "a pathological fear of confined spaces," going on to define pathological as "disordered in behavior." Looking back at my track record, my first job was as a baby-sitter at the age of thirteen. During the rest of my teens, I went on to work as a retail sales clerk, cashier, and food service assistant for a rehabilitation clinic. These may be taken merely as adolescent discoveries, learning experiences, monetary necessities, what have you. But as I reached my twenties, still without any sort of direction, I began to notice that the only consistency I maintained was that of inconsistency. I went on to work as a receptionist for a roofing company, a telemarketer, a quality assurance clerk, a saleswoman in a greeting card store, a data entry clerk, and a retail merchandiser for two different companies—all by the age of twenty-five. I could never seem to stay at one job for very long. Only recently, through participation in the research study, did I finally begin to understand what motivates me continually to leave my jobs.

When I am somewhere, anywhere, for a prolonged amount of time, I begin to develop certain symptoms: physiological, psychological, and emotional. My physical symptoms are minor, yet noticeable, and can consist of shortness of breath, rapid heartbeat, chills, and sweating. My psychological symptoms may consist of irritability, inability to concentrate, poor short-term memory, lack of interest, and eventually an overwhelming desire for solitude. I become so agitated at being in the same place for a long time that I must get out and need to be alone. I begin to feel overwhelmingly stifled and don't want to talk to anyone because I'm confused beyond a state of understanding how to explain what I'm feeling. This is different from the usual state of claustrophobia because I do not sense an immediate threat at being confined. I can see the door, and my way out. It's more of the silent, unannounced expectation that I am supposed to stay somewhere, the obligation that I have made to be there at a certain time, for a certain amount of time, to perform certain duties. It's not an immediate sense of urgency but one that seems to build up gradually. This also leads to a tremendous amount of resentment when I am reprimanded or instructed.

I have not held a job continuously for longer than three years. I believe the buildup of these feelings that I have just described escalates during the course of my employment and eventually leaves me feeling as if there is no other option than to find another job in another location. I find myself fervidly needing to get away from the place that I have been required to sit in for hours; I cannot look at the same view from the same windows another minute; I cannot listen to the same people say the same things everyday; I cannot perform the same tasks day in and day out. I also experience difficulty in arriving at a certain time every day, which becomes increasingly difficult as time goes on. I must get away from these consistently repetitive situations.

This sort of claustrophobia does not end with occupations. I feel this way in just about every situation I am in. I feel "emotionally cornered" by my roles of mother, wife, sister, aunt, friend, housekeeper, and even shopper. If I obligate myself to do something, I eventually feel the resentment building. And the longer I must wait to fulfill the obligation I have made, the stronger the resentment becomes. Even when I make an appointment for something in advance, I often find myself wanting to pace back and forth like a caged animal if I know I must stay somewhere, even though I'm well aware that I can leave at any time, which I have often done. This has occasionally given me the reputation of being irresponsible, even though my intentions were pure. Taking a trip to the doctor's office can become a nightmare if I am expected to wait too long. This feeling of dread over the commitments I have made often results in tardiness for appointments and even occasional, but rare, skipped appointments. My mind overemphasizes the "required" experience beyond what is actually expected, causing this tremendous amount of anxiety and unwillingness to go along with what is planned.

As you can well imagine, what I have been experiencing has caused extreme problems for me, as my symptoms interfere with what I would like to call an ordinary existence, one which seems more elusive to me with the passing of time. This only complicates things, causing further anxiety due to feelings of inadequacy and incapability. It has often left me feeling inconsolably depressed and constantly searching for direction.

After regarding all the symptoms I possess myself, I believe that a lot of people suffer from this same thing, which I call "emotional claustrophobia." This could possibly be related to the reasons why some men leave their families due to the pressures of responsibility, why some people can't hold down jobs, and others divorce often. In countless situations, this may play a role. The hardest thing is that it has gone unnoticed, and many people don't recognize it as a problem. It is merely labeled as indecisiveness or inability to settle down.

I am not at the point of understanding the direct cause and/or cure for this, though that is my ultimate goal. I believe that for something to be understood, its source must be discovered, which may ultimately lead to a solution. This may or may not be a direct consequence of PTSD. I do, however, strongly believe that my condition has resulted from being raised in extremely sheltered living conditions. I was not an overly social child, nor was I encouraged to be. In fact, it seemed as if any attempts I made toward "expanding my horizons" were discouraged. I was expected to stay home a majority of the time, going out only with my parents, which was not often. The view from my bedroom window was largely the extent of my range of vision.

As I've already said, I am not a doctor. I am merely looking for help or insight, for a potential solution, and/or possibly to help someone else who may possess the same problems. I was in psychotherapy for five years following my departure from my parent's home when I was seventeen. It has been a long road to get where I am now and I'm not about to stop here.

As a side note, I would like to mention that the job I presently hold is that of retail merchandiser. I work less than twenty hours per week, and though I am required to service the same store each time I work, I am not required to be there at any certain time or for any certain amount of time. My duties vary with each visit to the store, and I do not know what my tasks will be for the day until I arrive to see what's been delivered. It might also be interesting to note that I have enjoyed this job more than any other I've held, though it is still difficult at times.

Questions for Discussion

1. This woman is in a PTSD study. Does she meet the criteria for this diagnosis? What other diagnoses would you consider?
2. Do you think this woman has a mental disorder? Give reasons for your opinion.
3. How do the narrator's expectations and beliefs affect her self-image?

SELECTED READINGS AND ADDITIONAL RESOURCES

Anxiety Disorders

Obsessive-Compulsive Disorder

Abramowitz, J.S. (1997). Effectiveness of Psychological and Pharmacological Treatment for Obsessive-Compulsive Disorder: A Quantitative Review. *Journal of Consulting and Clinical Psychology* 65(1), 413-452.

Freeston, Mark H., Ladouceur, Robert, Gagnon, Fabien, Thibodeau, Nicole, Rheaume, Josee, Letarte, H., and Bujold, A. (1997). Cognitive-Behavioral Treatment of Obsessive Thoughts: A Controlled Study. *Journal of Consulting and Clinical Psychology 65*(3), 405-413.

March, J.S., Frances A., Carpenter, D., and Kahn, D.A. (1997). The Expert Consensus Guideline Series: Treatment of Obsessive-Compulsive Disorder. *The Journal of Clinical Psychiatry 58* (Suppl. 4).

Steketee, Gail (1993). *Treatment of OCD*. New York: Guilford Press.

Panic Disorder

Wilson, R. Reid (1996). *Don't Panic: Taking Control of Anxiety Attacks*. New York: Harper Collins.

Ballenger, James C. (1989). Toward an Integrated Model of Panic Disorder. *American Journal of Orthopsychiatry 59*(2), 284-293.

Phobia

Bourne, Edmund J. (1995). *The Anxiety and Phobia Workbook*. Oakland, CA: New Harbinger Publications.

Davey, Graham (1997). *Phobias: A Handbook of Theory, Research and Treatment*. New York: John Wiley and Son.

Goldman, Carol and Babior, Shirley (1996). *Overcoming Panic, Anxiety, and Phobias*. Duluth, MN: Whole Person Association.

Post-Traumatic Stress Disorder

Hansel, Sarah, Steidle, Ann, Zaczek, Grace, and Zaczek, Ron (1995). *Soldier's Heart: Survivors' Views of Combat Trauma*. Lutherville, MD: Sidran Press.

Matsakis, Aphrodite (1994). *Post-Traumatic Stress Disorder: A Complete Treatment Guide*. Oakland, CA: New Harbinger Publications.

PTSD Research Quarterly. Available from The National Center for PTSD, VA Regional Office Center (116D), 215 N. Main Street, White River Junction, VT 05009.

Schiraldi, Glenn R. (1999). *The Post-Traumatic Stress Disorder Sourcebook: A Guide to Healing, Recovery, and Growth*. Los Angeles, CA: Lowell House Publishers.

Wilson, John P. and Keane, Terence M. (Eds.) (1997). *Assessing Psychological Trauma and PTSD*. New York: Guilford Press.

Mood Disorders

Danquah, Meri Nana-Ama (1999). *Willow Weep for Me: A Black Woman's Journey Through Depression*. New York: Ballentine Books, Inc.

Goodwin, Frederick K. and Jamison, Kay R. (1990). *Manic-Depressive Illness*. New York: Oxford UP.

Jamison, Kay (1995). *An Unquiet Mind.* New York: A.A. Knopf.

McCraken, Anne and Semel, Mary (1998). *A Broken Heart Still Beats: After Your Child Dies.* Center City, MN: Hazelden Press.

Selene's Homepage for Bipolar Disorder and Depressive Illness. Recommended readings and resources, links, and poetry. <http://members.aol.com/faery116/depress.html>.

Stryon, William (1992). *Darkness Visible: A Memoir of Madness.* New York: Vintage Press.

Yapko, Michael, D. (1996). *Breaking the Patterns of Depression.* New York: Bantam Dell.

Schizophrenia and Other Psychotic Disorders

Munro, Alistair (1992). Psychiatric Disorders Characterized by Delusions: Treatment in Relation To Specific Types. *Psychiatric Annals 22*(5), 232-240.

Newhill, Christina (1990). The Role of Culture in the Development of Paranoid Symptomatology. *American Journal of Orthopsychiatry 60*(2), 176.

Penn, D.L. and Mueser, K.T. (1996). Research Update on the Psychosocial Treatment of Schizophrenia. *American Journal of Psychiatry 153*(3), 607-617.

Schiller, Lori and Bennett, Amanda (1994). *The Quiet Room: A Journey Out of the Torment of Madness.* New York: Warner Books.

Torrey, D. Fuller (1995). *Schizophrenia and Manic-Depressive Disorder: The Biological Roots of Mental Illness As Revealed by the Landmark Study of Identical Twins.* New York: Basic Books.

Dissociative Disorders

The International Society for the Study of Dissociation (ISSD). Guidelines for prescriptions, education, books, and conference information. <www.issd.org>.

Many Voices: Words of Hope for People Recovering from Trauma and Dissociation. (Newsletter) Cincinnati, OH: Many Voices.

Putnam, Frank, W. (1989). *The Diagnosis and Treatment of Multiple Personality Disorder.* New York: The Guilford Press.

Ross, Colin (1996). *Dissociative Identity Disorder: Diagnosis, Clinical Features, and Treatment of MPD.* New York: John Wiley and Sons.

West, Cameron (1999). *First Person Plural: Life As a Multiple.* New York: Hyperion.

Eating Disorders

Bambrilla, Francesca, Draisca, A., Pierone, A., and Brunetta, M. (1995). Combined Cognitive-Behavioral, Psychopharmacological, and Nutritional Therapy in Eating Disorders. *Neuropsychobiology 32*(2), 59-63.

Bullitt-Jonas, Margaret (1999). *Holy Hunger*. New York: Knopf.

Fallon, Patricia, Katzman, Melanie A., and Wolley, Susan C. (1994). *Feminist Perspectives on Eating Disorders*. New York: Guilford Press.

Kleifield, Erin I., Wagner, Susan, and Halmi, Katherine A. (1996). Cognitive Behavioral Treatment of Anorexia Nervosa. *Psychiatric Clinics of North America, 19*(4), 715-737.

Wolf, Naomi (1991). *The Beauty Myth: How Images of Beauty Are Used Against Women*. New York: William Morrow.

Substance Abuse

Agnew, Eleanor and Robideaux, Sharon (1998). *My Mother's Waltz: A Book for Daughters of Alcoholic Mothers*. New York: Simon and Schuster.

Davis, Charlotte, Kasl (1992). *Many Roads, One Journey: Moving Beyond the 12 Steps*. New York: Harper Collins.

Gorski, Terence (1989). *Understanding the Twelve Steps*. New York: Simon and Shuster.

Horowitz, Michael and Palmer, Cynthia (Eds.) (2000). *Sisters of the Extreme: Women and Drugs*. Rochester, VT: Inner Traditions.

Milam, James and Ketcham, Katherine (1981). *Under the Influence*. New York: Bantam Press.

Simon, David and Burns, Edward (1998). *The Corner: Life in an Inner City Neighborhood*. New York: Broadway Books (heroin addiction).

Diagnosis Problems

American Psychiatric Association (1994). *Diagnostic and Statistical Manual of Mental Disorders*, Fourth Edition. Washington, DC: Author.

Turner, Francis J. (1995). *Differential Diagnosis and Treatment in Social Work*. New York: The Free Press.

PART VIII:
FAMILIES COPING
WITH MENTAL ILLNESS

Fear

Elizabeth Howard

Night shadows still in control, a stranger rattles your doorknob, you in robe and slippers, not even a cup of coffee yet to start the day. He presses his face to the window, peering in at you. Frozen, you stare back at him—bushy beard, straggly hair, wild eyes, dirty clothes. Where did he come from? What does he want? Why your door?

You have to do something. Your mind lists possibilities. Call 911, but you could never get to the telephone before he broke down the door. Scream your lungs out, but who would hear in this closed-up neighborhood, not that your voice box would open, not that you could make a sound. Run, but he is much younger, and your breath is stifled at the moment. Besides, where could you go? How could you run far enough?

All at once, you realize it is indeed a stranger, yet not a stranger. It is your son, the stranger with schizophrenia, off his medication for weeks now, and the fear intensifies. He has walked more than twelve miles in the darkness. For what purpose, you do not know.

He speaks of demons, voices which scream his name, cracks in his face (he sees them in the mirror), the witch hiding behind the oak tree outside his window, the cat casting spells from the armchair, wenches who lust after him, black spots which speckle your face, iridescent colors which come and go.

A slavering dog chased him up the street, its eyes glowing fire. He ran like the wind to escape it, but it kept gaining on him. His neighbor, an angel of the devil, sent it after him. This neighbor grows psychedelic mushrooms, casts evil spells, spies on him. You know the neighbor is only a simple old woman, harmless as far as you can tell.

The cops are after him. They drive by, slow down, shine lights on him. They will plant marijuana on him, arrest him, lock him up. They creep along, talking about him, plotting. Their guns are unholstered, ready to fire if he looks around, if he runs. He tries to hide his thoughts, for they can read them. He has ripped out his telephone, thrown away his television, so they cannot eavesdrop on him.

He is a prophet like Moses. God speaks to him, tells him to go into the wilderness like Jesus. He wants a backpack for his journey. He has just returned from a hitchhiking trip to St. Louis, Missouri, weeks when you didn't know where he was, didn't know if he was alive or dead. But St. Louis was not the haven he'd sought, did not live up to its saintly name. He has told you of a nightmarish ride with a drunk man from St. Louis to Memphis, the car swerving swiftly through the darkness. Somehow, he found his way to his sister's door in a Memphis suburb, frightened her as he has just frightened you. She fed him and bought him a bus ticket home. But his travels are not over, God is not through with him; now he must go into the wilderness.

Determined that he will not disappear again, you buy him breakfast and drive him home. Once again, for the thousandth time, you argue with him about his medicine, which he says makes him crazy. You go through his complaints, explaining his illness, wondering why he can't just be rational, why he can't see that he's been through all of this before, that it's all just a vicious trick of his mind. You leave him at his trailer, knowing that he will indeed pack a few meager possessions, those he has not already thrown away, and head into the wilderness.

As soon as you get back home, you call the sheriff to have him picked up, go through the ordeal of having him committed. The nightmare is easier now, for he has a record of irrationality. Besides, his neighbors have complained about disturbances in church services (where he insists they are worshiping the devil, committing carnal acts with young girls), about his walking past their houses in the middle of the night (day and night, many miles a day, he walks; he cannot do otherwise).

You visit him in the hospital, but he curses you, will not see you. There is nothing you can do, but go home, heartbroken. You will try again and again, until after months of medication, he agrees to speak to you, though he never quite forgives you for calling the sheriff, for having him locked away.

That dirty, bearded face at the kitchen door at dawn, raving phone calls in the night, a steel guitar smashed into the wall, physical violence against his brother, so many kinds of fear.

Fear, another name for schizophrenia, paranoia, delusions, hallucinations. Your fear small in the face of his fear. Imagine demon voices that leave you no peace, visions of horror, your parents in collusion with the enemy, the whole world plotting against you, telling you that you don't see what you see, hear what you hear, that you can't trust your eyes, ears, reason.

What fear, the life of a schizophrenic, but what courage. To get up every morning to a fractured world, a world teetering on the brink of anarchy, to struggle everyday for sanity, to persevere in the face of adversity so severe most of us cannot imagine it.

You, too, must have courage, courage to answer the telephone in the middle of the night, to go to the door when a stranger knocks at dawn, to be calm and reassuring in the face of anxiety, to respond to ranting with a soft voice, to call the sheriff if need be, to arise each morning with thanksgiving for another day, another chance.

Questions for Discussion

1. Bearing in mind that this disorder happens not only to the patient but to the whole family, what kinds of support services would you like to see these families receiving?
2. Comment on the dynamics of having to report one's own child to legal authorities.

Mary and John

Bill Weiner

Those who do not complain are never pitied.

Jane Austen

> Mary is a good mother.
> She tries her very best.
> John is a good son.
> He does the best he can.

Paranoid schizophrenia. That's what the doctors call it. She doesn't know exactly what that means. It's got to do with a split personality or something, but she's not sure. Nobody ever really explained it to her. The doctors are always so busy . . . and she is only a mother. What she does know is that he is different. He hears voices in his head and sometimes he talks to himself. When he gets really sick he thinks people are talking about him behind his back. Sometimes he thinks she isn't his real mother and he can get a little rough with her, but he's a good boy and is usually very quiet and keeps to himself. He wasn't always this way. He was sweet and gentle and kind— God bless him—and so smart. Had a good head on his shoulders. He was such a good student before he got sick. Life has not always been easy, but God has been good to her. She counts her blessings, makes due with what she has, and takes one day at a time. She worked hard all her life. If she hadn't taken sick with leukemia she'd still be working. When John was three years old, his father walked out on them. He had his problems, too, but that's another story. She went back to work and Mother moved in to take care of John. Mary kept her nose to the grindstone, worked her fingers to the bone, but she was glad to do it. She scrimped and saved (had to watch every penny) to make a nice little home for John and her and Mother. Like they always say, God helps those who help themselves.

John is up in the county hospital. Again. John got a little rough with her. Again.

Mary is doing okay. She is feeling fine, thanks, and she can't complain. There is no use in complaining. What good would it do? You do the best you can. What else can you do? There was no harm done, really. He just got a little rough. He can't help himself. He's really a good boy, but he's sick. There were no bones broken. He just grabbed her and shook her and slapped her around a little. Well, yes, he was a little rougher this time. He didn't mean to be. He can't help it when he gets this way. The voices tell him to do it. He was screaming at her, saying all the bad words, and then he grabbed her and shook her and slammed her up against the wall, and then he banged her head hard against the kitchen cabinet. But she's okay now. Really. She is. She didn't need to see a doctor, nothing like that. Sure, she was scared to death. Who wouldn't be? But now she is fine, thanks. Well, yes, he is getting a little bit worse and she is scared to take him back home again. There is no telling what he might do. She is learning (the hard way). This time she did just what she was told to do. She didn't even argue with him when he said she was not his mother. That really hurts the most when he says that. (Why does he? It makes no sense.) Worse than when he hits her. But she didn't say a word— not a peep—'cause they told her, up at the county hospital, what to do and what not to do the last time. And she did just like she was told. Yes, she did. Well . . . not exactly. No, she didn't leave the house and call the cops when he started in saying all those bad words. It was late and she was scared and she was in her pajamas. But she didn't argue with him when he said that she killed Nana. And she didn't say a word when he asked what she did with her body. Not a peep. No, it's true she didn't call the cops like they told her to do, but she did walk away from him when he said the F word. She did what she could. She went into her bedroom and shut the door. She thought that would work. Walk away from him is what they told her to do. Getting away would calm him down. That's what they said to do and that's what she did. She didn't argue. She was scared to death—but she didn't let on. No, she just got up and walked away. She thought it would work this time. He didn't follow her. Not at first. She just calmly walked to her bedroom, quietly shut the door behind her, turned off the light, and got into bed. She heard him banging around out there, saying all those bad words, and put the covers over her head. She shook and shook. If it wasn't for all the commotion, she probably would have heard those bony knees of hers knocking. That's how scared she was. Soon he was right outside her bedroom door saying all those bad words, the F word. He even called her a whore (he never did that before). She pulled the covers even tighter. She shook and she shook. Then it got real quiet and she thought he was going to settle down—but she was wrong. He barged into her room and dragged her out to the kitchen and went berserk. Well, you know the rest of the story. There's no need to repeat it. The cops took him away. The guy who lives downstairs must have called them. He's black. John doesn't like him. He doesn't like black people—but she has nothing against them. John doesn't trust them. She tries to get along with everybody. Anyway, she is fine and John's doing nicely, thank you, and she'll tell John you were asking about him. She will be all right. There is truly no need at all to worry.

John called Mary last night. Again. He begged her to let him come home. Again. He said he wants to come home; he's ready to come home; he's really ready to come home. Won't she talk to the doctor? Won't she please just talk to the doctor? Please, all she has to do is talk to him, that's all, 'cause he's ready, really ready this time. He's been doing good, real good, and he's sorry, really sorry this time, and it won't happen again. No way, it will never ever happen again, never, 'cause he is so sorry and he's doing so good. You can ask anybody how good he's doing; he learned his lesson; he really has this time; he won't listen to the voices anymore; besides they went away and they're not coming back 'cause he's going to take his medicine every day. You'll see, and even if the voices do come back, he promises he's not going to listen to them. Just talk to the doctor, please, just talk to him. He'll tell you how good he's been; they didn't even have to tie him down once. He's been that good, and he wants to come home so bad, and he loves her and he misses her. Yes, he knows she comes to visit him every chance she gets, and, yes, he knows she loves him and misses him too, sure he knows that, but it isn't the same. It's not the same as being home, and it's his home too. If she really loves him as much as she always says she loves him, if she really means it, she'd give him another chance and let him come home. Please say yes. He'll do anything; he'll be so good, like when he was a little boy. PLEASE one more chance, just one more chance . . . NO, PLEASE, DON'T SAY NO, OKAY . . . okay, think about it, just think about it. OKAY? Okay, he'll call back again tomorrow.

Mary is afraid. Again. She is afraid to take a chance. Again. She doesn't want to live in fear anymore, but she doesn't know what do. There's no telling what he might do the next time. She is not as strong as she used to be, and she is not getting any younger. He seems to be getting worse. She used to think he would get better. She built her hopes up. She doesn't think that way anymore. She doesn't know what to think. She wants to do what's right. Everyone tells her he needs to be on his own. He would be much better off. He has to learn to do things for himself. Her lady friend, who is a teacher, says she needs to back off a little, he's got to find himself, he's a grown man, and he has to make his own way—he's fifty years old, for goodness sakes. She knows. She wants him to grow up—he needs to, and she's not going to be around forever . . . but it is so hard to let go and it's a little lonely without him. Up at the county hospital, they told her the same thing—plenty of times. They want to put him in some boarding home. But he doesn't want that—he wants to be in his own home.

And all she wants for him is to be happy. That is all she ever wanted. Tell her, is that too much for a mother to ask? And she tells him he's got to behave himself this time. He promises to be good. And take his pills. Sure thing—he doesn't want to be sick anymore. He wants to be Johnny again—the good son who always brought home a good report card and always went to church on Sunday . . . and she wants so badly to believe him . . . and in her heart of hearts she does believe him. Maybe this time it will be different. It just may be. And she will try her very best . . . and keep her fingers crossed.

Questions for Discussion

1. How would you address the issues of guilt and denial with this mother?
2. What other placement options, besides living with his mother, would you consider for the son?
3. What would you say to her regarding her need for and right to her own personal safety?

The Fool on the Hill

Carol Cochran

My son says he's "The Fool on the Hill." I've heard it so many times I believe it. In 1960 when John was born, the Beatles were becoming popular. It's difficult to imagine they wrote that song about him, a chubby baby in a three-bedroom split-level on Lynde Drive, near Moore Lake, in Fridley, Minnesota. Imagine. John Lennon said if only we can imagine. My son began imagining sometime in his late teens. He imagined he was on the Beatles' *Sgt. Pepper's* album cover, the one with the crowd of famous people. He would point to the various people and name them, some relatives and friends. John thought he was going to marry one of Paul McCartney's daughters and become rich. He's still at it twenty years later. John slips into imagining when his problems are too great for him to handle. The doctors call his illness schizophrenia: paranoid schizophrenia.

Except for brief stints in the hospital and Air Force, John has lived with me in Minneapolis most of his adult life. Our apartment in Cedar-Riverside, an urban area near the University of Minnesota, is too small for all of us. When I'm home, the Beatles are there with me, almost all the time. The apartment is definitely too small for six. Five, if I don't count Lennon. But he's there, too. John Lennon, Paul McCartney, George Harrison, Ringo Starr, John, and me.

"I wanna hold your hand," they croon loudly. "All you need is love. Love is all you need." I need peace and quiet. I need them to "get back to where you [they] once belonged." They belong on albums in America, in England, and around the world, but not in my son's head and not in my family. Most of all, I need a medical breakthrough in combating schizophrenia. John takes his medication regularly, something not always common among schizophrenia sufferers. But there's no magic pill for the "Magic Carpet Ride" (Steppenwolf) he's on. John's neuroleptic medication reduces his symptoms of paranoia and delusions, but it doesn't eliminate them.

Sometime in 1981, John called me from Ellsworth Air Force Base in Rapid City, South Dakota, and said he had changed his mind about the service and wanted to get out. Seven months had passed since his enlistment and basic training at Lackland Air Force Base in San Antonio, Texas. Minneapolis was gray and chilly that early morning when I drove John to the Armed Forces Recruiting Station and gave him to Air Force sergeants to finish what we had not been able to do. My tears could not provide what he needed, and neither could his dad and I.

My son's teen years during our drawn-out, four-year divorce battle included his using street drugs, becoming a sexual assault victim, dropping out of high school, losing direction, and the evaporation of family identity. John, his half-brother, sister, dad, and I were drowning, individually and collectively. Treading water is one of my strengths, and I managed to survive, at least on the surface. We all grabbed whatever floated by.

My son received a general discharge, under honorable conditions, and would proudly tell those who asked about his military experience. He emphasized the word honorable. A dishonorable discharge is unacceptable. And so is mental illness.

I noticed when John returned from the service that he was drinking too much beer and smoking too much marijuana. Nothing had changed. John's father and I had hoped the air force could become the structured family he needed—the mother and father who could keep him off the streets, protect, and provide for him. But the air force could not replace his fractured family. After a few weeks, I convinced my son to go with me for a chemical dependency assessment.

The massive, yellow brick building on the corner of Chicago Avenue and Eighteenth Street faces east on Chicago, a temple of hope, and spreads halfway across the long city block. The building runs deep in back, almost to Seventeenth Street, and reminds me of a hospital. The building houses the Detoxification Receiving Center (known by the regulars as detox) and other Hennepin County social services for the chemically dependent and mentally ill. My memory fails me regarding the exact details. I know I sat in a small waiting room on the other side of the closed wooden door where John and the counselor talked.

"Mrs. Cochran, would you like to come in?" he asked. The counselor had opened the door and was standing in the doorway. Through the doorway, I saw John sitting on a chair next to a desk piled with papers and books. John has always been good-looking, even as a baby. His blond, curly hair darkened to golden brown as he grew older. His baby fat stretched into a six-foot, well-proportioned frame that played football with a parks and recreation team and at West High School, until low algebra grades disqualified him. People tell me that he should have been a model. His nose is straight and his lips full. When he shaves the scraggly, reddish beard he grows every few weeks, he has almost a baby-faced appearance.

John's gray-blue eyes looked glazed. He stared just past me with that silly smile on his face, the smile he gets when he's self-conscious. When I see that look, I want to snap my fingers or clap my hands in front of him to get his attention. That look got him discharged from the air force, and that was before anyone realized he had a mental illness. My son's commanders thought he was not listening.

I walked inside the office and took the empty chair on the patient side of the desk, about three feet from John. The counselor, a slender African-American man who appeared to be in his late thirties, walked behind the desk and sat down.

"Mrs. Cochran," he began, "After talking with John, I believe his chemical abuse is secondary to a psychological problem. John uses alcohol and marijuana to self-medicate in order to cope. The world is difficult for him to understand. I recommend a psychological evaluation. I can give you the name of a psychologist." I was surprised, still confused, and relieved. John was finally getting attention.

Not knowing what to expect, I called Dr. Gross at the Pilot City Medical Center and was able to get an appointment for John within a few days. After the examination, Dr. Gross referred us to a Hennepin County Adult Mental Health Clinic psychiatrist. For this, I knew it was time to call in John's father.

After John's father and I divorced in the seventies, we all spent the next decade bobbing for air to stay afloat and searching for an anchor. John's older brother dropped out of college and followed Jesus, his younger sister dropped into the streets and was followed by pimps, his father developed life-threatening cancer, and I joined a commune and married a criminal. But those stories are for another time—a time when I am ready.

After examining John, Dr. Benninghoff called us into his office.

"Based on what you've told me about John's history and my examination, it's likely that John has latent schizophrenia." The words hung in the air and wouldn't go away. I felt that John might as well have received a death sentence. I was hit with something I could not change or fix. After I stopped sobbing, Dr. Benninghoff gave us some brochures that explained schizophrenia. John's father was stunned. His mother had schizophrenia and the diagnosis hit him like a bullet.

John began regular appointments with Dr. Benninghoff, but his denial of the illness interfered with progress and his keeping his appointments. He did not have a mental illness. He was The Fool on the Hill and was on the *Sgt. Pepper's* album cover. He and Paul were friends. Why didn't anyone believe him? They must be jealous because he was on the album and going to marry one of Paul's daughters and be rich. John was in the Bible, also, and had pictures to prove it. My son carried the Bible and the Beatles' album cover around with him to show others who he was. His denial of his illness led to a verbal threat toward Dr. Benninghoff, which not only ended that relationship but made it difficult for John to receive help elsewhere.

In 1987, I filed formal commitment papers, and John spent three months in the Regional Treatment Center at Willmar. After that he began taking his medications regularly and accepting the idea that he has some kind of a problem—not mental illness—but a problem that makes taking daily medications necessary for him to feel better. The unforgettable, painful process of commitment is still vivid in my mind. In the courtroom, John's father and I watched as John showed his pictures to the judge in defense of his sanity.

"I'm going to marry Stella, Paul's daughter," John tells me. I've heard it before.

"What if she decides to marry someone else?" I ask, trying to gauge his stability and reaction.

"If she married someone else, I'd marry Angie."

"Who's Angie?"

"My girlfriend in Florida."

John and I have conversations like this almost every day. I understand the solace he receives from an imaginary girlfriend. When I was a child, my mother told me that I had an imaginary playmate who filled my loneliness. Usually John tells me about his land in Florida that he bought because he's "The Fool on the Hill" and the land has "The Long and Winding Road." The Beatles' song confirms it. He explains the lyrics and how they refer to him. The Beatles are my son's obsession and delusion, but he is not exclusive and will include references to "Johnny Be Good" and the other Johns and Johnnys of music fame. When my son was a baby, his dad and I would bounce him on our knees and sing, "Big, Bad, John," a popular song in 1961. John was big, but he was not bad.

My son really does have land in Florida, almost. He paid $1,500 for one acre in the northern Florida panhandle. For over two and a half years, John paid Adamo $50 a month by stretching his meager income from low-paying jobs, government assistance, and family help. Getting title for the land is another story. John bought the land in 1983 after answering an ad in *Outdoor Life*. Adamo, a land wheeler-dealer, sold John one acre of land that was part of ten acres Adamo was buying. I had studied real estate law and knew it was impossible and illegal to sell land without holding the title.

What Adamo was doing wasn't right, but John wouldn't let me intervene. He had gone to Florida and seen the land. It had a "long and winding road that leads to your door . . . . " I can't interfere with that. I've tried. My son's trips to Florida and across the country in his rusty old vans were unstoppable as well as unwise. But, his resourcefulness and determination have protected him in his times of need. So have I.

My son's preoccupation with purchasing land is only one of his money-losing habits. Buying rusty old vans and cars is another. Whether land or cars, he buys high and sells low, which makes him, and others, feel good.

I could write a book about all the experiences my son and I have had. After all, "Your Mother Should Know." The other day when I walked past my portable radio-cassette player in the bedroom, a Beatles' tune was playing.

"Paperback writer. Paperback writer," I thought I heard faintly in the background. For my own sanity, I began tuning out those tunes long ago.

"John, are they saying paperback writer?" I asked.

"Yeah. Why?" he replied.

"That's my song," I said. "I'm the paperback writer."

"No, you're not," John said, looking at me strangely.

"Yes, I am," I said, and began dancing around singing, "I'm the paperback writer. I'm the paperback writer."

"You're having a delusion," he said. "I'm going to call Station 62 [the University of Minnesota psychiatric ward]," and he went to the phone and began dialing.

I rushed to the phone but didn't get there in time. Station 62 answered. John said, "Fool on the Hill and Paperback Writer" into the phone and hung up. Reminding me of my delusions and that I am the crazy one brings my son comfort and makes his life more acceptable.

"Oh, my God," I thought. "I hope they don't have Caller ID."

Imagine. Psychologists tell us that the images we hold and the thoughts we believe are powerful shaping forces and our reality. I envision myself a writer, including paperbacks. My son envisions himself a landowner, including land with a long and winding road. I ask myself if my vision is more sane that his? I have not written a paperback: John has purchased the long and winding road, almost.

Questions for Discussion

1. Discuss the relevance of genetics, drug and alcohol use, and family of origin stability as they relate to schizophrenia.
2. What part does the mother's guilt about the chaos of her divorce play in her behavior toward her son?
3. If you were to see the mother in this story for counseling, what issues would you address? What kind of support does she need?

Just Wondering

Ellen Turner

She wonders if he is alive
   or if he has a gun
she wonders
    if he is sticking a needle in his arm
    right now
    while she is making meat loaf

she walks the dog
brushes her teeth
takes a shower
kisses her lover
always
wondering

Sometimes I Pretend You Are Dead

Ellen Turner

I imagine the phone ringing
dead of an overdose
I plan your funeral
only wildflowers please
have Tim make a mix tape
punk rock, a San Francisco sound
invite your friends to speak
will your brother be up to it?
I choose photographs for the program
the one you love—makes you look so
gritty
and the one I love—wrestling with the
dog
my friends marvel—we haven't seen her cry
a state of denial they agree
but I am happy
your life is over
now mine can resume.

Questions for Discussion

1. What is it like to be the mother of a drug-addicted child? What feelings and reactions come across in these two poems?

Hostages

Karen de Balbian Verster

Sisterly love is, of all sentiments, the most abstract.

Ugo Betti

Big sisters are the crabgrass in the lawn of life.

Charles M. Schultz

As Kayla watched Cleo emerge from the Greyhound bus, she thought, where did she come from, this sister of mine? She may as well have been found under a cabbage for all they had in common. They embraced. "You look great," Kayla said. "Like a movie star." Cleo had gotten a surprisingly chic haircut, a twenties' bob, and had lost weight. After Cleo's second pregnancy, she had let herself go, but now she looked pretty, younger, better than she had looked as a teenager. Kayla was surprised to find herself jealous, a new emotion regarding her sister.

"Those are nice pants," Kayla said. "Stretch denims?" She hated her. But how could she, who had so much, hate one who had so little?

"Mom sent them to me. They were ninety dollars reduced to five. She left the price tag on—"

"Just like Minnie Pearl!"

"Yeah!" They laughed. "So I could show everybody at work."

Kayla steered Cleo to the subway entrance through the gauntlet of smelly men trying to open doors, clutch her suitcase, cadge money. She hated Port Authority. The only reason she ever went there was to meet Cleo, and, of course, whenever Kayla got there early the bus was late, and vice versa. Last time Kayla was late and it broke her heart to see Cleo standing there, trying to look relaxed and assured, but (Kayla assumed) totally helpless.

On the train, Cleo regaled Kayla with stories about her new job. She worked in a silk-screen factory where they made T-shirts. She told Kayla about Wilma who ran the C-press and Judy who operated the steamer, two small women in charge of big machines, something Cleo admired.

Kayla said, "That reminds me. Mother told me to tell you, 'Don't go back to work on Monday and brag about what a good time you had in New York or the people there will think you're a monster.' She said you should act depressed."

While Kayla was speaking, Cleo had gotten a set, mulish look on her face. She hated being the recipient of advice, yet she seemed to go out of her way to deserve this attention. Her husband, Tim, was currently in jail for driving while intoxicated, because the last time this happened his license had been revoked, and their children had just been picked up by the social worker and put into foster care until such time as Cleo and Tim could prove their ability to provide a stable home, which was starting to look like never.

"That's a bunch of baloney," Cleo exploded. "Mom don't know what she's talking about. Wilma told me when I come back she's going to kill me if I ain't had a good time. She said, 'You deserve to enjoy yourself with all the stress you been under. Just don't tire your sister out.'" This last was complete hooey as far as Kayla was concerned. She was convinced her sister didn't give a shit about her needs, except as a means to manipulate her to do what she wanted.

They got off at West Fourth Street and walked to Kayla's apartment, a challenge since Cleo had no awareness of the space her body took up. She constantly bumped into Kayla and other people. When Kayla made a turn, Cleo kept walking straight; when they got to an intersection, Cleo didn't look before crossing.

When they arrived at Kayla's apartment, her husband, Alec, was intently watching a football game.

"You men are all alike," Cleo said.

"Why do you say that?" Alec asked. He sincerely wanted to know.

Cleo couldn't answer. She turned to Kayla. The problem was that, for many years, she did nothing but stay home and watch TV, especially soap operas. Until she got a job, she based her sense of reality on their plots. As a result, she quoted a lot of lines that sometimes hit the mark and sometimes didn't.

"Did you eat on the bus?" Kayla asked. "You want something to eat?"

"I ain't hungry," Cleo said. "Could we go for a walk?"

"It's raining," Kayla said.

"I don't mind," Cleo said. "After sweating in that factory all day long it will be good to go out and get some air."

They stopped in a deli so Cleo could get some cigarettes, a Coke, and a candy bar. She ate half the candy bar, then lit up.

"Everybody at work tells me I eat too many sweets," she said.

"I thought you quit smoking," Kayla said.

"Last time Tim was in jail I needed something to calm my nerves. Could we go see Freddie?"

Freddie managed a restaurant where Kayla had worked when she was in college. They used to be buddies, but they didn't seem to have much in common anymore. For some reason, Kayla's mother and sister wanted to see him every time they came to visit, so Kayla reluctantly dragged herself over.

"You remember Cleo," Kayla said, when Freddie greeted them at the door.

"Sure, how are the Amish folk doing? Pennsylvania, right?"

"Still driving them buggies," she said.

Cleo stood idly by while Freddie and Kayla ran down old acquaintances. Cleo spotted a guy at the bar whom she thought was cute.

"The tall guy in the striped shirt?" Freddie asked.

"No!" Cleo said, affronted. "He looks like Big Bird."

Cleo wandered over to the bar. Great, Kayla thought. She dragged me in here so she could see Freddie and then leaves me alone with him. Kayla saw Cleo place the drink Freddie had bought her, watered-down and still full, on the bar. Kayla hated the way her sister could just take a bite or two of something and then toss it. Kayla had inherited their mother's fear of the Depression. She saved rubber bands, even those tight, useless ones from broccoli, never threw anything away when it could be passed on to someone and, of course, ate everything on her plate.

Kayla had once offered Cleo three pairs of shoes, identical in style, but differing in color. Cleo selected one pair.

"Why don't you take them all?" Kayla said.

"I only want that pair."

"But they're all the same."

Cleo shrugged. Kayla was really aggravated. She contemplated hiding the other two pairs in Cleo's suitcase.

"You don't have cable?!" Freddie said. "Listen, I'll give you the keys to my apartment and you can come over and watch something whenever you want."

Kayla felt the pull of Freddie's desire to re-enmesh her in his life. "Thanks," she said, "but I don't think I could handle that responsibility."

Kayla waved to Cleo, who was in conversation with the guy at the bar.

"It's time to go," she said, when Cleo finally sashayed over, leaving her drink on the bar.

"It's only eleven," Freddie said.

"Times have changed," Kayla said.

Cleo wanted to go to Washington Square Park and see if there was anything going on, but Kayla persuaded her to return home since it was raining harder.

The next day Cleo wanted to go to Tower Records. She picked out the sound tracks of *9½ Weeks* and *Pretty Woman*.

"Did you like those movies?" Kayla asked.

"They've got good dance music," Cleo said.

Their mother, Gwen, had told Kayla not to let Cleo spend any money while she was visiting her since the forty dollars Cleo brought with her was all she had until her next paycheck. Kayla used to take it for granted that it was her job to dispense important advice to her younger sister and it was Cleo's job to put it to good use. Now, Kayla just wanted to be a sister.

An IQ of seventy-seven entitled Cleo to an official classification of mental retardation. But since she didn't look or act in a stereotypically retarded fashion, it was only over time that one began to discern things were off. Still, people persisted in their expectations of normalcy: "Why doesn't she just pay her bills on time? Why doesn't she just change the cat litter? Why doesn't she just leave him?"

At the age of sixteen, she was given yet another evaluation which she "appeared to take very seriously, making a strong effort to succeed." She was reported as having immature social relationships and limited activities outside of school—she said she napped a lot and enjoyed playing with her kitten. Her unrealistic goal of wanting to study English literature and advanced history in "big textbooks" led to the conclusion that she did not accept her deficiency in reading and spelling skills.

It was hard for Kayla to watch someone who couldn't read, write, or perform simple math spend half her grocery money on tapes. She hauled out the older sister routine, which wasn't so dusty, and dissuaded Cleo from buying them. Cleo gave in, resentful that Kayla thought a thirty-year-old mother of two should have to be told how to manage her money.

Next they went to Saks Fifth Avenue so Cleo could try on evening gowns. This was tolerable for Kayla since it could be done without the assistance of a salesperson. Last time Cleo visited she'd insisted on going into The Fur Vault to try on minks, and Kayla had to fidget in the hoity-toity waiting room, writhing with embarrassment, while Cleo was led off by a sleekly coifed saleswoman. When Cleo returned, she excitedly related the story she'd concocted to fool the saleswoman. Kayla knew only too well that a saleswoman in such a place could take one look at Cleo and size her up in a minute, without even getting to her hands, chafed and red from the chemicals she handled at work.

Unfortunately, Cleo caught sight of some wedding gowns on display and began to examine them. Kayla wandered off and when she judged it safe, she returned to find Cleo standing before a large three-way mirror watching as a young saleswoman, like a lady-in-waiting, picked up the train of her gown and allowed it to float into its proper placement. As soon as Cleo caught sight of Kayla, she began to wave frantically and call her name. Kayla reluctantly made her way to within speaking distance.

"Where have you been?" Cleo said.

"Just looking around."

"I wanted you to see some of these dresses." Over her shoulder, Cleo said to the saleswoman, "Could I have the Cathedral veil?" Then back to Kayla. "The president of the company walked by while I was trying on another dress and he said I looked beautiful in it."

"That's right," said the saleswoman. "Do you want to show your sister?"

"That's okay," Kayla said.

"It'll only take a minute," Cleo said. "Alison's helping me try on the dresses."

"How nice," Kayla said, weakly. "Cleo, we have to go soon."

But Cleo was already striding away, Alison in her wake. Kayla hoped that Cleo was wearing a decent bra, not the scungy rag she'd had on last time. Cleo didn't seem to notice or care about things like that. On this visit, she'd managed to fill Kayla's whole apartment with the smell of cigarette smoke and cat urine from the three cats she refused to get rid of who regularly peed on the clothes which never made it from the floor beneath the washing machine to the closet.

Cleo came out with a silver lamé wedding dress. "What do you think?" she asked.

"I like the other one better," Kayla said. "We've really got to go or we'll be late."

"Just one more," Cleo said.

Her trailer was stacked with *Bride* magazines which she'd earmarked with dresses for herself and her five-year-old daughter, Kimberly. She and Tim had had a civil ceremony because she was six months pregnant, but on her eighth anniversary she renewed her vows with an elaborate ceremony, wearing a gown she found at Goodwill. Kayla went along with it, an aged bridesmaid, even agreeing to wear the bridesmaid dress Cleo had worn at her wedding, although Kayla thought the whole thing was just an excuse for Cleo to wear a wedding gown.

Kayla noticed a well-dressed, older woman seated at a dainty escritoire. She seemed oblivious to the scene as she flipped through the pages of an appointment book, but just as Alison turned to accompany Cleo to the dressing room, the woman called her over. Cleo sauntered over to Kayla while Alison talked to the woman.

"Why don't you like this dress?" she asked.

"I don't dislike it. I just like the other one better; it's more traditional. This one looks like an evening gown," Kayla said, only halfheartedly upholding her part in this inane conversation. She glanced over at the woman, certain she was telling Alison to get rid of them.

"Why don't I take your picture since I have my camera with me?" Kayla said.

"Photographs are not allowed," the older woman said sharply.

Now Kayla felt really slimy, caught red-handed in a conspiracy to defraud Saks Fifth Avenue. Finally, the last dress was tried on and they departed. Cleo reached into her pocket to retrieve her wedding ring, telling Kayla how she'd left her diamond engagement ring on to fool Alison into thinking she was serious about making a purchase. This wedding ring set cost several thousand dollars, about a third of the money Cleo got when her father died. The rest was spent on a king-size, canopied water bed with a mirrored ceiling; a top-of-the-line stereo system; and the downpayment on a living room suite, which was subsequently repossessed when Tim lost his job. At the time, Kayla tried to convince Cleo to get a cubic zirconia, since she'd lost her first wedding ring, a plain gold band. But Cleo haughtily refused, insisting that a diamond was a better investment.

They rode the subway in silence. At Cleo's request, they were meeting Alec at a Chinese restaurant since Tim hated Chinese food and never let her have it. She ordered her favorite dishes: dumplings, snow peas with water chestnuts, and sweet and sour chicken. Alec unsuccessfully tried to draw her out, but she seemed self-conscious and would only answer in monosyllables. When he went to the bathroom, Kayla said, "Cleo, I'm exhausted. I don't think I'm going to make it to the party tonight."

Cleo's face fell. "But you promised," she said.

"I know," Kayla said. "But I'm suddenly very tired and I just don't know if I can go dancing."

"Whatever you say," Cleo said, looking out the window.

"Well, don't pout," Kayla said.

When they got home, Kayla took a nap—she hated to disappoint Cleo—and when she woke she told Cleo they could go. It was a fifties prom night party, being held at the Center for Living, whose clients were mostly gay men. Kayla warned Cleo that she might not get asked to dance at this party since the last time Kayla took her to a party, she refused to dance unless a man asked her. Cleo got that mulish look again and told Kayla not to worry about her. Then she asked Kayla to help her attach her stockings to the Merry Widow she was wearing.

"Is this the one you bought at the lingerie party?" Kayla asked, knowing the answer but unable to help herself.

"Yes."

"Cleo, I don't understand how you can spend seventy dollars on something like this when you're broke."

"Well, Tim said I could. I called him up and asked him."

"You've barely been able to pay your bills since he lost his job and you know that. Just because he gives you permission doesn't magically make the money appear. You have to start being responsible for yourself. Tim's not your father."

"Well, he wrote the check out."

"Yeah, and it bounced. Wilma was your supervisor. You can't bounce a check on her. That outfit ended up costing a hundred dollars with the bank charges, so the money Mother sent to help pay the rent was wasted."

When they got to the party, Cleo immediately began cruising the men. She latched onto a handsome man in a white tuxedo jacket and plaid cummerbund. When they danced, Cleo flew around the room like a flamenco dancer. As she twirled around you could see everything: the Merry Widow holding up her stockings, a gratuitous pink satin garter around her thigh, and her gauzy black underwear. The men went wild, clapping and hooting.

After several dances, her partner excused himself. Cleo gave him a minute and then asked him to dance again. He said no. Kayla took her aside and told her not to make a pest of herself. For her pains she was rewarded with that mulish look.

As Kayla chatted with friends, she was happy to see Cleo had found a new partner who appeared delighted with her showgirl style of dancing. They even won the dance contest.

At midnight, when the party officially ended, Kayla hunted for Cleo to tell her she was ready to go. Cleo acted like she didn't see Kayla coming and walked off in another direction. Kayla followed her, calling her name, and when she finally caught up with Cleo, she grabbed her arm.

"Don't do this to me," Kayla said.

"What?"

"You know what I mean. You heard me calling you. Why are you acting like this?"

"I wasn't doing anything."

"Oh, really? I'm going to say good-bye to some people and then I want to go home."

When Kayla returned, Cleo and her dance partner were deep in conversation. Cleo turned to Kayla excitedly, "Peter wants me to go dancing with him."

"At The Monster," he said. "I'll take good care of her and make sure she gets home. She reminds me so much of my mother."

Poor guy! Kayla thought. But he seemed reliable, older and courtly, not like someone who would abandon Cleo for the first hot trick that came along. "Well, all right," she said.

"Goodie," Cleo squealed, clapping her hands.

Kayla jotted down her address and phone number since Cleo had no idea where Kayla lived or how to get there. As Kayla was writing, she heard Peter tell Cleo he was broke and heard Cleo say, "Don't worry, I got plenty of money."

Kayla restrained herself with difficulty from commenting.

"Well, good-bye," Cleo said pointedly.

"You don't have to got rid of me," Kayla said, annoyed. "I'm going."

Kayla walked home and wondered what it would be like to have a normal sister, one she could confide in and pal around with, one who didn't fill her with guilt and shame. Then she thought of Alec's sister, who was "normal" and had four children by three different fathers, lived in a teepee in New Mexico, and scrounged for food in the dumpster behind the neighborhood supermarket because she felt poverty was an attribute.

The next morning, Kayla said, "I was really hurt by the way you treated me last night."

"I don't like being treated like a child," Cleo said.

"Well, fine," Kayla said. "Then I guess you don't need me to cart you around today. You can just go off and do whatever you want and I'll stay here and get some work done."

Cleo went out onto their little terrace to smoke a cigarette. The phone rang. It was their mother. Kayla was so mad at Cleo's stubborn refusal to consider her feelings that she violated the agreement she'd made with Cleo not to involve their mother in their problems. Gwen said, "I guess Cleo was 'showing her ass,' as they say around here."

"In more ways than one," Kayla said, telling her about Cleo's twirls. "But you know, she's really a good dancer. She's so graceful."

"I tried to take her for lessons. I told the teacher about her handicap and he still said she had ability. But then your father left and we never got back to it."

"She said she practices at home, perfecting her moves."

Cleo walked into the kitchen and Gwen said to put her on.

"I don't want to talk to her," Cleo said. "She's just going to lecture me."

"No, she's not," Kayla said and handed her the phone, knowing full well that's exactly what Gwen was going to do.

When she hung up, Cleo came into the living room and forced herself onto Kayla's lap, like a dog thrusting its head under her hand for a pat. She curled up and started to cry. "I'm sorry," she said into Kayla's neck, her tears dripping down Kayla's back.

Kayla felt like a car crash survivor calmly waiting for firemen to saw her from the wreckage, about ready to cry herself and, at the same time, fighting off hysterical laughter because the mental picture of how they looked was so ludicrous. Kayla patted Cleo a little, feeling sorry for her, but also resentful. She told Cleo that it seemed like she came to visit only to be shown a good time, and she'd hated the charade with the wedding dresses.

"I just wanted to impress you," Cleo said, weeping again.

Every time Kayla made Cleo cry, she thought of the time she tried to teach her to play baseball. Cleo was about eight years old and Kayla was tossing her slow, easy pitches. Cleo kept missing and Kayla kept telling her to take her time, keep her eye on the ball, etc., until Kayla lost patience and shouted at her. Cleo started crying and told Kayla she was doing the best that she could. Kayla's exasperation immediately melted and she felt exposed—they were both exposed—Kayla as a relentless monster, Cleo as a handicapped nincompoop. Kayla learned that if she didn't say anything, didn't push, then her sister's defects were not as noticeable. If it weren't for those IQ tests, she could even forget Cleo's disability existed.

In spite of everything, Kayla loved her sister, so they patched things up and got on with their day. At the Metropolitan Museum, a staple of every visit, Cleo particularly liked the period rooms and houses that had been re-created. They also went through her other favorite, the armor section. Their last stop was the Rodin sculpture garden. The elevator opened onto a sunny rooftop terrace that overlooked Central Park. They'd never seen this before and they each moved toward what enchanted them.

Kayla joined her sister on a bench. From there, only the tops of the buildings were visible and the city looked like Oz. It seemed to encircle the park with loving arms, offering promise and protection to all in its embrace.

"Are you doing okay?" Cleo asked, referring to Kayla's breast cancer.

"Yes," Kayla said. "Chemo's a piece of cake."

"I've been worried about you. I didn't know what to do."

"Well, that letter you sent meant a great deal to me. I still have it."

"Deb wrote it for me. I told her what to say."

Cleo had signed her own name in her childlike scrawl and filled the bottom of the page with the word "kiss," written many times. Kayla saved this letter not only because it was the only one her sister had ever written to her but because it revealed a side of her Kayla often forgot existed.

She forgot it even then and thought, "If you can get someone to write a letter for you, I wish you'd send me a Christmas card or a birthday card once in a while." Her family had never questioned Cleo's illiteracy, but sometimes Kayla wondered if Cleo could read and write if she just tried harder. Yeah, like that time you taught her to play baseball, Kayla thought. She put her arm around Cleo and gave her a squeeze. Warmed by the sun, they shared a moment of quiet, effortless communion.

Questions for Discussion

1. What role has Kayla learned to take with her retarded sister, Cleo?
2. What changes would you suggest Kayla make in dealing with Cleo that might make the relationship easier for both sisters?
3. Do you think Cleo could care for her two children?
4. If her children were returned to her, what services would be necessary to help Cleo keep and raise her children? If you were her social worker, what would be your approach with Cleo?

The Pass

Edmund de Chasca

Julia, the sister, awakened exhausted. She had just finished breakfast when the telephone rang, as it always did about that time on Saturday. Her father spoke first—a bad sign—while her mother listened on the extension.

"Mary's got an overnight pass. You'll have to pick her up. I can't get the car out, the driveway's still glare ice."

"I have my folk dancing tonight," Julia said. "Besides, she's not well enough to come home."

"I know, but we've only got five more insurance days," said her father. "You know the doctor won't discharge her unless she's made it through a weekend first."

"You and your insurance days," her mother said. "We can afford to pay."

"Four hundred dollars a day? When I was starting up the business, I never made more than—"

"I will *not* allow my daughter to be put in the state hospital. They let them commit suicide there. Did you read about that boy who hanged himself in his room at Carver? He wasn't found for six hours. They leave them unattended."

Julia's heart began thudding. They'd had this discussion so many times. She felt like a towel that had been wrung through one of those old hand-operated clothes washers.

"You'll want me to stay overnight, I suppose," Julia interrupted.

"You know what's at stake," said her mother.

"This was my folk dancing night."

"Oh, I know, you're so good. We all have to rise to the occasion, though. This is a special weekend."

By the time Julia hung up, a new wave of exhaustion, like a parching summer wind, made her want to lie down again. All week she sold wallets and other leather products at the airport and at other stops all over the city. Then her weekends were absorbed by her aged parents and schizophrenic sister.

At her dressing table, Julia brushed her thick red hair, which was her best feature. It burned in striking contrast to her plain, colorless face and her lumpy figure. At thirty-eight, she was seven years younger than her ageless sister, yet few men took notice of her. She knew that still fewer would in the future.

She recalled once again the conversation with her parents. "You've sacrificed your life for us," her mother had said. "If anything should happen to Mary, we'll give you the money from the sale of the business and go to the Oakwood Retirement Center so you can travel and do some of the things you've always wanted to do."

A vision, like wisps of smoke, rose up. The woman in it did not have to settle for folk dancing clubs, attended by old maids and foreigners with curried breath, or church groups, with their widows and other marginalia. She shopped at Lord and Taylor and went to fund-raising dinners for the art museum and the symphony where her mousiness was forgiven by men with a sense of refinement, men who knew the importance of money in leading a dignified life.

But for now there was the grocery list, then Mary waiting for her at the hospital. Mary's latest suicide attempt, followed by a three-week hospitalization, had given them a much-needed break. She had almost succeeded several times in doing away with herself, but somehow always managed to fall short. Julia suspected the attempts were bluffs. Still, to give her credit, last month she had swallowed the whole bottle of aspirin. If her mother had not checked on her in the middle of the night. . . . Poor Mary!

Her sister had been moved out of the maximum security unit (also call the "lockup" or the "room behind the room") into the closed ward. When Julia saw her standing by the nurse's desk, the worm of contempt curled in her. She wore one stocking. The belt that was supposed to hold her dress together hung down like a hound's tongue.

"You forgot your stocking," Julia said.

Mary looked down at her bare foot and giggled through her tobacco-stained teeth. "I saw my diagnosis . . . depression and schizophrenia and anxiety and thirty dirty stories published. Sister abuse and interfamily conflict." This laugh was lower, like a car trying to start in the winter. "I got good news. Jane called me. She said I have so much akathisia, I ought to take Cogentin."

"You already take Artane."

"I said Cogentin," Mary replied in a belligerent tone.

Julia knew that the telephone call from Jane, a fictitious friend, had never taken place.

They passed an exercise bicycle in the hall and Mary flopped onto the seat and pushed down on the pedals. "Hey, Julie, I got more good news for you. Bad news. I got some muscle on my leg now." She rubbed it. "I'll kick little Julie's head against the cement."

Mary never had carried out any of her threats, at least not since she was an adolescent, when she would throw knives across the dinner table or press Julia down against the mattress, her full weight on top of her.

After signing out at the desk, Julia checked the nine packets of medicine. They were buzzed out the door. Julia was relieved to be outside, but her stomach still contracted. It was as if her sister brought the hospital with her.

They rode down the icy street. Mary fidgeted, then began raising and lowering her legs and rocking back and forth.

"I feel like jumping out of the car."

Julia drove on.

"Help! Help!' Mary cried out, opening a window.

"Practice your coping skills."

Mary took some deep breaths but at the same time thumped her leg against the underside of the dashboard. They stopped at a light and with unexpected agility Mary unfastened her seat belt and slid out of the car. Julia pulled over into a no-parking zone. Mary was walking against the wind, tilted forward, in the direction of the hospital. Julia caught up to her and towed her back to the car.

"I want to go back," Mary said.

"Just get in. Then we'll go back if you want to."

Julia removed a cigarette from the pack the nurse's aide had given her and handed one to her sister. Mary filled the closed compartment with smoke. Then she declared, "I'm all right now." She began singing. "Oh you take the high road and I'll take the low road, and I'll be in Scotland afore ye." The bile of disgust rose up in Julia. Her sister had cried wolf so many times, she could feel nothing for her. Like the paper clips they used to bend back and forth as children until they broke so they could sling them at squirrels with rubber bands, Julia had been bent back and forth and had broken.

They made it to their parents' house. Julia locked her arm in Mary's as they minced up the icy walk. Her mother stood at the door. The bright dress she had donned for the occasion contrasted with her wizened face. She greeted Julia and then her "sick one," as she sometimes referred to her elder daughter.

Mary dug a scrap of paper out of her pocket. "I won a prize at the talent show." Julia seized it. On the paper was printed, "First prize, banana."

"I'm so proud of you," their mother said.

Julia turned her attention to her father. He was slumped in his chair in a corner of the living room with a woebegone expression. He tried to lever himself up with his arms to meet her, but she reached him first and kissed him on the forehead.

"How is she?" he whispered.

Julia shook her head. "She panicked on the way home. We'll be lucky if she makes it through dinner."

"I told your mother she's not ready to come home. Another siege like the last one will kill me."

"I know," Julia said. "She always puts Mary first." Her father had suffered two heart attacks and had been warned to avoid tension.

They glanced toward mother and daughter. Mother was straightening Mary's collar. Then she unwrapped a candy bar and gave it to her.

Julia got back to business. "Did you check the bathroom?"

"The aspirin and razor blades are in the dresser under my handkerchiefs."

"I'd better double-check." Julia went into the bathroom and opened the door of the medicine chest. She spotted some extra Librium that her mother kept in case Mary ran short, but somehow did not see a bottle of phenobarbitol pills concealed behind some antacid. Julia locked up the Librium in one of the file cabinets in the study, where she kept all of Mary's medicine.

Meanwhile, her mother had gone to Mary's bedroom and returned with a ukulele. "Mary's going to sing for us," she announced.

Mary strummed the instrument, which was not in tune, and began "On Top of Old Smoky" in a loud, nasal voice. She forgot a chord and started over. As she sang, their mother moved her body from side to side, letting her arms rise and fall to the rhythm. When Mary finished, she clapped. Julia and her father joined in weakly.

Julia put the groceries away and fixed lunch. Her father and mother then took a nap. Mary, groggy from her medication, also lay down. Julia did the dishes, peeled carrots and potatoes for dinner, paid some of her parents' bills, and fixed Mary's four o'clock medicine.

They almost got through the afternoon without a crisis. All went well until the twilight. This often proved a shaky time for Mary, as if some eerie internal glow matched the failing outdoor light. They were in their familiar places—her father in his easy chair, Julia on the sofa near him, her mother to her left in the wing chair under the powerful lamp that aided her failing eyesight—when Mary made one of her many forages into the kitchen. A glass shattered. Julia hurried in and saw Mary standing over the fragments while the water spread on the floor.

"I thought it was alive," Mary said. "I was afraid it was going to hurt me."

Julia's stomach began churning.

"I'm depersonalizing." Mary turned in half circles, like a dog waiting to be let in the door.

"You'll cut your feet." Mary was not wearing any shoes.

Julie led her sister back into the living room. Her mother put her arms around Mary. Her father raised one eye over the rim of his glasses.

"You'll be all right, dear." Her mother stroked her hair.

"Maybe you should take her back," her father said in a quavering voice. He had a catch at the end of each breath.

"Help!" Mary screamed.

"I'll call the doctor," her mother said.

"She'll be all right." Julia adopted a cooing tone. "You want your roast beef dinner, don't you? You can have both of the bones. And a big ice cream sundae for dessert?" She patted her sister on the head. "I'll give you an extra Xanax."

"God, yes."

Mary gulped down the pill then curled up in her chair like a child, her hands pointed as if in prayer. Julia swept the glass from the kitchen floor. Her father, his eyes still wild and frightened, followed Julia out to the kitchen to fix a drink. He embraced her.

"Promise me that when we're gone, you won't let her ruin your life."

Julia caressed his back. "I won't, Dad."

Yet another dinner was spoiled. Mary was the only one with an appetite. She gnawed on the ribs, leaving a ring of grease around her mouth. Julia's mother smiled, as if in charge of a secret happiness.

Afterward, they watched a *Lawrence Welk* rerun. Julia thought of them gathering at the folk dancing club: Olivere, Roberto, Lars, Grunhilde, and the others. Later, they would have popcorn and lemonade. She looked at the used-up faces of her parents, lit by the glow of the television. They would all try to get through the night without another flare-up, then another day tomorrow like this one, then the midweek crisis over her discharge. Then more and more weekends of the same, like rows of flat grave markers.

Her parents retired early. Mary, freshened by her nap, was still going strong. Julia prepared the evening and morning medicine, dropping pills into two dishes, and then took the packets to the study to lock them up. As she was laying them in the file cabinet drawer, her sister called out from the kitchen. "Julie." She rushed out.

"What's wrong?"

"I feel sick." She steadied herself against the refrigerator. "I don't know where I am."

"You probably ate too much."

"You'd better take me back. I'm sorry." She grimaced, as if about to sob.

Julia took a deep breath and exhaled slowly. "Take your sleeping pill. I'll be here if you need me."

"I feel like killing myself."

Julia stared at her. Mary had uttered those words so many times. "Do you want me to wake Mom and Dad? Because I'd have to if we're going back."

Mary shook her head and lifted her knees several times, as if walking in place.

"Here, take this. You'll be okay."

Mary swallowed the chlorohydrate and meekly went to her bedroom. Soon afterward, Julia went to bed in her old room. She left the door open.

She awakened in the middle of the night. The hallway glowed from the light in the kitchen. The tap water went on, then a pantry door opened and closed. Footsteps came out into the living room where they were muted by the rug. There was a moan. It was Mary and she was in trouble again. A thin wail followed. Julia waited for her to appear in the door of her room and ask for help. The steps padded in a different direction, fainter, then inaudible. The vibration of a drawer made her start. It was the unmistakable sound of one of the file cabinets in the study where she had locked up Mary's medicine. Or had she? Julia remembered going to the study with the packets, then being distracted. The drawer closed. Julia told herself, "I should get up and check." She saw herself confronting Mary and waking up her mother and father. Her sister would have an extra Xanax in hand, or nothing, or all the packets. The possibilities were like filaments of a web that any action on her part would destroy. She lay there, unable to will herself to move. "I'm so tired," she thought. "Too tired. Besides, it's probably nothing."

The footfalls came nearer, then the light went on in the bathroom. The door of the medicine chest grated. Then the tap water ran. The light was left on and the footsteps faded into the bedroom. A mattress creaked. She thought, "If I had not awakened, then nothing would have happened. Because I was awake, it happened, but it didn't because I might have been asleep." She remained in a state of half consciousness for a while, then finally went to sleep.

At the funeral, Julia nodded her head as the minister sermonized about Mary's difficult life and how she would be exalted in heaven. The family shared the blame: her father for not having discarded the bottle of phenobarbitol that was found, empty, in the bathroom; her mother for allowing Mary to come home on pass before she was ready; and Julia for having slept through her sister's final act. When they checked the file cabinet in the morning, it was locked, as it should have been, with the packets of pills neatly stacked.

Julia urged her parents to remain in their home. Her mother admitted that the only reason she had kept it going was to provide a place for Mary. Her father repeated that the house was too much for him to take care of anymore. They gave Julia the option of living there after they went to Oakwood, but she said that a condominium would suit her better since she would be busy with her volunteer work and travel.

Questions for Discussion

1. What symptoms of mental illness does Mary demonstrate?
2. How does Mary's illness cause conflict within her family? How does each member of the family view her illness?

3. Siblings of schizophrenics sometimes show certain characteristics. How does Julia manifest these? Is she a sympathetic or unsympathetic character? Explain.
4. The author states that "The family shared the blame" for Mary's death. Who is responsible for Mary's death? In what way is the mental health care system at fault?

Shocking Mother: A Memoir
of Mental Illness and Recovery

Judith Beth Cohen

1. BIRTHDAY, 1992

For Mother's eightieth birthday, I ordered a cake covered with pink and purple sugar-spun roses. The baker who pushed the color scheme called it "very feminine." She also advised me against putting numbers on the frosting. How could she know that I needed to broadcast Mother's milestone, as proud as I would have been of a daughter turning thirteen. Yet I have neither daughters nor sons. My mother is my only child.

The streets were icy that February day I went to pick up the cake. When I noticed a crack in the frosting, the baker apologized, then whisked her creation off for repair, but the extra sugar and sprinkles couldn't hide the flaw. An imperfect cake would have to do. Mother sat in the sun-filled dining room of the Bay View Retirement Community, dressed in a smart blue blazer. Years ago I'd helped her buy "something nice" to wear to synagogue services, but the jacket languished in her closet through many breakdowns. Now the blue blazer had become a new outfit for a new life.

After she blew out her candles, the room full of "seniors" sang "Happy Birthday." A smiling, robust woman, dressed in a pink jogging suit bragged she'd soon be ninety-five.

"What's your secret for aging so gracefully?" Mother asked her.

"I've had a happy life," she said. "Nothing to complain about."

Even if she reworked all familiar definitions of happiness, my mother could not make such a claim. An image of her I try not to recall is this: freshly committed to a state hospital, she tears off all her clothes and runs naked down the gray corridors until they catch up and put her in restraints.

As I watched her unwrap her birthday gifts, her face seemed to glow in the winter light. She held up the pomegranate jeweled sweater for all to admire.

"It's beautiful—it must have cost you a fortune," she said.

"You know me, Mother; I always find bargains," I said.

"I hope I look as good as you do when I'm eighty," the waitress said as she kissed Mother's cheek.

"I was going to ignore this birthday," Mother joked. "Why call attention to being so old?"

Ten years earlier such a normal rite of passage as her birthday celebration would have been unimaginable. Five years ago I'd have done almost anything short of matricide to avoid standing at her side. That the woman I had known as my mother could bring me anything but misery was unfathomable; I had given her up for lost. Yet she had made a miraculous recovery from the intractable psychosis that had baffled all her doctors. What mysterious process left her healthier, more active, and more vital at the end of her life than she'd been for the past fifty years? As I watched the change unfold, I was untrusting at first, expecting more of the same. Then as the months passed, her unexpected rebirth dazzled me. After decades of frozen winters, it seemed as if Hades had returned her from the underworld.

2. MANIA, 1978

"I'm not staying one more day," my father said. "For almost forty years, I've put up with this, but no more. I can't be around her. Yesterday she even threatened me with a butcher knife. I almost called the police; instead I walked out. Last week, she left a pot on the stove and when the neighbors smelled smoke, they called the fire department. You can't imagine what I've been through. It would make your hair stand on end."

I held the phone in disbelief. Could she be driving him out of the house after all these years? Why couldn't I laugh at their dark comedy? "I'm not sleeping there," he said. "I only go home to get my mail. Maybe you can reason with her—I've given up. I don't have it in me anymore."

"What about Si?" I asked about her older brother.

"He's much too important to be bothered—you know that—and your sister's all the way out in California. Who else can I call?"

Who else? The eldest daughter—again it became my duty to drop my life, fly to them, and sort out the mess. No matter how far I fled, despite the distance I put between us, I was still their child. Every part of my body resisted, but I was no longer with Jerry, my husband of seven years. Didn't that mean I was freer, more available to bail them out? I'd better go, I told myself—paying dues now might buy me a few months of freedom.

As I stood in the chaos of their apartment, my sympathies were entirely with my father. How could I blame him for walking out? I had arrived directly from the airport with a clear purpose in mind: get her hospitalized. I'd lost count of the number of times she'd been in and out, but despite the familiarity of this cycle, it never became routine or easy. The house I'd grown up in sold, they were living in suburban Southfield—to me, one long indistinguishable chain of malls and garden units called Northgate, Kingswood, and Huntington Arms, interchangeable with the names of psychiatric hospitals she had been in.

When she answered my ring, she showed neither surprise nor pleasure at my sudden appearance—no warm greeting, no offer of tea or juice. She was so entirely self-absorbed, I existed only as an impediment to her mania. I left my bag in the guestroom. As I passed her room, I could see the bed covered with clothes in plastic bags, my father's suits, her two-piece printed silks. There wasn't a clear spot.

Wiry, frenetic in slacks and a bra, as if she'd been interrupted while dressing, she scurried around, filling brown paper bags with sweaters, jewelry, old *Reader's Digest*s. She stepped over serving dishes and vases randomly plopped on the living room floor. As I made my way around the maze, I tried to talk with her. I should have let her babble and poured myself a drink; instead I tried reason. "Mother, you need a doctor and I'm going to take you," I explained.

She laughed, that hysterical, mocking laugh. "It's all a lie. You can believe your father, but it's a lie." She headed for the front door, but I intercepted her, grabbed her arm, and tried prying her car keys from her hand. She pushed me away with all her might, so I lunged again. At thirty-five, I was stronger and more fit than she was at sixty-five, but mania had endowed her five-foot-two, hundred-pound body with extra stamina.

"Stop," she screamed. "You're going to break my arm."

"You've ruined my life, " I blurted as my rage bubbled over. "You've destroyed my marriage. You're the reason I don't have children. I've had to take care of you all my life . . . how could I become anyone else's mother?"

"All lies," she yelled, covering her ears as I snapped. I'd lost it. She had brought me to her level—I could hear myself screaming, sobbing, letting go as I never had in her presence. Yet, almost as soon as I'd uttered those words, even as they were forming, I began critiquing and revising. Throughout my tirade, part of me still observed, measured, strategized. Maybe I'd reach her, maybe my intensity would cut through her blockade. Rail as I might, I was still trying to be her therapist.

Finally, I managed to pry away her car keys. My plan was to get her to the psychiatrist (my father had alerted him) and admitted to a hospital, voluntarily, before we'd have to resort to the courts again. She had to be locked up so I could resume my life. I focused on my goal, my purpose, my raison d'être.

"That psychiatrist?" She laughed when she heard about the appointment. "That little twerp—he doesn't know his ass from his elbow. Besides, I have a hair appointment. I'm not going to any doctor before I get my hair done."

I pounced on the negotiating point she gave me.

"OK," I said. "I'll drive you to the beauty shop and we'll go to the doctor from there."

"No doctor," she said.

"Then no hair appointment," I insisted.

She pulled some fake-leather high-heeled boots from one of the bags—it would be a long walk in those heels. We headed out to the car together and I took the driver's seat. Just as I was about to turn the key, she insisted on going back to find her wallet. I followed, afraid to let her out of my sight. She rummaged through three drawers before locating it inside another purse. Then her pace changed to slow motion as she carefully applied lipstick, stalling.

"Let's go." I pulled her arm, and she shook me free and came along. From the passenger side, she barked out orders, directing me to the hairdresser. Finally, I pulled up to the beauty shop, and watched her walk inside—a moment of victory. Grateful for the time to collect myself, too frazzled to do anything but fiddle with the radio, I drove aimlessly around the mall, watching teenagers flirt. When I went back for Mother, she'd disappeared. Carefully, I described her to the woman at the desk.

"Yes, I know Evelyn, but she didn't have an appointment. She wanted us to squeeze her in, but things are too tight. I said we could take her at four. I really couldn't say where she went to."

3. CHILDHOOD, 1952

When I was nine, I lingered after school to finish my science project: a "Ming Garden" intended as a birthday gift for my mother. I imagined that my scrawny, pale tree would make her rise from her heap on the couch. The dwarfed twig seemed hunched and graceless as I labored, rearranging the moss, trying to turn my creation into a magical oriental garden. I didn't notice the passing time or the school emptying while little sister waited obediently. Frustrated, I put my unfinished project back on the shelf—it would have to wait. With my sister's hand in mine, I headed home along Outer Drive. When we crossed the large intersection alone, the afternoon sky was beginning to darken. Mother stood vigil at the door, her eyes so wild, her mouth so contorted, I knew something terrible must have happened—someone must be dead. So panicked, she could barely speak; she paced, wrung her hands, and wept. I soon discovered that the problem was all me, that my dallying with the garden had created this crisis. It was my death she had foreseen. From then on protecting her from such despair and guarding her fragile sanity became my most important life task, far more crucial than making gardens or celebrating birthdays.

Yet nothing about my childhood appeared abnormal: two parents, Mother home baking cookies, Dad's lawyer's income adequate, lots of family values in our synagogue-attending, holiday-celebrating household. Our brick, single-family house sat on a Detroit tree-lined street in a safe, middle-class neighborhood. Behind the picture window and the tall blue spruce, Mother's mental illness took center stage, rendering my father, my younger sister, and I bit players with no script to follow. One day I had an energetic "Mommy" redecorating the house, inviting strangers home for supper, filling the car trunk with packages she'd never open. Days later she would refuse food. Unable to rise from her bed, she'd lay curled in a fetal position, nearly catatonic. Then she would be hospitalized and I'd take over, her disease stealing my childhood.

4. SUICIDE? 1961

Though my bags were packed for college, I did not make it to Ann Arbor the fall after my high school graduation. In the weeks between the orientation and Labor Day, my mother became more and more withdrawn, refusing food, lying in bed until evening.

"I'll be all right. I'm just tired." she said. We sat at the kitchen table in the breakfast nook, the hamburgers and beans I'd quickly thrown together on our plates. In her bathrobe Mother watched us eat.

"You should make more of an effort," my father said. "Just try harder. You can do it."

"I'll be all right," she repeated over and over, staring at her plate, her food untouched. If she lifts her fork and swallows just a few bites, I told myself, it will be an omen meaning I'll be able to go.

She never said a word about my impending departure. One morning, the week before I was to leave, she didn't move at all.

"Wake up, wake up, Evelyn." My father sounded frightened. When he shook her, she didn't stir. He noticed the empty bottle of sleeping pills on her bedside stand. Immediately my sister and I plunged into the crisis. The three of us moved as efficiently as a professional medical team. My sister made coffee, my father phoned the ambulance and doctor, while I got her on her feet. Together we walked Mother around the room, dragging her weight. I slapped her face, while my sister poured coffee down her throat, getting it right, like a movie scene. We never did find out how many pills she'd swallowed—most of them went down the toilet, we suspected.

After she was settled in the hospital, I called my roommate. My father hadn't asked me to change my college plans; he didn't need to. Before he could make a request, I'd contacted Wayne State, a local university where I'd been accepted as a safety measure, and made arrangements to begin my freshman year in Detroit. I would stay and preserve the home I was too young to lose. The unknown that lay waiting for me at the University of Michigan less than an hour away couldn't compete with my mother. I explained over and over to friends that I had to stay—my mother was very ill. The name of her condition would remain a secret. Nobody I knew had mental illness in the family. I began to take a perverse sort of pleasure in the image I was creating: a suffering, romantic heroine with sobering responsibilities, much more serious than my frivolous friends. In truth, I probably could have gone to Ann Arbor if I'd insisted. It was as if we'd conspired to stay together, my mother and I. So submerged was I in her condition, it was as if I'd been trapped with her underwater, able to break the surface just often enough to gulp fresh air and keep from drowning.

During the quiet hours at my part-time job clerking at a textbook store on Warren Avenue, I'd probe psychopathology books, searching for descriptions of my mother's illness. As I scanned the entries on manic-depressive psychosis, I read on, hoping to find symptoms that didn't apply. But there she was, a classic case, just like the others. Furtively, I'd shut the cover if my boss approached, concealing my interest as if I'd been studying pornography.

After two years in Detroit I was determined to complete college in Ann Arbor. "Can't you stay one more year?" my father implored.

I was firm. "No. I can't wait until senior year. I can't switch schools with only one year left."

I moved to Ann Arbor that summer. By Christmas, Mother had been committed to Ypsilanti State Hospital, just a short drive from my campus. The General Hospital had refused to take her back again. My father said he had no choice. That's when she streaked the halls naked, almost taunting us all: if you think I'm so crazy, well, I'll show you what crazy is. On Sundays, my father and sister would pick me up and we'd visit Mother. In her way, she had managed to follow me to college.

5. ADAM MEETS MOTHER, 1988

Not long after my father's death, I took my new love to meet my mother. With trepidation, I went up to the ward with Adam. Would I find her depressed and hostile, challenging me that I wasn't really her daughter? Or would she be manic and chatty, giggling for no reason? Dressed and waiting, she looked very frail, her cheeks sunken, her mouth a puckered hole without the shape dentures provided, but she greeted me eagerly, gulping back tears. No longer on Haldol for hallucinations, she was back to antidepressants, meds for high blood pressure, and Tagamet for her stomach. Her powder blue cotton skirt and matching top hung loose on her small frame.

"Hello, Evelyn." Adam's musical voice made his cheerful greeting nearly a song. He gave Mother a generous hug, as if seeing her for the first time on a psych ward was an ordinary event.

"Nice to meet you," he said. I watched her as if she were my child, wanting to feed her the right lines, to climb inside her brain and make it work right. Inhaling deeply, I waited, hoping our presence would have a transforming effect.

"It's nice to have a son-in-law," she said shyly.

To forestall any paranoid delusions she might have about Adam being a stranger who meant me harm, I told her that we'd been married. Relieved that she had accepted him, I tried to relax as they carried on a polite conversation in the dayroom. She asked how the flight was, where we were staying. Had we seen her brother yet? The TV blared soap operas while an old woman mumbled and gestured at the air.

"That one's crazy." My mother pointed at her, making no effort to lower her voice.

The nurse beckoned me—Mother's doctor had appeared. I could speak with him in his office. I went alone to meet the expert, an Israeli psychiatrist, head of this research unit, where she'd been sent after all the other hospitals had failed, an institute said to be doing cutting-edge experimental work on geriatric mood disorders.

"I don't know why she's not responding." He shrugged his shoulders—a muscular man with very blue eyes, handsome in a clean-cut, preppy American way, despite his Israeli accent. "Can you tell me anything that might help me treat her?"

As I searched for clues, a piece of history he may have missed, my spirits drooped further—another expert with no answers, one more specialist who wasn't special. How I wanted to believe this would be different, that after all the moving from hospitals to nursing homes, that she was lucky to land here. There was another drug he could try, but if it didn't work, he had no more ideas. She could have more electroshock treatments, but that would have to be at a different hospital. They didn't do shock. Our brief interview over, I rejoined Mother and Adam with her pass in hand, smiling. We could leave—she'd been freed, at least for the day.

"He's good-looking, isn't he?" Mother said, as if she could read my face. Toothless, withered, this once beautiful woman still focused on appearances, oblivious to her own.

"Yes," I admitted. Before I could comment on her handsome doctor, she asked, "Did he make love to you?"

"What?" I looked at Adam, wondering if he'd heard the same words.

"Did he make love to you?" she repeated. "He tries it with everyone."

Adam and I exchanged nervous grins with the nurses and aides within earshot. Then, swiftly changing focus, Mother was on her feet.

"Let's go. Let's get out of this place. I can't take it one minute longer."

At lunch, she ordered vegetable soup while we ate club sandwiches. I watched her attack the carrots with her gums, while I forced myself to swallow.

"I can only eat soft food," she explained.

"What happened to your dentures?" I asked.

During one of her long hospitalizations, they had extracted her teeth, just as they would sterilize institutionalized women to prevent babies and eliminate the messiness of menstruation. They considered teeth expendable, like ovaries or a uterus. Mother's dentures presented problem after problem. She kept misplacing the uppers and never managed to wear the lower ones. She looked at Adam as if deciding whether or not to invent a story. Over the phone she had claimed that someone "stole" her teeth, that an aide had deliberately tossed them into the garbage, just to punish her. "They're like Nazis here," she had added. In her uncanny way she seemed able to choose either fantasy or the common experience we called reality.

"I lost them," she now admitted. "I don't know where they are. Ask my brother. Maybe he's keeping them for me."

On the ride back to the clinic, she didn't resist or refuse to return, though Uncle Si had warned me against taking her out. "You'll never get her back there," he said.

From the backseat of the rented Ford, she startled us with her announcement: "I'm changing my name—from Evelyn to Eve."

"Why?" I wondered.

She giggled like a mischievous child with a plan. "Because they're using my name," she continued. "You've heard of the Purple Gang, haven't you?"

I vaguely remembered the Jewish gangsters from Detroit active in the twenties—the restaurant must have summoned their ghosts.

"They've changed their name to mine. Now they're the Evelyn Berman Gang, so I'm going to call myself Eve Miller instead."

Adam tried to stifle his laugh, then gave up and let himself go—it was infectious, and I joined him. Mother chimed in, laughing with us, as pleased as if she'd deliberately made a joke. She gave us no trouble about going back to the ward—she thanked us for lunch and wished us a good trip back to Boston. I felt the tension leave my body as I grabbed Adam's arm and nearly skipped back to the car.

6. BOSTON, 1991

I helped Mother unpack her clothes. When she undressed, I averted my eyes, trying not to notice her protruding belly, her boney arms and legs, her curving spine. Once she'd been a model in her Hadassah chapter's annual fund-raiser. From the front row, I had watched, pleased that she was so much more beautiful than the other mothers, so svelte and lovely, her bare shoulders alluring in a swishy cocktail dress.

For twenty years, I had managed to keep some geographic distance from my mother. Finally there was no place for her to go, no more relatives left in Detroit to care for her. We had come full circle. I had no choice but to become her keeper. Would my relationship with Adam survive her presence in our daily lives? Fortunately, I got her into a new senior residence hungry for paying customers, only five minutes from our house.

After she settled in, Mother began wearing her teeth. Putting those dentures back into her head seemed to signify a passage—she would now bite and chew; she would seize hold of life. Her crises stopped—no depressed withdrawals, no more manic episodes or paranoid outbursts with Mother insisting someone had broken into the kitchen and replaced all the food with Jell-o. No more refusals to speak with me because I was "an imposter." As her life stabilized, we reinvented our mother-daughter relationship, transforming it in the process. I became her driver, her go-between in disagreements with her ceramics teacher, but, contrary to my fears, it was no grim nightmare. She had become a different person. No longer a helpless depressive or raving paranoid, she was simply an eccentric old lady.

To what can I attribute this transformation—her apparent recovery from a lifelong, debilitating mental illness? Everyone has a pet theory. Her last psychiatrist, the one we nicknamed "Sparky," would probably credit the year of maintenance electroshock treatments for reaming the depression (and a good deal of her memory) from her brain. But she'd had these treatments in the past and they failed to stabilize her. Endocrinologists might say that aging altered her brain functions. The sentimental would say it's me—that my attention wrought this miraculous healing, but I'm no shaman. My daughterly love hasn't produced any magical cure; we have no cleansing, intimate talks about our painful past. Much has been denied or lost in the cells destroyed by shock treatments or aging. Finally, I'll never know who she might have been if not for her illness.

In our daily phone chats she tells me funny stories: there's the woman who eats two desserts at every meal because she can't remember she's already had one. She keeps me up on Howard Stern's latest inanities ("He's disgusting, isn't he, but I did laugh.") or the article she read on Supreme Court Justice Ruth Bader Ginsburg ("Did you know her husband had cancer?"). She alerts me to department store sales, mortgage rate changes, suggests movies for Adam and me to see. She also keeps me posted on surviving family members. It's as if she's giving back some measure of what I lost so many years ago. Though it may appear that I've become her mother, our roles are, in truth, less fixed and more permeable as we nurture each other. Visiting our house, Mother looked out at the marsh; the ice chunks were melting fast and the Canadian geese were becoming more scarce. The marsh grass was just beginning to show green. Then, suddenly, we spotted the great blue herons; first one took off with a swooping of wings, then a second one glided after its mate. As I watch friends journey long distances to visit ailing parents, I stay put, enjoying those herons who return each year to rebuild their old nests on the wetlands behind our house. In her apartment five minutes away, Mother tends the plants that fill her place: tumbling ferns, delicate violets, and flowering azaleas. I have come to value the sense of rootedness and connection that her presence gives me. Above all I am humbled by the resilience of our bond. In our backward mother-daughter story, I am like Demeter whose daughter Persephone returned from the underworld for half the year. Together, we watch the gardens bloom again, if only for a season.

Questions for Discussion

1. The author does not mention having sought help for herself during the years of struggle. If she had come to you, what would you have recommended?
2. Comment on the interior dynamics of the child who stays near an ill parent. Could the author have had other choices, and how would they have impacted her?

My Mother Is Back

Juliana Rose

My mother is back. Not from Florida or California, where half of my friends' parents have retired to, and not from a cruise in Alaska, where half of the rest of the world seems to be. In fact, literally speaking, my mother has gone no place to return from. But for forty years, without having to leave her Manhattan apartment, she has been mostly "away"—wandering in the realms of addiction and its attendant madness. A recent hospitalization for asthma, though, led to her treatment with high-dose steroids, which led to wild psychosis, which led her to accept, once and for all, the psychotropic drugs she'd rejected for years. Once again, except for the gray and wrinkles, she seems the sweet amusing woman who forty years ago went away, leaving me in the care of a lunatic replacement.

Life has been too tough for me to wish consciously for happy endings, but for years, disarmed in sleep, I have dreamed of her return. Incredulous now that my dreams seem finally to have come true, I tell my husband, "It's happened. She's back. She's Mommy again!" I squeal like a joyous toddler, not a middle-aged cynic. "It's so wonderful, so wonderful."

And so it seems at first. This mother tells funny stories, listens to mine, shows generosity and gratitude, like the mother I once loved. She doesn't harangue me about a sweater of hers I lost in 1965 or five dollars that I forgot to pay back in the late seventies, proof positive of my worthlessness. Instead she freely hands out dollar bills to bums and overtips at restaurants after listening attentively to waiters' life stories. Proud, I take her to parties, allow her to stay in my apartment when colleagues are expected. What a great mom you have, they say, like kids used to say before she went away.

Not wishing to lose her again, I am super solicitous. My new/old mother barely acknowledges that she's been away, and I don't push it. She screwed up on the street corner we were to meet at and the next thing you know, forty years have passed. And I let it go, not wanting to depress her with the fact of squandered life. Not that she gets very depressed anymore. "Just like old times," she says, smiling brightly, with that juicy Rita Hayworth smile that helped me love her even in the worst of times, or at least to remember that I had. She rarely frowns—the new pills protect her from big aches.

But I ache, suddenly mourning the wasted years. I rip at myself—I should have convinced her to take the medications years ago. I should have tried harder, I tell myself, thinking only of this docile woman. But then I remember the crazed creature who roared at me for decades, and my guilt turns into anxiety. She turned over countless new leaves, only to toss them all about, in the furious chaos that was her specialty. Good intentions, followed by brief stints of normalcy, followed by the usual—amphetamines and barbiturates, spitting and scratching, 2 a.m. hate calls, 3 a.m. overdoses. Is this new leaf different, "for real" somehow? I ask myself, using the child's phrases and yearnings that have returned to me, with her. For real, for good, to stay?

And, in truth, after a while, it's clear that the good is not as it seemed in the first days of her return. She wants to be with me all the time. She loves me, I love her—that's all she seems to know. At work, her "urgent" calls interrupt meetings. "I missed my baby," she cries. "I thought you probably missed your mommy and needed to hear her voice." At home, her message bounces through the rooms again and again. "It's Mommy. Call Mommy. Mommy loves you." Sometimes, when she sees me talking with my husband and child, or my friends, her face twists, as if to say, "Who the hell are they?" And recognizing that mad pout, I brace myself. But the moment passes.

Some days the calls won't stop.

"What are you doing today?"

"I'm going to work."

"You go every day? Don't you ever give yourself a day off to . . . ?"

I finish her thought—a day off to be with your mommy?

"No," I say, remembering those years when I stayed home from school to make sure she'd wake up from her sleep, or to take her to the hospital, or to coax her to eat when the drugs killed her appetite and she grew so thin I thought she'd die. Or just to keep her company so she wouldn't be sad and need to take drugs. And she let me. Willing for me to give up my life for her.

"Never," I hear myself say.

"Well, it's nice that you like your work. I used to like my work."

I recall her magical dance classes—children galloping like beasts, falling softly like feathers. Then another memory—her in a red leotard, stoned, staggering across the concert stage, the curtain taking forever to come down, the audience murmuring, "Oh my, oh my."

"I mean I loved the dance. Maybe I'll return to the dance," she says. "What do you think of that? Maybe you can help me get started again. A few days off won't kill you. Or working part-time. You work too much."

I say nothing. If I speak, I will shout that she is no different. That she's not "back" at all. She's off the miserable drugs . . . but she's still hooked . . . on me now. On me again. I hear her old command: Make everything all right. And the latest version: Unbend my old body. Undo the twisted years. Banish time and consequence. I know you can do that for Mommy. If you just give up your life.

She will kill me this time around, I think, open to her as I haven't been in ages. Fooled by the sheep's disguise, I've let her come close—my devouring wolf. My heart pounding, I am tempted to put down the receiver, race to the front door, check that it's bolted. But, of course, she's far away, uptown, an old lady cooing into the phone, "I'm a believer in sharing and loving. . . . I raised you to be the same. . . . I was very nice to you when you were little. . . . "

Now her coos have turned to whimpers. And remembering how she'd lead my friends and me in synchronized water ballet, constructing perfect stars and flowers from the splashing bodies of chubby girls, how she taught me to ride a wild horse one summer, to fall and mount, again and again, I begin to lose it too. I remember the summer I was ten. My father screaming that he was tired of her phony arty meals, flipping over the table, just before he abandoned her for a young woman with "cracker-jack organizational and typing skills." Just before she abandoned me.

"I was very very nice," she says. "Don't you remember?"

"I do," I cry.

And then falling back, back, through canyons of time, I see her young eyes, wide with pride, as my wild horse takes off and I hold on tight.

Questions for Discussion

1. The mother in this story was using barbiturates and amphetamines to self-medicate. Though her abuse of these substances became a problem in itself, what do you think was wrong with the mother? What illness do you think she was trying to quell?

2. Speculate about some of the external factors that may have contributed to this mother's plunge into mental illness.

3. If this mother were referred to you for therapy, what information about her life would you want to inquire about? What issues might you focus on?

4. In families with an ill mother, the mother-daughter roles are often reversed. What issues do you think this may have caused for her daughter as an adult?

All Good Things Happen Below the Belt

Franz Weinschenk

All day long, Al had this nagging feeling that once again things weren't right with Grace. Her haziness, her preoccupation, her irritability that morning. He parked the car quickly and made his way through the clutter of garden tools and toys in the garage.

"Hi," he announced, turning the corner from the kitchen into the family room. "Hello, hello. . . . How's everybody?"

"Good, Dad," Shellie answered softly. She and Davie were lying on the rug in front of a subdued TV watching a kid's program, heads propped up on pillows.

At the other end of the room, past two yellow plastic tubs filled to spilling over with crumpled laundry, Grace was settled in her favorite chair next to the mahogany end table smoking a Slim—absorbed in her scrapbook.

"Hi, Grace. How ya doin'?" he asked, trying to sound cheerful.

"Oh, boy," she said excitedly, shaking her head. "I just got through listening to the *Joan and Jerry Show.* The whole program was about child abusers." She took a quick drag from her cigarette. "They molest their own children, Al . . . and beat them half to death! It's just like Marci used to tell us in group. Unzip a man's pants, and his brains fall right out on the floor. . . . Oh, these men, Al!" she shook her head again. "I can't believe you men."

"Hey, now, look-ee-here, Grace. Remember, I just got here. . . . Give me a little time to do something stupid before you start beating up on me, okay?" he laughed. "In the meantime, what's for dinner?"

At the mention of food, Davie turned round and asked, "Mo . . . Mo . . . Mom, c . . . c . . . can we have a snack?"

The question annoyed her. "All right . . . all right," she said. "Pressure . . . pressure! That's all I get around here." She drubbed out her cigarette. "You two children can get yourselves some Wheat Thins from the cupboard—but nothing else."

"Hey, come on now, Grace. Just relax." He raised both hands, palms down, as if he were smoothing down the waves in front of him. "Look," he said calmly, there's no pressure. We got all the time in the world. I'll wash up a little, change, and then we can talk about dinner, okay?" He turned and walked down the hall into their bedroom.

It was just five weeks ago that Grace was discharged from the hospital. As long as she was taking her medication and followed the program they had worked out with Lucille, their outpatient therapist, Al supposed things were going about as well as could be expected. They were just down there a couple of days ago. Lucille suggested that instead of having to come every week, they could wait a couple of weeks before their next visit. A good sign, he thought.

He was surprised to see her amble into the bedroom as he was putting on a T-shirt, a newly lit cigarette in one hand, her scrapbook in the other. Her mood had changed.

"Al, you know what happened today?" she said confidentially. "Marci called me this morning. 'Member Marci?"

"Oh, sure. Good old Marci."

"And you know what? Bob Ditweiler is getting a divorce. Boy, I just about keeled over."

"Bob Ditweiler? You mean the doctor from the hospital?"

"Yeah, Bob was in charge of group every day. He used to make you get your feelings out. You couldn't just sit there tight like a clam. 'Let your feelings out, Grace,' he'd tell me." She took a drag. "He was so funny . . . and always acted kinda flirty. And one day, one of the women said something about 'getting hit below the belt,' and you know what he told her? 'All good things happen below the belt.' That's just what her told her, Al." She laughed. "And then he did a number with his tongue . . . you know . . . licked his lips like this." She rotated her tongue around the inside of her lips. "And everybody laughed. Man, it gave me the goose bumps. . . . Marci used to call him 'the international type'" she giggled, "Roman hands and Russian fingers. . . . And you know what?" she went on. "One day after group, the two of us, him and me, we were walking out the door together and he asked me if I'd like to walk out to his car with him. . . . First he put his arm around my waist, kinda in fun, and as we walked, he sorta reeled me in close, and then he looked at me and he said, 'You know, Grace, you're a beautiful woman.' And when we turned the corner past the swimming pool down by the croquet court where nobody is ever around, he let his hand slide inside my Bermudas and inside my panties." She took a deep drag and exhaled slowly. "God, we walked that way for the longest time. . . . Al, it gave me such a great sensation."

"You mean a doctor down at that hospital did that to you? Right there on the grounds? Some damn nerve."

"Oh, I didn't mind, Al. . . . He was always foolin' around like that. You know, kinda sexy—free and easy—sorta naughty. And once we got out there to his convertible, man, I wanted to get into that automobile with that man so bad. . . . But he told me I had to wait till I got better. And you know what? Just today, after Marci called, I figured out why. . . . You know why, Al? Because, well . . . well . . . because they tell me I love him."

Al was taken aback. "Who tells you?"

"Oh, I don't know. I just get this feeling all over—you know, that I love him. Haven't you ever felt like that about somebody? . . . And he loves me, Al. I know he does. . . . Just thinkin' about it gives me the itchies."

"Oh, my God!" Al turned and started for the door.

"Al, Al, don't walk away. Please. You always do that—walk away when I'm trying to tell you something. I mean, he wouldn't be leaving his wife and kids if he still liked her, would he? And now that I'm better, he's ready for me, isn't he?"

Al remained silent, his back toward her.

"Al, Al, I'm talking to you," she scolded. "I am better now, ain't I?"

"You're not being very realistic, Grace," he said hesitatingly, the tone grim. "Look, he sees dozens of women down there. . . . And probably does more than just look at them, I'm sure. . . . Chances are he's already forgotten about you."

"No, he hasn't," she replied angrily. "Damn it! No, he hasn't." She pulled him around to face her. "Don't you dare ever say that again. I know he remembers me."

"Well, then why hasn't he called you? Or written? Or found a way to tell you?"

"But he does . . . he does love me. . . . You just never thought that somebody nice like Bob Ditweiler could care for me, did you?" She walked over in front of the mirror on the dresser and posed coquettishly. "And you know why he loves me?" She was talking to the image in the mirror. "Because I'm crazy about him. Gosh, I've been thinking about him all afternoon—he's so friendly, and sassy, and sorta sexy. Look," she said, picking up her scrapbook, "I got a Polaroid of him at the barbecue. Look, here he is roastin' a wienie."

Al stared at the tiny photograph—Dr. Robert Ditweiler, psychiatrist, middle-aged, thick glasses, paunchy, thinning curly hair, short pants, wearing a Snoopy T-shirt.

"Grace, doesn't it strike you funny that you're talking about a man you say you love, to me, your husband? I mean, look at me. . . . Look, this here is ol' Al, the guy you married."

"But that's just it, don't you see?" she cut in. "They told me to get in touch with my feelings. I never used to do that. Either my mother or my husband pushed everything inside of me—bottled it up like mental constipation. So now, they want me to let it all out—express my feelings—not be so damned anal. That's what made me sick in the first place—that's the reason I had to go down to the hospital. . . . It's just like they told us in dance class— oh, I just adored that class, Al—just listen to the music . . . pay attention to the melody inside your body . . . and your soul . . . feel the pulse of your life . . . and move to your inner rhythm."

"Well, then, I guess you need to tell all this to Lucille when we go in for our next meeting. Maybe she can figure out what the hell to do."

"I'm not going to see her," she said. "You go." Her tone was final. "You tell her. She's so prim and proper—so super professional." She affected a British accent, "Oh, we must spray the office with deodorant . . . so I, HER ROYAL HIGHNESS, won't have to smell someone else's farts!" And with that, she turned abruptly and walked into the family room.

As she passed the children who were still watching television, she bent over Shellie's head and smelled her hair. This was her way of checking to see if it was clean. As usual, it was not.

"Gee, Mom, can't I finish watching this program," she whined.

"Oh, your father would probably let you—he spoils you kids so. But I'm not having any daughter of mine go to school with grungy hair; so you just march your little butt out to that sink in the kitchen, young lady—and I mean right now."

The hair-washing rite opened old wounds between mother and daughter. Shellie had wanted it long like the other girls in the sixth grade, but Grace insisted that it be cut short. "First it's long hair," she told her, "then lipstick; next you'll be wanting to wear a bra—and before you know it, boys and sex and illegitimate babies!"

As usual, Shellie complained that the water from the faucet was too hot. She winced when Grace scrubbed her scalp too hard. She cried when the soap got in her eyes.

It bothered him for Grace to be so harsh with Shellie, but he was determined to stay out of it. In the past, whenever he had said anything, she had tuned on him and exploded.

"You're dividing parental authority," she had fumed. She was right about that, of course. So he ignored what was happening by the sink and turned to Davie.

"Davie, let's you and me go out front and throw the ball around for awhile."

Davie got out the ball and the baseball gloves, and as they were playing catch, every once in a while, they could hear some commotion from inside. He was hoping that the hair-washing thing would be over soon because it was getting dark and still no sign of dinner. Something was off with her again he thought; maybe she hadn't taken her medication.

He noticed that the front yard needed watering. "Davie, how's speech class?'

"Good."

"What does your teacher tell you?"

"Oh, she says I'm doin' f . . . f . . . fine."

"Okay, big guy, here comes a hot one."

Davie made a good pickup and fired the ball right back.

"Well, you are doing fine. I don't know what the hell they're talking about anyway. You don't really stutter. . . . I mean everybody stammers a little. I do it myself."

"I guess I get nervous."

Surely they're finished in there by now, he thought. "Tell you what, Davie. Take the hose and water the lawn and the shrubs around here a little bit. I'll go ahead and do the same thing in the backyard. Oh, yeah, and lemme see if I can hustle us up some dinner."

When he peeked in the kitchen door to see what was going on, he found that Grace had moved them into the family room for drying and combing. Each time she bore down on the tangled hair, Shellie screamed. "Listen to that!" was Grace's reaction. "A screamin' meemie. If you're this way now, Miss Hoity-Toity, what will you be like when you're a teenager?"

"But it hurts, Mom," Shellie cried. "Mom, you're hurting me."

Al closed the door quietly so she wouldn't know that he had been eavesdropping and made his way to the backyard. He watered the flower beds and the lawn for awhile; then set the sprinkler next to the bottlebrush. For a moment, he just stood totally still, listening. Nothing. "Thank Heavens!" he said to himself. "Now let's see if we can get something to eat." But once inside, he found Grace still shouting—though this time they were in Shellie's room. "That's it!" he said out loud. "That's fuckin' it!" and he bounded in.

Shellie sat on the edge of the bed, her eyes glistened with tears running down her face, her nose running, mouth wide open with spittle drooling all the way down to her lap. Her mother was standing over her, with yet another tirade in progress. The reason—the bottom of the parakeet's cage had not been covered properly.

"Look at this mess on the rug!" she bawled.

"All right," he burst in. "Give it a rest, Grace. . . . That's enough now."

She turned to face him, her eyes narrowing. "Oh, sure, I knew you'd be in here. You always take her side, don't you? And where does that leave me? Out in the cold."

"For Chrissake, Grace, just drop it now. You can't go on like this all night."

She made a frantic gesture of despair and stalked out of the room. When Al caught up with her, she turned on him in cold fury. "Some piece of work you are. I can't be responsible when you interfere. Do you hear? I CAN NOT AND WILL NOT BE RESPONSIBLE!"

"Grace, please. You've been at that child for hours now. Enough is enough."

"You bastard, you're dividing the authority around here. How do you expect me to get better when I've got a husband who is plotting against me?"

"Use your head, Grace. You can't get your kids to behave by yellin' and screamin' at 'em all the time. For God's sake, take it easy on all of us once in a while."

"You know, you're a real pile driver. A real throw up—a dumpster vomit!"

"Don't you see, you're comin' across like a bitchy fish wife? You don't want that."

"Who the hell do you think you are talking to?"

"You, that's who I'm talking to."

"Oh, no, you're not! You're talking to your mother. That's what you would tell her. You think I'm your mother, don't you?"

"Oh, bullshit! I'm not talking to my mother. I'm talking to my wife. You, Grace!"

"Get out!" Her tone was half wail and half demand. "Get out of here. You're abusing me, you son of a bitch! I know all about men who beat up on their women." And with that she started pushing him toward the door, but he resisted and wouldn't budge. When she realized that she couldn't move him, she suddenly let go of him altogether and fell limp into her chair, blubbering in great heaves. "Get out! Get out!" she pleaded. "Please."

"And you can stop with the phony crying," he told her flatly. "It doesn't impress me a bit."

"You! You!" she gasped, picked up the half-filled ashtray from the end table, and heaved it at him as hard as she could. It missed but splattered on the hearth in front of the fireplace, cigarette butts all over. Once again, she fell back in her chair, stared away from him, and sobbed, "Please leave. . . . Please . . . just go. . . . Please . . . please!"

He dashed into Shellie's room. She was still seated on the bed staring at the floor. "Get your clothes on, Shellie," he told her urgently. "You and Davie and me are gonna get us something to eat, goddamn it! . . . Now, Shellie! Get with it!"

As he was backing the car out of the driveway, he had the distinct impression that he had just blown a year's worth of therapy—all those sessions with Lucille and the rest of them; the tests, the medications; the trips down to the hospital; the interminable hours of waiting on those clammy Naugahyde couches; all the effort and frustrated hope, not to mention the money; and all that never-ending talk, talk, talk that the hospital people are so good at—all down the toilet. But wrong or not, he couldn't have stood it another minute. Damn her—and damn them—and damn Bob Ditweiler. The guy probably gets his kicks out of charming mental patients. All those "professionals" at that hospital—so glib, so all-knowing and super confident. Always with the snappy answers. Why can't they ever say, "We don't know" once in a while—because they really don't know. Always holding out the notion that there is some miraculous cure for poor Grace in there, when they knew from the very beginning that they don't have a clue as to how to fix a broken soul like hers. You'd think they would tell her to clean the house and have some dinner ready for her husband and her kids at the end of the day. Oh, no, she needs to be made over into a "woman of the twenty-first century with modern sensibilities." Always going round and round with their never-ending psychobabble, which in the end leads to absolutely nowhere anyway. Sure, they can zap the poor woman with electricity and give her zombie pills, but in the end nothing has changed. He should have pursued the divorce. But at the time that seemed so cold and heartless—to desert Grace when she was so sick and helpless. After all, he had loved her once—and not just a little. She hadn't always been like this; it wasn't her fault really.

Everyone in the car was silent. "Hey, you guys, how about some Italian? We haven't had Italian in a long time."

"F . . . f . . . fine, Dad."

He remembered how crestfallen he had been when his lawyer had told him that getting a divorce was one thing, custody another. "First of all," the lawyer had warned, "most judges will not grant you anything as long as one of the parties is considered so mentally unstable as to not understand the terms of the divorce agreement. So on that, you're gonna have to wait. And, of course, if she gets better, the whole custody thing is right up in the air. She might make a good impression on the judge or the social worker. Oh, sure, the kids might say that they prefer to stay with their father, but a good interrogator can trick or intimidate them. The truth is that fathers in this country have a hell of a time getting custody—even joint custody. In this society, taking children away from their natural mother runs against the grain. If you want to go ahead, sure, I'll do my best for you. . . . But I'm honor bound not to mislead you about your chances. It isn't all that infrequent that the courts choose a cuckoo mother over just about any kind of father. You've got to be prepared for that."

How could he even think about handing over Davie and Shellie into Grace's world?! After they got home, he put the two of them to bed. From the family room, he could look down the hall and see a sliver of light from underneath their bedroom door. Grace was in there. Normally, he might try to make some conversation, but not tonight. Tonight was too damned much. Good, he thought, let her stay in there. Besides, he was exhausted. He got some bedding from the hall closet, made up the couch, lay down, and turned on the TV.

Watching the news, he hardly noticed her come out of the bedroom. When she turned on the hall light, he thought she was headed for the children's rooms or the bathroom. But she came into the family room where he was. She was wearing her short, tight, leather skirt and a body-hugging cerise blouse. He noticed the pungent odor of her perfume. First she turned off the TV and started the CD player. He couldn't help but notice her wild makeup, like many of the women used to wear down at the hospital—deep olive eye shadow below the eyes, dark brown above, the eyes heavily outlined with a single line from the outside corner of each eye to the hairline—lots of rouge and fiery red glossy lipstick. The music started her dancing—in slow motion—like a strange dream ballet. After several turns, she stopped in front of him and posed gracefully up high on her toes, back arched, hips extended forward, arms reaching up to the ceiling.

"That's some makeup you got on, Grace."

"Oh, you like it?" She danced over to him, stopped, moved the coffee table aside, sat down on the edge of the couch, and bent over him. "Al . . . Al . . . do me a favor?" she said quietly. "For old times' sake, Al. Please?"

"Yeah, what?"

"Would you call her? You know, Bob's wife. Amelia—that's her name. You're so good on the phone. Tell her that your wife and her ex, are, you know . . . a number. And you would like to take her out on a date. She's probably a real nice chick. Al—such a nice name, Aa-mee-lia. And then you can take her out to dinner and a movie, and, you know, the two of you might hit it off." She smiled.

He was astonished at her cunning.

She took his head in her two hands and French-kissed him, her tongue rotating slowly inside his mouth. Then she took his arms and wrapped them around her hips. She kissed him again. He pulled her firmly toward him and buried his face into her silk blouse right between her breasts. The perfume was intoxicating. With all that makeup on, she didn't look like Grace at all—more like a delicious Geisha come to perform the ancient rite of pleasing her man. But whoever she was, she was soft, tantalizing, and willing—her fingers already searching for him under the covers.

"Al, you will call her, won't you?"

"Well, now wait a minute, Grace. I don't know if I . . ."

"Al, I'm sorry for the way I talked to Shellie," she said sincerely. "I don't know what gets into me. I'll try not to get on her so much, I promise."

"Well, that's good to hear."

For a moment they were perfectly silent. Then she whispered, "Al, let's do it tonight—you and me. Please, Al, come in and do it. Just do it to me good. Please, Al."

"Nothing would please me more."

"I mean, you don't have to love me or anything. Just as long as you do it. I'll make believe you're Bob Ditweiler."

"What?

"Come on, big boy," she cajoled playfully, pulling him up.

"Wait a second. . . . Wait. . . . You say you want me . . . so you can make believe I'm somebody else? And you want me to call this guy's wife for a date?"

"It's just a phone call, Al. No big deal. Come on now," she teased. "Come on, my big, beautiful, baby boy," and continued pulling him up. When he resisted, she became adamant. "I said to come on, Al." It all reminded him of how she had tried to push him out of the room earlier that evening, and then the whole thing about Shellie came back to him . . . and he lost interest.

"Grace, look, I'm not doing anything with you tonight. Go take a cold shower. I've had it . . . had it, you hear? Tomorrow morning, you can call that lover boy shrink of yours and tell him how much you adore him . . . because I'm fuckin' through . . . finished, do you hear?" He peeled away her fingers from around his wrist. "Just let the hell go of me."

She sat straight up. "Well, that settles it, mister," she shot back. "You had your chance. From now on, don't think you're getting any of your precious nookie when you want it."

Before he could think of anything more to say, she had already slammed the door to the bedroom. Click went the lock.

And now he couldn't get to sleep. Options? He wondered about his options. She was definitely off again—some kind of relapse. If only that fool Ditweiler hadn't screwed things up. But then again, Ditweiler might not have done a damned thing. It's standard procedure for patients to fall in love with their shrinks. He would have to call Lucille again and explain. . . . And see about getting her back into the hospital. Shit! Or maybe he should try another psychiatrist—somebody who could lay down the law and "manage" her instead of trying to cure the incurable—so it wouldn't all end up like this again. God, the kids are hurting, he thought. Hell, divorce is the only way out . . . for everybody. But the custody thing . . .

In the middle of his ruminations, he became aware of a rushing sound. The water, dummy! Damn! The sprinkler in the backyard from before dinner was still running. When he got there, the yard was flooded—water running everywhere—even into the neighbor's yard. As he stood there in his bare feet, mud squishing between his toes, he became fascinated with the stream of water that jettisoned itself out of the sprinkler nozzle, arching high into the moonlight. The droplets shimmered momentarily at their apex before plummeting back down to earth. Water to cool the fever, water to douse the fire, water to cleanse, to purify, to heal—water to drown in. He shut off the faucet and hoped it would all dry up by morning. On his way back, he looked in on the children. No sooner had he entered Shellie's room, than he became aware of an all too familiar acrid smell. The bed was sopping wet.

The next morning while shaving, he heard Grace running through the house. "They finally did it!" she shouted. "Dumped their garbage on the front lawn! I heard them, Al. Al, two great big truckloads full! Two huge loads. Al, come quick."

He fully expected to see several mounds of squishy kitchen waste, or trash, or whatever all over the front lawn. But there was nothing. She bent down and picked up three tiny rocks no bigger than pebbles and said, "See."

Davie peeked out the front door. "What's the ma . . . ma . . . matter?"

"Nothing, Davie. Nothing."

Questions for Discussion

1. What DSM-IV diagnosis would you give to Grace?
2. Comment on the husband's behavior throughout. How could he be helped or taught to help himself?
3. Though the wife's belief that her therapist is in love with her is probably a delusion, sexual attraction between therapist and client does occur. How should a therapist deal with the sexual attraction of a client? How should a therapist deal with his or her sexual attraction toward a client?

SELECTED READINGS AND ADDITIONAL RESOURCES

General

Adamec, Christine (1996). *How to Live with a Mentally Ill Person: A Handbook of Day-to-Day Strategies*. New York: John Wiley & Sons.

Johnson, Julie Tallard (1994). *Hidden Victims/Hidden Healers: An Eight-Stage Healing Process for Families and Friends of the Mentally Ill*. Edina, MN: PEMA Publications, Inc.

Lefley, Harriet P. (1997). *Family Caregiving in Mental Illness.*Thousand Oaks, CA: Sage Publications.

Families Coping with Schizophrenia

Adamec, Christine (1996). *How to Live with a Mentally Ill Person: A Handbook of Day-to-Day Strategies*. New York: John Wiley & Sons.

Atkinson, Jacqueline M. and Coia, Denise A. (1995). *Families Coping with Schizophrenia: A Practitioner's Guide to Family Groups*. New York: John Wiley & Sons.

Torrey, E. Fuller (1995). *Surviving Schizophrenia: A Manual for Families, Consumers and Providers*. New York: Harper Perennial Library.

Coping with a Mentally Ill Sibling

McHugh, Mary (1999). *Special Siblings: Growing up with Someone with a Disability*. New York: Hyperion Press.

Neugeboren, Jay (1997). *Imagining Robert, My Brother, Madness, and Survival: A Memoir*. New York: William Morrow and Co.

Simon, Clea (1997). *Mad House: Growing Up in the Shadow of Mentally Ill Siblings*. New York: Doubleday.

Coping with a Mentally Ill Mother

Berger, Diane, Berger, Lisa, Bergerm, Diane, and Vuckovic, Alexander (1992). *We Heard the Angels of Madness: A Family Guide to Coping With Manic Depression*. New York: Quill Publishers.

PART IX:
PRACTICE IN AN IMPERFECT SYSTEM

Rose Cottage

Catherine Quigg

Once a week, no matter what, we visited Rose Cottage, a grim place despite its pretty name.

As sheltered suburban women in the late 1960s, the four of us had limited experience with those less fortunate, especially the mentally ill. Now, as authorized volunteers in the back wards of Elgin State Hospital in Elgin, Illinois, we would encounter the bleaker side of life.

The first time we entered the cottage, we were shocked by the sights we encountered. At that time, and perhaps still today, the chronically "insane" were housed in one-story barracks, called cottages, with dreary thirty-bed dormitories and sitting rooms with bare floors, folding chairs, and wooden benches. Iron bars covered the dirty windows; sturdy locks secured the doors.

Female inmates of Rose Cottage wore nondescript cheap cotton housedresses; their hair dangled down their backs, stringy and unkempt. I say "inmates" because these forlorn women looked more like inmates than patients as they sat or lay on the hardwood benches, staring silently into space.

The young staff was sparse: one nurse and several attendants barricaded themselves behind a partially walled-off area at one end of the room. We saw them interact with the women, only on rare occasions. At the sound of a bell, all inmates lined up to receive their medications in paper cups. Sometimes they jostled for position, but there seemed to be no animosity between them—only solitary wretchedness.

We never observed a psychiatrist, or any kind of doctor, treat these mentally disturbed women in the five years we visited Elgin weekly. Only rarely did we see hospital staff comfort or even talk with these sick people. Some inmates had been given so much medication they had the shakes. Their tongues flapped uncontrollably, a common side effect of strong psychotropic drugs.

Staff attendants forced the overly agitated to wear football helmets to prevent them from injuring themselves when they banged their heads against the floor or walls. The heavy helmets only added to their misery.

Each time we went to Rose Cottage, we brought drawing paper, watercolors, paint brushes, colored pencils, Indian beads, magazines, flowers, coffee, and homemade cookies. We enticed the women to join us for several hours as we drew and painted pictures, made collages from cut-up magazines, strung beads for necklaces, worked on puzzles, read stories, planted flowers in plastic cups, and sang songs. Once a month, we brought cake and presents for the "birthday girls."

Despite our efforts, some of the women would remain slouched in their chairs, lying on benches or on the floor, minds and bodies frozen, numb. Sometimes they trudged back and forth in that long drab dayroom for hours on end.

Gradually, as they got to know us better, the ladies would wake up and clamor around us as we came in the door with our bags of crafts and goodies. We could sense they were starved for attention from the outside world. They had given up all expectation of help from those on the inside.

I remember two women in particular. One was Mary. Her parents had been missionaries in China during the years of the brutal Sino-Japanese War. Others hinted at the terror she experienced as a child, with stories of her parents being killed at the mission. Her sweet face belied her pent-up hostility, which displayed itself in sharp bursts of anger. She spoke only a few words. Mostly she just watched our activities. Once she painted a single red poppy surrounded by a jade border. When I complimented her painting, she gave it to me with a smile. I still have the painting, framed. Sometimes, I look at it and wonder what has become of Mary, if she survived life on Elgin's back wards and if her China experience goes on.

An attractive heavyset woman in her late thirties, Anna was almost catatonic when we first met her. She seldom participated—though we could tell she was watching our every move. Later, intrigued by our games and chocolate chip cookies, she began to join in. Over the years, Anna became more talkative and we learned that her father and mother had died at Auschwitz during the Holocaust. As teenagers, she and her younger sister came to Chicago to live with an aunt. When her beloved sister was killed in a hit-and-run auto accident, Anna went into a severe depression and was hospitalized at Elgin. She became another of Hitler's victims.

It has been over twenty-five years since I last visited Rose Cottage. Many things have changed in the mental health system in Illinois. Most chronically ill patients have been released to the community and to the streets. State hospitals have become only a revolving door for those in crisis.

I still visit Evelyn, one of the former patients, in a run-down suburban nursing home, surrounded by ill and broken people twice her age. With less potent medication, Evelyn's nervous twitching has ceased. She spends her days watching television as she waits for the next greasy meal to be served.

Anna, released to a nursing home, didn't fare well there. Her frequent bouts of anger and depression caused too many problems for other residents. Shifting between return visits to the state hospital and run-down hotel rooms, she has ended up in a Chicago sheltered home, a dumping ground for the unwanted.

Now years later, I drive past the state hospital on my way to my annual flower-buying spree in Batavia. I remember the women we befriended at Rose Cottage and their ability to rise above their desperate conditions, for even the few hours we visited. I wonder who lives in Rose Cottage today and if anyone from the "outside" ever comes to see them.

Questions for Discussion

1. What is lacking in this inpatient back ward? What is lacking in the care of the mentally ill today, most of whom live in the community? What is similar? What is different?
2. Looking at Mary and Anna today, what diagnosis would you give them? If they had been treated for this problem, do you think they might have avoided their lives as chronic mental patients? Give your reasons.

One Flew East, One Flew West

Kathleen Reiland Beck

The day I met her, I fell in love. But, of course, so did every other guy in maximum security that year, including the staff. It wasn't just the way she looked in her blue jeans and sweater—it was the way she looked at us. Something different. She would say I'm sorry when she shot our psychotic asses full of Thorazine. And I believed her.

At first we thought she was just a student. But Earl, the ward charge, held a meeting and said she'd been schooled as a psych tech someplace else. He said she was well qualified to be a new sponsor on our ward—the crisis ward. I wanted her to be my sponsor. Earl said he wouldn't be deciding until he'd had a chance to teach her a few things. In the meantime, if anybody thought about touching her, he'd kick our asses. Earl wanted to keep her all to hisself. But Earl couldn't stop us from thinking about her anymore than he could stop looking at her. Everybody seemed to be sitting a little straighter and talking a little nicer. At night, we ignored our poster girls and let thoughts of her help us ease our man needs. At least what was left of our man needs, after meds.

The first time she gave me meds, she watched me count the seventeen tablets at the bottom of my Dixie cup while the guys in line behind me yelled, like they always did, for me to hurry up. I tossed the pills back and swallowed 'em down without a drink. She looked at me with those blue see-through eyes of hers, and said, "How'd you do that?"

I told her, in my slow stuttering way, "L-lots of pr-practice."

She handed me a cup of liquid chalk and said, "No wonder you need so much Maalox."

In those days, I stood in line four times a day to get my daily dose of drug therapy. Before her, they'd given me liquid Thorazine, Stelazine, Elavil, and God knows what else mixed with orange juice. But whenever things had gotten rough on the ward, the mixture in my cup tasted less like juice. I accused 'em of giving me extra meds without doctor's orders, and things just got worse for me. They just added more meds to my cup until my juice looked like old cologne. Then I started spitting up blood, and they had to switch me to pills. I may not be bright, but at least I can count pills.

When we—the last eight guys at the end of the alphabet—found out she was gonna be our group sponsor, we high-fived one another until our hands hurt. The other guys said they was gonna change their names. For once, I was one of the lucky ones.

She called our first "group therapy" meeting. We sat, with our hair brushed and our khaki shirts tucked into our khaki pants, in a circle in the middle of the ward, while the rest of the guys chewed their Skoal tobacco and pretended to play cards and watch TV. She sat with her back to the puke-colored wall with the high-barred windows. After she introduced herself, smiling a time too many, she said she was happy to be with us, and she'd be meeting with each of us twice a week for individual counseling sessions. Her "program objective" was to help us become "competent to stand trial." We all looked at each other, then at the ground. None of us said nothing. She asked us to go around the circle, introducing ourselves and letting the group know if we had any issues we wanted to discuss. The guys shook their heads and got up to leave. She said, "Hey, wait—what's wrong?"

The guys sat back down on the edge of their chairs. Still, nobody said nothing. I could see Earl with another tech in the glass cage, watching us.

"Why doesn't anyone want to talk?" she asked.

I felt kind of sorry for her so I said, "W-we ain't n-never had n-no gr-group therapy before."

"Okay, how do you usually meet?"

"W-we don't meet, Mu-mu-mu-ma'am."

"But you meet for therapy? You have to meet . . ."

Nobody said nothing. Minutes went by; then she got up, looking a little less Pollyanna-ish, and said, "Okay. All right. This meeting is postponed until I find out what's going on."

We sat there, watching her shove open the door to the glass cage. Earl and Hank were laughing so hard, they were bent over in their chairs, slapping the floor.

"G-guys," I said, "we sh-should be n-nice to her. Sh-she's like, like our f-fairy g-godmother."

"Shut up, Danny T—you're our fucking fairy godmother; give me your coffee," said Simon Builds-a-Fire, who wore a red bandanna around his forehead. He'd shot and killed his pregnant girlfriend because she walked into his room holding a globe; he'd been convinced she was planning to take over the world. He'd only been on the ward for a few weeks, but already he was acting like all the other guys—always stealing my stuff. I stuck my plastic bag of instant coffee inside my pants. Simon rolled his eyes, "She's gonna help you be fucking competent? That bitch don't know what the fuck she's talking about—gonna help me, fuck!"

Jordan, who had a degree from Stanford in philosophy or psychology or something, sat with his ankle and wrist restraints on, talking more to his voices than to us. He said Simon Builds-a-Fire was wrong. She was a spy.

She'd been sent to us to uncover the conspiracy that kept us all there. Then he got up, went over, and pounded his head against the puke wall.

Antonio said, "Praise Jesus," which was the only thing he ever said.

Jack—Jack Nicholson (I can't remember his real name)—jumped up and started pacing. He didn't care why she'd been sent to us—she was a babe and he was gonna make the best of it. Jack had been arrested for impersonating the real Jack. He worked the airport, posing for pictures with foreigners. He accepted their wallets, luggage, and watches as gifts. The difference between me and him was speed: Jack was always moving. Sometimes, us guys just sat and watched him instead of the TV. He liked having an audience, I think.

John was a vet who was still at war. They found him "not guilty by reason of insanity" for killing people who looked Asian. He stood up and stuck the stub of a finger in Jack's face. "Boy," he said, "thy eye offends thee. Pluck it out—or I will."

Jack walked away, yelling, "Somebody, get these fucking fruitcakes away from me."

Old Man High-Tops, who'd been arrested twenty years or so ago for streaking with nothing on but red high-tops, laughed like an old ghost having fun at a haunting. He winked at Antonio and yelled, "Hallelu-u-jah! Praise Jesus! Hallelujah!"

But it was Clarence who said she must be into sadomasochism. Why else would a girl, not even old enough to drink, come work with us? He said he wanted her so bad, he was gonna have an "altercation" just so he could feel her hand pulling down the back of his pants and rubbing him with a wet cotton ball. Never mind who'd be holding him down, she'd be touching him.

Most of the guys already hated Clarence for molesting little kids and avoiding the penitentiary for four years now, but I'd lived with him the longest. I hated him the most. I got up and threw my chair at him. I knew he'd beat the shit of me, and I'd be helping him get his wish, but I couldn't let him say that kind of stuff about her. Clarence is seven feet tall and the top of my head fit right in his armpit whenever he grabbed me in a fucking neckhold. To take us both down took a dozen extra guards and techs who came running from other wards after a tech pushed the red button, sounding the alarm.

Clarence and I both ended up on the ward called STEP—as in the fucking bottom step—in full bed restraints and seclusion for a week. She came to visit me though. Only when I saw her look through that Peeping Tom window in the door, I felt some of the worst shame I ever felt in my life. The techs had forgotten to give me a piss bottle, and I'd pissed all over myself. When she unlocked the door, I thought she'd gag at the smell, but she acted like she didn't even notice. Somehow that was worse. With my hands belted to the bed, I couldn't stop the water, pooling up in my eyes like an idiot. She used a dry corner of the sheet to wipe my face; then she patted me on the shoulder. She and Michael, the other tech with her, changed the sheets. Michael gave me some clean clothes and apologized for the a.m. shift forgetting about me, and he promised to give 'em hell. I barely cared. I looked at her, looking at Michael, smiling like that: it made me want to kill myself. I made a useless effort to free my arms and legs. She leaned over with her sweet perfume, and said, "Danny T, please don't give them any reason to keep you here. We'll talk when you get out."

That was one of my shortest stays on STEP. To get me through, I kept thinking about talking to her, alone. What would I say? How could I tell her how I felt? I rehearsed little speeches, telling her that she was the first one who ever cared about me. But when the time came for us to meet, I sat there, saying nothing, nodding my thick head.

She said she'd been looking over my chart—the largest on the ward—and she couldn't find where it said what my crime was. I was twenty-four and I'd been institutionalized for fifteen years. I couldn't remember why they put me in, so I didn't say nothing.

She said, "Well, your chart says suspected schizophrenia, sociopathic behavior, and possible manic depression with borderline intelligence."

"I d-don't know wh-what th-that means."

"Have you hallucinated? Heard voices? Had delusions of grandeur?"

"N-no! I'm n-not cr-crazy. M-my mom just d-didn't know wh-what to d-do with m-me. I'm sl-slow, n-not crazy."

"That doesn't makes sense. Nobody puts people in maximum security because they're slow. You must have had some history of psychosis. I'll have to get your old files. But . . . Danny T, why do you think you're still here?"

"B-because, that tech l-lied. H-he already had a n-neck br-brace on th-that day."

"What tech?"

"A-at the other h-hospital. H-he said I br-br-broke his neck. I didn't d-do it."

"Oh, geez, you didn't?"

"No! H-he just w-wore that br-brace, said I did—but I di-didn't!"

"Hm. Seems like, if you broke a psychiatric technician's neck, that would be in your file. Wouldn't it?" She said she'd look into it and try to find out what it would take to get me back to court. Just like that, she was gonna help me, Danny T, who nobody never cared about. Whether she'd actually help me didn't matter. She didn't say that she didn't believe me.

It wasn't long after that, I heard the guys talking. Word was out—she was a hostage target for a group on another ward planning an escape. So I snitched. We had a shakedown; they found a gun and a few knives on the other wards but our ward was clean. Still, they didn't let her go anywhere alone no more. She always had to have another male tech or guard with her.

On the ward, we'd only talk alone as long as she had her back to the wall and a tech in the glass cage could see her.

Then one day, she said that she had finally got somebody to say what it would take for me to go back to court for a hearing: thirty days without an altercation. I told her that if guys didn't stop stealing my coffee, that wouldn't be easy. She said, "What if you got to come back on a higher step where nobody'd take your coffee anymore?"

"N-no. Everybody always take m-my stuff. Th-they m-mad at m-me for bu-bumping 'em."

"You do bump into people too much. And you fall down too much. But I think it's because you're on too many drugs. I'm going to recommend that they take you off all meds so we can determine whether there really is any psychosis or not."

"P-pardon me Mu-mu-ma'am. B-but do they have a pl-place like this for w-women? Cuz you gonna get yourself p-put in th-there."

She laughed and said I was probably right, but she didn't have much to lose.

It was a couple of days before the doctor visited the ward. I heard his voice in the back room. I'd been hanging around the door of the cage, sucking the meat off Earl's Kentucky Fried Chicken bones. All we ever had to eat was cafeteria food, but when Earl was in a good mood, he saved his leftovers from Taco Bell, KFC, or A&W for me. She'd said that I shouldn't be doing that anymore cuz she'd caught Earl in one of his laughing fits with Hank. He'd admitted to killing a fly and sticking it on a bone before I ate it without knowing it. She'd told Earl that if he ever did anything like that again, she'd report him all the way to the governor. But in case he did try it again, when she wasn't around, she said I should quit eating his garbage. From then on, I only ate those bones after I'd checked 'em real good, and she weren't around.

Anyway, I could hear the doctor, who hadn't seen me as a patient in what might have been years, yelling, "Who the hell is this new tech who keeps referring patients to me? Is she out of her mind, recommending Danny T be taken off meds? What the hell is going on here?!"

It was Monday morning and she was off. I felt it was my duty to get as much information as I could, but Earl slammed the door to the cage in my face.

Later, she told me the doctor had forbidden her from making any more recommendations to him. From now on, only the a.m. cosponsor, Bill, could make recommendations. And Bill said he wasn't nuts; he would never agree to taking me off meds, not with a history like mine.

She said the only trick left was for me to go thirty days without an altercation. So we made a plan. Every day, after shift change, she'd give me thirty minutes to tell her all about what had happened while she'd been off. If somebody took something from me, I was to let it go until she got there and we'd handle it together. I couldn't believe it. Thirty minutes. With her. Every day. I'd wait at the door of the ward for her to arrive. She always greeted me the same, "Hey, Danny T, how are we doing today?" Then we'd walk down the long hall together and she'd go to shift change. When she came out, we'd meet for thirty minutes. At first I talked a long time, telling her every little thing that'd been done to me, but after a few weeks, there seemed to be less to complain about.

Then Simon Builds-a-Fire stole my coffee and I slugged him. It was nothing serious, but my thirty days had to start over again, and I got myself an extra dose of Thorazine. I was lying on the floor mattress in one of our ward's seclusion rooms when I heard her come in, and I knew somebody'd be standing at the door, cuz she weren't allowed to come in alone. She was talking to me, apologizing for having to give me the shot. I was just lying there, making it easy for her. I barely felt the needle go in, but then Earl walked in behind her, and with what must have been his full weight, he shoved the needle into my ass as far as it would go. I yelled, but that was nothing compared to what she was doing. She yanked the needle out and shoved him against the wall, holding it like she was gonna stab him if he moved; she started yelling, louder than me, that she'd had it. That was it. She was reporting him. He laughed and told her to look at me. He said I was a worthless, stupid good-for-nothing nigger. He said nobody would care if she reported it, nor would they ever believe her over him. She didn't say nothing.

For about the next six months, I'd go ten, sometimes fifteen, days in a row without an altercation. Then I'd have a setback. The hardest days were her days off. If somebody stole my stuff, I'd have to wait two or three days to tell her. So when I'd gone twenty-three days without a fight, she said she wished she weren't going on days off. She was afraid something bad might happen. While she was preparing me for this, Jordan came over with only his wrist restraints on. He begged her to put on his ankle restraints. She asked him to try going a little longer without them; she said he had being doing so well, he didn't need them. Jordan walked away telling his voices to behave themselves, and she said to me, "As long as nobody tells Jordan that his parents are coming for a visit next week, he should be okay." And then to me, she said, "And you, you aren't to complain to anybody about anything while I'm gone—you got that? Nobody—including the techs. Nobody wants to give you what you want from them. So don't ask, don't whine, and don't make them mad. Save it for me. Seven more days to go, Danny T, only seven. Don't mess up. I'm counting on you."

More than anything else in the world, I didn't want to let her down. But Sunday morning, when things were real quiet on the ward, two of the techs walked out and turned up the TV and the radio real loud. One of the techs started yelling at Clarence to quit rolling his cigarettes cuz he was dropping tobacco all over the floor. The other tech grabbed my coffee and threw it across the ward. Then he yelled over at Jordan, who was sitting straight up, mumbling to himself, "Hey, Jordan, I hear your folks are coming Tuesday—be good to see 'em, won't it?" Jordan started yelling back at his voices, which must have started screaming at him from the sound of things. Clarence finished putting his tobacco and papers in his baggy; then he got up and flipped the table over on top of Simon Builds-a-Fire and Jack who were playing cards. Simon Builds-a-Fire started yelling, "Who the fuck do you think you are—I'm going to kill you, you motherfucker." I was trying to get to my coffee but Clarence picked it up. Jordan started kicking the crap out of Antonio who kept crying out between kicks in the gut, "Praise Jesus! Praise Jesus!" Had it been anybody but Clarence who got my coffee, I could have kept out of it. Things being the way they were, the two techs backed into the cage, and they watched me break my promise to her.

It was a long time before anybody pushed the red button that Sunday. I got so mad, I bit the guard who was trying to smother me with a pillow while about eight of 'em tried to take me down. I ended up on STEP again. That's where she found me on Tuesday afternoon when she came in. She'd heard Clarence had stolen my coffee and I'd bitten a guard, but she wanted to hear my side of it. I told her everything. As she listened, she loosened my restraints a bit and said that today was my birthday; she'd arranged a cake for me, but now it would have to wait. Before she left, she wiped her eyes and whispered, "I believe you. But it doesn't matter who picked the fight, Danny T; you finished it. I'm sorry. Happy birthday."

We started over. One day a few weeks later when I greeted her at the door, I said, "H-howdy, Mu-ma'am, it's good to s-see you. H-how are y-you doing t-today?"

She clapped her hands and said, "Well, I'll be . . . Danny T, that's the first time you've asked me how I am!" She looked straight at me, heating up the insides of my thighs, and then she said, "I think I'll tell you how I am. I just found out my next-door neighbor, whose been stalking me, used to be a patient here—for multiple rape; and Earl told me yesterday that the only way I can have Christmas off is if I 'put out' for him; and a patient on lockdown who saw me walk past his seclusion room with a guard while everybody else was at dinner assumed I was turning tricks with the guard, instead of shaking down Simon Builds-a-Fire's room, like we were really doing, and he's been mouthing off to the world; and protective services is conducting an investigation. Add that to the hostage thing and I'd say I've had better days. How about you, Danny T? How are we doing today?" She laughed when she said it, but it suddenly occurred to me that someday she would leave.

I couldn't bear the thought of her leaving me. But even more, if she did leave, I wanted her to be proud of me. I figured it was time for me to get serious about ignoring the bait, as she called it. If she left, my only chance to get out might be gone forever. Three more months passed before I was able to go thirty days in a row without an altercation. But I did it. And the doctor sent me back to court while she was out on her first vacation. She didn't even know I'd gone, and it was almost two more months before I was able to come back and tell her what had happened to me in court. I waited by the ward door like I always did for her to arrive for the afternoon shift. When she came in, she seemed more beautiful and more preoccupied than I remembered. She only nodded at me and continued down the long hall lined with doors. I said, "Howdy, Ma'am, how are you today?"

I thought she paused for a second, but she kept going. Over her shoulder, she said, "Welcome to the ward. I'm running late. We'll talk later."

I ran after her calling, "Ma'am, it's me, Danny T! I came to say good-bye."

She stopped and looked hard at me. "Danny T? But . . . your voice . . . sounds higher? Oh my god, you're not stuttering! You're thinner? Look at you; you're not stumbling around. How can you look so different . . . what happened to you?"

"The judge told them to take me off all medications. Can you believe it? Just like that, they took me off everything—well, almost everything; they didn't want me to go cold turkey."

"I can't believe it."

"And, I'm on Step Eight. Step Eight! They're really nice. They say they'll teach me communication skills and get me a job. It might take eighteen months or so, but someday, I could be an outpatient."

"What about the charges against you?"

"Dropped, no proof. The judge apologized for them keeping me so long."

"Really unbelievable. Are things not as bad as they seem to me?"

I didn't know what to say. Things were better for me than they'd ever been, with one exception. I planned to get myself put back on the crisis ward real soon, unless the rumor I'd heard was true. If it were true, my only chance of ever seeing her again was to get out. "I heard some of the guys in the yard saying that you're leaving."

"What you probably heard is that I'm giving up, like they said I would."

"Nobody said you'd give up, 'cept Earl. He said we didn't deserve you anyway. He's right."

"But I am giving up."

"No, you didn't give up on me."

"Yeah. You and me. Some group therapy. Don't let anybody know I was suckered in by you. They warned me that I was high risk. Said I was too young, altruistic, that I could get taken in by a bunch of lying sociopaths like you if I wasn't careful." She winked and turned to walk down the hall. Jordan, Antonio, and Jack were hanging around at the door of the cage, watching us.

I tagged along behind her for a minute; then I reached out and squeezed her elbow. Other than always bumping into her, it was the first time I really touched her. I think it scared me more than it did her. She just stopped and looked at me with her head tilted to the side. I stood up real proud and said, "Ma'am, in case I don't see you again, I wanted to say good-bye."

"Oh . . . good-bye?"

"Yes, Ma'am. More than anybody else in my whole life, I'm gonna miss you."

She eyed me for a long time before she said, "Yeah, I'll miss you too." She looked at the guys at the end of the hall, then back at me, and said, "Ah screw it, give me a hug." She wrapped her arms around me in the first hug I could remember. Jack and Jordan started hooting and Antonio praised Jesus. She held me close and whispered, "I don't know how you do it, Danny T. I can't."

"Do what?"

"Stay sane in such an insane place."

Questions for Discussion

1. What feelings does this story evoke?
2. What does the new psych tech offer Danny T that motivates him to go thirty days without an altercation? Does this make sense as a criterion for being "competent to stand trial"?
3. More like a third-world prison than a hospital, it provokes insanity from the psychiatrist down to Earl, the ward charge. How do you explain this situation?
4. Though all the patients are on psychotropic medications, no one is getting better. What do these patients need?

At the Bottom of the Ocean: Remembering the Psych Ward

Alison Townsend

The day I admitted myself to the psych ward at Baldy View Community Hospital I spent the morning writing out bills. After that I phoned my health insurance company one last time to reassure myself that this hospitalization would be covered. I got an agent I hadn't spoken to before. "Are you going to be confined?" he asked. My mouth opened and closed, a fish breathing air. I must have said something, must have stuttered some broken word. But what I remember is silence and the roar of biochemical static in my head and that word, "confined," hanging in the air between us. *Confined.* As in committed, incarcerated, crazy. As in point of no return.

In the hospital, one of the best around, I stare at the weave in the rose-carpeted hallway as I enter the psych unit with my fiancé. When I look up, what I notice is that there is chicken wire embedded in the windows and doors. What I notice is that the door clicks shut like a metal mouth, locking behind us, even on the "open unit." What I notice is that the nurse's station, its wrap-around windows webbed with more chicken wire, floats in the exact middle of the unit, an always-open eye I will learn to elude by hiding behind corners, leaving the door to my room ajar, shutting myself in the bathroom.

I am led to my room—white walls, white beds, white louvered shutters which are shut, casting everything into a permanent twilight. A nurse searches though my one small suitcase to be sure I haven't brought any sharp objects into the hospital with me. "I'm not suicidal," I tell her truthfully. My fiancé says good-bye, promising to come see me that evening. I know he'll come, but at the same time feel as if I am being abandoned in this place from which I am afraid I will never return.

I've been like this for weeks now, ever since the afternoon, when after a year of getting progressively more tired, I felt something literally snap in my head. Unable to sleep, unable to eat, I've turned our house into a hospital, which is why I've decided to come here, to this place at the bottom of the ocean where I float, feeling unreal as a plastic toy. Here at the bottom, there is nothing but darkness and the pervasive feeling that I am somewhere just outside myself. Later I will learn that there is a word for what I am feeling, *depersonalization,* a common symptom in clinical depression. But all I know is that I feel crazy, on the verge of psychosis, as if I am about to disappear into some kind of Marianas Trench where all contact with the world I love—southern California, the San Gabriel mountains, my job at the bookstore, my upcoming marriage to a man I love, my writing—will end.

This is when I see her for the first time. She is a tall graceful woman in a blue batik-print dress, her auburn pageboy swinging forward, concealing her features as she leans attentively toward the woman to whom she is speaking. I focus on the woman. She seems to emanate light, like one of those women in a Renaissance painting, busy doing something ordinary, pouring water out of a pitcher or sweeping a walkway. All she is doing is talking, paying attention to something, to somebody outside herself. But that is enough. It pulls me outside my own obsessive self-monitoring, my constant checking to see if I am "all right."

"Hi, I'm Sandy. You must be Alison. Katherine [a mutual friend] told me to look for you. She said you were a writer, too, and that we'd have a lot to talk about. Welcome to Wonderland."

She puts her hand over mine, saying, "I know. It's scary at first. But you'll get used to it. I've been at a place much worse."

I trust her immediately; we are friends by the end of my first day.

It's hard to hide in the psych ward. Something about the place insists on an intimacy which I am unaccustomed to with strangers. Patients talk about their diagnoses as easily as if they are discussing the weather. My diagnosis is ordinary, as ordinary as they come: major depression, single episode. Others are much more serious. After being misdiagnosed for years as a manic-depressive, Sandy has been diagnosed with multiple personality disorder (MPD) and, with what I will learn is typical passion, has thrown herself into learning as much about it as possible. Each day she appears with another thick journal article given to her by Sharon, the psychotherapist who has diagnosed her and who will later be instrumental in my own recovery. Sandy pours over the articles intently, underlining things and annotating the margins. Though I haven't known her long, I can tell she's hopeful. She tells me the diagnosis "explains everything": two closets full of clothes she'd never choose herself; all the times she's found herself somewhere in the car with no idea how she got there; the personality who tells her to hurt herself; the one who is a child, the little girl with no one to defend her; the one who remembers all the things she doesn't remember herself. Talking with her, I learn the jargon of MPD, become familiar with her "core personality" and some of her "alters."

"Write that down," I say sometimes, when one of her insights seems especially important. But the small spiral notebook Sandy carries everywhere remains blank. Sometimes she will sit for an hour or more in the atrium, notebook open and pen in hand, unable to write a word.

The hospital routine quickly becomes familiar. Breakfast. Inpatient psychiatrist and therapist appointments. Occupational therapy, where we are expected to work on "crafts," modeling a substance that looks like Play-Doh. I refuse, despite being told by the nurse, "This is going to go in your record." Then lunch, followed by more appointments and "group," to which we are assigned by diagnosis. Psychodrama is the focus of the afternoon, followed by quiet time. Finally there's dinner. Each night, after dinner, Sandy and I walk laps around the ward to stay in shape. Sometimes Sandy and I go outside, though she finds it scary.

Sandy is enthusiastic about her new psychiatrist, Doctor R.

"He hugs me after each session!" she says, glowing. She is so elated by him that for a while I hope to get to see him too. Maybe he can help me figure out what is really wrong with me. Then I see him hugging her one day outside one of the cubicle consulting rooms where the doctors have their appointments. He presses up against her full-length. I hurry past, feeling I've seen something I shouldn't. When I do see him, he pulls out his silver fountain pen and writes down on a prescription pad what he believes my problem is: "Dependence breeds hostility." What does this mean? I know my diagnosis. What I don't know is how his words can possibly help? I study his words silently, sinking down to the bottom of the ocean with them like a stone. I've never thought of myself as a dependent person. But he's the doctor. He must be right, mustn't he? It takes me a long time to figure out that the main "issue" on the psych ward is authority.

Of all the activities foisted upon us in the name of recovery, psychodrama is the worst. Directed by Ed and Shirley, two social workers whose knowledge of the psyche seems to begin and end with Psychology 101, the psychodrama sessions are, to anyone with a modicum of experience in psychotherapy, a travesty, a circus where people are forced into "confronting" disturbing experiences but given no apparatus with which to contain them. Patients joke about psychodramas, but the process itself is deeply frightening, and I dread the day I am "up." Sandy says with pride that they have never been able to make her participate, and she's been in and out of the hospital more times than she can remember.

One day Doctor R. writes it up as part of his orders.

"I can't do it," Sandy says over and over. "I can't do it. I know I'll have a rage attack." She proceeds to describe the nature of these attacks to me in horrifying detail. She rips her clothes, tears her hair out in lumps, hurts herself with any available sharp object, tries to die.

The doctor's orders stand. We meet in a small, darkened conference room made darker with the thick clouds of cigarette smoke that snake about the patients' heads into blackness. It's hot and close and hard to breathe. Ed begins the session by announcing that Sandy's doctor has ordered her to participate. Sandy pulls back, trying to hide, first behind me, then a chair.

"I can't," she pleads. "I can't. I'm too scared; I'll have a rage attack; please don't make me."

Ed jerks her to the center of the room. "You're not going to get way with wimping out this time."

Sandy, stiff as a rock wall, stands and weeps silently. Instead of nominating another patient as Sandy's partner (the usual procedure) Ed and Shirley both begin firing questions at her so fast it's hard to keep up with them.

Crouched in a corner, my mind hazy as a fogged-over window, I catch bits of what they say to her. Shirley has walked Sandy back in her memory, with a singsong litany about going down a long corridor and opening a door to see what lies behind it.

"I can't," Sandy says. "He's behind there. Please don't make me."

Ed is impatient. "Spit it out." He snaps. "Who's behind the door? What does he say to you? Where are you?"

Sandy twists and turns, but Ed holds her tightly, one arm jerked up behind her back the way boys attack in grade school.

"You're hurting my arm!" she screams. "Let me go!"

I keep thinking this is wrong, that I should do something, but I don't know what. I consider running out of the room and going to the nurse's station, but I know it wouldn't do any good. Who can I call for help when these are our helpers? My thoughts catch and hold for an instant, like an engine turning over. *This isn't right. This is wrong, wrong, wrong.* The thoughts vanish. The engine sputters and goes dead. Meanwhile, Sandy has, inexplicably, begun to talk. Words fall from her mouth.

"It was my pediatrician," she said. "He touched me; he put his hand in me and mother was there and she said if I ever told anyone she'd wring my neck like a chicken, and now I have told and she is going to get me and so is he, and it's cold. I'm so cold. I can't . . . "

Just as suddenly as she started, Sandy breaks off. She leans limply against Ed for a moment. The room is completely silent, cigarette smoke wafting around us like wraiths from everybody's past. Even Ed and Shirley seem disconcerted by what has happened. Ed releases Sandy's arm. In a single frantic reflex, Sandy leaps free and runs out the door. Snapping to, Ed pursues her, with Shirley behind him. Sensing that "psychodrama" is over for the day, first one, then another files out.

I don't see Sandy for the rest of the afternoon and she isn't at dinner. When I walk past her room, the door is ajar but something, some sense of respect for her privacy, keeps me from knocking. I can't even see if anyone is in there. It is as if Sandy has vanished, swept away from the unit like sea wrack from a beach. A terrible stillness emanates from the room.

It's later in the evening, and I'm on one of the four pay phones that line the wall between the open unit and the locked ward talking to my best friend when I hear the scream. It breaks everything.

"I'll call you back," I say quickly. "Something is happening." I drop the receiver and leave it dangling. The scream comes again, piercing, desperate. It reminds me of the time I saw a crow land in my yard and fly away with a baby rabbit in its mouth, the shrill keening, terrible in its helplessness.

Feet pound the hallway and the scream comes a third time. I see Sandy then, auburn hair streaming, running as if for her life. Her mouth is open, stretched around the sound she is making. But what happens next seems to occur underwater. I watch it, moment by wavering moment. Near the nurse's station two burly orderlies from the locked ward wrestle Sandy down to the floor. She collapses beneath them and lies so still for moment that I think maybe they've killed her. Then one of the nurses comes out with a hypodermic filled with clear liquid and jabs it into Sandy's exposed thigh, and the orderlies drag her away into the locked ward, where the solid metal door clangs shut behind them. My trance is broken by the sound. I rush to the nurse demanding an explanation. No matter how many times I ask what happened, she won't tell me the whole story. All I can discover is that Sandy did have a rage attack. Then she'd taken a piece of broken mirror she'd hidden in her room and tried to slash her wrists.

The unit is eerily still after she is taken away. Everyone has vanished, almost as if they are afraid of contagion, of being swept away as quickly as Sandy has been. I lie awake for hours, replaying the sound of her scream in my head.

Astonishingly, Sandy appears at breakfast the next morning. Pale and shaky, she is led in by the nurse from the locked ward and left, as if nothing happened. She stands completely still in the middle of the cafeteria, as if unsure where she is. Then habit kicks in and she moves toward the food carts. Her wrists are wrapped in gauze. Her forearms are chafed raw from the leather restraints they put her in, and her hands shake so badly the items she has begun to put on her tray dance as if on fire. Seeing her difficulty, I go and hold her tray for a moment, placing my hands over hers the way she did to mine the first day on the unit, as if my touch and the presence of corn flakes and orange juice can anchor us to all the possibilities waiting outside, in the ordinary world. I'm doing it for myself as much as for her, trying to reassure us both that there is something stable in this place, even if it is so small a thing as a breakfast tray. Sandy smiles and says weakly, "I guess I caused some excitement around here last night?"

I look into her guileless, almost violet eyes and say, "I guess so, Sandy. I guess so. But it's funny how they try to help you around here."

After the day of her attack, Sandy didn't have to go to psychodrama anymore. The tricyclic antidepressant they'd put me on, my own fierce exercise program, or some combination of both had begun to work. I was getting better, or at least better enough to leave the hospital. Sandy wasn't, though her serene appearance had returned. What she had endured lived in a place beyond words, a place where memory vanished down the long black corridor of forgetting, where we send the things that are too terrible to bear.

The day I left the hospital, Sandy was wearing the blue batik-print dress she'd been wearing the day I first arrived. When I complimented her on it, she said she had stolen it from her daughter. "But at least I knew I'd done it," she laughed, referring to the wardrobes at home her alters had selected.

"Sandy, how can I thank you?" I started to say, but she stopped me, putting her arms around me and whispering.

"Easy, you don't need to. Listen, you are going to be fine." And then, looking at me directly, her amethyst eyes glittering, she said. "You are going to write wonderful poems and a book. You are going to get married, move to Oregon, and blossom!" She hugged me again, hard, walked as far as the door with David and I, then stopped there, letting us enter the fierce sunlight of mid-July.

Questions for Discussion

1. For social workers, the code of ethics specifies what constitutes ethical behavior. Consult the code of ethics and name the ways the forced confrontation about Sandy's childhood experience violated this code. For those in other professions, consult your codes of ethics, and see if the behavior of the psychiatrist and the social workers violated ethical standards.
2. If Sandy had succeeded in killing herself, would the hospital, the doctor, and the social workers be held legally responsible?
3. The use of confrontation is a useful clinical skill. Under what circumstances should it be used? How should a clinician use this tool?

Kaiser Mental Health—1998

Ellen Turner

That tiny box of tiny tissues cannot dry my tears.

"Press 1 for seldom, 2 for often" leaves me helpless, enraged
"Please stay on the line. Your call . . ."

If I were well I could laugh.
But I'm not.

That's why I'm here.

If I had tiny tears I would not need your comfort.
My tears are endless and require more generous measures.

Our study shows that patients wipe their eyes once and discard the
tissue.
If you will just answer our telephone computer questionnaire we will
be better able to serve you.

You have managed me.
You have studied me.
You have prioritized me.

My body and soul are numb.

care

   for

      me.

Caseworker

Mark Dalton

Caseworker.
I'm supposed to see my
caseworker.
We're supposed to meet at a time
and a place.
I think his name is Dave.
Replaceable Dave.

I know a lady.
She had a caseworker
Loved to see her.
She'd come by and ask this and that;
Take this and that;
Do this and that;
How are You?

She didn't.
That lady, that is.
She didn't do.
Didn't take.
Didn't go.
But she did call her caseworker just to say "Hello."
"Come over. I'm feeling a little crazy today?"

She did
The caseworker, that is.
She stopped by.
She called up.
She went up.
She knocked on the door.

She opened.
The lady, that is,

the door.
Mumbling something about her Mama's cooking
with a carving knife in her hand
and chased her caseworker down three
flights of stairs.
Went back up and shaved her head,
staring in the mirror;
rocking foot to foot, heal to toe;
with her carving knife, saying,
"Come on.
Come on, dear, when's it gonna be on the table?"

   The Blues came to her door
the lady's, that is,
and knocked
and waited
and said,
"Come on lady, open up
or we're coming in anyway."

   She was rocking
When they popped the lock
and went in anyway.
And when she turned to face them,
they stayed away.
She told them dinner was running
A little late.
"Sit down
in the kitchen chair."

   The Blues got hold of two
kitchen chairs
and pinned her with them
against her own reflection.
The carving knife didn't get used.
"There was no food in the house anyway.
Mama was a lie."
But the state was gonna try
to take her place,
her mama, that is,
again.

I know what went down
'cause I was in the bathtub of my semi-private room;
omniscient as usual.
My caseworker will be by
At four.

Questions for Discussion

1. Describe the tone or feeling of this poem.
2. What is wrong with the system that is supposed to assist the chronically mentally ill?
3. How does the caseworker fit in? What impression does the poem convey about caseworkers?
4. Currently, most chronically ill mental patients live in the community, in halfway houses, shelters, hotels, single-room occupancy facilities, and on the street. Is this an improvement over state mental hospitals? What kind of care do the mentally ill need?

This One

Mark Dalton

This one is not quite like
the other ones.

He doesn't have a name—
Not that I know.
He hasn't got a smile—
Not that I've seen.
He doesn't have a prayer—
Not that I've heard.
But he's a person.

But not one to trust.

One to push you down the stairs.
One to run away and hide.
One to suffer with his loathing
'cause he never learned to love.

One who's strongest feelings
are pain
and numbing highs.

One alone.

So alone
he's afraid that others are just like him and he has nothing to give and
all that he can manage.

Questions for Discussion

1. If you were an outreach worker and "This One" were assigned to your caseload, how would you engage this client? What would be the biggest obstacle? What would your fears be?
2. What do you make of the title?

Case Summary: Homer Human

Mark Dalton

D.O.B.: 8-10-55   S.S.#: 228-49-2522

IDENTIFYING INFORMATION:
Homer Human is a 47-year-old homeless, mentally ill male with a long history of non-med. compliance and involuntary hospitalizations at state-operated facilities.

DIAGNOSTIC HISTORY:
Axis I: Schizoaffective disorder—Bipolar type. Alcohol abuse.
Axis II: Borderline personality disorder with paranoid features.
Axis III: R/O T.B. and S.T.D.s.

PSYCHO/SOCIAL HISTORY:
Despite repeated stays at state ops., very little is known. Mr. Human is a poor and reluctant historian who refuses to sign releases of information.

CURRENT PSYCHIATRIC HISTORY:
This is Mr. Human's 48th involuntary hospitalization. He was brought in on petition for reasons consistent with his history. While on the unit, he was initially combative and in need of some restraint. Over the course of the next few weeks, Mr. Human was stabilized on court-ordered medication. Although Mr. Human still exhibits some paranoid and delusional ideation, it is believed that he is currently functioning somewhat higher than baseline and is no longer considered to be a danger to himself or others.

PROGNOSIS:
Severe.

DISCHARGE PLAN:
Mr. Human has refused case management services and refused housing. His Social Security check is mailed to a Currency Exchange of his choice. He has been given an appointment at the community mental health center in his catchment area. He is being discharged to himself with two weeks of medication.

Questions for Discussion

1. How would having an axis III diagnosis of tuberculosis affect the type of case management services that would be required?
2. Some people think that an involuntary commitment for medication should be allowed for certain mentally ill people. What do you think?

Juniper and the Balance in Life

Frances Murphy

We were just ready to putt into the hubcap section of our miniature golf game when the cops rounded the corner by the soup kitchen. Juniper spotted them first.

"Elizabeth!" He whispered to me. The fear made his voice hoarse. Juniper says he can always feel the cops before he sees them. He says the air gets dangerous, full of invisible sharp fibers, and if you breathe it in too hard, you can cut the insides of your lungs.

There were two: Buckley, well-known on the street for his meanness, and a young one I didn't recognize. A rookie, judging by his walk. Long legged and eager, but awkward, as if his body didn't quite fit this new cop job.

We use the golf clubs Juniper found in the trash on Columbus Avenue. There's a plain silver one, slim as a blade, and a wooden one with the leather grip gone dark with heat and sweat from all the hands before ours. I like that one the best. The club part is wood, the size of a woman's fist. Heavy. A deep, brown, blood color with a wavery, black grain. I like to hold it in my hand and feel the nick. I like to think about the people before us who took time to line up shots and take practice swings with these clubs.

Juniper and I—members of the world's golf community.

Our game goes through an obstacle course: two orange crates, three tires, two bleach bottles, a zigzag of hubcaps, and a maze of cinder blocks. Eight holes in all. Sometimes we have prizes: a clean pair of socks, the silver feather earring, the autographed picture of Elton John. Maybe pills or cigarettes.

Buckley's heavy black shoes made a dull grinding on the gravel when the cops turned off the sidewalk and came over to us. Their long shadows spread into our game and onto our feet like stains. I could smell Buckley. It's a bad smell that comes off him in waves and breaks through the aftershave. It's his meanness, I've told Juniper. It's his little black olive-pit heart dying in his chest. Juniper says it's fear. Buckley's afraid, Juniper says. No question. I know the smell of it, he says.

Buckley looked us over, cleared his throat, and spat, right near Juniper's golf ball. Buckley plays himself, on his days off. I guess he doesn't like to think he's anything like us, or figures we don't deserve to play.

"So, Mr. June Bug," he said. "Another day eating up the taxpayers' money here at the inner-city country club. Killing time." He has a nasty voice, like a rusty can cover that cuts you jagged.

"Afternoon, Officer Buckley," Juniper said. He stood with the club in his good hand. He put his paralyzed hand—soft and curled like a baby's—behind his back. He stared over Buckley's shoulder, past him, the muscles of his face working. When Juniper gets nervous, his brown eyes get big, like wild horse eyes with too much of the whites showing. His caramel skin turns muddy and the deep dent in his forehead, where another cop, long ago, broke his skull with a nightstick, turns the dark color of a plum.

He swallowed hard, his eyes fixed on a place in the distance, and waited.

Juniper and I have been a pair for twenty years. When he found me, they had just let me out of the hospital again. Those were the years I spent searching the streets for the baby girl they took away from me when I was seventeen. From the very first day they took her, when my breasts were swollen hard and rocky, weeping a hot mix of milk and tears, I believed they had thrown her away.

The hospitals always wanted me to take medicine. They said it would help me to stop worrying about my baby and clear my thoughts. I didn't want to stop worrying about my baby, I told them. I wanted to find her. And I hated the medicine. It made you stop feeling altogether. It made you dead inside. I hated that.

The night Juniper found me was raw and cold, with a rain that tasted like pennies. I had spotted a pink blanket and a broken stroller in the trash near City Hospital where my baby girl was born. It fired me up with new effort. I had been searching for years, on a tired kind of hope, a desperation that had long given way to a dull trudging through the motions. The search gave shape to my days, gave a purpose to my life. If I didn't keep looking for my baby, I thought, then I should die. But I didn't die. Each new day was born and there I was, still breathing. So, I kept up the search.

I had sorted through half the block of barrels, article by article—bags of garbage, papers, cat litter—when Juniper appeared before me. The streetlight shone behind his mass of wild snake hair, making the water drops glow like animal eyes in the night. The shadows carved deep hollows into his cheeks and made a black hole of the dent in his forehead.

"You lose something?" he asked. His voice was soft as a blanket.

"My baby," I told him. "I lost my baby girl."

He stood very still and cocked his head, as if still listening after I spoke. A car swished a cold spray on our legs. "You lose this baby tonight?" he asked.

"No, not tonight."

"When?" he asked.

"I don't know," I said. "A long time ago, I think. But I know she's here." I dug into the barrel again.

Juniper watched me for a minute before he spoke again. "What's your name?"

"Elizabeth," I said, looking him over. He was wearing some kind of bright green high-top sneakers and baggy army pants.

"E-liz-a-beth," he repeated, carefully pronouncing every syllable and looking into my face. "What's your last name?"

"No last name. I dropped it," I said.

"I want to call you Elizabeth Doo-pray. I had a teacher, fourth grade, by the name of Lillian Doo-pray. She had hair the same color as yours. That reddish color. Maybe she's kin to you." He put his hands on his skinny hips and bent forward, putting his face close to me. "She wore these long, full skirts and big, wide, shiny belts. She'd ask me to erase the blackboards while she straightened out her desk at the end of the day. Then she'd say, 'Thank you for a lovely job, Juniper.' " He smiled. The streetlight caught a little gold star embedded in the enamel of his front tooth. "Miss Elizabeth Doo-pray," he said. "Kin to Miss Lillian Doo-pray."

"That's not me," I said. "I'm just Elizabeth. I'm not anyone else but myself. So don't try to make me into someone else you want. Someone you dream about."

Juniper gave a kind of surprised laugh. "Man, I wish I could be so lucky to dream about her," he said. He looked at me and then gazed down the row of barrels. He turned his face up to the sky, closing his eyes against the rain. He stood that way for what seemed like a long time, humming softly, his tall, thin body swaying a little in the drizzle. Then he opened his eyes and smiled at me. "Okay, Elizabeth," he said. "Just Elizabeth. I'm going to help you." He crossed his hands over his chest and made a little bow. "I am Juniper. Just Juniper."

We searched all night, sliding into alleyways when police cars passed. Juniper sang the whole time. "The Lion Sleeps Tonight" was the song. Over and over. Sometimes a sweet, clear falsetto, sometimes muffled and hesitating as he hunched over the barrels. Breathy. Interrupted. I began to fit myself to his music, waiting to hear the next phase, listening for him to take a breath, stopping my hands from moving when he interrupted the rhythm while he dug deeper into a barrel. I breathed when he breathed. His voice, carrying the music, carried me.

When the rain ended and the dawn breathed its fire upon the windows of the office buildings, Juniper looked up, blinking. We stopped our search and he stopped singing. Then, as the city pulled itself out of its tangle of sleep and pumped up its tired self for the work of the day, Juniper led me by the hand through the streets to his room. Not speaking, we walked hand in hand like schoolchildren while the morning sun turned the mica in the sidewalk to diamonds. City busses rolled by and people stared out with puffy, lonesome eyes. As I look back, I realize that what happened with Juniper was the most important event in my life. It was simply this: I was cared for so completely and carefully by another human being that I was restored, put back together. My soul got off its sick bed and did a slow waltz. The miracle of it! My stomach goes soft with the memory. My bones hum; my flesh rises up, soft and pliant.

"Gimme that," Buckley grunted. He grabbed the wooden club from Juniper and turned it over in his hands, hefting its weight. The rookie looked from Buckley to us and then to the corner of the lot where Juniper and I have our hooch in the ell of the warehouse. His eyes tried to take in everything without looking surprised.

The hooch is a kind of lean-to of plywood and plastic with a hole in the top so we can still see the sky when we're inside. It's dry and comfortable. Beside it grows a slender tree with heart-shaped leaves that tremble silver in the slightest breeze. Our friend Packy says it's a quaking aspen, rare for the city, usually found only in the high mountains. He says it's a good omen. It's the earth displaying her generosity, he says, and that we must only look up at the leaves to remember.

Buckley nudged the rookie and jerked his chin toward the hooch. "That's some shit shack, isn't it, Walker?" He spat again, near Juniper's foot.

The rookie said nothing.

Buckley moved right up in front of Juniper, his big, pocky face inches away.

"That little shit shack home of yours is going to be torn down end of next week, Mr. June Bug. All you people are being kicked off the streets and put in shelters where you belong." He jabbed the club in the air near Juniper's head. "You hear me?"

Juniper said nothing. He nodded, a jerky movement, and swallowed again, making his Adam's apple ride up and down in his throat, and kept staring past Buckley. Juniper hated shelters. The crowds and the trouble were too much, and when that happened the snakes came back. They coiled themselves in his stomach, waiting to eat him alive from the inside. He'd try to vomit them out. He'd cough and wretch all day and night until he was spitting up blood and stumbling. Since Juniper and I have been together, the snakes don't come as often. But when they do, I help him. We get off the street and hide out, and when he gets too tired to cough and throw up anymore, we lie down and I hold him. I take his tired, ropey-haired head and I put it against my chest. I promise to stay with him. I rub his head, deep in his wooly hair. I put my fingers, very softly, into the dark wound on his forehead and I say the Lord's Prayer, quiet and calm. I know it by heart, since the first grade. Juniper listens and at the end he says, "Say it again, Elizabeth." So I do, as many times as it takes. Finally, when I am repeating "for thine is the kingdom" for the seventh time, Juniper falls asleep.

Buckley walked over to where our golf balls sat in the dirt. His stride was heavy-footed and cocky, like he owned the place. He picked up the two golf balls, examined them for a minute, and thrust one in his pocket. He held the other and looked around until he found a small tuft of grass at the edge of the lot. He placed the ball carefully upon it. "Watch this, Walker," he said, grinning. He pulled his sweat-soiled hat lower on his head and gave a hitch to the black belt around his thick waist. "Check it out, June Bug," he said. He grasped the club, fidgeted a moment to adjust his grip and find his stance, cocked his knees, and threw his shoulders and arms back in a high swing. The ball sailed high over the next block, over the soup kitchen, over the lot for wrecked cars, over Hinkley's pawnshop. Buckley shaded his eyes with his hand. We all watched the tiny white sphere until it dropped out of sight. "Not bad," Buckley told himself. He placed the second ball on the tuft of grass and hit it in the same way. He was powerful; his bulky body moved with a surprising grace. "Now then," he said to Juniper, while he spit on his hands and rubbed them, "I'm all warmed up. You got any more balls in that collection of shit over there?"

I stepped in front of Juniper and looked up at Buckley. "No sir, officer." I gave him my biggest, phoniest, crinkly-eyed smile. "I guess you've got all the balls there is to have here. And aren't you proud of yourself, sir?

He looked me up and down. "Well, so Lady Elizabeth is talking today. Aren't we lucky?" He jerked his head back over his shoulder while his gaze held mine. "Walker, go check out the shack," he said.

The rookie cleared his throat and flushed. He looked as young as a high school kid. He walked over to our hooch.

"Look inside!" Buckley yelled.

The rookie lifted the plastic sheeting and bent over to look in. "Don't see anything," he said, pulling his head out. He walked back over to where we stood. "Nothing," he said and looked straight at me with the long kind of look you don't get very often—one you can feel a kind of pleasure in, which holds you like a good handshake. His eyes were as green as new leaves. Watching his face, I knew without a doubt that he had seen the big bucket of balls that Juniper keeps right inside the flap of the hooch. "Nothing," he repeated.

"Too bad," Buckley said. "I was in the mood to hit a few more." He turned his hard eyes on Juniper and me for a long moment, as if he were trying to decide what to do. "You people disgust me," he said. "Letting yourselves get like this. Living like rats. You disgust me." He twisted his mouth and shook his head. "Come on, Walker." He threw the club. It clanged against the brick wall of the warehouse. "Let's go."

Juniper moved close to me and I felt him let out his breath. The afternoon sky was turning lavender as we stood and watched the two cops make their way down the sidewalk and deeper into the city.

The rookie turned back once to look at us.

I worry about the balance of kindness and meanness in the world. I have worried about it since my baby girl was born. I fear that if the world tips too far in the direction of meanness that something bad will happen to my girl. I know she's not a baby now, but the only picture I have of her exists in my mind, and in that image she is tiny and red-faced with a small, dark, wet head and little fists that fly open when she is startled. At the moment of her birth, I was strong and round-armed and burning sore between my legs from delivering her. I thought I could fight anything and win. But then they took her away, and the pain in my chest—the ripped-out hole of her absence— broke two of my ribs. I thought I would die from the need for her. And I did fight. It got me into a hundred hospitals and months in isolation rooms with nothing but a bare mattress and my own voice. But over time the pain has grown quiet. I carry the yearning for my baby like a never-ending pregnancy. My strength is different now; it is not so much in the limbs but is carried deeper, way inside of me, a kind of bone knowledge. I am older, gray. Past the time of giving birth. And I know the exact weight of grief. My body has survived the hardships of the years and the streets and has healed its own broken heart. I have even learned to find solace in another human being and to give comfort, and for that great human miracle, for that most important life event, I thank Juniper.

The memory of our first day stays with me forever, is in the marrow of my bones, is stored in my very cells.

"Come with me," Juniper had said. And we went to his room, a small forest-green haven with an iron bed against the wall, one wooden chair, a hot plate, and a string of tiny Christmas lights up around the ceiling. Juniper sat me on the chair and washed my face and hands and made me a can of soup. Hot and spicy with beans and bits of carrot. He sat on the bed and watched and murmured while I ate. "Good," he said. Then he took his plastic bucket and gave me a warm sponge bath, all over. He used his good hand against the curled, small hand to wring out the cloth. He washed all of me, even my feet, and then wrapped me in a big, brown overcoat that had a satiny lining the color of coffee with cream.

"Elizabeth," he said finally. "Now you listen. I'm going to tell you about your baby girl. So listen careful. I know for sure she ain't in no rubbish barrel." He led me over to the single high window and stood behind me, put his hands on the flaps of the coat and opened it wide, like wings. "You see this, Elizabeth? You see how the light moves on this cloth?" The sun poured through the window and made the lining shimmer and change color—deep brown, bronze, silver—like light on the surface of a pond. "Just look at that, Elizabeth," he said. Then he closed the overcoat around me and took me to his bed. He took off his clothes and got under the blanket with me. "Your baby girl is right here, Elizabeth," he said. "She is right here in the color of that light moving on the cloth. She is here in the feel of that overcoat on your skin." He lifted the blanket and his long body was the color of polished walnut. Mine, beside him—peach and rose—shone like the inside of a shell.

"You see that?" Juniper asked. "You see those colors all shining? That's where your baby girl is. She is in those colors. She is right here with us." He stroked my face, my hair, and my head. "Now tell me what you hear," he said.

"I don't hear anything."

"Yes, you do. Try again," he whispered. "What do you hear?"

"I hear you breathing. I hear the breath coming in and out of your body."

He smiled. "What else?"

"My breath. I hear my breath. In and out."

"What else?" Juniper asked.

"I hear your hand making a sound on my hair and on my cheek." I listened again. "And when your hand covers my ear, I hear the ocean. And the wind around the tall buildings."

Juniper smiled and his eyes shone like chestnuts in autumn sunlight. "That's it, Elizabeth. That's where your baby girl is. She's in the sound of the ocean and the sound of the wind, the same wind that makes the breath between us. She's all around us."

I memorized Juniper's words so I always have them with me. And at the end of any day, when the dark falls upon us and I start to worry about the balance in life, I remember that first day, and I say to him, "Juniper, tell me about my baby girl. I am wondering where she is."

And Juniper will look up, deep into that place where there is a horizon I cannot see, and his face will become very still and very dark. Then he will whisper. "Listen," he will say. "Listen, Elizabeth, and tell me what you hear."

And I will be quiet as a stone. Listening. And then I will say, "I hear the wind rustling the leaves of the quaking aspen, Juniper."

He will nod, several times, still looking up and away. And I will touch his cheek and in the dark, under my hand, I will feel his face move into a slow smile. "That's your baby girl, Elizabeth," he will say, and his voice will be quiet and soft, pressing against me like the dark. "Oh, yes. That's her all right."

Questions for Discussion

1. How do Juniper and Elizabeth care for each other? What are their strengths?
2. Do you think Juniper and Elizabeth need intervention? If so, what kind?

3. What attitudes and skills would a mental health professional need to have in order to engage Juniper and Elizabeth?
4. In an ideal world, how should society care for people with chronic mental illness?

The Women's Group

Rebecca Rees

Two men are sitting in front of the clinic on an old sleeping bag with a basket of change between them.

"Spare change?" one says.

"Hi, baby," the other says.

I don't respond to either.

"Stuck-up bitch," one says, as I put my key in the clinic door.

Our clinic is one of the many neighborhood psychiatric clinics in the city that provide medication, individual and group therapy, and some social services. Our particular inner-city neighborhood is a tough one, where drugs, violence, and homelessness are common on the streets and where most of our clients live on SSI in hotel rooms or in shared studio apartments. One-third of our clients are women, and particularly vulnerable to the violence in the streets and in their homes.

Today is Women's Group day. Linda and Karen and I have our pregroup meeting in Linda's office under a framed photograph of two old women intently playing pool. Beneath them, we three middle-aged women sit, decades of feminism fermenting among us. Linda is a psychotherapist and group clinical supervisor and Karen and I are psychiatric technicians with years of experience, including group experience in hospital and crisis clinics. We're a hot team, and we know it, and we love our women's group.

The group is composed of six women. Bonnie and Debby are friends who frequently compare notes on their problem partners, men whose addictions eat up most of the money and energy in their relationships. Corinna is our highest-functioning member, with a job and a working husband. Althea is always quietly grieving her long-lost children. Louanne is the most withdrawn member of the group, but her silent misery makes a powerful statement. Grace is the newest member, a proud and reserved older woman I recently referred from my medication clinic.

"I feel so frustrated by the way we keep failing with Bonnie," I say. "She comes to the group complaining about her boyfriend, and we listen and support her, and she makes noises about changing things, but she never does. We're not helping her change; we're making her feel guilty and driving her away. And I don't know what else to do."

"She's just not ready to give up that relationship," Karen says.

I think about the in-service given last week by a feminist therapist.

"It's like Betsy said last week," Linda says. "We need to support Bonnie's strengths, not undermine them. And affirm the positive elements of being in a relationship—an important part of the female value system—and the positive qualities Bonnie brings to this particular relationship."

"And then, when she feels we haven't invalidated her whole life, she might find the strength to change," I say.

"Might," Karen says. "Maybe. I think it's a mistake to overestimate our power in these women's lives."

We talk about Althea's ongoing search for her lost children, how to integrate Grace as a new member of the group, and Luanne's reluctance to tell the group about being sexually assaulted last summer.

"She probably thinks nobody would believe her," Linda says. "Being forced to marry your own rapist at age fourteen is a major invalidating experience."

We head across the street to the support services hotel that lets us use their kitchen for our meetings, since two of our members with arthritis have difficulty climbing the clinic stairs. Only a locked and curtained glass door separates us from the street sounds and smells outside. The roar of a motorcycle almost drowns out Linda's opening announcements. We move into check-in, a quick summary from each woman of the highs and lows of the week.

Bonnie is the first to speak. A hearty red-haired woman who radiates warmth, she reminds me of the kind of waitress who makes every customer feel special. She is back after a two-week absence following her disclosure to the group that her boyfriend spends all their money on marijuana.

"I've been having a hard time, you-all. Mike's in the hospital for awhile—nothing serious, just treatment for an infection in his arm—and I've been alone. I thought I heard somebody call my name in the middle of the night, and then I just lay there like an egg until morning, waiting for my voices to come back. I thought I was going to get crazy as a Betsy-bug again and have to go back into the nuthouse. But I guess it was just crack dealers in the hall."

Debby always sits next to Bonnie like a skinny freckled shadow. They have developed a relationship outside the group, and it was a major victory when she came the last two weeks despite Bonnie's absence.

"He's feeling better, but he still stays home all the time," Debby says.

Debby always refers to her partner by the generic "he," and her check-ins are always about "him."

"He was a little nauseated from the AZT, but he did gain a little weight. He—"

Corinna interrupts, "It's only natural that you are concerned about your boyfriend's health, but you're the one we want to hear about, Debby. How are you doing?"

"Well, I enrolled in a mace class so I'll be able to take care of myself in case anything ever happens to him."

"Way to go girl!" Corinna nudges her in approval.

Corinna is a small spunky woman with long dark hair and a wild T-shirt collection. She has worked her way up from a life of addiction and prostitution to a stable marriage and a job as a nurse's aide in a senior citizen's home. Now she thinks she might have to get another job.

"I feel like I just can't win for losing," she says. "Julio spends that money as fast as we make it. He gave me beautiful diamond earrings for my birthday, but when I got the credit card bills, I realized I was paying for my own present. The worst thing is that Julio just won't cooperate with me on budgeting. I told him he's making me crazy."

We turn to Grace, a slender, elegantly dressed woman with hennaed hair. She is partially crippled with arthritis and carries a lion's-head cane she has used since a mugger pushed her down on the sidewalk last year.

"Well, I have the same low I always have. Someone sneaked into my apartment and messed up the pillows on my bed and ate some of the food in my refrigerator. And my refrigerator keeps talking to me. But that's nothing new. It's been going on for years."

The next to speak is Althea. A plump, pretty woman who dresses like a television housewife from the fifties, she seems continually stunned and mystified by the machinations of fate and the system that took away her children twenty years ago. During an episode of her illness, her children were placed in foster homes, where they gradually drifted away from her.

She did manage to contact one son, who spent one Christmas with her, and never called again.

"I guess it was hard for him to accept that his mother has showed up again after all these years." The pain is thick in her voice. "Still, if he doesn't show up again by next Christmas, I'm going to take that towel set I bought for him out of my bottom drawer and use it for myself."

"I wish my momma had loved me as much as you love your children, honey," Bonnie says. "They don't know how lucky they are."

"I appreciate your saying that, Bonnie. I sure feel blue a lot. Maybe it's just the menopause coming on."

"Well, we all have to go through it someday," I say brightly.

"Some of us already have," Grace says, and gives me a look.

I cringe inwardly. I have made her an outsider again.

The only woman we haven't heard from is Louanne. She is a big woman with perpetually hunched shoulders and graying blonde hair in a ponytail. She has barely lifted her head, even to watch the others speak. Although she comes to the group faithfully every week, she rarely speaks and rarely smiles, except when talking about her grandchildren.

"Nothing new," she says, her words barely audible. "Nothing I want to talk about."

"We'll check back with you later, Louanne," Linda says, "to see if you want to talk more."

Karen asks if there is any unfinished business. The women are silent. We introduced this part of the process to encourage the women to discuss their feelings about the interactions here in the group, but apparently the opportunity is too threatening. I decide to model the behavior.

"I have some old business," I say. "It happened about one minute ago. I want to apologize to you, Grace, for what I said about menopause. Thank you for reminding me that some of us have already experienced that stage."

"That's all right, dear." Her smile is as careful as her grooming.

"I guess I'm worried that I made you feel like an outsider to the group. I'm especially worried because you are the newest member, and I wanted to make you feel comfortable."

"Well, I'm kind of an outsider too," Althea says. "I'm the only black woman here. I'm glad you're here, Grace. Maybe you and I can talk about the menopause sometime."

Debby says, "And I'm glad you're here because now there's somebody besides me that has arthritis." Debby pats her knees. "I used to feel kind of funny, being the only one who couldn't make the stairs."

"Maybe we could all talk about the menopause and other health issues sometime," Linda says. "Sounds like that might be a good topic for our monthly discussion meetings."

"How do you feel now, Grace?" Karen asks.

"Better," Grace says.

We move on to the heart of the meetings: fifteen minutes each for the women who choose to work more intensively on a problem—Corinna and Bonnie today.

"I feel like even when I get a present, I pay for it," Corinna says, "but the part that really bothers me is that Julio and I can't discuss it rationally. We're not talking adult to adult anymore. There's a sly little boy in Julio who will go out and spend more money after we have a fight. It's like I'm being blackmailed. *Blackmailed.* I get so frustrated I don't know what to do. Last night I finally just told him he was making me crazy. And I kicked a chair so he'd get the point. I know he's afraid of me when I get crazy, so I get a little bit of power that way."

Bonnie nods her head in agreement. "Sometimes men back off me when I get crazy too. But it scares me, feeling out of control like that. I don't want to feel that way no more."

Corinna says, "I don't like that out-of-control feeling either. And it's not really power, you know. All of a sudden Julio starts acting like I'm a crazy woman he has to humor. And I really don't like being patronized. And I know that sooner or later he's going to pay me back by being a bad little boy again and spending too much money."

"Couldn't you just tell him you feel frustrated, Corinna?" Linda asks. "Do you have to act crazy?"

"It's the only way I get him to listen to me, if I'm bad too, if I act like I could go off and do something childish, just like he does . . ."

Her face changes.

"Hey, I just realized I'm blackmailing him, just like he blackmails me! I'm running the same game on him that he is on me! No wonder we can't get anywhere. Now I know I can figure out a better way to communicate than that. I'm going to have to think about this for awhile." She smiles and looks around the room. "It's not very often you put out a problem and start getting the answer right away."

It's Bonnie's turn to work.

"If it's voices in my head or voices in the hall, it's still scary. Scary being alone at night," she says. "In the daytime, though, I kind of like it, being on my own. I'm not having financial problems anymore. It's a wonderful feeling, not to be broke. And I visit Mike in the hospital every day. His arm is getting better."

"What's wrong with his arm?" Grace asks. She always focuses on physical frailty.

"It's abscessed. I guess it's his old problems acting up. He used to shoot heroin, but he doesn't do it no more, although they started him on methadone maintenance, for some reason. But no heroin ever again—he promised me that. I couldn't live with that again. And I couldn't live with him lying to me."

He's lying. Dump him! A voice in my head says.

As if she can hear it, Bonnie says, "I don't want to leave Mike, you-all! I love Mike! But he's killing my love, bit by bit. He spends all our money on marijuana, and we're always broke by the end of the month. Ten years it's been with Mike, and three years with my husband before that, and it's not getting better. I don't know what's wrong with me. It seems I can't have a good relationship with a man, no matter how hard I try."

Karen says, "I know relationships are very important to you, Bonnie, because you are a very loving person. I can feel it right here in the room. The group always feels like a warmer, safer place when you are here. And you've put a lot of effort into a relationship with Mike. I hope you are giving yourself credit for that. You're a warm, loving woman and you deserve a good relationship."

"Karen, that's very sweet of you to say that, honey. I never thought of it that way before."

Good work, Karen, I think.

"He does it too," Debby says. "He spends all our money on drinking. And if I say anything about it, he just goes out and drinks some more."

Corinna says, "Sometimes it seems like they all act like little boys. I love Julio, and I know we're supposed to support our partners, but I get confused. I haven't been able to figure out the difference between mothering and nurturing."

"They think they have a right to our attention all the time, just like children," Grace says. "There's a man in the hotel lobby who is always sitting down and talking with me about sexual things. I feel preyed upon, and I don't know how to get away."

For the first time, Louanne lifts her head. She watches Grace, her mouth slightly open.

"I don't want to have to spend all my time in my room," Grace says, gripping her cane tightly. "The lobby is my space too; they're always intruding into our space . . ."

We hear a spraying sound against the door to the street and a trickle of yellow liquid flows onto the linoleum floor of the kitchen.

"I don't believe it!" Corrina bangs on the glass door. "Go piss somewhere else!"

"Goddamn bastards," Karen mutters under her breath as we mop up the pee with paper towels.

"Just like dogs," Corinna says. "They think they can take their dicks out anywhere. But let a woman even wear jeans that look good on her and they act like she's asking for it and they have the right to do anything to her. They act like it's her fault for provoking them."

Louanne sits up straighter. Her face is red and contorted.

"Dog! That filthy dog. I let him into my room because he said he was gong to fix the lights. I didn't ask him to shove me down and tear my clothes! I didn't ask him to put his filthy hands all over me!"

Tears are streaming down her face.

"I feel dirty inside and dirty outside. I don't feel like the same woman, and no one believes me! No one believes it's not my fault."

"I believe you," Corinna says.

"I've been assaulted before, and it felt like it was my fault," Karen says. "Women are trained in our society to believe that. But it's not true! Men are responsible for their own actions."

"You are not the criminal, Louanne; you're the victim," I say.

"Who is it that doesn't believe you Louanne?" Linda asks.

"My ex-husband."

"Men just don't know," Corinna says. "But look around the room. We all believe you."

Louanne's fists are clenched.

"I am going to the police. I am going to the district attorney. This time the dog is not going to get away with it."

"Louanne, you've made a really powerful decision," Linda says. "Why don't you and I make an appointment tomorrow to talk about it some more?"

Bonnie says, "I hope you put him behind bars, honey. I never got a chance to get the man who got me."

A man poked his head into the kitchen. Our time is up.

Dazed from the intensity of the meeting, we spill out into the street. The women move off in a huddle, Corinna with her arm around Louanne.

Back at the clinic for the postgroup rehash, Linda and I flop on pillows on the carpeted floor of Karen's office while Karen rummages in her desk drawer for a bag of chocolate chip cookies.

"What a great meeting," I say. "And Louanne finally talked."

"I hope I didn't go too far in revealing that I have been assaulted too," Karen says. "I know we're not supposed to bring our private lives to the group."

"In this case, I think it was totally appropriate," Linda says. "That's the difference between ordinary group therapy and a women's group with a feminist perspective. There are times we have to let them know that their problems are not just intrapsychic. Sharing something from your own experience in this case made it even more obvious to Louanne that this is not just a personal problem or even a problem of women psychiatric patients, but part of the pattern of oppression of all women."

"I'm afraid Louanne just doesn't know what she's got in store for her," Karen says. "My experiences testifying against the man who beat me were horrifying. They even read my diary in court."

"She's going to need a lot of support," Linda says. "I'm going to be meeting with her frequently, starting tomorrow. It's a tough case, especially since she keeps looking to her abusers for support, like that ex-husband who used to beat her. It's part of her pattern."

Karen passes the cookies around.

"I think we did a good job with Grace today, too. I liked the way you raised the topic of being an outsider," Karen says to me.

"That was good process," Linda says. "I do feel a little bad that I didn't take the opportunity to pick up the cue Althea put out about being the only black woman in the group. I don't want her to think we don't consider that important."

"Bring it up next week as unfinished business," I say. "And I think there is another way we may be excluding some of the women. Did you notice that all the problems we worked on today were about relationships with men? I don't want the women who are not with men to feel like they are outsiders, or to feel that the only problems it is appropriate to discuss are relational problems. That focus particularly isolates older women."

"Maybe we could model that by helping the women identify other problems for discussion," Karen says. "Like Linda did when she suggested we talk about menopause and health problems."

"And Karen, you did great at supporting Bonnie," I say. "It was a perfect clinical demonsration of the principle Betsy brought up in her lecture."

"An how about that Corinna?" Linda says. "She gets stuff so fast. She's a firecracker."

"She gives me things to think about," I say. "I mean, what is the difference between mothering and nurturing anyway? I feel like Corinna's ready to graduate to the next step, but I don't know what it would be . . ."

"I've been thinking she would be good for one of the new peer counseling positions that are opening up," Karen says.

We look at one another.

"She'd be fantastic!"

"She's a natural!"

I reach up from my pillow to get another cookie in celebration and to admire my magnificent facilitators. Karen has her feet propped up on her desk like a slick female detective, and Linda is a miniature fertility goddess lounging on her cushion.

Linds gets a sly look on her face.

"And I guess we have to thank the man who peed under the door for his part in facilitating the meeting," she says.

I snort cookie crumbs. We all cackle.

There is a soft knock on the door and Mary Louise from the adjoining office bursts in, a big smile on her face.

"So this is what a women's group meeting looks like," she says.

Questions for Discussion

1. Where in the story do the counselors demonstrate the following helping principles:

   - Seeing each client as a unique individual
   - Supporting strengths
   - Supporting self-determination
   - Displaying caring
   - Displaying empathy
   - Displaying their own humanity
   - Modeling desired behavior

2. During the meeting, Karen discloses her own assault experience. Do you think this was helpful? When is it appropriate for a therapist to self-disclose? When is it not?
3. The therapists describe themselves as feminists. What does having a feminist perspective mean? What interventions come from that theoretical point of view?

SELECTED READINGS AND ADDITIONAL RESOURCES

Berman-Rossi, T. and Cohen, M. (1989). Group Development and Shared Decision Making with Homeless Mentally Ill Women. *Social Work with Groups 11*(4), 63-78.

Breggin, Peter, R. (1994). *Toxic Psychiatry: Why Therapy, Empathy, and Love Must Replace the Drugs, Electroshock, and Biochemical Theories of the New Psychiatry.* New York: St. Martin's Press.

Grob, Gerald N. (1991). *From Asylum to Community: Mental Health Policy in Modern America.* New Jersey: Princeton University Press.

Grob, Gerald N. (1994). *The Mad Among Us: A History of the Care of America's Mentally Ill.* New York: Free Press.

Grobe, Jeanine (1995). *Beyond Bedlam: Contemporary Women Psychiatric Survivors Speak Out.* Chicago, IL: Third Side Press.

Iii, Sydney (1997). *A Dose of Sanity: Mind, Medicine, and Misdiagnosis.* New York: John Wiley & Sons.

Howe, Gwen (1997). *Getting into the System: Living with Serious Mental Illness.* Bristol, PA: Jessica Kingley Publishers.

Kulman, Thomas (1994). *Psychology on the Streets: Mental Health Practice with Homeless Persons.* New York: John Wiley & Sons.

Moffic, Steven, H. and Rinzler, Alan (1997). *The Ethical Way: Challenges and Solutions for Managed Behavior Healthcare.* San Francisco: Jossey-Bass.

National Resource Center on Homelessness and Mental Illness, Web site address: <http.//www.NRC@prainc.com>.

Remer, J. and Worell, P. (1992). *Feminist Perspective in Therapy.* New York: John Wiley & Sons.

Rowe, Michael (1999). *Crossing the Border: Encounter Between Homeless People and Outreach.* Berkeley, CA: University of California Press.

Seager, Stephen (1998). *Street Crazy: The Tragedy of the Homeless Mentally Ill.* Westcom Press.

PART X:
OLD AGE

FROM THE PERSPECTIVE
OF THE ELDERLY PERSON

Time's Winged Chariot

Eleanor Capelle

My January birthday always seemed an anticlimax after three holidays. But turning three-quarters of a century old felt like a milestone.

At my age, I like living alone, doing just what I want to do after working and caring for a husband and children. Women friends in their sixties and seventies whom I've known forty or fifty years live nearby. We go to movies and plays together and to jazz concerts and clubs. They all live alone, separated from a husband, divorced, or widowed.

Last year, two friends had breast cancer, which reminded us of the hazards of life. During such times, we know we can count on our friends supporting us with loving concern.

In our age group, we are often reminded of our mortality, which we have to accept. My cousin had written in her last letter, "I'm just keeping on and smelling the roses." But after a stroke, she had fallen, been hospitalized with pneumonia, and died from a heart attack.

The morning after my birthday, I went for a swim. I swim laps at least five days a week and always feel my best after time in the healing element of water.

On reaching the shallow part of the pool after a second lap, I became disoriented, faint, my sense of balance gone.

What's happening? I thought fearfully. Am I having a stroke? Or an aneurysm like my mother?

Grabbing the edge of the pool, I stood there for several minutes until my head cleared. Then I cautiously let myself down into the comforting cradle of water and finished my thirty-minute swim.

After the pool experience, I felt lightheaded all day, unsure of my balance. That night, after a couple of hours sleep, I got out of bed to go to the toilet. Scared by my lack of balance, I clutched furniture and doorways on the trip to and from the bathroom. To my relief, the next morning, I could walk safely without support.

Friends told me I was crazy not to stop swimming when I became faint, that I should have immediately taken a cab to the hospital. So I went to see my doctor.

"Something happened that worries me," I said and told him about it.

"Have you noticed one side of your face affected?"

"I don't think so."

After testing my hand and arm strength, the doctor said: "You've had a slight stroke. Take an aspirin a day. They prevent blood clots that cause strokes and heart attacks. Because aspirin irritates the stomach, take a baby aspirin."

I read what he wrote on a form referring me to Neurology: "2 vertiginous episodes, facial asymmetry."

The report on the battery of tests ordered by the neurologist told me the triglycerides and cholesterol were in a high range, indicating a major risk of heart disease. For the first time in my life, I needed to go on a diet—a low-fat, low-cholesterol diet.

I drove to the Haight to see Emma, a retired teacher friend. We've known each other since we were in the Army Signal Corps in World War II. Both of us were English majors and we're addicted to reading.

As usual Emma is propped up in bed in her studio apartment with her cat and a book, a red knit shawl around her shoulders. She wears blue lace gloves because her hands are always cold.

I was her support friend through three long hospital stays. Emma is diabetic, and after congestive heart failure and kidney failure, she now goes to the VA Hospital for dialysis three mornings a week.

Emma is proud of weighing at last only 113 pounds instead of being a fat lady. Her Kewpie doll mouth looks tiny in her still-plump white Play-Doh face. Except for a topping of curly permanent, Emma's hair is a crewcut.

As usual, she is wearing silver rings on several fingers and her heavy Indian silver pendant and bracelets. She treasures the Indian jewelry because her husband, Bill, who died of cancer in December, had American Indian as well as black ancestors. For over twenty-five years, Emma lived apart from Bill, who was an alcoholic. But she never stopped loving him and kept kidding herself that they could get back together some day.

"A slight stroke is quite an attention getter," I say. "My kids are quite concerned."

"I am too," says Emma in her whispery voice. "You've always been such a tower of strength. Be careful now not to turn corners too quickly. I watch that so I don't lose my balance and fall."

After breaking bones twice in falls, Emma walks with a cane.

"Isn't it a bitch," she says, "losing your balance—and not from drinking?"

Emma is recovering from the flu and still has a hacking cough. She stopped taking antibiotic pills the doctor prescribed. "They made me crazy," she said. "I had hellish nightmares like when I was in the hospital."

I hate to see my old friend, who once was so lively, become frail. Since she went to Bill's funeral, she appears to have lost strength. I don't want to lose her.

"Can you remember," I ask, "what Andrew Marvell wrote about 'time's winged chariot'?"

Emma, whose memory ranges from John Donne poems to Bessie Smith lyrics, quotes Marvell:

> But at my back,
> I always hear
> Time's winged chariot hurrying near;
> And yonder all before us lie
> Deserts of vast eternity.

"I've been thinking," I say, "about why I finished swimming laps after a dizzy spell. I decided that when something happens like that, I don't let it stop me; I just go on; I survive. I become determined, cliché or not, to live every day to its fullest."

"I can dig it," says Emma.

Questions for Discussion

1. Betty Friedan, the feminist writer, said that old age is not for cowards. How does this story support that statement?
2. How are the narrator and Emma dealing with the physical deterioration of old age?
3. Comment on the process of watching one's peers weaken and its effects on the elderly.

Old Age

Anne Greene

He doesn't know if he should buy a myna bird or get a couch at Montgomery Ward. He isn't sure which day it is or if his shoes are on right. He doesn't know which daughter he prefers, although he doesn't like the one with the loud voice. He doesn't want the bank to get all his money, so he writes checks wherever he goes. He likes to be driven around slowly so he can see things, although he is nearly blind. He wants his wife back.

He doesn't know who all these strange women in his house are. He's not sure that he wants them there, except that they do offer some comfort. Pick the tomatoes, do the chores, fix him a little food. He resents his son for being a smarty-pants. The son seems to want to be in charge of the money.

He thinks that life has gotten difficult and dim. He doesn't understand how his eyes have gotten so bad. He thinks his hearing ought to be a little better, but it's worse than last year when he could clearly hear the sermon at his wife's funeral. His memory—that is, his understanding—has also grown dim. It's not quite like being in a long dark tunnel—he has heard that described in stories—but something like that. Certainly life is not like it used to be. It's sort of confusing.

Sometimes a lot of things will run together at once, like breakfast and dinner, night and morning, one daughter and the other. Is the sun just coming up at 5:45 or is it just going down? Was *Judge Judy* just on TV, or was *Judge Judy* on yesterday? If she was on yesterday then maybe that was Friday and today is Saturday, but Linda said it was Thursday and he trusts Linda, although to tell the truth he doesn't know her from Ana. Oh, he can tell them apart all right. I mean, he could tell if they were standing side by side, but when one comes in the morning and one at night and their voices sound so much alike . . . it doesn't make any difference. He tells himself that as long as there's someone there to reassure him, to fix his dinner, to watch television with him, that everything will be all right. He knows it won't really be all right; he's old and his wife is dead. One of these days he'll be dead too, so how could everything be all right? But he has to say that to himself. He has to say something to himself.

He says, "My cane is right over here. I'm looking for my wallet and Ana or Linda, or whatever in the hell her name is, will help me look for it. The phone is ringing, but my daughter is never home when I call her. I can go out in the car if someone else drives. I have to walk slowly. We have to park in the handicap space."

He says these things just to keep track of himself, to keep things in order, to keep it all going, this thing called life. But life is dim like the light in the TV room, like the sun going down in the evening. Like his thoughts when he tries hard to remember something specific, or place it in time. He's all right as long as he doesn't rush himself. If he just goes slowly, sometimes the thought comes back to him or he can remember what he's just forgotten. He doesn't always know that he's just forgotten it and so he repeats himself.

He goes on like this for days and everything seems all right, but since he knows deep down that everything is not all right, he gets tired of lying to himself. Actually he's disgusted, disgusted with his own body and its betrayals, with life as he's expected to live it. Why should he have to go out to dinner and pretend to be happy? Why should he want a pet? There's a story going around that old people are supposed to have pets to keep their spirits up and to boost their immune systems, but he sees that as a lot of nonsense. What it means is that you just have something else to take care of, and since it's not something familiar and easy, its just horrible and difficult, like cleaning dog shit out of the backyard or scraping a birdcage clean. He'd rather just tell everyone to go to hell; he'd rather die himself. But there's all this pretense; he has to keep everyone happy. They all seem to love him so. He doesn't know if it's really love or if they just want his money. He can hardly remember being a young father or a lumberjack or a soldier, although the photographs in his album prove that he has, indeed, been all of these things. He thinks true love is more like the big mommy, mommy of his wife's wide mouth and her huge breasts.

So he's settled on a plan. This is what it will be. He'll get the bird. Not a myna, although the conversation would be amusing. A myna is too expensive. A simple cheap blue parakeet will do, just to keep the family happy. He'll get the bird and pretend to like it, maybe he even will like it a little, but he'll pretend great affection and great improvement in his overall condition. He'll clean the cage. He'll talk to the bird and make faces at it. Then one day when he's home alone, he'll open the cage and let it fly out and away. He knows parakeets can't really fly that well, so it's more like he'll release it into the backyard, where it will make its way around the best it can and in no time at all be devoured by a bigger more aggressive bird. And when he's asked what happened, he'll say he can't remember.

He sees his own death as going something like that. He's not a big bird; he can't fly far—why, he can hardly fly at all. Pretty soon he'll just crumple up in the backyard and be devoured by death. He's not going to fly high in the sky or meet Jesus on the Internet. He's not going to hold hands with anyone in the afterlife, even though this is a nice thought. The things the priest said at his wife's funeral didn't make any sense to him, and he didn't believe any of it anyway. Belief is for children. The stories of Jesus with the baby lamb.

The Catholic hospital is a fraud too. A fraud with some bullshit thrown in. He is quite sure that they cheat people. And this hospice, what is hospice? Something to do with death and dying, something to do with a man and a woman who came to the house to see him and his wife while she was still living. A man and a woman. They came together, they traveled in pairs, they wore hats, they sat on the sofa. Every time he thinks of the man and the woman, these hospice frauds, he wants to spit on them, and he wishes them dead just as he wishes for the death of the bird he hasn't even purchased yet.

When he does buy the bird, he'll pay with a check and make his son go with him. Maybe they'll go to Vallejo and it might be on Sunday. Or if on a weekday, just an hour or so before *Judge Judy* comes on TV. And if there's any dispute, any problem with his son or with the bird store he'll just write a letter to Judge Judy and ask to be on her show. He's been wanting an airplane trip anyway—why not go to Chicago or New York and meet this TV judge? She's tough; why, she practically talks like a gutter snipe. Judge Judy doesn't take any nonsense. She could probably straighten out his son and the whole family. She'll tell them to leave him alone. She'll tell them to go to hell.

Questions for Discussion

1. What do you think this man really wants from his family?
2. What, if anything, would make his life happier?
3. How would you engage him in a helping relationship?

Cerebral Dust

Robin Famighetti

We enter the nursing home room of a seventy-three-year-old woman who has been placed here due to the progressive stages of dementia. In the midst of her confusion are fluctuating periods of clarity. It is during these lucid times that she tries desperately to make sense of what is happening and what she has lost.

My clothes, where are they? These are not mine. Who do they think they are? I know something's going on. They walk in and out of here. They don't think I see what they're doing.

Befuddled, she gets up and looks around the room, trying to ground herself to her surroundings. She paces slowly in the center and then moves to the bureau.

I used to know who I was but, now, I fear I'm not what I was. Before I could count on some certain simple things, like getting up, getting dressed, acknowledging the general routine of an everyday. Now, I look into this mirror and wonder that if I were to step away from it, will I lose track of myself? Will I lose sight of that very person who claimed a name, a history?

Now other people fill in the gaps of my life. They sometimes tap into what might be considered very intimate times for me. Not only do they tell me the facts which made up my existence, but they also tell me how I felt. How dare they rob me of this. I feel as though someone has taken hold of my spirit.

Frustrated and angry, she pounds her hand on the bureau.

There is no way to reason how this happened. How could anyone explain what is happening? Let alone me who is living it. Maybe if I listen to what they say about me, I can then piece together some of who I am. But if I can't feel it, then what connection have I made and, ultimately, what identity have I really assumed?

I am told that I am one from a family of two brothers and a sister. My parents were immigrants and they worked hard to immerse us in a new world with a new identity.

There are times when I have what seem like flashbacks of my life. They are often disjointed, fragmented, and people's faces loom large. They tell me that some of these people are dead, but I can't help but cry out to them. I seem to call for my mother; that is, I imagine I do because the people here come up to me and tell me, "Your mother is dead, and it makes no sense, dear, to keep calling out to someone who isn't here." What do they know of what restores some balance, some safety to my life, especially when I am feeling so unhinged? I thought I was going back to my home. Maybe being there will anchor me, restore some memories. Keep me from floating in this space which is unfamiliar and sometimes hostile.

There are days when I won't leave this room. Why should I? To pace a hallway which is some line leading nowhere. And if I do venture out, am I sure I will return, that I'll find my way back?

There was a time when I first sensed the insidious nature of this disease. It crept upon me like a fog slowly enveloping the land. Its movement, however, was not as peaceful. Its progress served only to distort my perceptions and cloud my senses. In some futile effort to protect myself, I denied that it was happening. I would try to cover up, and I guess no one else wanted to believe such a thing was happening either. Were we all colluding? And what were we conspiring to do—maintain an image, create an illusion that I was not greatly disturbed? While they were trying to keep me in the real world, I was beginning to enter something that is surreal. I could not fathom that one day I would not be able to enjoy a simple conversation. And now, when the words come out, they misrepresent my inner thoughts. They make a liar of me without my consent.

She walks slowly to her chair and sits.

Now I feel my senses shifting. I am beginning to rely more on touch and smell. It seems bestial, but my mind can't make sense to find the words I've always used. I now look to other sources that can engage me. Sometimes a smell comes to me and it evokes a memory. The smell becomes the pure essence of that person.

I remember when my father died. I would walk into his half of the closet and I would become one with him. I would inhale the smells of sweat and sweetness and come in touch with his very person.

Out of all the ungodly odors in this place, there are times when I can be in touch with that special smell that was on my mother's person. I feel transported and it makes me cry out to her, and I won't shut up despite their efforts to make me give her up.

Bracing herself on the arms of the chair, she raises herself up and goes to the bureau and looks into the mirror.

Although they tell me there is nothing wrong with my vision, why is it that I can't identify those people who come to me as though they've known me for many years? They embrace me and kiss me. I notice that they cry. I hear them say that I look like I'm peering right through them, as though there is no ability to discern. They say there is no life left in these eyes. Are they crying because they are mourning someone? Are they mourning me? Have I died? What is this thing that seems greater than God that it could take my very soul and leave me still breathing. God infused life. This has taken me from it.

Sometimes I wonder if I'm in a coma. If I'm in a limbo-like state and that one day I will awaken and everything will be restored. That I will be able to give a name and an emotion to those people who visit me and seem to cry for me. And when I look at one of them, I think, yes, you could be my child, for I vaguely remember looking somewhat like you when I was younger. And even for myself, when I look into that mirror and see my own eyes well up with tears, then maybe I, too, can find some meaning to all that has happened.

I would like to walk away as a decent person, with some dignity left. Maybe I can strike a deal with a higher power. It's been done before. Listen to me. I'm making no sense. Who am I to bargain? Well, if I can't say who I am or what I was, then I know that I don't want to be here. I want to get out of here, to get out of me. Why is it that others have chosen to take my life in their hands? I know I should trust. I have no choice. I can't make it on my own, anyway. I must rely on others who claim to have my welfare in mind. I'm sure some are kind and well-meaning, but most have no idea what it's like to be trapped in a mind that can exert no control. A mind that can make no sense of these surroundings.

Standing at her bedside, she becomes annoyed as she looks around her room.

I overhear people say that it's better that I am unaware. Do they think because I can make no sense of what is happening to me that I'm not in anguish? That every day I don't struggle to figure out that my socks are not my gloves or a fork isn't a comb. I imagine that maintaining a sense of humor is important, but there is such shame and humiliation.

Inspecting herself, she looks down at her dress and tries to assume a different posture. She stands erect, trying to give herself the dignity that has been taken away. She feels disgusted and ashamed.

So at seventy-three years old, I am the perpetual infant. Someone who is fed, changed, and guarded from danger. Unfortunately, I am not as cute and compact. It takes two people to lift me, and there is no one to sing to me the sweet songs my mother sang to me when I was bedded. They don't know that when the lights go out, the fears come in. Call them the dragons and the monsters a child conjures up in the dark.

She rocks gently in place, wrapping her arms around herself.

What comforts a child, would comfort me, too. Someone to hold me, rock me, tell me that they will go away. Someone to turn on the light and fully open the closet and show me that it is only my coat that is the menacing hooded figure. I guess I am one of many and there is not enough time or people to tend me in this way. I hear so many of us screaming. Is it as frightening to you as it is to us? Are there times when you would stay away because you can't understand or because you think that there is not much that we would understand? Please, don't stop talking to us even though we have lost our ability to communicate with words. Your presence can sometimes ground us.

There is a time of the day, twilight time. It's that time of the day when all the light begins to slowly leave the sky and all that is left are lines and shadows. The lines become menacing figures and they frighten me. It's a time when I feel like I have slowly immersed myself in a pool of dark water and I try to focus on some light that will direct me upward and out. It's that time of the day when I become so detached from my surroundings, so confused and scared that I scream and they tend me with medicines. Sometimes I hope for an overdose. To put it all to rest. Why is it that most people prefer not to talk about the preference to die? Does it incur shame or guilt to entertain such an option? At this point I'm slowly losing the ability to even think out the steps involved in such a feat.

Frightened, she moves away from the mirror and sits down on the bed. She pulls her pocketbook from under the pillow and rummages through it, trying to ensure that nothing has been lost. She clutches the bag tightly to her chest while staring blankly ahead.

* * *

Her middle-aged daughter has come to visit her. She enters the room with a shopping bag of different belongings. She is struck by the sparseness of the surroundings, contrasting it with the richness of her mother's former life. Her entry goes unnoticed, as her mother seems far removed. The daughter goes to the bureau and removes an object from the bag. The sound alerts and startles her mother, who then acknowledges her visitor.

MOTHER: How nice of you to come. Have you been waiting long?

The daughter goes to her mother, bends down and kisses her head.

DAUGHTER: You know I always come to see you on Saturdays. I got tied up and couldn't get here before lunch. I'm sorry I couldn't eat with you. How are you?

MOTHER: Nothing really changes, you know.

Daughter pulls off from around her neck a purple scarf which she has brought to her mother.

DAUGHTER: Look what I brought you. Remember this? It's your favorite color. I gave this to you several years ago for your birthday.

The daughter places it around her mother's neck.

DAUGHTER: Would you like to go to the mirror and see how you look?

The only reaction is a faint smile.

DAUGHTER: Oh, yes *(retrieving another object from the bag)*. Sharon wanted me to give you something special. It was the bear you gave to her when she was a child.

The mother takes it to her, kissing and squeezing it. She keeps it on her lap, stroking it in a repetitive way. Her daughter is touched yet disturbed by this behavior. She brings over a photo album, trying to interest her in something else.

DAUGHTER: Mom, look. I thought you might want to see these.

The daughter sits on the bed close to her mother's chair. She turns the pages slowly, pointing out different people.

DAUGHTER: There's the old house on Linwood Street. There's Michael and me at the beach. Isn't that a nice picture of Daddy?

The mother runs her fingers over the picture but says nothing.

MOTHER: There's Esther. She looks good, doesn't she? I can remember that time when she helped me with your party. We were so proud of you.

DAUGHTER: Were you? Why, yes, you're right. Aunt Esther was sweet. I remember that day. The two of you were frantically getting things together in time.

MOTHER: I've been wanting to give her an old set of dishes she loved so much.

DAUGHTER: Mom, you know Aunt Esther got very sick several years ago.

MOTHER: Perhaps you could wrap them carefully and drop them off to her.

DAUGHTER: Yes, certainly, whatever you say.

The bear falls to the floor.

MOTHER: I think I'll lie down.

The daughter attempts to engage her with another picture.

DAUGHTER: *[She sits by her mother's side.]* Wait, remember this day. You and Dad were going to a party. You looked so radiant.

MOTHER: *[becoming irritable]* Don't ask me to remember. There's not much that I can remember. I just seem to dream a lot.

DAUGHTER: Of what?

MOTHER: Nothing in particular and everything in particular. There are times when I sit here and there is absolutely nothing in my mind. I thought you were always thinking, even in your sleep.

DAUGHTER: I don't understand.

The mother goes under her pillow and removes her bag. As she lies down, she removes the scarf and places it on the pillow. She brings the bag to her chest as she lies down and slips into a dozing state.

DAUGHTER: I'll just put some things away.

The daughter goes to the bureau and puts her clothing in the drawers. She returns to her bed and stands over her mother, talking out loud to herself.

I see you lying there so untroubled as though you had made peace with those demons that invade your mind. When you are this calm I wonder if I made the wrong decision. How loyal could I have been to have abandoned you to strangers? Of course, people tell me that I did all that I could, that there are some things that are beyond our control. But what about you? Look at your life. There is no choice, no control. I look down at you and I see a woman whose body is healthy but whose mind is slowly dying. I'm afraid that what will be left is a shell, something that will hold the semblance of you, my mother.

She takes a magazine from her bag and sits on a chair by the door.

I remember taking her into my home after things started changing in her life. Locking herself out and misplacing her keys wasn't bad, but then things were left to burn on the stove. At first, we would laugh about some of the odd behavior, thinking that her eccentricities were just more pronounced as she got older. She was good in the beginning, covering up some of her mistakes. And even now, she has periods when she is clear and quite conversive, but then she can slip and lose sight of her words and just ramble.

The daughter recalls an earlier conversation.

DAUGHTER: I remember the day when there was such fear in your eyes.

MOTHER: I feel at times like I'm looking at myself but someone else has taken over. Is my mind so scattered, that I don't know me? I don't know what to feel. I get more and more mixed up. Should I say this or say that? I don't know if I can get out of wherever I am.

DAUGHTER: Tell me where you are, Mother.

MOTHER: I'm in a mess of thoughts where nothing intersects. I don't know how to get myself out of this pattern of thinking.

DAUGHTER: There are times when I do understand you. You can make sense. Just talk to me. I'll help you to figure it out. I'll point out things, draw pictures. We'll create a new language, one that we can both understand.

MOTHER: I will need you to tell me what I should be needing and wanting. I don't know what it is that will take care of me. But, Theresa, don't let me hold onto you beyond what is reasonable.

The daughter is brought back from this recollection and turns to watch her mother in repose.

I knew then that you had unwittingly tapped into that dark place which you are now entering. A place which they tell me you will never leave.

She moves to her mother's bed.

I thought getting older would bring the usual problems, but who would ever think that your mind could be so altered?

She moves to the backside of her mother's bed and kneels down, stroking her hair.

Even though I must become acquainted with a different person, I still have memories of you, the way you were, and that will never change. Of course, you would not remember events the way I do, but could you reach back and remember some of who we were when we were together?

Do you think if I whisper these thoughts about us in your ear that they will enter as a dream and mean something to you?

My God, what must it be like to have everything erased? You have no starting point from which to reference your life. And because I have these thoughts and memories of you and others, will I be assured that I will have them forever?

Oh, Mother, look at you. Clutching that bag even in your sleep as though your soul were locked in it.

She picks the bear up from the floor, holds it to her chest while absent-mindedly squeezing it.

I have gone over why you need to be here. I was told it would be safer. I can't argue with that since I failed in providing that for you. I remember that day. All I wanted was to ensure that all of your freedom wasn't taken away. How was I to know that your sitting outside would lead to a search for a missing person? Now that you are here, they put a bracelet on which sets off all types of alarms in case you wander off, or, maybe in a more sane moment, try to escape.

She gets up, dropping the bear to the chair.

Oh, this place, the smells, the monotony of such living, with TVs blaring, as though they were competing with one another for noise while the audience doesn't even hear. I see people herded into rooms, disengaged, even though they may be touching.

I have also heard the screaming. Those piercing sounds seem inhuman, and when you come closer to this noise, the scene resembles the frantic cries of wounded children who are unable to fend and figure out what would comfort them.

She returns to her mother's bed.

How can I leave you here? Daddy would have suffered, watching you lie here, taking in life so passively. You would be unrecognizable to him. Your passion and intelligence are leaving. He would have kept you with him.

She impulsively begins to unload the dresser and remove the pictures. She quickly realizes, however, that this feeble attempt will not alter things or absolve her guilt, so she slowly returns her mother's belongings to their proper places.

But how can I go through that again? I look at you now and there is a person in a bed which may very well serve as a crib. Like a child you need to take from others the simple things that would get you through a day. Although I am your child, I must now become the parent to someone who has become so childlike. I must watch out for your rights and speak in your defense.

I remember toward the end there was the constant watching to ensure your safety. I needed to calm your fears and suspicions. There were nights when neither of us slept. The dark seemed to frighten you. You would become wild. It reminded me of the night terrors children have when their eyes are wide open yet they cannot be reached by touch or sound.

The drugs would muffle the screams, but were the fears still there?

I would lie next to you until you fell asleep. I want that closeness again. Maybe lying next to you would bring me back to being your child. I know that you want those same feelings.

She sits down. She lightly touches her mother's arm.

May I lie down next to you? When you open your eyes, will you know who I am?

There is movement from her mother as she raises her head without turning it. She goes to touch the body next to her. She rests her hand on her daughter's arm.

MOTHER: Oh, Joe, I'm glad you're home. I was getting worried.

The daughter holds her mother's hand and momentarily kisses it. Her mother drops her head to the pillow and slips back into sleep. The daughter moves to the other side of the bed and removes the bag. She opens it up and finds a mass of tissues and other crumpled items. She returns it safely to her mother. With great sadness, she returns to the chair, takes the bear to her chest, and repetitively strokes it.

Questions for Discussion

1. If you worked in a nursing home, what changes would you hope to make in dealing with the demented person after reading this play?
2. There is guilt for placement of her mother in the nursing home as well as anger for how her mother's mind has been robbed of memories. How can the daughter be helped in managing and resolving some of these feelings?
3. Consider your position. What if she wanted to exert her final control and choose to die?

FROM THE PERSPECTIVE
OF THE CARETAKER

Growing Old in an Alien Land

Vicki Pieser

"Sex and violence! I hate movies with sex and violence. Always sex and violence!" my mother announced loudly, jarring the few others in the audience of the afternoon matinee.

While I gently shushed her, I looked around the theater to gauge the need for an apology. I felt greater distress over the futility of the outing than the embarrassment of my mother's outburst. The movie was the sweet and whimsical *The Milagro Beanfield War,* an innocent fantasy. The frustration of growing old in what had become an alien land caused this eruption. I knew that the general culture had finally segregated my aging parents and partitioned them off from the rest of the world.

It has become an intergenerational parlor game in our family. My siblings and our children and mates exchange anecdotes to define exactly when chaos and frustration replaced the stability and joy in our aging parents' lives. We need to know when my parents began to forget what they needed to do to manage the simplest day. When they began to lose the reasoning ability to make important life decisions. When they realized that their lives were darkening. And when we all knew that we were powerless to change this.

Was it when the nicks on the car grew to fist-sized dents and the sideview mirror became anchored by duct tape? Was it when they forgot which grandchild was having a bar mitzvah and which was attending college? Or was it when my father fell while I was visiting? The scare caused both of my parents to lose their English for the night, yet both remained in good spirits, giggling over my inability to communicate with them.

Our parents were still giants in our eyes. My mother was Queen Esther, her Hebrew name, stately and proud. She was born into an assimilated family in Prague. She spoke with reverence of her parents, whom we never saw but knew through my mother's description. Her father was, we believed, a successful businessman who dressed elegantly and wanted his daughters to have the finest of everything. Her mother, a second wife, was younger than her husband, although she looked plump and grandmotherly in the pictures with her young daughters. She taught them to love opera, dancing, literature, and to identify fiercely as Jews.

My father was a superhero—a combination of charm, intelligence, and bravery. He was, after all, a self-made man whose drive and ambition took him out of his uneducated family in a Russian shtetl, through medical school in a foreign land, and, finally, away from the clutches of Hitler. Especially at parties or with groups of people, he strove to be the center of attention, attracting others with his clever stories and risqué humor. His life experiences made him a fascinating man. We wanted to remain in awe of him.

And now that the headstones have been unveiled and all formal mourning long ended, we still try to understand the descent. We want to validate that they were complete and valuable persons in their prime and at their deaths. And to understand that their dying became as heroic as their lives.

For me, the difficulties began in that movie theater when they felt that modern culture and its values had abandoned them. My parents, like many European Jews, loved stories and the power of words, but they could no longer enjoy the oral and visual stimulation of art, literature, and music. Movies and television, the most available harbingers of culture, bombarded them with obscene language, nudity, violence, and cruelty. As my eighty-five-year-old father protested, "My eyes and ears are helpless and can't escape." When complicated by other issues of poor eyesight, fading hearing, lack of access to theatre and libraries, and with English as a second language, they were growing old in an alien nation. And what could we do? How could we explain grunge, blueberry bagels, e-mail, O. J. Simpson, or the growing acceptance of intermarriage? How could we communicate a thirteen-year-old's need to buy tennis shoes that cost more than the monthly salary my father happily earned when he arrived in this country in 1939? And why is it necessary that a liquor cart block the aisle of a two-hour flight when people with shrinking bladders need to go to the bathroom? There is no simple explanation as to why a society prizes youth and rewards it with many toys but speeds by its older citizens.

And so their three harried, aging children treated them as if they had slipped into a Rip Van Winkle state. We paid for items that they would consider outrageously priced. As the eldest of us had translated their neighbor's English for them fifty years ago, we all tried to interpret their world using PG movies, frequent synagogue visits, and a doctor who listened. We sought oversized print books, quiet museums, and user-friendly vacation sites to entertain and to calm. And we succeeded, for a while.

And then came the call we feared. Daddy had been in a car accident. No, Daddy *caused* an accident, pulling out of the parking lot of the grocery store less than a block from his home. The young woman and small child in the other car were unhurt. Daddy had a bad bump on his head and severe bruising on his legs and body but seemed alert, although an ambulance was transporting him to the hospital. The next call was not so optimistic. He was unconscious and hospitalized. There was a head injury, along with broken ribs and pelvis. My sister took charge of immediate arrangements, but there was no question that my brother and I would come home immediately. My sister, living in the same city as my parents and dealing daily with their increasing unhappiness, had hired a driver, but they rarely used him. After his surgical skills, my father most valued his driving prowess. We all knew that, without a car, he would feel shamed. The agreement that he drive only to the grocery store had been an uncomfortable compromise, now gone awry. We did not verbalize the feelings of guilt, only concerns for his life. What we did not realize was that this had precipitated another stage in their lives, a state of physical debilitation we did not anticipate. The kind gerontologist called in to help explained it simply. Elderly people frequently fell and broke a hip, or had a car accident, or suffered a head trauma, such as the one my father experienced. Full recovery was unlikely, and this usually marked the beginning of their decline. To wait and see was the only option, but we should know that it could be serious. Oh, and brain scans showed loss due to aging, an old brain.

In the intensive care ward, we all became involved in caring for his physical needs. They did not have the staff to control his thrashing and keep him in bed. One night, my brother had to make the haunting decision to put him on a respirator. One night during my shift, my father begged me to loosen his straps. Then he deftly removed his IV. As he awakened, his speech returned with hallucinations, a new unevenness, and agitation. With little warning, he was discharged into the general hospital population with minimal nursing services. To secure physical therapy and the care he required, we temporarily placed him into a highly recommended nursing home. There residents enjoyed a happy hour, expensive decor, wide halls, and no interaction with the staff. His buzzer went unanswered while he urinated in his bed. His prized 33rd Degree Masonic ring was immediately stolen, and the nurse physically wrestled with my frail mother in a medication dispute.

Every day brought us a new, unwanted lesson. He was not bouncing back, and my mother was losing ground. We had incorrectly assumed that she could make decisions for both of them, but she was willing to rely on a confused husband who was still the doctor and the head of his family. One day, he asked her to bring him the brandy bottle from the shelf on the wall. Without questioning, she tried to retrieve it for him. We all saw that there was no shelf, no brandy bottle.

As the doctor had warned, the physical decline was permanent and even escalating; my parents had entered a stage of physical and cognitive disability. If the first stage had been separation from the general culture, then the second—loss of health—led to a separation from friends and a total focus on physical care. The circle tightened. Caretakers became the center of our concern, just as baby-sitters had controlled our destiny twenty years before.

We ran the gamut of health care paraprofessionals, kind women who care for the elderly. Without complaint, my sister interviewed, researched backgrounds, and hired. The triangle of my mother, my father, and caretaker was uncomfortable; all three felt degraded. My mother became haughty, feeling displaced by this new person claiming authority in the kitchen. My father's gregariousness caused my mother to become resentful of the intruder. It was a battle zone. When one caretaker accompanied them on a visit to Minnesota, I exhausted myself nurturing the frazzled woman, bribing her with gifts and total sympathy. A week later, she left their house in tears in the middle of the night. Like misbehaving children, they could not get along with their employees even if the loss of their home was the outcome.

Moving them seemed like the best alternative to the caretaker dilemma. Lunch at the apartment for the elderly was delicious. Four choices of entrees, five types of pies, and smiling waitresses seduced me. The setting was gorgeous. Many of the residents were Jewish and, we believed, had similar tastes and expectations. My parents could have a social life and a private life without live-in help.

Trying to please them by accommodating their large European furniture, my sister arranged for two apartments to be combined, a wall removed. Her decorator placed the furniture as my parents silently moved to a new level, complete dependence. Within a day, we realized that they could not find the dining hall, could not dress themselves appropriately, and could not stand up to residents who bullied them for sitting at the "wrong" table. The apartment complex sold, quickly turning into a cold institution with poor food, inadequate services, and disrespectful staff. My mother cried daily, mourning the loss of her home. Frustrated, we, their children, wondered what was the last right decision we made.

Within a few months, my mother died, believing at the end that my father could still save her. "Help me, Eppie," were her last words to him, and his telling of her death plea was the last of his stories. A week after her death, he was unsure that she was gone and occasionally sought her. His eyes became vacant, and he was mostly silent. He was comfortable with his home health aides, enjoying a mothering that he may have needed as a lonely shtetl boy almost a century earlier. A kind and loving caretaker was with him when he died, less than a year after my mother.

If I liked and admired my siblings before, I liked and admired them even more after our parents died. As first-generation Americans, we thought we understood our parents' lives and experiences, but we probably made more irreversible mistakes with our parents than we did with our children. We did not make mistakes with one another. We talk more now, send family heirlooms back and forth in a strange exchange, and look after one another a little more. My parents would have been pleased that, in their last days, they brought about the closeness they always wanted among their children. Now as we age, we three do not face that alien land alone.

Questions for Discussion

1. How would you describe the experience of these middle-aged children who watched and tended to their deteriorating parents? What issues did they have to face?
2. With a family like this one, who did everything they could with the best of intentions, what kind of grief work would you do?

With Respect to Reba

Elayne Clift

Picture a young Indira Gandhi, smiling broadly and posing seductively in green satin lounging pajamas and a matching velvet jacket tied loosely at the waist, circa 1936, and you have my favorite image of my mother, from a picture taken long before I was born. Now imagine the same woman, forty-plus years later, in mismatched polyester pants and shirt, shuffling up and down a nursing home corridor, and you will begin to understand the agony of watching my mother in her last years at a nursing home.

The events of the intervening years are not important here. What matters is the memory of my mother—feisty, energetic, fun loving, intelligent—making paper flowers at Easter and styrofoam Christmas decorations in December (meaningless to a Jew), or being called "Dear" and "Sweetie" by people who meant well but who had no right to be intimate or patronizing. What matters is doctors and social workers and administrators who never knew her as vibrant and ripe with life making judgments about her ability to think, to act, to be. What matters is my mother's despair.

Here is my mother as person, not patient: She was born in the Ukraine sometime preceding the High Holy Days of Rosh Hashanah in 1904; her birthday was celebrated each year on August 25, although no one knew for sure if that was accurate. She came to America as an infant, learning, infamously, to walk on the boat that brought her to Ellis Island. She settled in a small town in south Jersey where her father, Samuel the Tailor, had a dry goods store, where her two younger brothers became pharmacists, where her mother lived a life of quiet desperation until one day, after her children were grown and gone, she walked into the shed and hung herself. My mother left school after eighth grade, went to secretarial college, became a crackerjack legal secretary, and worked for the law firm of Pepper, Bodine, Stokes and Schock until Mr. Bodine chased her around the office one day with a string of French pearls and a litany of promises. Beautiful and gregarious, she played the piano at parties, picnicked on weekends in Atlantic City, traveled to the Chicago World's Fair in 1936, and, finally, despairing of meeting Mr. Right, married my father in 1938 when she was well into her thirties. They had three children together, ran a men's haberdashery business, owned property, lost it all, and went bankrupt in the 1950s. My mother never got over that. Or suburban isolation. Or marriage to the wrong man.

Or the repression of creative, bright women in the age of "involutional melancholia" and electroshock therapy. Soon after her husband died in 1971, unable to rise above terror and despair, she entered a nursing home and, except for brief respites with her children, did not come out.

I could never decide which was worse, spending time with my mother when she was lucid, or when she was in such a disoriented fog that she seemed like a stranger, a foreigner who had just dropped in from nowhere, and whose language and culture were completely unknown to me. Either way I knew I was losing her, and in her moments of clarity, she knew it too.

"Something's very wrong," she would say, looking me in the eye more directly and fiercely than I had ever known her to do. "I don't know what it is, but something is not right in my head. When it comes over me, I feel lost. I don't like that." One night, she said something even more to the point. "I want you to promise me something," and that's when she looked at me so piercingly. "I want you to promise me that you will never—never, never!— let me be foolish. I am trusting you with something very precious to me, and that is my dignity. Do you understand what I am saying?" I did. And I promised.

She was sitting in a chair when I entered her room with a large bouquet of flowers in my hand after I'd been traveling for several weeks. Her thinning gray hair was brushed severely back from her face instead of in its usual chaotic heap on her forehead. She was dressed in a clean striped blouse and a plaid skirt, creating a jumble of color that assaulted her own good taste in clothes, and, worst of all, she had on knee-highs instead of proper stockings, and shoddy slippers. She stared straight at the flowers in my hand, and clear through me.

"Hi, Mom!" I managed. No response. "I'm here." Nothing.

"She's been like that all day, dear," a nurse said, coming up behind me. "Not to worry. She'll be herself again." A sickening feeling crept up from my stomach and into my throat.

"Can I see the head nurse?" I asked. "I'd like to review what's been happening this week." I moved toward the nursing station without waiting for a reply. No one was there. I looked at the charts hanging alphabetically on the carousel. I lifted hers from the rack. "Patient depressed. Not eating. Exhibiting signs of psychosis (catatonia). Psychiatrist called. 25 mg Mellaril ordered, q.i.d." My head swam. Here it was, happening before my eyes. Everything she had feared and I had dreaded. No. No, no, no!

I put the chart back just as an aide approached the station. "Can I help you?"

"Yes. I was just looking for a vase."

My mother never spoke to me the whole time I was there. I busied myself arranging the flowers, which now seemed a mockery, and made small talk, and all the while felt her anger like ice on the back of my neck.

Before I even had a chance to think what to do, the call came. "This is Donna, the nurse on 2 East. Don't be alarmed, but I thought you should know. Your mother made something of a suicide gesture last night. She didn't hurt herself. It was really just to get attention. But we thought you should know. She wrapped the nurses' bell cord around her neck, several times. She was actually pulling on it when we found her. Of course, we've called the psychiatrist."

"No!"

"Excuse me?"

"No psychiatrist. No more punishment. That was not the act of a crazy person. That was a gesture of utter sanity. My mother is in abject despair and she is trying to let you know. She is trapped! Physically and mentally trapped. Everything is gone, even her dignity. Can't you see? Don't do a thing until I get there."

I poured myself a drink and tried to calm down. What to do? What to do, not to break my promise to my mother?

When I got to the nursing home, I asked once again for the head nurse. "Clarence," the aide called out to my surprise. "Someone wants to see you. A relative." Clarence emerged from one of the rooms, hands in rubber gloves. His broad black face was kind.

"What can I do for you?" he asked in the lilting accent of West Africa.

"I want to ask you a question," I said. "It's just between you and me. Understand?" He didn't, of course, but he nodded assent. "What would happen if my mother were to say she didn't want to take her insulin shots anymore? I mean, I know what would happen, but would you honor that wish?"

Clarence's eyes grew wide and quizzical. His expression was trapped somewhere between shock and a smile. It was the face of someone when you have said to them, "Would it be all right for me to kill my mother?"

"This is a very strange question," he said. "Why would you . . . It would be . . . "

"Yes, I know," I said. "I know exactly what I am saying, but would you honor it if she said 'stop'?"

"Yes, we would honor it."

"Thank you. And remember, this is just between you and me, yes?"

"You mean you don't want me to write it down in the chart?" he asked with a gentle grin. And in that moment I blessed him for his connection, his humanity, his reverence for life.

"Tell me, Clarence," I said, turning toward my mother's room. "What do you do in your country, you who revere old age so much? How do you help your people pass peacefully into the night?"

"Well, we don't have institutions like this, for a start," he said, looking at me again with empathy.

Clarence's reaction to my question validated and put me deeply in touch with my own feelings. I wanted desperately to feel that my mother still had choices, could still control her life. This was important to me, for her. But beyond that, I think, I wanted a way out of watching her deteriorate further. I did not want her to become pathetic and grotesque, a shell of a person with only meaningless labels like "bipolar" and "geriatric." I'd grown up with a deep fear of her disappearing, literally and figuratively, lost to me in a world of mysterious hospitalizations, dubious therapies, and personality changes brought on by drugs. I shared her distrust of doctors and psychotherapists who didn't know anything about who she really was and what had triggered her panic and depression. Now, as the end of her life neared, I was absolutely committed to her dignity, for her, and for me. I would not allow the cold, impersonal, institutional life of a nursing home dictate how my mother lived . . . or died. I was protecting myself, as well as her.

Sometimes this resolution made me feel guilty and selfish. Was I really doing this for my mother, or only for myself? Was I ashamed of her? No longer able to cope with what she had become? Afraid of my own descent into inherited madness? I discussed these uncertainties with the friend and soul mate who had researched the Hemlock Society because of her own dedication to dignity for herself and her mother, and who had suggested the insulin strategy to me. She assured me my feelings were normal and appropriate and reinforced the idea that if my mother were to voluntarily reject her insulin, it would offer a self-directed option. Clarence's response seemed to support this perspective.

When I went back to her room, my mother was lying in bed, staring up at the ceiling, motionless. I took her hand, cherishing its warmth as I had done when I was a child. She squeezed my hand, then grimaced. A tear slid down toward her ear. "I love you so much," I said. Then, "You know, you could say you don't want your insulin. They can't force you. It's your choice. Or you could say you don't want to eat. No one will make you. It's up to you. Do you understand what I'm telling you?"

"So then what would happen?" she asked, childlike.

"You'd pass away."

"So who would make all the arrangements?" I wanted to laugh. My mother, the organizer.

"I'll take care of everything. You don't need to worry." She squeezed my hand again.

I went frequently after that. She was always in bed, eyes closed or staring at the ceiling. When I took her hand it was warm, despite the gradual wasting of her body. And day after day I told her again, "You could say you don't want your insulin. It's up to you. It's your choice." But she was tenacious about life. She told me once, after the bell cord episode, that she didn't really want to commit suicide; she just wanted the pain of living in this way to be gone. My mother, who loved life so much, just couldn't let go, not even when she was tormented. I think she was afraid she just might miss something worthwhile.

Clarence never mentioned our conversation to me again. He just smiled and spoke kindly to my mother whenever he entered her room. He left the nursing home soon after we had talked. I missed him very much and wondered if he'd told anyone else on staff about our agreement. There was no one I trusted enough to ask.

It was many months until my mother died, a slow, natural, wasting death. I was with her, holding her hand, and it was peaceful. I sat a long time by her side before telling anyone she was gone. Long enough to recapture the sight of her in those green satin and velvet lounging pajamas. Long enough to remember her laughter and her touch when I was small. Long enough to know it was my mother who had died.

When the men came to get her, I said, "Treat her with dignity!" And I watched until they boarded the elevator. Then I called the funeral home and said I wanted the Jewish orthodox ritual of bathing and prayers, which was the only way I could imagine her body being treated with respect. It was, in the end, the very least I could give my beloved mother, whose name, may she rest in peace, was Reba.

Questions for Discussion

1. The narrator talks about her mother as a person, not a patient. What are some ways a nursing home could deal with people as persons, not patients?
2. What kinds of support groups/programs for families could nursing homes offer? What do you think should be included in such programs?
3. What are your views on assisted suicide? What would you do in a situation in which it was handled in a way that conflicted with your views?

Peaches

Dennis Foley

Gramma Foley's brain didn't work so good, so she lived in the old folks home. She had some kinda disease that made it so she forgot most things, and since her mind didn't work so good, I never quite knew if I should believe a single word she said. Mom took us kids to visit Gramma three or four times a year. Johnny and Tim were ready to leave the old folks home the minute they set their teenage feet upon the beige linoleum floor. They'd park their butts on a couch, point their penny loafers at the front door, and hope the half hour moved quickly. That's how long we always stayed. One half hour. Never more than that.

Mom would always tell us kids to wait in the cafeteria while she went to get Gramma from her room. Sometimes it took Mom awhile to get Gramma ready. She might hafta help Gramma into her pajamas and robe, or Gramma might decide she wanted my mom to comb her hair. I never minded the wait though. There was always lots of old people to look at. They were staggered about the tables and chairs in the cafeteria like lost toys waiting to be put away. Some smiled at us, some just cried, some stared off at the lime green walls, and one guy—we called him Cow—liked to make mooing sounds all the time. When we got tired of starin' at the old people, we kids busied ourselves calling one another "jerk" or "spaz" and then chasing one another around the room. That usually got Cow to stop mooing. He'd open his mouth wide and cackle away at our antics.

If Mom was real slow getting Gramma back, we'd ask Cow to show us his false teeth. He was only too happy to oblige. Johnny and Tim even joined us at the table for this. Taking one's teeth out should've been a quick thing, but it wasn't for Cow. He'd shuffle back and forth before us like a magician ready to tout his finest tricks, a big smile on his face. Cow was short, thin, and wrinkly, and he had two wisps of hair that stood tall on his head. He'd start by bowing and then he'd pull a white hanky from his pants pocket. Cow always unfolded the hanky slowly until a perfect white square draped in front of him, and then he'd swing that hanky, in a figure-eight shape, through the air. Once he made a bunch of eights, Cow would let go of the hanky and we'd all watch it float down like a feather, drifting from side to side as it fell, until it landed on the table where we sat. Then came the pointing. Cow would aim a skinny, wrinkled finger at the hanky and keep that finger arrow straight as he circled the entire table. He never said a word as he walked around our table. He just pointed. But that wasn't much of a surprise cuz I never heard Cow speak during any of my visits to see Gramma. Not a word. The only sounds that came from his mouth were mooing and laughter. When the pointing was done, Cow'd stand about ten feet away from the table, arch his body back as far as his old bones would allow, and hold himself there a moment. Then he'd stretch his neck, thrust himself forward, and cough his teeth out. And when those teeth came out, it was a thing of beauty. It seemed they were moving in slow motion, tumbling and twisting through the air like the acrobats you see at the circus. Cow's teeth always landed on that white hanky, most times right smack-dab in the middle. That's when we kids would clap wildly for Cow and he'd take a final bow—nice and slow like. Then he'd grab his teeth, dry 'em up with that hanky, and hand 'em to one of us. They were his top teeth and they were perfect little pearls stitched to bright red gums. There wasn't anything ugly or scary about 'em. Each one of us kids would hold the teeth in our hands, take a quick stare at 'em like they were precious jewels that shouldn't be held for too long, and then pass 'em along. When we'd all handled the teeth, Cow would shove 'em back in place, walk away, and get back to his mooing.

We always knew when Gramma was getting near cuz we could hear her moaning at Mom. And then Mom and Gramma would appear from the hallway and Mom's right arm would be hooked around Gramma's left arm. Gramma always moved slow. She didn't so much walk as she shuffled, and her big fuzzy slippers didn't help her foot speed much. Her bathrobe was always wrapped around her and the strap was bow-tied at the waist. I figured Mom did that. Gramma wore a different colored bathrobe every year. Sometimes it was pink, sometimes white, and sometimes baby blue. And she always had matching slippers. That's what we kids gave Gramma every year at Christmas, a new robe and slippers.

Gramma would start up the minute she set her eyes on us kids.

"I want outta this place," she'd say, waving a finger at us. "I want out now."

"Easy, Mom. Easy," my mom'd say right back. "It's not so bad here."

"What do you know?" Gramma would look at Mom with pinched eyebrows, and her thick black-rimmed glasses would climb up on her forehead. Her white, thinning hair seemed to bristle. "Ah-h-h, you don't know shit from shinola." You could always count on Gramma for a few good zingers, and those zingers, along with Cow's teeth tricks, made the trip worthwhile for me.

"Have you ever eaten the food here?" Gramma would say. Her questions were the same every visit. I could rattle 'em off in the order they would come, if I set my mind to it.

"No, Mom. I haven't."

"Of course not. No one should. This slop isn't fit for pigs or even Italians." Gramma liked to throw darts at the Italian folks. She probably would've died if she knew Johnny was dating one. Then she'd let things settle in for a minute. That's when all of us kids would line up in front of Gramma like she was Santa Claus, ready to hand out some presents.

"What do you want?" she'd say, staring blankly at us.

"Hugs and kisses, silly," Donna would say. And then Gramma would give us those hugs and kisses and then all of us, with our backs turned to Gramma, would wipe the kisses from our cheeks and then sit down. And once we sat down, there would be a brief moment of quiet before Gramma started in again.

"And I suppose it doesn't stink in here either?" Gramma'd say. She had us there. Truth was, the place did stink. It smelled like pee and disinfectant everywhere. It was so bad your eyes felt like they were on fire. Mom always lied to Gramma and I liked that cuz when I got in trouble for lying, I always told Mom that I learned it from her. She never punished me too bad then.

"I don't know, Mom. It smells a little in here, but it doesn't smell too bad."

"Ah-h-h, what do you know? You couldn't smell a fart inside a pillowcase."

Another one to add to Gramma's list. And that's how our visits to Gramma usually went. I say "usually" cuz sometimes, every third visit or so, Gramma would talk about breaking out of the old folks home. She'd pull one of us little kids aside and say, "I'm breaking outta this place. You wanna help me?"

"Sure, Gramma."

"Bring me a hammer and a screwdriver next time. Got it?"

"Sure do, Gramma." By our count, Gramma planned to break out well over twenty times. But she never did. She's still in that home now.

Whenever she asked me to bring the hammer and screwdriver, I'd have a little fun with her. I'd say, "Should I bring a saw too, Gramma?"

"Did I ask for a saw?"

"No, Gram."

"What good would a saw do me? I'm breakin outta here—not cuttin' legs off."

"Right, Gram," I'd say and chuckle.

Mom said Gramma's brain went on shut down when her husband, Frank, died. That was way back in 1959, right around the time I was born. And things just froze up for her then. She remembered my oldest brother's name was Johnny, so she called all boys "Johnny." Gramma also remembered my oldest sister Jackie, so around Gramma, all three of my sisters answered to "Jackie."

She'd look at me and smile and say, "You're a fine boy, Johnny." Only thing was—my name wasn't Johnny. "You'll make someone a great husband one day, Johnny. You have the face . . . of a mortician. Maybe that's the line of work you should get into."

"Sure thing, Gram," I'd say.

"Lotsa money in that mortician stuff, ya know. A never-ending stream of clients. Remember. Shoot for the moon or it'll shoot you first."

"Right, Gram."

Gramma always left us with loads of things to talk about on the ride home, like, "What's a mortician, Ma?" or "How do ya fart in a pillowcase, Ma?" or "When's the last time you had some shinola, Ma?" By the time Mom got us home, she was ready for a breather. I don't know what wore her out more—Gramma or our stupid questions.

During one visit, though, a strange thing happened. Only Tim and I came with Mom that day to see Gramma. Tim played checkers with one of Gramma's friend's, a man friend. Gramma said he was her boyfriend. Sometimes she called him her "love jockey."

"That's mighty nice of Johnny to play with old Ed there," Gramma said to me and Mom as she pointed to her man friend. "It keeps him away from me and I like that. Heaven only knows there's nothing worse than havin' a soft, flabby dick chasin' ya around all the time." Mom knocked her styrofoam cup over and sprang to her feet. I nearly pissed into my shoes.

"I'll be right back," Mom stammered. "I'm gonna get a new cup of coffee. Do ya want anything, Mom?"

"No thanks, Jo. And take your time." Mom nodded. With Mom gone, Gramma leaned over the table. "I knew that'd get rid of her." She grabbed my hands and held them in her own. I looked at her hands. They were thin and wrinkled and full of bright blue veins. Brown spots that looked like huge freckles climbed all over her arms. She squished my hands and I stared into her eyes. For the first time in my life, Gramma looked as normal as any person I ever met. Just old. That's all.

"How come your father never comes with ya to visit, Johnny?"

I lied. "He's been busy at work, Gram." I lied some more. "Saturdays are his big workday." Truth was, my dad was sitting on a stool in a tavern somewhere. I knew it, but she didn't.

"Is he sick again?"

"No, Gramma." I decided to tell the truth. "He just came out of the hospital."

"What was he there for?"

"His ulcers. Liver. Lungs."

She shook her head and smiled. "He was always a sickly boy. Not like your Uncle Jim. He was always healthy. And most certainly not like Gene. That one was like a wild horse, even when he came outta me, kickin' and

scratchin' and clawin'. They had to open me up to get him out, ya know?"
She laughed. "Not your dad, though. He slid out like a stick of butter." She
laughed some more. "Got polio when he was fourteen." I didn't say anything. "You know that, right Johnny?"

"I knew he got it, Gramma, but I didn't know how old he was."

"Fourteen. I just told ya fourteen. Right?"

"Right, Gram."

"My God, Johnny. Get the Q-tips out and clean those wax mountains
outta your ears." I laughed. Gramma did too. But then the smile left her face
and her words came slow. "They told me, the doctors told me, that he'd
never walk again. I listened to 'em but you know what I told them?" I aimed
my eyes right at hers. "Bullshaven! That's what I said. He'll walk again, I
told them. And he did. Everyone stayed up around-the-clock to help. We all
covered a time slot. Frank, Ducky, and Jim. Even Gene pitched in, back
then, and he wasn't more than a half-pint like you."

"I'm no half-pint, Gramma. I'm ten."

She inched her face toward mine and turned her eyes into slits. "You're
what I say ya are, half-pint. Got it?" I nodded my head and then Gramma's
scary look went away. She smiled again. "Anyway, we worked in shifts, ya
know. We boiled towels in the water on the stove, wrung the towels out, and
put these hot towels on your father's legs as he slept. And we massaged his
legs with the hot towels when he was awake. It worked! They said it would-
n't work, but it did." There was a certain pride in Gramma's voice now. "We
made it work." She stared deep into my eyes. "I wasn't gonna just sit there
and let that son of mine be a cripple. No sir-ee, Bob! Two years after they
said he'd never walk again, he was running down the street with all the other
kids. Some nun thought up the remedy, ya know." She smiled. "Did you
know your Aunt Ducky wants to be a nun?"

Aunt Ducky, her daughter, already was a nun. She'd been a nun for over
ten years now.

"Yes, Gram."

"You have nuns teaching you?"

"Sure do."

"Thank God for nuns."

"Yes, Gram." And that's how I came to find out how my dad learned to
walk again, how he beat polio. He never said a word to me about those
times. Neither did my mom, other than to say that dad had the disease as a
kid.

Mom came out from the hallway and walked toward us. She had a new
cup of coffee in her hand.

"When's the last time you had a peach?" Gramma asked.

"'Bout two days ago," I said.

Gramma watched as my mom moved closer. "How'd it taste?"

"Good, Gram. Real good. Cold and meaty, sorta."

"I haven't had a peach in so long." My mom stopped about fifteen feet from us and fished through her purse. Then she pulled out the car keys. The half hour was up.

"I can bring ya one next time, if ya want, Gramma."

"That would be great Johnny. Just great."

A few moments later, Mom, Tim, and me kissed Gramma good-bye and as we started our walk toward the front door, Gramma wailed as usual.

"Traitors. All of ya. Leaving me here in this dump. You'll all go to hell in a handbasket." We pushed our way through the front doors and walked for the car. On the ride home we laughed a bit over Gramma's antics, but it was laughter mixed with sadness too. We would rather have her out of that home, but we couldn't. Not with that disease that made her forget. Mom said Gramma was far better off in there cuz she couldn't hurt herself with someone watchin' over her all the time.

We still visit Gramma at the home, but it seems we don't go as often anymore. Maybe just twice a year now. Gramma's not as feisty either. She's mellowed quite a bit. She likes to stare away at the lime green walls now and she doesn't say much. But whenever I visit, I always make certain I bring her a nice meaty peach. And I always give it to her just as we leave. She gets so wrapped up in that peach, she doesn't even see us leavin', and by the time she's done eatin' it, she doesn't even know we were ever there.

Questions for Discussion

1. What did the boy learn from his relationship with his "gramma"?
2. Do you think there is an appropriate age for children to visit a nursing home? What criteria, other than age, may be important?

Sounds

Elisavietta Ritchie

Great-Aunt Eleanora is giving us trouble these days. She wants to stay on her ramshackle farm. Alone.

"You can't even get good TV here!" argues the realtor, urging her to listen to a certain developer who wants to carve the farm into twenty-nine waterfront lots.

Reception is haphazard only because the house is down on the river.

Great-Aunt Eleanora has no time for television. Radio provides her news and good music. She listens as she paints—currently, murals. She started on murals when she had to stay within earshot of Great-Uncle Ramsey, and after thirty years could no longer hide out in the chicken coop, which Ben had helped her convert to a studio. There, she painted what she wanted, and when Ramsey was out, shipped the canvases off to a gallery in New York. Ben, and later I, transported the bigger paintings in the farm truck. Her works sold slowly over the years, but we quietly invested the proceeds in a fund, which now pays the taxes on the farm. So no need to sell it.

I'm one of the few people who know this. She assigned me power of attorney.

Now from the rafters a family of black vultures would observe every stroke of her brush, but she talks of working in the chicken house again, "once the weather warms and these darn murals are finished."

The murals are medieval scenes of knights and their ladies galloping or strolling around various picturesque European hillsides. Frankly, they aren't particularly well executed—proportions are off—not half as good as her earlier impressionistic passages, seascapes, and passionate abstracts.

Today she shows me the half-painted walls in the front hall. "Still some baffling blanks, and the moats look empty. Ramsey suggested lotus and Ben urged lilies—but it's old lady-ish to paint flowers. Last week a stag walked through the snowy yard, then obliged me by standing still—downright posing—under the English walnut while I sketched him onto that panel between the windows. But horses I need to study live again. . . ."

Great-Uncle Ramsey Leigh hates abstracts. A retired judge, he likes historic scenes and would wheel his chair, with Ben wheeling along in his wake, into whatever room she was painting. The fact that her eyesight and her hands were no longer as sure didn't matter to them: their own eyesight and coordination were failing too. That didn't stop them from advising.

Increasingly, Great-Aunt Eleanora cared for both old men, one black, one white. Ben's grandson, Percival, and I shoved the dining table against the wall and moved in their beds so they'd be easier to feed and keep an eye on while she was in the kitchen. On bright winter days, the sunporch heated up so they could all nap out there.

Then, even with Percy's help bathing and lifting them, it got too much for Great-Aunt Eleanora. Or so the county social worker insisted: "Judge Leigh and that old Ben are two big heavy men, and here you are, a little wren, trying to care for both of them day and night!"

A private room came available for Great-Uncle Ramsey at the Home, and for Ben, a bed in the ward.

I thought we'd have a time persuading them to move. But they consulted each other, just as they used to consult over the no-till way to sow soybeans while harvesting winter wheat, and did the barn need a new roof, the horse a new shoe. Finally, they agreed to visit the Home: each had cronies there already, hadn't seen them for ages. They let us sign them in.

"For one week," Uncle Ramsey said. "But just shove us both into the same room: that'll be cheaper, and we smoke the same brand of tobacco."

The admissions secretary blinked, but Aunt Eleanora and I okayed it so the matter was arranged.

Turns out, Uncle Ramsey and Ben rather like being sweet-talked by those pretty nurses, the large-screen color television beats the old black-and-white set at the farm, and though old ladies complain, in the common room, they can smoke without Aunt Eleanora coughing. Still, away from familiar surroundings, they've grown increasingly confused.

At home, though her eyesight is blurring, Aunt Eleanora continues to extend her murals throughout the downstairs. Cats brush against wet paint, leaving her pictures fuzzy and their tails purple and green. I wash the cats and her hair with tirpolene and baby shampoo, just as she used to wash mine when I was a child. While it dried in the sun, she would teach me to read from a tiny maroon-covered primer, and how to sculpt and fire my ungainly statuettes, which are lined up on an upstairs shelf like awkward anchors for my soul. While we shelled peas, baked cakes, or washed dishes together, she would tell me stories, usually about great dead artists.

Now she sometimes tells them aloud to herself as she cooks what she needs to feed herself and twenty-six (at last count) cats. The farmer who's leased the fields cuts fallen branches into logs small enough for her to put in the old stove. He also plows her road after it snows, and Wednesdays his wife brings groceries. I come by most weekends with a cake or casserole to last several days. Since her washing machine rusted through, I do her laundry in town. I lug my computer to catch up on my cases, and to manage her bills and the correspondence, which still comes in from galleries and other artists. I also bring new brushes and paints and, sometimes, friends for a picnic. She prefers young people.

At her request, every visit I check every inch of the farm, attempting to patch whatever needs patching. During my childhood summers here, Ben used to let Percy and me tag along to "help." Ben soon taught Percy to work with a wrench and saw, tractor and scythe, and I insisted on learning right along with him. So last week Percy and I shored up the sunporch, but another board's always rotten somewhere. The roof leaks into the upstairs bedrooms, though since she's had trouble with steps, she now sleeps off the kitchen, where Ben lived until his legs gave out. In winter the dinosaur furnace tends to die, or the chimney gets blocked. The electricity fails in storms, the circulating pump breaks, the septic system . . .

More than one midnight I've driven from the city at 65 mph to cope. And some night, it will be that Aunt Eleanora has tripped over a cat and broken a hip, or wandered to the beach and waded in too far. So of course I'm concerned about her, out here all alone now, fields on three sides, the river on the fourth.

"Just sell the place," people urge, "move her into the Home, and you won't have any more worries."

Since I am her closest relative, everyone is pressuring me. Sometimes I'm tempted. A terrible decision, to wrest her from her beloved riverside farm. Today I bring up the move.

"I am perfectly fine *here,* thank you."

January's wind methodically flaps the shed roof, beats magnolia boughs against the house, rattles windows—three panes slipped from their sashes as the putty crumbled, and the glazier is always coming *next* week. Cats meow to enter or exit.

"But don't all the odd noises bother you at night?"

"At night," she shrugs, "of course there are sounds. Most, I identify: From the woods, the hoot owl. From the cove, loons. Scratchings, shrills, chirps in the roof, wind spiraling down all three chimneys—each has a singular moan. And when I pry rot from a window frame, the squeal that freezes against the pane is explainable."

Since Aunt Eleanora is much alone, whenever she has company, she really talks.

"But . . ." she pauses to pour hot water into the pot, not noticing it splash on the worn Oriental rug, "it's the *voices* the farm has absorbed across three hundred years—from cries of love to quarrels over the lawn. Then this morning when I looked out the kitchen door to see if you had arrived, I noticed among the spindly figs and runaway vines covering the foundations of that shack burned in the Revolution—who knows which side lighted the torch—I noticed a child in a dark pink pinafore."

"What child?" The nearest house is a mile away, no children there. No picnickers land on her beach in January.

"A child . . . plump, about three. She was crying, her nose was running; she had a cold or was cold. Then, she was gone. . . . Or, was never there."

"Perhaps not . . ."

"But every spring when the garden is plowed, in a furrow near—remember that broken pipe which leads to the barn?—I always find one tattered rag doll. You might check in the pony cart . . ."

Except for Ramsey's ancient Packard and the farmer's tractor, the barn has stood empty for years. But the wood is good, and the stalls still bear the names of horses I learned to ride on—SMOKEY, STORM KING, OLD JESS.

Could raise horses again, someday . . .

Absently cradling an orange kitten named Titian, Aunt Eleanora stares toward the river. Can she see two black vultures in the moribund oak?

"But aren't you ever afraid here?" I pour tea into chipped china cups.

"Of . . . ghosts? Nonsense. I early learned to settle in with presences. As with the woodchucks in the cellar, raccoons in the roof, cats in the barn—their ancestors guard. In time," she smiles, "my voices too will merge with the farm . . ."

"Voices? Did you discuss this with the doctor?"

"This?" She looks puzzled. "The . . . voices? Whatever for? And it's not always voices. Mostly, it's like your computer pinging even if the power's off, or high-tension lines humming across the fields in a blizzard . . ."

"Ringing in the ears can mean something's wrong . . ."

"I meant to mention it to the doctor last week. Happens whenever I close my eyes. A hive in the brain." Her blue eyes focus on me. "You must hear them too. And, in town, there's always an ambulance down the avenue, fire engines across the park, jackhammers, traffic, that school yard six blocks away, hooves striking cobblestones."

"Except the cobblestones were asphalted over years ago, and there aren't horses in town anymore."

"Sounds pile up, you know, are stored. Volcanoes exploding decades ago remain in the air. Cathedral chimes, troubadours' plaints, street cries. High-pitched notes that set dogs howling. That's what I hear, when I wake in the night or try to nap after lunch. A music box under my pillow, roosters behind the drapes. I wonder, has my skull become one vast receptor? . . ."

Suddenly she looks troubled. "Do I also transmit?"

"Transmit?" The social worker may well be correct: incipient senility.

"I certainly don't generate. I doze in the armchair—no creaky rocker for me—radio off, phone off the hook. My necklaces which used to tinkle and jangle—I moved like a belled goat—have been stolen . . . or sold?"

"You gave them all to me, Aunt Eleanora. Don't you remember? One every birthday for the last twenty years. But I'll return them—you obviously miss them—I don't need more than one." Once she goes into the Home, any jewelry will disappear.

"Oh, don't worry about returning those baubles, dear. I can still hear their symphonies even on my bare neck. Lovely . . . Yes, the doctor suggested tests my next checkup, next year. Today"—she looks radiant—"today I'm tuned to a fishmonger's serenade . . . Now whistling swans . . . Sometimes, from farther waters, choirs of whales."

She settles back in her armchair. The piebald tomcat called Leonardo jumps onto her lap. She is content with her voices, her cats. And glad for my company.

Then she jumps up, spilling Leonardo and her untouched tea, gathers her splattered smock from its hook, her palette and paints from the kitchen.

"Swans—that's what I need for the moat. And a whale for the bay beyond. Would you mind shining that light there—just bend its neck—so I can see what I'm doing. Almost out of white paint—could I trouble you to bring me a tube next week?"

I jot "white paint" in my notebook. I'm forgetful of late if I don't write down—

"Now, child, I don't want to detain you. You have a long drive, your job tomorrow. Take those cookies for the road. There, in the Louis Sherry tin."

I look in the pantry. The tin, among shoeboxes marked ZIPPERS, FUSES (BLOWN), OLD SHADE PULLS, SHEEP SKULLS, ARROWHEADS, is empty. I write "Fig Newtons" on my list. When I was six, she taught me to arrange them into castles and battlements, as if they were dominos.

Given how the cats are scratching, I add "flea powder."

In the corner of the kitchen I notice a paper bag full of bread crusts. For the ducks. Although the weather has been too cold for her to venture outside, she still intends to go down to the inlet with them. Despite the cats, there is evidence the mice are taking their share on the way. She won't let me buy traps or poison.

Knowing I must be visiting, the social worker phones.

"Good news! Your aunt finally leads the waiting list for the Home. Could be a matter of only a week, at worst two, before . . ."

"How's your aunt doing?" the social worker asks cheerily.

"Great," I answer. "Let's let her stay here a bit longer. Someone else in more desperate need for a bed can take her place. If necessary, I can get leave from work for a few weeks."

Even years . . . Since I'm supposed to inherit this farm, *I'd* better get used to staying here, in season and out. Until one morning they discover me collapsed in the barn, or drowned on the beach, or shriveled and stiff in this wildly painted parlor, even with brushes dried in my hands. That's the way to go, Aunt Eleanora has said.

I thank the social worker and hang up.

"Next weekend," I promise Aunt Eleanora, "rain or shine, I'll drive you around to see horses. And if the weather should be warm I'll walk you down to the cove, and we'll feed some crusts to the ducks. I could even push you in a wheelchair all the way up the path to the lighthouse."

Preoccupied with outlining her swans, she seems not to pay attention.

I tape another sheet of plastic over the broken panes, then bank the fire, raise the thermostat, go outside with a broomstick to check the level of heating oil. . . . Enough to last till April. Afraid she'll forget the chicken on the stove, I cut the flame: she doesn't mind lukewarm soup. I wash and refill the dishes of the anxious cats—What would happen to them?

Despite the cold, I run to the cove with the bag of crusts. Mallards swim around the far side of a broken skiff caught in the ice rimming the shore. Waves are sparkling between ice floes.

"Here you are!" I fling the crusts: they skid across the ice toward the open water where the ducks retrieve them greedily. "More crusts next week, I promise."

I jog along the little beach. Around the bend, suddenly, twenty swans fly in line, they fracture the sun, then veer so low their feet and wingtips skim the water like skipping stones. One swan breaks formation, swerves off from the others, lands in the cove. At last the rest follow.

When I stop in the house to gather up my computer and Aunt Eleanora's laundry, I hear her humming. She is painting a whale into a cove between the tall clock and the fireplace.

The whole drive to town, the humming persists.

Question for Discussion

1. What would be your criteria for deciding when to remove someone from the home he or she loves?

Flying Time

Elisavietta Ritchie

"My father is walking today!" I hold him by his belt as he leans into the metal walker and shuffles one step. I'm startled to be able to see over the top of his head. He used to stand six-foot-two.

"Come on, just one more step."

Watitha Jones, the nurse in the doorway, applauds.

His mind also meanders streets he hasn't seen for years, and he is soon exhausted from the excursion.

Watitha and I guide him into his wheelchair, double loop canvas straps around the metal armrests, then tie them firmly behind the blue plastic back.

Climber of mountains, swimmer of seas, he always chafed at restraint. Lately, however, he no longer seems to notice the cotton vest oddly dubbed a "posey." Still, I hate to see him tied. But some days, with a sudden burst of adrenaline, or as if he could escape the pain, he tries to get up, and might fall again. The hip which splintered when he managed to take off on his own last July still aches.

How one's world shrivels when one is in pain. My back . . .

"He can only think of himself," my stepsister noted last week. "Existence is limited to his bodily concerns."

And yet . . .

"The Baron came to call this morning," my father tells me in a low voice. "He brought his whole entourage. We are still discussing negotiations. We had quite a party. Percy and Gustav and Vladimir and . . ."

He beams as he relates his friendships with the dead. Several seem still to be lingering over their cognacs and coffee. Then he tires of so much company and dozes off.

"He had kinda a bad night," the nurse says. "Like he was fighting some war."

"He was a colonel," I explain. "In the American Army, and before that, a recruit in a few other armies. He has indeed fought some wars."

Again a shell explodes and scatters light and alien finger bones. He shouts, screams. The other patients along the hall are terrified, or else unperturbed because they're accustomed, or deaf.

He wakes, embarrassed and confused: he was back at Anzio, Normandy, the Battle of the Bulge. Or the Ardennes, Verdun. Though years have

469

passed, his wars fight on. Shrapnel, rubble, and peculiar shards of flesh still litter the bedroom floor so deep he cannot find his slippers in the dark.

"Don't worry, Daddy, that war is over. Everything is all right now."

He looks relieved, but not convinced.

I too despise my patronizing tone.

He indicates discomfort.

"I think he—"

But Watitha is already half out the door. "I'll come back and change him soon as I finish down the hall. Won't you be staying with him a few minutes?"

I nod, though in fact it is late and I am desperate to leave. Desperate in part because I am agonized to see my father in this sad condition, and the other patients, some worse off than he. Whenever I leave the nursing home, I want to run, jog, bicycle, swim, make love, climb mountains—whatever is vigorous, exciting, reassuring. Then at home, I have a half-written manuscript waiting, a new job waiting, children waiting, a new lover who with luck is also waiting—multiple worlds waiting like wet canvases. Worlds lively and sane. Worlds that my father shared. Worlds to which, from my childhood, he introduced me. Some, he created.

For the moment, for this long hour, I am grounded by filial duty, and love.

With the nurse gone, in a whisper my father says he is concerned about my alimony. The whispering may be because it is not proper to discuss these personal, distasteful, monetary matters before strangers. Or because, since the nursing home lost his hearing aid in the laundry, he cannot seem to pitch his voice right anymore. Or simply, his voice is weak today. Some days he doesn't talk at all. Reasons vary from hour to hour.

"Yes, I guess I am getting alimony. It will help pay some bills."

We do not discuss the expense of the nursing home which is rapidly eating up what little he saved from a generous life.

"How much cash do you have with you?" He leans forward urgently. "I have to pay for the plane tickets. Last night three men waylaid me and beat me up and stole my wallet."

"No, Daddy, that was a bad dream. Your wallet's safe in the drawer. Here . . ."

He struggles to fit the worn cowhide billfold into his back pocket, but it slips between his trousers and the foam-rubber cushion. Of course there is no money in it: the lady down the hall shuffles in other people's rooms and takes what she thinks is hers, and the man . . .

"Your grandsons send their love."

I throw out the marigolds I brought him last week. The water is greeny black, odiferous, but does not mask the other nursing home smells.

He doesn't pick up on the grandsons. A rare day when I can cajole one into visiting. They cannot bear to come here. Hard for an adolescent to see old people, sick people, other young people incapacitated. "Grandfather wouldn't recognize us anyway. He is always all spaced out."

Great coughing and hawking from the other bed: The other half of his room is occupied by an eighty-year-old Italian mechanic with, among other ailments, emphysema. He still smokes on the sly in the bathroom, scattering ashes and cigarette butts and worse across the floor. But he is jolly, usually lucid, and his family never visits. I have brought chocolates for both men, but lunch is at noon, so I stash them in a cookie tin cockroaches can't pry open.

"We are facing superior numbers," my father whispers, "but with a little more artillery, we can win." His voice resonant now, he redirects the Battle of the Bulge and Tannenburg, confers with Genghis Khan, again shifts venue and instructs his broker to sell his Edsel fast.

Together we shuttle centuries and shuffle names. This is a good day, I remind myself: he is talking.

"Will you have dinner with me?" The old graciousness. His house was always full of guests. Some he might have met once in a foreign country but they would appear, stay a week, or a month.

Where are those friends now . . .

"I must get home soon, Daddy. I'm working on a science fiction or fantasy thing . . ."

He gets agitated, tugs at the straps of the posey, tries to abandon his wheelchair to climb Mount Fuji one more time.

"Too much snow up there at this season," I point out. "Let's wait until summer."

To calm him, I sing, the same old songs he used to sing to me when I was little: Irving Berlin's "Russian Lullaby," fragments of a Norwegian song, and even "The Old Gray Mare," and anything else I can remember to sing that used to amuse him. Then my voice cracks and I realize I am crying. Fortunately he doesn't notice.

He insists it is time to get properly dressed in his dark gray suit to receive the Queen of Belgium, some princess from Cleves.

"But, Daddy, you are already elegant." I try not to notice that his trousers need changing. Watitha the nurse promised to return quickly.

"Come on, till guests arrive, let's take a stroll."

I push his wheelchair down the long Lysoled hall to the common room, labeled "Solarium," although the curtains on the east side are perpetually drawn against a sun too brilliant for aging eyes. The television blares soap operas and commercials for snow-white laundry, action-packed weekends, and eternal beauty.

Parked before the set she cannot see, one ancient lady slips down in her wheelchair until all I can see of her is the untidy knot of white hair with its ridiculous pink bow. Beside her, a man with a gray-stubbled beard twisted on a sort of padded cot stares fixedly toward a moribund philodendron. In a yellow plastic chair, an old woman in a pink nightgown rocks a stuffed plush cat and tells it her troubles. A tense gray woman recites a litany of her needs, keeping time by banging the tray of her gerichair. Near the drinking fountain, propped in an angled-high chaise lounge and attached to plastic tubing, the twenty-year-old diabetic lies in an irreversible coma from a not quite fatal enough combination of alcohol and insulin. My heart tightens whenever I see him. Could be my own son.

I should get on home . . .

A man shuffles up and salutes. A woman chatters past and winks.

My father seldom seems to notice the other patients. Is the best solution to existence here a retreat into internal exile? Selective eyesight. Dying eyesight.

Meanwhile, in the solarium, I deal out double solitaire.

I can't stand the television and all these people talking to themselves and to the air. I'm feeling claustrophobic in here . . .

But the fat-faced clock shows noon. The first food cart is coming off the service elevator. My father's tray is always last; there's time to wheel him back to his room; he really needs changing but I can't manage it alone. Where . . .

Nella, the curly blonde medicine nurse flashing gorgeous crimson smiles in all directions, passes by with her cart full of pills and syrups and juices to wash them down. "I'll be over with your medicine in a moment, sweetheart."

With a grand gesture my father kisses her hand, then whispers to me, "Our guests are late! How's our sherry supply?"

The styrofoam cups stick together but I wrestle four free, set them in a row. The only juice at the nurses' station is prune.

Nella returns with a tiny pleated paper cup of crushed pills mixed with applesauce. "Something delicious for you, honey," she purrs.

I go out to see where Watitha is, she promised . . .

Out of sight. On her break.

Back in the solarium Nella is giggling. "He just asked me to fly to Bangkok with him!"

I picture my father's wheelchair growing wide aluminum wings, or his shoulders, skeletal under my hands, sprout feathers—scarlet, orange, green—like a swan sired by a parrot.

"I trust you agreed to fly with him," I answer. "He was once a famous explorer."

She laughs, slaps her broad palms against her white uniform. "Lord, what a crazy i-ma-gin-a-tion your daddy's got!"

"At eighty-five, he has license for madness."

Anxious, his blue eyes watch us. I smooth the wisps of hair on his skull. My mad daddy. . . . Here are the springs of my . . . imagination.

The last food cart is shoved off the elevator. I wheel his chair to the space at the table between old Mrs. Silverman incessantly screaming "I need sugar! More milk . . ." or anything for attention, and Muggsy sloshing soup on his neighbor.

I set the brakes and search for a nurse's aide. "My father's tired; he needs help eating. I must leave. Please . . ."

Most of the lunchtime shift seem to be on their own lunch hours. A kitchen worker sets down a special tray in front of my father. The nursing home lost his dentures months ago, and the dentist sees no point in new ones, so he can't chew ordinary food.

Although he would rather have smoked eel and vodka, or curry and beer, or beef stroganoff with good burgundy served in a real glass, I spoon the pureed liver, mashed lima beans, and fake grape Jell-o into his mouth quickly before his fingers explore the plate.

"Cheers!" I say, holding the styrofoam cup of prune juice to his lips.

He smiles. "And what about you, my dear?"

"I absolutely must leave, Daddy. I'll come back tomorrow."

The Indian orderly with a diamond in one earlobe promises to change my father as soon as he finishes the trays. Or perhaps he'll find someone else . . .

To hell with it. My father used to keep a sign on his desk: *"Nothing will ever be accomplished if all possible obstacles must first be overcome."* I wheel him back to his room, somehow hoist him onto his narrow bed, clean him up myself. Something that "residents'" families aren't supposed to do, a legality about what-if-we-should-drop-him, and for modesty, to spare their, or our, embarrassment. Wives—that should be no problem—but they don't do it either here. And daughters . . .

I suddenly recall the first and only time I saw my father naked was when I was four or five, and he hurried into the bathroom to shave while I was still in the tub, and he said not to look, then I closed my eyes tight until he left the bathroom.

Now his eyelids are heavy and he is exhausted by the time he is in fresh pajamas. Then he opens his eyes. "Thank you. Please inform the general I'll return to the front immediately." And he falls asleep.

Downstairs, on my way out, I detour to the ladies room, inadvertently find myself in the oversized stall with handrails, high commode, and the blue-and-white "Handicapped" sign.

When I too am . . . all spaced out . . . will there be room enough here for my wings?

Questions for Discussion

1. The father in this story had an interesting, event-filled life, as did many of the other patients in the nursing home. Think of some ways nursing homes can relate to patients in ways that tap into and honor their rich histories.
2. The daughter mentions that her father's dentures have been lost; the nurse's aid and the orderly don't come back to change her father's wet pants. What is going on? If our culture were committed to caring for the elderly, what kinds of changes would you want to see? What attitudes would have to change?

SELECTED READINGS AND ADDITIONAL RESOURCES

Berman, Claire (1997). *Caring for Yourself While Caring for Your Aging Parents: How to Help, How to Survive.* New York: Henry Holt.

Buckingham, Robert W. (1994). *When Living Alone Means Living at Risk: A Guide for Caregivers and Their Families.* Buffalo, NY: Prometheus Books.

Butler, Robert and Morris, Virginia (1996). *How to Care for Aging Parents.* New York: Workman Publishing Company.

Greenberg, Jerrold S. (1992). *The Caregivers Guide: For Caregivers and the Elderly.* Chicago: Nelson Hall.

Hagen, Brad, Gallagher, Elaine M., and Simpson, Sharon (2001). Nursing Home Placement Affecting Caregivers Decisions to Place Family Members with Dementia. *Journal of Gerontological Nursing 27*(2), pp. 44-53.

Holosko, Michael and Feit, Marvin D. (1996). *Social Work Practice with the Elderly.* Toronto: Canadian Scholar's Press.

Ilardo, Joseph A. (1998). *As Parents Age: A Psychological and Practical Guide.* Acton, MA: VanderWyk and Brunham.

Pipher, Mary Bray (1999). *Another Country: Navigating the Emotional Terrain of Our Elders.* New York: Riverhead Books.

Turner, Francis J. (Ed.) (1992). *Mental Health and the Elderly: A Social Work Perspective.* New York: The Free Press.

HAWORTH Social Work Practice in Action
Carlton E. Munson, PhD, Senior Editor

DIAGNOSIS IN SOCIAL WORK: NEW IMPERATIVES by Francis J. Turner. (2002). "This book is a useful resource for scholars and clinicians involved in clinical social work. It is thoughtfully written and well researched, and a timely additional to the professional literature." *Kathleen J. Farkas, PhD, Associate Professor, Mandel School of Applied Social Sciences, Case Western Reserve University, Cleveland, OH*

HUMAN BEHAVIOR IN THE SOCIAL ENVIRONMENT: INTERWEAVING THE INNER AND OUTER WORLD by Esther Urdang. (2002). "This book will serve as a superb introduction to human behavior, normal and pathologic, not only for graduate social work students, but also for anyone who is curious about the vicissitudes of the human condition....The students who use this book will be lucky, indeed." *Calvin A. Colarusso, MD, Clinical Professor of Psychiatry, University of California at San Diego*

THE USE OF PERSONAL NARRATIVES IN THE HELPING PROFESSIONS: A TEACHING CASEBOOK by Jessica Heriot and Eileen J. Polinger. (2002). "More than anything else, social work students need examples to connect theories with everyday practice. Here's a book that provides those examples. This book is not only valuable for teaching, it's also an absorbing and instructional pleasure to read." *Leon Ginsberg, PhD, Carolina Distinguished Professor, University of Maryland School of Social Work, Baltimore*

CHILDREN'S RIGHTS: POLICY AND PRACTICE by John T. Pardeck. (2001) "Courageous and timely . . . a must-read for everyone concerned not only about the rights of America's children but also about their fate." *Howard Jacob Kerger, PhD, Professor and PhD Director, University of Houston Graduate School of Social Work, Texas*

BUILDING ON WOMEN'S STRENGTHS: A SOCIAL WORK AGENDA FOR THE TWENTY-FIRST CENTURY, SECOND EDITION by K. Jean Peterson and Alice A. Lieberman. (2001). "An indispensable resource for courses in women's issues, social work practice with women, and practice from a strengths perspective." *Theresa J. Early, PhD, MSW, Assistant Professor, College of Social Work, Ohio State University, Columbus*

ELEMENTS OF THE HELPING PROCESS: A GUIDE FOR CLINICIANS, SECOND EDITION by Raymond Fox. (2001). "Engages the reader with a professional yet easily accessible style. A remarkably fresh, eminently usable set of practical strategies." *Elayne B. Haynes, PhD, ACSW, Assistant Professor, Department of Social Work, Southern Connecticut State University, New Haven*

SOCIAL WORK THEORY AND PRACTICE WITH THE TERMINALLY ILL, SECOND EDITION by Joan K. Parry. (2000). "Timely . . . a sensitive and practical approach to working with people with terminal illness and their family members." *Jeanne A.Gill, PhD, LCSW, Adjunct Faculty, San Diego State University, California, and Vice President Southern California Chapter, AASWG*

WOMEN SURVIVORS, PSYCHOLOGICAL TRAUMA, AND THE POLITICS OF RESISTANCE by Norma Jean Profitt. (2000). "A compelling argument on the importance of political and collective action as a means of resisting oppression. Should be read by survivors, service providers, and activists in the violence-against-women movement." *Gloria Geller, PhD, Faculty of Social Work, University of Regina, Saskatchewan, Canada*

THE MENTAL HEALTH DIAGNOSTIC DESK REFERENCE: VISUAL GUIDES AND MORE FOR LEARNING TO USE THE DIAGNOSTIC AND STATISTICAL MANUAL (DSM-IV) by Carlton E. Munson. (2000). "A carefully organized and user-friendly book for the beginning student and less-experienced practitioner of social work, clinical psychology, of psychiatric nursing . . . It will be a valuable addition to the literature on clinical assessment of mental disorders." *Jerold R. Brandell, PhD, BCD, Professor, School of Social Work, Wayne State University, Detroit, Michigan and Founding Editor, Psychoanalytic Social Work*

HUMAN SERVICES AND THE AFROCENTRIC PARADIGM by Jerome H. Schiele. (2000). "Represents a milestone in applying the Afrocentric paradigm to human services generally, and social work specifically. . . . A highly valuable resource." *Bogart R. Leashore, PhD, Dean and Professor, Hunter College School of Social Work, New York, New York*

SOCIAL WORK: SEEKING RELEVANCY IN THE TWENTY-FIRST CENTURY by Roland Meinert, John T. Pardeck and Larry Kreuger. (2000). "Highly recommended. A thought-provoking work that asks the difficult questions and challenges the status quo. A great book for graduate students as well as experienced social workers and educators." *Francis K. O. Yuen, DSW, ACSE, Associate Professor, Division of Social Work, California State University, Sacramento*

SOCIAL WORK PRACTICE IN HOME HEALTH CARE by Ruth Ann Goode. (2000). "Dr. Goode presents both a lucid scenario and a formulated protocol to bring health care services into the home setting. . . . this is a must have volume that will be a reference to be consulted many times." *Marcia B. Steinhauer, PhD, Coordinator and Associate Professor, Human Services Administration Program, Rider University, Lawrenceville, New Jersey*

FORSENIC SOCIAL WORK: LEGAL ASPECTS OF PROFESSIONAL PRACTICE, SECOND EDITION by Robert L. Barker and Douglas M. Branson. (2000). "The authors combine their expertise to create this informative guide to address legal practice issues facing social workers." *Newsletter of the National Organization of Forensic Social Work*

SOCIAL WORK IN THE HEALTH FIELD: A CARE PERSPECTIVE by Lois A. Fort Cowles. (1999). "Makes an important contrition to the field by locating the practice of social work in health care within an organizational and social context." *Goldie Kadushin, PhD, Associate Professor, School of Social Welfare, University of Wisconsin, Milwaukee*

SMART BUT STUCK: WHAT EVERY THERAPY NEEDS TO KNOW ABOUT LEARNING DISABILITIES AND IMPRISONED INTELLIGENCE by Myrna Orenstein. (1999). "A trailblazing effort that creates an entirely novel way of talking and thinking about learning disabilities. There is simply nothing like it in the field." *Fred M. Levin, MD, Training Supervising Analyst, Chicago Institute for Psychoanalysis; Assistant Professor of Clinical Psychiatry, Northwestern University, School of Medicine, Chicago, IL*

CLINICAL WORK AND SOCIAL ACTION: AN INTEGRATIVE APPROACH by Jerome Sachs and Fred Newdom. (1999). "Just in time for the new millennium come Sachs and Newdom with a wholly fresh look at social work. . . . A much-needed uniting of social work values, theories, and practice for action." *Josephine Nieves, MSW, PhD, Executive Director, National Association of Social Workers*

SOCIAL WORK PRACTICE IN THE MILITARY by James G. Daley. (1999). "A significant and worthwhile book with provocative and stimulating ideas. It deserves to be read by a wide audience in social work education and practice as well as by decision makers in the military." *H. Wayne Johnson, MSW, Professor, University of Iowa, School of Social Work, Iowa City, Iowa*

GROUP WORK: SKILLS AND STRATEGIES FOR EFFECTIVE INTERVENTIONS, SECOND EDITION by Sondra Brandler and Camille P. Roman. (1999). "A clear, basic description of what group work requires, including what skills and techniques group workers need to be effective." *Hospital and Community Psychiatry (from the first edition)*

TEENAGE RUNAWAYS: BROKEN HEARTS AND "BAD ATTITUDES" by Laurie Schaffner. (1999). "Skillfully combines the authentic voice of the juvenile runaway with the principles of social science research." *Barbara Owen, PhD, Professor, Department of Criminology, California State University, Fresno*

CELEBRATING DIVERSITY: COEXISTING IN A MULTICULTURAL SOCIETY by Benyamin Chetkow-Yanoov. (1999). "Makes a valuable contribution to peace theory and practice." *Ian Harris, EdD, Executive Secretary, Peace Education Committee, International Peace Research Association*

SOCIAL WELFARE POLICY ANALYSIS AND CHOICES by Hobart A. Burch. (1999). "Will become the landmark text in its field for many decades to come." *Sheldon Rahan, DSW, Founding Dean and Emeritus Professor of Social Policy and Social Administration. Faculty of Social Work, Wilfrid Laurier University, Canada*

SOCIAL WORK PRACTICE: A SYSTEMS APPROACH, SECOND EDITION by Benyamin Chetkow-Yannov. (1999). "Highly recommended as a primary text for any and all introductory social work courses." *Ram A. Cnaan, PhD, Associate Professor, School of Social Work, University of Pennsylvania*

CRITICAL SOCIAL WELFARE ISSUES: TOOLS FOR SOCIAL WORK AND HEALTH CARE PROFESSIONALS edited by Arthur J. Katz, Abraham Lurie, and Carlos M. Vida. (1997). "Offers hopeful agendas for change, while navigating the societal challenges facing those in the human services today." *Book News Inc.*

SOCIAL WORK IN HEALTH SETTINGS: PRACTICE IN CONTEXT, SECOND EDITION edited by Tobra Schwaber Kerson. (1997). "A first-class document . . . It will be found among the steadier and lasting works on the social work aspects of American health care." *Hans S. Falck, PhD, Professor Emeritus and Former Chair, Health Specialization in Social Work, Virginia Commonwealth University*

PRINCIPLES OF SOCIAL WORK PRACTICE: A GENERIC PRACTICE APPROACH by Molly R. Hancock. (1997). "Hancock's discussions advocate reflection and self-awareness to create a climate for client change." *Journal of Social Work Education*

NOBODY'S CHILDREN: ORPHANS OF THE HIV EPIDEMIC by Steven F. Dansky. (1997). "Professional sound, moving, and useful for both professionals and interested readers alike." *Ellen G. Friedman, ACSW, Associate Director of Support Services, Beth Israel Medical Center, Methadone Maintenance Treatment Program*

SOCIAL WORK APPROACHES TO CONFLICT RESOLUTION: MAKING FIGHTING OBSOLETE by Benyamin Chetkow-yanoov. (1996). "Presents an examination of the nature and cause of conflict and suggests techniques for coping with conflict." *Journal of Criminal Justice*

FEMINIST THEORIES AND SOCIAL WORK: APPROACHES AND APPLICATIONS by Christine Flynn Salunier. (1996). "An essential reference to be read repeatedly by all educators and practitioners who are eager to learn more about feminist theory and practice" *Nancy R. Hooyman, PhD, Dean and Professor, School of Social Work, University of Washington, Seattle*

THE RELATIONAL SYSTEMS MODEL FOR FAMILY THERAPY: LIVING IN THE FOUR REALITIES by Donald R. Bardill. (1996). "Engages the reader in quiet, thoughtful conversation on the timeless issue of helping families and individuals." *Christian Counseling Resource Review*

SOCIAL WORK INTERVENTION IN AN ECONOMIC CRISIS: THE RIVER COMMUNITIES PROJECT by Martha Baum and Pamela Twiss. (1996). "Sets a standard for universities in terms of the types of meaningful roles they can play in supporting and sustaining communities." *Kenneth J. Jaros, PhD, Director, Public Health Social Work Training Program, University of Pittsburgh*

FUNDAMENTALS OF COGNITIVE-BEHAVIOR THERAPY: FROM BOTH SIDES OF THE DESK by Bill Borcherdt. (1996). "Both beginning and experienced practitioners . . . will find a considerable number of valuable suggestions in Borcherdt's book." *Albert Ellis, PhD, President, Institute for Rational-Emotive Therapy, New York City*

BASIC SOCIAL POLICY AND PLANNING: STRATEGIES AND PRACTICE METHODS by Hobart A. Burch. (1996). "Burch's familiarity with his topic is evident and his book is an easy introduction to the field." *Readings*

THE CROSS-CULTURAL PRACTICE OF CLINICAL CASE MANAGEMENT IN MENTAL HEALTH edited by Peter Manoleas. (1996). "Makes a contribution by bringing together the cross-cultural and clinical case management perspectives in working with those who have serious mental illness." *Disabilities Studies Quarterly*

FAMILY BEYOND FAMILY: THE SURROGATE PARENT IN SCHOOLS AND OTHER COMMUNITY AGENCIES by Sanford Weinstein. (1995). "Highly recomended to anyone concerned about the welfare of our children and the breakdown of the American family." *Jerold S. Greenberg, EdD, director of Community Service, College of Health & Human Performance, University of Maryland*

PEOPLE WITH HIV AND THOSE WHO HELP THEM: CHALLENGES, INTEGRATION, INTERVENTION by R. Dennis Shelby. (1995). "A useful and compassionate contribution to the HIV psychotherapy literature." *Public Health*

THE BLACK ELDERLY: SATISFACTION AND QUALITY OF LATER LIFE by Marguerite Coke and James A. Twaite. (1995). "Presents a model for predicting life satisfaction in this population." *Abstracts in Social Gerontology*

NOW DARE EVERYTHING: TALES OF HIV-RELATED PSYCHOTHERAPY by Steven F. Dansky. (1994). "A highly recommended book for anyone working with persons who are HIV positive. . . . Every library should have a copy of this book." *AIDS Book Review Journal*

INTERVENTION RESEARCH: DESIGN AND DEVELOPMENT FOR HUMAN SERVICE edited by Jack Rothman and Edwin J. Thomas. (1994). "Provides a useful framework for the further examination of methodology for each separate step of such research." *Academic Library Book Review*

CLINICAL SOCIAL WORK SUPERVISION, SECOND EDITION by Carlton E. Munson. (1993). "A useful, thorough, and articulate reference for supervisors and for 'supervisees' who are wanting to understand their supervisor or are looking for effective supervision...." *Transactional Analysis Journal*

IF A PARTNER HAS AIDS: GUIDE TO CLINICAL INTERVENTION FOR RELATIONSHIPS IN CRISIS by R. Dennis Shelby. (1993). "A women addition to existing publications about couples coping with AIDS, it offers intervention ideas and strategies to clinicians." *Contemporary Psychology*

GERONTOLOGICAL SOCIAL WORK SUPERVISION by Ann Burack-Weiss and Frances Coyle Brennan. (1991). "The creative ideas in this book will aid supervisiors working with students and experienced social workers." *Senior News*

THE CREATIVE PRACTITIONER: THEORY AND METHODS FOR THE HELPING SERVICES by Bernard Gelfand. (1988). "[Should] be widely adopted by those in the helping services. It could lead to significant positive advances by countless individuals." *Sidney J. Parnes, Trustee Chairperson for Strategic Program Development, Creative Education Foundation, Buffalo, NY*

MANAGEMENT AND INFORMATION SYSTEMS IN HUMAN SERVICES: IMPLICATIONS FOR THE DISTRIBUTION OF AUTHORITY AND DECISION MAKING by Richard K. Caputo. (1987). "A contribution to social work scholarship in that it provides conceptual frameworks that can be used in the design of management information systems." *Social Work*

Order Your Own Copy of
This Important Book for Your Personal Library!

THE USE OF PERSONAL NARRATIVES IN THE HELPING PROFESSIONS
A Teaching Casebook

_____in hardbound at $49.95 (ISBN: 0-7890-0918-8)

_____in softbound at $29.95 (ISBN: 0-7890-0919-6)

COST OF BOOKS_____

OUTSIDE USA/CANADA/
MEXICO: ADD 20%____

POSTAGE & HANDLING_____
(US: $4.00 for first book & $1.50
for each additional book)
Outside US: $5.00 for first book
& $2.00 for each additional book)

SUBTOTAL_____

in Canada: add 7% GST____

STATE TAX____
(NY, OH & MIN residents, please
add appropriate local sales tax)

FINAL TOTAL____
(If paying in Canadian funds,
convert using the current
exchange rate, UNESCO
coupons welcome.)

❑ **BILL ME LATER:** ($5 service charge will be added)
(Bill-me option is good on US/Canada/Mexico orders only;
not good to jobbers, wholesalers, or subscription agencies.)

❑ Check here if billing address is different from
shipping address and attach purchase order and
billing address information.

Signature_____

❑ **PAYMENT ENCLOSED: $_____**

❑ **PLEASE CHARGE TO MY CREDIT CARD.**

❑ Visa ❑ MasterCard ❑ AmEx ❑ Discover
❑ Diner's Club ❑ Eurocard ❑ JCB

Account # _____

Exp. Date_____

Signature_____

Prices in US dollars and subject to change without notice.

NAME_____

INSTITUTION_____

ADDRESS_____

CITY_____

STATE/ZIP_____

COUNTRY_____ COUNTY (NY residents only)_____

TEL_____ FAX_____

E-MAIL_____

May we use your e-mail address for confirmations and other types of information? ❑ Yes ❑ No
We appreciate receiving your e-mail address and fax number. Haworth would like to e-mail or fax special
discount offers to you, as a preferred customer. **We will never share, rent, or exchange your e-mail address
or fax number.** We regard such actions as an invasion of your privacy.

Order From Your Local Bookstore or Directly From
The Haworth Press, Inc.
10 Alice Street, Binghamton, New York 13904-1580 • USA
TELEPHONE: 1-800-HAWORTH (1-800-429-6784) / Outside US/Canada: (607) 722-5857
FAX: 1-800-895-0582 / Outside US/Canada: (607) 722-6362
E-mail: getinfo@haworthpressinc.com
PLEASE PHOTOCOPY THIS FORM FOR YOUR PERSONAL USE.
www.HaworthPress.com

BOF00